CRITICAL TEMPER

on *English and American Literature*
to the Twentieth Century

MARTIN TUCKER
General Editor

Volume I

TO SHAKESPEARE

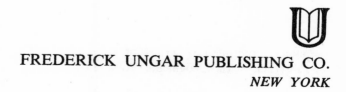

FREDERICK UNGAR PUBLISHING CO.
NEW YORK

Second Printing, 1973

Copyright © 1969 by Frederick Ungar Publishing Co., Inc.

Printed in the United States of America

Library of Congress Card Number: 68-8116

Standard Book Number for Volume I: 0-8044-3304-6
Standard Book Number for Volume II: 0-8044-3305-4
Standard Book Number for Volume III: 0-8044-3306-2
Standard Book Number for the set: 0-8044-3303-8

For material reprinted by permission
see Copyright Acknowledgments, Volume III.

CONTRIBUTING EDITORS

General Editor, Martin Tucker

OLD ENGLISH LITERATURE

Martin Tucker
Long Island University

MEDIEVAL LITERATURE

Robert Raymo
New York University

ELIZABETHAN AND JACOBEAN LITERATURE

Irving Ribner
*State University of New York
at Stony Brook*

SHAKESPEARE

Paul N. Siegel
Long Island University

MILTON, AND NEOCLASSICAL LITERATURE

John T. Shawcross
University of Wisconsin

ROMANTIC LITERATURE

Frances K. Barasch
*Bernard Baruch College
of The City University of New York*

VICTORIAN LITERATURE

Wendell Stacy Johnson
*Hunter College
of The City University of New York*

AMERICAN LITERATURE

Ray C. Longtin
Long Island University

v

CONTENTS

VOLUME I

FROM OLD ENGLISH TO SHAKESPEARE

ELIZABETHAN AND JACOBEAN LITERATURE   251
Irving Ribner, editor

SHAKESPEARE

Paul N. Siegel, editor

VOLUME II

FROM MILTON TO ROMANTIC LITERATURE

ROMANTIC LITERATURE
Frances K. Barasch, editor

VOLUME III

VICTORIAN LITERATURE, AND AMERICAN LITERATURE

VICTORIAN LITERATURE 1
Wendell Stacy Johnson, editor

AMERICAN LITERATURE   229
Ray C. Longtin, editor

FOREWORD

The present work, another in the series *A Library of Literary Criticism,* is an attempt to present a panoramic view of the best twentieth-century criticism on English and American literature from the period of Old English to the beginning of modern times. At the same time it aims to show the wide range of thought and perceptiveness within that criticism. To this end a committee of distinguished scholars, each an expert in his field, gathered material on specific literary periods. Each editor selected the criticism he considered to be the most significant and influential in his literary area.

The Critical Temper is thus a record of the taste of modern critics as well as a source for study of the writers included, who represent all periods with the exception of modern American and modern British literature. In form the work is parallel to *Moulton's Library of Literary Criticism,* recently published in an abridged and revised version under the same general editorship. *Moulton,* in its original eight volumes and in its abridged form, offered criticism of English and American literature gathered from various eras through the beginning of the twentieth century but largely of the nineteenth. A student examining any period of the literature thus could review it in the main only through the scholarship extant some fifty years ago. *The Critical Temper* now provides a much-needed supplement to the earlier *Moultons.* Like its predecessors, the original and the revised *Moulton,* these volumes are organized into literary periods and deal with particular writers within those periods. From the excerpts discussing individual writers the reader will, it is hoped, get an overview of the age and the influences and cross-currents within that age.

This work, however, is much more than a supplement alone. The present century has been called an age of criticism; certainly some of the most creative imaginations of modern times have produced remarkable works of critical theory and insight. These critical achievements, which in themselves form a kind of critical revolution, have not always been consciously schooled efforts, but often perceptions or immediate impressions put into permanent expression. It is with this kind of informal expression as well as formal criticism that the present work is concerned.

Under the stimulus of collective enterprise, the committee of editors worked with several general principles in mind. Writers were selected generally on the basis of commonly acknowledged reputation. Among experts, however, differences of opinion exist, and some authors were caught—more precisely, deleted—in this critical crossfire. This was particularly true of minor writers, some of whose reputations have risen and fallen, like quicksilver to quicksand, within a generation. Nor do these minor writers merely reflect the difficulty of judging one's contemporaries, an admittedly dangerous task, which in part is reflected in the original *Moulton*. The reader has only to compare the writers examined in that celebrated work with the writers in these volumes to perceive that the reputation of major *and* minor literary figures is highly volatile and elusive.

The editors have aimed to examine a major writer in terms of his work, his life, and his contemporary and posthumous influence. There are some difficulties inherent in this approach. The material available for the studies of major writers does not always appear in proportion to the needs of a student or scholar. Criticism has its vogues, and one good critical idea may occasion a hundred imitations. The result is that one writer may be treated many times from the same viewpoint while other aspects of his work or life remain untouched by the critical eye. Shakespeare, Milton, and Shelley, among others, have suffered from this myopia of critical attention in various periods. The editors have tried to avoid duplication of critical thought, except in instances of continuing controversy. For example: the section on John Donne, whose work has been voluminously explicated in the twentieth century, may seem short when measured against the extent of the writings about him. Because many modern works of criticism or exegesis on Donne are based on similar premises, only a representative sampling is printed here. Conversely, the ambiguities of Lord Byron continue to ignite the critical passions, and an attempt has been made to reflect the many-hued differences in judgment and opinion about him. A main principle, then, is to reflect quality and controversy rather than mere quantitative appearance in scholarly and popular publications.

For their material the editors have used three main avenues of research: scholarly and critical journals of literary history and opinion; monographs, textual editions, biographies and studies of a writer; and general books of critical interest on a literary period or esthetic movement. Their aim, like that of previous *Library of Literary Criticism* volumes, has been the simultaneous presentation of two frames of references, which lend themselves to division for study: the analytical or critical, presenting the major issues apparent in a writer's work and life, and the development or lack of development in his ideas, techniques, and style; and the historical, both in terms of the shifting viewpoints on a particular writer and the shift in critical values itself. Famous examples of barometric changes in the critical winds and storms are included here, at least in part, or else used as reference points to encourage the student to further study. Examples abound: T. S. Eliot's essay-review of H. J. C. Grierson's study of Donne that started a re-evaluation of Donne; the discovery and continuing interest in the manuscripts of the seventeenth-century poet Thomas Traherne; the resurgence of critical exegesis in Keats's work; the biographical revelations that at the very least have led to variant readings in the work of nineteenth-century American writers.

A word remains to be said about inconsistencies of style and form. In a century that has seen so many dramatic changes, it would be strange not to find many changes in literary style and forms. An attempt at general uniformity of presentation of material has been made in this work, but no attempt has been made to change the spelling of British locutions to fit American standards, nor have variant styles of punctuation and diction been sacrificed on the altar of prescriptive grammar and conventional expression. It is advisable to say, however, that what may appear as inconsistency is often part of a general style not immediately evident. Let us therefore lay our format on the page:

Each section may be divided into three or more subsections: Personal, General, and section(s) on a specific work or works. Major writers will have many subsections devoted to specific works (see Shakespeare, Chaucer, Milton, and Pope, among other). If criticism on a writer has been sparse, or if little need appears for a biographical (Personal) section on him—if, for example, the introductory headnote tells the essential facts about which no controversy or deepening of facts has been manifested recently—then the section may have no subheadings at all. Since such sections contain material of a general critical nature, passages are simply placed under the introductory headnote according to chronological order of publication. The reader will find such an arrangement in many sections on writers from the Old English and Neoclassic periods, and in the sections on Fulke Greville, Richard Hooker, Thomas Kyd, Wilkie Collins, Edward Lear, and Walter Pater, among others.

The order of critical material is by chronology of publication. This arrangement has been chosen because of its intrinsic value in dramatizing for the observer the critical history of a writer's reputation and the elevation or deflation of his reputation. Source notes indicate original date of publication. When an essay has been reprinted in book form or revised in a new edition, the later printed version, if the source was taken from this version, is notated as well. Dates of publication for journals are given in month and year, rather than volume number, a style adapted by the editors to give emphasis to the *currency* of critical observation. In some few cases, *n. d.* and *n. p.* are used to indicate a lack of date or place of publication in the original source material.

Titles of works have generally been placed in italics, except in the case of short poems or items in a collection. Although this procedure may seem to give equality to book-length works and to relatively short lyrics, it reflects the editors' aim to treat each work as equally worthy of serious critical attention. Subsections treating such individual works are arranged by order of publication of the subject-work. Thus, the discussion of each of Shakespeare's plays is arranged according to the accepted canon of date of composition of the various plays; the subsections on several of Thomas Hardy's novels are arranged according to the publication dates of the novels.

In a work that has taken several years to complete and has involved the cooperation of many colleagues and assistants, it is difficult to express a full measure of gratitude. Specific acknowledgments to authors, literary executors, and publishers who have kindly permitted the use of material will be found at the end of Volume III. I should also like to acknowledge, however briefly, my personal indebtedness. The committee of scholars responsible for these volumes worked not only well but at all times cooperatively. Special thanks go to Elizabeth Snyder and Edith Friedlander of the publisher's staff and to Shirley Helfman and Joyce Hergenhan for their assitance in the preparation of the manuscript. Many libraries—too numerous to mention here—made it possible for the committee to gather its material. John T. Shawcross, the editor of "Milton, and Neoclassic Literature" (the Section 5 in this work), was aided in his project by the Douglass College Student Summer Research Program and a grant from the Research Council of Rutgers University. Finally, I should like to thank Long Island University for its concrete encouragement of my participation in this project.

MARTIN TUCKER

New York, 1968

BIBLIOGRAPHIC NOTE

Below the introductory paragraph for each writer included in these volumes, the reader will find bibliographic entries of standard editions and biographic studies published through 1967. The scheme of these entries is as follows:

The standard edition (or editions) of the writer's work is placed first; in certain selected cases a study of a single work, as distinct from the collected edition of an author's work, will be found in the bibliographic listings; occasionally there is no listing when no standard work exists. Following the list of editions is the standard biographic study. In cases where scholarly biography has been particularly active, or literary issues remain in the realm of disputation and/or doubt, several biographical sources may be noted.

Abbreviations used in the entries are: *repr.* for reprint; *rev.* for revision; *ed. for* "edited by"; *tr.* for "translated by"; *n. d.* for no date of publication listed; *n. p.* for no place of publication listed.

The abbreviation BC/Longmans, Green means: published for the British Council by Longmans, Green of London The abbreviation *CHEL* means: The Cambridge History of English Literature.

In citation of books throughout the text, the place of publication is always given, with the exception of Oxford University Press and Cambridge University Press, where the places of publication are readily identifiable. Places of publication for The Clarendon Press at Oxford, as well as the New York offices of Oxford University Press and Cambridge University Press, are notated.

PERIODICALS USED

Listed below are titles, their abbreviations, if any,
and place of publication.

	The Academy (later The Academy and Literature), London
Adel	The Adelphi, London
ABR	American Benedictine Review, Latrobe, Pennsylvania
	American Imago, Boston
AL	American Literature, Duke University Press, Durham, North Carolina
AM	The American Mercury, New York
	The Proceedings of the American Philosophical Society, Philadelphia
AQ	American Quarterly, University of Pennsylvania, Philadelphia
AmR	The American Review, New York
AmS	The American Scholar, Washington, D.C.
	Anglia, Tübingen, Germany
At	The Atlantic Monthly (later The Atlantic), Boston
Boston Univ. Stud. in Eng.	Boston University Studies in English, Boston
	The Proceedings of the British Academy, London
BR	The Bucknell Review, Lewisburg, Pennsylvania
BJRL	The Bulletin of the John Rylands Library, Manchester, England
CambJ	The Cambridge Journal, Cambridge, England

CR	The Centennial Review of Arts and Science, Michigan State University, East Lansing, Michigan
CE	College English, Champaign, Illinois
	Commentary, New York
	The Commonweal, New York
CL	Comparative Literature, University of Oregon, Eugene, Oregon
Criterion	The Criterion, London
CQ	The Critical Quarterly, London
	Criticism, Wayne State University, Detroit, Michigan
	Delaware Notes, University of Delaware, Newark, Delaware
	The Dial, Chicago, then New York
	Discourse, Moorhead, Minnesota
DR	The Dublin Review, Dublin (since 1961 The Wiseman Review, London)
	Encounter, London
Eng	English, The Magazine of the English Association, London
	English Institute Essays, New York
ELH	English Literary History, Johns Hopkins University, Baltimore, Maryland
EM	English Miscellany, Rome, published for The British Council, London
ES	English Studies, Amsterdam, the Netherlands; also Englische Studien
	English Studies Today, Oxford (International Conference of University Professors of English, 1950)
Essays and Studies	Essays and Studies by members of the English Association, Oxford
EIC	Essays in Criticism, Oxford
Glasgow Univ. Publications	Glasgow University Publications, Glasgow, Scotland

Harpers	Harper's Magazine, New York
HJ	The Hibbert Journal, London
	History, London
HdR	The Hudson Review, New York
HLQ	The Huntington Library Quarterly, San Marino, California
	The Proceedings of the Second Congress of the International Comparative Literature Association, Chapel Hill, North Carolina
IER	Irish Ecclesiastical Record, Dublin
Irish Monthly	The Irish Monthly Magazine, Dublin
JAAC	The Journal of Aesthetics and Art Criticism, Cleveland, Ohio
JEGP	The Journal of English and Germanic Philology, University of Illinois, Urbana, Illinois
JHI	Journal of the History of Ideas, Princeton, New Jersey
JR	The Journal of Religion, Chicago
K-SJ	Keats-Shelley Journal, New York
KR	The Kenyon Review, Kenyon College, Gambier, Ohio
Library	The Library, London
LL	Life and Letters (later Life and Letters Today), London
List	The Listener (now The Listener and BBC Television Review), London
L&P	Literature and Psychology, University of Massachusetts, Amherst, Massachusetts
	Mediae ʳal Studies, University of Toronto, Toronto, Canada
	Papers, Michigan Academy of Science, Arts and Letters, Ann Arbor, Michigan
	Modern Language Association, see PMLA
MLN	Modern Language Notes, Baltimore, Maryland

MLQ	The Modern Language Quarterly, University of Washington, Seattle, Washington
MLR	The Modern Language Review, Cambridge, England
MP	Modern Philology, Chicago
Month	The Month, London
NR	The National Review, London
NEQ	The New England Quarterly, Boston
	News, A Review of World Events, London
	The New York Review of Books, New York
	Nineteenth-Century Fiction, Berkeley, California
NAR	The North American Review, Boston, then New York
NQ	Notes and Queries, London
	The Open Court, Chicago
PQ	Philological Quarterly, University of Iowa, Iowa City, Iowa
	Poetry, Chicago
Poetry R	The Poetry Review, London
PMLA	Publications of the Modern Language Association of America, New York
QJS	The Quarterly Journal of Speech, New York
QQ	Queen's Quarterly, Queen's University, Kingston, Ontario, Canada
QR	The Quarterly Review, London
	Research Studies, Washington State University, Pullman, Washington
RES	The Review of English Studies, London
PTRSC	The Proceedings and Transactions of the Royal Society of Canada, Ottawa, Canada
	The Transactions of the Royal Society of Literature of the United Kingdom, London
Sat	The Saturday Review of Literature (now The Saturday Review), New York

	Scrutiny, London
SwR	The Sewanee Review, University of the South, Sewanee, Tennessee
SQ	The Shakespeare Quarterly, New York
SS	Shakespeare Survey, Cambridge, England
	The South Atlantic Quarterly, Duke University, Durham, North Carolina
Spec	The Spectator, London
Sp	Speculum, Cambridge, Massachusetts
	Stanford University Publications in Language and Literature, Palo Alto, California
SN	Studia neophilologica, Uppsala, Sweden
	Studies in English, University of Texas, Austin, Texas
SEL	Studies in English Literature, 1500–1900, Tulane University, New Orleans
SP	Studies in Philology, Chapel Hill, North Carolina
	Studies in the Renaissance, New York
Texas Studies in Lang. and Lit.	Texas Studies in Language and Literature, University of Texas, Austin, Texas
TLS	The Times Literary Supplement, London
TDR	Tulane Drama Review (now TDR, The Drama Review), New York University, New York
Tulane Studies in Eng.	Tulane Studies in English, Tulane University, New Orleans
Univ. of California Publications in Eng.	University of California Publications in English, Berkeley, California
UKCR	The University of Kansas City Review, Kansas City, Missouri
UTQ	The University of Toronto Quarterly, Toronto, Canada

Univ. of Wisconsin Studies in Lang. and Lit.	University of Wisconsin Studies in Language and Literature, Madison, Wisconsin
	Victorian Newsletter, New York University, New York
	Victorian Poetry, West Virginia University, Morgantown, West Virginia
	Victorian Studies, Indiana University, Bloomington, Indiana
West Virginia Univ. Studies	West Virginia University Studies, Morgantown, West Virginia
	The Transactions of the Wisconsin Academy of Sciences, Arts and Letters, Madison, Wisconsin
YR	The Yale Review, Yale University, New Haven, Connecticut

OLD ENGLISH LITERATURE

Martin Tucker, editor

ALFRED THE GREAT
849-899

Born in Wantage, Berkshire. Fifth and youngest son of Æthelwulf, king of the West Saxons, and brother of Æthelred, whom he succeeded as king. Alfred ruled as king of the West Saxons during 871-901. Defeated Danes at Edington in 878, later was in the wars of 894-897, which led to the withdrawal of the Viking invaders. Alfred fortified London and built a superior English navy. Alfred's administration was marked by judicial and educational reforms, among them the codification of English law and the spread of learning in monasteries and schools. Alfred himself was a scholar who translated into Saxon the *Ecclesiastical History* of Bede, the *Epitome of Universal History* of Paulus Orosius, the *Consolation of Philosophy* of Boethius, the *Soliloquies* of St. Augustine, and the *Pastoral Care* of Pope Gregory. He was responsible for the compilation of the *Anglo-Saxon Chronicle*. He established Wessex as a new center of English scholarship and literary culture.

J. Stevenson, ed. and tr., rev. L. C. Jane, *Bede's Ecclesiastical History* (1954); Leo Sherley-Price, ed. and tr., *A History of the English Church and People* (1955)

W. J. Sedgefield, ed., *King Alfred's Old English Version of Boethius De Consolatione Philosophiae* (1899; tr., 1900)

Eleanor S. Duckett, *Alfred the Great* (1956). See also W. H. Stevenson, ed., *Asser's Life of King Alfred* (1904, repr. 1924)

If any one will look through the additions made by Alfred to the text of Boethius, which are very conveniently distinguished by italic type in Mr. Sedgefield's handy rendering of Alfred's version into modern English, he can hardly fail to notice how many of them consist in metaphors and similes; none perhaps so fine as that just quoted, but often of great interest and beauty. Even where the simile was suggested by something in the text or commentary which Alfred had before him, it is often developed at much greater length. This is a point of some interest, because it shows that Alfred's mind was of the class which delights in parable and figure, and makes it not unreasonable to look for deeper meanings in what he wrote and wrought.

I have said that the subject of fate occupies a prominent place in the *Consolatio* and in Alfred's translation of it. The relation of fate to providence, of divine foreknowledge to human freedom, the nature of evil, the existence of chance, these are the high themes round which much of the latter part of the argument circles. They are the themes which occupied the more intellectual spirits among Milton's fallen angels. . . .

There are other points which illustrate Alfred's studies, tastes, and circumstances; the saying that in the golden age no one had heard of a pirate host; the allusion to the wise goldsmith, Weland; the explanations about India and Thule.

And there are things in the text itself which evidently come home to Alfred; the beauty of gems, the fairness of the country-side—the fairest of all God's creations, the song of the birds in the woods, the worth of friends; the stories of kings reduced to poverty, of the sword of Damocles, the joy of a calm haven after storms. . . .

In regard to the translation as a whole no doubt has ever been expressed as to the authorship of Alfred; and it is the only one of Alfred's works which is mentioned by name by Ethelwerd, who wrote toward the end of the tenth century.

Charles Plummer
The Life and Times of Alfred the Great
(Oxford Univ. Pr., 1902), pp 182-85

The task of deciding upon the authenticity of the *Life* is by no means an easy one, and it has been rendered more difficult by the total destruction of the MS in 1731. The work is known to us therefore solely through the medium of printed texts and transcripts. Of the four editions through which it has run two only are based upon the MS. The earliest of these is filled with arbitrary alterations and interpolations, which are distinguished in no way from the readings of the original. The other affords us much aid in detecting these alterations and interpolations, but it occasionally makes the mistake of repeating as the reading of the MS alterations in the MS or misprints in the previous edition. Hence we are assailed with constant doubts as to its giving faithfully the reading of the MS. Owing to these interpolations and the imperfect manner in which they are distinguished in the existing editions, the work has had to bear not only the weight of its own sins, but also those of the authors of the interpolations and of the editors. . . .

We have thus examined the charges brought against the *Life,* and we have not found one dealing with facts that support the view that the work is of later origin than it pretends to be. Opinions that it ought to have contained certain information cannot in the nature of things command much consideration. We may regret that it does not tell us many things that we would fain know, but the absence of such information cannot fairly be advanced as an argument against it, more especially when we consider the time when it was written and the continental biographies that seem to have been the author's models. In the course of a microscopical examination of the work we have failed to discover anything that can be called an anachronism. . . .

This absence of anachronism is an argument in favor of the authenticity of the work. This argument is strengthened by the presence of several features that point to its being composed at least as early as the first half of the tenth century, and that are, so far as our scanty materials enable us to judge, compatible with an earlier date. . . . Agreeing with an earlier date, although not compatible with a slightly earlier or later one, are the evidence of the Welsh forms, the Latinity, the use of an old version of the scriptures, and of an earlier form of the *Chronicle* than any that has come down to us, and the reference to the monastery in the Island of Sheppey. The silence of the author regarding literary works that were ascribed to Alfred in the latter part of the tenth century, the absence of the mythical stories concerning Inguar and Ubba, which were in circulation in the tenth century, and silence regarding the numerous myths that centered round Alfred himself at a slightly later period, are difficult to reconcile with the view that the *Life* is spurious. . . . The information about Wales can hardly have come from any but a contemporary writer.

William Henry Stevenson
Introd., in *Asser's Life of Alfred* (Oxford Univ, Pr., 1904),
pp. xii-xiii, cxxv, cxxvi, cxxvii

From facts and details of history [his teachings of Othere and Wulfstan] Alfred now went on to the more difficult matter of thought and its discussion, into the sureties, and the questions, too, of philosophy and of religion. Here was increasing joy for him, in the turning of his mind to the high realities of his faith, in the more strenuous endeavor to bring these realities home to other men through words of their native speech. This time his choice of a Latin original for translation fell upon the book of a writer of the sixth century, the 500's after Christ, a writer and a book very different from Orosius and his *Histories*.

Yet again Alfred's choice was a natural one. The writer was Boethius, a leading minister of state and senate in the government of Rome under a barbarian king, Theodoric the Goth, ruler of Italy from 493 until 526; for by this time the Roman Empire in the West had fallen before the barbarian advance. In 476 Odoacer had driven from Italy's throne its last Roman possessor; in 493 Theodoric had marched with his Goths to wrest in his turn this throne from Odoacer, even, so men declared, to kill his fellow-barbarian with his own hand. . . .

Boethius, though a member of one of the most aristocratic and distinguished families of Rome, yet for that Rome's sake held office in its government under this barbarian conqueror of his land. The story of his fall from office and of his imprisonment and execution under Theodoric is well known. He was charged with treason against the king, a charge still unproved. If he was guilty, he was guilty for the service, he believed, of the

Rome and the Italy he loved so well. It may be that he died a victim to the fears of his less courageous associates in the politics of Rome.

In the nine months or so that he spent in prison, day by day uncertain of his final fate, which came upon him, with torture, it was said, in 524, he wrote that famous book, *The Consolation of Philosophy,* which, repeatedly read and translated into many tongues, has borne its influence and its tradition down the centuries of time. It is the story of a man's struggle with his rebellion against the pain which has come upon him, pain which he holds undeserved and, therefore, evil. Boethius cast his story in the form of a dialogue, of alternating Latin prose and verse. . . .

First, then, in this dialogue Philosophy allows Boethius to pour forth all his passion of complaint. Then slowly she begins to hold out before his wounded and darkened soul that light of sound doctrine which is to draw him back from the quicksands of unreality once more to safe lodging upon her rock of Truth. The argument passes from the unmasking of fickle Fortune, now kind, now adverse; from the revealing of the sure and lasting content known only to the soul that rests upon the One Unity, the One Good, and, therefore, the One Joy, which all men desire and which all men are seeking in their many, often foolish ways. . . .

The thought and the discussion in this book of Boethius, so far as King Alfred understood it, were of intense interest to him, first for its own sake and nature, then for its lesson to men in general. At the same time it must be remembered that Alfred was not skilled in the terms and the reasoning of classical philosophy; that the argument of Boethius here often eluded his grasp; that, moreover, the Latin itself of Boethius, formal and elaborate in its brilliance, offered to this English king difficulty at times insuperable.

Alfred, however, was eager, as before, to draw from these riches consolation and instruction for his own people, far removed from the learning of the Roman Boethius. He decided, therefore, in following the lines and the guidance of his original, to set himself here very largely free from adherence to its letter; to draw from it what he would and could; to add and change as he would. The result was really a book of his own, stamped from beginning to end with his own character, inspired by his faith: a vivid, warm, clear, and simple discourse on the Christian God as the Center and Foundation, the Life Eternal of all souls in this world and beyond.

As one looks back upon the Anglo-Saxon Alfred in his writings, it is impossible to forget that he was born and brought up, that he lived and wrote, in a Wessex which gave to him fully of its Celtic heritage. Inextricably mingled with the Anglo-Saxon traditions of his kindred were a Celtic consciousness of Nature, a love of solitude, a passion for learning, a spirit of sacrifice which called him from his youth until his death to give all that was in him, for his people, his country, and his God. These things, of course, were not peculiar to the Celt; but they rise from all Celtic life and literature to meet us with an intensity all their own. The learning of Wessex had been fostered under Aldhelm, in a monastery of Irish tradition; Alfred himself was taught day by day by a teacher he had called from Wales. These things surely had marked with their impress both the king himself and his work.

Eleanor Duckett
Alfred the Great and His England (London: Collins, 1957),
pp. 148-51, 163-64

The accession of Alfred was a very singular event. In the first place, it was surprising that he should ever have become king at all. His father Æthelwulf is known to have had six children: Athelstan, Ethelbald, Ethelbert, Ethelred, Æthelswith (his one known daughter) and Alfred. His eldest brother died before his father; the three others ruled Wessex in turn. When Ethelred died in 871, he left two sons; but both were minors, and only an experienced leader could hope to save Wessex from the Danes. Alfred's succession was undisputed, although one of his nephews tried to win the throne after his death.

In the second place it was singular that at the crucial moment Wessex should fall into the hands of the most inspiring king of his line; a man with the determination and imagination to plan a really successful defence, to leave his kingdom with some hope of future security. Even more surprising, Alfred found time to let his imagination roam in other fields; to think of monasteries and libraries and books which even laymen could read. . . .

It is clear that Alfred's life was even more difficult than we should expect. He was brought up to be pious and ignorant; he suffered constantly from fear of his own failings and shortcomings; and from physical disorders of a grotesque kind partly at least the result of mental anxiety. His career and writings were those of a man fundamentally healthy and sane; but Asser's marvellously confused account [*Asser's Life of Alfred*] of his illnesses and anxieties shows that this sanity was won at a price. The worst affliction struck him on his wedding day, and this, Asser plainly implies, was no coincidence. We are given a vision of a man of strong imagination, anxious and temperamental; always afraid of himself, afraid of illness and incapacity to the point of hypochondria, aware of a larger world than he himself lived in, desperately keen to live in it, and to enable others to live in it.

Christopher Brooke
The Saxon and Norman Kings (London: B. T. Batsford,
1963), pp. 116-17

ANGLO-SAXON CHRONICLE
891

> The *Chronicle*—the work of several chroniclers—provides information on early English history; its first entry notates the invasion of Britain by Caesar in 55 B.C.; its last entry describes the accession of Henry II in 1154. The *Chronicle* is preserved in seven different manuscripts, and consists of four distinctly separate parts. Poems and prose narratives are interspersed with more formal exposition. Alfred the Great was responsible in great part for providing the impetus and the means by which scholars arranged the *Chronicle*.
>
> George N. Garmonsway, ed. and tr., *The Anglo-Saxon Chronicle* (1953)
> Robert H. Hodgkin, *A History of the Anglo-Saxons* (1953), 2 vols.

Among the narrative sources of pre-Conquest English history, the *Anglo-Saxon Chronicle* must be given pre-eminence. It is a complicated record, surviving in seven manuscripts (not counting two brief fragments), and for the period covered in this volume it is accurate to describe them as containing versions of the same work, though each has some passages peculiar to it. In the later part of the work, which lies beyond the limit fixed for this volume, the manuscripts differ so greatly that a columnar arrangement of them is essential. . . .

In addition to the surviving versions, it is clear that some Latin writers had access to copies of the *Chronicle* which have not survived. Behind the twelfth-century work known as the *Annals of St. Neots* lies a version free from the chronological error from 756 to 845, which is in all the extant versions and in those used by Latin chroniclers. The West Saxon ealdorman, Æthelweard, a descendant of Alfred's elder brother, who wrote at the end of the tenth century a Latin chronicle for the benefit of his continental kinswoman, Matilda, abbess of Essen, had a version of the Chronicle which, while it had this error in chronology, was in some respects closer to the original than any surviving manuscript. For example, it had not lost by homœoteleuton a whole sentence from annal 885, as all our surviving manuscripts, and the one used by Asser, have done. This implies that Asser, who was writing his *Life of King Alfred* in 893, already had a version at least two removes from the original text. He shows no knowledge of the *Chronicle* after annal 887, an annal which could not have been composed before 889. The text he used sometimes supports the readings of the other manuscripts against "A," though there are places where his text, the version used by Æthelweard, and "A" all agree against the combined existence of "B," "C," "D," and "E," to an extent that suggests that all of these four manuscripts descend from a common version which contained several new features.

Dorothy Whitelock
Introd., in *English Historical Documents*, ed. David C. Douglas,
Vol. I (New York: Oxford Univ. Pr., 1955), pp. 109, 113

BEDE
671-735

Born near Monkwearmouth in Durham. Educated at the Benedictine Monastery of St. Peter's and of St. Paul's at Jarrow in Northumbria. Bede is most famous for his *Historia Ecclesiastica Gentis Anglorum* (*Ecclesiastical History of the English People*), a work which traces the history of England from 55 B.C. to A.D. 731. Bede, a monk at Jarrow, in addition distinguished himself in many intellectual areas. He wrote many works in Latin in the fields of medicine, astronomy, mathematics, philosophy, and biography.

A. Hamilton Thompson, ed., *Bede: His Life, Times and Writings* (1935)
J. Stevenson, ed., and tr., rev. L. C. Jane, *Ecclesiastical History* (1954);
Leo Sherley-Price, *A History of the English Church and People* (1955)
Eleanor S. Duckett, *Anglo-Saxon Saints and Scholars* (1947)

The *Historia Abbatum* was not known outside England. But his other historical writings had an even greater influence than the *Ecclesiastical History*. His *Martyrology* with its narrative parts gave material and, what is more, direction and character, to all the literature of this kind. The lucidity and clearness of both books on chronology made them favourites for centuries, as the multitude of manuscripts demonstrates. They were a mine of information to the later computists. In particular, the *Chronicles* joined to these manuals, narrow as their contents may seem to the modern historian, largely answered the needs of the Middle Ages. Certainly the chroniclers did not forget Jerome and his continuations, but they seized no less upon the shorter and handier text-books of Bede, which were transcribed until the fifteenth century, the appended chronicles being copied separately, summarized, augmented, and continued. Authors of new chronicles, like Frechulf of Lisieux, Ado of Vienne, and Regino of Prüm, and many of later times, made more or less copious extracts from them. Augustine's doctrine of the ages of the world owed its continuous existence in historiography largely to Bede.

He shows his creative powers most conspicuously in the *History of the Church*. . . . [W]here he lacks originality, he surpasses all others of his time in the manner in which he has transmitted traditional knowledge to posterity, "a brilliant example to all who, in dark ages, set themselves the task

of handing on the glimmering torch of learning to coming generations."
Through the *Ecclesiastical History*, moreover, he himself lighted a new
flame.

Wilhelm Levison
"Bede as Historian," in *Bede: His Life, Time and Writings,*
ed. A. Hamilton Thompson (Oxford: Clarendon Pr.,
1935), pp. 150-51

Even during his lifetime his reputation had spread far beyond the frontiers
of Britain, and St. Boniface likened his death to the extinction of a brightly
burning light. But in the centuries to come he was to exercise an influence
far greater than that of any other figure of his time. He has been described
as the Father of English History. He was much more than that; he was, in
the phrase of a German historian, the Father of all the Middle Ages. In
the age of Charlemagne his works were to be found in every cathedral and
monastic library in Western Europe. Historians and theologians relied on
him implicitly, incorporating large sections of his writings in their own
works. His astronomical calculations, his tables for the correct reckoning
of Easter, his *Martyrology* and his educational treatises remained for generations the standard and basic works on their subjects.

A. L. Maycock
HJ (April, 1935), p. 404

Lastly, there is the miracle of Bede's good Latin style. How exactly he
managed to escape the "Hisperic infection" cannot be explained. Aldhem
had caught it, though he had studied under Theodore at Canterbury. . . .
Nonetheless, thanks to his own good taste, to the sound Roman foundation
laid by Biscop or Ceolfrid, to the influence of Pope Gregory's writings and
to a northern feeling for simpler Latin, which is also apparent in the anonymous lives of Northumbrian saints, he somehow was able to set up a new
fashion of lucidity. . . .

Bede, like Theodore, was never acclaimed as a saint. But he was "the
master of the Middle Ages." From the first his writings were accepted as
the standard works on history, natural science, and grammar; and now,
while the earlier heroes of the Anglian race are mere names, or less than
names, Bede's is the first English mind which speaks to the modern world
fully and lucidly on a wide range of subjects.

R. H. Hodgkin
A History of the Anglo-Saxons, vol. I, 3rd ed.
(Oxford Univ. Pr., 1952), pp. 354-55

[I]t must . . . be remembered that it is probably in the eighth century that
the bulk of extant Old English poetry was composed. This poetry has its

roots in the heathen past, but little survives that is not Christian. Bede tells us how the inspiration came to Caedmon, a man of the *ceorl* class, to use the native metre for religious themes in the latter part of the seventh century, and how by the time Bede is writing he had been copied by many poets. Bede mentions expressly the didactic intention of Caedmon's work, and though only the hymn quoted in Bede manuscripts can confidently be assigned to this poet, much surviving Old English poetry is clearly intended to teach men the contents of Scripture and the duties of a Christian life. Its values for these purposes was realized by the missionaries to the Old Saxons, for it has long been recognized that the Old Saxon religious poetry, the *Heiland* and the fragmentary *Genesis* were inspired by English models, and their connexion with Liudger, who had studied under Alcuin at York, is becoming increasingly clear. But there is other religious poetry which is a more spontaneous expression of the poet's own religious emotion, notably the deeply moving poem known as the *Dream of the Rood,* and this personal note is visible in some of the work of a poet called Cynewulf, who lived in the later part of the eighth century or in the early ninth, while the poems called *The Wanderer* and *The Seafarer* . . . express the individual's response to the eternal truths in contrast to the temporal conditions of life.

Dorothy Whitelock
Introd., in *English Historical Documents*, ed. David C. Douglas,
vol. I (New York: Oxford Univ. Pr., 1955), p. 90

BEOWULF

650-750?

The author of *Beowulf* is by some scholars now believed to have been perhaps a chaplain in the service of a royal family, and one who lived in Northumbria or Mercia. Dates of his birth and death are unknown; some scholars believe he lived during 700-725; others date his life later into the eighth century.

The Manuscript: The *Beowulf* MS (Cotton Vitellius A. xv.) was one of those collected by Sir Robert Cotton. It was in Little Deans Yard, Westminster, when the fire which, in 1731, destroyed so many manuscripts took place, and was fortunately among those which were not fatally injured. In 1753, having spent some time in the old dormitory at Westminster, it was transferred to the British Museum. In 1705 Wanley, employed by Hickes, the Anglo-Saxon scholar, to make a catalogue of the old Northern books in the kingdom, discovered the poem of *Beowulf* in the Cottonian library and called it a *tractatus nobilissimus poeticè scriptus*. It is a parchment codex, and the handwriting of the two copyists is of the beginning of the tenth century. Thorkelin, a Danish scholar, had two copies of it made in 1786, and published the whole of it for the first time in 1815. This edition made the poem known, and it was discussed in

English and foreign reviews. Meantime, in 1805, Sharon Turner gave the first account of the poem in his history of the Anglo-Saxons. Turner again, in 1825, and Conybeare, in 1826, filled up that account and translated portions of *Beowulf* into English verse, and in 1833 and 1837 John M. Kemble edited and translated the whole of the poem and wrote historical prefaces. This scholarly book increased the interest of foreign scholars in the poem; since then, a great number of editions and translations have been published, and the essays, dissertations, articles, and notices on the poem and the subjects contained in it, fill a long list, and are written by English, French, German, Dutch, Danish and American scholars.

Stopford A. Brooke
The History of Early English Literature (1892), p. 12

Fr. Klaeber, *Beowulf and the Fight at Finnsburg,* 3rd ed. (1936), Supplements 1941, 1950; Charles L. Wrenn, ed., *Beowulf: With the Finnsburg Fragment* (1935); Julius Zupitza, ed., *Beowulf, with a Transliteration and Notes,* 2nd ed. (1959) (Facsimiles)

Charles W. Kennedy, tr., *Beowulf, the Oldest English Epic, Translated into Alliterative Verse* (1940); J. R. Clark, tr., *Beowulf and the Finnsburg Fragment,* rev. Charles L. Wrenn (1950) (prose)

Arthur G. Brodeur, *The Art of Beowulf* (1959); R. W. Chambers, *Beowulf: An Introduction to the Study of the Poem with a Discussion of the Stories of Offa and Finn,* 3rd ed., rev. Charles L. Wrenn (1959); Ritchie Girvan, *Beowulf and the Seventh Century* (1935)

The unique MS of *Beowulf* may be, and if possible should be, seen by the student in the British Museum. It is a good specimen of the elegant script of Anglo-Saxon times: "a book got up with some care," as if intended for the library of a nobleman or of a monastery. Yet this MS is removed from the date when the poem was composed and from the events which it narrates (so far as these events are historic at all) by periods of time approximately equal to those which separate us from the time when Shakespeare's *Henry V* was written, and when the battle of Agincourt was fought.

To try to penetrate the darkness of the five centuries which lie behind the extant MS by fitting together such fragments of illustrative information as can be obtained, and by using the imagination to bridge the gaps, has been the business of three generations of scholars distributed among the ten nations of Germanic speech. A whole library has been written around our poem, and the result is that this book cannnot be as simple as either writer or reader might have wished.

The story which the MS tells us may be summarized thus: Beowulf, a prince of the Geatas, voyages to Heorot, the hall of Hrothgar, king of the Danes; there he destroys a monster Grendel, who for twelve years has haunted the hall by night and slain all he found therein. When Grendel's mother in revenge makes an attack on the hall, Beowulf seeks her out and kills her also in her home beneath the waters. He then returns to his land with honour and is rewarded by his king Hygelac. Ultimately he himself becomes king of the Geatas, and fifty years later slays a dragon and is slain by it. The poem closes with an account of the funeral rites.

Fantastic as these stories are, they are depicted against a background of what appears to be fact. Incidentally, and in a number of digressions, we receive much information about the Geatas, Swedes, and Danes: all which information has an appearance of historic accuracy, and in some cases can be proved, from external evidence, to be historically accurate.

R. W. Chambers
Beowulf (Cambridge Univ. Pr., 1921), pp. 1-2

Some three centuries elapsed before the poem attained the extant form in which we now read it. What were its fortunes in the meantime? How often was it recopied and revised in other parts of Britain? Here evidence fails us; the varied dialectical forms are not, as they have sometimes been considered, trustworthy guides. By a series of fortunate chances *Beowulf* was spared in the Viking pillagings and burnings, and was ultimately put into the West-Saxon dialect in southern England, where it was copied, not far from the year 1000, by two careless scribes, and made a part of one of the manuscript codices which were the treasured possessions of the learned. The general characteristics of this final written form have been traced in an earlier chapter. The copying took place at a time when the lamp of Anglo-Saxon letters was burning low, when the traditions of native verse were kept alive by little original production, and the English spirit of the older days was enfeebled and irresolute. The age of Æthelred the Redeless was a sorry contrast to the glory of the Anglian kingdoms. Is it fanciful to imagine that the man for whom the final transcript of *Beowulf* was made saw, in its tragic tale of the vanishing splendors of great kingdoms and the extinction of royal houses, a reflection of the misfortunes of the English crown and the dangers assailing his native land, and, in its story of courageous struggles against heavy odds, a faint hope that his countrymen might win through in the end? The fulfilment was long delayed; but if the heroism of Harold at Hastings came to naught, the indomitable Anglo-Saxon temper so strikingly illustrated in *Beowulf* ultimately prevailed in England over all invaders, and proved the foundation of the greatness of the English nation.

William Witherle Lawrence
Beowulf and Epic Tradition (Cambridge, Mass.:
Harvard Univ. Pr., 1930), pp. 290-91

The subject of *Beowulf* is a conflict with two water monsters who are in turn despatched, and after a long interval a conflict with a dragon laying waste the country-side. It too is killed by the hero who, however, gets his own death in the encounter. Both conflicts, for the first, though double, is to be regarded as one, are set amid an historical environment at a definite time, and real people are introduced in person or by allusion. There are numerous references to historical events or events which profess to be historical, but the history is the frame and the background, and the canvas is occupied by a couple of folk-tales seemingly as old as humanity. We need not doubt that such subjects were cultivated from the beginning by the Germanic poet, and it is certain that they lingered on in the people's memory. Tales of dragons together with a belief in dragons survived till recent times, and the popular mind is apt to accept with credulity stories of water-monsters. The stories, moreover, are often attached to real persons and localized precisely in time and place. The habit is so well known that examples are superfluous.

The two folk-tales in *Beowulf* have parallels elsewhere. Several more or less close can be adduced for the dragon-conflict. Of greater interest is the striking parallel with the earlier conflict found in the Icelandic *Grettissaga*. In it we have the identical story with a different hero and in a different historical setting. There seems no doubt that the versions are independent, but that nevertheless the special form of the folk-tale is determined in both by a common source which cannot lie very far back. Differences in detail have developed, but these issue in part from the variant environment; in part they are due to a definitely rationalizing tendency more advanced in the later account. . . . I have spoken of a rationalizing tendency in *Grettissaga,* and we have, though in less measure, something similar in the poem. Someone has said that beast and monster stories take us back to the very heart of Germanic antiquity. They would if we could gather them in their primitive form, but in *Beowulf* we shall not find a primitive mentality, though the actual content may be unchanged. We have none of that attitude to the magical and supernatural which appears, for example, so strikingly in the Irish epic cycle *Táin Bó Cúalnge.* A changed outlook on life has left a deep impress on the folk-tale. Grendel and his dam may inherit cannabalistic features from the *eotonas* of old, but their position is explained and motivated in a manner to appeal to reason. Their outcast state has its root in descent from Cain, and the curse of Cain hangs heavy upon them. They are no longer embodied evil and destruction, motiveless malignity which men cannot explain, avoid, or appease. Everything about them has been reduced to the plane of reason and of experience, or at least all but one thing, that some of the limitations incident to humanity are removed, and the hero shares in part in the freedom from such limitations. We are, with few exceptions, in a world governed by the capacities and restrictions of human nature. To appreciate the distinction it is worth while to contrast Beowulf with the Irish hero Cuchulain in the *Táin Bó Cúalnge.*

Ritchie Girvan
Beowulf and the Seventh Century
(London: Methuen, 1935), pp. 57-59

Although the moralizing turn and also some of the maxims may be regarded as a common Germanic inheritance, the extent to which this feature as well as the fondness for introspection has been carried is distinctly Beowulfian and shows the didactic and emotional nature of the author himself. . . .

Although a poem of action, *Beowulf* is more than a narrative of notable events. Not that the author is lacking in the art of telling a story effectively. But a mere objective narration is not his chief aim. The poet is not satisfied with reciting facts, heroic and stirring though they be. Nor does he trouble to describe in a clear, concrete manner the outward appearance of the persons, even of the principal hero, though he sets forth, with eloquence, the striking impression he makes on others (lines 247ff., especially 369ff.). But he takes the keenest interest in the inner significance of the happenings, the underlying motives, the manifestation of character. He loses no opportunity of disclosing what is going on in the minds of his actors. He is ever ready to analyze the thoughts and feelings of Beowulf and Hrothgar, the Danes and the Geats, Grendel and his kind, even down to the sea monsters (lines 549, 562, 1431) and the birds of prey (lines 3024ff). Their intentions, resolutions, expectations, hopes, fears, longings, rejoicings, and mental sufferings engage his constant attention. In a moment of intensest action, such as the combat with Grendel, the state of mind of the characters is carefully taken note of.

Fr. Klaeber
Beowulf and the Fight at Finnsburg, 3rd ed.
(Boston: D. C. Heath, 1936), pp. lvi, lviii-lix

There is an historical explanation of the state of *Beowulfiana* that I have referred to. And that explanation is important, if one would venture to criticize the critics. A sketch of the history of the subject is required. But I will here only attempt, for brevity's sake, to present my view of it allegorically. As it set out upon its adventures among the modern scholars *Beowulf* was christened by Wanley Poesis—*Poeseos Anglo-Saxonicæ egregium exemplum*. But the fairy godmother later invited to superintend its fortunes was Historia. And she brought with her Philologia, Mythologia, Archaeologia, and Laographia. Excellent ladies. But where was the child's namesake? Poesis was usually forgotten; occasionally admitted by a side-door; sometimes dismissed upon the door-step. *"The Beowulf,"* they said "is hardly an affair of yours, and not in any case a protégé that you could be proud of. It is an historical document. Only as such does it interest the superior culture of to-day." And it is as an historical document that it has been examined and dissected. Though ideas as to the nature and quality of the history and information embedded in it have changed much since Thorkelin called it *De Danorum Rebus Gestis,* this has remained steadily

true. In still recent pronouncements this view is explicit. In 1925 Professor
Archibald Strong translated *Beowulf* into verse; but in 1921 he had declared: *"Beowulf* is the picture of a whole civilization, of the Germania
which Tacitus describes. The main interest which the poem has for us is thus
not a purely literary interest. *Beowulf* is an important historical document.". . .

Nearly all the censure, and most of the praise, that has been bestowed
on *The Beowulf* has been due either to the belief that it was something
that it was *not*—for example, primitive, pagan, Teutonic, an allegory (political or mythical), or most often, an epic; or to disappointment at the discovery that it was itself and not something that the scholar would have
liked better—for example, a heathen heroic lay, a history of Sweden, a
manual of Germanic antiquities, or a Nordic *Summa Theologica*.

J. R. R. Tolkien
Proceedings of the British Academy (1936), pp. 246-48

Reflective Englishmen of the seventh and eighth centuries, living under
the transforming influence of classical and Christian ideas, must have satisfied a special need by revaluating their Germanic patrimony in terms of
the new culture. In that process the Teutonic heritage naturally took on an
added lustre wherever it lent itself to Christian interpretation. *Beowulf* more
fully than any other English poem reflects that effort to assimilate and re-
appraise whereby the Germanic tradition from the Continent was ennobled
by the new theology, as by a light flashed backward into the heroic past.
Thus the career of the Danish king Heremod becomes an exemplum for a
Christian homily on pride; Grendel, creature of northern fantasy, is placed
in a Biblical lineage of evil reaching back to the first murder. The poet
probably recognized, however, that his illumination of the past stopped
short of perfect fusion of new and old, to say nothing of historical fidelity . . . .

As Klaeber comments, the heroic legends in the hands of the Christian
poet "assumed a markedly edifying character which requires to be analyzed
and explained." The solution is to be sought not, I think, in any dominant
message that the writer sought to convey, but rather in assumptions governing his vision of the past, imaginative moulds into which history or legend
must be poured before either might become significant or viable for him.

Among the beliefs that underlie the poet's treatment of his heathen narratives, the most inclusive is the Christian doctrine of Providence, the conception of God as having governed all races of mankind since the creation,
and as bestowing all favors, natural or supernatural, that men enjoy. Few
would challenge this truism concerning the poet's philosophy, notwithstanding his disturbing references to *wyrd*. But the orthodox view of Providence known to the English converts also included the dogma of election
and grace, which analysts of *Beowulf* have neglected. I wish to suggest

here that the theory of grace, alongside the doctrine of Providence, conditioned the poet's view of the past and influenced his interpretation of events and agents in his stories. Actual proof being out of the question, the only tests at hand are harmony with the prevailing tenor of the poem and congeniality to the intellectual climate in which it flowered.

Marie Padgett Hamilton
PMLA (June, 1946), pp. 309-11

This poem holds a unique place in the literature of Europe. Its fundamentally Christian orientation is now widely recognized, and needs no discussion in this paper. Nevertheless, one cannot properly classify it as a religious poem in any strict or narrow sense. The action of the poem takes place in a part of ancient Germania and at a time thought of by the poet as ancient and therefore pagan. The characters are not Christians and know nothing of Christianity. The hero is a virtuous pagan. He is made as Christ-like as the setting permits, but all his virtues can be explained quite naturally as growing out of the heroic ideals of conduct traditional among the English as among the other Germanic peoples.

The monkish author, devout Christian though he is, finds much to admire in the pagan cultural tradition which, as an Englishman, he inherited from ancient Germania. It is his purpose to glorify this heroic heritage, this spiritual heirloom, this precious birthright of his nation. He accomplishes his purpose by laying stress upon those things in Germanic tradition which agree with Christianity or at any rate do not clash seriously with the Christian faith . . . .

Let us now go back to the *Beowulf* poet. It would hardly do to think of him as an eighth-century humanist, born 600 years before his time, since his interest lay, not in the philosophy of life of classical antiquity but in that of Germanic antiquity. Nevertheless his case is not unlike Petrarch's, in that both authors, Christians though they were, sought and found spiritual as well as stylistic values in a pagan literary culture: each in the particular culture which was his own by inheritance. In this matter the *Beowulf* poet did not stand alone. The author of *Deor* taught the virtue of patience under affliction by exempla drawn from pagan Germanic story, and the author of *Maldon* sang a Christian lord and dright who fought and died for the faith, inspired and sustained by the same heroic ideals that their heathen forefathers had cherished. These ideals held their own to the very end of Old English times, and made many a man a hero in life and death not merely by force of ordinary tradition but also, and in large measure, by force of poetic tradition. The scops kept the old ideals strong by singing the heroes of the past. The very attack which Alcuin made on heroic story tells us that in his day the old songs were still sung even in the citadels of English Christian piety: the monasteries. Such performances became impossible, of course, after the monastic reform in the latter part of the tenth century, a reform which swept Western Europe and established a more rigorous pattern of monkish life wherever it went. But the English monk of that same century who composed the poem on the Battle of Maldon still knew and loved the traditional poetry of his people, and we may be sure that he was one of many.

Kemp Malone
ES (December, 1948), pp. 162-63, 164

One may reach the conclusion that the audience of *Beowulf* was a Christian company, and one which admitted that vengeance, in unavoidable circumstances and carried out in accordance with the law, was a binding duty. This second consideration is of no help at all in our dating of the poem; but the first, its Christianity, is. The depth of its Christian knowledge is for this purpose far more important than that of the poet himself, for his Christian education might be exceptional; it would be unsafe to argue from it to the general conditions of his day. Nor would the extent of the audience's Christianity be of much assistance in dating the poem if there were any reason to suppose that the poet was addressing himself to ecclesiastics alone. My choice of the term "audience" has already indicated that I do not believe that *Beowulf* was composed merely for people who could read, which is almost equivalent to saying, for the clergy. Nothing that is recorded of the ecclesiastics of Anglo-Saxon England lends countenance to a view that they were in the habit of composing long poems on secular themes solely for circulation among themselves. . . .

And now, perhaps, I may be allowed to indulge in speculation on how the poet wished to affect these men, and to consider why he chose for his central subject a story of monster-slaying, using heroic stories merely as illustration or as background. It is no longer usual for scholars to spend time regretting that he did so, or accusing him of a perverted sense of proportion. He was composing for men of his own day, and he doubtless had good reason for his choice of theme. Nor is it likely that it was forced on him because all the good "historical" themes had been used up. His main story would be as real to his audience as would have been an account of the strife for the Danish throne among the members of the Scylding dynasty; and in the course of it, the poet has placed the race of monsters in relationship to a Christian universe, and has shown that they can be overcome by human beings of courage and fortitude who fight them with faith in God. He has shown that humanity is not left helpless in the hands of the evil powers. That was no trivial theme to the men of that day. . . .

I do not, however, believe that the poet's intention was to pander to his audience's taste, in that he expected it to be more interested in human histories of the clash of personalities, of the conflict between ambition and duty, between affection and duty, between conflicting duties; nor that he was himself irresistibly drawn to such subjects and thus inserted references to them on the slightest provocation. If this were so, why should he have failed to emphasize similar situations in his hero's career? . . .

The tales he recalls are well known to his audience, but perhaps he is putting an unusual type of emphasis on them, stressing the suffering caused to innocent persons rather than the triumph of successful warfare and vengeance.

Dorothy Whitelock
The Audience of Beowulf (Oxford Univ. Pr., 1951),
pp. 19, 95-97

It seems generally agreed that *Beowulf* is a poem essentially about a hero and heroism. I believe that the elaboration of these important concepts in the poem is based on the old, widely recognized heroic ideal of *sapientia et fortitudo,* which so far has received only incidental attention in *Beowulf* studies; and that the *sapientia et fortitudo* ideal is accordingly the most basic theme in the poem, around which the other major themes are arranged and to which they relate in various ways. So far as I can see, this interpretation generally complements rather than opposes the most important *Beowulf* criticism of the past twenty-odd years. While it is perhaps no great novelty in the literature of any age or race to find an epic hero wise and brave, the formulary use of the *sapientia et fortitudo* ideal in *Beowulf,* as I hope to show it, seems to me to speak for a high degree of consciousness in its employment. . . .

I believe that in the *sapientia et fortitudo* theme itself we may find "the precise point at which an imagination, pondering old and new, was kindled" —that the poet has used this old ideal as an area of synthesis between Christianity and Germanic paganism. In a broad way, he seems first to draw on both traditions primarily as they relate to *sapientia et fortitudo*; and secondly, within this circumscribed area he seems to emphasize those aspects of each tradition that can be made reasonably compatible with the viewpoint of the other—somewhat like Dante's more complex synthesis of classical and Christian morality in the *Inferno*. . . .

We may notice in passing that a core of this kind in the poem helps account for some of its apparent large ambiguities, like the co-existence of eternal salvation and earthly glory as the goals of human life. If Beowulf is deliberately made to behave wisely and bravely according to both codes, then the very ambiguity of both the *sothfæstra dom* [judgment of the righteous] and earthly *lof* [praise, fame, glory] is not only relevant but in a way demanded. This same principle may perhaps help account for the roles of God and *Wyrd* in the poem, with emphasis on Beowulf's wise acknowledgement of the power of each.

R. E. Kaske
SP (July 1958), pp. 423, 426-27

This is, indeed, the tragedy of Beowulf: in all that human strength, courage, and wisdom may achieve, he is victorious; but against God's foreknowledge neither human might nor human wisdom may prevail. This is precisely what the poet tells us, and at a moment of high significance: Beowulf is dead; Wiglaf, unwilling to believe that the end is come, tries vainly to bring him back to consciousness. The poet comments: "He could not, greatly as he wished it, retain life in the chieftain, nor set aside anything ordained of God; the judgment of God insisted upon governing the deeds of each of men—as He still does!" (lines 2855-59.) Beowulf's death in victory was the work of Fate, operating as God's agent, to justify God's foreknowledge that the Geats are to be conquered in consequence of the hero's death.

This is not the first time in the poem that we have been reminded of the overruling power of God. It was God's will which had made it impossible for Hrothgar to approach his own throne after nightfall (lines 168-169); Beowulf, in his first speech to Hrothgar, had made the point that whichsoever is defeated in his fight with Grendel "must trust to the judgment of the Lord.". . .

The essential Christianity of the poet's thought resides, then, not merely in the piety of his utterances, or in that expressed by his personages, but in his persistent illustration of this underlying principle, that God's foreknowledge and God's will control all things, and control them for the best. There is no conflict here between God's foreknowledge and man's free will: as Hrothgar tells us in his long monologue, God is all good, and distributes all benefits in accordance with His wisdom; but through pride and covetousness man works evil; only through "eternal counsels" and through temperance may man win to happiness. Beowulf, with full freedom of will, sets out against the dragon with the noble purpose of preserving his people; but God's foreknowledge that the Geats are soon to be destroyed requires the hero's death. Although Beowulf has no clear knowledge that he is to perish, Fate touches him with feyness, a kind of instinctive apprehension of death; and in the face of this he goes, with unshaken fortitude, to his end, foredoomed by divine foreknowledge.

Yet his soul departs "to seek the judgment of the righteous"—a pretty clear indication that the poet thought of his hero as among the saved. . . .

The Christianity of the poem, then, is much more than "coloring." It manifests itself in the constant affirmation and illustration of a principle which underlies all the dealings of God with men. The primary sin of man against God is pride: through pride Heremod is brought low; through pride (*for wlenco*) Hygelac suffers death in Frisia; Hrothgar, in his monologue, attributes the persecutions of Grendel to Hrothgar's own pride, and he warns Beowulf against this sin. This sin motivates the envy of Unferth, and the usurpation and murder of kin of Hrothulf. From it Beowulf is free, and Beowulf is saved. God's will rules all creation; God's foreknowledge determines Beowulf's victories, failures, and death. Well is it with him who after death—like Beowulf—is permitted to seek peace in the embraces of the Father.

Arthur Gilchrist Brodeur
The Art of Beowulf (Berkeley: Univ. California Pr., 1959),
pp. 244-46

There are really two poems: one about Beowulf and the Danes, the other, roughly half as long, about Beowulf and the Geats. They have in common the same hero, first as a youth then as an old man, overcoming first two water-monsters and later a fire-drake. The earlier victories appear to be successful, though in delivering the Danes from Grendel and his Mother the hero has left them a prey to subsequent disaster; he has established his renown, which was paramount, but as the savior of a nation in distress his achievement was only temporary. His later victory has also a tragic irony: it brings his own death and so opens the way to disaster for his own people. Thus the two poems, or parts of the same poem, share a single theme: that beyond the hero's bravery there are forces which he cannot subdue. Valor is vanity in the end. So much any reflective reader may see.

The plan of Part I looks simple: the Danish setting, the hero's journey and reception, his fight and the celebration of his victory, his second fight and the following celebration, his return home and report of his adventures. But such is the poet's chosen method that he disguises the symmetry by making his concluding point (Hrothgar's plan to heal a feud with the Heathobards) look like an irrelevance. This is the result of pursuing two themes at once, the plight of the Danes and their deliverance by the hero—with the necessary interchange of background and foreground. For the rest, having not much story to tell and meaning to tell none *as* story, the poet took his raw materials from the old "lays," and combining them with history and with folklore created something new, not exactly a heroic poem (for there is less of that sheer delight in man-to-man fighting than we expect in heroic poems; compare the tone of the Finnsburgh Fragment with the poet's treatment of the same situation) and certainly not an epic, but a modification or adaptation to suit himself—a mixture of pagan matter treated in a somewhat non-pagan manner and of heroic matter from the legendary and historic past along with court ceremonies as he understood them. The actual fighting, including Beowulf's recapitulation, occupies less than one-tenth of the whole.

Part II, with less than a thousand lines, is another poem with the same hero. No significant differences in vocabulary, syntax, style or meter have been found, and in the face of an improbable assumption of two men writing at about the same time in the same, or almost the same manner, it must be taken for granted that both poems are by the same author. There are small linkages, but the subject and planning of the two Parts are different; there is a wholly new cast of characters, the emphasis is shifted, the polarity is altered. Part I had a beginning, a middle, and an end. Part II is less simple, it is more confused, the so-called digressions occupy relatively much more space (besides being more puzzling to the modern reader), and the whole is more gloomy, not only with the hero's death but also with the presage of disaster for his race.

Paull F. Baum
PQ (October, 1960), pp. 390-91

[Alan J. Bliss, *The Metre of Beowulf*, Oxford, 1958,] argues that the Heusler-Pope interpretations of Old English scansion, based on a chronometric assumption, are untenable; that Old English rhythm is more likely based on ordinary prose rhythm (like its musical contemporary, Gregorian chant); that the basic Old English verse rhythm is $\angle$ x (x) $\angle$ x (underlying 40 per cent of the verses in *Beowulf*); that if the stresses are shifted forwards or backwards only four other patterns are possible; and that these five patterns (the basic and the possible displacements) explain the types of rhythm which actually occur in the verse and no others. These types are those advanced by Sievers, and Bliss's theory is a return to, and an expansion of, Sievers' method of scansion. *An important book*, containing a complete index to the scansion of *Beowulf* and other relevant statistical data. For a detailed review, see W. P. Lehmann, *JEGP*, LIX(1960), 137-42.

Stanley B. Greenfield
Annotated bibliography supplement for David M. Zesmer,
*Guide to English Literature: From Beowulf through Chaucer
and Medieval Drama* (New York:
Barnes and Noble, 1961), p. 299

There is perhaps no other epic poem in Germanic literature in which anticipation has been so constantly used as in *Beowulf*. It is so characteristic a feature in the narrative element of the poem that it has been noted, of course, by almost every *Beowulf* editor and commentator. To quote one of our living authorities on *Beowulf*: "It is not a little remarkable that in the account of the three great fights of the hero, care has been taken to state the outcome of the struggle in advance."

But although carefully and frequently noticed, this trait has called for rather a modest amount of comment in comparison, say, with the use of repetition. It has hardly been considered as raising a real problem, whereas repetition, leading to apparent inconsistencies, has sometimes been eagerly fought over, the more so in that it provided arguments for pro- and anti-patchwork theorists. Indeed, the prevalent attitude towards anticipation is simply to regard it as an interesting device, remarkable for the fondness with which the *Beowulf* poet handles it, but common among heroic poems. . . . Nevertheless, is there not another kind of approach, allowing us to form an estimate of the use of anticipations from a different angle, in closer relation to the poem itself? Is it enough to think, what is quite true, that "evidently disregard of the element of suspense was not considered a defeat in story telling," and leave it at that, or should we think that the poet made such a lavish use of anticipation because it is very common in Germanic poetry? Or should we not perhaps inquire whether it has an actual relevance to the individual *Beowulf* poem as a work of art? In other words, is it possible to account for that remarkable use of anticipation in the poem strictly on artistic grounds, independent of a common tradition? . . .

For the sake of clearness we may consider that there are two main groups of anticipations, if we classify them according to the kind of events predicted. In the first group we have anticipations of events which we actually see happening later on in the poem, in accordance with the prediction. The second group consists of "allusive" anticipations (if we may call them so), *i.e.* anticipations of events which are supposed to happen in a near or distant future, but are never set forth in the course of the poem; they may refer, of course, to facts probably well known to the reader (or the audience) of *Beowulf*, but, in contrast with those of the first group, there is no single confirmation of them anywhere in the poem, apart from further allusions. This evidently involves a slight difference in the artistic value of the two kinds of anticipation which, we shall see, justifies the decision adopted here.

Adrien Bonjour
Twelve Beowulf Papers: 1940-1960, with Additional Comments
(Geneva: Librarie E. Droz. for Facultées des Lettres,
Université de Neuchâtel, 1962), pp. 11-12

Both epic and dramatic tragedy derive from and thrive on a tension between skepticism and faith; yet the tensions differ. They reflect the ages in which these genres predominate. Epic flourishes in the last days or in the aftermath of a nation or Weltanschauung, not in the heyday: "At such times a man surveys the recent past with its record of dazzling successes and asks if they can last; he analyzes its strengths, announces its importance, urges its continuance." [Bowra, *From Virgil to Milton*, p. 28] Dramatic tragedy flourishes at the peak of an era in which man has been apotheosized, but in which the events of the time give rise to doubts and uncertainties about his ultimate control of matters. Then man surveys his experiences, records his failures, and wonders at his presumption and audacity. A note of melancholy, of the elegiac, throbs through the tale of the epic achievement; of questioning wonder and asseveration through the dramatic enactments of defeat.

If the differences suggested in this paper have any validity, as I hope they have, then perhaps the question of whether *Beowulf* is epic, or heroic elegy, or heroic tragedy becomes academic.

Stanley B. Greenfield
"Beowulf and Epic Tragedy," *Studies in Old English Literature in Honor of Arthur G. Brodeur* (Eugene: Univ. Oregon Pr., 1963), p. 105

Unlike the twentieth century, the Middle Ages liked positive oaths. We know that, in contrast to modern servicemen, Germanic warriors of the early Middle Ages commonly took an oath to avenge their leader or die in the attempt if he should fall in battle; and the testimony of the *Anglo-Saxon Chronicle* suggests that they occasionally kept their word. In the Parker MS, for instance, the entry for the year 757 records that, after killing Cynewulf in a surprise attack, Prince Cyneheard generously offered to let his victim's followers go free; they, however, unanimously chose to fight until death rather than to survive their fallen leader without trying to avenge him. . . . *The Battle of Maldon*, likewise, reminds us that, as late as the end of the tenth century, Anglo-Saxon warriors swore in the hall heroic oaths which they were expected to keep on the battlefield. . . .

But the heroic oath was by no means one-sided. On the contrary, just as the warriors were expected to sacrifice themselves to avenge their leader, he in turn was expected to afford them all the protection in his power; he was their formal protector, their *æðelinga helm*.

We should not be surprised that the heroic oath is the principal source of action in the three greatest secular epics of the Middle Ages: the Anglo-Saxon *Beowulf*, the Old French *Chanson de Roland*, and the Middle High German *Nibelungenlied*. We should likewise not be surprised that it brings about the destruction of the virtuous character in each of the three poems.

Boewulf is beyond question the most virtuous character in the Anglo-Saxon epic; indeed, it has been convincingly argued that he is the only one to live up to the ideal of *sapientia et fortitudo*. The narrative makes him the only warrior honest enough to deserve Wealhtheow's confidence when she fears for the future of her sons (lines 1126b-31b) and wise enough to rule the Geats in peace for fifty years (lines 2207-9). We are told that his soul goes to Heaven (lines 2819b-20), and the concluding lines of the poem explicitly describe him as the most virtuous of all possible kings. . . .

The action of the first half of the poem comes about as the immediate result of his pledge to help out Hrothgar (lines 199b-201) and of his formal boast to fight the troll Grendel alone and barehanded (lines 429-45a; 601b-3a); the action of the second half of the poem comes about as the ultimate result of the implicit oath which requires him to act as his people's *æðelinga helm* like any other Germanic king, and his eventual destruction comes about as the clear result of his insistence upon carrying out this oath to the letter (lines 3532b-35a).

Alain Renoir
"The Heroic Oath in *Beowulf,* the *Chanson de Roland,* and the *Nibelungenlied,*" *Studies in Old English Literature in Honor of Arthur G. Brodeur* (Eugene: Univ. Oregon Pr., 1963) pp. 237-40

Finnsburg

The Finnsburg Fragment was discovered two centuries ago in the library of Lambeth Palace by George Hickes. It was written on a single leaf, which was transcribed and published by Hickes: but the leaf is not now to be found. This is to be regretted for reasons other than sentimental, since Hickes' transcript is far from accurate.

The Fragment begins and breaks off in the middle of a line: but possibly not much has been lost at the beginning. For the first lines of the Fragment, as preserved, reveal a well-loved opening motive—the call to arms within the hall, as the watcher sees the foes approach. . . .

Never, we are told, was there a better defence than that of the sixty champions within the hall. "Never did retainers repay the sweet mead better than his bachelors did unto Hnæf. For five days they fought, so that none of the men at arms fell: but they held the doors." After a few more lines the piece breaks off.

There are many textual difficulties here. But these, for the most part, do not affect the actual narrative, which is a story of clear and straightforward fighting. It is when we try to fit this narrative into relationship with the Episode in *Beowulf* that our troubles begin. Within the Fragment itself one difficulty only need at present be mentioned. Guthlaf is one of the champions defending the hall. Yet the leader of the assault, Garulf, is spoken of as Guthlaf's son. Of course it is possible that we have here a tragic incident parallel to the story of Hildebrand and Hadubrand: father and son may have been separated through earlier misadventures, and now find themselves engaged on opposite sides. This would harmonize with the atmosphere of the Finnsburg story, which is one of slaughter breaking out among men near of kin, so that afterwards an uncle and a nephew are burnt on the same pyre. And it has been noted that Garulf rushes to the attack only after he has asked "Who holds the door?" and has learnt that it is Sigeferth: Guthlaf had gone to the opposite door. Can Garulf's question mean that he knows his father Guthlaf to be inside the hall, and wishes to avoid conflict with him? Possibly; but I do not think we can argue much from this double appearance of the name Guthlaf. It is possible that the occurrence of Guthlaf as Garulf's father is simply a scribal error. For, puzzling as the tradition of Finnsburg everywhere is, it is peculiarly puzzling in its proper names, which are mostly given in forms that seem to have undergone some alteration.

R. W. Chambers
Beowulf (Cambridge Univ. Pr., 1921), pp. 245-47

Early scholars played with the idea of inserting the Fragment or selected portions of it into *Beowulf* as an essential part of the story. None would assent to that plan in these days, but perhaps most are still sufficiently under its influence to postulate the existence and the poet's use of a lay identical with the Fragment in its complete form. Protest has been rightly made against the use of quotation marks and attempts to make the lay begin at this line or that. In that sense the lay begins nowhere in *Beowulf*; the poet passes into an individual narrative, introduced by a string of allusions in accordance with the habitual method, and the content of his lengthy account is not to be reconciled with that of the Fragment or any single lay. A lay in Teutonic antiquity normally dealt with one incident, exploit, or adventure. On the scale in which the fight is given we should have an embryonic epic. Here is a series of happenings, casually connected and issuing in distinct and important incidents, themselves fit subjects for complete lays. It is further true and obvious that the story is regarded and told from a single point of view, that of the retainers defending the hall; the opposing party is just background to the picture. Nothing is said of Finn and nothing of Hildeburg, nothing explicit or implicit of the cause of the outbreak, and not a word about treachery.

If we are to understand the Episode I believe we must approach it on the aesthetic side. That its place is the deliberate effect of a conscious art is a belief which is insistent in my mind and as constant as the conviction that design governs the whole poem. That is what makes it so astonishing a performance, there our poet has his claim to greatness and is most original. I have called *Beowulf* an epic, and epic is the only acceptable term; from the Teutonic and Anglo-Saxon lays which preceded it, it differs as much in method as in content. We speak loosely of epic breadth, meaning perhaps a certain largeness and leisureliness in design and execution. There is more than that, a composite background against which the tale stands out in relief. It depicts a society, it has a sense of atmosphere, a suggestion of fateful events unfolding and appreciation of dramatic values. These are matters of content which I dismiss briefly because I wish to enlarge on method as touching our problem more nearly. Like all poets he has the design clear in his mind, but as the situation is more complicated than in the lay—not the story which may be simple enough—his method is different. He has an eye which looks not only forward but back, and the governing necessity is to work up his effects, motivate his situations and relate them to the general scheme. . . . It is not too much to say that the preparation is more moving than the physical struggle which follows and was by the nature of the case unavoidable. It is dismissed briefly. Some of the other matters are worth more detailed discussion. Consider the art of Beowulf's report to Hygelac and the whole scene at the Geatic court. Some have argued that the return of Beowulf is based on a precedent lay, but that can hardly be true. There is no centre to it and no issue, unless we can accept as such the recognition of Beowulf's merit at the end. In it there is and can be nothing doing, for it is all explanatory of things outside itself. Plainly we have an invention of the poet, a new thing in Teutonic poetry, a tale retold. Thus its character and content is determined. The account of the exploit is general and the hero minimizes it on the whole, as is natural in one of his modest demeanour, but he enlivens it with new and interesting detail which is strikingly in place at the court of Hygelac.

Ritchie Girvan
Proceedings of the British Academy (1941), pp. 10-11, 14-15

SUTTON HOO

At the same time, the close linkage between Sweden and England is not just one of casual trading; contact, for the secondary pieces, such as gold buckle, show the Swedish traditions transmitted into English forms. And yet in the ship-burial, places of high honour were given to the ancient Swedish pieces, which were carefully refurbished for the ceremony. This close interlocking of Swedish and English traditions for at least a century makes impossible the suggestion that it could have been a memorial to a visiting Swede. As we have already seen, the cenotaph must have been in honour of an East Anglian king, Æthelhere being the most probable choice. But the Swedish past is none the less real and the status of this Swedish ancestor was royal. If then Wuffa—and perhaps his father, Wehha—be seen as an adventurous Swedish prince who had gathered around himself a largely Danish war-band, we have just what is needed to explain both the Swedish links shown by the royal burial and the Danish influences visible in the grave-goods of the Sandlings commonalty, which also show evidences of Anglicisation. The continued contacts with the Baltic shores also confirm the retention of seafaring habits by these settlers, habits which we have seen were discarded by the earlier Anglian settlers when once they had found their new homes. All these conclusions may be reached from a study of the archaeological evidence of the Suffolk graves. And when we turn to *Beowulf*, though this is but a "heroic" story blending fact and fiction, there is in its background of history and its choice of heroic figures just that evidence needed to explain the reason for this early Scandinavian migration and to place in his former royal setting its leading actor who became the eponym of his English descendants.

Charles Green
Sutton Hoo: The Excavation of a Royal Ship-Burial
(London: Merlin Pr., 1963), p. 137

In the eighteen years since the discovery of the Sutton Hoo ship-cenotaph a quite considerable literature of descriptive material and various discussion has been published. This is conveniently listed up to 1954 in F. P. Magoun Jr.'s *Chronological Bibliography* in *Speculum*, vol. XXIX of that year. Since then, in three successive years, the fullest cultural and historical background has been provided in the monumental *Herrschaftszeichen und Staats-symbolik* of P. E. Schramm and his contributors in the 3 parts of vol. XIII of the *Schriften der Monumenta Germaniae Historica*. An admirable popular account of the actual course of the findings by C. W. Phillips has appeared in Bruce-Mitford's *Recent Archaeological Excavations in Britain* (London, 1956). Miss Evison's study of *Early Anglo-Saxon Inlaid Metalwork* in the *Antiquaries' Journal* for 1955 provides a useful addition to the background for the study of the traces of silver wire-work discernible on the Sutton Hoo helmet, and makes clearer indirectly the remarkable parallel between the helmet of Beowulf [ll. 1030-31] with its *walu wirum bewunden,* and that of Sutton Hoo. . . .

It may now seem appropriate to ask what new light the discoveries at Sutton Hoo may throw on the still quite unsolved problems of the date and place of the composition of *Beowulf.* Sune Lindqvist, in his now famous article "Sutton Hoo and Beowulf" . . . looks for the explanation of the apparent confusions and anachronisms in the poet's account of the passing of Scyld Scefing and of the funeral rites of Beowulf himself in the idea that phenomena like the Sutton Hoo ship-burial were still remembered at the time when the poem was composed. . . .

Such a view would tend (a) to place the date of the composition of *Beowulf* as early as possible; and (b) to suggest a search for the exact connexion between the making of the poem and the royal house of East-Anglia. At the beginning of the eighth century, the frequently accepted date for *Beowulf*, there would still have been living old men who could remember that public burial of the Sutton Hoo treasures whose actuality the British Coroner's Inquest of Aug. 14th, 1939, had accepted as fact. So that whether we accept the statement of Nennius that the house of the Wuffingas was founded in East-Anglia by Wehha, Wuffa's father, or the implication of Bede that it was Wuffa himself who was the first Anglo-Saxon East-Anglian king, it would be a legitimate inference that there was a real link between *Beowulf* and East Anglia.

C. L. Wrenn
"Sutton Hoo and Beowulf," quoted in *An Anthology of Beowulf Criticism*, ed. Lewis E. Nicholson (South Bend, Ind.: Univ. Notre Dame Pr., 1963), pp. 311, 325-26

CAEDMON*
ca. 657-80

Almost nothing known of his life, except what Bede tells the reader of him. Caedmon's *Hymn* is the only extant work today still generally accredited to him. The *Hymn* is found in several Northumbrian and West Saxon manuscripts and is paraphrased by Bede in Latin. The large body of poems ascribed to Caedmon is now generally credited to imitators and disciples of Caedmon, who are known as the Caedmonian school of poets.

George P. Krapp and Elliott V. K. Dobbie, eds., *The Anglo-Saxon Poetic Records* (1931-1953), 6 vols., see vol. I, *The Junius Manuscript*; A. H. Smith, ed., *Three Northumbrian Poems* (1953)
Charles W. Kennedy, ed. and tr., *The Caedmon Poems* (1916, repr. 1965); Robert K. Gordon, ed. and tr., *Anglo-Saxon Poetry* (rev. 1954) (prose)
Charles L. Wrenn, *The Poetry of Caedmon* (1948)

In the process of destructive criticism that has gradually nibbled away the body of poetry first ascribed to Caedmon, the *Hymn* alone has endured challenge. In the case of this poem the weight of critical opinion is in favour of crediting Caedmonian authorship. The *Hymn* has been preserved to us, aside from the Latin version of Bede, in a Northumbrian version, and in a West Saxon version in the English translation of Bede's *Ecclesiastical History* which is usually accredited to Alfred. The question has of course been raised in connection with this hymn whether the Northumbrian poem, written at the end of a manuscript of Bede's *Ecclesiastical History*, is to be considered an authentic poem or a translation of Bede's Latin version. . . . On the whole, the judgement of critical opinion has been that in the Northumbrian version of the *Hymn* we have a genuine bit, perhaps the only genuine bit remaining, of the work of Caedmon.

Charles W. Kennedy, tr.
The Caedmon Poems (London: George Routledge, 1916), pp. xxi-xxii

Cædmon's *Hymn*: The name *Cædmon* is of British origin and this has been taken to imply that Cædmon himself was a Briton or of British extraction.

---

*The spelling of Caedmon has been normalized. It is reproduced with a ligature, Cædmon, when spelled in this manner in the original passage.

But the survival of such British personal names in Anglian Northumbria was not uncommon and all that they show is that there had once been a fairly close contact between the native Britons and the invading Angles in that district.

The only biographical information we have about Cædmon is recorded in Bede's *Historia Ecclesiastica* (Book IV. cap. xxiv). There we learn that in the monastery of Hild (abbess 657-80) at *Strenæshalc* a certain brother had lived in the secular habit until he was well advanced in years, never having learned anything of the art of versifying, and, lacking that skill, he usually left those entertainments (at which for the sake of mirth each should sing) as his turn came round. On one such occasion he went out to the stable where that night he was in charge of the horses and at the proper time he went to sleep. "But someone appeared to him in his sleep and addressing him by name said, 'Cædmon, sing me something.' But he replying said, 'I know not how to sing; that is why I left the entertainment and came here, for I could not sing.' He who spoke with him then said, 'Nevertheless, you shall sing.' He replied, 'What must I sing?' And the other said, 'Sing of the beginnings of created things.' Thereupon Cædmon began to sing to the praise of God verses he had never heard." Here Bede gives a paraphrase of the *Hymn* and adds that, on waking, Cædmon remembered all that he had sung. In the morning he related this to the steward, and after being taken to the abbess he was commanded to tell of his dream and to repeat the verses; it was concluded that heavenly grace had been conferred upon him and the abbess instructed him to enter the monastic life. He was then taught sacred history and this he converted into the most harmonious verse. . . .

The main fact that Cædmon composed the *Hymn* there is no need to doubt, for in more recent times it has not been uncommon for peasants to compose verse of great merit in their native dialect, but the originality is less in the verse-forms than in the subject matter and diction. The supernatural explanation of Cædmon's poetic inspiration was probably suggested by Bede or by Bede's informants or by other stories, to show why an aged farmhand had been endowed with the faculty of composing verse. Yet doubt of a divine inspiration does not imply that neither the poet nor his work was real. . . .

In its relationship with the rest of Old English poetry Cædmon's *Hymn* appears to display no great originality, for, though it is technically accurate, nine or more of its eighteen half-lines can be paralleled in other poems. But in Cædmon's time when Northumbria had been converted to Christianity for only half a century these phrases belonging to Christian poetry could scarcely have become conventional, as they certainly were in later Old English; on the contrary, the poem represents the beginnings of such a diction and its freshness and originality must have been felt a generation or more after its composition; no mere assembling of clichés would have called for inspiration, divine or otherwise.

A. H. Smith, ed.
Introd., in *Three Northumbrian Poems* (London:
Methuen, 1933), pp. 10-11, 14-15

The justification for treating these two poems together [Cædmon's *Hymn* and Bede's *Death Song*] . . . lies in the homogeneity of their manuscript sources and their common association with the name of the Venerable Bede. Although Cædmon's *Hymn*, in its original Anglo-Saxon form, is not an integral part of the *Historia Ecclesiastica*, a Latin translation of it was inserted by Bede in his story of Cædmon, and it is in the manuscripts of Bede's *History*, both Latin and Anglo-Saxon, that all the extant copies of the Anglo-Saxon text of the *Hymn* are preserved. The *Epistola Cuthberti de obitu Bedae*, of which Bede's *Death Song* is a part, has only a fortuitous connection with the *Historia Ecclesiastica*, in that it is found more frequently in manuscripts of that work than anywhere else; but of its great historical value as a contemporary source for Bede's biography there can be no doubt. The problems of textual criticism presented by the *Hymn* and the *Death Song* are also strikingly similar. Both poems were composed in the Northumbrian dialect, and both are preserved—if not abundantly, at least adequately—in the original linguistic form. Like all the other Northumbrian poems which have survived to the present day, both the *Hymn* and the *Death Song* were translated into West Saxon during the revival of English scholarship in the late ninth and tenth centuries. The Northumbrian texts of the two poems are found only in continental manuscripts, or in manuscripts of continental origin; all the extant copies which derive from insular sources are in West Saxon.

Elliott Van Kirk Dobbie
The Manuscripts of Caedmon's Hymn and Bede's Death Song
(New York: Columbia Univ. Pr., 1937), pp. 1-2

In the Latin text, . . . Bede says that he is giving only the *sensus* of Cædmon's Old English *Hymn*. But the Old English poem must quickly have become popular in the houses of religion, for versions of it are preserved in seventeen manuscripts: four in the Northumbrian dialect native to Cædmon, in manuscripts of the Latin text of the *HE* [*Historia Ecclesiastica*]; eight in the West Saxon dialect in manuscripts of the Latin text; and five in West Saxon in texts of the late ninth-century Old English translation of the *HE*. These manuscripts date from the early Moore MS of 737 to the late fifteenth-century Paris MS. . . .

We may consider here a few of the major problems this apparently simple poem of praise has occasioned. First, what is the nature of the miracle that

Bede felt to be present in Cædmon's song? Shepherd sees it in the light of *prophetism's* connection with song, calling the *Hymn* "the first of a long line of English writings in the prophetic tradition"; Huppé thinks that the miracle to Bede lay "in the concrete, empirical truth . . . that a man unlearned in Scripture, with its great intellectual demands, had the insight to proclaim what he never formally learned"; most critics feel it resided in the linguistic feat which enabled Christian thought to be expressed for the first time in the native alliterative meter. In connection with all these views, we should remember that Cædmon composed about 670, and his *Hymn* is the earliest extant poem, secular or religious (apart possibly from some Charms, segments of *Widsith*, etc.), that we possess; further, that it was composed less than one hundred years after Augustine's Christianizing mission landed in England and only about fifty years after the conversion of the Northumbrian King Edwin at York. A second problem concerns the nature of Cædmon's linguistic accomplishments. Recently Magoun has challenged the older view that Cædmon was responsible in his following of native tradition for the coining of new vocabulary and formulas necessary for his Christian purposes, claiming that oral formulas develop slowly and that those in the poem must have had prior existence and simply lain in solution in Cædmon's mind from his having heard them recited many times. Even more recently the cowherd's source of inspiration in vocabulary as well as in content and form has been seen in the Psalms rather than in native tradition at all.

The *Hymn* would seem to pose few critical problems as such, yet one scholar has felt it incumbent to provide a lengthy interpretation in terms of Patristic exegesis, a view of the poem as Trinitarian in doctrine, structure, and stylistic development; and a further theological explication of *modgethanc* (1.2b) as God's design, an externalizing in the Son of His internal eternal thought, has continued the doctrinal-literary school of criticism. That the untutored cowherd could bear in mind such subtle doctrinal notions may be explained, if not by the miracle Bede thought it was, by his having absorbed some of the intellectual discussions current in the monastery; that he could express these ideas in such felicitous poetic form I prefer to leave unexplained, as part of the miraculous stream from which all true poetic compositions flow.

Stanley B. Greenfield
A Critical History of Old English Literature (New York:
New York Univ. Pr., 1965), pp. 169-172

CYNEWULF

ca. 8th Century

Almost nothing known of his life. Probably an Anglian cleric of the late eight or early ninth century. Cynewulf signed four of his poems—*The Fates of the Apostles, The Ascension* (also known as *Christ II*), *Juliana,* and *Elene*—in runic letters within the text of the poems themselves. Cynewulf's poems show a sophistication and intellectual awareness far in advance of the poetry of the Caedmonian school.

Henry Morley, in *English Writers,* vol. II (1888), p. 206, says, "Cynewulf the poet was unknown until the runes were read by which he had worked his name into his poem of *Elene.* These runes were first read in the year 1840 by two independent workers—by Jacob Grimm in his edition of *Andreas* and *Elene,* and by John Mitchell Kemble in his essay upon Anglo-Saxon Runes, published that year in the *Archaeologica.* Each discoverer of the names endeavored also to find who Cynewulf was, and when he lived. Grimm placed him in the eighth century. Kemble placed him in the end of the tenth century and beginning of the eleventh, by suggsting that he was the Cynewulf who was Abbot of Peterborough between the years 922 and 1006, who succeeded Ælfeage as Bishop of Winchester in the year 1006." Kemble's theory, and other judgments rendering Cynewulf a Bishop, are no longer held credible.

George P. Krapp and Elliott V. K. Dobbie, eds., *The Anglo-Saxon Poetic Records* (1931-1953), 6 vols., see vol. II, *The Vercelli Book,* vol. III, *The Exeter Book*; Jackson J. Campbell, ed., *The Advent Lyrics of the Exeter Book* (1959)

Claes Schaar, ed., *Critical Studies in the Cynewulf Group* (1949); Kenneth Sisam, *Studies in the History of Old English Literature* (1953)

[I]f Cynewulf is a student of poetry and a lover of learning rather than an improvisator such as we hear of in the *Beowulf,* who on the completion of the hero's first exploit immediately celebrates it in hall; and if everything points to his maturity as the epoch in which he developed the reflective habit, and practised his exacting art, there can be no difficulty in assuming that he had experience of military adventures in his youth. In this way he would have accumulated the fund of exact knowledge concerning war, and all its pomp and circumstance, which he exhibits in his poems, while at the same time he would be performing the deeds of valor for which he was to receive guerdon from his lord. That he was familiar with armies and battle can hardly be doubted by any one who reads the opening of the *Elene,* and who bears in mind that of all the splendor and movement depicted by the poet there is virtually nothing in the original. . . .

But Cynewulf has not merely, nor even chiefly, the soldier's enthusiasm for war. He has the poet's love for beauty—the beauty of the world, the splendor of art, the loveliness of woman, the glory of manhood. His eye is caught by the gleam of gold in ornaments or on apparel, and he mentions a second time the golden gates which serve him as metaphor. To him the earth is all green. . . .

I have said that Cynewulf loves the beauty of the world. This is shown by the fact that, though he has a utilitarian sense of the earth as bringing forth food for men, and as producing wealth of all kinds, he yet conceives of it in its array—no doubt as dressed in living green, with grass and trees, and among them flowers and fruits.

A. S. Cook, ed.
Introd. in *The Christ of Cynewulf* (Boston:
Ginn, 1900), pp. lxxxiv-lxxxvi

Cynewulf, the chronological and perhaps the literary successor to Caedmon and his school, is not superior as an essential poet to any of his predecessors; but he is a man much more deliberate and conscious as an artist, and his ear is much more delicately attuned to the tonal qualities of his rough Anglo-Saxon language. It seems probable that Cynewulf's education was much more intensive than that of the shadowy Caedmon, whatever the facts about the latter's life. The Cynewulfian poems certainly exhibit a much more obvious impress of the monastic churchman. But while one can assert with some degree of confidence that Cynewulf actually wrote this or that poem, the personality of the author is only a little less vague than that of Caedmon. . . .

Cynewulf appears to have been a man from the north of England, but whether a Northumbrian or a Mercian is uncertain. The general tendency has been to follow Sievers's theory that he was a Northumbrian, a theory which was based chiefly upon the Northumbrian texture of his meter and assonance; but scholars are free to concede that such a belief is based almost equally upon the altogether negative point that our state of knowledge concerning the Mercian dialects is still far from satisfactory. Yet all except the very earliest critics like Grimm accept the fact that he was Anglian and not Saxon. The usual assumption is that his life fell somewhere between 750 and 825. His "signature" is now *Kynewulf* (or Cynewulf), now *Kynwulf* (or Cynwulf). . . .

Essentially it matters very little whom we select as the real Cynewulf. Certain qualities in his poems are their own excuse for being. This love of the sea is one, and perhaps it is the most poetically appealing. Religiousness is another; there could be no possible doubt that he was a cleric, and all his poetic purpose is the poetic purpose of a churchman who is fired with a zeal to propagate the faith. Along with his religious inclinations and poetic feelings, he is something of a mystic and an ascetic. Perhaps it is proper to regard this trinity of mysticism, asceticism, and poetic insight as a typical combination in the literature of the medieval Church.

The historical significance of Cynewulf, then, as the first English author to sign his name is clear enough, as are the variant forms of that signature and their probable dates. The four poems bearing the signature (*Juliana, Elene, Christ,* and *The Fates of the Apostles*) survive in separate manuscripts—*Christ* and *Juliana* are in *The Exeter Book*; *Elene* and *The Fates of the Apostles* are in *The Vercelli Book*.

George K. Anderson
The Literature of the Anglo-Saxons (Princeton, N. J.:
Princeton Univ. Pr., 1949), pp. 123-25

Two main motifs are discernible in religious verse, revealing themselves in epic plots and lyrical reflections: the martial theme and the pious theme. The former is not restricted to accounts of struggle between human powers, as in the Cædmon group, or between human and inhuman powers as in Beowulf, but also recurs when the poets devote themselves to the problem of good and evil, as in the Cynewulf canon. Just as Alcuin regarded the Lindisfarne brethren as surrounded by enemies of the soul, waiting for an occasion to take possession of mind and body, so Cynewulf imagined the domination of sin over the mind as a successful siege, the decisive attack of a fiend after the breakdown of the moral fortifications. The pious theme is often logically bound up with the martial theme: the mind engaged in the moral struggle, as well as the military forces fighting the enemies of God, derives the strength to make resistance from an ecstatic devotion to the Lord. Just as the inhabitants of the ravaged monasteries resort to God in their distress, so the persecuted Israelites in Exodus, the tormented and imprisoned saints in *Juliana* and *Andreas,* the tempted hermit in *Guthlac A,* and the lonely seafarer on his perilous voyage, take their refuge with the Lord.

This double attitude to life is, of course, a feature in common with the Christianity of the early Middle Ages. However, it seems as if the insistent emphasis with which the first theme is carried through in Anglo-Saxon poetry is due to special circumstances. There is, first, the Germanic descent, the inherited heroic tradition, which made it natural for Christian poets who were aware of the past to select subjects that came as close as possible to the old sagas about the adventures of the Germanic tribes. Hence the predilection for Old Testament episodes in the earliest poetry; the message of the Gospels as a subject of literary treatment was a stage in a later development. There is, no doubt, a further and more patent reason for the warlike key in the poetry of the Anglo-Saxons. The heroic fashion must have been favoured by the demands of an aristocratic audience, to whose interest contemporary poetry certainly owed much practical support and stimulus. But it is less probable that the heroic style was inspired by contemporary events: the optimism concerning the inner conditions of the country in his own time that is manifest at the end of Bede's History . . . must have been comparatively justified also in the days of Alcuin and Cynewulf, and serious violence and disorder things of the past—and of the future.

If, then, the martial theme may be looked upon as rigidly conventional, the pious theme was less probably so. Even if there are numerous signs of dissolution of monastic discipline and of laxity of faith in the eighth century, a genuine fervour is unmistakable in many of the religious poems, and the expressions of religious ideas did not become petrified to the same extent as the numerous heroic formulas. On the contrary, the frequent reminiscences from the Bible and the Fathers indicate that the Anglo-Saxon poets eagerly searched the Christian Latin literature in their endeavours to find new and more dignified ways of moulding their thoughts and feelings. And probably, from the existence of detailed legends about the famous saints, we are entitled to conclude that the tradition about the great hermits and missionaries of the first one hundred and fifty years after the conversion was still fresh in the minds of the age.

It would seem natural if there were only little room for individual modifications in the religious poetry of the Anglo-Saxons, weighed down by the pressure of this double tradition. The situation of the poets in the vernacular was, no doubt, the same as that of the contemporary Latin ones. . . . For we must here make an important distinction. Even if we cannot perceive any conscious endeavours, on the part of the poets, to assert their personalities (except for Cynewulf's successful attempts to hand down his name to posterity), it is nevertheless clear that in fashioning their style the poets have escaped the bonds of anonymity and are exposing their own individualities.

We have chosen, as the object of our analysis, a group of poems which will be termed "the Cynewulf group" and which comprises the four poems signed by this author (*Elene, Juliana, Christ II,* and the *Fata Apostolorum*); further *Andreas, The Dream of the Rood, Christ I* and *III, Guthlac A* and *B,* and the *Phoenix.* These texts occupy an intermediate position in time between the earliest poetry (the Cædmon group), and late texts such as the *Metres* of Boethius and the *Psalms*; the Cynewulf canon is generally held to date from the end of the eighth or the beginning of the ninth centuries. The search for individual characteristics is of special interest in these poems since a discussion of priority and attribution relevant to them has been going on for a long time.

Claes Schaar
"Critical Studies in the Cynewulf Group," *Lund Studies in English*,
vol. XVII, ed. Olof Arngart (Copenhagen:
Agnar Munksgaard, 1949), pp. 7-9

ELEGIAC POETRY

Nora K. Kershaw, ed., *Anglo-Saxon and Norse Poems* (1922)
Charles W. Kennedy, tr., *Old English Elegies* (1936)

Of unknown authorship and uncertain date these Old English elegies differ markedly in mood and pattern from the personal elegy. They do not bewail the death, or eulogize the life, of an individual. They have little in common with modern elegies of the type of *Lycidas* and *Adonais*. In detail and design they owe no debt to the pastoral idyll. Their range of interest is universal, deriving from a moving sense of the tragedy of life itself— *sunt lacrimae rerum*—a consciousness of the transience of earthly joy, and the fleeting glory of earthly strength. Their rhythm is tuned to the ceaseless flow of time and change. Their pathos springs from knowledge that all life moves with frail feet and fragile wings. Their dignity clothes a recognition that man's years of breath are first a hope and brief struggle, then silence, memory, and the ruin of time.

The mood of the Old English elegies is the mood of undaunted reflection upon the universal lot of mankind, the inexorable limitation of man's existence by the mutable and mortal. Written, in all probability, in the eighth, or early ninth, century, these lyrics must have been responsive to dominant elements in the life of that troubled era. The turbulent wars of the Northumbrian and Mercian kings, with their attendant destruction of records, and ruin of monuments, of the past, must have sharpened in sensitive minds a sense of the unsubstantial nature of worldly power and achievement. The influence of spreading Christianity, and its emphasis upon the transience of earthly, and the permanence of spiritual, values, furnished a background of thought fitted to exhibit and interpret the elegiac mood. . . .

Not the least characteristic quality of these elegies is the temper of the stoic endurance whereby their emotional intensity never weakens to sentimentalism, nor their meditations upon mortal fate to self-pity or despair. Their genius blends a sensitive perception of human woe with an acceptance of a mortal destiny in whose grip man's virtue is less to struggle than to bear.

Charles Kennedy
Old English Elegies (Princeton, N. J.:
Princeton Univ. Pr., 1936), pp. 2-4

The Exeter Book, the largest and probably the best known of the four great miscellanies of Anglo-Saxon poetry, receives its name from the fact that it is preserved in the library of Exeter Cathedral, having been given to the Cathedral by Leofric, the first bishop of Exeter, who died in 1072. . . .

Although the two poems entitled the *Wanderer* (fol. 76b-78a) and the *Seafarer* (fol. 81b-83a) are found at different places in the manuscript, they present similar problems of structure and literary history, and may profitably be considered together. In each of these poems a relatively specfic treatment of the subject matter—in the one case the desolation of a man who is lordless, in the other case the joys and hardships of a seafaring life— is followed by an epilogue in more general terms, Christian and homiletic in spirit. This apparent lack of structural homogeneity has led to the suspicion of composite origin for these two poems, and to a number of attempts at critical dissection of the texts.

George Philip Krapp and Elliott Van Kirk Dobbie, eds.
The Exeter Book (London: George Routledge; New York: Columbia Univ. Pr., 1936), pp. ix, xxxvii

The lyric qualities which we have noted in the *Wanderer* are exemplified in almost equal degree in the *Seafarer*. Its lines reflect the actualities of ocean life and seamanship with such faithful directness that, save for the idiom, the poetic rendering is as expressive of the emotions and attitudes of the nineteenth century as of the ninth. The sailor's intimate struggle with elemental forces of ocean and air; the rigor, loneliness, and danger of wintry voyages in uncharted seas; the lure and fascination that intertwine even with knowledge of peril, and strip it of repelling force; these attributes of the sailor's life and mood are set forth in the *Seafarer* with sensitive faithfulness.

Charles W. Kennedy
The Earliest English Poetry: A Critical Survey
(Oxford Univ. Pr., 1943), p. 109

The three poems [*The Wife's Lament, The Husband's Message,* and *The Ruin*] . . . have given rise to endless discussion of their form and meaning, mainly because they present situations without localisation of the settings or identification of the characters. The fondness of Anglo-Saxon poets for generalisation may be seen in *The Fortunes of Men,* in the series of gnomic verses known as *Maxims* I and II, and in many passages from poems with otherwise specific settings such as the elegy of the last survivor in *Beowulf,* lines 2247-66 and the father's lament in lines 2444-62 of the same poem. In accordance, therefore, with this habit of generalisation, the three poems might be regarded as studies in the expression of atmosphere, emotions and principles of behaviour, the characters and backgrounds being little more than sketched in, with no more substance than is necessary for the immediate situation. Each poem, however, contains sufficient concrete detail to make it clear that it is founded on a particular experience. Since they lack named characters and the precisely stated social and historical contexts of poems such as *Beowulf,* the key to their interpretation is to be found in a fuller understanding of the semantic overtones of those words and phrases which appear to have had a deep social or aesthetic significance for the Anglo-Saxons. . . .

The Ruin stands rather apart from the other two poems; its theme is an imaginative nostalgia for a glorious past, stimulated by a particular scene spread out before the poet's eyes. Both *The Wife's Lament* and *The Husband's Message* are psychological studies. They contain too much detail for them to be readily explained as lyric passages isolated from longer poems and, at first sight, too little to allow them to stand by themselves. In view of their allusive style and the wealth of meaning packed into words and phrases, the answer to the problem may well be that the characters and their circumstances owe their truth to the fact that they represent typical situations in which the emotions they call forth can be most powerfully displayed. The enmity of the husband's kin towards the wife in *The Wife's Lament* and the necessity for the husband to send a messenger instead of coming himself for his wife in *The Husband's Message* are then seen to be, not loose ends, but circumstances enhancing the particular dilemma which is the starting-point for each of the elegiac studies.

R. F. Leslie, ed.
Introd., in *Three Old English Elegies* (Manchester, Eng.:
Manchester Univ. Pr., 1961), pp. 2-3

RIDDLES AND GNOMIC VERSE

George P. Krapp and Elliott V. K. Dobbie, eds., *The Anglo-Saxon Poetic Records* (1931-1953), 6 vols., see vol. VI, *The Anglo-Saxon Minor Poems*; Paull F. Baum, tr., *Anglo-Saxon Riddles of the Exeter Book* (1963); Robert K. Gordon, tr., *Anglo-Saxon Poetry* (rev., 1954)

Frederick Tupper, *The Riddles of the Exeter Book* (1910); Blanche C. Williams, *Gnomic Poetry in Anglo-Saxon* (1914)

Among Anglo-Saxon poems which have received comparatively small notice from scholars of the present day are the *Gnomic Verses* of the Exeter Book and the Cotton Manuscript. They have not entirely escaped observation, for they have been printed in collections and have been given passing glances in articles dealing with other topics. But only once have they formed the subject of a separate work. Practically no attempt has been made to relate the *Gnomic Verses* with the gnomic mood revealed in sententious sayings of epic and lyric. Some writers of literary history, it is true, indicate that they recognize the relation, but they have lacked space for detailed study. No writer has at once pointed out the significance of the gnomic reflections which occur so often in early Anglo-Saxon literature, traced their gradual decadence as the Anglo-Saxon period declined, brought together the most prominent examples, and from them drawn inferences regarding Teutonic life and thought. Although the present volume is avowedly indebted to all predecessors who have in any one of these particulars contributed notes on gnomic poetry, it claims for its individual achievement the modest attempt to perform the varied task just indicated.

At the outset it becomes necessary to define terms. . . .

From combining and sifting [various definitions] we may say, in general, a gnome is a sententious saying; in particular, it may be proverbial, figurative, moral. The various types, possessing each its individual characteristics, account for diversity of definition. But . . . the meaning has been, on the whole, pretty constant from the time of Aristotle to the present. . . .

Blanche Colton Williams
Gnomic Poetry in Anglo-Saxon (New York:
Columbia Univ. Pr., 1914), pp. 1-3

Versified wisdom, like versified tags and name-lists, is old in England, older than the language indeed. But it had to pay for the privilege of written record. The clerics who wrote down what we have made of it made fewer changes, interestingly enough, in the spells than in the sayings. They presumably feared that a spell would not work unless they kept the old wording, while they knew a saying would hold good whatever the wording. . . .

Our spells make a literary group of their own, not only in subject-matter but also in versification and style. They reflect a tradition independent of classical poetry, but allied to legal verse and to pre-classical end-stopped linear verse. Nearly all our twelve spells include prose as well as verse. In the verse parts a line may be followed by a short verse, a short verse by a line. Alliteration may be heaped up, or may be wanting. . . . The familiar classical device of variation is avoided. We find, instead, repetition, and serial effects not unlike those achieved in the thulas of *Widsith* or in certain passages of *Beowulf* (e.g., lines 1392ff; 1763ff). The *epitheton ornans* and other commonplaces of the classical style are likewise rare in the spells. These vary much in literary merit, but they all have freshness and go. . . .

The term *sayings* is here taken to mean versified words of stock everyday wisdom: short, pithy, homespun generalizations about the common concerns of life, whether proverbial, descriptive, or moralizing. The sayings that won record in Old English are found (1) embedded here and there in a number of texts, and (2) brought together in gnomic poems. Four such poems are extant. Three of them are recorded in the Exeter Book, a MS of circa 980; they go by the collective name *Exeter Gnomics* (66 lines). The embedded sayings must first, of course, be winnowed out. . . . A gnomic passage once found, we need to know besides (if possible) whether the generalization was original with the author or common literary property. The latter is normally to be presumed, in virtue of the traditional and conventionalized character of Old English literary art. . . .

In studying the four gnomic poems we have to consider not only the individual saying which these poems embody but also the poems as such. These are primarily compilations of traditional sententious wisdom, but the clerical compilers have more or less remodeled their material to make it fit the classical run-on linear style (though now and then they fail to do this and the older versification stands out). Sometimes, too, we find a single saying expanded or developed at some length, and not a few passages are homiletic or reflective rather than gnomic in character. Christian piety has made its way into the gnomic matter besides, and the poems as a whole give us a remarkable mixture of old and new. While the nature of the material makes a clean-cut structural pattern impossible, most of the sayings fall more or less loosely into groups, and certain passages are built up systematically enough. The sayings are so little organized in the Cotton Gnomics that the old term "gnomic verses" seems appropriate; the gnomic monuments of the Exeter Book, however, are properly poems rather than mere collections of verses. [1948]

Kemp Malone
A Literary History of England, 2nd ed., ed. Albert C. Baugh, vol. I
(New York and London: Appleton-Century-Crofts,
1967), pp. 38-39, 43-44

The founder of riddling in England was Aldhelm (ca. 640-709), abbot of Malmesbury and later bishop of Sherborne, one of the most distinguished pupils of the great school of Canterbury. Under Irish influence (the abbey of Malmesbury was founded by the Irish scholar Maildubh) he cultivated an elaborate Latin style, which tends to obscure his great learning. In his prose work *Epistola ad Acircium* (695) he included one hundred *Ænigmata* in hexameters, ranging in length from four to eighty-three lines, on a great variety of subjects meant to glorify God's creation. They begin with Earth, Wind, Cloud, and other natural phenomena, and end fittingly with the longest, *Creatura*, or Creation. They are unlike riddles in that they do not pose a problem and ask for an answer, but are each headed by self-explanatory titles. Aldhelm acknowledges as his model the one hundred *Ænigmata* of one Symphosius (of uncertain date) about which nothing is known beyond his work. Aldhelm was followed in England by Tatwine, archbishop of Canterbury (d. 734), and Eusebius, generally identified with Hwætberht, abbot of Wearmouth and a friend of Bede. Between them Tatwine and Eusebius produced another one hundred *Ænigmata*. Aldhelm is known to have composed poems in the vernacular, admired by King Alfred; and there is a story reported by William of Malmesbury (who had it from a lost work of King Alfred's) of how Aldhelm would stand at a bridge and by reciting like a minstrel hope to entice passersby into the church. Thus it would not be suprising if he had composed riddles in the vernacular, but none in the Exeter Book can be reasonably attributed to him—unless possibly the Storm riddles. Riddles *II* (K-D 40) and *50* (K-D 35) are translations of Aldhelm.

Paull F. Baum, tr.
Introd., in *Anglo-Saxon Riddles of the Exeter Book*
(Durham, N. C.: Duke Univ. Pr., 1963), p. xi

WIDSITH

650-700?

Parts of *Widsith* may be the earliest poetry extant in English. The poem is a long narrative of heroic deeds and legends told by a "scop," who has travelled to distant lands and foreign kingdoms and is now sharing his golden hoard of adventures and words with his audience. The poet of *Widsith* is unknown, and he is certainly full of loud boasts and historical impossibilities, but his sense of joy in his narrative and his attention to the craft of the "scop" are impressive.

Kemp Malone, ed., *Widsith* (1935)
Kemp Malone, tr., *Ten Old English Poems, Put Into Modern English Alliterative Verse* (1941)
R. W. Chambers, *Widsith: A Study in Old English Heroic Legend* (1912)

A survey of the geography of the poem has emphasized the contrast between the stamp of definite locality borne by the undoubted portions, and the chaos of names found in the doubtful passages. A study of the grammar of the poem has shown that such examples of late usage as we do find occur in just those passages which the earlier critics, on grounds quite other than those of metre or language, had suspected of later additions. The poem as a whole, and still more the undoubted portions, taken by themselves, we find to be more primitive in grammar and metre than the poems usually regarded as the oldest in English literature, such as *Beowulf* and *Genesis A*. Above all, the habit of always concluding the sentence with a line, never with the half line, dissociates these undoubted portions of the poem from Old English epic poetry, and connects them with a small group of poems which, in subject matter, all seem to go back to a more primitive people than that of the courtly or learned epic, as we know it.

Reason has been shown for believing that these undoubted portions of the poem fall into two sections, originally distinct, the Catalogue of Kings, and the language of Ealhhild and Eormanric which we may regard as the essential *Widsith*. *Widsith,* alike on the grounds of legend and of geography, cannot be the work of a contemporary of Eadgils and Ealhhild who really visited the court of Eormanric. The Catalogue of Kings is older than *Widsith* proper, yet on account of the names it contains it can hardly be earlier than the middle of the sixth century, and may be considerably later. *Widsith* seems to belong to a period later than this, but earlier than *Beowulf* or *Genesis*: that is, to the seventh century.

This too is the date which has already been approved by those who have studied the poem chiefly from the point of view of heroic legend and of geography: it has been widely accepted, but not universally, because the view has hitherto been entertained that the language and metre of *Widsith* pointed rather to the eighth than to the seventh century. This view has been shown to rest partly upon a miscount, partly upon a failure to differentiate from the rest of the poem those parts which (on grounds not grammatical or metrical) had been already suspected of later interpolations.

R. W. Chambers
Widsith (Cambridge Univ. Pr., 1912), pp. 177-79

The Old English poem *Widsith* is recorded in one MS only, the *Exeter Book,* an English poetical miscellany transcribed "early in the period 970-990." *Widsith* begins with the eleventh line of fol. 84b and ends with the eighth line of fol. 87a. It is 143 lines long. The poem consists of (1) a prologue and an epilogue, each nine lines in length, and (2) a speech put in the mouth of a fictitious scop, Widsith by name, who gives a learned lecture on Germanic political history and tells something of his personal experiences as a wandering gleeman. The speech itself falls into well-marked divisions: (1) an introduction and a conclusion, of four lines each; (2) the Hwala-Alexander passage (lines 14-17), grammatically tied to the introduction but hard to reconcile with the structural scheme of the poem; and (3) the body of the speech (lines 18-130). The last is made up of three *Fits*. The First Fit (lines 18-49) differs from the other two in that here the scop does not profess to relate experiences of his own, but is content to give information to his hearers, speaking throughout in the third person. The Second Fit (lines 50-111) has a character all its own, by virtue of its unusual if not indeed unique construction. . . . The Third Fit (lines 112-130) shows greater kinship to the First than to the Second, in structure and tone alike, but has definite peculiarities. . . .

If now we look at the body of the speech from a somewhat different point of view, we find that it consists of (1) three name-lists (and one fragment of such a list), to which I will refer by the technical name *thula*, taken from the Icelandic; (2) four sections, hereafter called *episodes*, in which we are given more informaiton about certain kings than would have been possible had the poet held strictly to the thula pattern; and (3 five sections, more or less lyrical in character, which I will group under the name *yed* (See NED s.v.)....

From the foregoing analysis it seems evident that the *Widsith* poet was a literary artist of considerable skill in composition. Certainly he produced a poem remarkable alike for its complexity and for the balance and proportion of its parts. And if his structural achievement be set aside as mere architecture, there remain poetical passages which "give an unsurpassable effect of fusion of thought and form." As a stylist our poet is notable above all for his success in making the complex seem simple. His elaborate periods are so cunningly wrought that the unwary reader marks neither artifice nor art, or hears at most a flow of words as limpid as a folk-song's. Conventional stylistic devices are not wanting, it is true, but these devices (like those to be found in a folk-song), by virtue of their very familiarity and obviousness, only add to the effect of simplicity at which the poet aims throughout.

Kemp Malone, ed.
Widsith (London: Methuen, 1936), pp. 1-3

The most important thing about a poem is that it is poetry—or at least intends to be. The poem *Widsith* has long been a magnet of immensely attractive power to every sort of criticism except literary criticism. History, geography, archeology, philology—and what else?—have been drawn so voluminously into its discussion that it might easily seem no room was left for aesthetic appreciation. And this is not surprising. When almost every line is a puzzle for the learned, literary criticism might well be daunted; and in any case, it might be asked, what could it make of a composition that appears to consist mainly of a perfunctory cataloguing of obscure proper names? But if *Widsith* does seem to be that, or anything like that, surely it must be because literary criticism has not done its duty by it. It is a fair assumption that the man who composed the poem meant to create a work of art. If so, should not all criticism, literary or not, start from that intention, and come back to it? But, though it would certainly be untrue to say that the art of the author has been ignored (how could [R. W.] Chambers, of all men, possibly have done that?), yet it is true, on the whole, that literary criticism of the poem has tended to be merely incidental to its scientific criticism. In its discussion, the poem has seldom been *seen* as a poem, until it has been considered as a collection of scientific problems; and when these problems have been answered, to the satisfaction of this critic or that, the poem, instead of a work of art, had become a concourse—aesthetically speaking, a fortuitous concourse—of pieces of information, extremely varied in their provenance; and its author a disembodied spectre, flitting from one age to another.

It is the grand merit of Professor Kemp Malone's edition of *Widsith* [1936] that it avoids this serious methodological mistake. The result is not only singularly beneficial to literary criticism, which now, almost for the first time, finds the artistic purpose of this most remarkable composition credibly elucidated; it is perhaps equally beneficial to the scientific interpretation of its many fascinating but troublesome problems. . . .

What Dr. Malone's aesthetic analysis of the poem brings out is not, of course, absolutely new. It has often been noticed—it is, indeed, unmistakable—that the poem has some sort of strophic structures; and again that the quality of its substance varies somewhat sharply from "personal" to "impersonal." Working out these two lines of suggestion, with the most scrupulous nicety, and combining them together, Dr. Malone shows the poem to be, first, an elaborately complex and cunningly balanced piece of poetic architecture. This, at any rate, is, to me, completely convincing. Such beautiful and masterly craftsmanship does not happen by chance; we are in the presence of a great artist, thoroughly conscious of his art and using it with supreme assurance. There is nothing "primitive" or "native" here. But further this poet is using, for his own purposes, considerable masses of poetic material which have descended to him from a much earlier age, combining this with lyrical *intermezzi* (the feeling of which colours the whole), and setting boundaries to the consistent shape of it all by means of Prologue and Epilogue. The poem is an imaginative reconstruction of the great English heroic tradition, and at the same time (as the focus of this) an imaginative re-creation of the profession and ideals of the scop, in whose personality the author's purpose is dramatized. The kind of interest in heroic legend which the poem implies is not that of the heroic age itself, but of what we may conveniently call "culture." "The author of *Widsith* was a cleric at home in vernacular poetry, sacred and profane."

Lascelles Abercrombie
SwR (January, 1938), pp. 124-26

If Widsith is not the actual poet but an ideal bard, he is used by the poet to make certain claims for his art. This, it seems, is what poetry does and is. It enables the poet to be acquainted with the whole world as it is known to heroic song and gives him rich rewards. The kings and peoples enumerated are the subjects of which an ideal bard would be able to sing, and indeed suggest an enormous range of possible themes. In presenting his ideal bard in this way the poet may perhaps imply something of an old view that the bard has a special knowledge denied to other men. He may have felt, dimly and uncertainly, that the bard is a kind of shaman, who can somehow transcend the limitations of space and time and see all the kings of the earth. That traces of such a belief may have survived in Anglo-Saxon poetry is not impossible. The old Norse religion had its mantic aspects, which were associated with Othin and practised by skalds who were often singers. Be that as it may, it seems probable that *Widsith* is not intended to be taken literally but gives a picture of an ideal bard and his range of subjects. In that case it shows how many subjects were available to a bard in the heyday of Germanic heroic poetry.

Widsith's range is indeed large, and as R. W. Chambers' learned study has shown, it draws on many branches of Germanic legend—on Goths, Burgundians, the sea-folk, Franks, and Langobards. Yet wide though the range of subjects is, it is limited in two ways. First, there are many places and peoples which the poet omits. He knows nothing about the Herulians or the Slavs or the Avars or the Sciri or the Turcilingi, though these peoples would have been known to any Gothic poet who lived in central Europe. The English poet draws on a different range of geography, and, though he derives it from continental sources, those sources probably belong to some region not far from the North Sea. It is the kind of world that would be known to Angles and Frisians before they crossed the water. Secondly, the poet has his own taste in stories. He does not mention any monsters, nor even Beowulf. His taste is not for the supernatural but for human relations, and especially for tales in which character and passion play a large part, like Ermanaric's vengeance on his young bride; the strife between Hagena and Heoden, between the young chief and the father of his betrothed; the mischief caused between Ingeld and Hrothgar. Especially he likes tales with contrasts of devotion and disloyalty, like the retainers of Guthhere who fall round their lord; the loyalties aroused for Hnaef and Finn; the contrast between Hrothgar and Hrothulf. The poet of *Widsith* shows how large a choice of themes may lie open to a heroic poet in a living art of song.

C. M. Bowra
Heroic Poetry (London: Macmillan, 1952), pp. 436-37

GENERAL CRITICISM OF OLD ENGLISH LITERATURE

The theory that all the poetry of the early Old English period was of Northumbrian origin has been generally accepted. But what is the basis for the belief that Northumbria was the only center of poetic composition? It is true that philologists have discovered in certain poems definite evidence of northern origins. But does this imply that all the poetry is northern? It has been rather easy for handbooks to carry on the tradition, to repeat the generalization, with little consideration given to possible exceptions to the rule; early scholars of the type of Stopford Brooke, who loved the old English traditions, painted such appealing pictures of the cultural life of Northumbria that their successors merely accepted the fact without examining the evidence. The south, we know, produced scholars and teachers. . . .

The Ruin, one of the most interesting poems in the *Exeter Book,* presents the most striking case for West-Saxon authorship. . . .

. . . the manuscript [of the *Exeter Book*] shows every sign of having emanated from an especially well-developed scriptorium of the southwestern section of England, possibly Glastonbury Abbey, at that time one of the most important and renowned churches in all England; finally, several individual poems in the *Exeter Book,* notably the *Wanderer,* the *Seafarer,* the *Exeter Gnomes,* some of the Riddles, the *Guthlac,* and *The Ruin,* the only poem for which identification with a real city is possible, inasmuch as they bear no relation to Northumbria but point rather to southern England, may, with the possible exception of the *Guthlac,* be regarded as West-Saxon production.

Cecilia A. Hotchner
Wessex and Old English Poetry, with Special Consideration of The Ruin
(Lancaster, Penn.: Lancaster Pr., 1939), pp. 1, 9

It is during this period of the seventh and eighth centuries when this scholarship of Latin Christianity was gradually spreading through England, that we see the rise and flowering of English religious poetry in the vernacular. It seems likely, indeed, that these same cultural influences stimulated the rewriting of older poetry rooted in the Germanic traditions of the Continent. It is probable that behind the *Beowulf* lay an older Continental epic, or series of epic lays, which later in England a Christian poet reshaped into the poem as we know it.

Charles W. Kennedy, tr. and ed.
Introd., in *Early English Christian Poetry* (New York:
Oxford Univ. Pr., 1952), p. 7

I should like to comment on the possible relation of one aspect of the physical preservation of our Anglo-Saxon poems that may reflect their oral background, namely, the fact of their all being written out as prose. It is a not uncommon view that this method was employed as a measure of economy, that the vernacular poetry was perhaps felt not quite worth, or worthy of, as much parchment as writing the poetry out as we today print it would require. I find it hard to believe this to be the case and suspect it was written in prose merely because neither scribes nor singers understood in a formal sense the metrics of the verse, even when they may have had an understanding of Latin verse studied in monastic schools. That tenth-eleventh century scribes at times separate verses (not our typographical lines) by dots may merely reflect a feeling for the basic rhythm, the onset of a down-beat, comparable to a musically unschooled person's tapping time with foot or finger though knowing nothing of the writing of music or of musical composition.

Francis P. Magoun, Jr.
Sp. (July, 1953), pp. 462-63

Old English poetry was composed in a flexible type of four-stress, alliterative line consisting of two half-lines of two stresses each separated by a strongly marked caesural pause. The stressed syllables established the rhythm, and the two half-lines were bound into a unit by the convention of alliteration. Variation in the relative positions of stresses within the line, and a convention of subordinate stresses, produced delicate and subtle currents of mutation and change of rhythm. The recitation of this alliterative verse was usually accompanied by chords struck on the harp.

The occurrence of rhyme is infrequent. Cynewulf uses it in a passage of fifteen lines near the end of the *Elene,* and a more extended passage is found in the eighty-seven lines of the *Rhyme Poem* of the Exeter Book. In a few other poems the rhyme occurs in brief passages. Its occasional use may perhaps be traced to an influence of rhyming Latin hymns familiar to religious poets.

Estimated as a whole, Old English poetry expresses in many ways the changing spirit of the age. It was a period during which the limited perspectives of a pagan world were being gradually widened by the Christian philosophy. The stark and primitive social codes expressive of Germanic folkways were being transformed by the spiritual demands of Christian ethics.

Charles W. Kennedy, ed.
Introd., in *An Anthology of Old English Poetry*
(New York: Oxford Univ. Pr., 1960), pp. xiv-xv

The Phoenix . . . represents a valiant attempt by a sensitive poet to produce an Old English poem out of a mixture of a late classical Latin poem and some Christian themes. The attempt is not altogether successful for the poet has not been ruthless enough in selecting and arranging his material. Though he has substantially altered the *Carmen*, he has not tailored the allegorical interpretations adequately to the measure of the story that he adapted from the *Carmen*. The poem is composed in a simple, fairly plain style, the major fault of which is a tendency to repetition. The poet repeats too many of his favourite phrases. . . . He can, however, at times make use of striking similes and words. The poem's beauty lies in its idyllic tone, in the picture of a terrestrial-heavenly paradise, and in the gracefulness with which some of the allegorical interpretations are linked with the story of the phoenix. It has indeed a quiet charm and simple dignity which are not found elsewhere in the whole of Old English poetry.

N. F. Blake, ed.
Introd., in *The Phoenix* (Manchester, Eng.:
Manchester Univ. Pr., 1964), p. 35

MEDIEVAL LITERATURE

Robert Raymo, editor

JOHN BARBOUR

ca. 1320-1395

Little is known of the life of John Barbour. He appears to have travelled to England and France, perhaps as a student, and sometime before 1357 to have been appointed Archdeacon of Aberdeen, a post which he retained for the rest of his life. For his services to the Scottish crown as auditor and ambassador he was granted a series of pensions between 1378 and 1388. His long verse chronicle of Robert Bruce's career was composed about 1375. A collection of saints' lives in verse, a fragmentary *Siege of Troy*, and a *Buik of Alexander* have been attributed to him, all on insufficient authority.

William Mackay Mackenzie, ed., *Bruce* (1909)

The *Brus* (1376) is a narrative in rhymed octosyllabics extending to nearly 14,000 lines, and divided into twenty books, the subject being the exploits of the remarkable man who at once vindicated the independence of Scotland, and established himself securely on the Scottish throne. Barbour calls it a romance, and there are statements in it manifestly erroneous . . . , as well as others which historical scepticism would bid us pause before accepting. But, on the whole, . . . there is no reason to question his substantial accuracy and good faith; and he is the source whence we derive our knowledge of all those pleasing and picturesque traits in the career of King Robert I, which are, or ought to be, familiar to every child in Scotland. The *Brus* is better entitled than any other work to be called the national epic.

That there should be a want of artistic unity about the poem as a whole was an almost inevitable consequence of Barbour's choice of a subject. He cannot be said to be strong in the matter of construction. It is in episodes rather than in plot that he shows what he can do; and his episodes are truly admirable. There he shows fire, enthusiasm, "gusto"; yet his fervent patriotism is never disfigured by acerbity. He is astonishingly fair to the other side, and displays a warm appreciation of chivalry and courtesy wherever he finds them. Nevertheless there is no touch of sentimentality or self-consciousness about him; and the simplicity and dignity that mark a noble spirit are reflected in his style. He is never "aureate," and his best passages are distinguished by an unaffected straightforwardness which is more impressive than the most elaborate ornamentation. . . . Barbour's comments upon the events and actions he narrates are usually shrewd and to the point. He saw life steadily, and would not have dissented from the view that virtue is a happy mean. . . . The mixture of daring and policy which he saw exemplified in his hero must have possessed a strong attraction for him. And it is not surprising to find in this connection that he was blessed with a sense of humor, not, perhaps, very highly developed, but genuine and kindly enough.

J. H. Millar
A Literary History of Scotland (London:
T. Fisher Unwin, 1903), pp. 15-17

Again, the style of Barbour, though less correct than his contemporary, Gower, proves how well the spirit and manner of France had been appropriated. The *Bruce* is a poem of the same kind as the French life of William Marshall; in verse, in grammar and diction, it follows the French school; it has the same simplicity of language, the same ease of narrative as the *Roman de Thèbes* or any other of the romances that Barbour loved.

W. P. Ker
Essays on Medieval Literature (London:
Macmillan, 1905), p. 110

Barbour was not of the order whose "eye in a fine frenzy rolling, Doth glance from heaven to earth, from earth to heaven." He was a God-fearing churchman and statesman, who thought it well to put on record his country's deliverance, before, in the inglorious days of Bruce's successors, its memory should have perished. And what he aimed at he achieved. Like Scott, whose poetry he inspired, he finds his metre so facile that, at times, he falls into the merest commonplace. The battle of Bannockburn occupies an altogether disproportionate space in the poem. Nevertheless, the description of the battle is Barbour's masterpiece. He must often have talked with men who had fought at Bannockburn; he obviously had a very clear conception of the manner in which the day was lost and won. In his narrative he combines the qualities which Matthew Arnold assigns to the highest epic style; he is rapid in movement, plain in words and in style, simple in ideas and noble in manner. The only one of these characteristics which can be disputed is the last.

Peter Giles
"The Earliest Scottish Literature,"
CHEL, vol. II (1908), p. 107

Barbour's function was that of the bard—when the work was finished, when men had witnessed the birth of a nation out of conflict and blood, to step forward and brand upon the heart of the people the true meaning of the fight for freedom which had just been ended.

The poem [*Brus*] has not fire for us today, but for the poet himself and those of his day whose feelings would be stirred by the memories the verse could kindle, it must have had an effect which we cannot fully grasp. Its natural movement, the short narrative iambic beat of its lines, the clear-eyed vision, impart to it an epic place in virtue of its own right. Scott's debt to it is written large over his work.

Lauchlan Maclean Watt
Scottish Life and Poetry (London: James Nisbet and Sons,
1912), pp. 52, 58

Apart from its greatly superior humanity, *The Bruce* is of much the same quality as Minot's songs. Barbour, too, dispenses with the finer elements of poetry—those elements that distinguish poetry from verse. He is not without imagination, but it is imagination of a crude, popular sort, inherent in the material. Of fancy blossoming into metaphor, of the myriad little arts that poets know, he is wholly guileless. It is a *musa pedestris*, but for that very reason better suited than a more conscious and cultivated style for a work of such amplitude. . . . No doubt in a truly poetic soil . . . beauties arise unbidden, but Barbour was by nature an historian, and only by accident a poet.

F. J. Snell
The Age of Chaucer (1346-1400) (London:
G. Bell and Sons, 1926), pp. 15-16

Barbour's *Bruce* seems fittingly to commemorate the attainment of nationhood; it mingles epic and romance, its hero is a national hero, and the poem appeals to national feeling. But the work lacks the splendour of epic, it might be described in the words used by Wordsworth to describe Scott's poetry, "localized romance." The appropriateness of the title suggests that the type of theme and treatment represent some definite Scottish characteristic. The appeal lies in the theme: the poem deals with serious and interesting emotions and events, and paradoxically, because it is based on reality, it escapes the monotony of many old romances. Barbour describes simply and vividly heroic and warlike scenes and speeches. He shows himself a poet in his vivid narrative, and in the appreciation of brave and magnanimous thoughts and actions. Bruce's praise of freedom is, justly, the most famous passage in the poem; and the passages which are most truly poetic are those in which something deeply felt is expressed with simple directness and sincerity. . . . There is in the poem little of the beauty of phrase, or the beauty of musical verse; and of beauty visible to the eye only one manifestation appealed to Barbour: the beauty of a great army splendidly equipped.

M. M. Gray
Scottish Poetry from Barbour to James VI (London:
J. M. Dent and Sons, 1935), pp. v-vi

The *Brus* is not exactly a great poem; vivid as it is in description and shrewd in characterisation, its verse is rather unmelodious and its diction rather pedestrian. But if it is not exactly a great poem, it is a noble piece of work, animated by a chivalrous spirit worthy of its subject. The image of Bruce that Scotland still carries in her heart, the wise, patient king, high-hearted, high-minded, humorous, and kindly, is the Bruce that Barbour drew.

Herbert J. C. Grierson and J. C. Smith
A Critical History of English Poetry (London:
Chatto and Windus, 1944), p. 50

The long struggle waged by Scotland for her independence made itself felt in literature for a long time, and here in the *Bruce* Scottish themes and personages are the life of the poem. Barbour writes more as an historian than as a teller of romance, and his object is to preserve for posterity the exploits and patriotism of Bruce and of those who fought with him for Scotland's freedom. The aggressive spirit of the English is contrasted with the defensive attitude which animates the Scots, and Barbour infuses into his poem the temper which went to the making of Bruce's Scotland. Thus it is that the poem is a strange amalgam of the old *chanson de geste* and the chivalric romance. The actions of the hero are often as bloody and violent as those of earlier warriors such as Gautier d'Arras or Raoul de Cambrai. The heroic element is stressed: Bruce is sagacious in council as he is unmatched in the field, while Douglas exhibits even more of the primitive hero. He is harder and more determined than his leader, since his personal wrongs have inflamed him more fiercely against the English. It is the national cause, however, rather than individual wrongs that animates Bruce and most of his followers. A sense of responsibility controls their actions; loyalty to Scotland, not as in chivalric romance to a lady, or a king, or to a remote ideal.

H. S. Bennett
Chaucer And The Fifteenth Century (Oxford Univ. Pr.,
1947), p. 166

. . . The traditional view that Barbour's theme is "freedom" is the most adequate. He is not, like Chaucer, a subtle analyst of human nature; but with the chronicler's concern for accurate reporting he combines a strong interest in the motives and aspirations behind action. Abstract reflection and suggestive explanation abound in the *Bruce*. Beneath the coherent story of a single heroic career lies the deeper unity of an ideal expressed and realized in action. A passionate desire for independence is the mainspring of the whole story.

The *Bruce* is the work of a man with a dry humor and shrewd appreciation of character; an honesty in weighing evidence and judging friend and foe; a thoughtful and fundamental patriotism; and a masculine enjoyment of bloody conflict. Barbour used the techniques of romance critically and imaginatively to perpetuate the fame of a national hero, and contrived to be true to the demands both of history and of art.

James Kinsley
"The Medieval Makars," *Scottish Poetry: A Critical Survey*
(London: Cassell, 1955), pp. 4, 7

There is no doubt that Barbour is very far from the verbal and poetic art of the French romances which he took as his model, but it is equally true that his seriousness, his moral or psychological depth, and the high aim of his poem have created a work of greater weight than all the romances. Up north in Aberdeen Barbour was living on the fringe of the literary conventions of his time, but he left a poem whose message still carries weight, if only as the first literary document concerning self-determination and the rights of small nations, as well as the right of the individual to participate in all decisions by which he himself is vitally affected.

K. Wittig
The Scottish Tradition in Literature (Edinburgh:
Oliver and Boyd, 1958), p. 32

Of course, for Barbour the story is the thing. He is a great narrative poet, adept at creating tensions, rejoicing in the dent of sword on shield, the prodigies of valour. But the springs of the action are patriotic, philosophic, religious. The repository of those ideas, the medium in which they became articulate, was the Catholic and Scottish church, the political and moral architect of Scotland's freedom.

T. H. Kean
Month (October, 1959), p. 214

Barbour has the artist's eye for the small image and frequently stops to note details like the blinking of the sun upon the shields of the warriors and the glitter of their armour and trappings. He gives us a vigorous account of Bannockburn which, though rougher-hewn than Scott's description of Flodden and gaining its effect mainly through the accumulation of detail, maintains a dignity which Scott never reaches. Barbour is at his best as a scenario-writer, describing scenes of action and vigorous combat in a succession of flashes. The work is essentially masculine in temper, and its vocabulary is somewhat cryptic and limited in range, as might be expected of any report on a military expedition, yet the poet does not lack the felicitous touch that saves the *Bruce* from baldness. The atmosphere of the poem, evoked by the economy of its language, the episodic quality of its narrative, and its occasional flashes of lyricism, indicates that Barbour's poetic technique is that of the ballad-singer, not of the cloistered scholar.

A. Kinghorn, ed.
Barbour: The Bruce, A Selection (Edinburgh:
Oliver and Boyd, 1960), pp. 11-12

WILLIAM CAXTON

ca. 1421-1491

William Caxton, England's first printer, was born in the Weald of Kent. His apprenticeship to a London mercer brought him to Bruges where in due course he became Governor of the English Nation of Merchant Adventurers in the Low Countries. This position he relinquished in 1469 and soon embarked on an English translation of Raoul le Fevre's version of the history of Troy, completing it in 1471. From 1470 to 1472 he lived in Cologne and studied the art of printing. Returning to Bruges, he published, in 1475, the first book in the English language—the *Recuyell of the Histories of Troy*. The following year he returned to England and set up his press in Westminster. Here, for the next fifteen years, he edited, translated, and published nearly one hundred works of a widely varied nature, among them, the "classics" of Middle-English literature—Chaucer, Gower, Lydgate, and Malory.

W. J. B. Crotch, ed., *The Prologues and Epilogues of William Caxton* (1928)
William Blades, *The Biography and Typography of William Caxton* (1882)

GENERAL

Though he expresses admiration for the virtue of compactness in Chaucer, Caxton himself cannot be said to have eschewed prolixity. He has only one device for elevating his style, and that is the multiplication of words. For form and structure his feeling is rudimentary. He escapes the monotony and simplicity of the medieval narrative style, but he does so at the expense often of being obscure, labored, and clumsy. He sought fullness, but the harmonious arrangement of parts in the structure of the sentence, which was to be the chief contribution of the classics to English style, was beyond his grasp. On the other hand the "fayr and straunge termes" of the originals from which he translated were within his comprehension, and these terms he brought over freely into English. When he was blamed for this, his answer on one occasion was that the "olde and homely termes" of the language were no longer intelligible, and furthermore that he translated not "for a rude uplondysh man to laboure therin," but for the clerk and gentleman. [1915]

George P. Krapp
The Rise of English Literary Prose (New York:
Frederick Ungar, 1963), p. 279

Caxton's prose sentence is of the "Journeyman" character, of a type calculated to convey his meaning in a manner as intelligible as his particular skill in rhetoric was able to make it. It is evident that his rhetorical skill was not advanced; but he made an earnest attempt at a serviceable prose which often falls below, and sometimes rises above, its norm. He could be very wooden; his outline of chapter divisions in his edition of Malory's *Le Morte Darthur* lapses into a most mechanical series with not the slightest attempt at variety; where it is convenient, he plays safe. On the other hand when he relates an anecdote like that of the dean and the poor parson in the epilogue to *Aesop* . . . he becomes direct and almost vigorous, with a quaint conversational vivacity that sits odd among his great structures. For the moment he drops his endless strings of clauses and writes a simple coordinate prose which is a relief to read. This is the exception.

Caxton marks the first step in a conscious, unintermittent effort to "improve" English prose of the near-modern type. He felt the inferiority of his English instrument and the superiority of the French. He struggled to express himself adequately in a prose made largely by himself. Though the degree in which he succeeded may have been small, he began and sent forward a movement toward "cultivation" which has grown stronger with the years. The drab and somber colors of Middle English become brighter; there is a growth in variety of expression; there is a stimulus to achieve definite rhetoric and a settled structure. When Caxton feels vaguely that French is a fair language and that, as *he* writes it, his own is not, a desire for better things has sprung up, and progress is under way.

Robert Ray Aurner
Univ. of Wisconsin Studies in Language and Literature
(1923), pp. 57-58

Caxton's work as a translator was even of greater value than his work as a printer. Much of the best literature was only to be had in French, and long before he ever thought of learning to print he had been moved to translate books into the English tongue. Translating was more or less a hobby with

him, and he seems to have begun at a fairly early age. He probably translated many things that never appeared in print.

Henry R. Plomer
William Caxton (London: Leonard Persons; Boston, Mass.: Small,
Maynard, 1925). pp. 174-75

An interesting parallel might be drawn between the literary work of Caxton
and that of King Alfred. Both were preeminently translators and diffusers
of knowledge. One brought into existence the first body of written prose in
the English tongue; the other first put in print, and enormously extended the
possibilities of, English prose with the effect of greatly increasing both the
writers and readers. Both were popularizers in the best sense of the term.
They were eager to extend knowledge beyond the limited circle of nobles
and scholars "to thende that many myght come to honoure and worshyppe".
Both took books which they thought "most needful for the people to know,"
and made them intelligible and interesting to the ordinary individual.

Nellie Slayton Aurner
Caxton (London: Philip Allan, 1926), p. 204

Certain words of his on Chaucer are his title-deeds as a critic . . . in his
favourite poet Caxton saw his own literary ideals fulfilled. The humble
craftsman in letters, conscious of many bunglings, could admire the sure
hand of the master. In Chaucer he found a true mean between the rude and
the ornate, and a model for economy of workmanship. His praise of the
poet's "high sentence" does indeed betray the didactic bias which lingered
long in Ascham and others, holding back Elizabethan criticism from the
aesthetic way. But a negative ideal for the literary workman of all time is
found in "he writeth no void words," and behind the saying be the struggles
of Caxton's own career as a writer. More clearly personal still, and more
portentous, is the simple statement: "he excelleth in mine opinion all other
writers in our English." Wise after the event, we may patronisingly commend this verdict, forgetting perhaps that Caxton wrote thus of a poet
whose language was outmoded, whose prosody was misunderstood, whose
fame was outshone in contemporary eyes by the verbose Lydgate. But those
words "in mine opinion" are most significant of all. Here at last a writer has
forgotten what medieval authority may say; the Church, the learned, for the
time being count for nothing. He has given a personal literary judgment,
which lifts him clear out of his age and points to the best criticism of the
Renaissance, to the days of freely expressed conviction, of artistic enthusiasm and discovery.

It was a phenomenon typically English that the man who spoke the first
quiet word of true criticism in our country should have been no scholar, but
a simple-minded craftsman who, having done well in trade, did well, too, in
printing, and set himself to give his countrymen something good to read. He

gave them Chaucer and Malory; he showed the language the way it should go. He prepared humbly for the coming of a greater age and was himself a herald of its dawn. All this was indeed an achievement for one who is usually thought of in terms of sales and record prices, or as the pioneer of a mechanic art in this country, or even, sometimes, as a name of no importance in literature.

W. Wright Roberts
BJRL (July, 1930), pp. 421-22

Cultured noblemen stimulated the progress of literature by ordering and supervising translations of their favourite works and by demanding courtly literature of entertainment. Supply of these demands by printers such as Caxton called for the careful exercise of both literary and linguistic judgment. Caxton had to pay due attention to the requests of his influential patrons and work according to their tastes in the polished style which they preferred. . . . Caxton feels himself unequal to the handling of the appropriate ornate language. Deference to the wishes of his noblest patrons cannot compel this Kentishman, "a symple person," to relinquish his own conviction that plain speech is the best. He willingly acknowledges his lack of instruction in rhetorical models. . . . He distrusts the craze for ornamentation which results in obscurity. . . . Caxton's importance as a critic of language lies in his trust in his own independent judgment, his refusal to be harried by his patrons into a cast of speech which is alien to this character and preference. As an Englishman of the southeastern counties he is familiar with the language in its London form and with dialectal variation. As printer and translator he examines older English and foreign languages. Working for aristocratic circles he is *au fait* with all the more fantastic fashions of speech. From all these strata of language he selects the plain style as comprehensible and acceptable for all purposes and thus anticipates at this early date the later judgment of scholars such as Castiglione in Italy, Wilson and Cheke in England. He says, ". . . in my Judgemente" when he explains his preference for "the comyn termes that be dayli used" and he consciously tries to find a middle style between the uncouthness of very plain English and the aureate terms. . . .

Caxton's comments on literature and language are so discriminating, his attitude to translation so thoughtful that they point to a mind alive to the many currents of thought in his age, a mind which deliberately selects and formulates its decision. He was no scholar and is therefore untouched by any intimation of the intellectual progress of the next phase of the Early Tudor period. There is in him a genuine manifestation of the critical spirit, independently developed and consistently sustained.

Elizabeth J. Sweeting
Early Tudor Criticism (Oxford: Basil Blackwell,
1940), pp. 9-11, 14

He did not have a natural and instinctive sense of form. He seems never to have grasped the function of the sentence as a unit of thought. His ideas, unless controlled by his original, are joined one to another in a loose and at times unending chain, often without logical or syntactical cohesion. Compared with Trevisa, or Malory, or even Pecock, he cannot be said to have advanced the art of English prose. But for making available to English readers the most popular and useful books of his day—a truly noble five-book shelf—his service to English culture is inestimable.

Albert C. Baugh, ed.
A Literary History of England (New York:
Appleton-Century-Crofts, 1948), p. 308

In his writings, Caxton displayed a genuine zest, wanting in many of his colleagues; his prose is rich with promise of the Tudor brilliance so soon to follow. Caxton understood full well the value of this form of literature, and he obviously endorsed the view proclaimed by Trevisa . . . that "communly prose is moore cleere than ryme, more easy and more playne to knowe and understand." Naturally enough, his style improved with practice and with the passage of years, but happily without loss in the charming freshness of its content. Slyly, here and there, his dry, quiet (sometimes teasing) humor crops out. . . . There was a sanguine realism in his outlook upon everyday life and he seems to have been an excellent judge of character; yet he never stooped to vulgarity. Quick perception and a fine sense of the value of detail heightened his vigorous powers of description. Through the charm of his narrative, Caxton helped materially to keep alive an interest in that common store of traditional stories upon which, in the next century, the great poets and dramatists of the Renaissance were to draw so heavily.

Curt F. Bühler
William Caxton and His Critics (Syracuse, N. Y.:
Syracuse Univ. Pr., 1960), pp. 16-17

He [Caxton] was not a systematic thinker. His attitude toward ideas is marked by an ambivalence typical of the practical man in a time of changing values. Instinctively and by training he adhered to the old order and the old values. His choice of texts included little that was not the common stock of late medieval culture. The two orations of Cicero, alone among the products of his press, represent an unmedievalized antiquity; and the *Declamacion of Noblesse*, published . . . together with the works of Cicero, alone represent the influence, rather indirect, of the Italian Renaissance. But these remain items of considerable importance, and his comments on them reflect a high regard for scholarship, for the example of the ancients, and for a liberal education. He was, moreover, on terms of respectful intimacy with John Skelton, a fact which if it does not link him directly with the New Learning, links him at least with a man to whom humanistic learning was by no means a closed book.

Arthur B. Ferguson
The Indian Summer of English Chivalry (Durham, N. C.:
Duke Univ. Pr., 1960), pp. 202-3

EDITING AND PUBLISHING

It is impossible for many reasons to consider the books issued by Caxton as quite representative of the popular demand. His position was entirely different from that of the ordinary printer or publisher. The best part of his life had been spent abroad in business connected with the woolen trade, he had risen to a high position and was, doubtless, a man of very considerable wealth. When he settled in England as a printer, he was able to consult his own tastes in the matter of what he should print, and this clearly lay in the direction of English poetry and prose romances. The reading public was not then very large, and Caxton directed rather than followed the popular taste. A third of the books he printed were translations made by himself, and he carefully edited all that he printed. At the same time, it cannot be supposed that he neglected the popular demand. He printed service books for the clergy, school books and statutes, but his own interest lay elsewhere. In especial, he was an admirer of Chaucer. He took pains . . . on the printing of his works, and expressed his admiration and appreciation in several prologues and epilogues. He did even more, for, as we learn from the epilogue to *Boethius*, he placed a memorial tablet to the poet in Westminster Abbey.

E. Gordon Duff
"The Introduction of Printing into England and the Early Work
of the Press," *CHEL*, vol. II (1908), p. 317

The mannerisms of the Middle Ages are still noticeable in Caxton's work: in his irresponsible moralising, his quotations from old authority, his conventional excuse for writing a book (to keep himself from idleness, which is the nurse of sin), his arrant inaccuracy as to names, his profession of incapacity "to smattre me in suche translacions"; but his definite claim to have embellished the older authors, his quiet pride in his own authorship and the interest taken therein by his noble patrons, his conscious appreciation of language, are of the new world, not of the old. The days of anonymous compiling are over; and, henceforth, not the substance, alone, but its form will challenge attention. Prose is no longer to be merely the vehicle of information, but conscious literature.

Alice D. Greenwood
"English Prose in the Fifteenth Century," *CHEL*,
vol. II (1908), p. 334

His [Caxton's] position was like that of a modern dealer in costly biblio-graphical rarities, or pictures, or *objets d'art,* who know in advance where he can place a purchase, who owes a great deal of his business success to his talent in forming friendly connections with wealthy customers, and who does not simply manufacture for a quantity public. A little of this intimacy of relationship between printer and patron continued to Caxton's immediate successors, but with rapidly lessening energy, until it died out entirely. A book to Caxton was something of a miracle wrought by his own hand or by the hands of his workmen. His intimate comments on his work, his colo-phons, fixing the exact day of the completion of the printing of the book, are in spirit and form like the similar expressions of the closeness of a manu-script copyist to his familiar and beloved, though wearying, labour.

H. B. Lathrop
Library (September, 1922), pp. 89-90

The names of eighteen English men of letters are inscribed round the rotunda of the British Museum reading room. The first is Chaucer's, the second Caxton's. Yet, though Caxton has never lacked homage as the first English printer, it has not always been so clearly acknowledged as it might have been that he was also the first of the arbiters of English literary taste, and in some respects the most important of them, since he came in the March of our renaissance and influenced enormously the kind of book that Tudor England was to read, and, in consequence, the kind it was to produce. It also needs emphasis that with Caxton the press was only a means to an end and that end the spread of letters.

K. N. Colvile
QR (January, 1927), p. 165

It was fortunate for England that her first printer was not a mercenary trader, but a man of vision and high ideals. He had typically English respect for rank, but he reserved his truest devotion for the aristocracy of the mind, the poets and thinkers whose works he multiplied in the hands of his readers. In his original writings he shows the quiet strength, the modesty, the insist-ence on the highest standard of excellence, that characterize a great man.

A. T. P. Byles
Library (June, 1934), pp. 24-25

His title to a place among the immortals rests upon the fact that he was the first to introduce the art of printing into his native England, and upon the further facts that:

1) He printed the first book ever printed in the English tongue. . . .

2) He produced the first known piece of printing to be issued from a press in England. . . .
3) He printed the first book in England. . . .
4) He designed and used Caxton Black, an extraordinarily beautiful face of type, and was the first printer in the world to use a type that was different than the old Latin face.

John Charles Terr

William Caxton: The Man and His Work (Salt Lake City, Utah: Porte Publishing Co., 1934), p. 55

As our first printer Caxton is worthy of our undying regard. The sneers of Gibbon and Disraeli, and any modern attempts to write down his services to English literature, must be regarded as ignorant and unworthy. Except that he omitted to print *Piers Plowman*, Caxton showed a real understanding of what was best in the available literature of his time. The printer of the first editions of the *Canterbury Tales, Troilus and Criseyde, Confessio Amantis, Morte Darthur*, to say nothing of various smaller works of Chaucer and Lydgate, deserves our warmest praise. But Caxton's services to literature were not confined to one class of writing. He showed an admirable catholicity of taste, while retaining a preference for certain kinds of books. The works of the great writers of antiquity he did not attempt to print in their original languages. That was being done by countless continental presses, and Caxton preferred to translate afresh, or use the translations of others. Prose romance was represented by *Godfrey of Boulogne, Charles the Great, Paris and Vienne, Blanchardyn and Eglantine, The Four Sons of Aymon*, and *Morte Darthur. The Recuyell of the Histories of Troy, The History of Jason*, and *Eneydos* contained much classical myth and story, while the favourite beast fable was represented by *Reynard the Fox* and *The Fables of Aesop*. Other instructive works of a more austere nature were to be found in the translations of Boethius and Cicero. Morality and piety were the informing qualities of another large group of which . . . the *Dicts or Sayings of the Philosophers*, and the *Golden Legend* are outstanding examples. *The Book of Good Manners, The Moral Proverbs* of Christine de Pisan, *The Curial* of Alain Chartier, *The Book of the Knight of the Tower* were among works published by Caxton which have a didactic purpose. . . . Books of a more informative nature were not neglected: Trevisa's translation of Higden's *Polychronicon*, as well as a *Description of Britain, The Chronicles of England*, and an encyclopaedic work, *The Mirror of the World*; books on chivalry and war . . .; and books of elementary grammar and vocabularies. In addition to works in these categories Caxton also published service books, indulgences, statutes of the Realm, and other minor pieces.

This was an impressive body of work for a pioneer printer to have accomplished between 1475 and 1491. We may discount any denegation of Caxton's services to literature so far as quantity, range, and quality of his output is concerned.

H. S. Bennett
Chaucer And The Fifteenth Century (Oxford Univ. Pr., 1947), pp. 205-6

One hundred books in all were made and published by Caxton, ninety-seven of them at Westminster. His literary task was catholic and covered many subjects: games, morals, religion, poetry, and history. Indeed his "list" though small would earn the respect of any modern publisher both for its variety and quality. In addition to the books there were a number of indulgences which prove that Caxton was not only our first printer-publisher, but also our first jobbing printer. Eight different type-faces were used, all . . . following closely the Gothic lettering. . . . The extent and variety of this product both as regards works and typography prove that Caxton was a man of energy and resources. His range of types alone is an achievement. But more than that, more than his inventiveness and enterprise, must be reckoned the bookish foresight and intelligence of this pioneer of a new craft. What faults his typography possessed were outweighed by that honesty of purpose by means of which he opened the way to the building of a great common language for his countrymen. The very fact that he was a man of sound sense and general intelligence rather than a highly specialized scholar helped him in his task and assured his success. He himself had no illusions on that point, and more than once confessed that he was "not lerned ne knowynge the arte of rethoryk ne of suche gaye termes as now be sayd in these dayes and used." His aim was to be "understonden of the redars and herers" for, he said, "that shall suffyse." It not only sufficed them but it is an example which every defender of the English language . . . follows to this day.

Holbrook Jackson
William Caxton (Berkeley Heights, Calif.: Oriole Pr., 1959), pp. 19-21

Caxton draws attention to himself simply because he brought printing to English. Yet he was more than a printer. He was a publisher and editor, a translator, and essayist. To an unusual degree for his time he was a literary critic, a professional litterateur, intelligent, educated, remarkably moved to express his own judgment. We know also that he came to these activities only after a successful thirty-five year career in business.

What he did for England is great enough that there is no need to claim that he did more. Caxton had no conception of the future of printing. He had no notion of its democratizing power. He used the press to provide copies of books of a restricted, non-commercial subject matter and of interest to an audience so limited that it might be described as a subscription list. Because his clientele was small, because of the slowness of the printing process, he published his books in small editions, smaller than those being issued on the continent, and each book, though cheaper than a manuscript copy, was costly. His own activity, rather than leading him into the print shop, kept him at his desk reading, editing, translating. These things he was engaged in during the first ten years. After 1485 the output of the press is slimmer, consisting of reprints of several earlier publications, a few books major in size but historically less important, and more of what might be considered commercial job work. The change might indicate a loss of patronage, or a loss of personal interest, or a slight participation in the growth of commercial printing.

None of this suggests to me a crusader, an educator, a democrat, a journeyman printer, or a business man. Rather I see a rich man with an avocation, providing for his friends among the nobility and wealthy middle class copies of books which they wanted. He was a man of taste and education who did not foresee that a new social order was coming in, and who admired the literature and the people of the old order so much that a great part of his concern and effort was to reform England in the image of the past. He was a serious man, a moralist and propagandist, and would have had England revive the virtues and practices of early chivalry. Such virtues and the literature asserting them, which bulks large in his press's production, are the virtues and literature of an aristocracy or of those who can aspire to becoming aristocrats. To this reform and to this literary service for his betters Caxton devoted his intelligence, knowledge, and scholarship.

Murray F. Markland
Research Studies (Washington State Univ.,
June, 1960), pp. 47, 59-60

That Caxton was the first English printer is sufficient reason for successive generations to treasure whatever he ran off his press. But Caxton valued his work for its excellence, not its novelty of method. Early printers, we remember, produced books closely imitative of the best work of contemporary scribes. The management of lineation and margins, the use of founts of type cut on the pattern of the book hand, and the rubrication, or the supplying by hand of important capital letters, make a folio page of Caxton resemble closely one from a professionally produced hand-copied book. Caxton's zeal for fine presswork is but part of his quest for excellence. Especially important to him was the selection of books worthy to be copied in type. His search for the best was comprehensive, unrestricted by age or by literary kind: he sought to print standard authors of his time. . . . His criteria seem clear enough: each book he chose was (1) long established in reputation or very popular, (2) well-written, (3) instructive, and (4) if the subject permitted, delightful.

William Wells
The One Millionth Volume: The Poet and the
Poem: The Printer and the Book (Chapel Hill, N. C.:
Univ. N. Carolina Library, 1960), pp. 13-15

He [Caxton] has made a coherent whole from his somewhat unsophisticated original, providing his reader with an interesting explanatory preface, book and chapter divisions that are usually well-chosen, rubrics for the chapters, and reasonably consistent punctuation. Above all his text is careful and accurate; and most of what appear to be editorial liberties, especially the substitution of more modern equivalents, are either perfectly justifiable or too slight to cause serious objection. Caxton's text does not need re-editing: it is sufficiently professional to stand on its own and deserves not to be forgotten.

Sally Shaw
"Caxton and Malory," *Essays on Malory*, ed. J. A. W. Bennett
(Oxford Univ. Pr., 1963), pp. 23-24

GEOFFREY CHAUCER

ca. 1340-1400

Geoffrey Chaucer, the foremost English poet of the Middle Ages, was born into a prosperous bourgeois London family closely connected with the wine trade. Nothing is known of his early life and education. He first appears in history as a page in the household of Elizabeth, Countess of Ulster, in 1357. When Edward III invaded France two years later, Chaucer joined the expedition. He was soon captured by the French near Rheims and ransomed in March, 1360. Sometime near 1360 he married Philippa, daughter of Sir Payne Roet, demoiselle of the Queen's chamber, and became a member of the royal household. In 1370, and intermittently for the next decade, he journeyed to France and Italy on a series of diplomatic missions for the crown. His visit to Italy in 1372 is of particular significance, for it brought him into contact for the first time with Italian literature which was to exert such a decisive influence upon his work. In 1374, he was appointed controller of customs on wools and hides, and, in 1381, controller of the petty customs, in the port of London. These two positions were apparently relinquished in 1385-1386 when he became a justice of the peace and a knight of the shire for Kent. A year or two later his wife died, and there is evidence to suggest that he soon found himself in straightened circumstances. From 1389 to 1391 he served as clerk of the king's works at Westminster, the Tower of London, and elsewhere, and from 1391 possibly until his death, as subforester of the king's park in North Petherton, Somersetshire. Despite these appointments, financial difficulties continued to beset Chaucer until Henry IV, soon after his accession to the throne in 1399, made him an annuity of twenty marks and confirmed the pension granted him by Richard II. He died in London October 25, 1400, and was laid to rest in Westminster Abbey. It is around his tomb that the Poet's Corner has grown. His chief works are *The Book of the Duchess* (1369-1370), *The House of Fame* (1375-1379), *The Parlement of Foules* (1378-1382), *Troilus and Criseyde* (1385), *The Legend of Good Women* (1385-1388, revised after 1394), and *The Canterbury Tales* (1387-). He is also responsible for a *Treatise on the Astrolabe*, a prose translation of Boethius' *Consolatio Philosophiae*, and a partial verse translation of the *Roman de la Rose*.

F. N. Robinson, ed., *The Complete Works of Geoffrey Chaucer* (1957)
Neville Coghill, *The Poet Chaucer* (1949)

PERSONAL

By a gracious whim of circumstance, the earliest English poet of the first order, Geoffrey Chaucer, had in his blood nothing austere or somber; his song was the spring-note of our verse, and into it he freely wove spring only of all the moods of nature. A light-hearted, gracious-humored man, the blown rose and withered leaf had no place in his poetry. His constant charity of temper at no time allowed him to look upon the tragic follies of human affairs for more than a brief moment. When the conduct of his story leads him to the contemplation of sorrow or ruined frailty, he makes a simple statement of the happening and passes from it without elaboration. But when he is singing, as he usually is, of laughter and good luck, he waits on them delightedly, and then it is that he turns continually to nature for colours whereby to heighten his expression and bear witness to his exultation in the beauty of health and the sanctity of joy.

John Drinkwater
Prose Papers (London: Elkin Mathews, 1917), pp. 66-67

There are two types of tale, one from the Human Imagination of the complete being, the other from the Animal Imagination of the natural man. The concept of the two bound together upon a pilgrimage is that of a great poet, summing up the Middle Ages. The variant from that concept, that of Cervantes, is that of a great Renaissance gentleman mocking the Middle Ages.

John Masefield
Chaucer (Cambridge Univ. Pr., 1931), pp. 33-34

The one limitation in Chaucer's vision is his disdain, for it seems no less, of the popular and native traditions. While he gave so much else to poetry, he stunted the native forms at a time when they might have been transformed with the aid of his genius. Apart from this rejection Chaucer's outlook seems one of happy open-mindedness. To exploit one form, he does not reject others. He brings into his conceptions of poetry, and into the criticism which his experiments imply, a sense of compromise, of the union of opposites, which has been one of the most distinguishing and characteristic features of our poetry.

B. Ifor Evans
Tradition and Romanticism (London: Methuen, 1940), pp. 23-24

Chaucer's optimism consists in stressing the positive, more than in denying the negative, but his didacticism is none the less real for all that. He spreads the contagious propaganda of a kindly view of human nature. In the four-teenth century it is noteworthy that he extends this kindly view to the lower classes, even when he is talking with kings; and his influence inevitably would tend to create a broader social sympathy. Gower and Langland give all the necessary evidence that they pitied the poor. Chaucer without sen-timentality appears to have loved them.

Howard Rollin Patch
On Rereading Chaucer (Cambridge, Mass.:
Harvard Univ. Pr., 1948), pp. 193-94

Chaucer was a man of voracious intellectual curiosity, and a man who obviously delighted in the exercise of this curiosity. What he read and remembered leaps into his work, so that when he looks most directly at life some analogy from letters of science jumps to his mind, and the illusion or comparison, suffused with his humor or his irony, is as fresh in its novel context as a bush that blooms all over again in new ground. His delight in applying a proverb is the same as his delight in applying a text from Augustine or St. Paul; it gives him pleasure to recognize any relation be-tween thought, whether homely traditional wisdom or the "authority of learned clerks," and the experiences of men and women in the common world. . . .

With all his intellectual curiosity, Chaucer was of course not an original mind, and not a profound one; he did not add new ideas to the world nor did he supply from his own mind ideas of intrinsic intellectual difficulty. Few if any poets ever have, nor is it the office of a poet to do so. The profound dimension of poetry is the emotional dimension; poetry is profound when it relates a particular image or character to the whole of life, or to the comic or tragic sharpness of life. In such ways Chaucer is profound enough. What he added to the world was what a poet should add, new imaginary people, new expressions of human feeling, an all but unique personal style. But it is remarkable that his people are seen not merely as direct observations of the shrewd and estimating eye, not merely as projections of understanding personal insight, not merely in the light of literary tradition, but also in such light as the nonliterary sciences at the time could furnish, or believed that they could.

Theodore Morrison, ed.
The Portable Chaucer (New York:
Viking, 1953), pp. 27, 29

The Book of the Duchess

[In *The Book of the Duchess* Chaucer] introduced into the most factitious of all poetic styles [the dream vision] a sense of reality and a dramatic force, which brought life and colour to the conventions he dealt with. Instinctively, and thanks to the natural and easy swing of the dialogue, Chaucer rediscovered and brought to the allegory qualities which were to be found in the old verse romances. Under what proves here to be the beneficial influence of Machaut's *dits*, he substituted human beings for the personified abstractions of the *Roman de la Rose*. But he went much farther than Machaut in the way of realism. It is a conversation, on the whole brisk and natural, which takes place between him and the unknown knight. Moreover, the dramatic tone of the narrative, it should be noticed, counteracts defects which are even turned to account and which add to likelihood. The verbosity of the bereaved knight, his repetitions, the desultory way in which he enumerates the virtues of his mistress, are certainly in keeping in a spontaneous effusion like his. Thanks to these, the narrative loses its stilted and didactic character. The very fact that his confidence is so prolific and disconnected imparts to it a certain pathos. Moreover, in the attitude of the confident, who is none other than the poet himself, we can already detect the Chaucerian humor. For the first time he describes himself as the man "of little wit," slow of understanding, who marvels at a great passion, the lyrical elevation of which is beyond him. So that nearly all the characteristics of Chaucerian poetry can be found indicated here in this still somewhat clumsy poem, which closes the period of his youth.

Emile Legouis
Geoffrey Chaucer, tr. L. Lailavoix (New York:
E. P. Dutton, 1913), pp. 81-82

The *Duchess* is not an ironical poem, yet is there any other elegy in the language with such playful passages and with such a general effect of lightheartedness? From what we know of Gaunt's character, and specifically of his readiness to remarry, it is likely of course that the husband's grief was more chivalric than intense; certainly Chaucer's lament seems delicately adapted to just such polite mourning. All the conventions of the dream genre and the lover's threnody are not so much obeyed as they are lightly greeted and quickly forgotten.

However whimsical, the poem is nevertheless an elegy, and it is not surprising to find running through it threads also of tragic irony. The very device of the "daswed" dreamer heightens the knight's sorrows by sharpening his loneliness; he has but one listener, and between even them there is a gulf, as between Tolstoi's Ivan Ilyitch and those who listen by his deathbed. Chaucer never emphasized these darker ironies here, however; he manages to draw more attention to his Dreamer-self than to the black mourner. We are distracted, a little shocked, but yet amused and permanently interested in a Dreamer who is such a bourgeois as to blame Dido because she died for love. . . , [or] be delighted and surprised to find neither holes nor cracks in his dream-windows (321-25), [or] imagine that a lady's beauty is relative to the observer (1047ff.). These social "breaks" of the Dreamer have narrative function, of course, but their mildly ludicrous effect must have been calculated. Chaucer is developing the role he was to play throughout his literary life, that of amateur entertainer to a courtly audience in a time when bourgeois heresies were common enough to be amusing and yet not influential enough to be treated with alarm.

Earle Birney
PMLA (September, 1939), pp. 643, 645-46

Chaucer . . . is not only eulogizing Blanche by presenting her as a symbol of the ideals of courtly love, but is also lamenting the departure of such ideals—with the result that not only love is debased but the virtues consequent to the concept of love as an ennobling power are no longer practiced. Chaucer laments the death of Blanche and of those things of which she herself is the embodiment. This is why the Man in Black's sorrow is so great that he can claim he is Sorrow; this is why the dream was worth recording and "for to be in minde/While men loved the lawe of kinde" (ll. 55-56).

Stephen Manning
CL (Spring, 1958), p. 105

The Book of the Duchess, with all its defects, is a very beautiful poem. There is a haunting charm about it that eludes analysis, but subdues our mood to a gentle and vaguely troubled passiveness. The mind is purged, not by the tragedy of life, with its pity and terror, but by a sense of the sadness which pervades its beauty and its joy. Ours is a pleasant world . . . and life in such a world is gracious and desirable, and nothing is so good as tender and faithful love, which is its own reward. But the glory of it all is for a moment. . . . Now this thought—that life and love and happiness are transitory —is not, with Chaucer, a commonplace reflection, with which he has only a concern that is conventional and impersonal and external. Nor is it, again, a dogma of experience, to which he has dispassionately adjusted his philosophic scheme. It is an element in his nature: it beats in his heart, and flows in his veins, and catches in his throat, and hammers in his head. All men are mortal, no doubt, but seldom do we find one in whom mortality is a part of his consciousness.

George Lyman Kittredge
Chaucer And His Poetry (Cambridge, Mass.:
Harvard Univ. Pr., 1960), pp. 71-72

All the dream-vision poems of Chaucer are in some way poems of discovery: even *The Legend* seems to promise to be. And they are all dramatic in method. Unlike the dreamers of poems such as *The Pearl*, or *Piers Plowman*, . . . the poet-dreamer is given the qualities of a "character." The dreamer of the *Pearl* poem slips from the world of loss into a dream about the lost; the dreamer of the fair field of folk observes with critical and satirical eye the corruption and decadence of the dream world that corroborates his view of the real world. None of the other dreamers has much potential for comedy, none of them exists in the middle distance as a figure of interest in his own right. What makes Chaucer's dreamers essentially comic is their purblindness, which is not, I think, in the situation of the dream, merely a pose. They are neither figures to be laughed at, nor figures who laugh, but are ones in possession of partial knowledge who arrive at full knowledge in the course of the dream-experience; or at some awareness of the degrees of their purblindness. What that full knowledge is, is never hidden from the reader; indeed, it is that which gives meaningful form to the structure of the dream itself. That the Duchess is dead is clear from the moment the "man in black" speaks; that the Dreamer must find out that this is really so provides the dramatic movement of the poem. That Love is many things is proclaimed in the opening lines of *The Parliament;* the dreamer's vision of the actuality of the fact is the action of the poem.

Why the discovery of truth is, in these poems of Chaucer, comic and not tragic, or at least "non-comic," is difficult to answer in any simple way. Certainly, the discovery of truth is not, *per se,* comic; indeed, it is also the process of tragedy. . . . In every instance what the Dreamer discovers in Chaucer's poems is something of happy import. Though the knight has lost, he has loved greatly; though Fame is fickle and unjust, she is sometimes just; though contention and order threaten order and harmony, they are never a fatal threat. And all those values that please us in the contemplation—order, harmony, reward, love—become translated into possible reality through the complex workings of the poems. Such a simple observation that literature is not nearly as interesting as life, for instance, becomes a pleasing reality in each of these poems, though ironically the world of the book is the waking world, the world of life is the dream world. And always, there is the perspective established between us and the action of the poem, as our somewhat superior view of the dreamer and his experience gives us the right and the power to understand the two together.

Helen Storms Corsa
Chaucer: Poet of Mirth and Morality (South Bend, Ind.:
Univ. Notre Dame Pr., 1964), pp. 38-39

The Hous of Fame

The House of Fame is one of the most puzzling of Chaucer's productions. . . . In some respects, the piece is a reversion—in metre, to the octosyllable; in general plan, to the dream-form; and, in episode, to the promiscuous classical digression; the whole story of the *Aeneid* being most eccentrically included in the first book, while it is not till the second that the main subject begins by a mysterious and gorgeous eagle carrying the poet off, like Ganymede, but not to heaven, only to the House of Fame itself. The allegorical description of the house and of its inhabitants is brilliantly carried on through the third book, but quite abruptly cut short; and there is no hint of what the termination was to be. The main *differentia* of the poem, however, is, besides a much firmer and more varied treatment of the octosyllable, an infusion of the ironic and humorous element of infinitely greater strength than in any previous work, irresistibly suggesting the furthering of the vein first broached in the character of Pandarus. Nothing, before, in this respect in English had come near the dialogue with the eagle and parts of the subsequent narrative.

George Saintsbury
"Chaucer," *CHEL,* vol. II (1908), p. 200

There is no need to speculate very seriously on the various possible reasons why Chaucer left the poem unfinished—if he did do so. He must have been always the kind of poet who writes only when the mood is on him, when the spirit moves. The air often of improvising, the apparent absence of severe discipline in all but his best work, the number of other incomplete poems, the very enthusiasm and élan of so much of his verse—all point in this direction. There had been no flagging in the gaiety here, but he had reached his climax and proved his point, and it is likely enough that he felt there was no occasion to go further. The whole has sufficient unity, if not proportion. He represents at the outset that he is in search of news—news of the actual quotidian affairs of love such as are not to be had in his books. He goes to the place where all the news of the world is concentrated. He finds all fame a travesty, renown fickle, and rumor a mockery. The ultimate tidings of love from the man of authority would have inevitably been a similar disappointment and disillusion. He returns to his books, with the conclusion that in love, if not in all life, the poetic dream is preferable to the earthly reality. This was his *lore* and his *prow*, presented to us without sting or malice and with the greatest virtuosity he could command.

Paull F. Baum
ELH (December, 1941), pp. 255-56

. . . What did Chaucer do with the literary material he used in composing this poem? His matter was mainly representative or symbolic in kind. Instead of presenting this matter in the usual cut-and-dried fashion, with everything neatly arranged and labeled, and the symbolism carefully explained, Chaucer tried to present it as a series of real events, things that had really happened to him. He either left it to the reader to draw a given moral or, if he drew it himself, he did so incidentally and by the way, putting his comments into the narrative quite unsystematically as the spirit moved him. He made his descriptions as lively as he possibly could, and strove always first for entertainment, with edification as a by-product. In so doing, he brought new life into bones long dry and dead.

Kemp Malone
Chapters on Chaucer (Baltimore: Johns Hopkins
Univ. Pr., 1951), p. 60

The *House of Fame* is not a masterpiece, though it contains a masterly flight. Within his development, it is Chaucer's great *loosening*. It has a swifter verse-movement than before, and sometimes a new freshness of imagery. . . . The poem is addressed not simply to another audience, but to more than one audience at once, and is thus a preparation for the Chaucer of the *Canterbury Tales*.

Raymond Preston
Chaucer (New York: Sheed and Ward, 1952), p. 42

A close reading of the work should convince the most reluctant reader that Chaucer was here, if not in complete possession of his artistic powers, nearing the goal of facility and force such as are to be seen in the structural strength and psychological validity underlying his major poetry. . . . The steadily expanding compass of the successive books of the *House of Fame* demonstrates, in small, Chaucer's whole development as an artist as he masters a literary type, absorbs a new and liberating philosophy from Boethius, and creates a new form. Book III is an attempt to stay within the tradition of the love-vision while at the same time widening its scope to include more direct observation, more invention and detail. None of Chaucer's early poetry seems so clearly to discover to our eyes the poet utilizing convention but putting it aside for larger and profounder patterns of thought.

Paul G. Ruggiers
SP (January, 1953), pp. 16, 27

To argue that *The House of Fame* shows the closeness of construction, the consistency of imaginative logic, or the thematic unity which are often found in post-Renaissance poetry would be absurd. There is, however, no mistaking the fact that the poem preserves a sustained interest in the nature of literary art. The dreamer whom Chaucer has created, partly in his own image, records a series of experiences which are drawn together by a recurring motif. This motif . . . emerges with some clarity from the lines of the poem and need not be sought in Chaucer's sources or in occurrences at the court of Richard II. We are safer in looking for the "man of gret auctorite" among the purveyors of love-tidings than anywhere else; and a poet like Boccaccio, whose *Teseide* and *Philostrato* were full of love-tidings soon to be repeated by Chaucer, is as likely a candidate for the position as anyone yet suggested if the purpose of the serial journey is kept in mind. Even without the solution of this celebrated riddle, it is possible to share Geoffrey's wonder, curiosity, and delight in the journey in search of "newe thinges" which love vouchsafed him in his dream. Such unity as the poem has must be related to the journey, and it is heightened by the poet's sustained interest in the nature and treatment of poetic material.

Robert J. Allen
JEGP (July, 1956), p. 405

The *House of Fame* relates an amusing adventure; yet beneath the surface we can clearly distinguish the conflict between *auctoritee* and *truth*, between what is handed down and a man's personal experience; this is a theme that runs through the whole of Chaucer's early work. The early poems start from a background of literary tradition, conventional subjects, themes already moulded by much treatment in the past; yet all this material is presented in a spirit directly contrary to convention. Undoubtedly there is more than a humorous or ironic intention in all this; for in itself it postulates a new critical attitude to poetry, a new consciousness, a new freedom. In other words, the *House of Fame* is a typical poem of a transitional period. A new content is to be expressed within a traditional framework; and fresh motives replace what had governed the use and purpose of former themes.

Wolfgang Clemen
Chaucer's Early Poetry, tr. C. A. M. Sym (London:
Methuen, 1963), pp. 113-14

The Parlement of Foules

. . . If you take the pretty tradition of St. Valentine's Day as the day on which birds choose their mates, and if you endow the birds with varied human qualities and have them speak in Parliament, Chaucer's parliament is the kind of mix-up you will get, human nature and social barriers being what they are. Place the quarrelsome parliament in the Garden of Love, place the Garden against Africanus's asceticism, touch the Garden itself with humor, and place the quarrel against the principles of order and co-operation in Cicero and in Nature—and you have the *Parlement of Foules*. The *Parlement* is a comedy of medieval manners and ideas adapted to the framework of the love-vision. Like all good comedy, it had something to teach its audience about their ideas, attitudes, and behavior. Its comment was light, witty, and impartial. It seems unlikely that such comedy could be the vehicle for a compliment to individual persons. It is much more likely that Chaucer's audience delighted in his poem much as an Elizabethan audience delighted in *As You Like It*, as a Restoration audience delighted in Congreve, or as a present-day audience delights in Shaw.

Gardiner Stillwell
JEGP (October, 1950), pp. 494-95

We can see in the poem [*Parlement of Foules*] . . . an approximation of the four levels of medieval allegory. The literal is the simple story of the narrator's experience, the reading, the dream, the unenlightened awakening. The allegorical is what this represents in the narrator's life, the victory of impulse and passion, frustrated though they may be, over the idealism suggested by his reading. The moral level is represented by the implied criticism of the parliament in Scipio's "commune profyt" and the comment on the complicated pretentiousness of the nobler birds in the simple happiness of the matings and the roundel. The fourth level, the anagogical, is approached if not actually reached by the contrast between the two dreams in the poem and the freedom for man implied in this conditioned triumph of nature and instinct.

Charles A. Owen, Jr.
CE (February, 1953), p. 269

Chaucer's picture of human disagreements, against the background of Nature's simple plan, constitutes the main point of the poem. . . . Topical allegory there may be . . . but a topical allegory is rarely the central one in a good poem. . . . The *Parlement* may have been written to celebrate the betrothal of Richard and Marie of France. There would be no want of compliment in it if it were, for, though the aristocratic attitude toward courtly love may be faintly satirized, the touch is delicate, no more than Chaucer directs towards his amorous Squire, and this view of love is clearly superior to the others. It is just such an occasional poem as *Midsummer-Night's Dream,* which celebrates a wedding with a play about the irrationality of love! But whatever topical reference is present is of secondary importance to the delightfully satiric view of the human situation that emerges when birds begin to argue about sexual mores.

Dorothy Bethurum

"The Center of the *Parlement of Foules,*" *Essays in Honor of Walter Clyde Curry* (Nashville, Tenn.: Vanderbilt Univ. Pr., 1954), p. 47

. . . The poem has as its subject matter love, but love considered from a very special point of view—that of an entire spectrum of varying types of love experience which the poet is trying to define and analyze. Through the use of contrasted pairs—the golden *versus* the black side of the garden gate, the lush natural beauty of garden *versus* the sterility of the abstract personifications, Priapus *versus* Venus, and the birds of low degree *versus* the "foules of ravyne"—this spectrum of love experience is set up. Through the idea of "commune profyt," and particularly through the figure of Nature, a norm is established by which these types of love can be viewed in their proper perspective and the extreme ends of the spectrum may be treated with a delicate humour and irony. This is the essence of the poem in which Nature plays the role of a tolerant mediator between apparently contradictory points of view, and in which the usual roles of the naive and sophisticated are delightfuly reversed.

Charles O. McDonald

Sp (July, 1955), p. 444

Chaucer is smiling . . . at more than a literary form in the *Parlement of Foules.* The three-part structure of the poem and the careful projection of a view of love in each are evidence that attitudes towards love amuse him most. . . . Taken alone, each attitude can make a convincing case for itself. But when they are placed side by side they make one another look slightly ridiculous. That is what Chaucer has done in the *Parlement of Foules.* Among these views he has, in the poem at least, no favorites and no special targets. Each view is presented with the same artistic care, so that each one will have its convincing moment. Scipio's dream, the garden, and the parliament each in turn seems real enough. What amuses Chaucer, and should amuse us, is the seriousness with which each view is held, and the denial of any other view. This comedy of attitudes, I believe, gives the poem its unity. Each attitude is partial and incomplete, each attitude distorts and does an injustice to the great fact of natural, physical love which it professes to control and to assign to its proper place and value in the scheme of things. Natural, physical love is a force too powerful, complex, and irrational to be completely contained by any one attitude or philosophy in the poem. What emerges, finally, is a sense of love's power. The seemingly conventional lines about the power of Love with which the poem opens comes to have an unsuspected literal truth by the time the poem ends. In its own wonderfully comic way, the *Parlement of Foules* pays tribute to love, offering as sacrificial victims on its altar a literary form too restrictive to do love justice and the conflicting, inadequate attitudes toward love of Chaucer's fellow men.

Robert Worth Frank, Jr.
PMLA (June, 1956), pp. 538-39

Some thirty years ago an anonymous reviewer of Mr. Eliot's *Tradition and the Individual Talent* remarked that a poet makes the best use of tradition when he continues the exploration both of what may be said in terms of poetry, and of the manner of saying it, beyond the point to which the exploration has been carried before: "he poeticises complex experiences that have never been poeticized before." This is precisely what Chaucer attempts, however modestly, in the *Parlement of Foules*; the complex experience being that of the poet himself when he ponders the problems and paradoxes of love, and in particular the relation of personal love to the common weal and to the laws set in the universe by Nature, vicar of God. The poem differs in scope from earlier explorations of a similar kind partly, at least, because some of it concerns the relation of men and women not only to each other but to society: a concern that is ultimately to issue in the collective pilgrimage to Canterbury foreshadowed at the close of the *Hous of Fame*, where the poet begins to turn from his books to those "neyghebores that dwellen almost at thi dores," and where the "tidings of love" are to be sought amongst the crowd of shipmen, pilgrims, and pardoners that is to crystallize into the company at the tabard.

J. A. W. Bennett
The Parlement of Foules (Oxford: Clarendon Pr., 1957), p. 23

What, however, is the total effect in the *Parliament?* Chaucer, like other medieval writers of debates, deliberately leaves the problem open—he is no propagandist. But the satirical humour of parts of the debate should not blind us to the genuine seriousness beneath. The strain between the two ways of life, the way of Acceptance, the way of Denial, he does not finally resolve till the end of his life, when, old and tired, he takes the way of Denial and condemns his non-religious writings. But in this fruitful period of manhood, conscious of and delighting in his powers and the richness of the world, he very strongly leans towards the way of Acceptance. Nature is good, and genuine love is good, since ordained by her—that is the overwhelming impression left by the *Parliament*.

Chaucer himself called the poem *The Parlement of Foules* and the debate has always and rightly been thought the heart of the poem. The whole poem is itself as it were a debate about the nature of love, though the movement of thought is by association and contrast, rather than by direct logic. *The Dream of Scipio* gives a world-picture in which the world is despised—a view of great authority in Chaucer's day. By contrast, the park of Nature represents the world as God's own creation, and under his law. Within the park the pictorial or dramatic descriptions of Venus and the noble and common birds all show contrasting aspects of or attitudes to love. It is typical of Chaucer's methods of writing poetry that he presents these contrasts in the form of descriptions with a high degree of surface decoration, and that he leaves an appreciation of them and of the underlying principle of connexion to the reader's wit and imagination. He creates a set of "states of feeling" which interact and come to function in the reader's own mind. He does not argue a case—it is no lecture on love's philosophy. Even the birds' arguments are more dramatic than logical; they are contrasts in attitudes. Although the ostensible subject of debate is who should marry the formel, the real subject of what the common birds say is the nature and value of love. And the delightful comedy of their argument only enhances the genuine seriousness of the fundamental issues. *The Parliament* is beyond question the richest and most remarkable poem of its length in the English language.

D. S. Brewer
Chaucer, 2nd ed. (London: Longmans, Green, 1960), pp. 86-87

Troilus and Criseyde

Of all the poems of Chaucer, not excepting the *Canterbury Tales,* none is more characteristic of his genius than is *Troilus and Criseyde*. In some ways it is his supreme masterpiece; for it is the only work of large dimensions, requiring a sustained effort of the poetical imagination, which he brought to completion. In mastery of constructive art, in perfect finish of execution, in portrayal of character and easy flow of action, above all in its dramatic objectiveness and vivid actuality, it will bear comparison with any narrative poem in the language.

Hitherto Chaucer had written, gracefully and wittily, in the school of French allegory and dream-vision. With *Troilus* he becomes the poet of living humanity. Though ostensibly a tale of Troy long ago, it makes but the scantest attempt to suggest the world of classical antiquity. Only the names are ancient; the characters, the manners, are modern and contemporary. Troy is but mediaeval London, besieged as it might have been by the French. The parliament which King Priam convenes is an English parliament. Troilus might as well be son to Edward II. Its spirit and temper is that of the modern novel rather than of the mediaeval romance. Were it written in prose, it would be called the first English novel.

To the taste of the modern reader, particularly at a first reading, it may seem in places tediously prolix; for considering its length there is comparatively little action. Its interest lies not in rapid action, but in a keen, minute, almost Richardsonian portrayal of character and situation. Its appeal grows with a second reading or a third. One ceases to be impatient at the slowness of progress, and looks eagerly in every stanza for subtle revelations of character and motive, for flashes of that ironical humour with which Chaucer has enlivened his essentially tragic theme, for lines of haunting poetic beauty. Perhaps the poem would be more effective still if it were somewhat condensed; but it is none the less true that from beginning to end there is not a stanza which is really irrelevant.

Robert K. Root
The Poetry of Chaucer (London: Archibald Constable,
1906, rev. 1922, repr. 1957), pp. 87-88

The narrative stanza of *Troilus and Criseyde* is a technical triumph. Even the rich harmonies of *The Faerie Queene* hardly dispute its eminence; for they are adjusted rather to description. Chaucer's stanza is narrative in sure and fluent onwardness. It so furthers the movement of the story as rarely to invite separate attention, so deftly merges with the other means of narrative suggestion that its values transpire not from quoting this stanza or that, but from reading on and on. No other verse narrative is more satisfying to read aloud. The subtle harmonies of *Pearl* are adapted to lyric reflection. The easy movement of *Childe Harold* pauses again and again on picturesqueness. A fairer comparison is Byron's triumph of fluency, *Don Juan*. Those stanzas have the same achievement of onwardness where Byron gives himself to the story. Chaucer's story, deeper, more consistent, more progressive, is always his main concern. His distinction is in making his stanza constantly serve this.

Charles Sears Baldwin
Medieval Rhetoric And Poetic (New York:
Macmillan, 1928), pp. 284-85

. . . *Troilus and Creseyde* never reaches the stature of the greatest tragedies in the Greek or Christian European traditions. Chaucer finds his fable in a love story told with all the myopic attention to the details of tender individualized emotion that romance demands. He sees its narrowness. He does much to widen the story by making us feel the tragic fate of this one man and this one women as part of the tragic fate of Troy. But still the events of the fable insist upon eddying far too closely about the absorbing interest that Troilus has merely for Cressida and that Cressida has merely for Troilus. . . . A still further widening of the fable to give it participation in the universal drama of struggling forces, in a drama pitting right against wrong, or duty against desire, or one good against another good, is neither attempted nor hinted at by Chaucer. When Troilus debates free will, the argument does not reach to the higher issues; and all through the poem we feel the influence of that courtly love code which is inherited from the *Filostrato* and which excludes itself from any ethical consideration except the loyalty of lover to beloved. In the *Troilus*, as in his other mature work, Chaucer often shows the final authority of genius in searching the springs of human action, but that searching of his which rouses our highest admiration is in the direction of Shakespearean comedy rather than of Shakespearean tragedy. Perhaps the ethical depths reached by the greater tragic poets were waters which Chaucer would have had neither inclination nor ability to sound, even if models of their kind of tragedy had been available to him.

Willard Farnham
The Medieval Heritage of Elizabethan Tragedy (Berkeley, Calif.:
Univ. California Pr., 1936), pp. 158-60

The end of *Troilus* is the great advantage in our literature of pathos pure and unrelieved. All is to be endured and nothing is to be done. The species of suffering is one familiar to us all, as the sufferings of Lear and Oedipus are not. All men have waited with ever-decreasing hope, day after day, for some one or for something that does not come, and all would willingly forget the experience. Chaucer spares us no detail of the prolonged and sickening process to despair: every fluctuation of gnawing hope, every pitiful subterfuge of the flattering imagination, is held up to our eyes without mercy. The thing is so painful that perhaps no one without reluctance reads it twice. In our cowardice we are attempted to call it sentimental. We turn, for relief, to the titanic passions and heroic deaths of tragedy, because they are sublime and remote, and hence endurable. But this, we feel, goes almost beyond the bounds of art; this is reason. Chaucer is letting the cat out of the bag.

C. S. Lewis
The Allegory of Love (Oxford Univ. Pr., 1936), pp. 195-96

The comedy in *Troilus and Criseyde* is never so overt as to make it pos-- sible for one to seize upon a passage and say: It is here. It is not alone in Chaucer's asides to the reader, though they make their contribution. It is not alone in the character of Pandar, that older Mercutio to a still more youthful Romeo. It is not alone in the devious, the seductive Criseyde. In nothing can it be alone, for comedy is social, and occupies all of the available air. The comedy of *Troilus and Criseyde* is in the tone of the whole, a tone so delicately maintained that if we hear it at all we understand the legend that comedy is divine: the gods know best how, when, and why to smile. Troilus is denied a tragic death; it is Achilles, not Diomede, who kills him in battle, though it was Diomede who stole his mistress from him. But even that is not it. No single item is. The genius of the poem enjoys itself constantly and everywhere. For this is a poet who knows perfectly how "to walk both light and soft"—as Shakespeare did not choose to do when he retold the tale in *Troilus and Cressida*, his most savage and least successful comedy.

Mark Van Doren
The Noble Voice (New York: Henry Holt, 1946), pp. 264-65

Having chosen a pagan love story for his theme, he [Chaucer] set about spiritualizing it by first of all giving it a setting in the courtly love tradition as Boccaccio had, to some extent, done previously. In no instance does he present Troilus to the reader as a weak, effeminate, or vacillating lover. The hero's agony, his secrecy, his forbearance, his unwillingness to expose Criseyde publicly are all in keeping with the rules of the Court of Love. His manliness, his gentleness, his magnanimity, his bravery are the marks of the perfect knight. Throughout the entire poem we find a dovetailing and overlapping of these principles and virtues which were upheld jointly by courtly love convention and medieval Christianity. Similarly, Chaucer emphasizes the virtues of Criseyde, and although he feels constrained to reveal her weakness of character in her "slyding corage," he carefully refrains from judging her; in fact, the reader carries away with him the feeling that the poet was deeply moved by the tragedy of this lovely woman.

After having chosen his subject and its setting, Chaucer carefully selected from his original sources only those parts which contributed to a spiritualization of the theme. Not finding these sufficient to elevate the tone to the desired sublimity, he inserted original passages designed to undergird the spiritual quality of the poem still further. Critics have noted that at each crisis or high point in the *Troilus* there is a passage of great power and beauty, skilfully inserted by the author. Many of the poet's small, but subtle additions make use of ecclesiastical terms or refer to the Deity, some are Biblical references, direct and indirect, yet all are instrumental in leading the reader's mind away from the merely physical aspect of love to a contemplation of that unending and all-enveloping higher love which fills the universe in spite of the presence of tragedy. From this point of view the epilogue is an integral part of the poem, contributing to the final spiritualization of a pagan theme. Surely Chaucer, the careful artist, made these changes and additions purposely, with an eye to their cumulative impact and to the total effect of a satisfying artistic production.

Marion N. Green
Delaware Notes (1957), pp. 91-92

It is well to remember how far *Troilus* was below the horizon of appreciation for the general reader in the whole period from Dryden to Ker; Scott could pass over it as "a long and somewhat dull poem." One thing we [moderns] have found fascinating in it is the expression of a highly formalised way of thinking about human behaviour, this expression in turn being to a great extent conventional: "heigh style," the lover's complaint, the *alba* or dawn song of the lovers with its Provençal derivation: all this appeals to that element in modern taste which, having learnt in its catechism that good poetry is nurtured in a tradition, is ready to worship the most highly stylised conventions it can find. . . .

The poem has another claim to special favour in the twentieth century. It is the celebration of a love that goes wrong, not simply the story of an unhappy love or of unfaithfulness, but of a supreme happiness that turns sour. . . . It is undeniable that some of the poem's peculiar attraction for the modern reader is due to this disenchantment; the love that is treated so tenderly in the Third Book is remorselessly destroyed by the progress of the fable, until when he sees the brooch, his love-token, worn by his rival Diomede, Troilus can say

Who shal now trowe on any othes mo?

The simplicity of disillusion here, a simplicity of profound shock, is, not surprisingly, close to the poetry of disillusion Shakespeare developed out of his reading of Chaucer in *Troilus and Cressida*. . . . It is the idea that spiritual maturity implies suffering and that a mature understanding of human love must penetrate to the canker at the heart of the rose. . . . It fits in with the current abuse by reviewers and others of the world "adult" as a critical term.

Finally, . . . Chaucer's *Troilus* presents the intriguing challenge of the problematic, that fatal Cleopatra for both modern critics and sophisticated readers. The motives governing Criseyde's conduct and prompting her fatal weakness are now endlessly debated; with her charm and complexity she comes to be seen as an enigmatic "character" demanding analysis. Chaucer deliberately treats her later behaviour from the outside, as if he were sure only of the bare outline of what passes with Diomede in the Greek camp. By putting the kindest construction possible on the reasons for her surrender, he leaves it open for later readers to try their hand at further psychological analysis. But this vagueness in presenting her state of mind in the Greek camp, in contrast to the detailed treatment of her falling in love with Troilus in the Second Book, is due to tenderness; he is not really puzzled in the face of the enigmatic, but oppressed by his responsiiblity as story-teller, like a Dumas coming out of his study weeping because he has killed Porthos. . . .

Roger Sharrock
EIC (April, 1958), pp. 126-27

An understanding, sympathetic yet dispassionate, pervades the *Troilus,* an understanding which encompasses diverse manifestations of human nature, finds all of interest, discriminates smilingly or gravely but never with severity, and can therefore communicate to us a view of the whole in which tolerance and critical perception are harmoniously blended. Until the Epilog, the oppositions which Chaucer effects are oblique rather than polar whether between virtues and defects in individuals, between persons, or between the endeavors of these mortals and what is celestially decreed for them. . . . And even the polar opposition in the Epilog of heavenly to mundane affection cannot obliterate our memories of the fine if soon withered fruits which the latter yielded to the hero. Our zest unspoiled by the finale, we begin the poem again and again, which as its author prayed with some worldliness has been spared the ravages of time.

Sanford B. Meech
Design in Chaucer's Troilus (Syracuse, N. Y.:
Syracuse Univ. Pr., 1959), p. 427

This dramatic narrative, founded ultimately upon a mediaeval philosophy, occupies a sort of middle ground artistically between the ancient Greek tragedy and the modern tragedy of Shakespeare. It is wholly like neither, yet it participates spiritually in the characteristics of both. In Greek tragedy, on the one hand, we sense a mysterious and unalterable Fate or Necessity back of human action, imposing its judgments arbitrarily from without upon men and women whose criminal actions, intentional or otherwise, have brought them into conflict with these destinal powers. In Shakespearean tragedy, on the other hand, while one may dimly glimpse a shadowy fatality connected with a mysterious moral order, the principal destiny which rules the fortunes of men is the fatality of character. In other words, in Greek tragedy the emphasis is put upon the mystery of those powers which force men to destruction; in Shakespeare the emphasis is laid upon the fact that a man is the architect of his own fortunes. Now Chaucer, in the *Troilus,* has placed approximately equal stress upon the external and internal sources of human happiness and misery. No one can help perceiving that Troilus's fortunes are in large measure the result of the action and inter-action of character upon character—which, it must always be remembered, is itself one aspect of destiny. But it is one of the glories of Chaucer's tragic art that he should have dignified his drama of human experiences by linking them up with those more mysterious and awe-inspiring forces of destiny [Nature and the stars] which govern both men and the universe. No purely psychological work can ever have such a powerfully tragic effect as does the tragedy in which human actions are made to have cause-and-effect relationships with whatever external forces there are in the world. . . . [Chaucer] has gained such an effect in the *Troilus* by creating back of his tragedy the mystery which shrouds the activities of Nature, and the stars. And this deterministic tragedy is entirely complete when Troilus is brought to his death by an inescapable destiny (V, 1806).

Walter Clyde Curry
Chaucer and the Mediaeval Sciences, 2nd ed. (London:
George Allen and Unwin, 1960), pp. 292-94

Dryden long ago defended the artifices of the stage against the rigid prescripts of neo-classical rationalism with the profound observation that since we know all art is illusion, no art can succeed unless we are at least partly conscious parties to the maintenance of the illusion. Thus the best art contrives to create in its audience a sense of participating in its illusions, without destroying the simultaneous awareness of a detachment sufficient for perception and enjoyment. So if the poet strikes the balance exactly, he can keep our consciousness of his artifices just sufficiently focused to prevent empathy from becoming sentimentality and usurping judgment, and at the same time hold us in the poem enough to prevent detachment's becoming moral arrogance and encouraging unjustified conclusions. Exactly so Chaucer, by keeping The Poem—its sources, history, techniques, inspiration, management, and inherent limitations—always just within our field of perception, gives us a reference point for the correlation of the various perspectives in *Troilus and Creseyde*. It is this more than anything else which so differentiates the work from psychological novel, and makes it impossible to define as drama. And the poem as a reference point becomes, for a variety of reasons, a reminder of the limitedness and partiality not of its ultimate moral principles but of any particular man's application of them. In that sense, what it establishes first of all between the poet and his audience is a very special commitment to humanity.

Robert O. Payne
The Key of Remembrance (New Haven, Conn.:
Yale Univ. Pr., 1963), pp. 220-21

Chaucer's most famous love story, the tragedy of *Troilus and Creseyde*, is neither a tale of true love . . . nor of courteous love. It is, rather, a tale of passionate love set against a background of Boethian philosophy. Those familiar with the *Consolation* and its major themes will realize at once that it is impossible to idealize passionate love for a gift of Fortune in Boethian terms. . . . The Boethian elements in *Troilus* and their implications were . . . easily recognizable to the members of Chaucer's audience. And no one reminded of the doctrines of Fortune and Providence, fate and free will, the love of God and the love of worldly goods, or the Herculean nobility and heroism of virtue, could possibly regard passionate love for a fickle woman with anything but disfavor. This disfavor might appear either as amusement at the antics of the lover or as pity of the kind that one should, from a Boethian point of view, bestow on any sinner. If Chaucer had shown any inclination to doubt the wisdom of his philosophical master, we might have reason to approach his poem with something like a romantic point of view. But such doubt would have been strange indeed in fourteenth-century English court circles, and the poem itself is one of the most moving exemplifications of Boethian ideas ever written.

> D. W. Robertson, Jr.
> *A Preface to Chaucer* (Princeton, N. J.: Princeton Univ. Pr.;
> Oxford Univ. Pr., 1963), pp. 472-73

The Legend of Good Women

In Hoccleve, Chaucer's *Legend* is referred to as Cupid's "Legende of Martres," in Lydgate as "The Legend of Cupide," and as a "legende of parfit holiness," and in the Lay Folks' Mass Book as "The holy legende of martyrs of Cupydo." To modern taste, this title seems paradoxical, as all the stories concern heathen women and as the medieval and technical meaning of the world "legend" is the life of a saint who is often also a martyr to the Christian religion. The solution of the difficulty lies in the very conception of the poem. Chaucer has borrowed from the Court of Love literature the idea of a religion of love of which Cupid is the God. Just as Christian saints have suffered martyrdom for their religion, so those whom the worship of the God of Love has brought to their deaths may be thought of as martyrs to the god Cupid. Just as the stories of Christian saints are called legends, so the stories of those who died because of their devotion to love become legends of the saints of the God Cupid. In this poem, Chaucer is creating a collection of the legends of Cupid's saints and martyrs.

> D. D. Griffith
> "An Interpretation of Chaucer's *Legend of Good Women*,"
> *Manly Anniversary Studies* (Chicago: Univ.
> Chicago Pr., 1923), p. 32

. . . The G Prologue, the revision of his later years, shows Chaucer emerging from, and even finding subject for amusement in, the courtly poetry and doctrine in which he served his apprenticeship. It is of unique importance, moreover, because alone in the whole body of his poetry it shows him consciously revising an earlier work to bring it in accord with the artistic attitude toward such material which finally dominated his writing. And the key to that revision is not a desire for greater structural unity, nor a growing sense of reverence for established religion, but only the wish to cast off the out-grown shell of courtly love convention in both style and intellectual content.

Robert Estrich
JEGP (July, 1937), p. 337

The Canterbury Tales

I. THE WHOLE WORK

The pilgrimage is a kind of open forum, in which every one speaks his mind, and gives his views on a variety of subjects under color of story-telling. These people debate as well as narrate, as various questions arise—social, moral, religious, and literary—which claim their interest. And these debates are carried on most informally; every one has a right to be heard, the commons as well as the gentlefolk. A thoroughly democratic spirit prevails. This is one of the most striking things about the *Canterbury Tales*, that here, for the first time in English literature, all classes meet in mutual sympathy and fellowship on a common footing as human beings. . . . Despite this democratic spirit, no effort is made by the various pilgrims to adapt their tales to the taste of the company as a whole. On the contrary, each offers a story of the kind which he has been accustomed to hear, addressing himself to those of the party who care for the same sort of entertainment as he does himself. . . . There is rarely any hint of insincerity among the pilgrims; they are frank and unabashed at all times. What they have to say is thoroughly characteristic of their breeding and their tastes. Thus their tales afford a comprehensive view of the principal types of medieval narrative, as developed by the different classes of society; they illustrate vividly the aristocratic and democratic tendencies in the life of the times.

William Witherle Lawrence
Medieval Story, 2nd ed. (New York: Columbia
Univ. Pr., 1931), pp. 206-8

The very fidelity with which the poet paints his own time shows us the Reformation in embryo. We have in fact here, within the six hundred pages of the *Canterbury Tales*, one of the most vivid and significant of all scenes in the Great Legend of the Ages; and his pilgrims, so intent upon the present, so exactly mirrored by Chaucer as they moved and spoke in their own time, tell us nevertheless both of another age that was almost past and of a future time which was not yet ripe for reality. The Knight is still of course the most respected figure in such a company; and he brings into the book a pale afterglow of the real crusades; but the Host now treads close upon his heels, big with the importance of a prosperous citizen who has twice sat in Parliament side by side with knights of the shire. The good Prioress recalls faintly the heroic age of monasticism; yet St. Benedict and St. Francis would have recognized their truest son in the poor Parson, whose puritanism brought him into such vehement suspicion of heresy, and upon whom the pilgrims called only in the last resort. The Monk and the Friar, the Summoner and the Pardoner, do indeed remind us how large a share the Church claimed in every department of daily life; but they make us ask at the same time "how long can it last?" Extremes meet; and the "lewd sots" who went "goggling with their heads," gaping and disputing at the painted windows on their way to the shrine, were lineal ancestors to the notorious "Blue Dick" of 250 years later, who made a merit of having mounted on a lofty ladder, pike in hand, to "rattle down proud Becket's glossie bones."

G. G. Coulton
Chaucer and His England, 6th ed. (London:
Methuen, 1937), pp. 171-72

The idea of a pilgrimage was masterly. Since "pilgrims were they alle" Chaucer was able to assemble the greatest possible variety of people, all linked by a common purpose, and to allow them to jog forward with a certain loosening of the stricter rules of etiquette and precedence which divided them in everyday life. As the hours proceed they mix together, lose their shyness, and in intercourse, or rivalry, or sheer exhibitionism reveal themselves, and often much more than themselves—the whole social *milieu* which contains them. We are privileged, in short, to see this group of fourteenth-century men and women, not as in a picture, or in the stiff attitudes of a tapestry, but as they laughed and talked, unconscious that the sharp highly trained eye of Geoffrey Chaucer was upon them. The result is not the story, but the *drama* of the *Canterbury Tales*.

H. S. Bennett
Chaucer And The Fifteenth Century (Oxford:
Clarendon Pr., 1947), p. 68

Honour corruption villainy holiness
riding in fragrance of sunlight (side by side
all in a singing wonder of blossoming yes
riding) to him who died that death should be dead

Humblest and proudest eagerly wandering
(equally all alive in miraculous day)
merrily moving through sweet forgiveness of spring
(over the under the gift of the earth of the sky

knight and ploughman pardoner wife and nun
merchant frere clerk somnour miller and reve
and geoffrey and all) come up from the never of when
come into the now of forever come riding alive

down while crylessly drifting through vast most
nothing's own nothing children go of dust

E. E. Cummings
XAIPE (New York: Oxford Univ. Pr., 1950), p. 63

. . . Nowhere in the *Canterbury Tales* does Chaucer commit himself utterly to an exploration of the implications of personality. He adapts the tales to their tellers. He invents excuses for introducing the literary citations of which he was so fond. . . . He sometimes slyly uses his learning as it would have been used by one of his pilgrims had the pilgrim been able to possess it. He shows an extraordinary and precious awareness of idiosyncratic appearance and behavior. But he does not, except by way of introduction in the *General Prologue,* keep the focus very long upon men. About the intellectual and emotional tensions that underlie outward eccentricity he knows chiefly what an impersonal medieval science and philosophy have taught him. More important still, he does not seek tirelessly by direct observation to learn more. He has no really profound curiosity about the individual soul. His strongest interest is in the general —in what is not (as it would have seemed to him) self-limiting and therefore trivial. He is not a patient searcher of men's hearts, but a docile scholar who imposes upon his perceptions . . . a framework of systematized notions.

Wayne Shumaker
ELH (March, 1951), p. 88

In the area of motivation, the portraits seem to propose, ultimately a fundamental, inescapable ambiguity as part of the human condition; prayer for the purification of motive is valid for all the pilgrims. And the pilgrims who move, pushed by impulse and drawn by vows, none merely impelled and none perfectly committed, reflect, in their human ambiguity, the broad problem of origins and ends, the stubbornness of matter and the power of spirit, together with ideas of cosmic resolution and harmony in which source and end are reconciled and seem to be the same, the purposes of nature and supernature found to be at one, the two restorative powers akin, the kinds of love not discontinuous, Saint Venus and Saint Thomas different and at odds yet not at war, within the divine purpose which contains both.

Arthur W. Hoffman
ELH (March, 1954), p. 5

. . . Within the structure of the book as a whole Chaucer employed a principle which includes three stages of dramatic presentation.

A. Simple suiting of tale and teller. . . .

B. Simple suiting of tale and teller, plus an externally motivated dramatic situation. . . .

C. Simple suiting of tale and teller, plus an externally motivated dramatic situation, plus internally motivated and extended self-revelation of which the teller is not fully aware. . . .

Although there is some minor overlapping among and within these three categories, such an arrangement represents an ascending order of complexity in the employment of the dramatic principle involving the relationship between tales and tellers. Thus, in the first category, the Second Nun and the Squire have a single predominant trait; the Prioress, the Knight, the Franklin, and the Physician are presented in the General Prologue as characters with double traits or interests, and their tales mirror both sides of their characters; then, as in the cases of the Sergeant of the Law, the Shipman, and the Cook—the instances in which Chaucer's dramatic intentions are least clear—we find some appropriateness of tales and tellers, and, in addition, a hint of the kind of controversy present in the performances which make up the other two categories.

In the second category the Monk and the Parson deliver material aimed at discomforting the Host; the Manciple expediently tries to smooth over his error in dealing with the Cook; the Friar-Summoner and Miller-Reeve pairings represent open conflict; the Nun's Priest slyly defends the Host; the Pilgrim Chaucer exposes the Host on two counts; and the Clerk delivers a surprise burlesque of the Wife's views.

In the four performances making up the third category, the Merchant's remarks about his unhappy married life are cautiously brief; the Canon's Yeoman is freer in his personal revelations; and the Wife of Bath and the Pardoner give unabashed, detailed pictures of their lives, both past and present.

. . . The principle which seems to control the dramatic interplay among the Canterbury Pilgrims leads to a further important conclusion concerning Chaucer's narrative artistry in the book. There can be no doubt . . . that upon occasion Chaucer sacrifices absolute literary criteria in favor of dramatic decorum. In plainer words, Chaucer at times purposefully includes in the *Tales* a story not possessed of consistent literary merit because a tale lacking such merit is demanded by the dramatic context. The Parsons Tale is a good example of this.

R. M. Lumiansky
Of Sondry Folk (Austin, Tex.: Univ. Texas Pr., 1955), pp. 247-49

The Canterbury Tales

II. The General Prologue

That Chaucer's character sketches represent not so much types as individuals—typical no doubt of their status and occupations, but typical only as the happily chosen individual may be—will, I think, readily be admitted by anyone who bears in mind . . . that Chaucer's poetry was not written for the world in general nor was it "published," in the modern sense of that term. It was written for a comparatively small social group, to the members of which the persons, places, and experiences hinted at were thoroughly familiar. Allusions which to us mean little or nothing were instantly intelligible to the hearers and readers for whom he wrote. . . . We can understand the spirit and guess at the success of many of Chaucer's sly "digs" and "hits" only if we think of his work as conceived and received like a local Christmas revue or revel that banters and satirizes persons and incidents familiar to every member of the audience. Chaucer was not writing for posterity or even for the whole contemporary population of England, but for a handful of courtiers, gentlemen, churchmen, professional men, officials, and city merchants. There was no need to give them a systematic view of fourteenth century life.

John Matthews Manly
Some New Light on Chaucer (New York:
Henry Holt, 1926), pp. 74, 76

That there were here and there through the Prologue allusions which some of Chaucer's hearers would catch and savour there can be no doubt. But that is not to say that the portraits of the Prologue, as portraits, had living models to such a degree that contemporary listeners would exclaim when they heard them: "That is the man!" Persons of every sort and condition represented in the Prologue had been intimately known to Chaucer through years crowded with experience and observation. What the portraits actually do, all conjecture aside, is to strike the delicate balance between the *character,* in the technical, Theophrastian sense of the word, and the individual —a balance which preserves at once the typical qualities of the one and the human idiosyncrasies of the other. Observation, in a word, has been caught up into the moulding energy of the creative act. Chaucer may well have had that piratical rogue John Hawley of Dartmouth in the back of his mind when he drew the Shipman. But if so, the Shipman assuredly has ceased to be John Hawley. He is the incarnation of the type to which John Hawley, and a score of his congeners, belonged. And one line alone—"With many a tempest hadde his berd been shake"—sets him, like the Flying Dutchman and the Ancient Mariner, among the immortals who in their spheres are every one and no one. [1934]

John Livingston Lowes
Geoffrey Chaucer (Oxford: Clarendon Pr., 1961), pp.162-63

Readers or hearers of the General Prolog in the year 1387 would . . . have felt that on another vital controversy of the time Chaucer was deliberately taking sides and shaping the evidence. Three years after Wyclif's death Lollardy was still powerful and popular in London; though partially suppressed at Oxford, it was still alive there; it found favour with a party of the lesser nobility and knights, including Sir Lewis Clifford, Sir Richard Stury, and other friends of Chaucer's. Now if Chaucer displays any bias in his selection of characters for idealization or satiric treatment, it is in this very matter. . . . It has not been brought out . . . how heavily the scales are weighted in the General Prolog in favor of the supporters of Wyclif and against the classes who opposed him.

The General Prolog of the *Canterbury Tales* . . . furnishes three wholly ideal portraits; of these one [Parson's] is plainly sketched in accordance with Wyclif's ideas, and the other two [Knight's and Clerk's] represent members of classes known to be sympathetic to his program. On the other hand, the Prolog furnishes portraits of several rascals. The rascality of the Miller and the Merchant is briefly and lightly touched upon; that of the Shipman is offset by admiration for his hardihood and seamanship; and that of the Reeve and the Manciple is offset by admiration for the cleverness with which they cheated their wealthy masters. But there are three rascals whom Chaucer seems to have labored to make morally repulsive—the Friar, the Summoner, and the Pardoner—and the two latter he made physically loathsome as well. . . . If contempt and loathing can be expressed in words, they are found in these three portraits. Now, of course, satire on clerical scoundrels was no monopoly of the Lollards; Catholics in good standing were loud in their denunciation of these same traitors to the faith. But the fact remains that Wycliffite literature is full of attacks on the mendicant orders, ecclesiastical courts, and the veneration of relics.

The impression made by the General Prolog on the public of Chaucer's day may perhaps be appreciated if we imagine a novel published in 1936, say, in which three characters were idealized—a Middle Western farmer, a college professor, a Democratic politician of liberal views—and three characters were pilloried—a journalist in the employ of Hearst, a syphilitic banker, a homosexual stockbroker. Though the novel contained no downright New Deal propaganda, would a modern reader have any doubt as to where the author's sympathies lay? Neither can there be much doubt as to where Chaucer's sympathies lay when he wrote the Prolog of the *Canterbury Tales.*

Roger S. Loomis
"Was Chaucer a Laodicean?" *Essays and Studies in Honor of Carleton Brown* (New York: New York Univ. Pr., 1940), pp. 137-38, 145-46

The pilgrimage was undoubtedly a common occurrence in Chaucer's day, and he had in all likelihood seen a good many groups of pilgrims among whom were to be found close analogies to the characters in the Prologue. Scholars have been concerned to establish that he lived in Greenwich on the Canterbury road, where he could have seen groups of pilgrims passing before his window, perhaps while he was writing the *Canterbury Tales.* Kittredge is willing to wager he had undertaken a Canterbury pilgrimage himself. The argument is that what he found day after day in real life he needed no literary precedent to invent. But this is not so. It is not the direct observation of murders and of the process of detection that leads to the construction of a detective story. Nor was it the perception of violent death in high places that prompted the Elizabethan dramatist to compose a tragedy. What a writer finds in real life is to a large extent what his literary tradition enables him to see and to handle. . . . The literary form to which the Prologue to the *Canterbury Tales* belongs and of which it is a special realization is the form of the dream-vision prologue in the tradition of the *Romance of the Rose* and of the associated French and English poems of the subsequent century and a half. This is certainly to find the answer in the most obvious place, to find it, like the purloined letter, in plain sight. For if one were to look for the source of anything in Chaucer, the first place an experienced scholar would look is in the *Romance of the Rose* and its tradition.

J. V. Cunningham
MP (February, 1952), pp. 173-74

. . . Many readers, too much influenced by Chaucer's brilliant verisimilitude, tend to regard his famous pilgrimage to Canterbury as significant not because it is a great fiction, but because it seems to be a remarkable record of a fourteenth-century pilgrimage. A remarkable record it may be, but if we treat it too narrowly as such there are certain to be casualties among the elements that make up the fiction. Perhaps first among these elements is the fictional reporter, Chaucer the pilgrim, and the role he plays in the Prologue to the *Canterbury Tales* and in the links between them. . . . He is not really Chaucer the poet—nor, for that matter, is either the poet, or the poem's protagonist, that Geoffrey Chaucer frequently mentioned in contemporary historical records as a distinguished civil servant, but never as a poet. The fact that these are three separate entities does not, naturally, exclude the possibility—or rather the certainty—that they bore a close resemblance to one another, and that, indeed, they frequently got together in the same body. . . . He is, to place him in his literary tradition, merely an average man, or mankind: *homo*, not very *sapiens* to be sure, but with the very best intentions, making his pilgrimage throughout the world in search of what is good, and showing himself, too frequently, able to recognize the good only when it is spectacularly so. . . . The pilgrim belongs, of course, to a very old—and very new—tradition of the fallible first person singular. His most exact modern counterpart is perhaps Lemuel Gulliver. . . .

Artistically the device of the *persona* has many functions. . . . The most obvious . . . is to present a vision of the social world imposed on one of the moral world. Despite their verisimilitude most, if not all, of the characters described in the Prologue are taken directly from stock and recur again and again in medieval literature. . . . It was left to Chaucer to turn the ancient stock satirical characters into real people assembled for a pilgrimage, and to have them described, with all their traditional faults upon them, by another pilgrim who records faithfully each fault without, for the most part, recognizing that it is a fault and frequently felicitating its possessor for possessing it. One result . . . is a moral realism much more significant than the literary realism for which it is sometimes mistaken; this moral realism discloses a world in which humanity is prevented by its own myopia, the myopia of the describer, from seeing what the dazzlingly attractive externals of life really represent.

E. Talbot Donaldson
PMLA (September, 1954), pp. 928, 933-35

Chaucer shares some characteristics with Horace, though there is no certainty whether by influence, or by coincidence and some affinity of temper. He has in common with Horace the easy tone of a man talking to friends who share his assumptions and sympathies, though usually with a deceptive twist: for when Horace meets the characters in his satires, he expects his audience to sympathise with his misery, whereas Chaucer . . . pretends that the situation was delightful and the characters to be admired. He shares with Horace too . . . the use of comic images and, above all, the quick observation of human affectation, and the suggestion of a recognisable personality. . . . Chaucer, however, extends Horatian ridicule to the kind of objects satirised in the Juvenalian tradition, and modifies it by the tone of pretended naivete, not found in Horace's style, but almost certainly learnt, at least in part, from Ovid, whose works Chaucer had undoubtedly read and who might indeed be called Chaucer's master.

Rosemary Woolf
CQ (Summer, 1959), p. 156

As we pass from pilgrim to pilgrim we respond to each as a distinctive sort of person, but also to the distinctive way in which he is drawn; and the relation of one of these kinds of portraiture to another strengthens and multiplies the artistic comparisons and contrasts from which the structure of the series is built up. The difference between the kinds is often a difference of degree; this means that there are various gamuts on which a particular portrait can be assigned its position: the gamut in characterization from the purely typical to the much more individualized, for example; or the gamuts in tone and humour and satire

From grave to gay, from lively to severe.

In consequence, it is easy for Chaucer to keep from marshalling the portraits on a single principle, such as social rank. His arrangement satisfies the sense of order, without being reducible to formula. It is related to regularities much simpler than itself, of which the social scale and the moral scale are, naturally, the most evident. For though he will not allow either to become a formula, Chaucer does not neglect them; he combines them variously with each other, and with his gamuts of tone, humour, individualization and the like. By the very fact that all these are scales or gamuts, with their highest and lowest points, they afford him possibilities of emphasis and significant order; while by their number and the way he combines them, they help to save him from what Blake would have called "mathematical form" and enable him to create for his portraits an order of his own, an artistic order that places every portrait to the best advantage.

Harold F. Brooks
Chaucer's Pilgrims (London: Methuen, 1962), pp. 9-11

The Canterbury Tales

III. INDIVIDUAL TALES

Not only in its unity—of time, of place, of action, of plot, of characters, of impression—but also in its concreteness, does the *Reeve's Tale* anticipate the modern short story. It is dramatic in its use of dialogue to carry on the action, to suggest character or past events; in its wealth of vivid and concrete incident and detail; in its tendency to avoid analysis or epithet, to depend rather upon words, actions, dress, effect upon others, to indicate character or emotion. . . . The remarkable thing is that Chaucer elaborated and developed in the *Reeve's Tale* the already excellent technique of the Old French fabliaux, and, in so doing, anticipated the . . . "dramatic concentration" of the modern short story.

Walter Morris Hart
PMLA (March, 1908), pp. 43-44

In several respects the dramatic irony of the *Merchant's Tale* is unique in Chaucer's works. First of all, and as far as such things can be measured, the ironies of life seem to play here an even larger part than, let us say, in the *Reeve's* or the *Pardoner's Tales*. A larger part, and also a more essential one, for that mood of intense bitterness that makes the *Merchant's Tale* stand apart in the Canterbury collection is due primarily to Chaucer's handling of the irony of action. His success in using the device with such effectiveness is due largely to the intensity and subtlety of the individual strokes, but even more to their number, to that inexhaustible power of invention which allowed Chaucer to keep up through his long tale the mood of fierce irony so boldly pitched at its highest point in the opening pages—another feature unparalleled in the other works. And finally, though well-presented dramatic irony always implies appreciation by the narrator, that of the Merchant is unique in its continual and exceptionally definite suggestion of the teller's resentful and embittered state.

Germaine Dempster
Dramatic Irony in Chaucer (Stanford, Calif.: Stanford Univ. Publications in Language and Literature, vol. IV, 1932), pp. 57-58

. . . Both Chaucer's depth of emotion and the extreme subtlety of his art are generally underestimated. What, for instance, is the general opinion of *The Miller's Tale*? A brilliantly told piece of bawdry, no more: coarse fun plus one of the familiar Chaucerian features, narrative power. Actually it is a consummate piece of obliquity, yet so elusive, so apt to turn another front to you when you read it again, that to explain the obliquity is terribly difficult. And yet *not* to call it oblique at once lands you in worse trouble. Of all great English poets Chaucer is the most patently sane; but if he lavished his utmost skill of plotting and character-drawing on mere pleasant "harlotrye" he must have been temporarily mad. For it is the most brilliantly plotted of all the *Tales* and the character-sketches in no way yield to those of the Prologue. It is in the clear, economical style of Chaucer's maturity: the earlier padding or rambling have disappeared. What was he after that he should take so much trouble? . . . Comedy deals with individual caprice at variance with society; and society, implying a norm and limitations, must win in the end. These limitations can be expressed in more than one way. Restoration comedy expresses them by the code of manners implied by what the characters say. Chaucer too expresses them, but far more obliquely, through the perfect orderliness of his plot, and also by the elegant economy of his language. Against this order his charming but offending victims are set, and they get their reward. Not that he judges them morally, but he shows them up against the normal background of what the world insists on being. Chaucer's extreme sensitiveness and sympathy extend the comic view of life to a very unusual range. But . . . the meaning of the *Miller's Tale* goes beyond the normally comic. . . . The quality it most expresses is a strong, acute, and eager sensibility. The vehemence with which Chaucer absorbed and was absorbed by the characters of those around him was amazing: the kind of vehemence Keats showed towards pure sensation and D. H. Lawrence towards his birds, beasts, and flowers. Supplemented by the sensibility, vouched for, as it were, by it, the plot of the *Miller's Tale* acquires an abstract significance analogous to that of good music or of the Martyrs and Virgins in S. Apollinare Nuovo at Ravenna. And when Chaucer delivers his master-stroke, bringing back the carpenter into the story through Nicholas's yelling for water, he gets beyond the limitations of comedy and sets the mind wondering and expanding as it does in the contemplation of all the greatest art.

E. M. W. Tillyard
Poetry Direct And Oblique (London: Chatto and Windus,
1934), pp. 215, 223-25

For unrelieved acidity the *Merchant's Tale* is approached nowhere in Chaucer's works, and rarely anywhere else; it is one of the most surprising pieces of unlovely virtuosity in all literature. Without a trace of warm-hearted tolerance or genial humor, expansive realism or even broadly smiling animalism, it is ruled by concentrated intelligence and unpitying analysis. Its dexterity may be diverting to the reader, but that is not the teller's mood. His utmost is to cast a lowering smile. There is little of the external; none of that description of people's looks or dress which is so brilliant in others of the bawdy tales, little of interior or outdoor scenes; even January's garden is vaguely dismissed—the author of the *Romance of the Rose* could not do it justice, nor Priapus himself (suggestive deity). Though the tale contains greater obscenity than any other of the *Canterbury Tales*, . . . all this sounds as if due to the kind of savagery which makes one bite on a sore tooth; it serves as an insolently deliberate counterirritant to the cruel feeling, and is neither easily humorous nor rawly animal. The basal refinement of the speaker is shown by disclaimers and apologies at the coarsest points. One might feel half-ashamed of so greatly enjoying so merciless a tale. . . .

J. S. P. Tatlock
MP (May, 1936), p. 367

The *Melibeus* is a serious work, to be seriously regarded. It may not be to our present jigging taste, but that is no reason for not taking it at its face value. The reader must acknowledge the presence in it of a fine and lofty dignity, nobility of thought, and a moral earnestness not unworthy of its high themes. It deals with the tempering of justice and mercy in a statesman, with the nature of good counsel, and the way to determine wise policy in accordance with Christian forgiveness. That Chaucer thought well of this treatise is sufficiently proved by his translating it. If he wished to represent himself as a serious member of the Commonwealth, deserving of the weighty responsibilities which had been entrusted to him, he could have done worse than to have made himself the mouthpiece of this "moral tale vertuous." The principles enunciated in the *Melibeus*, as a model for statecraft in a troublous time, are no discredit to their sponsor. The fundamental solidity of Chaucer's character, the deeper seriousness of his inner nature, could hardly be better revealed. The only thing of comparable weight in the *Canterbury Tales* is the Parson's sermon, and Chaucer thus compliments himself as one of the two persons on the pilgrimage who are soberly concerned with the conduct of life in its most essential aspects.

Bertrand H. Bronson
Univ. of California Publications in English (1940), pp. 40-41

Ten Brink's statement that Chaucer wrote in the Indian summer of chivalry applies with special emphasis to the literary convention of courtly love. And he is, in the "Wife of Bath's Tale," . . . the Meridithean Comic Spirit presenting and observing its incongruities.

George R. Coffman
Sp (January, 1945), p. 45

The story [The Man of Law's Tale] is obviously a low order of romance. It is repetitious, pedestrian, and lacking the glitter and finish of that order of composition. It has little of the psychological analysis or decorative detail that we expect. . . . [Chaucer] adapted a pious story, made certain changes in its handling so that it might share in some of the appeal of the romantic genre, but bent his efforts mainly toward producing a sentimental tale. . . . The story would have satisfied middle class taste. While its tone is distinctly above that of the *Miller's Tale*, its very combination of a pseudo-genteel awareness of manners with the rawest kind of sentimentalizing may remind us fleetingly of the servant-girl literature of a latter day. That Ker should have classified the story as a romance, but a bad one, was a fit judgment. The trappings of the *genre* are there. But, Chaucer worked most obviously toward improving his original where the improvements would most count. Blatant emotionalization, a show of verisimilitude, common piety, and broad, trite characterization are clothed incongruously in a semblance of the romantic manner. This incongruity is the chief characteristic of the tale's art and the prime clue to its intention.

Bernard I. Duffey
ELH (September, 1947), pp. 192-93

No doubt *The Merchant's Tale* makes strenuous demands on the maturity of its readers; but, equally without question, it ranks, both in substance and in form, among the very best and most original of Chaucer's works. One sign of rank is the fact that it is out of category. It uses a fabliau as part of its structure, but as a whole it isn't a fabliau at all; or if it is one, it is unique in its kind. In it are found . . . most known devices of satire; but in its total effect, it is unlike any other satire. . . . If, in the terribly hackneyed phrase, *Troilus and Criseyde* is the first "psychological novel," *The Merchant's Tale* may quite as justly be called the first psychological short story. In complexity of texture, like the Wife of Bath in person, it passes "hem of Ypres and of Gaunt."

G. G. Sedgewick
UTQ (July, 1948), p. 337

. . . The *Knight's Tale* is essentially neither a story, nor a static picture, but a poetic pageant, and . . . all its materials are organized and contributory to a complex design expressing the nature of the noble life. . . . The story is immediately concerned with those two noble activities, love and chivalry, but even more important is the general tenor of the noble life, the pomp and ceremony, the dignity and power, and particularly the repose and assurance with which the exponent of nobility invokes order. Order, which characterizes the framework of the poem, is also the heart of its meaning. The society depicted is one in which form is full of significance, in which life is conducted at a dignified, processional pace, and wherein life's pattern is itself a reflection, or better, a reproduction, of the order of the universe. And what gives this conception of life its perspective, its depth and seriousness, is its constant awareness of a formidably antagonistic element—chaos, disorder —which in life is an ever-threatening possibility, even in the moments of supremest assuredness, and which in the poem falls across the pattern of order, being clearly exemplified in the erratic reversals of the poem's plot, and deeply embedded in the poem's texture.

Charles Muscatine
PMLA (September, 1950), pp. 919-20

. . . The conventions of courtly love form the basic structural patterns for the Merchant's Tale and the Franklin's Tale. . . . The two stories mutually enrich each other, and that enrichment is the result of their parallel structure. Either consciously or unconsciously, in the *Merchant's Tale* and the *Franklin's Tale*, Chaucer employed courtly love conventions to comment on what men and women make of institutions. The framework of these two tales is the pattern of Andreas' Rules of Love, yet the stories are recto and verso of the same richly embellished sheet on which the poet has written his faith that human dignity and sincere love create the true beauty, grace, and charm of life.

C. Hugh Holman
ELH (December, 1951), pp. 251-52

Instead of being an intricate bundle of oddments, as a too exclusive study of the sources used might make her appear, Dame Alison is one of the best integrated characters in fiction. The more closely one scrutinizes her words and ways, the better one sees that the contradictions in her are contradictions proper to a full-blooded human being. She is quick of tongue and sharp of wit, but she has no other interesting quality of mind except common sense, and common sense has not prevented her from making extravagant pilgrimages and marrying imprudently. Though argumentative, she is controlled by instinct and feeling rather than by reason; and she proves nothing whatever by her elaborate prologue and tale except that women can subjugate their menfolk if they will make the effort. Presumably that was what Chaucer intended to convey. She is a convinced feminist because she enjoys the sense of power that any sort of mastery can give and because she rather despises the dominant but indispensable male.

Gordon Hall Gerould
Chaucerian Essays (Princeton, N. J.: Princeton
Univ. Pr., 1952), pp. 79-80

In the *Manciple's Tale*, the thesis [exalting expediency rather than morality] is the thing of primary importance. To this consideration, Chaucer subordinated all others as his imagination shaped and modified the story. Character was developed only to the extent and in the direction consonant with this aim; rhetoric was employed liberally but always in ways calculated to contribute to the large effect; plot was freely subjected to excisions, interruptions, and digressions which would help to develop values necessary to enforce the thesis. Chaucer's formula was pared plot, simplified characters, and much interspersed comment by the narrator. The result . . . is effective. . . . For the kind of thing which Chaucer set himself to do, it is a success. The double standard that Chaucer put upon every line in the stories of the *Canterbury Tales*—that is, artistic appropriateness in the tale itself and to the character telling it—is achieved at least as successfully in this tale as in most of the others. Though the *Manciple's Tale* is not among the most memorable told on the Canterbury pilgrimage, it nevertheless has its virtues, and it is only proper that we should grant them the commendation which they deserve.

J. Burke Severs
JEGP (January, 1952), p. 16

Chaucer can hardly be blamed . . . if his attempt to expand the limits of human nature by poetic fiat has misled some of his readers to defend him by asserting that the world of the *Clerk's Tale* is the real world and that there have, too, been men like Walter and women like Griselda. Wiser readers have noted that Griselda's strength, in the world which Chaucer and the others created for her, is made believable by repeated scriptural echoes that remind us of its source. These echoes are heard, for example, in Griselda's farewell to her daughter and in her words to Walter at their separation. . . . God's grace, our knowledge of Walter's secret pity and repentance, and the narrator's broad hints that all may yet be well, combine to take the edge off Griselda's sufferings and to assure us that Walter is not so ruthless as she might believe; and as the carefully ordered tests grow more severe, the re-assurances become more obvious. Griselda is tested first by the loss of her daughter and then of her more precious man-child, only less dear to her than her tormenter: but the scene in which the boy is taken from her is deliberately left undeveloped; we are promptly told, quite bluntly, that "al fil for the beste"; and if Griselda thinks her children dead, we know that they are safely cared for. More concentrated suffering is imposed on Griselda by her dismissal, by the summons to welcome her successor, and last by the order to praise the second bride; yet we really cannot worry too much about the children, or Griselda, or the Pope himself, for even before the dismissal, the grand restoration is already being prepared. Whatever other merits the *Clerk's Tale* may have, it does not operate through variety or surprise. Chaucer takes every opportunity for pathos, but comfortable pathos; and he hurries over those parts of the story, such as the twelve long years of Griselda's separation from her children, which any but a summary and objective treatment would make too painful. Gross sentimentality would indeed be a more likely charge against the Clerk's Tale than that of improbability, which takes a last blow from Walter's words at the reconcili-ation: " 'This is ynogh, Griselde myn,' quod he," precisely as he had received her promise of obedience before the marriage; and the repetition of the line seems to suggest again that the story is all of a piece. It is far from a perfect tale. . . . If sentimentality is one likely charge against it, plain dulness is another, for interesting complications . . . cannot be expected from a story of how the marvelous patience of a pious wife converts a husband from cruel suspicion to the ultimate conviction that she is really what she seems. Through it all, Griselda must remain immutable, and Walter's activity consists solely in teasing her and wondering how she stands it. Chaucer does his best to make Griselda a convincingly human embodi-ment of patience and Christian humility, and he makes the most of her big situations without allowing them to become grotesquely painful; but I do not wish that the *Clerk's Tale* were longer.

James Sledd
MP (November, 1953), pp. 80-81

The type of writer represented by Chaucer is to a considerable extent the vernacular counterpart of the Latin man of letters, raised to eminence by new social forces. Far from acknowledging ancestral voices from the minstrelsy of the early Middle Ages, these writers seem to have found their chief inspiration in the world of books. By their reckoning, the minstrels were barred through sheer ignorance from the practice of literature and had properly to limit their activity to the spheres of music and frivolous entertainment. This conception, nowhere gainsaid by Chaucer, seems implicit in the representation of minstrel art in *Sir Thopas*. . . . *Sir Thopas* is much more than a dig at the Flemings or a burlesque of popular romances. Taken in conjunction with the Host's remarks and the contrasting *Melibee*, the piece fairly reflects the opinion of a perceptive man of letters of perhaps the most familiar type of oral literature in the fourteenth century, sets forth the conspicuous defects of this art, and finally signals the collapse of minstrel pretensions on the literary level. The *Thopas-Melibee* unit deserves consideration as an essentially critical exercise, doubly valuable because Middle English affords so little literary criticism of any kind and no other work which represents the predicament of the minstrel as litterateur near the point at which he was permanently eclipsed by the type of writer whose art and matter came rather more from books than from oral sources.

Arthur K. Moore
JEGP (October, 1954), pp. 544-45

The treatise [*Parson's Tale*] is authoritative and orthodox. It is dull only to those who regard the posing and discussion of such questions as the sport of, in Bacon's phrase, *sectores cymini*, as a sophistry. It holds no general appeal for the modern reader, and even the Chaucerian scholar reads it for the most part out of a spirit of dedicated drudgery. . . . But, word for word, principle for principle, it is not too much to say that Chaucer himself might have claimed it the most meaningful, and in a dialectal, perhaps even a dramatic sense, the most artistic of the *Tales*. To insist that a sermon is dramatic may seem at first blush tendentious, but the *Parson's Tale* can be considered non-dramatic only if it is regarded in itself, completely detached from the *Tales*. Yet such a reading of the *Parson's Tale*, or the complexus of the *Tales*, would pervert the work. For we know that Chaucer never allows us to forget for long that each story is part of a total situation, and if indices of structure, with emphatic expression of intent, mean anything, then the *Parson's Tale* is not only the capstone of edification but of drama as well. For when its pulsing relationship and organization with the rest of the *Tales* and the pilgrimage proper is marked, it becomes, in its own way, very dramatic. The *Parson's Tale*, or treatise, if you will, has been carefully articulated with the rest by Chaucer in its Prologue. Its importance and place have been emphasized. Implicitly it recapitulates and musters into dramatic unity all the silent symmetries of the other tales and the image as such.

Ralph Baldwin
The Unity of the Canterbury Tales (Copenhagen:
Rosenkilde and Bagger, 1955), pp. 98-99

A fourteenth-century Englishman such as Chaucer or Langland could scarcely have questioned the laws and social forces that had excluded the medieval Jew from Christian society. The time had not yet come to condemn anti-Semitism in the way Pius XI was to do. . . . But there is in Chaucer's treatment of the Prioress a clear-eyed recognition of the inhumanity of her Tale, its violation of the deepest sense of charity which fourteen centuries of Christianity had been laboring to develop, and its failure to carry the burden of charity which is enjoined on all Christians but especially on religious. The Prioress is not condemned, however, rather is the poem's objective view one of understanding pity of her: further than this all of Chaucer's compassion could not go. But how great a thing it was in such a complex social and cultural environment for a poet to insist that anti-Semitism could be viewed through the recognizable frame of such a woman as the Prioress, one who succumbed too easily to the worldly concern with things and manners, and whose charity was too much of this world.

R. J. Schoeck
"Chaucer's Prioress: Mercy and Tender Heart," *The Bridge:
A Yearbook of Judaeo-Christian Studies,* vol. II, ed. John W.
Osterreicher (New York: Pantheon Books, 1956), pp. 254-55

The *Merchant's Tale* is not only a poem of clarity, critical observation, and disgust—a medieval *Madame Bovary.* There is an opposing impulse, an impulse to approach and understand, which appears in a tendency to *generalize.* . . . this generalizing impulse (characteristic of allegory) exists side by side in Chaucer with the ironic or satiric impulse (characteristic of fabliau) which tends to isolate its object and to particularize it. It is this dual impulse which makes the *Merchant's Tale* a saner and more balanced poem than the conventional account might suggest. It is unlike the *Summoner's Tale* in having a significance beyond its anecdotal content, in having a "meaning." The irony is controlled (and this is surely characteristic of Chaucer) by a recognition that January's case illustrates general human weakness—a suggestion that is rigidly excluded in the treatment of the Summoner's Friar. It is a knowledge of "fantasye" which informs the poem and gives it its moral framework within which the irony works. This knowledge appears in the unobtrusively allegorical treatment of the story, notably of the garden. The poem owes as much to the allegory as to the fabliau, bringing to the anecdotal quality of the latter a scope and significance which belong to the former tradition. This seems to be one of the secrets of Chaucer's best narrative poems. They grow in the mind without losing the precision of their outline.

J. A. Burrow
Anglia (1957), pp. 202, 208

. . . The most conspicuous characteristic of the world with which the poem [*Knight's Tale*] deals is one of mutability, transmutation, and incessant fluctuation between radically juxtaposed extremes. . . . This principle of order in the form and movement of the poem pervades every aspect of its structure. . . . But the principle of mechanical order is not, of course, the only one in the poem. There is also in the poem's form and world the principle of human order. Unlike the first, this order—as the product of the human mind and will—is purposive rather than mechanical. Its purpose is the fulfillment of human nature as conceived by the human mind. And it seeks to move toward that fulfillment by harmonizing the diverse forces within man and those which, as he conceives them, operate upon him from without. Its aim, in one sense, is stability rather than incessant change, and in another sense, development rather than repetition. Ironically, therefore, its chief figurations are, first, a purposely fixed and unified design of diverse parts, rather than unpurposive fluctuation between discordant extremes; and, second, a progressive movement of line, rather than a closed circle. This principle of human order, while antithetical to the order of the mechanical, seeks to transcend it by accommodating it to human design and progression. . . . The poem is finally . . . the poet's theatre, world, and tale, in which he images the form and principle not only of Fortune and of man but, encompassing and transcending these, the universe of divine order. But unlike the principle of human order, which reveals its disorder through apparent order, this divine world reveals its order through apparent disorder. This is in part to say that its logic, like the order of Fortune, is non-human. But it is so because it is super-human and, therefore, in the words of Dame Philosophy, "almost impossible" for the human mind to comprehend. Again like the principle of Fortune, and unlike the principle of human order, its executing movement in time and things is cyclical. But unlike Fortune and like the order of man, this movement is at the same time a progressive and unfolding line. . . . The ups and downs of Fortune . . . are finally the ups and downs of the order decreed by the First Mover.

Dale Underwood
ELH (December, 1959), pp. 456-58, 466-67, 469

[*The Franklin's Tale*] . . . is the most gracious of all *The Canterbury Tales* with its glowing illustration of the virtues of generosity and of fidelity to a plighted word and its complete freedom from any rascality. The plot delights by its shapeliness, its maintained suspense, and by the twist at the end. The characters are all likeable, sensitively depicted, and subtly contrasted as they react to situations and to each other. Their experiences are unfolded with a consistent logic and with a variety in the telling of imaginative description, spirited dialogue, philosophical reflection, sentimental colloquy, parody, humour, pathos and irony. . . . The tale, moreover, warmed by Chaucer's sympathy for his fellow-creatures and conditioned throughout by his astonishingly wide cultural interests, bears the unmistakeable impress of the poet's individual genius in the full maturity of his art. It is provided with a setting unusually comprehensive even among *The Canterbury Tales*, for in the development of his plot Chaucer has not only drawn extensively upon his lively reading in contemporary French and Italian literature, Boethius' *De Consolatione Philosophiae*, and in the works of some of the Church Fathers, but he has also made masterly use of particulars of oceanic and geographical lore, astronomy, astrology, and the craft of magic.

Phyllis Hodgson, ed.
Chaucer: The Franklin's Tale (London:
Athlone Pr., 1960), pp. 7-8

The Reeve is only one of a series of pilgrims who expose their fellows mercilessly; the Summoner, the Friar, the Manciple, all do the same thing. Each provisionally brings himself under the retributive economy which the Reeve so ably dramatizes. But the cruel judgment under which Oswald brings himself and them is not inevitable. His tale also promises, by implication, mercy to the merciful. The quarrel between the Reeve and the Miller comes immediately after the Knight's affirmative of a providential world bound together by love, and the Parson, in asserting that the pilgrimage is part of a pilgrimage to the celestial Jerusalem, presumably is urging the pilgrims toward the love in which that city dwells. By its condemnation of the vindictive man, the *Reeve's Tale* drives men toward a realization of the love to which the Knight and the Parson would draw them. The tale, more than a simple joke, thus takes its place in Chaucer's ordered view of man's moral experience.

Paul A. Olson
SP (January, 1962), p. 17

The material out of which the [Summoner's] tale is composed provides almost a compendium of the standard abuses for which the friars were criticized. An essential feature of the use of this criticism within the tale is its dramatic presentation. None of the abuses are obtruded merely for the sake of exposing the abuse; all are integral parts of the story and inseparable from the narrative situation. Each criticism is dramatically realised through the character and action of this particular friar. And it is this realisation, achieved indirectly through internal structure, which proves most devastating.

John F. Adams
EIC (April, 1962), p. 126

What impresses the reader, first and last, about the *Knight's* and *Clerk's Tales* is the variety, both of style and attitude, which Chaucer provides within such relatively limited art-forms—the chivalric romance and the moral tale. Neither poem takes in large areas of human experience, large areas of the social scene. As they were received by Chaucer, in their original state, they were certainly more anxious to exclude certain elements from their vision than to widen it, and with all the changes he made, Chaucer preserved a good deal of this "exclusiveness" of form and vision. The outer shape of the poems is conventional: by their own definition, they are still concerned to speak of "royal linage and richesse," and of "sharpe scourges of adversitee" in language which more often describes the rituals of secular and religious life than the accidents, the casual disorder of human existence. But variousness there is, in spite of this. . . . The *Knight's Tale* mingles formal lament and address, offhand comment, dramatic exchange, sumptuous description and philosophic comment with no hint of self-conscious display. Even in richest poetic modes, Chaucer gives no impression of indulgence. . . . The *Clerk's Tale*, in fact, shows that he can use vocabulary quite as barely and functionally as Langland, in *Piers Plowman*, harnessing his poetic strength for religious purposes. In the same work, however, and with the same lack of self-consciousness, dramatic, intimate, and sentimental styles are given a part to play, and contribute to the total effect and meaning of the poem. When we consider not only the range of language but the range of approach to subject matter—by turns reverent, serious, admiring, sceptical, indignant, facetious and sorrowful—we might once more, even for these two tales alone, endorse Dryden's comment:
. . . Tis sufficient to say according to the Proverb, that here is God's plenty.

Elizabeth Salter
Chaucer: The Knight's Tale and The Clerk's Tale
(London: Edward Arnold, 1962), p. 66

The Shipman's Tale has a sound farcical plot but one which lacks both the physical action and the downright improbability necessary to great farce. This is why the conversations, despite their interest and liveliness, seem like Chaucer's compensations for the story's shortcomings: he cannot give us action, so he gives us talk, and the tale remains somewhat bodiless. It is not long, yet it might be shorter without much loss. Likewise, though

Chaucer tells the story in such a way as to bring out every comic feature of its situations, the situations themselves are of limited variety; and the climax, being wholly an intellectual one, is not comparable with the fantastic actions which dramatically conclude the Miller's tale or the Reeve's, and which Chaucer has made not only plausible but inevitable.

T. W. Craik
The Comic Tales of Chaucer (London: Methuen, 1964), p. 70

No matter how many of Chaucer's tales we know before we come upon *The Canon's Yeoman's Tale* for the first time, it must come as a slight surprise. One could almost assume that the poet expected readers to wonder why a new narrator had been sprung upon them, and to go on to wonder how many others might be necessary before the book was completed. Although it does not stand in the highest rank of tales, it has a considerable originality and as an attempt at explaining some of the actions of scientists of the period it is far too valuable to ignore.

Maurice Hussey, ed.
The Canon's Yeoman's Prologue and Tale
(Cambridge Univ. Pr., 1965), p. 3

Short Poems

Truth

One of Chauncer's most impressive poems is a "Ballade de Bon Conseil," entitled *Truth*. "Flee from the press, and dwell with soothfastness;" "tempest the not all crooked to redress;" "work well thyself, that thou canst others rede;"—these are words of counsel that he spoke with conviction, revealing his own creed. . . . Truth evidently meant to Chaucer, not merely veracity, but, above that, loyalty, verity, and highest of all—symbolically—the truth that makes one free. Truth, indeed, is the very keynote of Chaucer's poetry—truth in description, which we call realism; truth in sentiment, namely poise; truth in imagination, that is art; truth to human nature; truth to truth. "Truth," Chaucer affirmed, "is the highest thing that man may keep."

W. H. Schofield
Chivalry in English Literature (Port Washington, N. Y.:
Kennikat Pr., 1964), pp. 27-28

General

One of his special qualities, indeed, is the amazing ease, the unconscious grace, with which he passes from light facile verse to poetry of noble sweetness, lovely melody, high imagination. He does not, as some poets do, give the impression of being subject to waves of inspiration which now raise his poetry to a high tension, and now fall away and leave it mechanical or uninspired. It rather seems as if he used, varyingly and capriciously, a poetical gift that always came when he chose to call for it, and of which he never lost control. One reason why he is always interesting is that the moment anything ceases to interest him he drops it.... He has much of the spirit of the child, easily pleased and easily fatigued, prone to follow the suggestions of an alert but vagrant fancy.... And so we may see Chaucer writing sometimes with a grace and charm that are quite idle and irresponsible, and then kindling to some piteous or tragic motive, some beauty of situation or splendour of passion, until the bird-note thrills us by turning into the song of an angel.

J. W. Mackail
The Springs of Helicon (London:
Longmans, Green, 1909), pp. 5-6

Technically, he showed how to write a story which combined rich description, incisive comment, lyrical emotion, and a good plot, in one reasonably harmonious whole. As an artist, he raised the whole craft of story-telling from a level at which a graceful beginning, a flowing middle, and a dignified end constituted the whole duty of a minstrel. With him commences, at least in England, most of the subtleties of plot arrangement, most of the "busy care" for truth to life and character, which mark the artist working in full maturity and in an original vein. Precedent is everything in story-telling, which is the most conservative of the arts. Chaucer clung to precedent, retold old tales, held to ancient forms, ranged through the old fields of intrigue, adventure, and misfortune. Yet he broke the bonds of servitude to plot; showed that Malkyn of the dairy, Thomas of the mill, and Hugh of the cloister, might step into the narrative and turn it into English life. He showed, too, that the homeliest tale could be made excellently humorous, tremulously pathetic, or surpassingly beautiful, if only the writer could see it as it would have happened. Much of this achievement is due to personal genius; but some of the most characteristic excellencies remain, and these denote him a transitional writer, his accomplishment pointing ahead to the bursting of the shackles of medievalism, yet in itself mature, harmonious, unperturbed by excess, and the best of mediums for the strong English thought which at last had come to its own in narrative literature.

Henry Seidel Canby
The Short Story in English (New York:
Henry Holt, 1909), pp. 76-77

With Chaucer's poetry, we might say, English was brought up to the level of French. For two or three centuries English writers had been trying to be as correct as the French, but had seldom or never quite attained the French standard. Now the French were equalled in their own style by an English poet. English poetry at last comes out in the same kind of perfection as was shown in French and Provençal as early as the twelfth century, in German a little later with narrative poets such as Wolfram von Eschenbach, the author of Parzival, and lyric poets such as Walther von der Vogelweide. Italian was later still, but by the end of the thirteenth century, in the poets who preceded Dante, the Italian language proved itself at least the equal of the French and Provençal, which had ripened earlier. English was the last of the languages in which the poetical ideal of the Middle Ages was realised—the ideal of courtesy and grace.

W. P. Ker
English Literature: Medieval (New York: Henry Holt;
London: Williams and Norgate, 1912), pp. 220-21

To Chaucer the interest lies in the study of normal men and women, and in comparing his narratives with their originals nothing is more striking than the air of homeliness and naturalness with which he contrives to invest the most amazing incidents. Dorigen and her husband strike one as simple, natural folk whose nice sense of honour leads them to keep their word though it were to their own hindrance. We hardly notice the absurdity of the situation itself, and are little troubled by the magic arts which enable her persecutor to remove all rocks from the coast of Brittany. Constance is no tragedy-queen, but a true-hearted, simple woman; and the fact that she lives in a world of miracles never obtrudes itself. We accept her adventures without a qualm since our interest lies in her personality, and the odd thing is that her personality, attractive as it is, strikes one as so little out of the common. Writers of the day, as a rule, desired either to point a moral or to thrill their readers by sheer force of adventure. Chaucer took the accepted conventions of his day, and pierced through them to the human nature underneath.

Grace Hadow
Chaucer and His Times (London: Williams and
Norgate, 1914), pp. 104-5

He [Chaucer] is the poet of earth, supremely content to walk, desiring no wings. Many English poets have loved the earth for the sake of something—a dream, a reality, call it what you will—that lies behind it. But there have been few, and, except for Caucer, no poets of greatness, who have been in love with earth for its own sake, with Nature in the sense of something inevitably material, something that is the opposite of the supernatural. Supreme over everything in this world he sees the natural order, the "law of kind," as he called it. The teachings of most of the great prophets and poets are simply protests against the law of kind. Chaucer does not protest, he accepts. It is precisely this acceptance that makes him unique among English poets.

Aldous Huxley
On the Margin (London: Chatto and Windus, 1923), pp. 205-6

Chaucer, it seems, has some art by which the most ordinary words and the simplest feelings when laid side by side make each other shine; when separated, lose their lustre. Thus the pleasure he gives us is different from the pleasure that other poets give us, because it is more closely connected with what we have ourselves felt or observed. Eating, drinking, and fine weather, the May, cocks and hens, millers, old peasant women, flowers—there is a special stimulus in seeing all these common things so arranged that they affect us as poetry affects us, and are yet bright, sober, precise as we see them out of doors. There is a pungency in this unfigurative language; a stately and memorable beauty in the undraped sentences which follow each other like women so slightly veiled that you see the lines of their bodies as they go. . . .

Virginia Woolf
The Common Reader (London: Hogarth Pr., 1925), pp. 33-34

The artistic development of Chaucer may be briefly stated: he passed from complex to simple forms, and from simple to complex matter.

Walter Raleigh
On Writing and Writers (London: Edward Arnold, 1926), pp. 106-7

Chaucer had certain essentials of artistic mastery as completely in his grasp as had the Greeks from whom he differed so widely. He knew the superiority of balance over symmetry; he understood and practiced restraint in expression; he studied contrast as no man but Shakespeare, in England, has studied it; he recognized the power of the selected detail; his senses were alert and keen. But neither these essentials nor his amazing technical mastery of his material could be communicated, and his touch was too light and shrewd to guide his followers. In that technical mastery no comparison with his English predecessors is possible. His management of verse-flow, the vigor of his imagination, his perfect acquaintanceship with the creatures of his art and his power of bringing his readers into their presence, his understanding of his audience, have no prototype in England. We term such qualities "modern"; yet medieval Chaucer is as well. He used unhesitatingly and naturally many themes and forms which seem to us absurd; but by using this familiar material he kept himself understanded of the many, as Shakespeare did. In both of them was the "communication" with their fellows, and in both of them the "separate-ness" of genius.

And in yet another way Chaucer was a composite. He worked often with an eye on the aristocratic patron, used often aristocratic themes; but more and more, as he grows older, is the power released in him bourgeois. His kinship is with Boccaccio, with the French fabliau-makers, with Chrétien de Troyes or Jean de Meun. Like them his perceptions are quick, shrewd, amused; like them his study is by preference of human situation. Like them he excels in the smaller structural qualities; like them he makes little or no attempt to raise the pitch of life, as romance and allegory do, and as the bourgeois spirit never does. Yet simply and solely bourgeois, of the bourgeois ignorance of letters, the bourgeois-Philistine contempt for whatever it fails to understand, Chaucer was not. Always he is the composite, bourgeois enough to meet the bourgeoisie, courtly enough to meet the courtier, of genius sufficing to understand and to fuse both and to carry both into permanent literature. Bookman by taste and business man by profession; not deeply read but passionately addicted to reading; neither philosopher nor thinker, yet observer of everything human, interested in everything human, tolerant of everything human, without desire to teach or to preach; pliant to the literary customs of his times, yet understanding how to comply and to surpass with the same gesture—Chaucer, like Shakespeare, struck a balance between individual assertion and conserva-tive acceptance.

E. P. Hammond
English Verse between Chaucer and Surrey (Durham, N. C.:
Duke Univ. Pr., 1927), pp. 11-12

Both writers [Chaucer and Jane Austen] enjoy the contrast between characters with a romantic point of view and characters with a prosaic, wordly one, and enjoy playing such types in opposition. This contrast runs through Chaucer's *Troilus and Creseyde*. . . . The use of different phases of this contrast became a characteristic of Chaucer's narrative; sometimes it is between sense and sensibility, sometimes between disinterested feeling and wordly wisdom, sometimes between a fantastic ideal and a rather sordid reality.

TLS (August 25, 1927), p. 565

Who can say how much of the delicious freshness and perfume that hangs about Chaucer's loveliest lines is due to the presence of all those French words, many of them employed in English for the first time in the passage we are reading, and nearly all of them comparatively new to the language?

Owen Barfield
Poetic Diction (London: Faber and Gwyer, 1928), p. 191

There was never a man who was more of a Makar than Chaucer. He made a national language; he came very near to making a nation. At least without him it would probably never have been so fine a language or so great a nation. Shakespeare and Milton were the greatest sons of their country; but Chaucer was the Father of his Country, rather in the style of George Washington. And apart from that, he made something that has altered all Europe more than the Newspaper: the Novel. He was a novelist when there were no novels. I mean by the novel the narrative that is not primarily an anecdote, but is valued because of the almost accidental variety of actual human characters. The Prologue of *The Canterbury Tales* is the Prologue of Modern Fiction. It is the preface to Don Quixote and the preface to Gil Blas. . . . It is not too much to say that Chaucer made not only a new nation but a new world; and was none the less its real maker because it is an unreal world. And he did it in a language that was hardly usable until he used it; and to the glory of a nation that had hardly existed till he made it glorious.

G. K. Chesterton
Chaucer (London: Faber and Faber, 1932), p. 15

He [Chaucer] is a master-romancer; his *Troilus and Creseyde* is the greatest long poem between *Beowulf* and the *Faerie Queene*. Still, the world of romance is not Chaucer's true or final scene of operations, which is the world of men. He is the first free and brilliant intelligence among our poets, the first artist to show the open life of mankind upon a generous scale and in a clear mirror; the first portrait-painter, and the first true comedian. And he is so in the company of Shakespeare, that he too presents character and the human scene impartially, and in a way that we can trust. These two are the friendliest of our great poets. After Shakespeare, there is no such showman of the English roads and their population until we reach Fielding, with whom Chaucer has much in common. Both of them sit familiarly in the midst of their own *dramatis personae*, and yet apart from them, observers unsuspected. At first sight, Chaucer may seem to treat his pilgrims with detachment, as delightful material for his picture, but very soon, like Shakespeare and Fielding, he lets us know where his own sympaties lie—with Troilus, with the Knight and Parson, or with the constant Dorigen. Fielding, however, is not a poet; and the union of the narrative and portraying gift with the poetic gift is Chaucer's characteristic.

Oliver Elton
The English Muse (London: G. Bell and Sons, 1933), p. 56

The vital independence of his [Chaucer's] genius is clearly shown in the emergence at once, along with a delicate metrical art, and an occasional high-wrought phrase, of a native English simplicity of style. His diction is everywhere vivid, nervous, racy—the language of prose raised to poetry by its vitality and by its music. He seems to be seeking only the aptest expression of his thought, to say everything just as one would wish to say it in talk, and yet, somehow or other, he finds it with rhyme and metre, giving it that graceful ease which is the highest art. At times, indeed, he achieves, irrespective of its meaning, an unforgettable melody . . . and he can write a lyric which owes more to its music than to its intellectual content: but he avoids fine writing as studiously as many seek to achieve it. . . . His style reflects everywhere his love of things real and natural. . . . Tricks of fashion change with a generation, and, as we say, "date," a writer. But the simple and the natural are never antiquated. The best of Chaucer has still the freshness of an April morning.

E. de Selincourt
Oxford Lectures on Poetry (Oxford: Clarendon Pr., 1934), pp. 26-28

Chaucer had a deeper knowledge of life than Shakespeare. . . . Chaucer . . . was a man with whom we could have discussed Fabre or Fraser; he had thought considerably about many things which Shakespeare has not very deeply considered. Chaucer really does comprehend the thought as well as the life of the time. . . . Chaucer was the greatest poet of his day. He was more compendious than Dante. . . . Chaucer and Shakespeare have both an insuperable courage in tackling any, but absolutely any, thing that arouses their interest. No one will ever gauge or measure English poetry until they know how much of it, how full a gamut of its qualities, is already THERE ON THE PAGE of Chaucer. Logopoeia, phanopoeia, melopoeia; the English technique of lyric and of narrative, and the full rich flow of his human contact. . . . Chaucer is aware of life. . . . He is informed, and understands the intellectual conquests of Europe. . . . He is open minded, let us say to folk-lore. . . . You would not be far out if you chose to consider Chaucer as the father of "litterae humaniores" for Europe.

Ezra Pound
ABC of Reading (London: George Routledge and Sons, 1934), pp. 85-90

Chaucer is the type of the tolerant ironist: the defects in the society of his day are not separated, for him, from the defects in human nature, and he has learned to tolerate human nature, to stand outside it, as it were, and look on, half sad, half amused. In such a mood he paints what he sees, selecting those features of the scene which in combination will give the picture as it presents itself to him. If his mood shifts, his selection of detail changes.

David Daiches
Literature and Society (London: Victor Gollancz, 1938), p. 63

Chaucer's method of characterization is . . . essentially static: a character is presented, that is, shown as made up of certain characteristics such as pity or generosity; and then, by the events of the story, it is placed in various circumstances in which it always acts in accord with these characteristics. Chaucer's characters do not change or develop under the impact of experience; they display various aspects of an established set of characteristics as the progress of the narrative places them in varying circumstances. Conversely, the events of the narrative are not determined by the particular moral qualities ascribed to the characters. It would not occur to a mind who conceived of the relationship and event in this fashion to ask how a person who exhibited a certain character in one set of circumstances could possibly have acted so as to get himself into certain other circumstances; because in this conception the personages of the narrative do not get themselves into circumstances; the circumstances are primarily determined by the necessities of the action.

Arthur Mizener
PMLA (March, 1939), p. 68

Chaucer is the first great example in literature of that Franco-British marriage which the *Petit Parisien* the other day urged should be made indissoluble. He is the mouthpiece of an Anglo-French ideal of knighthood, which, extending also to neighboring lands (to Scotland, for example, or to Flanders), was the noblest product of the Middle Ages.

R. W. Chambers
TLS (April 20, 1940), p. 194

The critical spirit of the fourteenth century becomes most clearly apparent [in Chaucer]; and with him vernacular criticism assumes its most notable form. Of direct and explicit literary criticism, it is true, he supplies no trace. Yet his work is suffused throughout by the critical temper, which is visible not only in his attitude to contemporary life, with its foibles, its hypocrisies, its superstitions and the like, but also, and more constructively, in his reasoned artistic treatment of his borrowed material, and in his numerous experiments in verse-form and expression. Nor was this critical tendency without effect on his development as a poet; for he is seen to advance from the cramping technique of medieval poetic, with its rhetorical artifice, its conventional mechanical processes, its elaborate descriptions, apostrophes, and *exempla*, to creative methods of a freer kind, in which scope was given to the dictates of genius, wherein imagination, a sense of fitness, and a knowledge of human nature, all played their part.

J. W. H. Atkins
English Literary Criticism: The Medieval Phase
(Cambridge Univ. Pr.; New York: Macmillan, 1943), p. 151

Chaucer had no great lyric gift, nor much invention in the narrower sense. But give him a skeleton of plot and elbow room, and he can tell a story with any going. As a teller of merry tales in verse he has been equalled in our literature only by Burns, and by Burns only in *Tam o' Shanter*. Looking back over the years that lie between him and Layamon, we may truly say that he found English poetry brick and left it marble. His services to English metre and diction were immense. He had a firm grasp on the true way of wedding the stressed and syllabic systems, by accommodating metrical ictus to natural accent. Above all, he naturalised the iambic pentameter, first in stanzas of eight or of seven lines—the latter the famous rhyme royal; then in the still more famous heroic couplet.

Herbert J. C. Grierson and J. C. Smith
A Critical History of English Poetry (London:
Chatto and Windus, 1944), pp. 34-35

With *Troilus and Criseyde a*nd the *Canterbury Tales* Chaucer inaugurates the English novel; and, moreover, the Great Tradition of it. In these two great dramatic-poetic novels we see the English novel actually in being, with the characteristics of our eighteenth- and nineteenth-century masterpieces. Chaucer's preoccupations here are those of the great novelists. He explores the theme of the individual's relation to the society he is part of. He launches the comedy of the clash of character and the conflict of interest and moeurs. He shows the comic and ironic effects obtainable from the class distinctions felt by the newly emerged bourgeoisie associated with the growth of town life and of the trades and commerce (the Wife of Bath is the new bourgeois wife asserting her independence). He observes, as do Jane Austen and George Eliot, the changes in manners and outlook between the older generation and the new—between the Knight and his son, and the Franklin and his—and, like these novelists and Richardson before them, he explores feminine psychology. He develops to the highest artistic level what is only visible in an elementary form elsewhere in his contemporaries (in the play-cycles and Langland) the kind of characterization which distinguishes the English novel from Bunyan to Henry James—characters which, while exquisitely realistic in detail, are morally and socially typical.

John Speirs
Chaucer the Maker (London: Faber and Faber, 1951), pp. 201-2

Doubly strengthened by a concrete philosophy—a temperament of mind rather than a set of ideas—and by a clear intuition of its own psychological process, Chaucer's humor is so rich and full that it reaches at one stroke a stage of development far beyond that of his own time. His art will be lost by his successors, and will have to be rediscovered; no one before

Addison, except Shakespeare, will equal the delicacy of its shades, and no one before Sterne will add substantially to its background. . . . The humour of our age is heir to a much vaster range of potential effects. But the form of Chaucer's humor can hardly be improved upon; it is perfect, within its limits and of its kind.

The matter and even the manner of his pleasantry are no doubt very often derived from France. But the temper of his humor, or of his method in handling those comic elements, and of his whole reaction to life, does not need to be explained by a fictitious French descent. There never was in France before Chaucer a humorist like him; there never was one in England either, but a deeper affinity to humor was in his time fast becoming a trait of the English character. He took many and invaluable lessons from his French masters; but in the field of humor, as in most other fields, he improved very much upon their example. . . . Not only through his more vigorous intuition of the virtue that resides in concreteness, through his wonderful sense of life, but through his humanity and his genial tone of feeling, he is as a humorist in line with his English successors, not with his French predecessors.

Louis Cazamian
The Development of English Humor (Durham, N. C.:
Duke Univ. Pr., 1952), pp. 68, 79-80

Chaucer's play on words . . . is quite in accord with medieval rhetorical practices. It is essentially the studied application of an artifice which he had learned from such thirteenth-century theorists as Geoffrey of Vinsauf and from his models Guillaume de Lorris, Guillaume de Machaut, Eustace Deschamps, and others. He never abandoned the stylized, often mechanical repetition of words according to the formulas of *traductio* and *adnominatio*, but his first enthusiasm for this kind of writing as revealed in *The Book of the Duchess* and *The House of Fame* seems to have abated to some extent in his later works; perhaps he found the English language less pliable than the French for contortive manipulations. . . . ; perhaps his common sense told him to use the artifice sparingly in the type of stories he was writing—who can tell? Yet, only a poet with a keen sense of humor like Chaucer could occasionally transform this formalized word-play into a display of wit, sometimes subtle, sometimes coarse. In this sense he becomes a precursor of the Elizabethans, even though their punning should probably be regarded as a spontaneous development in the spoken language itself rather than the outgrowth of rhetorical word-play. Some of Chaucer's own puns, too, in particular his double-entendres, reflect the same colloquial background—the chit-chat of the office and the tavern, at street-corners or in the market place, afforded many opportunities for the exchange of sallies. Whatever their genesis, in the language of the fourteenth-century poet well versed in medieval rhetoric, they acquire the labels *traductio, adnominatio,* and *significatio.*

Helge Kökeritz
PMLA (September, 1954), p. 952

Of all our poets, Geoffrey Chaucer is the most courteous to those who read or listen to him; he seems ever-conscious of our presence and charmed to be in such perceptive company. He never threatens or alarms us, as Milton can, intent upon his great theme; nor ignores us, as Wordsworth can, intent upon himself. He addresses his readers as if he could wish for none better, he exchanges experiences with them, consults them, and begs them not to take offence at what he is about to say, touching his show of courtesy with an elegant but ironic wit. . . .

There is so much fun in Chaucer, and so little reproof, that his appeal to moralists . . . is not immediate. Yet he is one of those rare poets who can strongly affect, not only our passions and intelligence, but our wills too; he creates generosities in them. A sense of welcome to the created world, to men and women, and to the experience of living, flows from his pen.

Nevill Coghill
Geoffrey Chaucer (London: BC/Longmans, 1956), pp. 22, 60

His poetry [Chaucer's] is everywhere the same in the first power: that of good judgment. He sees the whole work which he is writing from the outset, and sees everything in its place. The effect is not only progressive; it is collective also; the entire poem has the clear and calm look of a fine painting.

Edmund Blunden
Addresses on General Subjects (Tokyo: Kenkysisha, 1958), p. 135

There are few places in Chaucer's whole work where we can securely trust that he is speaking for himself; he was not a "subjective" poet; and even where we may think we have found something revealing we face the alternative possibly that the views were second-hand, or we recognize an undertone of irony. For the rest, he speaks for his characters as their attitudes or situations require. Dreams are safe to believe or not according as Chanticleer or Pertolote, Troilus or Pandarus, is speaking, and in the *House of Fame* Chaucer refuses to commit himself because the hesitation is pertinent there. On the subject of Fortune he follows tradition. On the subject of gentilesse he echoes Boethius, Dante, or the *Roman.* On the subject of freedom and necessity . . . he borrows from Boethius direct and has Troilus decide for necessity, as the poem demands, but nowhere does he present the "solution" for which Boethius argued in his Book V; and in the Nun's Priest's Tale he succinctly reviews the three possibilities, with citation of authorities, only to brush the question aside as unsuitable for the story of a cock. His whole attitude on such doctrinal and philosophical questions is to let the *clerkes* worry. . . . It may mean that he has no fundamental principles of his own, or that the artistic situation of any context was best served by not taking sides or airing his private views. Thus he lays himself open to the charge of wanting high seriousness. . . . But Chaucer has a vital quality the springs of which lie elsewhere. He may never have attained to a synthesis which without paradox or over-subtlety comprehends in a unity the multitudinousness of life; he was not greatly concerned with spiritual values or the mysteries of the soul. . . . So far forth he was an unfinished man, just as so much of his literary work betrays an unfinished artist. . . . Ecstasy and exaltation and inward illumination he seems not to have known, and does not give. His was not casement opening on the seas of perilous thought. His gaze was on this world, such as it is. It is his praise that he saw so much of it and reported it so faithfully, its changes and chances, the curiosities of human behavior, while he stood back from its painful anxieties and tragic suffering, with no desire to penetrate their dark recesses. . . . When he came near to tragedy at the end of the *Troilus*, he turned aside with a pious platitude. It may be, it may well be, that his tolerance, his Laodiceanism reflects his personal unrest, his unwillingness to accept the violence and viciousness he could not help seeing, his protection against the climate in which he had to live. His gift was not for tragedy, but for comedy. . . .

Paull F. Baum
Chaucer: A Critical Appreciation (Durham, N. C.:
Duke Univ. Pr., 1958), pp. 208-9

Chaucer's balance is a delicate one. The Neo-platonic terms in which his favorite authors saw the universe—the Immutable has expressed himself in change, but the mutable is his work and lovable—is in agreement with his own delight in the visible world. But that is not the whole story. After the first ardor of youth he begins to find in learning the stability the world of human relations lacks. His interest in science, in philosophy, his critical sceptical mind, his absorbed delight in a fine book . . . define the kind of man to whom learning is an absolute necessity. The heart of Chaucer's position as narrator is to set off the contrast between books and experience, between the stable world of learning and the fragile world of love. He knows another kind of stability also, a belief in an immutable God who "nyl fasten no wight," and this becomes most valuable to him when love brings most pain. But his trust in the stable did not lead him to undervalue what he seems to have considered mortal man's best experience on this earth. From his appreciation of *both* worlds comes his incomparable poise.

Dorothy Bethurum
PMLA (December, 1959), p. 520

Just as Chaucer fully subscribes to the doctrine that the true height and sublimity of love is found in adherence to the Code, so he assumes that the greatness of literature stems from the due observance of rules and regulations and from the mastery of that medieval art of rhetoric whose requirements were as complex and exacting as those of Courtly Love itself. "The lyf so short, the craft so long to lerne." The famous line refers directly to love as well as indirectly to literature, and Chaucer's extraordinary sophistication and his no less extraordinary originality can only be understood in relation to these twin poles on which they turn. His "perpetual fountain of good sense" flows from his agile but reverential attitude towards precepts and ordinances which often strike as singularly lacking in freshness, intelligence, or vigour. He is like one of those dolphins of which one reads in accounts of great salt-water aquaria, disporting itself among an apparatus of tunnels and bars, a mechanical structure which is none the less essential to the brilliant and lively display. The game depends on sticking to the rules, and by their indifference and rigidity . . . the rules encourage exhibitions of freedom and feeling.

John Bayley
The Characters of Love (London: Constable, 1960), pp. 58-59

Geoffrey Chaucer produced what English had lacked since Anglo-Saxon times—literary creations worthy to rank with the best works of contemporary European literature. . . . Chaucer had his limitations; he lacked the profundity of a Dante or the spiritual vision of a Bunyan. But his breadth of sympathy and understanding of character, his tolerance and humour, his powers of construction and description, his sense of drama and of vivid imagery, all combine to make him one of the greatest writers in the English language. He was the first Englishman who was a man of the world and created poetry out of what he saw around him. Moreover, his mastery of dramatic characterization was something new in English literature; Criseyde is in many ways the first real character of English fiction.

A. R. Myers
England in the Late Middle Ages (1307-1356) (Baltimore: Penguin Books, 1961), pp. 85-86

In the work of Chaucer and some one or two of his successors, such as William Dunbar and Robert Henryson, are to be found so many of the characteristics of the poetry, variously, of Spenser, Shakespeare, Milton and Pope that it is clear why Dryden called Chaucer the father of English poetry. In the earliest, consistently accomplished instances of the characteristic English verse line, Chaucer achieved the confident and expansive copiousness of the sonnets and dignified stanzas of the Elizabethans. And though, as has been said, the poetry of Chaucer is in the same tradition as that in which many of the early secular lyrics were written, there is no reason to think Chaucer was aware of continuing in it: he made a fresh start, in many respects, learning direct from France and also from Italy.

R. T. Davies, ed.
Medieval English Lyrics (London: Faber and Faber, 1963), p. 34

Chaucer is more sober, more domestic, more reflective even, than Ariosto; both give us the delight of living through the lives of their characters, while we can watch them also acting out their stories in a brightly coloured world beyond ourselves. It may be that our familiarity with the modern novel, with its tendency to confused richness and lack of perspective, inclines us to exaggerate the sense of intellectual mastery, the exercise of choice and discrimination, in such a treatment of, say, love as we find in Chaucer and Ariosto. Perhaps their concentration on the object is not the result of penetrating intelligence, as it would be in, say, Benjamin Constant or Stendhal, but of inherited tact: an instinct, not a conscious discipline. However, we have in Chaucer, and I would say also in Ariosto, a wonderful feeling for what is interesting, for what matters and what does not, within the limits of the *genre*, if we are to be made to participate in the pleasures, passions and strivings of their fabulous beings. What matters is their peculiarly clear insight into moments of intense experience: Criseyde in the garden with her ladies, musing on the possibility of taking a lover; Ruggiero lying awake in bed, impatiently awaiting the coming of the bewitching Alcina. One feels that, again and again, these poets, coming at the climax of a long tradition of romantic narrative, have achieved in their own way as exact a transposition of emotional experience as Stendhal claimed to do by his "exact chemistry."

F. T. Prince
"Gravity and The Long Poem," *English Studies Today*, Third Series, ed. G. I. Duthie (Edinburgh: Edinburgh Univ. Pr., 1964), pp. 83-84

GAVIN DOUGLAS
1474-1522

Gavin Douglas was born at Tantallon Castle in East Lothian, Scotland, the son of a powerful feudal lord, Archibald Bell-the-Cat, fifth Earl of Angus. After graduating from St. Andrews University in 1494, he probably proceeded to the University of Paris for the study of law. On his return to Scotland, he became active in ecclesiastical and political affairs. In 1515, through the influence of the Queen Dowager Margaret (whom he served as counsellor) and Henry VIII, he was elevated to the Bishopric of Dunkeld. The appointment was unpopular, and the subsequent downfall of the Queen coincident with the reversal of his family's fortunes resulted in his flight to England, where he died an exile. His literary reputation rests upon a long moral allegory, the *Palice of Honour* (1501), and a translation of Vergil's *Aeneid* (1513).

J. Small, ed., *The Poetic Works of Gavin Douglas* (1874), 4 vols.

Aeneid

In the translation itself, Douglas justifies his claim to fidelity to the Latin. His chief fault is a certain diffuseness and elaboration of the original, the bulk of the translation being much greater than that of the *Aeneid* itself. But that was characteristic of the period in which he was writing. He keeps faithfully to the "sentence" even if he is forced to change the expression at times because of "sobtell wourd or the ryme." Francis Junius accused him of making many errors, but in reality there are very few. . . . Sometimes he inserts a phrase in explanation of an unusual word . . . or in personal comment on the situation. . . . On the whole, however, this first version of the great Roman epic is a good translation. It has failed to catch quite the elevation of tone that marks the Latin, but it is frankly a rendering in a vernacular which is "imperfite" beside the Roman tongue, couched in "haymly plane termes famyliar." While it sometimes lacks dignity, however, it is spirited and full of vigor.

Elizabeth Nitchie
Vergil and the English Poets (New York:
Columbia Univ. Pr., 1919), p. 84

Douglas was frankly a Scottish poet in his intent, with little thought of a wider audience than the readers and teachers of his own land and race. Yet at times there are gleams of a larger hope, that by his work he had loosed a music bound hitherto in the chains of ancient phrase, and given an example and incentive to others. The Scottish poet hoped by his method to make what was a world classic, a classic of the Scottish folk, and a guide to Scottish thought and action, in familiar phrase, vocabulary, and idea. Professor Henry Morley says of Chapman's translation of Homer, that in it "the *Iliad* is best read as an English book." And in this sense Douglas's is a great Scottish poem, while at the same time a translation of a very great Latin work. If, as Montaigne said, Amyot in France made Plutarch speak French, truly Douglas made the refined Augustan speak Scots, though as a dignified schoolman, with a Scottish tongue still in his mouth, might speak it, standing between the scholar of his day and the peasant, touching now the one and now the other, but never quite together at once.

Lauchlan Maclean Watt
Douglas's Aeneid (Cambridge Univ. Pr., 1920), p. 119

Virgil came to life again in 1514 partly or possibly because Gavin Douglas knew the sea better than Virgil had. . . . Gavin Douglas . . . made something of the Aeneids that I, at any rate, like better than Virgil's latin.

Ezra Pound
ABC of Reading (London: George Routledge, 1934), pp. 29, 42

That word [*Eneados*] is notable, not only as the first translation of Virgil into the vernacular in Britain, but also for its considerable poetic merits, which are particularly apparent in the lengthy prologues that the Bishop added to each book—verses of wide range and varying form, sometimes full of keen observation and pungent colloquialism, sometimes raising to the power and dignity of a hymn to the Godhead.

J. A. W. Bennet
MLN (February, 1946), pp. 83-84

. . . Though . . . Douglas was a Goth rather than a man of the Renaissance . . . and though his *Aeneid* itself is like a vast Gothic cathedral with gargoyles swarming round the doors and windows, and covered with fretted and frequently monstrous ornament both of language and matter, yet, especially, in his famous Prologues to Bukes VII, XII, and XIII, he appears as the first poet in Europe since the "enammelit" and aureate decoration taken over from the medieval French romances. In fact, it is when he is describing landscape and weather which he could see out of his window that his style becomes easier, using words almost entirely from the vernacular with hardly any Latinisms or coinings.

Douglas in these Prologues is breaking new ground in the Renaissance manner much as the almost contemporary Pintoricchio and Perugino were doing by introducing naturalistic Italian landscape as backgrounds to their paintings, but his method is still medieval, Gothic (and Celtic). His effects are gained by the piling up of a multiplicity of detail, . . . which method is diametrically opposed to the lapidary classical statement (whose essence is proportion) and, surely, most un-Virgilian.

Sydney Goodsir Smith
LL (November, 1947), pp. 116-17, 121

It is not the history of Aeneas, but the myth of Aeneas which engages Douglas. . . . And the idea of Aeneas as the embodiment of manly virtue and political sagacity becomes the informing principle of the entire translation.

In Douglas' *Eneados*, then, appears a prototype of the ideal prince who is to occupy so much of the attention of the poets of the English Renaissance. While in Boccaccio's *De Casibus Virorum Illustrium* and in Lydgate's *Fall of Princes* the melancholy tales of princes and noblemen come to grief are taken as examples of the mutability of fortune, Douglas' rendering of Vergil insists upon the superiority to fortune of a prince who possesses humanity, integrity, and resolution. In his typically Renaissance view Douglas looks to and beyond the *Mirror for Magistrates,* which concerns itself not only with "how frayle and unstable worldly prosperity is founde, where fortune seemeth most highly to favour," but with the manner in which "vices are punished in great princes and magistrates." . . . the real focus of Douglas' attention, however, is upon the ideal ruler and the virtues to be imitated, using by way of contrast the vices to be eschewed. And it is more plausible, as well as more generous, to find in Douglas' approach to the *Aeneid* evidence of a scholarly understanding and appreciation of his original rather than proof of naivete and a quaint medievalism. . . . That original . . . was designed to glorify Rome and Augustus through identification with the epic hero. Aeneas is held up as a moral and religious ideal, and it is not too much to say that in his championship of peace, reconciliation, law and piety, rather than military color, Vergil is writing as a political apologist for Augustus. Evidence that Douglas the humanist knew well enough what Vergil meant Aeneas to represent to the Romans appears in one of his own notes inscribed on the Cambridge manuscript: "Bot ye sall knaw that the principall entent of Virgill was to extoll the Romanys, and in specyal the famyllye or clan Julyan, that commin from this Ascanyus, son of Eneas and Creusa, otherwais callyt Julus: because the empryour August Octavyan, quhamto he direkkit this wark, was of that hows and blud, and sistyr son to Cesar Julyus. . . ."

Though Gavin Douglas is throughout his translation deliberately emphasizing the political lessons to be gleaned by a sixteenth-century prince from the pages of Vergil, and though topical political allegory lay ready to hand, it is noteworthy that he gains his emphasis not by perverting the original, but by making unmistakable the *sentens* that could be obscured by a merely literal rendering of the Latin. The result is not merely a textbook for schoolboys, nor a tale interesting only for its fable, nor a mere exercise in scholarship, as various scholars have styled it. It is instead a prototype of the Renaissance cultural and political epic.

Bruce Dearing
PMLA (September, 1952), pp. 854-55, 859

Douglas shocks us by being closer to Virgil than we. . . . Time after time Douglas is nearer to the original than any version could be which kept within the limits of later classicism. And that is almost another way of saying that the real Virgil is very much less "classical" than we had supposed. To read the Latin again with Douglas's version fresh in our minds is like seeing a favourite picture after it has been cleaned. Half the "richness" and "sobriety" which we have been taught to admire turns out to have been only dirt; the "broun trees" disappear and where the sponge has passed the glowing reds, the purples, and the transparent blues leap into life.

C. S. Lewis
English Literature in the Sixteenth Century
(Oxford: Clarendon Pr., 1954), pp. 83-84

That Douglas's *Aeneid* . . . is one of the great translations is undoubted; but there may be now the danger of making too much of it. When Ezra Pound calls it better than its original, we need not take him seriously. But when he couples Douglas with Chaucer as the two medieval poets writing in English who matter most and illustrates abundantly, it is time to reflect and ask questions. There are splendid things in the passages Pound quotes, and there are splendid things all through Douglas's *Aeneid*. But what of the whole poem? Many people have read the original *Aeneid* from beginning to end with pleasure. Some people may have read Douglas's *Aeneid* right through with pleasure in his own day. But how many of those who have praised it recently have read and enjoyed the whole. The knottiness of Douglas's language, admirably effective for certain passages and in small doses, does not make for intelligible narrative and wearies the reader after a few hundred lines. Douglas's prosody, admirably expressive in some passages, often collapses into incoherence; leaving the reader doubtful how to read lines, and having no particular point on any reading. . . . In spite of these weaknesses Douglas's *Aeneid* is a very distinguished work, probably the best translation of one of the great epics till Dryden and Pope. It is permeated throughout, even if spasmodically, with passion, and a passion which, different from the Virgilian, gives the work a character. Virgil can deal with quick and violent action surpassingly well, but it is not his special and central concern. Douglas has the keenest sense for close and rapid action. He pictures happenings so vividly that he constantly adds particular strokes that are missing in Virgil. Often when he appears to err by breaking the taut, packed, yet exquisite quality of his original, he compensates by infusing his own special vigour through greater amplitude and circumstantiation.

E. M. W. Tillyard
The English Epic and Its Background (London:
Chatto and Windus, 1954), pp. 338, 340

Douglas's *Eneados* is one of the great Renaissance translations. In it he makes it his purpose to bring one of the very great classical authors within reach of the common reader. He shows a respect for the letter of his original that is wholly new; and such is his reverence for Virgil, both as a man and as a poet, that he reviles Caxton's so-called *Aeneis,* and even censures the liberties that Chaucer had taken with his author (Prol. I, II. 14). In many ways the Prologues of the *Eneados* represent the beginnings of literary criticism (Prols. I, V, VI, IX), and Douglas ponders the problem of choosing between a literal translation and one that attempts to reproduce the style as well as the meaning of the original. . . . He quotes his authorities, and adopts the educated Renaissance man's slightly patronising attitude towards the unlearned; yet he includes a translation of the "Thirteenth Book" of the *Aeneid*, by Mapheus Vegius (Maffeo Veggio). His style and his theory of epic show a similar mixture of old and new. Douglas retains the Christian interpretation of Virgil and the Catholic system of thought, and he writes allegories—but he fills them with a new meaning, and he comes within striking distance of Sir Philip Sydney's theory of an epic as a sugar-coating for a moral pill. . . .

K. Wittig
The Scottish Tradition in Literature (Edinburgh:
Oliver and Boyd, 1958), p. 77

Douglas translating the *Aneid* accomplished something that we have to call modern, because it established an idea that has lasted until today. This idea, the idea of translation, is so fundamental to our understanding of the epic that only by looking backward can we realize that a time existed when that idea was not important. The middle ages, to understand the *Aeneid*, developed the technique which Hugo of St. Victor expressed as "modus legendi in dividendo constat," and which gave the understanding a particular characteristic, the separation of *dulcis* and *utilis*. As long as these functions remained separate we could have the allegorical analyses on one level, the level of reason, and the various adaptations on the other, the level of the senses. For the middle ages the value of the *Aeneid* lay partially in the variety with which an author could utilize its story. Gavin Douglas turned his back on the technique of division and thought of the *Aeneid* as a single, individual work in which Virgil "miscuit utile dulci." As a result of this unified understanding, Douglas not only translated as accurately as he could, but he also simplified his interpretation. Instead of changing the text to suit the ideas of his own times, he took his times back to the text. Before him were the adaptations, and after him the translations.

Louis Brewer Hall
Studies in the Renaissance (1960), p. 192

The movement of Douglas' verse is characteristically impeded; the heavy, loaded, clogged lines do not flow. This is not artistic incompetence: it is simply another kind of verse, having affinities with the alliterative verse.

It can be most expressive when what is being communicated *is* a sense of effort and struggle, strain and stress. It is not at all like Chaucer's verse—and it is not at all like Virgil's. . . .

Douglas . . . is a close translator. His whole endeavour, clearly, was to be faithful to his much respected original. Yet the miracle is that the result again is a new, a different poem. The whole effect could not be more different from that of the poetry of Virgil's *Aeneid*. The differences are radical: the differences between two languages (Douglas' Scots and Virgil's Latin), between two civilizations (medieval Christian and Augustan Roman).

J. Speirs
The Scots Literary Tradition, 2nd ed. (London:
Faber and Faber, 1962), pp. 165-66

Douglas must be regarded, then, as a competent poet in his own right—beyond this as a great translator. He had doubts about Scots, for it had not been dignified by age and use as Latin had. But he faced the difficulty of language with individuality and vigour, asserting the rightness of Scots as it was right for Virgil to use Latin, and aiming at a vitality unrestrained by the stately decorum of Neo-classicism. History on the whole has been kind to his reputation, and it would be an error in taste to find now nothing in his work except an archaic level of sensibility. His *Aeneid* differs from Virgil's, being less sensuous and melodic, more spirited and lively, and, above all, more nautical. But if the reader can accustom himself to the curiosities of Scottish orthography, then he may find here the most satisfying translation of the Latin original.

David F. C. Coldwell, ed.
Selections from Gavin Douglas (Oxford:
Clarendon Pr., 1964), pp. xviii-xix

GENERAL

The Palice of Honour, Douglas's earliest work, is an example, in every essential sense, of the later type of dream-poem . . . illustrated in the *Goldyn Targe*. It is, however, a more ambitious work (extending to 2166 lines); and it shows more clearly the decadence of the old method, partly by its over-elaboration, partly by the inferior art of the verse, partly by the incongruous welding of the pictorial and moral purposes. The poem is dedicated to James IV, who was probably expected to read between the lines and profit from the long lesson on the triumph of virtue.

G. Gregory Smith
"The Scottish Chaucerians," *CHEL*, vol. II (1908), p. 295

Neither in vocabulary nor style could Douglas accommodate himself to the vulgar. He was a man of the study, a disciple of Chaucer, "a judge and master of polite learning." He belonged to the advance guard of that noble army of translators who in the fifteenth and sixteenth centuries did more than any original writers could at that time have done for the cause of learning and civility in Britain.

TLS (April 1, 1920), p. 210

If Dunbar is akin to Skelton, Douglas is akin to Lydgate and to Hawes, though a much larger man than they. Certain of the conventions obeyed by them he has; his *Palice of Honour* is as heavily allegorical as the *Court of Sapience* or the *Flower and the Leaf*; and in much of his work there is a straining for "aureat language" which, as in Hawes, speaks the rhetorician rather than the poet. This connects Douglas with such Frenchmen as St. Gelais and Molinet; indeed, his likeness to Octavien de St. Gelais, also bishop, rhetorician, and translator of Virgil, is marked. But wholly a pedant Douglas was not. The interesting escapes of personal expression and of nature-feeling in his prologues to the Aeneid, and his harsh but not systematically harsh treatment of the five-beat line, give him advantage over Lydgate, even over the nature-bits of the Troy Book.

E. P. Hammond
English Verse Between Chaucer and Surrey
(Durham, N. C.: Duke Univ. Pr., 1927), p. 25

Douglas is one of the most redundant of poets, but he is a real poet and an allegorist of remarkable ingenuity. His longest, and apparently earliest, independent poem, *The Palice of Honour* (1501), fills eighty pages of intricate nine-line stanzas and hardly yields in imaginative merit to any of the other offspring of the *Romance of the Rose*.

Douglas's translation of the *Aeneid . . .* was his greatest and most famous labor. Preceded among English renderings only by Caxton's *Eneydos*, towards which Douglas is justly scornful, it has the virtues of accuracy, clearness, and, save for the dialect, readability. Naturally the copious Scot was no man to emulate Virgil's great compactness; he normally requires two lines for each line of the Latin, but the result is seldom incorrect or heavy.

Albert C. Baugh, ed.
A Literary History of England (New York:
Appleton-Century-Crofts, 1948), pp. 319-20

WILLIAM DUNBAR

ca. 1460-1515

William Dunbar, Scottish poet, descended from the powerful earls of Dunbar and March. He probably attended St. Andrews University; at any rate, he is thought to be the William Dunbar who took a "Batchelor's" degree there in 1477 and a Master's degree in 1479. By 1504 he had become a priest, but the tradition that he was a Franciscan is apparently unfounded. Between 1500 and 1510 he received a series of pensions for his services to the court and crown as poet and diplomat. His chief works are *The Thrissil and the Rois*, a political allegory; *The Tretis of the Tua Mariit Wemen and the Wedo*, an antifeminist satire; *The Goldyn Targe*, a love allegory; *The Dance of the Sevin Deidly Synnis*; and *Lament for the Makaris*, an elegy lamenting the passing of poets from Chaucer's day to his own. All these poems were probably composed between 1503 and 1508.

W. Mackay Mackenzie, ed., *The Poems of William Dunbar* (1932)
J. W. Baxter, *William Dunbar* (1952)

PERSONAL

The world of Dunbar is very limited. His "anamylit" meads have few far glimpses; his angry sphere of folly and spleen does not invite to profounder invasion. . . . Dunbar's anxieties and interests were, on the whole, of a commonplace kind. He was a bourgeois, thoroughly overcome by the municipal glories of London, and longing above all things for a settled place in a comfortable world. He was, however, born on the wrong side of the Cheviots to be content with this aspiration. He is a man of talent; and he has some gifts that should have gone with genius, an extraordinary passion for words, an effortless dexterity in metre, and most of all, a power of extravagant mirth, which went ill with his bourgeois part. . . . There is no actual tragedy in this makkar, and so none of the reconciliation and assent of the soul in beauty by which, in so many diverse ways, we recognize the presence of great art. His restless spirit could not pause in the eternal moment by which and only by which we escape the tyranny of time. Sometimes, perhaps, when the rhythms that besought him became smooth and yearning in his ear, did the mystery approach him; but he could not listen long enough for the inevitable image to follow its cadence. He was content to take the first that came, so that there is often much incompatibility between the image and the chord even in his most serious poems.

Rachel Annand Taylor
Dunbar the Poet and His Period (London:
Faber and Faber, 1931), pp. 71-73

The many-mooded William Dunbar . . . is the best executant of all the Scottish poets before Burns. He is a "virtuoso," one who loves to sport with his instrument and show off its powers. Not like Burns a singer, he has the same gifts of raking satire, of speed and concision, and a similar freedom of mind. Dunbar does not care what he says; at times he hath a devil, and there is a light in his eye that mocks at decorum. Then comes revulsion, and no bard is more sober and religious. Also he is a fertile inventor and bequeather of poetic forms; both a courtly and a popular writer.

Oliver Elton
The English Muse (London: G. Bell, 1933), p. 85

GENERAL

Dunbar was undoubtedly a man of genius, but a reference to the poets who immediately preceded him will make large deductions from the praises lavished on him by his eulogists. He struck no new notes. *The Thistle and the Rose* and *The Golden Targe* are mere echoes of Chaucer and Lydgate, and, in some degree, of the author of *The King's Quair*, and are indeed full of plagiarisms from them. *The Dance of the Seven Deadly Sins* is probably little more than a faithful description of a popular mummery. His moral and religious poems had their prototypes, even in Scotland, in such poets as Johnston and Henryson. His most remarkable characteristic in his versatility, which ranges from the composition of such poems as *The Merle and the Nightengale* to the *Twa Maryit Wemen and the Wedo*, from such lyrics as the *Meditation in Winter* to such lyrics as the *Plea for Pity*. Mr. Smeaton calls him "a giant in an age of pigmies." The author or authoress of *The Flower and the Leaf* was infinitely superior to him in point of style, Henryson was infinitely superior to him in originality, and Gavin Douglas at least his equal in power of expression and in description.

John Churton Collins
Ephemera Critica (New York: Dutton;
Westminster: Constable, 1902), pp. 189-90

Though the bulk of Dunbar's work as it has reached us is not large, there is great variety in his subjects and in his modes of treatment. His range extends from devotion to buffoonery, from courtly panegyric to scurrilous invective. And whatever he touches is handled with the success which comes of the poet's complete control of his medium of expression. There is nothing in Dunbar of the tyro or the fumbler. He never appears to be tentatively groping for new effects. He approaches his work with perfect confidence in his own accomplishment, and that confidence is never betrayed by the result. In a word, he is a conscious and consummate artist, whose "finish" is comparable, without exaggeration, to that of Virgil, or Pope, or Tennyson.

The most abiding impression left upon the mind by a reviewal of Dunbar's poems as a whole is that of his immense resources and of his splendid prodigality in employing them. Never was poet less parsimonious of his means, less troubled with care for the morrow. He squanders his treasure with a princely generosity, yet he never reaches the bottom of his purse. To rhyme he adds abundant alliteration, and, when pure alliteration is his choice, he must needs, of his bounty, provide a very superfluity of the device, carrying on the use of the same letter to a second line, and supplying an even larger number of alliterating syllables in one line than the rules of the metre require. The more tasks of this nature he sets himself, the more adequately he performs them; the more formidable the obstacles he places in his own path, the more triumphantly he surmounts them; the heavier the fetters with which he loads himself, the more graceful and easy becomes his every movement. His vocabulary is practically inexhaustible. In pieces like the *Brash of Wowing* and the *Flyting,* he pours out a perfect torrent of words, and leaves you wondering that the stream should ever cease. But it is in the command of every sort of measure that Dunbar's mastery of his craft is most noteworthy. . . . No sort of metre, however difficult—no interweaving of rhymes, however intricate—can appal Dunbar. . . . It may safely be asserted that no one of Dunbar's contemporaries who wrote in the literary dialect of the Southern portion of the island could boast anything like the dexterity and nimbleness with which his fingers swept the keys.

J. H. Millar
A Literary History of Scotland (London:
T. Fisher Unwin, 1903), pp. 67-69

Dunbar has been called the "Scottish Skelton." There is some justice in the likening, but the reasons are not consistent with those which give him the title of the "Scottish Chaucer." His allegiance to Chaucer is shown in literary reminiscence, whether of *motif,* or phrase, or stanza—a bookish reminiscence, which often helps us to distinguish the fundamental differences in outlook. There is a spiritual antithesis; but there are textual bonds. With Skelton, on the other hand, who must have been the borrower, had any contact been possible, he stands in close analogy, in two important respects. In the first place, both poets, in their unexpected turns of satire and in their jugglery of words, anticipate the Rabelaisian humor in its intellectual audacity and inexhaustible resource. . . . In the second place, their metrical purposes have much in common. The prosodic variety of both is always our first impression—of Dunbar, without parallel in range and competence in any English writer before his time. The interest of the matter in him, as in Skelton, is that the variety is not the effect of mere literary restlessness, but the outcome of experiment to extend the capabilities of English verse in counterpart to what was being done by "aureation" and other processes for poetic diction and style. . . . Dunbar borrows from all quarters, chiefly from Chaucer, but also from older popular forms, and from French models found in that other Bohemian genius, François Villon. Yet he is not a mere copyist: his changes in the groupings of the lines in the stanza, his varying the length of the verses and his grafting of one form upon another, are evidence of the literary artist at work. . . . The remarkable range and resource of his technique and the vitality of his imagination must redeem his work in the eyes of the most alien modern of the charges which have been brought against the art of Lydgate and Hoccleve. His was not the heavy-headed fancy of a moribund medievalism.

G. Gregory Smith
"The Scottish Chaucerians," *CHEL*, vol. II (1908), pp. 292-93

The difference between Henryson and Dunbar is very strikingly seen in the quality of their humor. Henryson's is quaint, gentle, and with the soft touch of a kindly personality in it. Dunbar's is fierce at the heart. It has the snap of gleaming teeth in it. He is, in fact, a satirist wielding the lash of wit, which knows the secret of the tenderest place on his subject. One has only to look at his satire on Edinburgh, his mockery of the Friar of Tungland, whose attempt at flying was frustrated because the feathers of the barnyard fowls which he had used sought the level of the kitchen midden most familiar to them. His fun is comicality dancing wild, and frequently spotted with the blood it draws from the tender skin with which it comes in contact, and from its own hands and feet wounded by flint and thorn. His fancy has the sheen of running streams by moonlight upon it. He is the Scottish Rabelais, with a touch of Villon sometimes in his work. . . . Dunbar is in other things as personally expressive of his emotion and purpose—a master of prosodic art, with variety of form and music in his verse. He holds a unique place in Scottish poetry. A priest, unpriestly in his life at the unclean court of a king, his humours had not the freshness of the flocks and fields. His *Robene and Makyne*, if he had written one, would have achieved an immortality very different from that which they won from the quaint pen of Henryson. Yet verily he knew the inmost heart of man, having first taken lessons in his own; and sometimes when he laughs the very echo of his laugh has the terribleness of dreadful memory about it. The pity is that he so often chose unsavoury topics, and presents them in the uniform they wore when he met them in the broad and narrow ways of the remarkable world he moved in.

Lauchlan Maclean Watt
Scottish Life and Poetry (London: James Nisbet, 1912), pp. 105-6

It is of some interest to compare him with other poets who have adopted another old and widespread fashion—the lyrical satire or lampoon. If Dunbar had been a Greek he would have been among the Iambic poets—those who launch the dart directly, in short attacking poems, not, as generally in the Roman satire, working in their attacks as parts of a long discursive essay. And this poetry of the lyrical satire goes along with poetry of light occasional verse. It is so in the poems of Catullus and Burns; it is so with William Dunbar. To compare Dunbar with Catullus is possibly idle. But still, is it not of some interest to find the same modes of poetical work in two authors far apart, and can it be denied that Catullus and Dunbar are both fond of attack, and both, at other times, ready to make poetry about anything that comes into their mind, without troubling to search for a large heroic theme? Dunbar is one of the first modern light horsemen, the lyrical journalists of the passing day.

W. P. Ker
Form and Style in Poetry (London: Macmillan, 1928), p. 89

In estimating Dunbar's place in the history of our poetry is it possible to find in him promise or foretaste of the Renaissance? A man who spent so many years abroad, in France certainly, and probably farther afield, must have been in contact with the new scholarship and the new creative work, but there is little to show for it in his poetry; the only poets he acknowledges as masters are English. The individualism of his work is marked, but one suspects this quality would have appeared in him in any age. It is on the side of prosody that some promise of the new age of literature can be detected in Dunbar. His accomplishment shows he had taken this element of his poetry seriously, had studied, experimented, invented; his versification is more distinguished and original than the content of his poetry. . . . The attention to diction, too, suggests some knowledge of the beginnings of literary criticism and literary theory, for, whether the aureate terms be a defect or a beauty, their use implies a new attitude on the part of the poet. Yet, allowing these hints of the new, Dunbar is a medieval poet; Scottish poetry could only develop by receiving inspiration from outside, by passing through the same stages as English poetry: it was Chaucer's influence that quickened the fallow ground, and the poetry that blossomed was medieval poetry. "The spring comes slowly up this way."

TLS (April 10, 1930), p. 306

Over all, then, Dunbar is one of the poets who illuminate the life of their time but do not idealistically transform it. Robert Browning in an essay distinguishes the class of poet as "fashioner," or as the Scots, after the Greeks, would say, "makar," from that of the poet as "seer"—the objective from the subjective type. Dunbar is of the former class; he does not proffer "intuitions" as reflections of an "absolute mind," as Browning held himself to do. Poetry was for him a social art, not the functioning of a seer or diviner, the latter being an assumption which by now surely dates itself as does Dunbar's "mellifluate" diction. This restriction may or may not be a disparagement, but other poets, from Aristophanes and Juvenal onwards, flourish in spite of it. Further, he is without the sentimentalism incident to Burns, though, like him, he tended to become, at times, "literary" in the prevailing fashion. Most poets carry dead weight of this character. But he and the rest of his school saved their share of the island literature from the blight which fell upon the successors of Chaucer in the southern kingdom. And so they worthily repaid the debt they owed to that great master.

W. Mackay Mackenzie, ed.
The Poems of William Dunbar (Edinburgh:
Porpoise Pr., 1932), pp. xxxiii-xxxiv

He [Dunbar] has a fine intellectual quality; an intense degree of the "more than ordinary organic (= sensory) sensibility" that Wordsworth considered the essential of the creative temperament; and a spectacular technical accomplishment. But he comes in an age that all over Europe is almost devoid of spiritual intensity, and his experience rarely brought him the intensity of emotion that, poetically speaking, might have made up for it. He was a priest and a courtier together, one of

> Those gay abati with the well-turned leg
> And rose i' the hat-brim, not so mush St. Paul
> As saints of Caesar's household

—the type of the eighteenth century abbé de salon. Now, priests have written great poems, and so have courtiers, but the combination is a hampering one for the highest kind of poetry. The man who is both can never be wholly either, can never, at heart, desire wholly what is of either, with a sense that the desire, however far from his power, is within his right. Dunbar thus remains below the pinnacles: he writes superb court-poetry, but though he can dance divinely he seldom roars. And partly because of that very limitation it is he of all Northern European poets who most fully expresses the spirit of his own age, its intricate, rather brutal gorgeousness, its hard intellectual quality, its intense vitality of the will and the senses and its numbness of the finer spiritual perceptions.

Agnes Mure Mackenzie
An Historical Survey of Scottish Literature to 1714
(London: Alexander Maclehose, 1933), pp. 81-82

Dunbar never copied the *Rhétoriquers'* manner of twisting and playing with ideas, and though he does imitate their vocabulary and their elaborate rhymes, he does not go far with their tortuous verbal conceits. In "Haile, sterne superne!" he uses the Latinised diction and the internal rhymes popular with the French poets, but the sense is perfectly simple, and he preserves the lyrical quality of the Latin hymns—a quality which had practically disappeared from contemporary French. Even Dunbar's religious *ballades* are unusually lyrical. "Roiss Mary most of Vertew Virginall," is full of aureate diction after the manner of Chastellain, but the others are really quite simple, and express a genuine religious feeling.

Janet M. Smith
The French Background of Middle Scots Literature
(Edinburgh: Oliver and Boyd, 1934), p. 76

Dunbar undoubtedly owed much to Chaucer: at the same time he lacks the genial humanity, the width of view, and the inspiration of the English "makar"—Chaucer's dramatic talent found no counterpart among the many gifts of Dunbar who is one of the most self-centered of bards, always brooding over the good fortune of others, and the ill luck of William Dunbar. It would be more to the point to compare him with his greater descendant, Robert Burns—the Burns of satiric humour, who wrote *The Jolly Beggars* and *Tam O'Shanter*; but a Burns deficient in passion and pathos, who wrote not for the people but for the Court, and certainly not the best-loved Burns, the Burns of the songs.

James Kerr
Poetry R (September, 1938), pp. 376-77

The ribald priest, parasite on a rude and dissolute court, is not so estimable a character as Henryson nor so solid a poet; but he had more fire in his belly and more arrows in his quiver. His versatility and virtuosity are amazing. Whatever vein he writes in—pious, courtly, satirical, cynical, or merely abusive—he is always the artist, with the artist's delight in language and metre for their own sakes. He has command of two distinct vocabularies— "aureate diction" bejewelled with French and Latin for pious and courtly work, and for satire and abuse an arsenal of the broadest, coarsest Scots, hard, concrete words that hit his victims like clods of earth. He is master of all Chaucer's metres and some of Villon's—heroic couplet and rhyme royal, French octave, common rondeau, rime couée, and kyrielle all come alike to him; and his *Tua Mariit Wemen* is a brilliant exercise, the last of its kind, in the old alliterative verse.

Two foreign influences meet in Dunbar: his pious and courtly poems are in the Chaucerian tradition, though grandiose beyond the modesty of

Chaucer; from French, the contemporary French of Villon, he learned some
of his metres and the clean-cut terseness that marks his shorter pieces. These
influences played on a genius characteristically Scottish—fervid to excess,
pungent, realistic, and strong in visual imagination. One national trait he
lacked: he was a Scot, but not a kindly Scot. He has been compared with
Burns, sometimes of late to Burn's disadvantage. "Not back to Burns, back
to Dunbar," our young lions roar. Certainly Dunbar was the greater virtuoso; he had more strings to his lyre than Burns. But for all his wealth of
words and metres he had not Burns's gift of phrase, nor his singing voice,
nor a drop of his warm humanity. The people of Scotland, clannish as they
are, have never taken Dunbar to their hearts: "he wants the natural touch."

Herbert J. C. Grierson and J. C. Smith
A Critical History of English Poetry (London:
Chatto and Windus, 1944), pp. 56-57

Freshness, metrical facility, and variety are Dunbar's great merits. . . . Liveliness is the keynote of all Dunbar's work. Even in his allegories the woods
are noisy with the din of birdsong, and the landscape splashed with exuberant color. . . . Till we reach Robert Burns we shall hardly find a poet more
animated than Dunbar in his dealings with nature and human nature.

Albert C. Baugh, ed.
A Literary History of England (New York and London:
Appleton-Century-Crofts, 1948), pp. 317-18

The worthlessness of the available models taken into account, Dunbar's
achievements are by no means slight. He worked of necessity within the
medieval tradition, but rebelled frequently against the standards of *vers de
société*. With the lugubrious pose of the humble lover, the Scot had no patience, and he abhorred the slovenly rhetorical and metrical habits of the
period. What has come from his pen is characterized by concise and logical
statement; he wrote little effusive verse and nothing that is completely
shoddy. In all likelihood, due recognition has been withheld, because, in the
first place, the overshadowing connection with Chaucer emphasizes the
longer and satirical pieces, and, in the second, scholars have been reluctant
to differentiate between the uninspired work and the lyric with some
originality.

The lyrical verse of the gifted Middle Scots poet is unequal in conception,
not in execution; the most fastidious of craftsmen, he polished all that he
wrote. Possessed of a good ear for rhythm and a prominent flair for sharp,
bold phrasing, the Scot was often as not occupied more with "termis" than
with "sentence." An artist with vast technical power, Dunbar unfortunately
lacked the capacity to interpret his age or to give the eternal truths brilliant

restatement. When he attempts profundity in religious and didactic lyric, he is merely tedious. But then, a mind cast in the medieval mold had no message for a world at the threshold of a new era. Save in his individualism, the northern poet has little of the spirit of the Renaissance. Nevertheless, Dunbar, as many learned men of his day, felt an increasing tension, the conflict of old and new, although he did not resolve the struggle within himself. Devoted to the material world "off sangis, ballattis, and of playis," he was yet acutely aware that this life is "A fre chois geven to Paradice or Hell."

Dunbar anticipates the Renaissance, then, not as a seer, but as a poet, the wholly self-conscious artist risen after three centuries of experimentation with lyric form and style. If courtly lyric in the insipid manner is abundantly represented in the extant work, the reason is that he could not consistently ignore his literary inheritance, sterile though it is; the atypical poems are symptomatic of rebellion. The poetry of generalized experience, diffuse and often insincere, contrasts sharply with the lyrics which confess an emergent sensibility. *All Erdly Joy Returnis in Pane*, for example, belongs to the medieval world of selfless contemplation of Heaven. . . . As certainly, *My heed did yak yesternicht* is occupied with a particular man and his ills in the material world. *To a Ladye*, though provided with conventional garden imagery, differs from polite complaints in form and spirit, having a hard, witty core and a tight organization. These less conventional poems of Dunbar illustrate his developing concept of lyric as a medium for wholly personal expression, for the assertion of the intrinsic interest and importance of the poet's own experience. . . . It is probably correct to say that his lyric succeeds in proportion as this impulse is unfettered.

Rebel and conformist by turns, Dunbar completes a cycle in which form triumphs over spirit, at the same time expressing discontent with the abominable practices of a century of formalized art. If not a great poet, the Scot is historically important as a transition figure, in whose work the blossoming of modern lyric is foreshadowed. . . . With the sardonic Scot, medieval lyric may make an honorable, if not a distinguished, end.

Arthur K. Moore
The Secular Lyric in Middle English (Lexington, Ky.:
Univ. Kentucky Pr., 1951), pp. 197-98, 214-16

Nowhere else does Dunbar rise to quite such felicitous expression. Had he written nothing else, *The Thistle and the Rose* would alone have established his fame. The poem harmonises the arts of the courtier and the poet. The traditional dream-form, decked with gems of Chaucerian phrases and imagery, combines with allegory and pageantry to express the rejoicings of a nation. If a modicum of moral advice is intermingled, it is fitting to the priestly office of the poet and to the impulsive character of the royal bridegroom, and the skill with which it is introduced is equalled by its delicacy and restraint.

J. W. Baxter
William Dunbar (Edinburgh: Oliver and Boyd, 1952), p. 115

What is immediately noticeable in his work is the *display of poetic energy,* in forms that have considerable technical and craftsmanly interest, rather than the *distillation of poetic situation,* in personal emotional encounters. His first mark is a certain effectual brilliance that may commend him more keenly to the practising poet than to the ordinary reader—an agility, a virtuosity in tempo and momentum, a command of rhythm. His poems were produced by cooperating with and transforming the linguistic trends of his age rather than by relying (as Henryson did) on the ancient common fund of human situation and story from which poetic feeling can be summoned with less expenditure of the specifically poetic verbal gift. If Dunbar has at times "words with no matter," Chaucer and Henryson in their less satisfactory passages have matter (the story) and form (the careful metre) but no word-energy. These are complementary wants; and if we sometimes sigh for a Henryson-leavened Dunbar we can also wish, more heretically perhaps, for a Langland-leavened Chaucer. The fusion of the two elements had to wait for Shakespeare. Dunbar's character as a poet—his wild imagination, his quickness of response to particular situations in a humorous and mocking spirit and to general ideas in a serious spirit, his evident delight in gesture, in presentation, in fanfare and march and rout and climax—fitted hand-in-glove with all those tendencies which in Scotland supplemented the influence of Chaucerian poetry. His work shows how far a writer could go at that time whose poetic energies could be released so largely by formal preoccupations.

Edwin Morgan
EIC (April, 1952), pp. 147-48

It is pleasant to trace the things Dunbar and Chaucer had in common and how, even in these, they differed. The difference is almost climatic—between the Thames-side garden and the bleak ridges of Edinburgh and Stirling. Both men disliked the regular orders of clergy. . . . Both were much about courts. . . . Both had fits of melancholy. . . . Comparison comes to a speedy end. *Troilus and Criseyde* stands clear of all comparisons, then or afterwards. *The Parliament of Foules* should be compared with Holland's *Buke of the Howlet* . . . rather than with anything in Dunbar. Dunbar took warning, if he needed it, not to begin anything like *The Legend of Good Women* or *The Monk's Tale,* he was incapable of anything like the Prologue to the *Legend,* or, for that matter, the Prologue to the *Tales.* On the other hand he could manage a fabliau with anybody; and he was possessed of a riotous and fantastic devil that never haunted Chaucer or the banks of Thames. It is a familiar spirit of the north, lewd, foul, comic both in joy and in despair, infinitely vigorous. Skelton knew it, but Skelton's is a ragged double-shuffle compared with the accurately-executed enormities of Dunbar when he set himself capering. It is not satire, nor burlesque, but something on the far and windy side of both. Turn the page, and in *Suete Rois of Virtew*, or *Rorate Coeli Desuper*, the torchflare changes to cool summer morning or the light of altar-candles. Dunbar's moods are as incalculable as his attitudes: aristocrat, sinner, worshipper at the feet of Our Lady, painter by turns in the school of Hieronymous Bosch and Holbein, he postures, kneels—and disappears. If there are two men to study in all our history from Beowulf to Skelton, they are Chaucer and Dunbar.

W. L. Renwick and Harold Orton
The Beginnings of English Literature to Skelton 1509, 2nd ed.
(London: Cresset Pr., 1952), p. 119

Some of Dunbar's finest work was done in religious poetry of a more ordinary kind. He does not deal much in solitary devotional feeling, like the Metaphysicals or the Victorians; he is public and liturgical. His two supreme achievements in this vein are his poems on the Nativity and on the Resurrection. The first of these (*Rorate celi desuper*) might almost claim to be in one sense the most lyrical of all English poems—that is, the hardest of all English poems simply to *read*, the hardest not to sing. We read it alone and at night—and are almost shocked, on laying the book down, to find that the choir and organ existed only in our imagination. It has none of the modern —the German or Dickensian—attributes of Christmas. It breathes rather the intoxication of universal spring and summons all Nature to salute "the cleir sone quhome no clud devouris. . . ." I would hesitate to read Milton's Hymn on the same evening with this. The "Resurrection" is equally, but differently, excellent. It is speech rather than song, but speech of unanswerable and thundering greatness. From the first line ("Done is a battell on the Dragon blak") to the last (*Surrexit Dominus de sepulchro*) it vibrates with exultant energy. It defies the powers of evil and has the ring of a steel gauntlet flung down.

C. S. Lewis
English Literature in the Sixteenth Century
(Oxford: Clarendon Pr., 1954), pp. 95-96

Dunbar is much more, however, than a wild court poet with fire in his belly. He is a keen and humorous observer of a part of the human pageant, a moody but finely reflective moralist, a word-hurler and castigator on the grand scale, and a persistent experimenter in an age when the English poetic tradition had hardened into derivative formalism. The vocabulary of his poems awaits critical analysis; but it is clear at least that he had a sense of the weight and colour of words, and a resourcefulness in marshalling and deploying words, unequalled in his generation or the next. Whether through some inner inadequacy or because of the circumstances of his life at court, he is too often deficient in matter. His intellectual interest is more restricted than Henryson's; he has neither the humour nor the humanity of a Henryson or a Burns. . . . Yet in linguistic and metrical variety, assurance and exuberant imagination he is the richest of our poets.

James Kinsley
"The Medieval Makars," *Scottish Poetry: A Critical Survey*
(London: Cassell, 1955), p. 32

In craftsmanship Dunbar surpasses most medieval poets and all other Scots poets—a passion for form and finish is not conspicuous in Scottish literature. Has he anything more to offer his reader? His eye seldom reached beyond the fringe, or his mind beneath the surface, of that now remote Stewart court which was his milieu. He does not share Chaucer's (or even Henryson's) interest in philosophy and letters. His didactic and reflective verse is smooth without depth, subtle only in style and changing mood; he expresses the melancholy temper of his age with fine simplicity, but there is no provocative questioning, no restless seeking "after the whyes." He has little of the compassion of a Chaucer or a Burns.

Yet he has two important qualities besides sheer style—an original humour, and imagination; and in him the two are complementary. He had not Chaucer's facility for making conventional dreams seem real. His "aureate" visions are not seen and felt; they are constructed in paint, and the artist's preoccupation is with what is on his canvas and not with the visual reality. The seething life of town and court, on the other hand, he depicts with delight—the throng of charlatans and eccentrics about the king, the bustle of market and law-court, whores and gallants and rogues in the street, a fat gossip wheezing by a tavern fire, the revealing capers and gestures of those that danced in the queen's chamber, and the disorderly rabble that "claschit" Kennedy.

Realistic genre-painting is not, however, his natural mode (and here he stands apart from the main tradition of Scottish poetry). What is most distinctive in his genius is a wild comic fantasy, an extravagance of vision and expression which appears fitfully in some anonymous pieces of grotesquerie from Dunbar's time, but almost passed out of Scots poetry at the Reformation.

James Kinsley, ed.
William Dunbar: Poems (Oxford: Clarendon Pr., 1958), pp. xviii-xix

In "The Flyting of Dunbar and Kennedy" Dunbar exploits to the full the cacophonous possibilities of Middle Scots and achieves a kind of comic violence that bespatters his opponent with dirt and disgrace. . . . "Poetry should surprise by a fine excess," Keats once wrote. . . . "It should strike the reader as a wording of his own highest thoughts, and appear almost a remembrance. Its touches of beauty should never be half way, thereby making the reader breathless, instead of content." If we substitute the word "ugliness" for "beauty" and the words "lowest thoughts" for "highest thoughts," we come near to understanding the macabre effectiveness of Dunbar's invective. I doubt if we really want 250 lines of it, but the effect is necessarily cumulative; one stone flung through one window is good in its way, but a whole volley of stones breaking every window in the building is the natural and desired consummation, and can make a stupendous and unforgettable impression on the mind. Dunbar, of course, is not throwing anything so clear as stones.

James Sutherland
English Satire (Cambridge Univ. Pr., 1958), pp. 26-27

Dunbar affords the clearest indication of what is really meant by "Chaucerian." Chaucer invented a poetic diction when he translated *Le Roman de la Rose* and Dunbar is fully conscious of that; his "aureate style" and, later, Gawain Douglas' "sugarit sang" is the result of the Scots poets' own experimentation with European rhetorical conventions and Chaucerian modifications of them. In his freedom of expression Dunbar is lively and modern, and his ability to turn his hand to almost any kind of verse on almost any subject makes him the first Scottish poet to impress his readers with a dynamic mental agility.

A. M. Kinghorn
Texas Studies in Lang. and Lit. (Spring, 1959), pp. 77-78

The rhetorical figures and ornate diction in Lydgate and his followers are for the most part strictly decorative, being added to make palatable and ostensibly poetic the underlying prose sense, which has the place of honor. But in all of Dunbar's poems the prose sense is negligible and the decoration, the poetic artifices, are everything. Where the typical poem of the Lydgatian school rambles interminably, finding what structure it has in a preconceived logical plan or in a vague narrative thread, Dunbar's poems are static, ending where they begin, but are made tightly unified by technical poetic devices.

Denton Fox
ELH (September, 1959), p. 333

Within it, there are immediately apparent two styles, two dictions; one could almost say, so great is the difference, two poets. The one is ornate, artificial, and English; the other colloquial, natural, and Scottish. Of the former, the two allegorical poems, *The Golden Targe* and *The Thrissill and the Rois,* are the most complete examples. In one thing, at least, these poems are remarkable: they succeed in enclosing, in small compass, virtually every commonplace of their age and *genre,* the allegorical poem of the Middle Ages. They are both dreams, both dreamed on a May morning. Both use a quasi-religious language; both assemble companies of mythological personalities; both draw up lists of allegorical abstractions. Both, above all other resemblances, are written in that medieval "poetic diction" which is just as lifeless and conventional as the worst that the eighteenth century can show and which, indeed, in many ways resembles it. "Fresh anamalit termes celicall" is Dunbar's own phrase for it (praising Chaucer in the *Goldyn Targe*)—"animalit" (enamelled) is one of his favourite epithets when he writes in this style. . . . And the word is unintentionally appropriate: this diction *is* like enamel, applied from above, rootless, indiscriminate. It abounds in clichés. . . . In such a diction, fixed and prefabricated, living poetry can hardly be made. . . . It is not in such writing that the greatness of Dunbar makes its true contribution, but in his other style. . . . One poem in this style . . . the *Tretis of the Tua Mariit Weman and the Wedo* . . . is perhaps the finest of all his poems, and it is certainly the most remarkable. There is nothing like it in the language.

Patrick Cruttwell

"Two Scots Poets: Dunbar and Henryson," *The Age of Chaucer*
(Baltimore, Md.: Penguin Books, 1961), pp. 175-76

Dunbar's two poetic voices, one given to pasquinade and the other to panegyric, show in their separation the range of his artistic imagination, which could juxtapose, without the slightest impropriety, the gargoyle and the angel. His poetry is like the decoration . . . of a medieval cathedral. In part, there is the remote, marmoreal serenity of saints and holy men. . . . In part, there is the richly bedevilled world of *ylfes, orcneas, woodwoses,* and calibans lurking on corbel, misericord, and water spout. . . . Idealization and reverence produced the divine, while ridicule and contempt produced the grotesque, one beautiful, the other ugly, one proportioned, the other misshapen, one god-like, the other demonic, one that inspired aspiration and the other that tickled laughter.

In the one voice he could sing with the sublime, disembodied detachment of Apollo. . . . In his other voice he could also sing, indeed, some would say, could sing with greater power, with the grotesque and heart-exposed cry of Marsyas. For, despite the pain, or, perhaps because of it, the heart laid bare has a power to move the emotions, a power arising from the agony and horror of exposure, which the dispassionate harmony of disembodied divinity, for all its sublime beauty, has not. These two voices are especially clear in Dunbar's poetry because he employed a markedly different poetic diction for each.

John Leyerle
UTQ (April, 1962), pp. 316, 317-18

What gives him [Dunbar] his extraordinary power, whereby he is perhaps the greatest Scottish poet, is his skilled command of the rich and varied resources of language open to him, and, related to this, his command of varied metres adapted from what were by his time the rich accumulations of medieval French and medieval Latin verse, as well as, and often united together with, indigenous alliteration and assonance used as Hopkins rather than as Swinburne uses it. This variety of language and of metres has its counterpart in a variety of modes so bewildering that our first difficulty must be to determine where the center of Dunbar's work as a whole is. Dunbar's technical skill and versatility are what may first strike the reader. It may be that his poetry appears to be more various than it really is. There is a variety of modes and moods, a vigour and directness, but not a Chaucerian large view of experience.

J. Speirs
The Scots Literary Tradition, 2nd ed. (London: Faber and Faber, 1962), pp. 54-55

THE GAWAIN-POET

fl. 1375–1400

The author of *Sir Gawain and the Green Knight* is also considered to be the author of *Pearl, Purity, Patience,* and, possibly *St. Erkenwald.* His identity is unknown. It has been suggested that he was a cleric, possibly a chaplain, in a noble's household, but of this there is no evidence. All that can be safely asserted about him is that he haled from the Northwest Midlands and was conversant with its baronial life. His work is marked by wide learning and a remarkable refinement of moral and religious feeling.

John R. R. Tolkien and E. V. Gordon, eds., *Sir Gawain and the Green Knight* (1936)

Eric V. Gordon, ed., *Pearl* (1953)

Hartley Bateson, ed., *Patience* (1918)

Robert Menner, ed., *Purity* (1920)

Israel Gollencz, ed., *St. Erkenwald* (1922)

The charm of *Sir Gawayne* is to be found in its description of nature, more especially of wild nature; in the author's enjoyment of all that appertains to the bright side of medieval life; in its details of dress, armour, wood-craft, architecture; and in the artistic arrangement of the story, three parallel episodes being so treated as to avoid all risk of monotony, or reiteration. . . . But, much as *Sir Gawayne* shows us of the poet's delight in his art, the main purpose of the poem is didactic. Gawain, the knight of chastity, is but another study by the author of *Cleanness*. On the workmanship of his romance he has lavished all care, only that thereby his readers may the more readily grasp the spirit of the work. Sir Gawain may best, perhaps, be understood as the Sir Calidor of an earlier Spenser.

Sir Israel Gollancz
"Pearl, Cleanness, Patience and Sir Gawayne,"
CHEL, vol. I (1907), p. 328-29

He is a writer with a gift for teaching, of a peculiar sort. He is not an original philosopher, and his reading appears to have been the usual sort of thing among fairly educated men. He does not try to get away from the regular authorities, and he is not afraid of commonplaces. But he has great keenness. His memory is well supplied from all that he has gone through. The three sporting episodes in *Sir Gawain*, the deer-hunt (in Christmas week, killing the hinds), the boar-hunt and the fox-hunt, are not only beyond question as to their scientific truth; the details are remembered without study because the author has lived in them, and thus, minute as they are, they are not wearisome. They do not come from a careful notebook; they are not like the descriptions of rooms and furniture in painstaking novels. The landscapes and the weather of *Sir Gawain* are put in with the same freedom. The author has a talent especially for winter scenes. "Grim Nature's visage hoar" had plainly impressed his mind, and not in a repulsive way. The winter "mist hackles" (capes of mist) on the hills, the icicles on the stones, the swollen streams, all come into his work—a relief from the too ready illustrations of spring and summer which are scattered about in medieval stories.

W. P. Ker
English Literature: Medieval (New York: Holt;
London: Williams and Norgate, 1912), pp. 139-41

The English romance of Gawain and the Green Knight is a very distinguished piece of work. The plot is one of the best that an age of good stories has transmitted to us, and the unknown author handles his material with a combination of power and delicacy rare even in the best periods of literature. His sense of fitness and proportion entitles him to high rank as an artistic writer. His descriptive ability is extraordinary; yet he does not allow description to clog the narrative. His ideal of life is noble, and his knowledge of human nature is at once minute and sympathetic. Finally, his command of a difficult metre, and the ease and felicity with which he handles an amazingly elaborate diction, bending its conventions to his will and never impeded or dominated by its inherited mannerisms, mark him as a master of expression. Some of the best of the Middle English romances are rough and artless compositions: they live by their freshness and naive energy, or by the bare fact that they embody a good tale, whose merits are independent of phraseology. But for *Gawain and the Green Knight* no allowances need be made. Both in plan and in execution, in gross and in detail, it would be a credit to any literature. The author was a poet and an artist as well as a lively raconteur.

George Lyman Kittredge
A Study of Gawain and the Green Knight (Cambridge, Mass.:
Harvard Univ. Pr., 1916), p. 3

This poet knew the frailty of human flesh and the self-complacency of the human spirit. The moral of his poem is not merely that man should curb his fear or rein his lust or keep his word; it is deeper and simpler. It is the moral of a poet who has become long familiar with the very heart of life. It is the vanity of human pride—the pride of magnificent kings, of gray-eyed queens, of perfect knights whose perfection is illusory.

George J. Engelhardt
MLQ (September, 1955), pp. 223-24

A comparison with Chaucer is not, indeed, wholly to the disadvantage of the lesser-known poet, for he surpasses Chaucer in some things—in architectonics, for instance, and perhaps in natural description—and, though his range is narrow, within it he shows himself a subtle delineator of character. In outlook he is as civilized as Chaucer, but sterner, much more of a moralist, a great deal less of a humorist. But there is humour of a sort in his presentation of the Green Knight's play-acting in Arthur's hall, and in some of Gawain's rueful remarks; and the poet has some of Chaucer's capacity for seeing his story and his characters from both inside and out, so that his readers can sympathize with the hero and at the same time see him and his doings in perspective.

Dorothy Everett
Essays on Middle English Literature (Oxford:
Clarendon Pr., 1955), p. 85

The Gawain poet . . . is presenting us, within a deliberately limited form, a microcosm, or better said, a semi-allegorical presentation of the whole history and meaning of the Round Table. Morgan attempts reform; Gawain fails in keeping faith with Bercilak; treacherous Guinevere remains alive. The form of the poem is thus quite consciously limited in time and in space in order to facilitate a unified and complete presentation of the progress of the Round Table; only in a single, complete adventure could the poet achieve any unified design which would reflect the whole of the tragedy. In this sense the poem is semi-allegorical in method in that we are presented with a segment of action, but with a miniature version of the whole action. The gay light tone, which reflects the ignorance and pride of Arthur's court, is maintained throughout the scenes which take place within the safe precincts of Camelot, but once the poem moves to the outside world, the tone changes radically. The journeys are always difficult and dangerous, the terrain rugged and foreboding. The scene of the final encounter, the Green Chapel, is, to Gawain, the "corsedest kirk" that he ever saw. . . . Certainly, the prevailing tone is that of Christmas, but we must remember that the court is in "her first age" and that all the knights are ironically ignorant of Morgan's attempts to forestall the fate which will overtake them and ignorant also of the dangers outside the court which must be a part of any spiritual quest. Only the returned Gawain, who has himself made the initiatory journey, sees the imminent destruction which he expresses in his condemnation of women, and which he attempts to forestall by the institution of the green baldric. . . . The *Gawain* poet is using the myth of the hero's quest to develop a theme which lies at the core of medieval literature: that the tragedy of the Round Table, and of the secular society of which it is a symbol, was inevitable and that the seeds of that tragedy were present even in the "first age" of the youthful and joyous court at Christmas time.

Charles Moorman
Mediaeval Studies (1956), pp. 170, 172

As a metrist the author of *Pearl* and *Gawain* must stand very high. . . . There are hundreds of lines . . . that evince their writer's knowledge of vowel and consonantal quality, his awareness of that elusive, but very real, nexus between sound and sense, the quickness of his imaginative powers. One runs upon them in every one of the poems attributed to this unknown poet. Keen sensitivity to the values of consonant and vowel, meticulous care in the arrangement of the alliterative syllables . . . skill in the employment of the caesura, and in the manipulation of the double caesura or long pause, all these exalt our author above his less gifted brethren of the school. Nor did he dread comparison with Chaucer as a metrist; for he seldom wrote a line lacking in zest, or imagination, or rhythm—and Chaucer sometimes did. To say so much is simply to say that he was past master of his medium.

Henry Lyttelton Savage
The Gawain-Poet (Chapel Hill, N. C.: Univ. North
Carolina Pr., 1956), pp. 22-24

Our poem is clearly a midwinter festival poem. The seasonal theme . . . is the poem's underlying, indeed pervasive theme.

The Green Knight whose head is chopped off at his own request and who is yet as miraculously or magically alive as ever, bears an unmistakable relation to the Green Man—the Jack in the Green or Wild Man of the village festivals of England and Europe. He can be no other than a recrudescence in poetry of the Green Man. Who is the Green Man? He is surely a descendant of the Vegetation or Nature god of almost universal and immemorial tradition (whatever his local name) whose death and resurrection are the myth-and-ritual counterpart of the annual death and rebirth of nature—in the East the dry and rainy seasons, in Europe winter and spring.

Sir Gawayne and the Green Knight is of course a Christian poem. But it is Christian rather as some of the medieval Christmas carols are, as Christmas itself is; Christian in harmony with pre-Christian nature belief and ritual, a Christian re-interpretation of these. It is Christian to about the same depth as it is a courtly romance. The value of "courtesy"—Sir Gawain is among other things the pattern of courtesy, the most courteous of Arthur's courtly company—is certainly one of the values defined in the poem and brought out in relation to the other values in their order, Christian and pre-Christian; and these other values are pre-courtly.

The fundamental *knowledge* in the poem, the hidden source which the poet has tapped, the ultimate source of the poem's actuality, strength and coherence, is the knowledge, which the age-old experience of the race has turned into an assured knowledge, that there is life inexhaustible at the roots of the world even in the dead season, that there is perpetually to be expected the unexpected spring re-birth. The whole poem is, in its very texture—its imagery and rhythm—an assertion of belief in life as opposed to winter deprivation and death; and it seems finally to discover, within the antagonism between man and nature, between the human and the other-than-human, a hidden harmony, expressed in the kind of humorous understanding that develops between the Green Knight and Gawain.

John Speirs
Medieval English Poetry: The Non-Chaucerian Tradition
(London: Faber and Faber, 1957), pp. 219, 220-21

... Gawain and the Green Knight is basically a study of the contrast between two aspects of life. It tells us of man's struggle against tendencies which would draw him back to the state of nature, and of his uncertain efforts to maintain a hold on the comforts and codes of civilization. The poet suggests that at best life is but a truce between natural impulses and allegiances to the virtues which civilized creatures are pledged to uphold. As is surely the case with many literary masters, this poet reveals his profound grasp of his subject—and at the same time he renders more effective his commentary —by means of consummate skill as a stylist. We come away with images which haunt the imagination: the harsh seasons hold before our eyes the force of nature and the pressure it exerts to make man's attempts to secure comfort, ease, and courtliness only partially and imperfectly realized. Inside the warm dining-hall, all is warmth and gentle, refined comfort; outside, one hardly dares venture, for the risk is great and one might too easily succumb.

William Goldhurst
CE (November, 1958), p. 64

As an artist the *Gawain*-poet had the habit of close visual observation and an exceptional sense of form, proportion, and design. As a connoisseur familiar with costly things and courtly taste and custom, he pauses to describe exquisite trifles of embroidery and jewellery, rich fabrics, fine armour. He dwells on the architectural details of the great castle that Gawain first sees shimmering through the distant trees, then in all the glory of its chalk-white, many-towered magnificence. The poet accents social sophistication; manners are polished, talk is an art. The conversations between Gawain and the lady suggest the advances, the retreats, of a courtly dance. Within the set pattern of perfect courtesy, wit meets wit; a gracious comedy of manners is enacted. Temptation is offered to Gawain and refused largely in the tone of light social badinage. One has but to read other society romances in Middle English to recognize the difference between them and the greater elegance, the more assured touch, of the *Gawain*-poet. Moreover, in this romance, unlike many others, there is no inchoate rambling, no waste. The episodes move directly from cause to consequence, and individual act and character are finely linked. Situations are repeated, but with skilful, deliberate variety and contrast. Court scenes at royal Camelot are different from those at Bercilak's castle; the three temptations of Gawain have subtle differences of tone and temper; the three hunts, whether they have allegorical significance or not, are as different from each other as are the hunted beasts; each hunt implies expert familiar knowledge. The rich indoor revels, whether at Arthur's court or Bercilak's castle, are effectively alternated with cruel winter realities without, and so is the gay fellowship indoors with Gawain's stark loneliness as he goes by desolate crags to seek his death. The romance has superlative art in its fashioning; it is mature, deliberate, richly seasoned by an author who never suggests minstrel servility or even compliment to those who hear him. He wrote in his own way and apparently for his own delight in a provincial dialect and in the alliterative verse which belonged to that same north country which he pictured with such startling vigour.

Laura Hibbard Loomis
"Gawain and the Green Knight," *Arthurian Literature in the Middle Ages*, ed. R. S. Loomis (Oxford: Clarendon Pr., 1959), p. 539

The author of *Sir Gawain* appreciated the aims and virtues of French romance as few English romancers did. His poem is as human, as skillfully diversified, and at all times as courtly as the best French romance. In these very qualities he probably surpassed his original, as he undoubtedly surpassed the existing romances of the beheading and temptation. He has, further, a special gift for description, and has elaborated the whole setting with a richness of detail unusual in French romance. He handles the story with a moral sensitiveness not to be matched in any of the analogues. His work indeed is not mere reproduction: it is a fresh creation.

> J. R. R. Tolkien and E. V. Gordon, eds.
> *Sir Gawain and the Green Knight* (Oxford:
> Clarendon Pr., 1960), pp. xv-xvi

Sir Gawayne is a poet's treatment of a myth. What is the meaning of the myth, thus treated and transformed?

In the poem the main contrast is between the social joys of the court . . . and the savagery of Nature's winter. . . . The contrast is dramatic. It first implies and then promotes a conflict, and the conflict is then resolved, and the highly formal mechanics of plot and stanza . . . are essential features of this resolving pattern. For the form and narrative cannot be separated. The poem in its cyclic form corresponds to that cycle of the year which forms the essence of the narrative. . . . Such an imaginative appreciation of the rhythm of the seasons involves a recognition of the indivisible process of getting and spending. . . , of fluorescence and deliquescence, begetting and dying; of enjoyment of harvest and of the deliberate letting of blood or sacrifice that is a premium for the enjoyment of harvest. Some such principle of sacrifice, or expenditure, is implied in the beheading incident. . . . But there are other examples of spending in return for getting. The hard journeys over inhospitable country are measures of payment for the court festivities they follow; Gawain, in return for his getting of the green girdle, has to pay for it by the spending of a token of blood. And so on. But this principle of adjustment between getting and spending is chiefly embodied in the figure of the Green Knight himself. He is huge in the richness of his personal resources and capacities of enjoyment, and in the bounty of his entertainment. But in Fitt iii, while Gawain is recuperating his energies in bed, he hunts wild beasts; we see him curb the excesses of Nature, redressing its economy. This dramatic contrast between humanity (especially in its finest aspect of the court) and harsh Nature is solved by imposing a pattern, and this pattern of narrative is itself the poet's transmutation into artistic terms of his perception of the balance and adjustment between winning and wasting, between growth and deliquescence.

> Francis Berry
> "Sir Gawayne and the Grene Knight," *Age of Chaucer*
> (Baltimore: Penguin Books, 1961), pp. 152-55

Sir Gawain is soaked in time in all its aspects, and this rich chronological perspectivism is one of the strongest elements in the sense of solidity we get from reading the poem. It, along with the rhetorical descriptions, is part of the richness against which these strange, tense, and comic events of the plot play themselves out. These many dimensions of time are part of the bulwarks of life; they give security and strength. They are the framework of the human universe into which fantastic and puzzling irrationality penetrates and which it seems to wish to destroy. Here we have a cosmic humor in which the fragility of life and honor are threatened against a solid and rich background akin to the density of reality itself. Except when he deliberately violates the illusion, the poet endeavors to maintain a distance between his poem and the reader which is necessary to true comedy. Time is functional to this purpose. It helps to create the impression of another world both similar to and different from our own which keeps the reader away from the events taking place. They are far enough to preserve their integrity and strangeness and near enough to interest us. If the reader were to get too closely involved, he might find a tragic horror too great to be borne. The wonder would turn to fear and the delight and curiosity which are always a product of objectivity would be lost. Occasionally, however, especially in the temptation and journey scenes, we are deliberately brought into the poem by being told what the hero is thinking. Those passages are, I believe, deliberate and are justified by the circumstances. We get close to tragedy for the heart of Gawain's predicament. . . .

Morton W. Bloomfield
PMLA (March, 1961), p. 18

Bercilak is as vivid and concrete as any image I have met in literature. He is a living *coincidentia oppositorum*; half giant, yet wholly a "lovely knight"; as full of demoniac energy as old Karamazov, yet, in his own house, as jolly as a Dickensian Christmas host; now exhibiting a ferocity so gleeful that it is almost genial, and now a geniality so outrageous that it borders on the ferocious; half boy or buffoon in his shouts and laughter and jumpings; yet at the end judging Gawain with the tranquil superiority of an angelic being. There has been nothing really like him in fiction before or since. No one who has once read the poem forgets him. No one while reading it disbelieves in him.

C. S. Lewis
"The Anthropological Approach," *English and Medieval Studies
Presented to J. R. R. Tolkien*, eds. Norman Davis and C. L. Wrenn
(London: George Allen and Unwin, 1962), p. 222

The language of *Sir Gawain and the Green Knight* is thoroughly traditional. Where he is original, the poet may rather be said to add to the tradition than to depart from it. The store of stock phrases, of set patterns, of ways of building the line, of modes of reference, of qualitative adjectives, which was drawn on by the *Gawain*-poet was drawn on equally by the other poets. These characteristic features of style are historically determined: the *Gawain*-poet was born into the tradition in which he wrote. But from the point of view of criticism of style, features become devices. The superiority of *Gawain* over other poems belonging to the same tradition is not in the devices themselves but in what they accomplish. In the hands of the mediocre poet the technical resources of the alliterative style merely made possible the construction of the line. In the hands of the *Gawain*-poet these resources take on poetic power: the technical problems of the line are not merely solved but transcended. The result is "þe best boke of romaunce."

Marie Borroff
Sir Gawain and the Green Knight (New Haven, Conn.,
and London: Yale Univ. Pr., 1962), p. 90

All the best qualities of the [Alliterative] *Morte Arthur* appear heightened in *Gawain and the Green Knight*—a rich vocabulary, clear visualization, shapely structure, vivacity, seriousness, and the worst features are absent—monotony, coarseness, chauvinism. When one discovers in the Gawain poem refinements of technique and subleties of feeling, one is not likely to contest the verdict of critics that here is the masterpiece of medieval English romance. It combines the sturdiness of epic, the fantastic charm of romance, and the sophistication of the country-house novel.

It is the perfection of plot in *Gawain and the Green Knight* which is most surprising—a plot which brings into causal relationship a complex of apparently disconnected facts; which creates suspense and maintains it to the end; which rounds out the action by bringing the hero back to the court from which he had started. This impression of completion is accentuated by the echoing of the opening lines in the concluding ones.

Roger Sherman Loomis
The Development of Arthurian Romance (London:
Hutchinson's Univ. Library, 1963), pp. 152, 155

Everywhere in the poem is balance, contrast, and antithesis. Things are arranged in pairs—there are two New Year's days, two "beheading" scenes, two courts, two confessions; or in threes—three temptations, three hunts, three kisses, three strokes of the ax.

This elaborate parallelism, with its multiple contrasts, helps produce the game-like, ironic tone of *Sir Gawain*. Its effect is comic. The ritual balance of incidents does, in the end, what comedy always does—it purges extremes of conduct and brings the reader comfortably back to a norm; it restores the *status quo*. Gawain returns to the starting-place, and, however chastened, is greeted with laughter which dispels his sobriety. The symbolism of shield and girdle suggests an essential and inescapable conflict between chivalry and Christianity; but this conflict is treated throughout in a spout of amused and ironic detachment, as if the poet meant to suggest that these contrarieties of medieval thought, being irreconcilable, should be taken in good humor as a condition of life in an imperfect world. The mysterious and marvellous, which in tragedy remain ultimately incomprehensible, are here explained rationally away; we are asked not so much to feel the hero's experience as to think about it, to understand. The symmetrical world of the poem is at once unreal and substantial—far in the past and idealized, and yet plainly the world of real human conduct, of uncertainty and self-deception. It is too neatly balanced to be like the flux of history itself, yet it is an unpredictable world full of surprises; and, from the long view, it is ordered and right.

Donald R. Howard
Sp (July, 1964), pp. 425, 433

. . . *Cortaysye* was a leading ideal among the aristocratic classes of medieval Europe. . . . It meant the kind of behaviour current in or appropriate to courts, and it would cover the whole range of behaviour from politeness (what *we* should call courtesy), through elegant conversation about love with persons of the opposite sex, to the conduct of a real love-affair. . . . The unifying element in this range of activity seems to be an attitude towards women: deference, or even devotion. Historically the development of *cortaysye* appears to be connected with the rise in importance of the Blessed Virgin as an object of devotion: the lady to whom deference was supremely due. Thus Christianity and *cortaysye* could fuse into a single aristocratic way of life, with no sense of incongruity. It is such a way of life that we see exemplified in the Camelot of the poem, where Christmas is celebrated first with the singing of mass and then with games. . . . In this, Camelot is only an idealized version of a medieval European court: the court of Edward III or Richard II, or that of the provincial lord for whom *Sir Gawain and the Green Knight* was perhaps written. The effect of the poem . . . is to undermine the pious gaiety or gay piety of Camelot, by driving a wedge between courtliness and Christianity. Gawain is chosen as the supremely courtly or *cortays* representative of a courtly society to go on what seems an exploit demanding physical courage only. But the exploit turns out to be a moral test demanding the power to resist a woman: and *cortaysye* is based on devotion to women. The test that Gawain undergoes at the castle is one that sets his *cortaysye* against his chastity.

A. C. Spearing
Criticism and Medieval Poetry (New York:
Barnes and Noble, 1964), pp. 35-36

Pearl

The wealth and brilliancy of the poet's descriptions have been the subject of criticism. But surely the richness is what one would expect in a poem, the inspiration of which is mainly derived from the visionary scenes of the Apocalypse, with its pictorial phantasies, and the *Roman de la Rose* with its personifications and allegory. The poet's fancy revels in the richness of the heavenly and earthly paradise, but it is subordinated to his earnestness and intensity. The heightened style of *Pearl* responds, moreover, to the poet's own genius for touching vividly his dream-pictures with rich imagery and bright colour. The wealth and brilliancy pervading *Pearl* may still delight those theorists who seek in our literature that "fairy dew of natural magic," which is supposed to be the peculiar gift of the Celtic genius, and which can be discovered as "the sheer inimitable Celtic note" in English poetry. It would, I think, be fair to say that the Apocalypse has had a special fascination for the poet because of its almost Romantic fancy, and that he has touched certain scenes of the book with a brilliancy of colour and richness of description altogether foreign to the Germanic strain of our literature. *Pearl* finds its truest counterpart in the delicate miniatures of medieval missals, steeped in richest colours and bright with gold, and it is just those scenes of the apocalypse which the old miniaturists loved to portray, one might better say lived to portray, that seemed to have been uppermost in our poet's mind. . . .

Sir Israel Gollancz, ed.
Pearl (Oxford Univ. Pr., 1921), pp. xxvi-xxvii

The *Pearl* I take to be a very beautifully wrought account of an experience in interior desolation. It opens with a real case of spiritual "blues," followed by a consideration of God's grace, elaborated by a number of natural and characteristic digressions and brought to a perfectly consistent change, the contemplation of heaven. It ends with the poet's complete resignation to the will of God, which is both the ideal cure for his malady and the ideal conclusion for the poem. The fact that autobiography dons the lonely role of symbolism and walks incognito in allegory may suggest resemblances to the *Romaunt of the Rose*, the only secular poem with which it has been seriously compared; it points much more significantly to kinship with the great body of religious writing, prose and poetry. . . . Spirituality, even more than love, has always spoken a symbolic language, and without parable its speech almost does not exist. I believe that the author of the *Pearl* was a religious who, if not young himself, was recording the experience of one young in religion. As to wife, and child, and bereavement, I say there was no wife, there was no two-year-old daughter and consequently no bereavement. . . .

Sister M. Madeleva
Pearl, A Study in Spiritual Dryness (New York:
Appleton, 1925), pp. 89-90

Viewed as a personal elegy the *Pearl* is a poem of deep feeling, the poet's grief yielding gradually to resignation and spiritual reconciliation. In its sensuous beauty, its artistic restraint, its skilful manipulation of a complex and difficult metrical pattern, and its imaginatively beautiful descriptions of the garden, the pearl-maiden, and the New Jerusalem, it is in its best parts unsurpassed by anything in Middle English poetry.

Albert C. Baugh, ed.
A Literary History of England (New York:
Appleton-Century-Crofts, 1948), p. 235

The symbol of the Pearl may be thought of on four levels. Literally, the Pearl is a gem. Allegorically, as the maiden of the poem, it represents those members of the Church who will be among the "hundred" in the celestial procession, the perfectly innocent. Tropologically, the Pearl is a symbol of the soul that attains innocence through true penance and all that such penance implies. Anagogically, it is the life of innocence in the Celestial City. The allegorical value presents a clear picture of the type of innocence; the tropological value shows how such innocence may be obtained; and the anagogical value explains the reward for innocence. To these meanings the literal value serves as a unifying focal point in which the other values are implied to one who reads the book of God's work on the level of the *sentence*.

D. W. Robertson, Jr.
MLN (March, 1950), pp. 160-61

To the unprejudiced student, willing to take the trouble to acquaint himself with its language and tradition, the poetry of *Pearl* should need no special pleading. He will probably find in the artificial form a setting admirably suited to the richness of the jewel it encloses. And beyond its decorative value he will feel the force which the verse pattern lends to the argument: the refrain in each stanza-group underlines the particular stage of thought with which that group is primarily concerned, and this is especially effective in a poem in which there is so much discourse. But, above all, he will feel the emotional effect, as moving as music itself, which the verse pattern adds to the feeling. . . . It is difficult, of course, to separate the musical effects of poetry from the significance of the words, but it is probably true to say that the verse-form plays no small part in conveying both the poignancy of the dreamer's grief and the transmutation of it which comes with his relief from doubt and assurance of hope. The repetition and variation on the verbal theme, of the separate stanza-groups, drive home to us with an emotional insistence the different stages of thought and feeling through which he passes until he reaches the peace which accepts immediate loss with faith and hope. So moving is the verse that, if its difficulties strain the poet's powers too far, the occasional lapses of precision or taste seem trivial in the light of the general achievement.

E. V. Gordon, ed.
Pearl (Oxford: Clarendon Pr., 1953), pp. xl-xli

As the educated person of the Middle Ages would surely have been expected to perceive, *Pearl* is, in brief, a Christian *consolatio*. Although the specific coloring of each is not identical, in theme, situation, roles and treatment *Pearl* is analogous to Boethius's then-revered *Consolation of Philosophy*. Whether, in the conventional sense, *Pearl* like the *Consolation*, is semi-autobiographical, we shall apparently never know nor . . . need we ever know. In fact, probability compels the conclusion that the secular age of the virgin is to be accounted for parabolically rather than realistically: as a datum that allows the author of *Pearl* to enforce maximally a point concerning salvation, a point of which the typical sinner always needs to be reminded—that ultimately salvation depends upon God.

John Conley
JEGP (July, 1955), pp. 340-41

What is the import of the story? Pearl, at the centre of her defense of her rank as a queen in God's kingdom, gives a resumé of the Fall and the Redemption (637-660): Mankind, created for perfect happiness, forfeited it through Adam, and so was condemned to death and the pain of Hell; but there came a remedy. Water and noble blood flowed on the Rood. The blood delivered us from Hell and "the second death"; the water is baptism. . . . Consequently, no barrier remains between us and bliss, and bliss itself is restored "in sely stounde." The whole of *Pearl* is a finely wrought elaboration of this theme, the Biblical epic of the soul in delicate miniature, seen in the epitome of one man's passionate experience. The hero is not literally the poet, but "a type of the whole race of fallen man, called to salvation," like Dante, the pilgrim of the *Commedia*, though less learned than Dante. . . . In the English poem the dreamer's awareness is constantly moving toward Pearl's, as hers approaches the author's. Indeed, the dreamer is presented as one conventionally naive in theology, so as to call forth the inspired maiden's account of the plan of salvation, the plenitude of the divine grace, and the blessedness of souls wedded to Christ; for the poet's design, identical again with Dante's, is "to remove those living in this life from a state of wretchedness and lead them to the state of blessedness."

Marie Padgett Hamilton
PMLA (September, 1955), pp. 810-11

Viewed in the light of Catholic thought, . . . the *Pearl* becomes luminously beautiful, a jewel of religious inspiration whose central theme is Christian justification, the regaining of Paradise. Like a pearl, it catches the rays of the theological lights of its time and sends them on to us in lines glowing but mystical, not so plain as they might be in prose. But plainness is not the intention or function of the poet; art is not science. *Pearl* is an art of a high order, filled with connotations, hints, gleams, setting forth in symbols the deepest longings of the human soul in search of peace and salvation. It is the finest poetic treatment of Paradise in our language, and it grew from the Catholic soil of fourteenth-century England.

Bruno McAndrew
ABR (Autumn, 1957), pp. 249-50

Patience

Patience presents us in its greatest moments with a story that has passed through the alchemy of imagination and received the impress of a strong poetic art. We have a tale recorded with a bold and vivid realism, and the moral pleaded with a dignity not austere and at times a quiet pathos. There are moments when the vigour of the music is softened by tremors of tenderness, by a plaintive and lyrical undertone which sweetens the pleading of the moralist. But the fabric of *Patience* is of varying colour. . . . at times it descends in less sublime moments to the lower plane of medieval homilies.

Hartley Bateson, ed.
Patience, 2nd ed. (Manchester: Manchester Univ. Pr.;
London and New York: Longmans, Green, 1918), p. xxxviii

Patience, whether classified as a paraphrase of the Scriptures or as a homily, must occupy a high place in either category of Middle English works. Perhaps the most striking feature of the poem is its artistic unity; it is a perfect whole. In the short prologue the writer introduces to us his *theme*—the virtue of Patience, which he says may often be displeasing at the time but in the end brings its reward; his *text*, the Beatitudes, then follows with a special stress upon Patience as underlying the whole of Christian life. His *sermon* illustrating this virtue takes the form of a recounting of the story of Jonah the prophet, and the version given is as simple and severe as that in the Vulgate. It is, of course, much fuller, for the poet had a vivid imagination which made of the storm a mighty tempest visualized in its every detail and which pictured the interior of the whale realistically. The poet loved to narrate his story, and had also the ability to write with power.

He was equally successful in his portraying of human nature; the character of Jonah was fully developed in his original, but the poet has given us delightful sidelights on the hero; the hero does not easily forget Jonah's musings to himself against God or his ponderings as he sits in a nook of the whale's entrails. The largeness of the poet's heart is admirably reflected in the final speech of God to the prophet which brings the work to its dramatic climax; it is the poet who speaks through the mouth of God and appeals for the little children who never did any wrong, for many who cannot discern between their right hand and their left and for all dumb beasts who know not how to sin. Out of a single verse of the original the poet has made a speech

of thirty lines throbbing with human sympathy. No long moral is appended
—the story must speak for itself—and the poet wisely draws his poem to a
close, leaving us a masterpiece both in construction and in execution.

J. P. Oakden
Alliterative Poetry in Middle English, vol. II (Manchester:
Manchester Univ. Pr., 1935), pp. 67-68

He uses the bible as a foundation on which to build his poem and as the
building material. Often, he literally translates, but more often he must paraphrase and elaborate in order to make the moral more vivid to the common
man. People do not like to be preached to concerning their sins. The poet
must devise a method whereby Biblical lessons could be forced home while,
at the same time, men are being entertained. The *Pearl* poet, seeing in the
story of Jonah a perfect vehicle for enforcing the duty of obedience and
resignation, uses his source effectively. He elaborates what he wishes to
emphasize. He presents a Prologue and Epilogue in which he directly
states his purpose. Then, in the narrative proper, in order to make the terror
of God more convincing, he presents the storm and the whale incident in
graphic detail. The descriptions are pictorially vivid. The mercy of God
(one must never forget that the Jonah story is essentially concerned with the
idea of mercy) becomes brighter when we witness His ability to be terrible.

Normand Berlin
SN (January, 1961), p. 85

GENERAL

By far the largest part of the lines not dependent on the Vulgate are elaboration of detail and ornament. It is significant that the poet does not modify
or add to the narrative in order to enforce his moral, or call attention to the
particular application of his story. To be sure, he tells us the significance and
point of each narrative before he begins it; but once embarked on it, he
depends for his moral effect solely on the vividness of his presentation of
the doom of the wicked. The brief outline of Belshazzar's story that he
found in the fifth chapter of Daniel, he fills out with all the trappings of
medieval chivalry, the sound of trumpets and gay revelry, the lavish ornament of precious jewels, and all the splendor that God shatters in a single
night. Out of the few verses which relate the destruction of Sodom and
Gomorrah, he forms a picture that in its terrible grandeur is unsurpassed by
any poet of his time. It is, in fact, the gorgeous color and swift movement
of such passages of *Purity* that make the poem worthy to endure.

Robert J. Menner, ed.
Purity (New Haven, Conn.: Yale Univ. Pr.;
Oxford Univ. Pr., 1920), pp. li-lii

Craftsmanship . . . is not this poet's only gift. *Cleanness* and *Patience* contain Bible stories, and here the literary tradition of the Lives of the Saints may have helped. . . . The Saints' Lives preserved, while French example dwindled into prettiness and triviality, an inherited portion—little enough sometimes, but genuine—of the grand style of the Old English heroic poets. In the hands of a poet who possessed the sense of magnificence and the sentiment of grandeur, the tradition revived. Here was a poet whom wind and rain elated, who knew the strength of the seas and the pride of kings, and who believed in God. He was not the professional preacher who tells an impressive tale and appends a lucid moral: he was a poet like Spenser and Milton and Wordsworth, a poet of wide powers and wide knowledge, guiding his fellow-men in the way of good, seeking purity of heart and submission to the divine will.

W. L. Renwick and Harold Orton
The Beginnings of English Literature to Skelton
(London: Cresset Pr., 1939), pp. 67-68

JOHN GOWER
ca. 1330-1408

John Gower, Esquire of Kent, a wealthy landowner and real estate investor, was descended from the Gower family of Langburgh Wapentake, Yorkshire. Most of his life was spent in and around London where his professional and literary activity brought him into close association with Chaucer and other contemporary men of letters. His voluminous writings, mainly on moral themes, in French, Latin, and English, include *Cinkanta Balades* (before 1374), *Mirour de l'omme* (1374-1385), *Vox Clamantis* (1374-1385), *Confessio Amantis* (after 1385), and *Traitié pour esampler les amantz marietz* (after 1385).

G. C. Macauley, ed., *The Works of John Gower (1899-1902)*, 4 vols.
John H. Fisher, *John Gower* (1964)

Confessio Amantis

The success of the work [*Confessio Amantis*]—for a success it is in spite of its faults—is due to several merits. The first of these is the author's unquestionable talent for story-telling. He has little of the dramatic power or the humour which distinguish Chaucer, but he tells his tales in a well-ordered and interesting manner, does not break the thread by digressions, never tires of the story before it is finished, as Chaucer does so obviously and so often, and carries his reader through with him successfully to the end in almost every case. His narrative is a clear, if shallow, stream, rippling pleasantly over the stones and unbroken either by dams or cataracts. The materials of course are not original, but Gower is by no means a slavish follower in detail of his authorities; the proportions and arrangements of the stories are usually his own and often show good judgement. Moreover he not seldom gives a fresh turn to a well-known story. . . . There is no doubt that this gift of clear and interesting narrative was the merit which most appealed to the popular taste . . . and that the plainness of the style was an advantage rather than a drawback.

However, the literary characteristic which is perhaps most remarkable in the *Confessio Amantis* is connected rather with the form of expression than with the subject-matter. No justice is done to Gower unless it is acknowledged that the technical skill which he displays in his verse and the command which he has over the language for his own purposes is very remarkable. In the ease and naturalness of his movement within the fetters of the octosyllabic couplet he far surpasses his contemporaries, including Chaucer himself. Certain inversions of order and irregularities of construction he allows himself, and there are many stop-gaps of the conventional kind in the ordinary flow of his narrative; but in places where the matter requires it, his admirable management of the verse paragraph, the metrical smoothness of his lines, attained without unnatural accent or forced order of words, and the neatness with which he expresses exactly what he has to say within the precise limits which he lays down for himself, show a finished mastery of expression which is surprising in that age of half-developed English style, and in a man who had trained himself rather in French and Latin than in English composition.

G. C. Macaulay
The Complete Works of John Gower, vol. II (Oxford:
Clarendon Pr., 1901), pp. xii, xvi-xvii

The artistry of the *Confessio Amantis* has not always been recognized. Gower told us that his design was to . . . combine "profit with delight." Delight, for a fourteenth-century poet, almost inevitably meant courtly love, and "lore" would naturally include both ethical diatribe and information, both wisdom and knowledge. The work is to be moral, yet also encyclopedic, and the whole is somehow or other to be given a courtly and amatory colouring. In other words, Gower is proposing to do for his countrymen what Guillaume de Lorris and Jean de Meun had already done in France, and the impulse behind his work is the same which drove Chaucer to undertake a translation of the *Roman* itself. It is by considering the *Romance of the Rose* as Gower's original that we first become conscious of the technical problem involved in the *Confessio Amantis* and of the success—imperfect indeed but none the less astonishing—with which Gower has solved it. For in his original all was in confusion. The design of the first writer was incomplete; and, in the continuation, the amatory, satiric, pedagogic, and religious interest jostled with one another untidily and unprofitably. If Gower had been nothing more than the mere man of his own age with a talent for verse which he is sometimes supposed to have been, he would have been content to reproduce this confusion; for architectonics were not the strong point of the Middle Ages. But Gower everywhere shows a concern for form and unity which is rare at any time and which, in the fourteenth century in England, entitles him to all but the highest praise. He is determined to get in all the diversity of interests which he found in his model, and even to add to them his own new interest of story-telling; but he is also determined to knit all these together into some semblance of a whole. And he almost succeeds.

C. S. Lewis
The Allegory of Love (Oxford: Clarendon Pr., 1936), pp. 198-99

It is obvious that as a framework for a collection of tales [*Confessio Amantis*], Gower's plan is much inferior to Chaucer's. But to criticize it on this score is quite unfair. It assumes that the framework is an excuse for telling a series of stories, whereas in Gower's case the stories are secondary, a concession to his public. He is still the moralist and preacher; he has not abandoned the didactic purpose, but is attempting to make his teaching more palatable by a liberal use of tales and anecdotes. Under the circumstances it is surprising how well he can tell a story. He is neither dramatic nor humorous. His nature was essentially sober, but his narrative is always fluent, generally rapid, and at times marked by genuine grace of both language and metre. . . . Gower is not a great poet. He is an earnest man with a message for his times. He is alarmed at the way the world is going. He exhorts the King, preaches to the public. He is for reform within the established order. He is opposed to Lollardry, and the Peasants' Revolt fills him with horror. What more can the serious and thoughtful layman do than try to arouse his contemporaries to action?

Albert C. Baugh, ed.
A Literary History of England (New York:
Appleton-Century-Crofts, 1948), pp. 265-66

. . . the *Confessio Amantis*, though it aims at being a sort of *codex* of the rules of Courtly Love, is so confused by the sombre temper of its "moral" author as to be rendered almost unreadable wherever it strays from straightforward narrative. Gower seems not to have realized that in choosing to "go to the middel weie/ And wryte a bok between the tweie,/ Somewhat of lust, somewhat of lore" he was mixing oil and water. Nor does he seem to have anticipated that his Confessor, who sees it as his duty 'not only to tell the "propretes" of Love but also "The vices forto telle arew," though he does indeed commit (in respect of the Courtly Code) treason enough for

God's sake, would be unlikely to equivocate his way to Parnassus. The task he set himself was almost prohibitively difficult. Yet when we observe the medieval habit of christianizing secular ballads like "The Nutbrown Maid" or tales from the *Gesta Romanorum*, and the poets' fondness for ending any poem (even a purely political prophecy or a merry tale about a ploughman and a parson) with a brief prayer to God to admit both his reader and himself "unto ever-lasting Ioie," it is difficult to feel that its author considered the *Confessio Amantis* an uncongenial undertaking.

John Peter
Complaint and Satire in Early English Literature
(Oxford: Clarendon Pr., 1956), p. 52

The poet who is perhaps neareast to Chaucer . . . is Gower. Gower's verse . . . certainly implies the same social and cultural *milieu* as Chaucer's. In Gower's English book, *Confessio Amantis* (1300-1303) . . . we recognize again the well-bred, easy conversational tone and manner that we are familiar with in Chaucer, and the smooth-flowing—perhaps in Gower's work, too smooth-flowing—verse. Yet *Confessio Amantis*, for all its great length and considerable achievement in workmanship, is a pale shadow compared not only with *The Canterbury Tales* but also with the other poems of Chaucer.

Here, more than 300 years before the eighteenth century, is a kind of poetry which has the prose virtues, which is, in fact, more prosaic than a great deal of prose. What we are given by Gower is seldom more than simply the adequate statement. His modesty or sobriety of style must be allowed its due; his is the middle way of style. But it is hard to be sure whether, in Gower's case, the middle way is not simply the way of mediocrity. Gower's lack of emphasis, whether studied or not, becomes in time monotonous.

John Speirs
"A Survey of Medieval Verse," *The Age of Chaucer*
(Baltimore: Penguin Books, 1961), p. 52

It was at one time the fashion to compare Gower and Chaucer much in the manner of the school examinee comparing Keats and Shelley. This is an unrewarding pastime, for Gower's aims were quite different from those of his friend: more modest, more sober, more serious. Gower has less wit and humour, less drama and panache, not only by nature but also by choice. Nevertheless, these qualities are by no means absent. And, when he chooses, Gower can rise to real eloquence and splendour—as in his many descriptions of weather, or in the "Prayer of Cephalus" and the "Tale of Ceyx and Halcyone" (both in Book Four). He is capable of real pathos, as in the "Tale of Canace" (Book Three), and of genuine excitement, as in the

"Tale of Medea" (Book Five). His most remarkable quality, however, is his tireless ease and fluency—all in meticulous rhyme and metre—while avoiding both monotony and "bittiness." He was a lesser poet; but he was, in his chosen way, almost as great a craftsman as was Chaucer in his.

Terence Tiller, tr.
Introd. in, *John Gower, Confessio Amantis* (Baltimore: Penguin Books, 1963), p. 12

GENERAL

There is nothing unreasonable in the opinion . . . that Gower had a quality of style for which there is no better term than "natural." It is an old fallacious term in criticism, but it expresses what people mean. Gower "followed Nature," inasmuch as he did not overload, or bluster, or, at any rate in his English work, go raking for ornamental phrases out of books. . . . But his natural utterance is the result of a long process, in which the study of rhetoric had its place, during the generations that formed the courteous art of poetry in France. The beauty of it was that the rhetoric had been thoroughly assimilated and the school processes forgotten before Gower took in hand to write. . . . Gower's language is never strained, and it is never anything but gentle. Wordsworth's ideal of poetical expression might be exemplified from Gower, and justified; for though Gower's vocabulary is not taken from the "humble and rustic life" which Wordsworth recommended, it is natural and unaffected; there is no artificial rhetoric in his phrasing, there are no ornamental words daubed over his page; there is, in short, nothing remarkable about his diction. It is attractive purely through its simplicity and ease, "as clean as hill-well water."

W. P. Ker
Essays on Medieval Literature (London: Macmillan, 1905), pp. 106-7

. . . As a story-teller he is far above contempt. Perhaps narrative never runs much more smoothly than in the best of his easy, four-stress couplets. . . . No digression, no emotional outbursts, no comments clog his stories. The style is as unimpeded and as lucid as that of the French, whose tongue was as familiar to him as his own. If the narrative is seldom so artfully handled as to gain by what is cut away, yet there are no monstrous introductions of disjointed climaxes to ruin the uniform excellence of proportion. Nothing could be more fluent than his telling of Ovid's tale of *Actaeon* for example, and, though he makes no attempt to realize and vivify the story, yet another prime requisite of tale-telling, a flowing well-ordered narrative, must be accorded him. Never so vivid as Chaucer's the descriptions everywhere are adequate and effective. . . . And last, Gower possesses the art which in a story-teller is to be prized above rubies—he knows when to stop. These merits, in origin, are not entirely unrelated to certain faults in the tales of the *Confessio Amantis*. . . . It is, in part, because they are *exempla*, that brevity, lucidity, and freedom from interruption are enjoined upon the narratives. Each story illustrates its point; great length, digression, complexity, all impair efficiency for such a purpose. To this didactic purpose, however, may be assigned a certain lack of climax in many of the stories, a fault speedily felt, though not easily shown. Unlike Chaucer, very unlike the moderns, but in close resemblance to the medieval homilists, Gower drifts through his tale, not assembling his forces for a climax, sometimes not pointing the story at all. One often feels the plot die away as one reads, until it fades into the moralizing. . . . The fault is rhetorical; its cause an undue preoccupation with the illustrative possibilities of the stories; its presence only another evidence of how completely Gower wrote in the school of the exemplum, of which, in England, he is the head.

Henry Seidel Canby
The Short Story in English (New York:
Henry Holt, 1909), pp. 61-62

In a certain sense, its age and its accomplishment being taken together, it is the capital example, in English, of the unequivalenced variety of the [octosyllabic] metre. It has less vigour and variety than Chaucer's, but runs much more easily; it seems to be written as much *con amore* as Chaucer's was written against the grain. It was, I have little doubt, directly in the eye and mind of Wither and Browne when they wrote in the early seventeenth century, and while it may have had direct influence, as well as through them, on Keats, in the admirable *Eve of St. Mark*, it certainly influenced directly, as well as through him and them, Mr. William Morris, the actual author of the greatest examples of it in English, taking bulk and merit together. . . . The immense length of his poem and the heterogeneous character of its contents, have no doubt, in modern times, done him at least as much harm as they secured him respect in his own, and those immediately following. He deserves, equally beyond doubt, no small credit for his accomplishment in a certain kind and degree of style, and for the almost complete manner in which he has mastered and applied his own conception of the metre which he uses. And I am bound to say the more I read Gower . . . the less I am inclined to think him merely an example of polished longwindedness and accomplished monotony. But I do not think that he can ever be entirely cleared from these charges, and though it may seem unfair, I believe that his conception and execution of metre had a good deal to do with this. . . . Gower . . . has followed the French in rejecting foot-elasticity, with the result of meeting the same—"disasters" is perhaps too strong a word, but—inconveniences which they met. The liability of the French octosyllable to a sort of skipping-rope monotony, insignificant and even a little irritating, has been acknowledged in its own country, and certainly cannot escape anyone out of it. And Gower generally does nothing to obviate or evade the danger. . . . But we must never forget or undervalue the immense value of the example of accomplished prosody which Gower set so far as he went.

George Saintsbury
A History of English Prosody, 2nd ed. vol. I (London:
Macmillan, 1923), pp. 139-42

There is perhaps nothing of the highest poetry in Gower. He does not make us see visions, or feel more intensely any of the great emotions of human life. He does not light up the dark places of man's soul, laying bare motives or analysing thoughts. He tells his stories plainly or prettily, wisely and, at times, wittily, turning aside not at all to elaborate the character of any of his personages or theorize on the why and wherefore. . . . Yet Gower is a true poet. He feels for and with the personages of his tales; and by his choice of words conveys to us not the bare facts only, but something of the atmosphere in which his imagination sees them happen, something, too of his feelings of pity or scorn.

K. N. Colvile
Fame's Twilight (Boston: Small, Maynard, 1924), pp. 29-30

Gower's little light has been dimmed by the brilliance of Chaucer. He cannot rival Chaucer's lively comedy and vivid realism, his variety and amplitude, nor has he the force and passionate sincerity of Langland; but he deserves to be remembered not only for his share in establishing the new tradition in English poetry and his faith in the future of the English tongue but for his actual achievement. He has a quite characteristic, and at times charming, vein of poetry; his best stories are told so easily and clearly that we are hardly conscious of the poet's art, the story appears to tell itself, there is nothing to come between it and the reader. But to create this impression of absolute ease was, at the end of the fourteenth century, a real distinction. We remember, too, the quiet, pleasant melody of his verse like his river "rennende upon the smale stones," the charm of his old romantic tales, suffused with tender feeling, awakening echoes of sorrows "far-off and very long ago."

TLS (August 18, 1932), p. 574

He [Chaucer] is Le Grand translateur. He had found a new language, he had it largely to himself, with the grand opportunity. Nothing spoiled, nothing worn out. Dante had had a similar opportunity, and taken it, with a look over his shoulder and a few latin experiments. Chaucer felt his chance. The gulf between Chaucer and Gower can be measured by Gower's hesitation, by his proved unwillingness to "take a chance." He had a go at metrical exercises in all three of the current tongues, English, French and Latin. Books, used in the wrong way. The hunt for a subject, etc.

He was the perfect type of English secondary writer, condemned recently but for all time by Henri Davray with his: "Ils cherchent des sentiments pour les accomoder à leur vocabulaire."

They hunt for sentiments to fit into their vocabulary.

Ezra Pound
ABC of Reading (London: G. Routledge, 1934), p. 88

He is a poet with neither the genius nor the intelligence to support a long poem, yet worthy, as a teller of stories, to rank second only to Chaucer in his time; a writer who, in the course of the *Confessio,* seems able to avoid most of the pitfalls of the medieval writer, only to fall into the biggest pit of all at the end, a patently didactic purpose; a master of the plain style, excellent for story-telling, yet often prosaic; one who, in spite of these contradictions, is well worth reading and deserves to be better known than he is. As a commentator on the social scene he can be studied as a corrective to Chaucer, but he also deserves reading for his own undoubted merits as a poet.

D. S. Bland
Eng (Autumn, 1947), p. 290

Whenever one turns to Gower's writings and studies them in fourteenth-century historical relationships, he will find the poet repeatedly going through the same cycle: a ruler is responsible for the welfare of England and for its morality in civic, religious, and political life as exemplified in the individual citizen. He brings to bear upon what he writes the heritage of political and ethical practice to give the document permanent significance concerning all rulers, hereditary or elected, who govern constructively. He urges their reliance on good counsel and sound judgment and not on progress through parliamentary procedure for developing representative government. With a humourless intensity he interprets the corruption and perversity of all classes. For this state of affairs he holds Richard II ultimately responsible. His hope for the future of England he mirrors finally through his hero, Henry IV, for whom he becomes poet laureate.

George R. Coffman
PMLA (September, 1954), p. 964

For if the basic brick of Gower's poetry is the block of lines rather than the individual phrase, it is unrewarding to pick out one sentence more striking than the rest; the overall effect is the object. He could never have created that brilliant series of cameos in the Temple of Mars where Chaucer catches a salient point as in a flash of lightning. . . . Neither, however, could Chaucer have conveyed the impression of Pope Sylvester in the Tale of Constantine, where, though not a single line may be isolated *in vacuo,* the sense of the man dominates the whole legend. Because for Gower, as for Dryden or Byron, it is the final impact of the story as a whole that counts; and it is of Dryden amongst later poets that he most reminds me. Nothing is less likely to appeal to any of the critical schools of today than his controlled and effortless smoothness that prefers to sacrifice an individual beauty rather than to upset the balance of the whole.

Peter Rison
EIC (January, 1958), p. 21

The *Vox Clamantis* does not emerge as a great work of art, despite much serious effort on Gower's part to make it one. Like the author of *Piers,* like Spenser, in a long poem he lacks architectonic ability. He erects an imposing but sprawling and shaky framework and then fills in the pieces as best he might, with some backtracking, rambling, and repetition. There are nevertheless effective areas in the mosaic, such as some of the descriptions scattered here and there in the poem. Some examples are the banquet of the gluttonous prelates . . . ; the sarcastic portrait of that stock figure the hunting parson . . . ; and the picture of London commercial life. The retelling of the creation of Adam in Book VIII, Chap. 6, is well done. There is an occasional touch of wit. . . . Unfortunately, Gower often pursues the rhetorical ornament of *amplificatio* to extremes, wearily dilating whatever he has to say. He takes to heart the medieval view that every author ought to beautify his verses in as many ways as he can.

Eric W. Stockton, tr.
The Major Latin Works of John Gower (Seattle, Wash.:
Washington Univ. Pr., 1962), p. 30

Though . . . the Anglo-Norman lyric begins in obscurity and the earliest survivals are not of the highest order, its end is magnificent, and the last writer surpasses his French contemporaries by a long way. John Gower shows what French poetry in England might have become if Chaucer had not flung his cap over the windmill and plunged into the English language. Gower . . . is usually refused a place as an Anglo-Norman writer on two grounds—that he wrote good French and that he struck out a fresh line. Neither of these reasons will stand scrutiny. Gower wrote an Anglo-Norman dialect, influenced, as had been the case from 1066 onwards, by continental

French. . . . The *Mirour de l'Omme* . . . follows the tradition of Anglo-Norman religious literature. All that is new and might be considered un-Anglo-Norman is his use of the balade. But this is ridiculous. The balade was not adopted in northern France until the time of Gower himself, and its best exponents, Charles of Orleans and Villon, wrote after his death. It is with Deschamps and Machault alone that he can be compared as a lyric poet, and he is their superior. It is a curious fact that the balade does not well survive its transference into English—even Chaucer's experiments with it are not very successful, and his use of the form is another reason, besides his use of the French language, why Gower would have been ranged with the "attardés et égarés," supposing Lanson had ever written a history of literature in England.

M. Dominica Legge
Anglo-Norman Literature and Its Background
(Oxford: Clarendon Pr., 1963), p. 357

The most striking characteristic of Gower's literary production is its single-mindedness. The similarity in the method, structure, and content of his major pieces was what made it possible for Macaulay to identify the *Mirour de l'omme* as Gower's work when it turned up in a defective, anonymous manuscript. This external similarity is the outgrowth of an inner consistency in purpose and point of view. In a very real sense, Gower's three major poems are one continuous work. The *Mirour de l'omme* he renamed *Speculum Meditantis*, presumably to harmonize with *Vox Clamantis*, and he called his English poem *Confessio Amantis*. . . . The three works were intended to present a systematic discourse upon the nature of man and society. For this they do. In spite of their length and involution, they provide as organized and unified a view as we have of the social ideals of England upon the eve of the Renaissance. This view may be subsumed under the broad headings: individual VIRTUE, legal JUSTICE, and the administrative responsibility of the KING. The three works progress from the description of the origin of sin and the nature of the vices and virtues at the beginning of the *Mirour de l'omme*, through consideration of social law and order in the discussion of the estates in the *Mirour* and *Vox Clamantis*, to a final synthesis of royal responsibility and Empedoclean love in the *Confessio Amantis*. But while this evolution provides a pattern, the social consequences of individual sin are kept constantly in view at all times, and the importance of law and the functions of the king are given specific attention in all three works.

John H. Fisher
John Gower (New York: New York Univ. Pr.,
1964), pp. 135, 137

ROBERT   HENRYSON
fl. 1450-1500

> Little is known of Henryson's life. A late but probably authentic tradition
> styles him "Master Robert Henryson, schoolmaster of Dunfermline." His
> works show him to have been a warm, witty, and well-educated man with
> a considerable knowledge of law. He wrote three long poems—*The Morall
> Fabillis of Esope the Phrygian, The Testament of Cresseid, The Complaint
> of Orpheus*—together with a dozen short, miscellaneous pieces, including
> a charming pastourelle, *Robene and Makyne*.
>
> H. Harvey Wood, ed., *The Poems and Fables of Robert Henryson* (1958)
> Marshall W. Stearns, *Robert Henryson* (1949)

. . . Henryson's most successful and characteristic work is to be sought in
his version of *The Morall Fabillis of Esope the Phrygian*, one of the happiest
performances in its kind which the English language has to show, and
distinguished by a humanity and a tolerance which our national poetry, in
so far as it bears to be a "criticism of life," has sometimes lacked. The plot
of the *Taill of the Uplandes Mous and the Burges Mous*, for example, is
familiar to everyone, but the inimitable happiness of its adaptation to
Scottish life and manners, and the dexterous mingling of the animal and
the human element, give it an irresistible claim upon our attention. . . .
But, indeed, all the *Fables* are good, and stamp Henryson as a master of
fluent and easy versification, a man of insight into character, and the
possessor of the same wide and generous outlook upon men and life which
are not the least among the many memorable excellences of his model,
Chaucer.

J. H. Millar
A Literary History of Scotland (London:
T. Fisher Unwin, 1903), pp. 33, 35

Henryson's longest and in some ways his best work is his *Moral Fabillis of
Esope*. The material of the book is drawn from the popular jumble of
tales which the Middle Ages had fathered upon the Greek fabulist; much
of it can be traced directly to the edition of Anonymus, to Lydgate's version
and to English Reynardian literature as it appeared in Caxton's dressing.
In one sense, therefore, the book is the least original of Henryson's works;
but in another, and the truer, it may take precedence of even *The Testament
of Cresseid* and *Robene and Makyne* for the freshness of its treatment,
notably in its adaptation of hackneyed *fabliaux* to contemporary requirements. Nor does it detract from the originality of presentation, the good
spirits, and the felicity of expression, to say that here, even more than in his

closer mutations of Chaucer, he has learnt the lesson of Chaucer's outlook on life. Above all, he shows the fineness of literary taste which marks off the southern poet from his contemporaries, and exercised but little influence in the north even before that later period when the rougher popular habit became extravagant.

G. Gregory Smith
"The Scottish Chaucerians," *CHEL*, vol. II (1908), pp. 245-46

In the history of literature the writer of good short stories stands forth either for his technical skill and originality in handling his chosen form of expression; or for the influence his work exerts upon successors; or for that residuum of personality which, as Lanson puts it, remains when from his writings has been subtracted all that belongs, "à la race, au milieu, au moment," and to "la continuité de l'évolution du genre." Chaucer's fame rests upon all these qualities. Henryson is technically excellent, but not so to the point of great originality. His influence is not easily traceable, although it may well have a share in that tradition of homely realism, and of a close observation of nature, which has well nigh ever since belonged to the poets of the "northern lede." But his quaint and delightful spirit, his sensitiveness to pathos and to humor, make him a personality in literature, and thus one of a genus rare in all periods, rarest in his own late middle ages. It is personality that gives the feeling heart which, with the seeing eye, makes the great story-teller. The seeing eye imparts the rare power of imaginative insight into the actions which stand for character. . . . But even more important is the feeling heart that knows which to retain of all the vivid whirl of events driving through the imagination. Here is a test of essential genius, and it is by means of a successful choice that the warm sympathy of a Cervantes, or a Shakespeare, or a Chaucer, beams out in some little phrase or incident. Of this rare humor, perhaps no writer before the Elizabethan dramatists possessed so much as Henryson, save only his master, Chaucer. In force, in fire, and possibly in beauty of verse, Dunbar exceeds him, as his own *Cresseid* certainly exceeds the fables of which we make so much. In pathos, Gower, never his superior, is sometimes his equal. In satire of the cudgeling variety, Langland is more proficient. But in the kindly humor, that plays about the little things of life, and shows us men's hearts as often as not under the control of their spleens or their stomachs, in this humor the Scottish story-teller has won the title of "Maister," which tradition, for another cause, has given to him.

Henry Seidel Canby
The Short Story in English (New York:
Henry Holt, 1909), pp. 96-99

He reveals in all his works a charming personality moving through a still atmosphere of musical thought. In his poems the true man speaks beautifully, shadows running over the sunny gold of his humour, like the wind across the wheat.

He has a keen outlook upon Nature, and the art of painting a picture. . . . In such matters he observes for himself. His pictures have not the conventional touch, and he stands forth as a great poet with the three graces that mark out such an one always—namely, humour, truth, and interpretation.

It was a life unstirred by passion, far from the din and ambition of courts, that this poet lived, within sound of the abbey bell; and as fancy looks on at the window of his school, we can behold him dreaming of the green knolls, and the sheep, and the whims of rustic lovers, while the monks chant their orisons in the cloisters near, and the boys hum their Latin, which was the key to all the wisdom of their world.

> Lauchlan Maclean Watt
> *Scottish Life and Poetry* (London:
> James Nisbet and Sons, 1912), pp. 96-97

His *Testament of Cresseid* . . . is, although a bit laden with mediaeval machinery at the start, one of the most peaceful and affecting poems of the century, as his *Robyn and Makyn* is one of the most graceful and pleasing of pastorals. The thirteen Fables are perhaps an even more significant accomplishment, for to this time-honored theme Henryson has brought so much vivacity and acute, sympathetic observation of men and beasts, that no fables have more flavor than his.

> W. A. Neilson and K. G. T. Webster, eds.
> *Chief British Poets of the Fourteenth and Fifteenth Centuries*
> (Boston: Houghton Mifflin, 1916), p. 434

As for *Robene and Makyne*—arch and fresh and jolly as a small idyll by Theocritus—it is in all the anthologies and deserves to be: with the possible exception of Victor Hugo's *La Coccinelle*, the prettiest perfect thing ever written on the theme of "he that will not when he may."

> Sir Arthur Quiller-Couch
> *Studies on Literature, Second Series*
> (Cambridge Univ. Pr., 1923), p. 272

The greatest, and the most original, of Henryson's works is that one which would appear least likely to have that quality—his translation of the *Moral Fables of Aesop*. In his rehandling of popular and traditional material, the reader has the best opportunity of assessing the classical nature of Henryson's originality—the originality that makes all things its own, the originality of Chaucer, and of Shakespeare. Not only in tales for which no original is known (like *The Fox, the Wolf and the Cadger*), but in well-worn pieces like *The Town-mouse and the Country-mouse*, the story is told as though it had never been told before, with a wealth of personal observation, simple pathos, and lively humour. The dead bones are made to live. Aesop, the slow-pacing moralist of medieval tradition, is barely recognisable. Like the cadger of the fable, "As he had hard ane pyper play, he gais"; and the moralising, which is admittedly dull, is confined to the postscript. Henryson's most Chaucerian gift, though it should be recognised as one distinctively Scottish, is his power of turning from pathos to humour, from the sublime to the ridiculous, in a line or phrase which breaks in upon the narrative like a spoken comment in the voice of the poet. When the two mice, seated at their alderman's feast, and singing, "Hail, Yule, hail!" for very joy, are startled by the entrance of the steward with his keys, how is their scuttling to safety described?—

"They taryit not to wesche, as I suppose!"

It is the perfect art, of the same kind as Chaucer's chat with the eagle in the *House of Fame*.

H. Harvey Wood, ed.
The Poems and Fables of Robert Henryson
(Edinburgh: Oliver and Boyd, 1933), p. xv

Robert Henryson, the earliest of the group of poets to whom pre-eminently the title Scottish Chaucerians is given, has more of the element of greatness in his themes and treatment than the others.

Henryson alone, in poetry other than lyric, approaches in his subjects and characters the high seriousness of great poetry. He presents tragic situations and characters stirred by deep feelings, he creates moving and pathetic speeches, he alone seems to have been able to infuse into the new poetry some of the passion and tragedy of the ballad, and thus to create something individual in his *Testament of Cresseid* and his *Orpheus and Eurydice*. He also has a more genial humour, and a power of giving very real and animated representation to everyday things, as in the *Fables*. He has more creative power; he is, to use the old Scottish word, a greater *makar* than the others.

M. M. Gray, ed.
Scottish Poetry from Barbour to James VI (London:
J. M. Dent, 1935). pp. viii-ix

So strong, and so self-possessed, is Henryson's personality, that the title of "Scottish Chaucerian" seems unnecessary. He exists in his own right, sober, devout, quietly observant of beasts and people. Both his meditative sadness, as in *The Abbey Walk*, and his humour, as in that admirable "pastourelle"

Robyn and Makyn and in the *Fables*, seem restful in comparison with the black melancholy and the noisy rough-and-tumble of his compatriots. These quiet traits are indeed Scottish, but they stand outside the common literary habit that was handed down to Burns; and they are more difficult of expression.

W. L. Renwick and Harold Orton
The Beginnings of English Literature to Skelton
(London: Cresset Pr., 1939), p. 118

It is in the Fables, I think, that one finds Henryson's gifts—easy narrative, playful humour, poetry and gravity—in happiest balance. But his most original poem is the *Testament of Cresseid*. There is a little over-elaboration in the aureate style, especially in the description of the gods. But it is to my mind perhaps the most original poem that Scotland has produced. It was no light thing to come after Boccaccio and Chaucer, and to succeed in making a real addition to a great dramatic story, something that without needless challenging of comparison does, in its impressive way, complete that tragic tale.

As a lyrical poet of the Swinburnian kind, a master of every variety of rhyming technique, Dunbar is the greater, but in dramatic power, in gravity of temper, Henryson is the first of early Scottish poets; and his humour, if not so boisterous as Dunbar's, is finer, shyer, more Chaucerian and more Scottish.

Sir Herbert Grierson
Essays and Addresses (London: Chatto and Windus,
1940), pp. 111-12, 116

Henryson was sage and serious. It was part of his Scottishness. The Scots seem to have a capacity for finding sap in what to more southern minds is dry fare. . . . The Scots find in a high sentence, in a *moralitas*, a nutriment which they can sustain themselves on richly. This may have been a more widely spread capacity in the middle ages than now. What was then the taste of Christendom may since have shrunk to Scotland. But even then Chaucer had less of it than Henryson. In the tales of the Parson and Monk, Chaucer can be sufficiently dramatic to deal out *moralitas* generously as porridge in Scotland, but his view of life demands some formula less simple. To Henryson the world and its people are controlled by form and uncomplicated moral machinery. Human life for him is thoroughly governable, both in theory and practice. . . . There is nothing in Henryson to confuse the moral issue as the Prologue confuses it, or as the whole Canterbury pilgrimage confuses it—a pilgrimage on which the tales of Hugh of Lincoln and of the miller meet and kiss each other. Chaucer sees to it that he keeps the issue confused. He advances beyond an accepted morality into a morality which is finer and more difficult, rather of the New Testament than of the Old. Chaucer, who appreciated the complex cross-purposes of human minds, has no place for a moral. The real difference between his "Cock and the Fox" and Chaucer's is that Henryson is seen to be working towards his *moralitas*. It is during three stanzas only of his twenty-seven that Henryson wanders. . . . His telling of the fable of how the swallow preached to the other birds and preached in vain is moralist let loose. Here there are three sermons, two of which are long ones, and a moral elegy. But this does not suffice. In his own person he introduces the story with thirteen stanzas of theological argument, stately as Boethius. To balance this he concludes with a *moralitas* of nine stanzas. . . . This capacity for loaded-up edification has remained strong in Scotland. The marvel is, in Henryson as in Scottish preachers generally, that the *moralitas* can be so vigorous, its images so rampant. . . .

Geoffrey Tillotson
Essays in Criticism and Research
(Cambridge Univ. Pr., 1942), pp. 3-4

Of all the Scottish Chaucerians, Robert Henryson . . . is likest the master in temper. Being only a Dunfermline dominie, he had not Chaucer's wide knowledge of the world nor his brilliant, urbane wit; but he knew men well within his narrower horizon, and he had something of Chaucer's *bonhomie*, with a keen sense of the comic and a vivid, sometimes poignant realism that is all his own.

Herbert J. C. Grierson and J. C. Smith
A Critical History of English Poetry (London:
Chatto and Windus, 1944), p. 54

Although Henryson learnt much of his craft from Chaucer and although his poem continues and assumes in the reader a knowledge of Chaucer's *Troilus and Criseyde*, he does not really compete with his master, nor does his poem suffer when compared with its source. In temper the *Testament of Cresseid* is tragic and as such it is nearer akin to some of the ballads and to the later books of Malory's *Morte Darthur* than is the essential comedy of Chaucer. And through being truly tragic it takes itself right out of its medieval setting and allies itself to the tragic writings of all ages. True, when Henryson calls the poem "this tragedie" he meant no more by "tragedie" than the simple medieval notion of a human being, of whatever character and by whatever sequence of events, falling from prosperity into adversity; but in actual fact his poem fulfils more exacting tragic standards. Cresseid's character is not subtle or complicated but it is sufficiently mixed to approximate her to the requirements of Aristotle. She is far from being a saint but she is no villain. Indeed, in herself she is more good than bad, but her errors of weakness and vanity co-operated with the turn of events in causing her ruin. We pity her misfortune and we are afraid because her own misfortune is the type of what may befall the run of humanity.

The tragic emotion is swift and concentrated and can only be conveyed by corresponding poetic means. Henryson is free from the besetting medieval vice of prolixity and joins the successfully tragic writers of all ages by the economy and the emphasis with which he tells his tale. When he is ornate (and he can be so after the fashion of his age) it is in the pauses of the action.

E. M. W. Tillyard
Five Poems 1470-1870 (London:
Chatto and Windus, 1948), pp. 5-6

The Moral Fabillis of Esope the Phrygian is [Henryson's] great humorous, and *The Testament of Cresseid* his great tragic work. During the last century *The Fables* have been overshadowed by *The Testament*, and their beauties neglected. But to appreciate the sweetness and harmony, the endlessly lively and inventive quality of Henryson's poetry, it is necessary to know them both; otherwise he runs the danger of being considered a poet of moderate capacity who, by a piece of good luck, wrote one great poem. . . . Henryson's humour is not quite like anything else in Scottish literature, more subtle and pervasive than the humour of Dunbar or Burns or Scott, more urbane, more indirect, less specialised, and saturated with irony. It is an assumption more than anything else; it remains implicit in the selection of detail and the choice of expression, and rarely comes to the point of statement.

Edwin Muir
Essays on Literature and Society (London:
Hogarth Pr., 1949), pp. 8-9

Henryson observed the life around him with a keen, kindly, and sometimes indignant eye. The chief fruits of his observation may be found in his version of Aesop's *Fables*. At the outset, the poet suggests that it is profitable to mingle "merie sport" among earnest subjects, "to light the spreit, and gar the tyme be schort." Not that Henryson cannot moralize with high serious-ness and fire when he so desires. But in his *Fables* he relegates most of his moral *sentence* to the end of each story, and it is difficult to escape the impression that he intends his fables to be at least as entertaining as they are instructive.

Marshall W. Stearns
Robert Henryson (New York: Columbia Univ. Pr., 1949), p. 107

He [Henryson] extended the bridgehead of cultivated style established by the author of *The Kingis Quair*. Some critics have denied that he owed any substantial debt to the Chaucerian tradition; but he learnt from Chaucer what no Scots poet of his own day could have taught him—tonal contrasts and the subtle uses of rhetoric, an appreciation of stanzaic pattern, and above all the art of mirroring his own personality in his work. . . .

Henryson is the first considerable Scots poet to draw his inspiration from Chaucer, and yet he is, within the Chaucerian tradition, a highly independent writer. He stands apart from Chaucer in many important respects. He shows a constant moral concern in his work, perhaps even in the lightsome "Robene and Makyne." Despite his heavy debts to Chaucer the rhetorician, he continues the native tradition of simple narrative and colloquial dialogue with a new subtlety and subdued grace. To conventional poetic themes he brings a whimsical and sometimes sardonic humour very different from Chaucer's and unmistakably Scots.

James Kinsley
"The Medieval Makars," *Scottish Poetry: A Critical Survey*
(London: Cassell, 1955), pp. 16, 24

By modern, if not contemporary, standards *Robene and Makyne* is the finest jewel in the debris of the fifteenth century. The pastoral is a miraculous hybrid: a ballad plot interfused with the whimsical sensibility of a good poet. Scores of sentimental ballads from later periods suggest the difficulty of the experiment and by contrast emphasize Henryson's achievement.

Arthur K. Moore
The Secular Lyric in Middle English (Lexington, Ky.:
Univ. Kentucky Pr., 1957), pp. 193-94

Robert Henryson's debt to Chaucer is great, and he is the first to acknowledge it. . . . But he does not imitate. He assimilates Chaucer's conception of poetry and creates from his artistic centre. In a more limited field he achieves (as Tillyard observes) the same artistic level as his master, and there are even passages where Henryson surpasses Chaucer, as in the introduction to the *Testament* or the meeting of the lovers. He fertilizes Chaucer's heritage with his own native tradition and achieves a new subtlety which is totally his own.

K. Wittig
The Scottish Tradition in Literature (Edinburgh:
Oliver and Boyd, 1958), p. 34

Much of his work is infused with a genial but retiring quality . . . and, although in terms of quantity he did not write much, in emotional content he surpasses his contemporary makars and did not shy away from realistic treatment of a tragic theme. His masterpiece is "The Testament of

Cresseid," in which his direct debts to Chaucer are limited to the skeleton of the plot itself and to the use of the English poet as a model for rhetorical composition. Whereas Chaucer translated and developed Boccaccio's *Il Filostrato* in order to make his *Troilus and Creseyde*, Henryson took up the old story at the point where Chaucer left off and applied his talents to the creation of an original imaginative work. Cresseid has broken the moral and the theological laws and her sin is punished by the physical affliction of leprosy, but through her eventual repentance and her testament relinquishing earthly things she is permitted to die in the purified state of an aspirant to the conventual life. Whereas Chaucer saw the real values of life as religious and makes his Troilus see human efforts as wasteful, Henryson promotes sympathy for Cresseid's miserable lot on this earth, but the stern moralist is always in control and, as a matter of principle, displays little sympathy for the shortcomings of fallen humanity. Chaucer's inconclusiveness may be closer to life, but Henryson's strong and unyielding sense of justice in the Platonic sense of giving each man his due is aesthetically more satisfying.

The *Moral Fabillis* . . . are in a lighter vein. They are rehandled versions of *Aesop's Fables* but include others. . . . The heavy, moral Aesop is transformed in his hands and a fresh cast is given to the old stories, which now become the vehicles for political and social commentary. Historical investigations into the subject matter of the fables suggest that they were closely connected with the vicissitudes of the times. . . .

Henryson's language is a good deal less "literary" than that of other makars, in the *Fabillis* at least, and is more clearly rooted in the speech of the peasantry. Unlike the others, he was not strictly of the Court circle and is often thought to have been little affected by Chaucer, though such a view fails to take into account the more subtle direct influences of tone, rhetoric, and verse-formation, as well as the art of reflecting his own personality in his poems without seeming to do so, itself a strong characteristic of Chaucer. The *Fabillis* emphasize character and action rather than setting, for Henryson gives only slender hints of the Northern landscape; but his straightforward narrative and colloquial dialogue are squarely in the native Scots tradition. Though he may lack the versatility and the glitter of his fellow poet William Dunbar, Henryson reveals a more profound poetic character that is less prone to enslavement by the wizardry of words. . . .

A. M. Kinghorn
Texas Studies in Lang. and Lit. (Spring, 1959), pp. 76-77

The *Moral Fabillis* consist of thirteen animal-fables. Most, though not all, are taken from Aesop; with the modesty incumbent upon a medieval author, Henryson represents his work as a mere translation, but he is, in fact, as original as Shakespeare: like him, he takes the bare bones and nothing else. The Fables are completely re-created; they emerge as a product conceivable only in the time and place that produced them, in medieval Scotland; and in them, better than in any other work of art, its life is preserved. A first reading will probably pick out the obvious qualities: the life and quickness of narrative, the charm of personal details, and the wealth of discursive comment. But of Henryson as of Chaucer it can be said that the picturesque detail owes its effectiveness to the solidity and seriousness of what it grows from. Henryson's *Fables* (like La Fontaine's—they deserve the comparison) do more than present types of human beings in animal guises and animals comically behaving like human beings; they build up a total and consistent *society,* both rendered and criticized. The types of humanity are shown in their relationships as well as their individualities; they form the particular pattern of the society that Henryson lived in.

   . . . there is a real kinship with Chaucer. Henryson leaves an impression somewhat similar to Chaucer's, of a man who has no deep quarrel with his world and no real difference with the ideas of his age, and who did not find it too difficult to love his fellow creatures, but who was not made complacent, unobservant, or uncritical by his conformity and his tolerance. He is, in fact, the only "Scottish Chaucerian" who is at all like Chaucer, and he is so by a genuine temperamental affinity much more than by literary discipleship.

Patrick Cruttwell
"Two Scots Poets: Dunbar and Henryson," *The Age of Chaucer*
(Baltimore: Penguin Books, 1961), pp. 183-84

The jasper and swallow fables have an obvious resemblance: in both of them birds turn aside from a proffered higher good in order to seek food, and so incur loss or destruction. This plot, which can be paralleled in many of the other poems, indicates very neatly the fundamental conflict of the *Fables,* the conflict between man's carnal and spiritual sides, between the natural and the supernatural worlds, between the actual and the ideal. One can see easily enough why Henryson found it advantageous to use animals in dealing with this theme. The birds scratching busily in the dirt or chaff are powerful symbols for appetite, and ones which convey vividly its bestiality. In the same way, all of Henryson's animals, not only those who choose blindly or arrogantly the worse course, or who escape after great perils and torments, present a graphic image of the folly and vicissitudes of the natural world. But since Henryson refuses to oversimplify the natural world into an easy target for invective, he describes his short-lived and suffering animals from a sympathetic viewpoint; the *Fables* are filled, for instance, with pathetic and occasionally valiant sheep and mice. So the animal kingdom that Henryson gathers together forms a symbol for man-

kind that, if unflattering, is far from harsh. Yet the final value, in each
fable, is not the mortal world but some absolute, whether perfect justice,
divine wisdom, or eternal life.

Denton Fox
ELH (December, 1962), pp. 355-56

Henryson takes as his starting point Chaucer's *Troilus and Criseyde,*
perhaps (especially in its first four books) the most diffuse poem of the
least diffuse of Middle English poets; and since Henryson's conciseness
seems the very opposite of his model's prolixity, a comparison of the two
poems may be helpful. The diffuseness of the *Troilus* is not a fortuitous
stylistic quality, but is closely related to the action presented and the poet's
attitude towards it. Chaucer is diffuse in order to maintain until the last
moment a balance between a wide variety of possible attitudes towards his
Criseyde and Troilus's love for her. He builds up an iridescent structure,
showing a different light at every moment, and his story enables him to do
this, for it is not until the end of the fifth book that Criseyde's treachery
is made certain, and not until Troilus dies and looks down from the with-
drawn distance of the eighth sphere that he realizes how absolutely he has
been betrayed. Only then is there a reduction in the variety of possible
attitudes towards the situation. In Henryson's poem we have the coldly
objective vision of the eighth sphere transferred to the earth, and the
reduction is present from the beginning. Henryson's narrator . . . has, like
Chaucer's Troilus, undergone the experience of human love and its decay
. . . and then, by withdrawing from involvement in it, has been able to
see it in clearer perspective. Troilus withdraws to the eighth sphere, the
narrator of the *Testament* to the comfort of a private room. And it is
made clear that this narrator's withdrawal is only part of a more general
withdrawal from youth into age, and that the cold of a winter night is also
the cold of an old man's blood. . . . The *Testament* is presented as the
poem of an old man, free from the magnificently idealizing illusions of the
young Troilus, and seeing in his story no complication of issues and attitudes. . . . The "mistie cloudis" of Chaucer's diffuseness have been swept
away, and with them what they express: the variety of contradictory
perspectives suspended in the mind of a garrulous and enigmatic narrator.

A. C. Spearing
Sp (April, 1962), pp. 220-21

Henryson is on the whole more "popular" than either Chaucer or Dunbar.
This is less immediately obvious in the *Testament* than in the *Moral Fables*
and certain of the minor poems. The majority of the *Fables* are based on a
Latin text of Aesop. But a number are drawn from the popular Reynardian

cycle, and a broad folk element is present throughout. The Chaucerian refinement of the verse, French and Italian in origin, is crossed in the *Fables* and in the *Testament* by the native alliterative type. . . . The verse is reinvigorated . . . from this source. Certain of the minor poems, on their part, bear an obvious relation to the ballad. The more "popular" quality of Henryson is both his strength and his weakness. He is more "popular" because he is more "local." He is further from the European centre than either Chaucer or Dunbar (perhaps partly because he is a "clerk," not of the court).

J. Speirs
The Scots Literary Tradition, 2nd ed. (London:
Faber and Faber, 1962), pp. 37-38

If the expression "Scottish Chaucerian" is to be applied to Henryson, it must connote qualities of wit, control, urbanity, ironic juxtaposing, sympathy, and engaging demand for the cooperation of the audience, and fluency of metre and diction. But his poetry also manifests a faculty to express moral attitudes in varying ways, now dichotomized, now more subtle, but always with sincerity and independence. He is less precious and more fundamental than James I, less immediately impressive and more practical than Dunbar, less "allegorical" and more succinct than Douglas.

Charles Elliott, ed.
Robert Henryson, Poems (Oxford: Clarendon Pr., 1963), p. xv

THOMAS HOCCLEVE (or OCCLEVE)
ca. 1370-1450

Thomas Hoccleve, poet and friend of Chaucer, was employed in the Office of the Privy Seal for some 24 years. His chief works are a version in 5488 lines of Aegidius Romanus' *De Regimine Principum* dedicated to Henry Prince of Wales (Henry V), an autobiographical account of his youthful dissipations, *La Male Regle*, two verse-stories from the *Gesta Romanorum*, *The Emperor Jereslaus's Wife* and *Jonathas*, and an *Ars Sciendi Mori*.

F. J. Furnivall, ed., *Hoccleve's Works* (1892-1925), 3 vols.

There is no doubt that Occleve—like Pepys and some other, but not all, talkers about themselves—has found himself none the worse off for having committed to paper numerous things which any one but a garrulous, egotistic and not very strong-minded person would have omitted. Nor can it exactly be counted to him as a literary merit that he does not seem to have been at all an unamiable person. Nor, lastly, is his wisdom in abstaining from extremely long poems more than a negative virtue. Yet all these things do undoubtedly, in this way and that, make the reading of Occleve less toilsome than that of Lydgate: though the latter can, on rare occasions, write better than Occleve ever does. . . . Though lesser in every sense, one merit Occleve may claim—that he has some idea how to tell a story. Neither *Jereslaus* nor *Jonathas* is lacking in this respect. . . .

George Saintsbury
"The English Chaucerians," *CHEL*, vol. II (1908), pp. 207-8

If Occleve had only been as much interested in other people as in himself, he might have given us some famous narratives. In his dialogues and confessions he is a perfect Pepys. No shame withholds him from recounting how he stuffed, drank, and made after the girls, "that so goodly so shaply were, and feir"; or how pleased he was when the boatmen called him "maister." He has an eye for London life and considerable freshness in describing it. Furthermore, his personality, querulous, and rather contemptible though it is, makes itself felt in his style with results not common in Lydgate, or, indeed, in the middle ages. But Occleve imitated the style, and only the style, of the master in his story-telling. He might have duplicated *in petto* the lively personages of Chaucer's stories. He did not, perhaps because of his narrow egoism. The little failings, the lovable virtues, which make the individual, were interesting to Occleve only when they were his own, and there was usually no room for Occleve in the plot!

Henry Seidel Canby
The Short Story in English (New York: Henry Holt, 1909), p. 85

Both Hoccleve's production and his range of production are very much smaller than those of Lydgate. There are in his work no long romantic-epic narratives, no lives of saints, no allegories, no tapestry or fresco-poems, no courtly love-addresses, no beast-fables, no mummings. The religious-didactic is Hoccleve's theme whenever he is not autobiographic; but his constant tendency to the autobiographical is the most interesting of his qualities. *La Mâle Règle* is a deliberate and frank self-confession, used as lengthy prelude to a begging-letter. The two long tasks undertaken for Henry V and for Gloucester are each preluded by a lively piece of dialogue in explanation of their origin. In the one case it is a friend, in the other a wise old beggar, who receives Hoccleve's laments over his muddled life and counsels him how to proceed. Where Lydgate would compose a prologue in imitation of Chaucer or in praise of the original he was translating, Hoccleve plunges awkwardly but vitally in another method. His dialogue is real dialogue, not alternating set speeches. He is limited enough in his handling; there is no setting for his two speakers . . . ; the voices, though lively in tone, are bodiless. And as soon as they cease, and the business of Jereslaus' Wife or the Regement of Princes begins, Hoccleve drops into the stereotype of his period.

What recommends Hoccleve to us is his deep and genuine respect for Chaucer, the candid, even if contrite, relish with which he talks about himself, and his direct commonsense handling of his work. He has no "aureate language," no rhetorical colors; he is too honest to delay his advance about his business by playing with words, and too clearheaded not to see the way to state that business. If Chaucer tried to teach Hoccleve to write, it was because Chaucer saw in Hoccleve the possibilities which are still to be seen. In studying him we study someone who was very little of a writer, but a good deal of a man.

E. P. Hammond
English Verse Between Chaucer and Surrey
(Durham, N. C.: Duke Univ. Pr., 1927), pp. 54, 56

His works . . . are much more limited in character than those of Lydgate. They are in the main of a moralizing, didactic nature, plentifully interspersed in the large works by refreshing personal anecdotes and reflections. We are always in touch with the poet: we do not feel that his poems are mechanic exercises, but the reflection of the poet's own ideas and personality. That does not give his verses value, for on the whole Hoccleve has not a sensitive alert mind. He is an egoist, and the naïve outpourings of his own hopes and fears are presented to us in all their crude immediacy. What his mind thought his pen set down without much preliminary attempt to control or refine his matter in a clear picture; yet his dialogue gives the illusion of life. . . . This immediacy gives what little value may be found in Hoccleve's work. He does not pierce far below the surface, nor has he a very poetic view of life, but his poems move to their conclusions without the padding and syntactical confusions of Lydgate. Hoccleve never rises to any heights—even such a passage as Lydgate's verses on his conversion is beyond him, and he has no feeling, or liking, apparently for nature. Fortunately he never tries to cover up his poetic weaknesses by the use of "aureate" language, but is content with a limited vocabulary which he occasionally uses to good effect by the inclusion of some colloquial phrase . . . or by a striking line. His control of rhythms and the verse forms which he adopts is very imperfect, but at times he gets beyond a mechanical counting of syllables and marking of stresses. On the whole, however, the Chaucerian music, which he tried to imitate, eluded him completely. . . . Hoccleve, then, cannot claim any high place in the poetic heavens. Indeed, this "crimeless Villon," as Saintsbury calls him, survives mainly for two reasons. First, because his devotion to Chaucer endears him to all lovers of poetry. . . . Secondly, Hoccleve's work is full of interest for the student of social history. The extravagant costumes of his time; the debauchery and riotous behaviour of the "man about town"; the starvation endured by those broken by the wars; the decay and partiality of justice; pluralism and absenteeism; the abuses of child-marriages—these and many another topic find expression in the pages of Hoccleve, and help to create the picture of the world in which the poet lived, and in which poetry could hope for but a casual and fugitive hearing among the many distractions of the time.

> H. S. Bennett
> *Chaucer and the Fifteenth Century*
> (Oxford: Clarendon Pr., 1947), pp. 149-50

Hoccleve does not have Lydgate's fatal fluency, or Gower's social and moral urge. He does not write for the sheer love of writing, and he seldom rises to the level of poetry. Yet his complete frankness, his many personal revelations, and his frequent references to current events make his verse almost always interesting. In poets of the fifteenth century, or indeed of later centuries, this is no small merit.

> Albert C. Baugh, ed.
> *A Literary History of England* (New York and London:
> Appleton-Century-Crofts, 1948), p. 298

Self-revelation . . . is one of Occleve's personal tendencies. . . . The main attraction of Occleve is that he has something to communicate about himself and his feelings; and so, in spite of his technical shortcomings, he is refreshing; for it is better to read about good fellowship or even about personal infelicities, than to be confronted with extensive moral commonplaces expressed without mitigation of earnestness.

> George Sampson
> *The Concise Cambridge History of English Literature*, 2nd ed.
> (Cambridge Univ. Pr., 1961), p. 85

WILLIAM LANGLAND
fl. 1370-1400

> William Langland, one of the two or three foremost poets of Medieval England, a native of the West Midlands, lived with his wife, Kit, and their daughter, Calote, in the Cornhill district of London. He was a clerk of the Church, in minor orders, and supported himself and his family as a singer of masses. His masterpiece, *The Vision of William Concerning Piers the Plowman*, originally composed in 1362-1363 (A-text), was revised and expanded about 1377 (B-text) and again about 1392 (C-text).
>
> George Kane, ed., *Piers Plowman: The A Version* (1960)
> E. Talbot Donaldson, *Piers Plowman: The C-Text and Its Poet* (1949)

PERSONAL

Two things are evident in his self-revealing verse—a passionate sincerity and a sensitive heart. The one compelled him to look at what was around him and the other taught him the full horror of what he was. Still further to aggravate his agony he was gifted beyond any of his contemporaries with the insight of a prophet. He saw and plainly stated that some terrible vengeance must fall upon that ecclesiasticism which had betrayed its sacred trust. Langland knew and taught that the military and naval victories . . . , with the glory of which the nation rang, must be paid for in long years of poverty. The decline of Feudalism registered itself in his deepest consciousness. He was living in the death-chamber of a whole civilization. As Dante's fellow-citizens pointed to him as one who had been in Hell, so might the London of Richard II have learned that the lanky, disreputable, indigent Poet who slouched in torn gown along the London streets had visited that Hell which it was preparing for itself. Is it any wonder if sometimes he might have been heard muttering to himself and that to many he seemed mad?

Stanley B. James
Month (March, 1932), p. 225

When those things in Langland that give him rank as an artist with Pieter Brueghel the Elder have been listed, such as are rough laughter, a gift in proverbs, peasant sympathy, Christian faith, irony, skill in visualizing (crowds especially and tumultuous landscapes), a rich colour-sense, a deep pity, and so forth—it still remains to praise his best power (and Brueghel had it too), namely a strong architectural instinct for planning and carrying out a great composition, a design enormous in itself and wild with detail. It is not he who loses himself in a tangle of digressions, or if he does it is seldom; the unaccustomed modern reader, missing some association of idea, may cry out that he is lost, that the poet has no control; but however many and however long his digressions, he seems like a man giving himself more room, rather than like one who has lost his way.

Nevill Coghill
Proceedings of the British Academy (1945), pp. 8-9

Piers Plowman

Langland's aim is to bring religion out of the palace and the pulpit into direct contact with common humanity. He wants to strip it of its rich vestments, its pious knick-knacks and its load of useless learning, and set it to work in the slums and the highways, clearing up the mess that had been accumulated by generations of neglect. This ideal is embodied in the symbolic figure that has given its name to the whole poem. While Dante, a

type of the political idealist, puts his faith in the coming of a prince . . .
Langland finds the man who will put the world right in the shape of an
English farmer, ploughing his half-acre by the wayside. Piers Plowman is at
first simply the type of honest husbandry, a mediaeval John Bull who does
his duty by Church and State and has no use for beggars or lazy workmen.
But he is John Bull spiritualized, "Truth's pilgrim at the plough for poor
men's sake," whose mission it is to bring Christendom back into the ways
of salvation.

Christopher Dawson
Mediaeval Religion and Other Essays
(New York: Sheed and Ward, 1934), pp. 177-78

Scholars more interested in social history than in poetry have sometimes
made this poem appear much less ordinary than it really is as regards its
kind, and much less extraordinary as regards the genius of the poet. In fact,
its only oddity is its excellence; in *Piers Plowman* we see an exceptional
poet adorning a species of poetry which is hardly exceptional at all. He
is writing a moral poem, such as Gower's *Miroir de l'homme . . .* , and
throwing in . . . a good deal of satire on various "estates. . . ." Like Chaucer
he reverences knighthood. Even as a moralist he has no unique or novel
"message" to deliver. As a cure for all our ills he can offer us only the
old story—do-wel, do-bet, and do-best. His advice is as ancient, as "conventional," if you will, as that of Socrates. . . . It is doubtful whether any
moralist of unquestioned greatness has ever attempted more (or less) than
the defence of the universally acknowledged; for "men more frequently
require to be reminded than informed." As a politician, Langland has
nothing to propose except that all estates should do their duty. It is unnecessary, I presume, to state that his poem is not revolutionary, nor even
democratic. It is not even "popular" in any very obvious sense. . . . Langland is a learned poet. He writes for clerks and for clerkly minded gentlemen. The forty-five manuscripts, and the presence of quotation from
Langland in Usk's *Testament of Love,* prove that he did not write in vain.
It would have been strange if he had. He offered to his educated contemporaries fare of a kind which they well understood. His excellent satiric
comedy, as displayed in the behaviour of the seven Deadly Sins, belongs
to a tradition as old as the *Ancrene Riwle*; and his allegorical form and
pious content were equally familiar. What is truly exceptional about Langland is the kind, and the degree, of his poetic imagination. His comedy,
however good, is not what is most characteristic about him. Sublimity . . . is
frequent in *Piers Plowman*. The Harrowing of Hell, so often and so justly
praised, is but one instance. . . . In a quieter mood, the great vision wherein
the poet beholds "the sea, and the sun, and the sand after" and sees "man
and his make" among the other creatures, is equally distinctive. There is in

it a Lucretian largeness which, in that age, no one but Langland attempts.
. . . It belongs . . . to what has been called the "intellectual imagination";
the unity and vastness were attained by thought, rather than by sense, but
they end by being a true image and no mere conception.

C. S. Lewis
The Allegory of Love (Oxford: Clarendon Pr., 1936), pp. 158-60

Despite the antiquity of its metre, the anxious, inquiring spirit of *Piers
Plowman* is strangely modern. We might call its poet the "morning star of
the Reformation" with more truth than Wyclif, whose outlook was in many
ways very medieval. In that case, however, we must use the word "Reformation" in no narrow-minded sectarian sense, but to include the Counter-
Reformation as well as the Protestant Reformation; in fact to signify that
renewal of the spirit which has to come from time to time to most forms of
organized religion.

R. W. Chambers
Man's Unconquerable Mind (London:
Jonathan Cape, 1939), p. 94

Piers Plowman was a semi-mystical political tract intended to be committed
to memory by the uneducated commons—written in verse-form for greater
verbal emphasis. But for a strong sense of social injustice, probably sharpened by the humiliation of his bastardy, Langland would never have come
to be included in the roll of English poets; what he wrote was not a poem,
but something between a work of philosophical speculation on possible
remedies for the ills of the day and a diatribe against those who seemed
immediately responsible for them.

Robert Graves
The Common Asphodel (London: Hamish Hamilton, 1949), p. 280

His style is almost violently direct in address and manner, never ornate or
artificial; it contains no formal rhetoric in the accepted sense of the term,
and no literary tricks of expression that could not conceivably have been
acquired by a man with a good ear and a retentive memory from acquaintance with liturgy and stage and sermon or developed from his attitude
to life and mode of thinking. Moreover his fluency has an air of distinction;
however slovenly he may seem in the manner of his writing, and however
careless about alliteration, or overloading his lines with unstressed syllables,
his verse is never quite ordinary, or trivial, or as lifeless as corresponding
work in other contemporary literary dialects can be, for its shortcomings
never suggest incapacity, but only neglect, and, good or bad, it is always
charged with his emotion. His fluency endows him still further with several
extremely useful special gifts, skill at composing dialogue, the art of giving

rapid accounts of action so vivid that one regrets the little scope his subject allowed him in this direction, and a knack of making even the most far-fetched allegory come to life. Whatever its origin, whether it was developed and trained in a literary apprenticeship the early results of which are lost or hidden in the anonymity of the fourteenth century, or whether it was an unschooled natural talent, his fluency is of the utmost importance to the style in which his poem was written.

After this fluency the next important quality in the author's character as an artist is an unusually powerful visual imagination. This quality in him has not been sufficiently remarked; it is stronger and clearer even than Chaucer's, and functions with unbroken ease even when he is dealing with allegorical characters. In consequence *Piers Plowman* has a most graphic style and a more completely pictorial effect than most Middle English poetry, despite the abstract nature of a good deal of its subject.

I have mentioned in connexion with the poet's irony a habit which constitutes his third and probably most individual stylistic feature: the practice of the striking or startling metaphor or figure in which, whatever other quality it may have, the element of incongruity is prominent.

George Kane
Middle English Literature (London:
Methuen, 1951), pp. 235-36

Medieval thinkers realized to the full that without some concept of value it is impossible to lend the events of everyday existence significance beyond animal satisfaction. To the poet it was of utmost importance that the system of values which he found symbolized in Jerusalem be maintained, lest the vision fade away entirely from the sight of man. The fears of the poet were justified. What the poet was witnessing and attempting to counteract was the beginning of the great intellectual chaos which produced the Waste Land, a country which has become so much more terrifying than the poet's Field of Folk that the modern reader is apt to overlook as insignificant some of the poem's bitterest portrayals of evil. *Piers Plowman* is the epic of the dying Middle Ages.

D. W. Robertson, Jr., and Bernard F. Huppé
Piers Plowman and Scriptural Tradition (Princeton, N. J.:
Princeton Univ. Pr., 1951), pp. 235-36

. . . The revelation of moral values in the delineation of character and action is one of the things that places our great writers in their high rank. The poet of *Piers Plowman* is one of these. Everywhere, of course, he upholds a strict adherence to the doctrine of the Catholic Church and no-where does he condone heresy. Yet he could be adduced in support of the Reformation, because he reveals and reproves the abuses that spring, not from doctrinal error, but from lapses in the common standard of good social conduct which originates in charity and love. His sympathy lies with the poor and the oppressed; yet he can castigate them for their idleness and bad husbandry. His fierce condemnation of corruption in the Church is not an attack on the established Faith; it is rather on the Church's failure to inspirit the practice of its religion with love, grace, and forgiveness. With the rich it is their lack of charity; and with all who seek material advancement, it is bribery and excess that call forth his reproof. The standard by which he measures mankind is a moral one, and his finest and most moving verses are those aroused by love and charity, which are the fulfilment of the moral outlook. . . . Though there is a layer of allegorical nomenclature in his characters, the realism of description furnishes them all with human quality. Though many are enshrouded in human weakness, even as in the case of Sir Glutton to the point of grossness, his satirical reprobation invests his work with a propriety inspired by his moral attitude, which we can accept as one of the marks of his greatness.

A. H. Smith
Piers Plowman and the Pursuit of Poetry
(London: Constable, 1951), pp. 19-20

There is indeed only one work in medieval English that has serious epic pretentions: Langland's *Piers Plowman*. And for this poem I do, quite unequivocally, demand the status of epic; not indeed of relatively flawless epic, but of epic nevertheless.

It is idle to deny Langland's faults of construction. He was obsessed with the sufferings of the poor and with the sins of the rich; and he voices his obsessions in and out of season. There is a major structural tautology in that the opening section, the Vision, which deals with contemporary England in the main, concerns the same active realm of life as the second section, on Do-Bet, does. H. W. Wells seeks to prove that these sections concern different portions of the active life and that hence there is no tautology. Technically he may be right in the main; but, in our reading, this technical rightness makes very little difference, and we do not feel a sufficient progression of subject to enable us to grasp these two sections as part of the growing whole. Ye we never quite give up the effort, and even in the most confused sequences we never really doubt that Langland has a clearly formulated end in view. He has ultimately, however much he abuses it, that control of his multifarious material that is essential to the true epic effect. He reminds me of his own parable of the man in the boat. The man may stagger dangerously through the boat's motion, but these staggerings do not interfere with the boat's direction to its goal unless they are such as to force him to neglect the rudder altogether. In the allegory the staggerings are the venial sins, the neglect of the rudder mortal sin. Well,

Langland is extremely prone to venial sins of construction; at one point
he is near the mortal sin of letting go the rudder altogether: but in the end
he steers a straight and magnificent course. I am thinking above all of the
masterly evolution leading to the climax. Out of the theme of various
trinities emerges the Pauline trinity of Faith, Hope, and Charity. Faith is
represented in the person of Abraham, Hope in that of Moses, Charity in
that, not of any Old Testament character, but, of the Good Samaritan
whose deed of mercy is described. It is then that the progress of the
dreamer's mental pilgrimage, one of the main themes of the poem, reaches
a definitive point. The dreamer wishes to be enrolled as one of the Good
Samaritan's, or Charity's, servants, and his wish is granted. But the Good
Samaritan turns out to be another pilgrim, a knight who is on his way to
joust in Jerusalem: in other words Jesus on his way to his final battle with
death on the cross. And the old idea of Jesus as the warrior knight is caught
up and amplified, when, as Christ the Conqueror of death, he enters Hell
and hales out Adam and Eve: the first deed of salvation under the new
dispensation. This sequence of changes from the abstract idea of Charity
to Christ·the Conqueror, the harrower of Hell, is a sublime display of
architectonic power, capable of redeeming a multitude of subordinate lapses.

E. M. W. Tillyard
The English Renaissance: Fact or Fiction?
(London: Hogarth Pr., 1952), pp. 90-92

The *Visio* . . . is concerned with the *animalis homo* and with the first stage
in his regeneration. The *Vita de Dowel, Dobet, et Dobest* is concerned
with the spiritual life proper. And at the end of Dowel, the people in the
plain of Passus V are recalled in the person of Haukyn; and we are reminded that the pilgrimage to Truth has been, in fact, for some time under
way, but in a different mode—the only possible one. In this manner, the
two parts of the poem are intimately bound together as one whole.

T. P. Dunning
RES (July, 1956), p. 232

The poet's artistic vision is moralistic rather than raptly prophetic, realistic
rather than mystical. The poem closes with both a warning and a note of
hope. There is neither universal darkness nor the supernal vision. The
climactic battle with the sins and Antichrist has produced splendid Bee-
thovian thunder, but the final chords are muted and unresolved. This is
neither a tragedy nor a comedy, for the drama of salvation continues as
long as mankind exists and as long as there is a Piers Plowman, a goodness
and a divinity in man. There is nothing trivial, however, in this conclusion
in which nothing is concluded. Conscience's cry for grace which closes the

poem is nothing less than a cry for a faith in the salvation of man. And the salvation of man is the great theme of the whole poem. It is the poem's reason for being.

Robert Worth Frank, Jr.
Piers Plowman and the Scheme of Salvation (New Haven, Conn.:
Yale Univ. Pr.; Oxford Univ. Pr., 1957), p. 118

Piers Plowman offers us a congested canvas of late fourteenth-century society. The value of the poem as a source for social history has been widely recognized, more widely, perhaps, than its poetic quality. Yet, in contrast with *Troilus,* or the *Canterbury Tales,* or even with *Confessio Amantis,* the figures are two-dimensional, we do not see them in the round; we seem to look at a medieval fresco, rather than to mingle with a medieval crowd. Perhaps by reason of its form—for the Old English alliterative line was burning itself out—the whole poem has an archaic air. It is none the less impressive for that. But, whereas Gower presents us with the conventions of a polite society, and Chaucer with human nature as we know it, Langland speaks to us from a forgotten world, drowned, mysterious, irrevocable.

May McKisack
The Fourteenth Century 1307-1399 (Oxford:
Clarendon Pr., 1959), p. 527

The hall-mark of Langland's work is a special authenticity, deriving from visionary power not at variance with but sustained by a penetrating realism. His poem . . . succeeds in communicating the very pressure of experience itself. The arguments are there, and they come with varying force—and relevance. But what is also there is the sense that nothing less than the highest is at once required and made possible. *Piers Plowman* is no merely didactic work, nor is it simply a confession of faith. Its essential witness is to the whole need of man—to make sense not merely of a scheme of things considered as external to ourselves, but of the riddling and evasive heart of man himself. Newman, we may recall, once said that he did not "care to overcome" the reason of his auditors "without touching their hearts." The stubbornness of the Dreamer, in the *Vita de Dowel* especially, demonstrates a similar unwillingness to accept for truth what must be divorced from the pressure and complexity of experience. . . . Just such an inseparability of doctrine and practice is fundamental to any "grammar of assent." It is Langland's great gift; and his poem is therefore peculiarly resistant to any attempts to abstract or simplify.

John Lawlor
Piers Plowman, An Essay in Criticism
(London: Edward Arnold, 1962), pp. 317-18

It is Langland's peculiar distinction that, at one and the same time, he can keep us fully in touch with the great metaphysical consequences of human existence and with the tangible realities of our humorous, corrupt, frustrating and yet desirable life on earth. The language in which he conveys deep spiritual truths . . . is often as simple and familiar as that in which he invites his reader to share the experience of the mediaeval peasant's harsh life in wintertime, the warm, raucous atmosphere of the alehouse. . . . Praising Christ who "blewe alle thi blissed into the blisse of paradise," he achieves that blend of reverence and vigour which few religious writers after the mediaeval period were capable of, and which was not put to such high poetic uses by any of Langland's contemporaries. Sharp forthrightness of diction and spontaneity of verse-movement give us often a direct entry into *Piers Plowman*: much of the verse provides reading quite as unhampered as any we are likely to meet in the work of Chaucer, for instance, or in the Miracle Plays. And because of the return of many twentieth-century poets to the use of the free, unrhymed, accentual line which is Langland's verse form, we can often respond to the movement of *Piers Plowman* as to a contemporary verse pattern. . . . Moreover, the conviction that no theme and no vocabulary are to be debarred from poetry on account of their closeness to everyday, ordinary life is one from which spring some of the finest passages in *Piers Plowman* as well as some of the finest in compositions nearer to our own day. "For the modern poet nothing is inherently unpoetic"; this observation could be made equally well about Langland, as he presses sights, experiences and words, with little or no special selection, into the service of his urgent and dedicated purpose.

Elizabeth Salter
Piers Plowman, An Introduction (Cambridge, Mass.:
Harvard Univ. Pr., 1962), pp. 2-3

GENERAL

The spirit of Langland's verse was not that of the school. Although the style was not without its technic, it was a free and easy technic. It called for the readiness and copiousness of the improviser, rather than the care and forethought of the literary artist. If impassioned prose had been possible in his day, Langland might well have chosen to write in that form, but lacking such a medium, he developed in his free metrical rhythms a form that approaches prose. By means of this form he expressed himself with an astonishing ease and abundance. There is a power in the mere sweep of his thought which would have been impossible in the regular rimed meters of Chaucer. And yet Langland's eloquence seldom reaches the lofty heights of great poetry. [1915]

George P. Krapp
The Rise of English Literary Prose (New York:
Frederick Ungar, 1963), pp. 17-18

Half a century and more of learned criticism has been expended on Langland's famous *Vision*. But, through modern contempt for a pulpit now shorn of its ancient glory, the one complete clue to the poem is still persistently ignored. In reality, it represents nothing more nor less than the quintessence of English medieval preaching gathered up into a single metrical piece of unusual charm and vivacity. Hardly a concept of the poet's mind, an authority quoted, a trick of symbolism, or a satirical portrait but is to be found characteristic of the literature of [sermons]. The fact applies equally, and indeed adequately, to the loosely-quoted references from "great clerks," or from Scripture, the quaint "saffron" of French and Latin phrases, the knowledge of legal or commercial practices, the mildly conservative attitude towards Authority as divinely constituted in Church and State, the passion for reforms, the biting satire of the classes, the criticisms of the churchmen, the whole apparatus of imagery, the stress on Love and good works, the unqualified praise of the virtuous labouring poor.

J. R. Owst
Preaching in Medieval England
(Cambridge Univ. Pr., 1926), pp. 295-96

The *Visio* is a study of the life of the laity both as it is and as it should be. We have in this part of the poem that which the common communicant ought to know, and nothing more. We have no abstruse theological or philosophical problems, no allegory of learning, no account of the saintly life and no thorough and detailed analysis of the functioning of the church as the coordinating principle in society. On the other hand, we have such social satire and such an account of man's religious duties as the humblest medieval reader might be expected to understand. If he follows the road here traced by the poet, he is considered to be sure of salvation. With the *Vita* the theme is changed. We have an account of the world as seen by the thinker who has passed through the medieval disciplines of learning, asceticism and priestly responsibility. He has known the intellectual life, the mystic and the active life, and so fulfilled the more arduous duties which heaven imposes upon its specially chosen warriors. In this part of the poem the satire falls not upon delinquencies in secular duties, but upon faults peculiar to persons dedicated to the life of scholarship and religious practice: upon those who, like the gluttonous Doctor, the feigning Hermit and the over-indulgent Confessor, betray learning, devotion and the institution of the Church. This part of the poem deals with ideals superfluous to and improper in a layman, but to which God's select soldiers must conform if they are to remain loyal and in turn win their salvation.

Henry W. Wells
PMLA (March, 1929), pp. 124-25

The identification of God and nature is perhaps more marked in him than in any other medieval poet. Yet his uniqueness, his greatness, does not lie in this: it lies in his power to relate the world of nature to the world of the spirit, man's inner life to the life of society, the life of study and contemplation to the life of action; and to express these relations in vivid terms.

J. A. W. Bennett
List (March 2, 1950), p. 382

What is there actually in Langland for the ordinary reader, in a world already overcrowded with good literature? As a whole, his poem is impossible—floundering, unintelligent, as out of date as a dinosaur. Allegories and sermons we find to-day almost unreadable at best; certainly when, as here, they topple over one another in seething queries to get at us, there is nothing for it but to run. . . . And if Langland's method has lost its appeal, so too, for many of us, has his message. His theology has become mythology. . . . Why then read Langland? Partly for his human interest. A character like his, which never relaxes its stern sincerity to trifle even for a moment, is apt to grow boring; yet it is interesting also. Naked souls are rare; most men go masked beyond recognition; but Langland, whatever his faults, always stands stark and bare. And together with himself he has revealed a great deal of this strange mediaeval world that bred him. But Langland is more than food for historians. He is also a vivid artist in his own way—a poet gifted both in eye and ear. To think that he would one day be read for his style, would doubtless have filled him with rage and despair at human frailty. Yet such is the common lot of preachers and moralists.

F. L. Lucas
Studies French and English (London: Cassell, 1950), pp. 51-52

. . . Langland's work offers a remarkable combination. His theme is of the greatest solemnity: man is a creature destined for regeneration. Hence we have the distinctive appeal to imagination—vision must show forth what remains hidden to discursive thinking. But it is Langland's genius to imitate and conduct his poetic argument by showing us man as determinedly ratiocinative, seeking the causes of all things, and overlooking what lies nearest home. The kind of poem we are dealing with is thus not easily determined. If we approach it by asking what is the poet's dominant faculty, we must answer, in however unfashionable terms, the satiric intelligence.

John Lawlor
RES (May, 1957), p. 121

Langland was, in fact, a great poet, and the quality of his greatness throws some light upon the nature of the English contribution to poetry. The greatest English poets have been those who have followed the genius of the language in resisting false convention. Shakespeare and Donne, in their day, were great poets because they freed English from the bondage of a dead scholarship and restored to it expressiveness and idiomatic strength; and Gerard Hopkins, in his, when he praised Dryden for stressing "the naked thew and sinew of the English language" was only giving critical formulation to their practice. Their idiom was similar to that of Langland, whose language was living English and the alliterative metre in which naturally fell the vital vehicle for it. Driven underground after the Norman Conquest by versifiers who, for a long period, could neither make a foreign medium live nor retain the life of the old, it revived in the fourteenth century as a natural framework for the English language. . . . The full alliterative verse represents values more important, not, indeed, than those of *Troilus and Criseyde* and *The Canterbury Tales*, but of the Chaucerian version of *The Romaunt of the Rose*, and by virtue of these values its influence deserves to survive in later English literature. In particular, Langland's verse achieves a peculiarly fruitful relation of rhythm to feeling, the same relation which allowed Shakespeare to play sense and stress in infinite variety against the restraining influence of the traditional blank verse line.

Derek Traversi
"Langland's *Piers Plowman*," *The Age of Chaucer*
(Baltimore: Penguin Books, 1961), pp. 132-33

. . . Langland is a prophetic poet—a poet who felt himself privileged to reveal to his fellow men a coming renewal of justice and love that would transform society and through it the individual. Like Dante . . . he believed in and wished to hasten the day of a return to a pristine state of justice that would regenerate Christian social life; and *alta fantasia* [imagination] was an important force in enabling him to grasp and communicate this news to his fellow men. I do not wish to give the impression that Langland and Dante envisaged themselves as prophets in exactly the same way. Langland is fundamentally involved in the search for Christian perfection; Dante gives us the Christian truth, the next world, against which our present world must be measured. Langland is oriented towards the transformation of this world; and although he no doubt believed the same fundamental Christian truths as Dante did, it is the quest for them in this world that is his major concern. The quest is basic to Will, Langland's heirs, and on a further quest the poem ends. The *Divine Comedy* comes to rest at the end, and the quest is under authoritative guidance. In Dante it is a true means to knowledge. Will's problem is to find authorities in this world to whom he can turn and on whom he can model himself. Christian perfection is Dante's theme; the quest for Christian perfection is Langland's.

Morton W. Bloomfield
Piers Plowman as a Fourteenth-Century Apocalypse
(New Brunswick, N. J.: Rutgers Univ. Pr., 1962), p. 173

JOHN LYDGATE

ca. 1370-1450

John Lydgate, the most prolific and influential English poet of the fifteenth century, was born at Lydgate in Suffolk and at an early age
entered the monastery of Bury St. Edmunds. Much of his life, however,
was spent far from his cloister as a student in Oxford, as a court poet in
London, and as a traveller in France and Italy. He was made prior of
Hatfield Broadoak in 1421; in 1432 he resigned the position and returned
to Bury where he passed his remaining years. He received a pension from
the crown in 1439. The Lydgate canon is still uncritical and incomplete;
it now comprises more than 150 works, both secular and religious, running
to nearly 150,000 lines. Among his most important compositions are
Reson and Sensuallyte (ca. 1408; 7000 11.), *Troy Book* (1412-1421;
30,000 11.), *Siege of Thebes* (1421-1422; 4700 11.), *The Pilgrimage of
the Life of Man* (1426-; 25,000 11.), and *Fall of Princes* (1431-1438;
36,000 11.). In addition, he wrote numerous shorter works on religious
and didactic themes as well as a number of saints' lives together with a
Life of Our Lady.

H. Bergen, ed., *Fall of Princes* (1924-27), 4 vols.

F. J. Furnivall, ed., *The Pilgrimage of the Life of Man* (1905)

H. Bergen, ed., *Troy Book* (1906-35), 4 vols.

A. Erdmann, ed., *Siege of Thebes* (1911-1930), 2 vols.

E. Sieper, ed., *Reson and Sensuallyte* (1901-1903), 2 vols.

R. R. Klinefelter and V. F. Gallagher, eds., *Life of Our Lady* (1961)

H. N. McCracken, ed., *Minor Poems* (1911-34), 2 vols.

W. F. Schirmer, *John Lydgate* (1961)

PERSONAL

While we must remember that Bury was one of the most important monasteries in England, and that its library was immensely rich with its two
thousand and more volumes of sacred and profane literature, yet we cannot
but realize that Lydgate lacked that "precious experience of life" of which
Langland speaks, and a little reading will convince us that this is reflected
in Lydgate's works. Unfortunately, he showed distinct powers of welding
together words and phrases into collocations which had all the appearance
of verse, and he must have had an intolerable glibness and an indomitable
energy, which enabled him to essay tasks which a more sensitive man, or
one "charged with children and chief lordes rent," would not have dared
to attempt. Hence, in the quiet of the monastic scriptorium he turned out
works in the utmost profusion and of the greatest variety. Nothing seems
to have been beyond him: "a mumming by London merchants before the
Lord Mayor," a "letter" to accompany Christmas gifts to the King, an
explanation of the Mass for a pious Countess to keep in her chamber, a

set of stanzas to serve up as a "subtlety" at a banquet, a complaint for a love-sick squire to offer his lady, the "histories" to accompany figures in a fresco or in tapestry, a classical translation of Boccaccio's "tragedies"—all went through the same process, and the same dreary tale of verses poured out. As M. Jusserand says, "Rien que la mort ne put le faire taire; son dernier poème étant de 1446, ses biographes en ont unanimement conchi qu'il dut mourir cette année-là." Lydgate's importance for us . . . is not because of the quality of his work, but by reason of the conditions which enabled him to gratify his literary fecundity. In the first place it will be noticed that much of his work is not of a predominantly ecclesiastical nature, and a little investigation shows us that he was employed by a variety of patrons to write on various subjects. His translations, done to satisfy some patron's desire, were innumerable and voluminous. His history of the Trojan wars (the *Troy Book*) runs to some 30,000 lines, and was commissioned by Henry V while still Prince of Wales. Again, his translation of Deguilleville's *Pèlerinage de la Vie Humaine*, made for the Earl of Salisbury, occupied 25,000 lines, while his translation of a French version of Boccaccio's *De Casibus Virorum*, made for that prince of patrons, Humphrey, Duke of Gloucester, had the correspondingly princely length of 36,000 lines. . . . His smaller works . . . were obviously *pièces d'occasion*, and no doubt were paid for by the London merchants, or the pious countess, or the love-sick squire at rates satisfactory to the poet. Hence in the course of an industrious lifetime Lydgate turned out something over 130,000 lines of verse.

H. S. Bennett
Essays and Studies (1937), pp. 13-14

GENERAL

Now, of Lydgate, . . . it is not too much to say that he was one of the most richly gifted of our old poets, that as a descriptive poet he stands almost on the level of Chaucer, that his pictures of Nature are among the gems of their kind, that his pathos is often exquisite, "touching," as Gray said of him "the very heartstrings of compassion with so masterly a hand as to merit a place among the greatest of poets." His humour is often delightful, and his pictures of contemporary life . . . are as vivid as Chaucer's. In versatility he has no rival among his predecessors and contemporaries. Gray notices that, at times, he approaches sublimity. His style often is beautiful— fluent, copious, and at its best eminently musical. The influence which he exercised on subsequent English and Scotch literature would alone entitle him to a prominent position in any history of English poetry.

John Churton Collins
Ephemera Critica (New York: Dutton; Westminster:
Constable, 1902), pp. 198-99

The truth is that there is hardly any whole poem, and exceedingly few, if any, parts of poems, in Lydgate so good that we should be surprised at his being the author of even the worst thing attributed to him. He had some humour. . . . But his humour was never concentrated to anything like Chaucerian strength; while of Chaucerian vigour, Chaucerian pathos, Chaucerian vividness of description, Lydgate had no trace or tincture. To these defects, he added two faults. . . . The one is prosodic incompetence; the other is longwinded prolixity.

A little Lydgate, especially if the little be judiciously chosen, or happily allotted by chance, is a tolerable thing: though even this can hardly be very delectable to any well-qualified judge of poetry. But, the longer and wider that acquaintance with him is extended, the more certain is dislike to make its appearance. The prosodic incompetence cannot be entirely due to copyists and printers; the enormous verbosity, ignorance of how to tell a story, the want of freshness, vigour, life, cannot be due to them at all. But what is most fatal of all is the flatness of diction . . . the dull, hackneyed, slovenly phraseology, only thrown up by his occasional aureate pedantry— which makes the common commoner and the uncommon uninteresting. Lydgate himself, or some imitator of him, has been credited with the phrase "gold dewdrops of speech" about Chaucer. He would hardly have thought of anything so good; but the phrase at least suggests an appropriate variant, "leaden splashes," for his own.

George Saintsbury
"The English Chaucerians," *CHEL*, vol. II
(1908), pp. 199-200, 205

The enormous amount of verse of all kinds, except the very good, which he produced in his lifetime makes it impossible not to join, though for different reasons, with his contemporaries and immediate successors in assigning him an important place in his literary generation. A high level in poetry, and in story-telling, had just been reached. No genius arriving to lift it higher, the strenuous workman, who sincerely imitated what he could not exceed or equal, was invaluable, for he kept his generation aware of a great past. Such a worker was Lydgate, and his accomplishment was like the wall of sand which the child builds frantically about his pool lest all the water run back before the advancing tide brings in the new wave.

Although but a small portion of Lydgate's work is imitative of the Chaucerian short story, yet in this portion his services as a conservator are even more notable than elsewhere. The style and method of the greater story-teller are always evident—utility aside, too evident. The elaboration, the visualizing, the comment, which made Chaucer's narrative so much better than the old *lais* and *fabliaux*, is always consciously striven for, and sometimes attained. Hope of success never rests entirely with the plot, and proper names do not serve for characters. The tale is told with an eye for its beauty of effectiveness, while the circumstances of real life appear whenever they are needed—and the author is able to command them. . . . But when all is said, Lydgate is not a good story-teller. In spite of his rich commentary upon plot and character, and his glimmering appreciation of "atmosphere," he is not so good a narrator as old Gower. His prime fault lies in the literary sense which was at the same time his saving virtue. Like the Elizabethan novella-writers, he was too anxious to adorn. He thought by phrases, or by stanzas, not by episodes. Hence his stories drag, are overladen with rhetoric, and fail to catch fire at the climaxes. The crudities of his verse make this defect more pronounced, for while he caught at the phrase of his master's work he never learned its rhythm. His lines are monotonous, no verse movement carries the narrative forward, and it is usually easier to stop than to go on.

Henry Seidel Canby
The Short Story in English (New York:
Henry Holt, 1909), pp. 81-82, 84

Naturally, as one would expect in an author so "voluminous," his style is both prolix and careless. Written *currente calamo*, his sentences are accretions of afterthoughts, illustration piled on illustration and epithet on epithet until the thought is exhausted. In the same way he runs to catalogue. It gives the effect of having been composed impromptu. This is increased by the manner in which, to fill up his verse, he interjects stock phrases, and unnecessary words. In like manner, his scansion is entirely by ear. His accent shifts without much regard for the number of syllables on the line. A peculiar trick is to treat the caesural pause as equivalent to a weak syllable, thus bringing two accented syllables together. As he is also apt to omit the first weak syllable in the line, the effect is one of two short lines. . . . The result of this peculiarity of scansion, in combination with the uncertainty of the language, caused some of his imitators to write little more than rimed prose.

John M. Berdan
Early Tudor Poetry (New York: Macmillan, 1920), p. 62

A writer who usually contrives to spoil even his most felicitous passages before he has done with them, who systematically pads out his lines with stock phrases and rhyme tags, and pours out unending streams of verse during apparently the whole of a very long life, cannot well be taken seriously as one of the great poets. We search his works in vain for evidence either of imagination or originality, of sympathetic insight into character, sensibility, delicacy of feeling or a fine instinct for form; nor is he distinguished for more purely intellectual qualities. On occasion he shows that he

has power and rises to a somber dignity of manner, well seen in parts of the
Fall of Princes and in the *Daunce of Machabree*, and this, together with a
strain of melancholy, which was in the air at the time and a few years later
inspired François Villon to his finest work, is perhaps his strongest point.
No doubt in his day he was highly commended for both pathos and humour;
but the latter when not unconscious is as a rule little more than clumsy
playfulness, and the former too obvious and exaggerated to make any deep
impression on the reader . . . , and neither is sufficient to make a poet. However, considering his intellectual environment, his position, and his public,
he surely did all that can reasonably be expected of him. The rude men
of action of the time were slow-witted and uneducated; even the clerks, if
we are to judge, as we must, by their literary performances, were a singularly prosaic lot, and taste was evidently unknown in their circles. As Gray
remarked, "it is a folly to judge of the understanding and of the patience of
those times by our own. They [the reading public] loved, I will not say
tediousness, but length and a train of circumstances in the narration." They
got both in the *Fall of Princes*. Even Boccaccio laid aside much of his
genius when he began to write histories for the edification of the men of
the world of his day; and whatever qualities of greatness the world possesses lie rather in the hammer blows of its subject-matter than in the
art of the author or of his translators.

Henry Bergen, ed.
Lydgate's Fall of Princes, Part I (Washington, D. C.:
The Carnegie Institution of Washington, 1923), pp. xxi-xxii

The student who had never read a line of his work might suspect, upon
hearing of its enormous amount, that its quality was strained. It is indeed.
And with Lydgate the period of life at which he writes has less to do with
his power of expression than has his subject. The *Testament* may have
been of his later years, but it contains fine stanzas of deep religious feeling.
. . . Yet other late verse by Lydgate, such as the *Secrees,* has no value;
and other religious verse by him, when done to order, as *St. Albon* was
done to order, can drop to a very low level, not so low as *Guy of Warwick*,
but weakly monotonous. In Lydgate's many and respectful allusions to
Chaucer he pleases us; but when he attempts to imitate the Prologue he
makes a lamentable failure. If the *Flower of Courtesy* be his . . . he was
capable of grace and sweetness of expression on a hackneyed subject; but
his epithalamium to Gloucester is a wooden piece of work. His sunrises
and spring settings were not unjustly praised by Warton; compare the picture of Spring in *Reson and Sensuality* 101ff, and many passages in the
Troy Book . . . , pictures much better and more detailed than the monk
permits himself in the *Fall of Princes*. . . . In this respect, as in others, the
Troy Book is the most successful of Lydgate's longer works; in vivacity, in
self-expression, in knowledge of life, it is much superior to the *Siege of*

Thebes, although it be a commissioned task and a translation. If a religious emotion be absent, and if Lydgate lacks the restraint of a compact stanzaic original, such as he had for the *Dance Macabre*, he easily wanders; the slender substance of his meaning dries into the sands of his fluency, and he blunders among words, unable to advance to a goal which he does not clearly see. He spoils Canace's lament by a tastelss allusion to Cupid as causer of the tragedy; he cannot let Paris relate his dream, in Priam's family council, without a pedantic explanation of the attributes of Mercury. He can no more deny himself a digression, especially a didactic one, than could Browning; but it is not Browning's pressure of bounding vitality . . . which drives Lydgate to utterance; it is a sort of "total recall," the inability to stop until a whole series of familiar and related phrases have been not only ruled off, but repeated. This verbosity, when joined to a lack of structural sense, is disastrous; and Lydgate had little or no structural sense. He had no notion of the value of brevity, of selection among details. Indeed, his proclaimed theory is to the contrary. . . .

The remark of Gosse, that Lydgate appears better in selections than in wholes, means of course that the monk's inability to conceive of structure, to treat any part of his work with reference to any other part, or to get from one episode or mood to another, is disguised by the process of selection. No writer is at once so slow and so breathless as Lydgate; his discourse advances at a crawl, with constant returns upon itself, but marks time with such volubility that the reader is bewildered.

E. P. Hammond
English Verse Between Chaucer and Surrey (Durham, N. C.:
Duke Univ. Pr., 1927), pp. 79-81

Of the earlier Chaucerians Dan John Lydgate . . . is probably the most interesting. If voluminousness be in his case, as in so many others, a concomitant of genius, he may hope to stand better with posterity. . . . His authentic remains run to nearly one hundred and fifty thousand lines. An historian might reasonably despair of thoroughly digesting this mass, and might be tempted to travesty the pious sentiment of Benedict Burgh—

"Off John Lydgate how shulde we the sotyl trace";

but it is more than likely that no evidence will ever be forthcoming to alter the estimate based on an enforced selection. The extent of his work, coupled with the fact that most of it was done to order and that he seems on that account to have been compelled to return from his priorate at Hatfield to the Bury of his early days, gives an almost professional flavour to this literary life.

G. Gregory Smith
The Transition Period (Edinburgh: William Blackwood
and Sons, 1927), pp. 7-8

. . . Chaucer enriched his style with many new and unusual words, not because he was deliberately seeking them, but because each in its place suited his artistic demands. Lydgate, like many other imitators, felt the potency of Chaucer's verbal innovations but failed to comprehend the artistic taste and discretion which gave them charm. He repeated the device mechanically and as a deliberate means to an end, which naturally gave barren results. It was his custom to adopt some phrase which Chaucer used on rare occasions and repeat it *ad nauseam.* . . . So, following the same habit, he laboriously paraphrased and amplified "dulcet speche" in his master's work, not hesitating to coin many new phrases himself. This is evident from the fact that he added approximately eight hundred and thirty new words (including many new formations based on old words) to the English vocabulary of his day. Consequently his style became, in its way, effective; but not Chaucerian, since for truly artistic diction he had substituted a *repertoire* of far-fetched, decorative monstrosities. Thus by exaggerating the dangerous propensities and failing to reproduce the fundamental virtues of his master's diction, the old monk evolved the basic models for the extreme aureate effusions of the Scottish-Chaucerians.

Pierrepont Herrick Nichols
PMLA (June, 1932), p. 517

In his style, and in the construction of his poems, he is the pupil of Chaucer. . . . In his conception of allegory, again, Lydgate hardly modifies the practice of Machault and Chaucer. He is rather inclined to go back behind Chaucer, or at least, to go back to Chaucer's earliest work. He uses allegory merely as a frame-work for effusions which are unallegorical or which, at the most, reintroduce allegory only in the form of rhetorical personifications. The amorous complaint, or letter, or prayer, is the form in which he is really most at home. Thus in the *Black Knight* the spring morning and the bird-haunted garden serve only to introduce the Knight's soliloquy which constitutes the real body of the poem. In the *Flour of Curtesye* they are merely the setting for the poet's letter. In both poems, indeed, it might be argued that there is no allegory at all: the landscapes probably have a *significacio* in fact, but it is unimportant and uncertain. In the *Temple of Glas*, again, we are brought "ful fer in wildirness" to a "craggy roche like ise ifrore," not mainly that we may witness an allegorical action but that we may hear the long soliloquies and conversations of the Lady, the Lover, and the Goddess. And Lydgate was wise to concentrate on these; for nothing is more striking in this poem than the superiority of the stanzaic speeches and dialogues over the poet's own narration in couplets. Nearly all that is of value is in the former. No doubt with Lydgate, as with most minor poets, the choice of a metre almost determines the quality of the work; the couplet offers no obstacle to his fatal garrulity (the first sentence of the poem lasts for nine, and the third for eighteen, lines) while the stanza compels him to "grow to a point." But a difference of metre goes with a difference in content. The slow building up and decoration, niche by niche, of a rhetorical structure, brings out what is best in the poet.

C. S. Lewis
The Allegory of Love (Oxford:
Clarendon Pr., 1936), pp. 239-40

Both Hoccleve and Lydgate admired the artificial diction of Chaucer's dream-allegories and tried with little success to imitate it. The effort carried Lydgate to the extreme stylistic affectation properly called aureatism. Polysyllabic Latin and Romance forms, which were valued for sound, sense, or rhyme, had been entering the language since several decades before Chaucer, but Lydgate carried the practice to excess. He is credited by the *New English Dictionary* with introducing about eight hundred words. This in itself is not fatal to the monk's verse, no more than to Chaucer's *Troilus*; it does, however, disclose in Lydgate an effort to conceal the poverty of ideas with rich ornamentation. Yet, Lydgate realized, if his century did not, that he fell far short of his master. . . .

Arthur K. Moore
The Secular Lyric in Middle English (Lexington, Ky.:
Univ. Kentucky Pr., 1951), p. 137

. . . He [Lydgate] remains a massive figure and quite central to the English literary tradition. His output was large and he exploited nearly all the major literary types of contemporary English poetry. He was well versed in foreign learning. . . . He must have had an exceptionally swift and assimilative intelligence to have seized on and adapted so large a bulk of literature that was genuinely congenial to his contemporaries. But his effort was not so much poetical as what Arnold would have called critical. Through a competent, agreeable, but not often poetically exciting verse he made known to his countrymen much of the genuine cultural fare of contemporary Western Europe. It was not his fault that no man came after him capable of profiting by this "critical" effort, of making great poetry out of the learned material he supplied.

E. M. W. Tillyard
The English Epic and Its Background (London:
Chatto and Windus, 1954), pp. 172-73

He [Lydgate] may have considered himself a thorough Chaucerian to the bitter end, but—at least in respect to classical antiquity, to the regiment of princes, and to nationalism—he spoke the language of the Renaissance as often as that of the Middle Ages. It is no wonder, then, that his *Fall of Princes* should have yielded *The Mirror for Magistrates*, and his *Serpent of Division* should have influenced *Gorboduc* and Spenser's *Ruines of Time*; that scholars should have argued in his works the influence of the Italian humanists, of Virgil, of Seneca, and even of Plato, and demonstrated his influence upon Shakespeare, Bunyan, and Milton—for John Lydgate was *the* poet of the transition between the Middle Ages and the Renaissance, and, conversely, if we admit that he ever lived and wrote, we must also admit the existence of such a transition.

Alain Renoir
EM (1960), p. 19

It is wrong to apply modern criteria of judgement, and to consider Lydgate's obscure and involved diction as jarring, deplore his introduction of abstract terms, and maintain that he had no feeling for the poetic quality of words and did not use language in an imaginative, lively, and creatively artistic manner. It is not that Lydgate was incompetent, or that he was an aberration, or a singular phenomenon; we have here a new poetic style adapted to the taste of the fifteenth century, and Lydgate was its most characteristic exponent. *Florida verborum venustas* was also the ideal of the early humanists who wrote in Latin. These are the words used by the author of Archbishop Chichele's *Registrum* to describe the florid style as taught by John de Norwick in his *Tractatus de modo inveniendi ornata verba* and used by Abbot Whethamstede in his letters to the monks of St. Albans. These efforts to produce an artistic, exuberant, and refined Latin style are identical with Lydgate's efforts in vernacular poetry. Lydgate's position as a court poet and as a protégé of Duke Humphrey of Gloucester, who was highly esteemed as a patron, as well as his voluminous work, made him a model for others. For this reason the tradition that he also exerted an influence as a teacher, by founding a school of rhetoric at Bury St. Edmunds, even though not in strict accordance with the facts, nevertheless points the way to a correct appreciation of his achievement.

Walter F. Schirmer
John Lydgate (Berkeley, Calif.: Univ. California Pr., 1961), pp. 76-77

SIR THOMAS MALORY
ca. 1410-1471

All that we know for certain about Sir Thomas Malory is that he was a knight and that he was in prison when he completed his great collection of Arthurian romances between March 4, 1469, and March 3, 1470.

Numerous efforts have been made in recent years to identify this knight-prisoner more closely. The likeliest candidate is a Sir Thomas Malory, knight, of Newbold Revell, Warwickshire, a wealthy landowner, soldier, and supporter of the Lancastrian party, who from 1450 onwards turned to outlawry and was accused of such crimes as robbery, rape, extortion, and attempted murder, with the result that for the last two decades of his life he was as frequently in as out of jail. Whether such a man would have had the motive, let alone the opportunity, to write about the adventures of King Arthur and his knights is a matter of grave doubt. A version of these adventures was first published by William Caxton in 1485 under the misleading title "Le Morte Darthur."

Eugène Vinaver, ed., *The Works of Sir Thomas Malory* (1948), 3 vols.

PERSONAL

Malory was himself a man of action and dispatch, and his style suggests such a man. He converted the long and involved periods of his French originals into simple, idiomatic prose. Where his original is diffuse, Malory is terse and forthright. Yet his short, firm sentences . . . are seldom abrupt, but flow in a naturally modulated prose rhythm. The style of the *Morte Darthur*, when all is said and done, is Malory's greatest distinction, and it is wholly his own. But he has also preserved for subsequent generations a matchless body of romantic stories which might otherwise have remained the property of the Middle Ages, forgotten by modern poets and readers in the English-speaking world, as they have been forgotten in France.

Albert C. Baugh, ed.
A Literary History of England (New York:
Appleton-Century-Crofts, 1948), p. 307

When one considers the circumstances of Malory's life—his aristocratic lineage and profession of arms, his training as a gentleman and a soldier, his experience of foreign and civil war, the vicissitudes of his own fortunes, and finally, the fact that he wrote late in life, probably suffering in prison, approaching death—one understands better why the *Morte d'Arthur* is what it is: a work of retrospect, tinged with sadness for the passing of the good old days; a work of idealism, troubled with knowledge of miserable facts daily divulged; a work of patriotism, written when the land was being wasted by civil strife; a work of encouragement to the right-minded, and of warning to the evil-minded, among men of that class in which the author lived and moved.

William Henry Schofield
Chivalry in English Literature (Port Washington, N. Y.:
Kennikat Pr., 1964), p. 87

GENERAL

To call Malory a humorist of the first order is perhaps a trifle paradoxical, for truly none are more devoutly and supremely serious than he. Yet therein lies the humour; for this very devoutness, this grand seriousness, this superb unconsciousness of absurdities, yields for the sceptical modern most exquisite diversion. The absolute belief in the events narrated which is stamped upon every line of the book, the august air of history with which every impossible episode is surrounded, have a cumulative effect far more subtle than any conscious humorist could have designed.

The Academy (January 4, 1902), p. 657

Indeed, Malory has that without which the highest art does not exist—a sense of the mystery of life. He is far from being confined by fact as most writers of the eighteenth century were from getting beyond it. From the beginning of his tale, with the love of Uther Pendragon for the lady Igraine, to its conclusion, the death upon a good Friday in the Holy Land of the last four knights of the Round Table, who have gone thither to do battle "upon the miscreants or Turks," Malory is never unconscious of the poetic wonder of this world, of the truths which we feel rather than know.

Howard Maynardier
The Arthur of the English Poets (Boston:
Houghton Mifflin, 1907), p. 243

Medieval stories were, naturally, negligent of causes in a world where the unaccountable so constantly happened in real life, and a similar suddenness of adventure may be found in tales much older than this. Malory, however, on the threshold of an age which would require dramatic motive or, at least, probability, saved his book from the fate of the older, unreasoned fiction by investing it with an atmosphere, impossible to analyse, which withdraws his figures to the region of mirage. The indescribable conviction of magic places Malory's characters outside the sphere of criticism, since, given the atmosphere, they are consistent with themselves and their circumstances. Nothing is challenged, analysed or emphasised; curiosity as to causation is kept in abeyance; retribution is worked out, but, apparently, unconsciously. Like children's are the sudden quarrels and hatreds and as sudden reconciliations. The motive forces are the elemental passions of love and bravery, jealousy and revenge, never greed, or lust, or cruelty. Courage and the thirst for adventure are taken for granted, like the passion for the chase, and, against a brilliant and moving throng of the brave and fair, a few conceptions are made to stand forth as exceptional—a Lancelot, a Tristram, or a Mark. Perhaps most skillful of all is the restraint exercised in the portrayal of Arthur. As with Shakespeare's Caesar and Homer's Helen, we realise Arthur by his effect upon his paladins; of himself we are not allowed to form a definite image, though we may surmise justice to be his most distinct attribute. Neither a hero of hard knocks nor an effective practical monarch, he is not to be assigned to any known type, but remains the elusive centre of the magical panorama.

Alice D. Greenwood
"English Prose in the Fifteenth Century,"
CHEL, vol. II (1908), pp. 336-37

The final quality of Malory's art lies deeper than cadence or dramatic narrative; it is his power of suggestion. Through the early part of the Morte a sense of hidden meaning is intermittent. It is conveyed largely through omens, prophecies, and hints of under-rhythm in the events. As the work goes on, the impression grows, till the whole story seems to move to some unheard music from secret places. To read it is like watching a complex dance, controlled by some orchestra which fails to meet the ear. Such quickening suggestiveness is the hallmark of romance at its conclusion rather than its inception. . . . In Malory, the process is complete and one gazes into the flux of life with an intuition that its depths are unsounded and its source is far. The Morte Darthur is as the Faerie Queene of those echoes which "roll from soul to soul, and live forever and forever." It has more affinity with Keats and Coleridge than with Chrétien de Troies.

This impression of significance is not only conveyed by the detail of style, it is inherent in the whole conception. . . . A sense of secret intention is rarely absent even in the most care-free and offhand passages; beneath the happy spaciousness, the apparent rambling, which impart surface charm, the whole story moves as Maeterlinck would put it in the shadow of a great expectation. And the explanation of Malory's heightened art is that the principle of causality has taken full possession of his mind.

Vida D. Scudder
Le Morte Darthur of Sir Thomas Malory (New York: Dutton;
London: Dent, 1921), pp. 399-400

But in the very midst of the Transition muddling of structure and blurring of vision, the Transition's blindness to the method of Chrétien or of Renaud or of Chaucer, a greater than Henryson, in England, laid his hand upon the almost stiffened mass of romantic narrative, and raised the Arthurian story to permanent life. Malory's imagination was of far larger calibre than that possessed by Henryson; and to his sense-perception, his power of seeing, hearing, and feeling his personages, the way in which his eye holds the picture while his figures move, Malory adds a strong sense of structure. Perhaps the huge compilations of the latter Middle Ages brought gain to narrative in the sense of Causality which was pressed out of event by the sheer weight of material. Malory's greatest service to English narrative is here, a greater even than his character-portrayal, than his prose. He bound the Arthurian stories together by a sense for causality, for the unescapable consequences of human conduct; through the juxtaposed mass of separate narratives he drew the bursted thread of the three great Loyalties, to sovereign, to the beloved lady, to God; and by the shattering of the Round Table he showed that no man held those three in equal reverence, that no man served the Ideal, that punishment for such failure came here upon earth.

Malory removes our world and substitutes his. The integrity of his conviction, his feeling, his imagination, is such that we return from him with difficulty to that smaller and meaner life which we have called normal.

E. P. Hammond
English Verse Between Chaucer and Surrey (Durham, N. C.:
Duke Univ. Pr., 1927), pp. 34, 36

There are . . . in Malory two distinct aspects: an archaic cadence and crisp idiom, an "alluring archaism" and an almost colloquial straightforwardness. These correspond to the two common methods of telling an old tale in a modern tongue; that of restoring the old manner and avoiding conflict between form and matter; and that of using modern idiom and deliberately creating a contrast between matter and form. . . . For men of little genius there is no third alternative: they imitate or they ridicule; they lack the skill of reproducing the spirit of an old story without being artificial; and they cannot adapt it to their own times without being consciously or unconsciously coarse. Malory is one of the few writers who found a "third way" and steered clear of both coarseness and artificiality. His fundamental merit is not so much his Latin fluency and facility as his art of combining pathos and simplicity, romance and epic straightforwardness. His language has all the strength of an oration, all the ease of a popular tale. It is traditional and fresh at the same time, and this is why it is so well fitted to its theme. Malory's subject was conventional; the world in which his characters lived and acted was artificial. Any less able author treating it artificially and bombastically would have rendered it unreadable; or, by using an inappropriate, popular manner, would have parodied the original. Malory avoided both dangers, and without being unjust to the old Romance endowed his story with a wide and undying appeal.

Eugène Vinaver
Malory (Oxford: Clarendon Pr., 1929), pp. 103-5

Shakespeare in his Henry IV and V gives us Elizabethan England in a garb of Lancastrian names and events; Malory gives us the first half of the fifteenth century masked in the characters and incidents of the traditional Round Table tales. When he had completed the reducing of his "Frenssche Boke" he had achieved an allegorical presentation of the use and downfall of a united English chivalry under the Lancastrian dynasty. He had traced the coming of order and harmony from discord; he had pictured the joy and the glory of a social organism acting with perfect esprit de corps under a great leader; shifting attention from the leader, he had dwelt upon outstanding achievements of individual knights and had projected a vivid contrast of the English and French kingdoms under the guise of Logres and Cornwall; he had shown how from the highest earthly attainment the human soul moves toward the accomplishment of a spiritual quest, and then how inevitably the transfer of vital interest in the best members of the group from worldly to spiritual aims left affairs free from self-seeking, ambition, and envy to control.

Nellie Slayton Aurner
PMLA (June, 1933), p. 389

How Sir Thomas Malory, who seems to have been an ordinary unscrupulous man-at-arms fighting in a most unchivalrously-conducted war, was inspired to produce the first monument of artistic prose since the days of Aelfric is . . . a mystery. It was one of those happy accidents that occur to men of genius like Sidney and Fielding and Walpole. This we can say, however, that the new qualities that come into Malory's prose come from his working over poetic originals. These new qualities are harmony of rhythm and emotional power, qualities neglected by men whose only use for prose was exposition, but so vital to the poets that they infected the translator and informed his prose with their power and grace, just as the great, grave tradition of liturgical Latin was to infuse its qualities into the Bible of Tyndale and the Prayerbook of Cranmer. But that assumes that Malory could feel and appreciate the qualities of his originals, and it merely defines, without explaining, his achievement of a new art, "the other harmony of prose."

W. L. Renwick and Harold Orton
The Beginnings of English Literature to Skelton
(London: Cresset Pr., 1939), pp. 67-68

While the majority of writers of the fifteenth century were busy endeavoring to make use of prose for new ends, here and there we meet with a writer who holds firmly to the old ways. Such a one was Sir Thomas Malory. In one of the most fortunate moments for English literature he decided to make use of his tedious leisure as a prisoner of Edward IV by reading and reducing into English the vast compilation of stories about Arthur which he found, in the main, in his "French book. . . ." By the fifteenth century whatever had existed of the chivalric life mirrored in the *Morte Darthur* had long since passed away. The age of Malory was no fruitful soil in which to replant the ideal of chivalry; his own experiences in the Wars of the Roses must have taught him that. Occasionally he exclaims against the times, but for the most part he retires into a world of long ago. It is a world of heroes —and one into which few but heroes are admitted. It is unconcerned with getting and spending. Kings and knights serve queens and ladies in court or in the field in an unending series of settings designed for the most part to show them to advantage. It is a world wherein the ordinary sordid affairs of business and politics are not allowed to intrude. Many battles are fought: many quests undertaken. Love and war are the twin poles of man's existence. In the course of relating much concerning these matters Malory also contrives to tell some of the greatest stories of the world, and in one of them—that of Lancelot and Guenevere—rises to the height of his great argument. Malory's conduct of the final books of the *Morte* has long been recognized as a masterpiece of story-telling. The movement is splendidly controlled and maintained, while the figures of Arthur, Lancelot, Gawaine, and Guenevere move in and out ineluctably pressing forward to the great final scenes and the break-up of the Round Table and of all Arthur's dreams.

H. S. Bennett
Chaucer And The Fifteenth Century (Oxford:
Clarendon Pr., 1947), pp. 200-201

If we feel that Malory is slow in getting under way with his high theme and too often allows the earlier part of his narrative to be unduly clogged with episodes, there can at least be no doubt as to the singular beauty of his prose. He is free from the desire to "augment" the English language with "aureate" terms, which is the bane of so much contemporary writing, and comes nearer to the vernacular tradition which Dr. R. W. Chambers has traced back . . . to its Anglo-Saxon beginnings. But he gives it a wider scope by applying it to secular material, and here, of course, he is much under the influence of his French models. . . . One may add that Malory, unlike Caxton, does not share the love of his French predecessors for linking synonymous words in doublets, and that he makes no attempt to reproduce in English those elaborate periods of carefully linked subordinate clauses which they favoured. He prefers to proceed, both in narrative and in dialogue, by a succession of simple sentences . . . and to obtain his rhythm by balancing these with longer ones. . . . The diction is fairly modern. . . . Dialogue is apt to come to an abrupt conclusion. The knights are men of their hands and have no turn for a prolonged debate.

E. K. Chambers
English Literature at the Close of the Middle Ages, 2nd ed.
(Oxford: Clarendon Pr., 1947), pp. 198-99

The predominant ethical tone of Malory's work is certainly not the bourgeois, still less the proletarian, morality of our own day. And, on its own showing, it is not the Christian rule of life; all the chief characters end as penitents. It is aristocratic. It does not forbid homicide provided it is done in clean battle. It does not demand chastity, though it highly honours lifelong fidelity to the chosen mistress. Though it admires mercy it allows private war and the vendetta. And it has no respect at all for property or for laws as such. It is distinguished from heroic morality by its insistence on humility. It can be very accurately called nobility if the noble is defined as the opposite of the vulgar. It does not condemn all whom we would now call "criminals"; its displeasure is primarily for the cad. It is magnificently summed-up in Sir Ector's final lament, which, so far as we know, is Malory's own invention: "Thou was the mekest man and the jentyllest that ever ete in halle emonge ladyes and thou were the sternest knyght to thy mortal foe that ever put spere in the rest." There is the real, and indispensable, contribution of chivalry to ethics.

TLS (June 7, 1947), p. 273

Malory was more than a generation younger than Lydgate and yet he is less touched by the literary happenings in Italy that promoted the Renaissance. He is thus at the very tail-end of a tradition. . . . Malory's chivalric world is not ineffective because by then antique and outmoded. It is indeed highly effective, but only in expressing an individual vision. Set *Morte Darthur* alongside *Piers Plowman* and you will see how little group-feeling Malory possesses. He creates no picture of general life; he almost makes us forget that there are other classes in the world than the knightly. Even his notion of chivalry is less true to his age, than is, for instance Spenser's to the Elizabethan. . . . Malory's notion of chivalry is nostalgic and not expressive of the actual England of the Wars of the Roses. That is, in the main; for it may be that something of contemporary gloom has got into the account of Arthur's final battle.

E. M. W. Tillyard
The English Epic and Its Background (New York:
Oxford Univ. Pr., 1954), p. 176

Malory was, of course, not depicting the troubles of his time directly; he was giving an imaginative form to them only. Unlike the poets of the alliterative tradition, Langland and the rest, he has no counsel to give. The grace and beauty of the Morte Darthur spring largely from its freedom from any reflection, any complicated tangle of social or of emotional repercussions. It is a splendid holiday from all such teasing questions as our living in the daily world implies.

M. C. Bradbrook
Sir Thomas Malory (London: BC/Longmans, 1958), p. 26

The pure Malory is the prose-writer whose language has given new life to a dying tradition. Exactly how this happened we shall never know; but there is in Malory's prose the same aesthetic principle at work as in his method of composition. Both the literary English of his time, and the language of his French Arthurian books were, like the books themselves, reminiscent of a woven fabric. Alternating themes, cross-links and over-lappings were characteristic of the language of some of the best among his sources. More than that: there is much the same contrast between their style and Malory's as between the two types of structure: the same kind of structural evolution leads to a break with the traditional forms of writing. Hence Malory's natural falling back into the even tenor of familiar dis-course and the characteristically haunting "elegiac tone or undertone which never fails in romance or homily to bring its sad suggestions of the vanity and transience of all things, of the passing away of pomp and tradi-tion, of the fall of the princes." What makes his prose live is his way of subordinating his verbal material to a rhythm all his own, his instinctive discovery of a new stylistic pattern. The smooth symmetry of the French période disappears and in its place we find a succession of abruptly divided clauses, some of them strikingly brief and compact, and all of them spoken rather than written. . . . For the first and perhaps the last time in the history of Arthurian literature the power of language raises the story to the level of tragic action.

Eugène Vinaver
"Sir Thomas Malory," *Arthurian Literature in the Middle Ages*,
ed. R. S. Loomis (Oxford: Clarendon Pr., 1959), pp. 550-51

Malory's prose style, which moves with a simple cogency always perfectly adapted to the narrative line which he is developing, is not easily placed in the history of English prose. He is outside the tradition of English devotional prose which continues from Anglo-Saxon times to the Tudor and Eliza-bethan translators of the Bible. He begins by capturing something of the rhythms, and using some of the alliterative devices, of Middle English al-literative verse as represented by the verse romance *Morte Arthur*; he sim-plifies, tightens up, adds weight and precision and, at the same time, a conversational flow. He learns as he writes, and the later books show a fine ease in dialogue together with a dignity and eloquence which derive at least in part from the heroic element in the *Morte Arthur*. The flow is simple enough, marked by such conjunctions as "and," "for," "but," "then," and "therefor." The underlying rhythms provide a quiet emotional ground swell to the narrative; the dialogue is lively and often captures the individual quality of a character; the accounts of action rise and fall with a restrained epic movement which has quiet gravity without magniloquence. The result of it all is an impressive summing of the "Matter of Britain" as seen through

the perspective of the Indian summer of the Age of Chivalry; excessive sentiment, the pure devotional note, and over-abundant narrative complication
are equally pruned away, and Malory gives us the Arthurian stories set to
an uncomplicated chivalric morality. But the epic note does not really
belong to these nostalgic stories of a lost way of life; the defects of the code
are manifest in the actions which are based on it, and in the end the
heroic key is modulated into elegy.

David Daiches
A Critical History of English Literature, vol. I
(New York: Ronald Pr., 1960), p. 141

If it was, even incidentally, Malory's purpose to use the example of chivalric
tradition to point the way toward a better England, he was undertaking an
ambitious and from our point of view a not very realistic task. . . . His own
experience in the Wars of the Roses, we are told, must surely have taught
him the futility of such a project. But did it? Malory was, after all, a man of
his day. He could not see, as the historian can, that he was already leaving
the medieval countryside and nearing the outskirts of a new era. He was no
more able than any of his contemporaries to recognize the signs of social
change or to interpret the obvious decline of chivalric morale as anything
more than the spiritual decay always to be expected in the society of sinful
mankind, a society ordained in a fixed framework in which the only variable
factor was the frail and fickle nature of man himself. If he looked to the past
for the Golden Age of chivalry, that was no more than social critics did
habitually in the later Middle Ages. . . .

Arthur B. Ferguson
The Indian Summer of English Chivalry (Durham, N. C.:
Duke Univ. Pr., 1960), pp. 56-58

In the difficult task of retelling an old tale he [Malory] achieves a wonderful
blend of archaism and straightforwardness, pathos and simplicity, majesty
and ease, cadence and clarity. . . . His book is England's first work in poetic
prose.

A. R. Myers
England in the Late Middle Ages (Baltimore:
Penguin Books, 1961), p. 233

At the end of the Middle Ages and the end of the long efflorescence of
medieval romance in many languages, Malory endeavoured to digest the
Arthurian romances into English prose, using as his source chiefly an assort-
ment of French Arthurian prose romances. But this traditional material has
not been organized so as to convey any coherent significance either as a
whole or, for the most part, even locally. Malory persistently misses the

meaning of his wonderful material. The comparison with *Sir Gawayne and the Green Knight* is in this respect—as indeed, in nearly all respects—fatally damaging to Malory's *Morte D'Arthur*. The modern reader does best to accept the book as essentially episodic, a book to be dipped into rather than read right through. Once we have fallen under the spell of such an episode as that concerning the Maid of Astolat, it is to it that we shall return.

What is it, then, that constitutes the charm of the book, that draws readers back to parts of it again? Partly it is the magic of its style—those lovely elegiac cadences of the prose, that diffused tone of wistful regret for a past age of chivalry, that vague sense of the vanity of earthly things. Yet the charm of the prose is a remote charm; the imagery is without immediacy; there is a lifelessness, listlessness, and fadedness about this prose for all its (in a limited sense) loveliness. There is also the fascination of the traditional Arthurian material itself, even though we feel it is not profoundly understood. The material fascinates the reader in spite of Malory's "magical" style, which seems to shadow and obscure rather than illuminate it. Malory's Grail books, for example, include some of the most fascinating of his traditional material. We find here once again the Waste Land, the Grail Castle, the Chapel Perilous, the Wounded King, and so on, but reduced to little more than a succession of sensations and thrills. The recurrent appearance of the corpse or corpse-like figure on a barge and the weeping women— fragments of an ancient mythology though they are—become in Malory merely tedious after a number of repetitions, and the final effect is one of somewhat morbid sensationalism rather than of mystical vision.

John Speirs
"A Survey of Medieval Verse," *The Age of Chaucer*
(Baltimore: Penguin Books, 1961), p. 42

The whole book is bound together in various ways: by the unity of atmosphere and the continuous moral concern; by the chronological continuity of the main events and characters. . . ; by significant references backward and forward to important characters and events; and by links between the various tales. Some of this binding together is due to the inherent nature of Malory's material, and some of it to Malory's personal contribution. . . . Malory's method is the same both for the lesser arrangements within the tales, and for the major arrangements of the tales themselves. The smaller sections within the main tales correspond structurally to the major sections within the whole book. Often there are no close links between the subsections of a major tale; but no one doubts that they are parts of a larger whole. The subsections have a high degree of autonomy, just like the major sections.

D. S. Brewer
"The hoole book," *Essays on Malory*, ed. J. A. W. Bennett
(Oxford: Clarendon Pr., 1963), pp. 61-62

Malory's greatest original passages arise when he is most completely absorbed in the story and realizes the characters so fully that they begin to talk for him of their own accord; but they talk a language he has largely learned from his sources. The very ease with which he wanders away from this style into that of some inferior source or into a language of his own (which he may have thought "higher") suggests that he hardly knows what he is doing. Thus, while in one sense it would be monstrous to say that he "has no style" (he has written prose as musical, as forthright, as poignant, as was ever heard in England), it would be true in another. He has no style of his own, no characteristic manner. (If you were searching all literature for a man who might be described as "the opposite of Pater," Malory would be a strong candidate.) In a style or styles so varied, everywhere so indebted to others, and perhaps most original precisely where it is most indebted, one cannot hopefully seek *l'homme même*. Here also Malory vanishes into a mist.

C. S. Lewis
"The English Prose Morte," *Essays on Malory*, ed. J. A. W. Bennett
(Oxford: Clarendon Pr., 1963), pp. 23-24

Like the Bible, the *Book of King Arthur and His Noble Knights* is an assemblage of materials from different peoples and epochs, and looks at life from shifting points of view. There is a fascination in watching the kaleidoscopic changes in colour and dominant pattern as one passes from tale to tale. The first, comprising Books I to IV, is pervaded and controlled by the heathenish magic of Merlin; the account of the Roman war is charged with the chauvinistic passion roused by the Hundred Years' War; the doctrine of divine grace furnishes the leit-motif of the quest of the Grail; a series of fatalistic accidents combines with the faults of the chief characters to bring about the downfall of the Round Table. To the serious student of medieval culture this variety can be of absorbing interest, and to the casual reader it affords relief from monotony. When battles and tournaments pall and magic and marvels lose their charm, there are heavenly visions and powerful scenes of psychological conflict and grim tragedy.

Roger Sherman Loomis
The Development of Arthurian Romance (London:
Hutchinson Univ. Library, 1963), p. 173

The French prose that determines this English style [the anonymous *Merlin*] is also the source for Malory's *Le Morte Darthur*, and it would be a confident judge who could be sure that any short sample of the anonymous translation was not Malory's work. This is not to deny that Malory's own tastes and his techniques of drastic abbreviation by jumping from one key statement to the next did not lend distinctive qualities to his book and his style: a somewhat synoptic narrative that stresses action more than description o.

analysis and so achieves greater energy and directness (and also occasional confusion); an emphatic manner that accompanies his fondness for front-positioning adverbials; slightly more dialogue; a less involved characterization and interpretation; an Englishry that proceeds from these simplifications as well as from his strong preference (despite a sprinkling of Gallicisms) for native vocabulary; and a personal cast of language that comes from the reiteration of favorite words and phrases. Such traits, however, become obvious only with extended reading. The bases of his style, like the matter itself, come from the French romances—the forms of the sentences and their continuing even rhythms, the simplicity in diction, the ordering of events, and their disposition between exposition and dialogue—these are almost as much indebted to the French sources as is the style of the unadventurous translation of the *Merlin.* . . .

William Matthews, ed.
Later Medieval English Prose (New York:
Appleton-Century-Crofts, 1963), p. 20

For Malory's is indeed a world of dream, even though he is engaged on the apparently prosaic task of translating a "French book" in which the *Morte* itself is only one of a number of stories with different heroes, all members of the Round Table. This change of focus from book to book adds to the sense of an enchanted and fantastic world. Amid these green forests of remote kingdoms, the sunlight and the banners and the spears, the brilliantly coloured pavilions, stories slip mysteriously into one another, knights pass and reappear or are wholly lost. But most readers are content to accept the unexplained, to be carried forward with the flow of pageantry and the rhythmic enchantment of words. There is flux in that world, but no bewilderment, for the theme of all the stories is one. The whole, as Malory presents it, is an intricate study of the pattern of "noblesse" or magnanimity.

Not even Spenser has studied it with more passion or more subtlety; and certainly Spenser had no such intractable material to subdue. For Malory lives between two worlds. The earlier magnanimous hero, whether the pagan Alexander or the Christian Arveragus, followed a straight course; the ideals of his class and time were accepted without question. Spenser's heroes were in a faery land where, to some extent, they create their own ideals. But the knights of the *Morte Darthur*, for all their marvellous adventures, represent the highest of a real but passing world in an age which has begun to question its values. Galahad and Lancelot are types of magnanimity indeed, but magnanimity measured by two mutually exclusive standards, which Professor Vinaver would call those of Carbonek or Camelot—the fortress of the Christian soul or the palace of courtly love. Malory is always conscious of both; and it is the conflict of the two, each so lovely and beloved, which haunts the very rhythms of the *Morte Darthur* like the echo of the passing-bell.

Margaret Greaves
The Blazon of Honor (London:
Methuen, 1964), pp. 51-52

Malory is concerned with the Round Table as the attempt to embody on earth spiritual as well as human virtues, an attempt to keep God in England so that all may remain right in the English world. But earth is not heaven, and men on earth are not yet saved, as any medieval author knows. Dante shows how man can successfully progress toward paradise by degrees of purgation, and the result is a comedy. Malory shows how human society can only fail in trying to bring paradise down to earth, and the result is tragedy. Like Dante, Malory shows, however, the way out of this tragic state: the path of salvation can be trod by individuals alone, and its summit can be reached only after death. But Malory's method of presenting this view of man and his society is not an attempt to exhort, to preach, or to teach. . . . Malory seeks not to be hortatory but to be dramatic, to display the tragic shortcomings of earthly life while dramatizing the final solution to them.

Wilfrid L. Guerin
" 'The Tale of the Death of Arthur': Catastrophe and Resolution,"
Malory's Originality, ed. R. M. Lumiansky (Baltimore:
Johns Hopkins Pr., 1964), pp. 272-73

SIR THOMAS MORE

1478-1535

Sir Thomas More, English humanist, born in London, the son of a distinguished jurist, Sir John More of Lincoln's Inn, received his early education at St. Anthony's School in Threadneedle Street and in the household of Cardinal Morton, archbishop of Canterbury. At fourteen, he was sent to Canterbury College, Oxford, where he acquired a knowledge of Greek, and, two years later, to New Inn and Lincoln's Inn for the study of law. In 1501 he was called to the bar and appointed reader in Furnivall's Inn. At the same time he gave for Grocyn a celebrated course of lectures on St. Augustine's *De Civitate Dei* in the church of St. Lawrence Jewry. In 1504 he was elected to parliament and successfully led the opposition to the king's claim for feudal aids. His marriage to Jane Colt took place the following year. Their home at the Old Barge in Bucklersbury attracted a distinguished coterie of humanists, among them, Erasmus, who completed his *Praise of Folly* there in 1510. For more than a decade More pursued a highly successful legal career, and it was not until 1518 that he was persuaded (or more likely compelled) by the king to relinquish it in favor of a life at court. Public offices and honors soon followed. He became a Privy Councillor (1518), a Master of Requests (1518), Undertreasurer of the exchequer (1521), Speaker of the House of Common (1523), Chancellor of the Duchy of Lancaster (1525), and Chancellor of England (1529). He had been knighted in 1521. His opposition to the king's proposed divorce and antipapal legislation necessitated his resignation of the Chancellorship and his retirement from public life in May, 1532. Silence and seclusion, however, failed to satisfy the king. More was summoned to Lambeth on April 13, 1534 and required to take an oath to the Act of Succession. He refused and four days later was committed to the Tower. His trial for High Treason took place at Westminster on July 1, 1535. He was convicted and five days later executed on Tower Hill. In 1886 he was beatified by the Roman Catholic Church and in 1935 canonized by Pope Pius XI. Apart from his masterpiece, *Utopia* (1516), his chief works are *Life of John Picus* (1510), *History of Richard III* (1513), *Epigrammata* (1518), *Four Last Things* (1522), *Answer to Luther* (1523), *Dialogue Concerning Heresies* (1528), *Supplication of Souls* (1529), *Confutation of Tyndale* (1532), *Apology* (1532), *Debellation of Salem and Bizance* (1533), *Dialogue of Comfort Against Tribulation* (1534), and *Treatise upon the Passion of Christ* (1534).

W. E. Campbell, ed., *The English Works of Sir Thomas More* (1927-1931), 2 vols.

R. S. Sylvester, ed., *Complete Works of Sir Thomas More* (in progress)

R. W. Chambers, *Thomas More* (1935)

PERSONAL

He always saw the comic element in life. He loved a joke. . . . That is the secret of his wonderful family life and the affection which his children bore him. It is the secret, too, of most of his writings, particularly the *Utopia*. No one can hope to understand that work who does not remember that More could never be serious or stern for long. He was always jesting and if a great deal of what he wrote in the *Utopia* reveals the man's indignation at things as they were it is important to bear in mind that much was purely mischievous fear deliberately written for the enjoyment of his colleagues. . . .

C. H. Williams
The Open Court (September, 1917), p. 525

. . . The best friend of the Renaissance was killed as the worst enemy of the Reformation. More was a humanist, not only in the sense in which many crabbed and pedantic scholars earned that name by their real services to Greek and Latin scholarship, but in the sense that his scholarship was really both human and humane. He had in him, at that relatively early date, all that was best in Shakespeare and Cervantes and Rabelais; he had not only humour but fantasy. He was the founder of all the Utopias; but he used Utopia as what it really is, a playground. His *Utopia* was partly a joke; but since his time Utopians have seldom seen the joke. . . . The Great Humanist was above all a Superhumanist. He was a mystic and a martyr. . . . But he was not, like so many mystics of his time, one who lost his common sense in face of the mysteries. And it will remain a permanent and determining fact, a hinge of history, that he saw, in that first hour of madness, that Rome and Reason are one.

G. K. Chesterton
"A Turning-Point in History," in *The Fame of Blessed Thomas More* (London: Sheed and Ward, 1929), pp. 63-64

Four things were killed when they killed More. First, they killed learning, for More and Fisher were the two most learned men in England. By killing them Henry declared war on scholarship, and he dealt it such a blow that it was not until more than a century later that English scholars were to be able to bear comparison with the scholars of the Continent. . . . Secondly, they killed justice. . . . Thirdly, they killed laughter. . . . But fourthly—and it was what mattered most—they killed holiness. Before that colossal fact all the excuses and explanations fade into nothing. It is the mark of a Christian saint that he possesses the imagination that jumps back across a thousand or two thousand years of history. . . . Such a man was More—a man of the world, indeed, a lawyer and a statesman, but one to whom law and statesmanship and literature were only important in so far as they could be used to further the purposes of Christ.

Christopher Hollis
Sir Thomas More (London: Sheed and Ward, 1934), pp. 298-99

When Thomas More's career is understood as conforming to the pattern established by the typical humanist-diplomat of Renaissance times, it gains unity and a meaning which . . . it otherwise lacks. He is then no longer a succession of rather dimly related Mores: an amateur humanist and lover of good letters; a lawyer unhappy in his profession; an under-sheriff of the city of London; a diplomat, secretary, and orator in the service of the king; a writer of voluminous anti-Lutheran tracts. His career is rooted, not in amateur, but in professional humanism, and from that root stem most of the activities of his life. As a teacher of the discipline of grammar he lectured on historical subjects, wrote commendations for an elementary text-book for Latin students, in collaboration with Erasmus published a translation of Lucian which was much used in the schools, and, if the identification of the Thomas More of the Oxford register be accepted, sought the right to instruct in the humanities at the English universities. His humanistic training, in addition to his legal services, made him valuable as interpreter and orator to the merchants of London. The English government claimed him because he could make speeches, write letters, and discharge diplomatic functions. Finally, he turned his rhetorical talents to the service of his conscience.

William Nelson
PMLA (June, 1943), p. 352

He [More] tried to break away from the unhealthy conditions of the Middle Ages in two ways: by asserting against the underlying pessimism he had inherited an optimism and confidence in the goodness of the universe and its creator; by asserting in the face of this empty pomp and magnificence the virtues of simplicity and inwardness. The result is a precarious balance, not a neat system. The contradictions in More are not pressed home to what might be thought their logical conclusions: More does not reject the extreme ascetic ideal, nor does he subordinate to it the cult of sensual pleasure. They are held together without resolution.

H. A. Mason
Humanism and Poetry in the Early Tudor Period (London: Routledge and Kegan Paul, 1959), p. 139

. . . What first attracted me was a person who could not be accused of any incapacity for life, who indeed seized life in great variety and almost greedy quantities, who nevertheless found something in himself without which life was valueless and when that was denied him was able to grasp his death. For there can be no doubt, given the circumstances, that he did it himself. . . . Another thing that attracted me to this amazing man was his splendid social adjustment. So far from being one of society's sore teeth he was, like the hero of Camus' *La Chute*, almost indecently successful. He was respectably, not nobly, born, in the merchant class, the progressive class of the epoch, distinguished himself first as a scholar, then as a lawyer, was made an Ambassador, finally Lord Chancellor. A visitor's book at his house in Chelsea would have looked like a sixteenth-century *Who's Who*: Holbein, Erasmus, Colet, everybody. He corresponded with the greatest minds in Europe as the representative and acknowledged champion of the New-Learning in England. He was a friend of the King, who would send for More when his social appetites took a turn in that direction and once walked round the Chelsea garden with his arm round More's neck. . . . He adored his life, for he accepted and enjoyed his social context.

Robert Bolt
"Preface," *A Man for All Seasons* (New York: Random House, 1962), pp. xiii, xv

Utopia

The *Utopia is* . . . interesting because it is one of the most inconsistent of books. Never were the forms of Socialism and Communism animated by so entirely an Individualist soul. The hands are the hands of Plato, the wide-thinking Greek, but the voice is the voice of a humane, public-spirited, but limited and very practical English gentleman who takes the inferiority of his inferiors for granted, dislikes friars and tramps and loafers and all un-disciplined and unproductive people, and is ruler in his own household. He abounds in sound practical ideas, for the migration of harvesters, for the universality of gardens and the artificial incubation of eggs, and he sweeps aside all Plato's suggestion of the citizen woman as though it had never entered his mind. He had indeed the Whig temperament, and it manifested itself down even to the practice of reading aloud in company. . . . He argues ably against private property, but no thought of any such radicalism as the admission of those poor-peons of his . . . to participation in ownership ap-pears in his proposals. His communism is all for the convenience of his Syphogrants and Tranibores, those gentlemen of gravity and experience, lest one should swell up above the others. So too is the essential Whiggery of the limitation of the Prince's revenues. It is the very spirit of eighteenth-century Constitutionalism. And his Whiggery bears Utilitarianism instead of the vanity of a flower. Among his cities, all of a size . . . , the Benthamite would have revised his sceptical theology and admitted the possibility of heaven.

H. G. Wells
Social Forces in England and America (New York:
Harper, 1914), pp. 216-17

The *Utopia* is the result of wide reading in classic authors. . . . The various opinions are gathered from almost the whole range of classic literature. It is not of much value to endeavor to trace back any detail to its peculiar source. Usually the idea expressed is a modification of, and sometimes a reaction from, the possible original. This is but another way of saying that More's mind had assimilated and made its own the product of the past. And that, also, is the condition of modern culture. The similarity between many of More's ideas and those of the man of to-day is due to the fact that the roots of both reach down into the same past. The *Utopia* is a striking example of the advantages of a classical education as experienced by Newman. The unique position of the early Tudor humanists is due to the fact that they put into practice Newman's argument four hundred years ago.

John M. Berdan
Early Tudor Poetry 1485-1547 (New York:
Macmillan, 1920), p. 274

The *Utopia* is entirely free from the blemishes that mar More's polemical treatises. Whereas these are of inordinate length . . . and written in a tone unfortunately as coarse as is habitual to the scholars and theologians of his time, More's masterpiece is remarkable for its concise and condensed form; nor are its pages sullied by any abusive or opprobrious language. Yet, in spite of this condensation, the style is lucid and clear. . . . From a stylistic standpoint the *Utopia* is nothing but a series of essays on a wide range of various topics. There is no intrigue to link the different subjects together or to impart an idea of unity to the whole. The dramatic element which occurs in the first part is almost lacking in the second and yet, in spite of all this, the reader's interest never flags for a moment. This is for no inconsiderable part owing to the perfect way in which the writer conducts the vivid dialogue between the fictitious traveller Raphael Hythloday and well-known living persons. . . . Nor is it only for the vivid and animated dialogues that the style of More's masterpiece deserves special mention. There is in his fiction that subtle irony, that tender humour, those brilliant flashes of wit that so typically and characteristically reflect More's nature, but there is also in it that biting satire which strikes deeper than the most direct and fierce attack.

Gerard Dudok
Sir Thomas More and His Utopia (Amsterdam:
H. J. Paris, 1923), pp. 176-78

If in his lectures on the *De Civitate Dei* he had distinguished, as St. Augustine does, the State or the city of men from the Church or the City of God, it was with the city of men, the State, that *Utopia* dealt. He therefore in nowise handles in it the wider conception of St. Augustine that ultimately and in every real sense the true State is the Church. That this was More's central position his whole life is a witness not less than his death. Like St. Augustine he felt the demand for absolute authority in a capricious world; the State must merge in the Church, the civil power become the weapon of the Church, legislator and magistrate be but sons of the Church, bound to carry out the Church's aims; the Empire must be the instrument and vassal of the Church. If this is a fair statement of the practical teaching of the *De Civitate Dei* it is none the less ultimately the principle for which More gave his life. With this higher conception More is not concerned in his *Utopia*: he is dealing only with the city of men. His *Utopia* is the criticism of the social and political life of the day, by the Hellenic standards of one who has the shrewd practical instinct of the reformer. He applies in a somewhat Lucianic manner the philosophy he had learnt from Plato and the ideas he had got from Plutarch to conditions and problems that he found at his door. But it is as a citizen of the city of men, and not as a citizen of the city of God, that he takes his stand.

A. W. Reed
"Sir Thomas More," *The Social and Political Ideas of Some
Great Thinkers of the Renaissance and the Reformation*,
ed. F. J. C. Hearnshaw (London: G. G. Harrap, 1925), p. 138

What did More aim at in his *Utopia*? . . . More designed to show how England would look, and what shape her relations with abroad would assume, if she were communistically organised. . . . Historians and economists who are perplexed by *Utopia* perceive in this name a subtle hint by More that he himself regarded his communism as an impracticable dream. In all the discussions about the Utopians there is only one element of a fantastic nature, and that is not the goal that was aimed at, but the ways and means of achieving it. More saw only one force which could carry communism into effect, and this he mistrusted. He has shown us in *Utopia* in what manner he conceived that communism would be enforced. A prince named Utopus conquered the country, and impressed on it the stamp of his mind; all institutions in Utopia are to be traced to him. He thought out the general plan of the commonwealth and then put it into execution.

Karl Kautsky
Thomas More and His Utopia, tr. H. J. Stenning (New York:
International Publishers, 1927), pp. 247-49

Throughout the book [*Utopia*] . . . More maintains an attitude as intellectually sceptical as it is sentimentally sympathetic; and we shall not perhaps fully resolve this contradiction unless we remember that, whilst the porch and facade and decoration of the Utopian edifice are of a date contemporary with the discovery of the New World, the framework of the structure is markedly medieval.

Algernon Cecil
A Portrait of Thomas More (London: Eyre
and Spottiswoode, 1937), p. 129

The Utopian commonwealth is ingeniously built up from suggestions in the narratives of Vespucci and Peter Martyr, combined with hints from Plato's *Republic* and *Laws*, the *Germania* of Tacitus, and other sources which describe the workings of a primitive society, if by primitive is meant a society living according to the law of nature. All Utopian institutions are founded on reason, and on reason alone. More has been careful never to exceed this self-imposed limitation. The Utopians have learned everything that the ancient philosophers can teach us, and even in their religion there is nothing for which there is no precedent in classical antiquity. Like their institutions, their philosophy and religion also are founded on reason. Their virtue consists in living according to nature, and the law of nature regulates their private and public life, their actions in peace as well as in war. As a synthesis of the best pagan customs and philosophical systems, of the political and religious thought of the pagan world, *Utopia* is an achievement of no small significance, a *tour de force* which delighted the humanists of the Renaissance and gained for its author a position among the foremost men of learning in Europe, excelling in wit, erudition, and style. To the learned it was not least for its scholarship that *Utopia* became an object of admiration.

With a consistency that must impress minds trained in the school of the Platonic Academy of Florence and stimulated by the constructions of Pico and Reuchlin, More assigned to the Utopians a definite place in the order of the universe and in the history of mankind. To the common reader no such complexities need distract from his enjoyment of the book as a production of humanist wit, a *jeu d'esprit* of an uncommonly accessible nature.

The *Utopia* does not attempt a final solution of the problems of society . . . but it contains an appeal addressed to all of us, which allows of no refusal, that we should try and do each one his share to mend our own selves and ease the burden of our fellow-men, to improve mankind and prepare for the life to come. In this lies its enduring power, that however high we may fix the ideal, to whatever perfection we may attain, More points higher still, from matter to the spirit, and from man to God.

H. W. Donner
Introduction to Utopia (London: Sidgwick
and Jackson, 1945), pp. 75, 83

The great key . . . to the understanding of More and his *Utopia* is his attitude toward the common working man. This is not an attitude of mere pity or kindliness for the wretched poor—the good-natured, half-contemptuous paternalism that so often passes as liberal, enlightened, and progressive— instead it is an attitude of indignant sympathy, appreciation, respect, and faith. It is thus that we know More to be a true democrat rather than a benevolent aristocrat. . . . Not only does More show the poor man to be superior to the rich and mighty in individual morality but he also . . . extends the superiority into social values and economic theory. . . . Perhaps the most important evidence of the democratic intention of *Utopia* comes from the first book. There More gives to us a description of the struggles, the pains, and the tragedies of the English working people—with a scientific explanation of the causes of poverty, crime, and injustice—which has no equal in English writing. This, rather than his invention of Utopian society, is More's highest artistic and intellectual achievement. He does not find the causes of human misery in the mind or soul, in Fate, infallible and unchanging "human nature," or in the mental and moral weaknesses of the workers. Instead, More finds the causes of human mistery in material conditions. Human beings do wrong under social *compulsion.*

Russell Ames
Citizen Thomas More (Princeton, N. J.:
Princeton Univ. Pr., 1949), pp. 174-76

One simple fact should be firmly grasped by every reader of the *Utopia* from the very outset—namely, that it was written in the form of a *dialogue.*

For subsequent disregard of this fact has made fair judgment upon the book itself, and also upon its author, almost impossible.

W. E. Campbell
Erasmus, Tyndale and More (London: Eyre and Spottiswoode, 1949), p. 87

Two essential elements of Christian humanism bear on the question of the relation of Utopian religion and philosophy to Thomas More's own opinions. In the first place like other Christian humanists More believed that the gentile writers of antiquity had arrived at certain profound moral and perhaps even religious truths. But he also believed that the ultimate truths, religious and moral alike, were fully revealed only in the New Testament, that without the light of Revelation the whole truth can be glimpsed but partially, through a glass very darkly indeed. Now as we have said, More probably intended Utopian philosophy and religion to represent the nearest approach natural reason can make to Christian truth. The trouble is that *in any particular matter* we have no way of telling how near he believed natural reason came to Christian truth or how far he believed it fell short of it. . . .

Because quite a few present-day academic prestidigitators have felt impelled to make More's conception of the community of property and goods, recently become politically embarrassing, softly and silently vanish away and never be heard of again, I have felt justified in taking special pains to indicate the central importance of that conception in *Utopia*. But it is unjust to More and to the scope of his conceptions to summarize and dismiss the Utopian social economy with the bare flat phrase: community of property and goods. For in the bare idea there was nothing new in More's time or long before. There were a number of variations on the idea both in theory and in practice available in More's day and well within the bounds of his knowledge. On the theoretical side he was familiar with Plato's *Republic*, with Seneca, and with the great Latin Fathers; on the practical side he knew about the way of life of the early Christian groups and especially about the prescriptions of the Benedictine Rule.

More's originality then—and he was one of the very few original social thinkers in the two centuries before Calvin—lay not in the bare idea of a community of property and goods; it lay in the exactness, the precision, and the meticulous detail with which he implemented his underlying social conceptions, proposing all the basic rules of law and methods of adminstration necessary to make community of property and goods one of the motor forces in a going polity. But his achievement in this matter rests on a prior feat of the mind. For More proceeds to his Utopian—in some ways even Draconian—remedies only after he has made a careful diagnosis of the evils of society, and not of society in the general and abstract sense, but of sixteenth century Christendom as it lay before his sharp probing eyes.

J. H. Hexter
More's Utopia: The Biography of an Idea (Princeton, N. J.:
Princeton Univ. Pr., 1952), pp. 54, 62-63

Certainly More was gay as well as pious in his youth and to the scaffold he took his gaiety as well as his piety; but it is hard to reconcile the liberal tone of *Utopia* with the austerities practiced by More at various periods of his life and the tolerance of *Utopia* with the attitude toward heretics which he adopted in his later years. The truth seems to be that at one time More, like Erasmus, hoped to see a liberal reformation inside the old church, and that experience convinced both men that reform as it gathered force would tear down many things which seemed to them holy and precious. Confronted with a choice, they decided for the old and the known; Erasmus was deaf to the plea of Dürer: "Hear, thou knight of Christ! Ride forth by the side of the Lord; defend the truth, gain the martyr's crown!" More gained the martyr's crown, but not as a protestant.

J. D. Mackie
The Earlier Tudors 1485-1558 (Oxford:
Clarendon Pr., 1952), p. 265

Living at the time when he did, More could not go beyond mental projection of an imaginary ideal society (which is so characteristic of utopian socialism). In sixteenth century society he could not, of course, discover a force capable of removing the social contradictions which he noted and condemned. For socialism as a science the time was not yet ripe. But for its period, "Utopia" is a work amazing in its depth and discernment. . . . But then More was a man of exceptionally wide intellectual vision. Besides a fine classical education, he had a profound knowledge of contemporary writings. . . . At the same time, he was keenly alive to social developments in the world around him, and was affected most by the misery wrought by the enclosures. Under the impact of the stirrings of the dispossessed, he proved able to draw up a complete design for an ideal society free of the evils of his time. All those centuries ago, when the bourgeois order was just coming into being, More subjected its principles to penetrating criticism and proclaimed in their stead the principles of social equality and community. He must indeed be acknowledged the father of utopian socialism and one of its greatest exponents.

Vyacheslav Volgin
News, A Review of World Events (February 15, 1953), pp. 14-15

Utopian philosophy, Utopian education, and Utopian communism are ...
seen to hang together as a coherent and systematic unit. With reason and
philosophy alone to guide them and without revelation and faith to light
their path, the Utopians have chosen good and upright pleasure as the end of
human existence and activity. As a practical result, their life is one of
physical health, intellectual enjoyment, and moral recititude. To secure a
minimum of pain and a maximum of pleasure for their citizens, they have
adopted communism as the most practical and equitable means for the
distribution of the matter of pleasure, namely, the commodities of life. As
for learning and education among the Utopians, it is not merely the source of
real pleasure, as in the discovery and absorption of Greek literature: it is
also the means for the transmission and preservation of their hedonistic
philosophy, theistic religion, and democratic communism. It is not extravagant to say that the whole Utopian state is waiting breathlessly, as it were,
for fulfillment in the reception of Christ's faith and morals. Christ would
not come to destroy the Utopian law and the Utopian prophets but to fulfill (Matt. v. 17). Little would have to be discarded: nearly all could be
retained. If by reason and philosophy pagans could devise and maintain a
natural commonwealth of such perfection, ought not Christians to be
ashamed that, although aided also by the incomparably superior gifts of
revelation and grace, they have failed to provide a life of greater happiness
for the individual and to establish a system of greater prosperity and justice
for their people as a whole? *Utopia*, in the last analysis, is a cry of distress
over the exploited poor and a call to reform in every department of human
endeavor in England and in Europe.

Edward L. Surtz
The Praise of Pleasure (Cambridge, Mass.:
Harvard Univ. Pr., 1959), p. 199

Its structure, its use of characters, its rhetorical techniques, its purpose, its
subject, its tone—all these accord with the conventions of a literary genre
firmly, if ambiguously, fixed in literary history. *Utopia* has the shape and the
feel—the form—of satire. It is useful to think of it as a prose version with
variations of the formal verse satire composed by Horace, Persius, and
Juvenal.

Robert C. Elliott
ELH (December, 1963), p. 320

History of King Richard III

In the fragmentary *History of King Richard the Thirde* are displayed a skill
in narrative and description, a freshness of style, a keen appreciation of

human character, an easy handling of dramatic situations, all combining to produce a moving and readable story. . . . The characters are shown as living people; their speeches—though extremely long—are probable; their actions consistent; every detail contributes to form a convincing picture.

E. M. G. Routh
Sir Thomas More and His Friends 1477-1535
(Oxford Univ. Pr., 1934), pp. 48-49

The *History* is the most consistent in style of More's English writings; he did not, unfortunately, write *Utopia* in English, and his later vernacular works were of a controversial character that called for argument rather than for narrative and description; all contain passages that are memorable; there are humorous digressions, and interludes of vivid narrative, but there are also long, complicated sentences and involved passages that make hard reading. These blemishes do not occur in the *History*, but his style is rarely simple; he likes to bring together many details to form his pictures, a kind of literary pointillism, and he delights in picturesques similes and phrases. More had a quick sense of drama and his best writing was done when this sense was called into play; the turbulent reign of Richard III provided rich material on which to work. So outstanding is this characteristic, it is not idle to speculate that had he lived in Elizabethan times, he could have found his natural form of expression in the drama.

E. E. Reynolds
Saint Thomas More (New York: P. J. Kenedy
and Sons, 1953), p. 84

Thomas More's *History of Richard III* . . . is all the more noteworthy, considering its brevity, for being not only the first attempt at English biography and history on what may be called philosophical principles, but also the first English prose in which the methods of the modern novel, and, indeed, of poetical drama, appear at large.

A. I. Doyle
"A Survey of English Prose in the Middle Ages," *The Age of Chaucer*
(Baltimore: Penguin Books, 1961), p. 81

What Sallust and Tacitus gave him was a form, a set of techniques and analogues, a literary pattern according to which he could develop his own historical vision. The basic elements in that vision were defined by the source, oral and perhaps written, which were available to him. More took the new material that they furnished and shaped it into an historical narrative of compelling power, utilizing, as he proceeded, all that he had learned from the classical authors. The result was a truly humanist history which, combining old forms and new subject matter, often suggested that the present could best be understood when seen in terms of the past. The vision . . . was characteristically double. His Richard is no mere usurper but a grand villain whose figure draws much of its literary strength from the similarity which it bears to the tyrants of tradition; the usurping protector is seen in terms of a broad historical metaphor that allows More to emphasize the moral patterns implicit in the story of his reign. The basic technique was commonplace enough during the Renaissance when the new interest in the classics turned every potential patron into a Maecenas and could make a Hannibal of Charles VIII, a Ulysses of Louis XII. More, however, converts the normal eulogistic process, finding his analogues not in the virtuous rulers of the past—they would be enshrined in Utopia—but rather in the vicious corruption of decaying Rome.

Richard S. Sylvester, ed.
The Complete Works of St. Thomas More, vol. II (New Haven,
Conn., and London: Yale Univ. Pr., 1963), p. xcviii

MINOR WORKS

More's distinction as an epigrammatist is twofold. First, he had a sharply defined sense of what he conceived an epigram to be: a short poem, normally in elegiac couplets, terse, witty, and satirical. His book contains a few poems which deviate from this rule, but ninety per cent of them conform to it. Secondly, he banished from his writing both the licentious Ovidianism of the Italian poets and the dull religiosity of the northern humanists. In their place we find true wit and a keen eye for the ridiculous in many fields of life. It was doubtless his choice of fresher and livelier subject matter which accounts for the immediate popularity of his poems, resulting in the appearance of three editions in two years.

Leicester Bradner and Charles Arthur Lynch, eds.
The Latin Epigrams of Thomas More (Chicago:
Univ. of Chicago Pr., 1953), pp. xxvi-xxvii

The historical significance of the *Dialogue of Comfort* will, perhaps, constitute its chief interest for the general reader. It leads us into the penetralia of a statesman's mind at a crisis when the world, of which he was a foremost figure, was undergoing an epochal transformation. But it would be an error to suppose that the value of the work is merely documentary. It is beyond any doubt one of the most charming spiritual treatises in the English language. It is divided into three books, of which the contents may be roughly outlined as follows: I. The Function of Suffering in Human Life; II. Various and Common Kinds of Affliction, Principally Temptations of the Soul, with Corresponding Remedies; III. Temporal Evils and the Way They are to be Encountered. Under these broad headings is collected a mass of weighty practical philosophy garnered from a career unusually crowded with rich and multifarious experience, and presented with an instinct for literary form which, in England at least, was the most highly cultivated of the age. Like Sir Thomas himself, it is a synthesis of unexpected excellence, with surprises around every corner. It is to be noted, too, that, while the *Dialogue* is intensely Catholic in tone, it carefully avoids all controversy. In this respect it is a singular exception among the writings of Sir Thomas in the vernacular.

James J. Daly
A Cheerful Ascetic and Other Essays (New York,
Milwaukee: Bruce, 1931), p. 58

Compared with the great mystics and saints—St. Augustine, St. John of the Cross, St. Ignatius—there seems to be a lack of genius in the spiritual life of More. He was a literary, not a spiritual genius; and he did not plumb the uttermost depths of the spirit. Above all, he was a great *man*, a concrete character, in which imagination, feeling, judgment, knowledge and will were singularly balanced; a highly cultured man of the world, a "true humanist . . ." who led a life of intense holiness and simplicity and became a saint. By no stretch of the imagination does he rank with the great spiritual giants of hagiology; hence his appeal to us today. . . . But it was not so much in his holy and dutiful life that More was great, but in his death; and it was because he was willing to give up so much that his martyrdom became of such profound significance. He was in the prime of his life, possessed of almost everything that the world could give—the highest position in the State, a legal reputation respected by lawyers and by rich and poor clients alike, a literary and philosophical genius recognized all over Europe ("the wisest man in Christendom," Erasmus called him), a brilliant circle of friends, a good wife and adoring family, and a noble and expansive estate; yet he gladly gave up everything to languish in the Tower and to die on the block, for what in those days was regarded by most people as a very small point of conscience. . . . More's willingness to suffer and die is the more remarkable when we consider his literary genius and social position: for great men have proved sorry figures in the times of crisis. There is always the tendency for the creative artist to regard himself as a being apart from his fellows, one who, by reason of his superior gift, is able to stand outside the everyday restrictions, and behave as though he were a law unto himself. The pitiful egotism of the great is a blot on the history of creative genius; yet it is in a way excusable. For if it is hard for an ordinary ungifted individual to transcend his personality, it must be far more difficult, well-nigh impossible for the genius, imprisoned as he is, in the microcosmic universe of his creative ego. . . . What was the secret of More's power over himself? It was, he tells us, the frequent meditation upon the four last things—death, judgment, hell, and heaven, particularly the first of these, since death is the key to the understanding of all the rest. . . . He embodied his most profound and intensive thoughts on this subject in the fragment of an uncompleted work entitled *The Four Last Things*. His duties at Court prevented him from ever getting beyond the first; but it was enough: and what remains is among the most important of his writings.

Robert Hamilton
IER (May, 1941), pp. 452-54

More's treatise [on the *Four Last Things*] seems to belong entirely to that world of thought which conceived the *Vado Mori* poems, the *Memento Mori* verses, pictures, prints, devices, emblems, medals, jewels, rings, and rosaries—More himself, like Erasmus, possessed a *Memento Mori* seal—the *specula hominis*, the moralities of *Everyman*, the many versions of the *Three Living and the Three Dead*, the *Ars Moriendi*, and, most formidable of all, the *Dance of Death*. . . . More lived in the world of Villon and Dunbar: "Timor mortis conturbat me."

H. W. Donner
EM (1952), p. 38

GENERAL

They [More's works] are long: his usual prose has the easy elastic abundance of Boccaccio, and a lawyer's love of proving a point exhaustively in controversy. But he has all the qualities of a great prose style: sonorous eloquence, less cumbersome than Milton: simplicity and lucidity of argument, with unfailing sense of the rhythms and harmonies of English sound. He is a master of Dialogue, the favourite vehicle of that age; neither too curiously dramatic in the *ethopoia* of the persons, nor yet allowing the form to become a hollow convention: the objector in his great *Dialogue* . . . is anything but a man of straw. We can see that if Lucian was his early love, he had not neglected Plato either. Elizabethan prose is tawdry and mannered compared with his: at his death Chaucer's thread is dropped, which none picked up till Clarendon and Dryden. With his colloquial, well-bred, unaffected ease he is the ancestor of Swift. His style—so Erasmus tells us—was gained by long and careful studies and exercises; he took a discipline in Latin of which the fruits were to appear in English when the increasing gravity of the times warned him that it would be well to speak to a larger public than Latin could reach. Even where he is prolix . . . his merry humour is not long silent. For his controversies are enlivened with humorous stories, illustrations and recollections. . . . The man who joked on the scaffold till the very moment when he laid his head on the block . . . was not likely to forget the great truth that wit is another mode of thinking, and piety need not wear a sour face.

J. S. Phillimore
DR (July, 1913), pp. 18-19

As a writer of English prose, More followed now one and now the other of two tendencies. The first of these was a tendency towards an informal easy style which rests directly upon colloquial discourse, and the second towards the use of a structurally elaborated form after the classical tradition. It is characteristic of the experimental stage in which English style found itself in More's day that he developed neither of these tendencies into a consistent and harmonious style of his own. But on the whole his writing stands much closer to colloquial discourse than to the artificially elaborated periods of the classical stylists. For though More was partly driven and did not voluntarily choose to use English in order to oppose a popular movement, he shows his customary wisdom and open-mindedness in his frank acceptance of the native idiom for literary purposes. His range of expression in English is consequently wide. When it suits his purpose he can assume the familiar, even the broadly popular style. And in his more literary moments, he has command over a carefully cultivated and organized form of expression. But even when he is most literary, he is not manneristic. All such tricks of style as alliteration, the use of doublets, of strange and learned words, of ingenious figures of speech, he consistently avoids. His diction is admirably simple and idiomatic and he seems to have felt no difficulty in expressing learned matters in plain English. He rises superior to the naive medieval sentence, with its sprawling members held together by a sprinkling of temporal and coordinating conjunctions, and he does so by giving his sentences body and structure as well as length. But his periodic sentences are not often highly elaborated, and the order of clauses, though not always natural, is seldom stiff or mechanical. The most modern English writer to develop and to maintain a dignified literary style, without being pompous or overcharged with literary mannerism, More shows a much more certain feeling for English expression than any of his learned contemporaries.

[1915]

George P. Krapp
The Rise of English Literary Prose (New York:
Frederick Ungar, 1963), pp. 100-101

The truth seems to be that in writing he cares little what words he uses, whether Romance or Anglo-Saxon, so long as they serve his purpose. He moves amongst words as a master and even a creator. Language is subject to him, not he to it, and at his bidding and magic touch it becomes living, expressive and beautiful. The *History of Richard III,* one of the earliest of his English works, shows what perfection he could have attained had he cared merely for style. . . . Stapleton testifies that he wrote the Latin version to practise his pen, and perhaps we may assume the same for the English. But those early days of comparative leisure were to pass and give place to the busy hurly-burly of controversy. He could not now afford to be a mere stylist or purist, but had to write with a most definite practical aim. His chief concern was no longer fine writing, but clearness, vigor, and persuasiveness.

He was probably the most brilliant English orator of his age and the qualities of the orator are evident in his prose. As the cleverest lawyers of his day he knows how most persuasively to display his arguments and as a keen dialectician he is relentless in his logic. . . . We could best express the truth by the paradox that his books are the spoken rather than the written word. He will not have his meaning mistaken, he is never in a hurry, he is not afraid of repetition if thereby he can impress upon his hearers the strength of his case. Sometimes his sentences run to enormous lengths, but they are so skilfully constructed, so well balanced, so cleverly supported by frequent summaries of what has gone before, that they become quite manageable. From his longest and most involved sentences he emerges triumphantly at the end.

P. E. Hallett
DR (July, 1932), pp. 121-22

It has always been difficult to explain the sudden brilliance of Elizabethan prose and drama: they seemed to have sprung from nowhere, for they could not be traced back on the one hand to such known writers as Pecock, Malory or Berners, each highly individual and of limited range, nor on the other hand, in certain important respects, directly to the mediaeval miracles and moralities. But when More is restored to his place all becomes clear: he is seen not only to fill the gap himself in a remarkable manner as the centre of an important group of writers who are restored with him, but also to bridge it, enabling the lineage of English prose to be traced beyond him into the mediaeval period. Coming at the opening of the modern period, a hundred years after Chaucer and some fifty before Shakespeare, he is an essential link between mediaeval and modern. And in his English writings there is a richness and variety of matter and style that makes the 1557 volume a worthy precursor of all the glories of the seventeenth century.

W. A. G. Doyle-Davidson
ES (April, 1935), p. 53

For in spite of his intense personality, and in spite of his deep affection for those he loved, perhaps even because of these, there is in all the writings of More, in his letters as well as in his books, a certain objectivity, a going out and forgetfulness of himself, which is characteristic of him as it is, it would seem, of no other writer in his own genre. In the *Utopia*, in the *Dialogue of Comfort*, with its outlook on the Europe of his time, in his correspondence and conversations, More is so occupied with the vision before him, and especially with what lies on the distant horizon, that he forgets his own existence; with the result that, perhaps, excepting Shakespeare, no writer in the English language has more unconsciously, and therefore more truly, described himself.

Alban Goodier
Month (August, 1938), p. 109

Writing racy English for the larger audience, More tolerated the looser aggregative habit of English prose in his time. But his English, as well as his Latin, shows clear grasp of the period, and even occasional strict conformity. Current English still lagged in this respect throughout the century. Before Hooker English prose is generally less controlled than Italian. On the other hand, More uses balance and epigram discreetly, not for decorative display, but strictly for point; and his shifting from longer aggregations to sharp short sentences gives pleasant variety.

Charles Sears Baldwin
Renaissance Literary Theory and Practice (New York:
Columbia Univ. Pr., 1939), p. 220

What it means to have St. Thomas More as one of the great figures in the literature of the English language has not been sufficiently emphasized. . . . He teaches us that an admirable style and literary enthusiasm may be combined with a profound Catholicity. In him, literature is freed from all dilettantism. . . . And St. Thomas More discovers to the literary man the great secret of their mutual art; a cause to which one can unreservedly dedicate oneself. And to all who would make literature an exclusively aesthetic preoccupation . . . St. Thomas More stands as a warning and a reproach. For in his writings, all of man's powers conspire to create a living entity that reflects the multiple interests and potencies of its creator.

Gerald Kerman
Thought (June, 1942), p. 301

. . . It is impossible to do justice to the leading issues of to-day—Nationalism, Church and State, Patriotism and International Unity, Secular and Sacred—without giving close attention to what More said and did. His figure grows in stature as the relevance of his principles to present-day controversies becomes increasingly apparent.

F. Brompton Harvey
Church, State and Letters (London: Epworth Pr., 1943), p. 122

More is the presiding genius of the mediaeval comic spirit in the early English Renaissance. His writings often show a wise love of folly. We find in them a defence of what he calls "fond chyldyshe tales" and a declaration that he thinks "no tale so foolishe, but that yet in one matter or other to some purpose it may hap to serve." He kept a household fool. . . . He furthered the cause of comedy, both in life and on the stage. He handled the difficulties of life with never-failing humor. And because his soul was at peace, he met his martyr's death in a spirit of grim Gothic foolery. . . . More's comic spirit is comparable to that found in sincerely religious moral plays of his period, plays such as he loved. It is of finer grain but it is of the same order. Because it is of that order, it seems sometimes to be incompatible with seriousness and yet is happily married to seriousness. We may take *The Praise of Folly*, over the writing of which More's spirit may be said to have presided, as giving perhaps the best insight into the religious accompaniment of More's genius. Its sentences on God's love of foolishness makes us think of the saint who loved foolishness, and loved it wisely, St. Thomas More.

Willard Farnham
"The Mediaeval Comic Spirit in the English Renaissance,"
Joseph Quincy Adams Memorial Studies, eds. James McManaway,
Giles E. Dawson and Edwin E. Willoughby (Washington, D. C.:
Folger Memorial Library, 1948), p. 431

Great claims have in modern times been made for More's English prose; I can accept them only with serious reservations. . . . The man who sits down and reads fairly through fifty pages of More will find many phrases to admire; but he will also find an invertebrate length of sentence, a fumbling multiplication of epithets, and an almost complete lack of rhythmical vitality. The length of sentence in More is quite different from the fullness of impassioned writers like Cicero or Burke or Ruskin, or from that of close thinkers like Hooker or Coleridge. It is not even the winning garrulity of Montaigne, or not often. Its chief cause is the fact that More never really rose from a legal to a literary conception of clarity and completeness. He multiplies words in a vain endeavor to stop up all possible chinks, where a better artist forces his conceptions upon us by the light and heat of intellect and emotion in which they burn. He thus loses the advantages both of full writing and of concise writing. There are no lightning thrusts; and, on the other hand, no swelling tide of thought and feeling. The style is stodgy and dough-like. As for the good phrases, the reader will already have divined their nature. They come when More is in his homeliest vein: their race and pith and mere Englishry are the great redeeming feature of his prose. They ring in our ears like echoes of the London lanes and Kentish villages. . . . They belong to the same world as his merry tales. Nearly all that is best in More is comic or close to comedy.

C. S. Lewis
English Literature in the Sixteenth Century
(Oxford: Clarendon Pr., 1954), p. 180

More's claims to distinction are very various. He was a member of that earliest group of Greek scholars, with whom English humanism begins. He was High Steward of Oxford and Cambridge, an educational pioneer, particularly enthusiastic about the education of women. As a writer of English prose, his position is specially important. It was not till long after his day that anyone could rival his mastery of many different types of English: dramatic dialogue and rhetorical monologue, narrative and argument combined in a style at once scholarly and colloquial. More's *History of Richard III* remained a pattern of historical writing unequalled for a century. His death as a martyr "for the faith of the Catholic Church" was at the same time a protest against the claim of the civil power to dictate religious belief, and should make him the hero of all who care for religious liberty. For over twenty years he exercised important judicial functions of different kinds, and it was his promptitude and incorruptibility as a judge that most impressed his countrymen. It is as "the best friend that the poor e'er had" that his fellow Londoners remembered him, in the old play of *Sir Thomas More*. Swift had learnt from *Utopia* many of the things which make *Gulliver's Travels* remarkable, and he repaid his teacher by giving him the magnificent testimonial, of being the person "of the greatest virtue this kingdom ever produced."

R. W. Chambers
"Sir Thomas More," *The Great Tudors*, ed. K. Garvin
(London: Eyre and Spottiswoode, 1956), pp. 81-82

JOHN SKELTON

ca. 1460-1529

John Skelton, Tudor poet and satirist, was born probably in Norfolk and educated at Cambridge. He was employed by Henry VII as court poet and tutor to Prince Henry. In 1498 he took Holy Orders and held the rectorship of Diss, Norfolk, from about 1503-1504 until his death. He remained in residence at Diss, however, only until about 1512, when he returned to court, describing himself as *orator regius*. Cambridge, Oxford, and Louvain Universities honored him with laureation. He wrote *The Bowge of Court* (1498), *Speke, Parrot* (1521), *Colyn Cloute* (1522), *Why come ye nat to courte?* (1522-1523), all satires directed against the court or clergy, particularly Cardinal Wolsey, *Magnyfycence* (1516), a morality play, *The Tunnyng of Elynour Rummyng* (1508), a description of an ale-wife and her friends, *The Garlande of Laurell* (1523) in praise of himself, *The Boke of Phyllp Sparowe* (1508), a delightful mock elegy on the death of a pet sparrow, and other short miscellaneous pieces. He was highly esteemed by his contemporaries as a scholar as well as a poet. His extant translation of Diodorus Siculus' *Bibliotheca Historica* and his moral treatise, *Speculum Principis*, may provide a measure of his classical learning.

A. Dyce, ed., *The Poetical Works of John Skelton* (1843), 2 vols.

R. L. Ramsay, ed., *Magnyfycence* (1908)

F. M. Salter and H. L. R. Edwards, eds., *The Bibliotheca Historica of Diodorus Siculus,* translated by John Skelton (1956-1957), 2 vols.

H. L. R. Edwards, *Skelton* (1949)

PERSONAL

Skelton was almost the last classically educated English poet who could forget his classics when looking at the countryside and not see Margery Milke-Ducke as Phyllis and Jolly Jacke as Corydon, or find "behind every bush a thrumming Apollo" (John Clare's criticism of Keats).

Robert Graves
The Common Asphodel (London: Hamish Hamilton, 1949), p. 255

Of his poetry I have given some typical samples, and you will agree that he is entertaining and not quite like anyone else, that he has a feeling for rhythm, and a copious vocabulary. Sometimes—but not often—he is tender and charming, occasionally he is devout and very occasionally he is wise. On the whole he's a comic—a proper comic, with a love for improper fun, and a talent for abuse. He says of himself in one of his Latin verses, that he sings the material of laughter in a harsh voice, and the description is apt; the harshness is often more obvious than the laughter, and leaves us with a buzzing in the ears rather than with a smile on the face. Such a row! Such a lot of complaints! He has indeed our national fondness for grumbling—the government, the country, agriculture, the world, the beer, they are none of them what they ought to be or have been. And although we must not affix our dry little political labels to the fluidity of the past (there is nothing to tie them on to), it is nevertheless safe to say that temperamentally the Rector of Diss was a conservative.

E. M. Forster
Two Cheers for Democracy (New York: Harcourt, Brace and World, 1951), p. 152

Skelton does not know the peculiar powers and limitations of his own manner, and does not reserve it, as an artist would have done, for treating immature or disorganized states of consciousness. When he happens to apply it to such states, we may get delightful poetry: when to others, verbiage. There is no building in his work, no planning, no reason why any piece should stop just where it does (sometimes his repeated envoys make us wonder if it is going to stop at all), and no kind of assurance that any of his poems is exactly the poem he intends to write. Hence his intimacy. He is always in undress. Hence his charm, the charm of the really gifted amateur (a very different person from the hard working inferior artist). . . . He has no real predecessors and no important disciples; he stands out of the streamy historical process, an unmistakable individual, a man we have met.

C. S. Lewis
English Literature in the Sixteenth Century
(Oxford: Clarendon Pr., 1954), pp. 142-43

Energy, wit, originality, individualism; a mastery of vernacular idiom and rhythm; a capacity for direct observation which resembles that of a Dutch Old Master—every quality, in fact, most directly at variance with the general trend of his age, and remarkable at any period—these are what we associate with Skelton. He is, moreover, an eccentric in the great English tradition, a figure of prickly and paradoxical humours who would have appealed strongly to G. K. Chesterton. There are few characters from the Early Tudor Age of Austerity who come across to us with more immediate impact. Skelton stalks through his own pages with egotistical panache, flaunting his laureate's robe. . . . , quarrelling, laughing, swearing, blasphemously devout, a master of polyglot abuse and political allegory, equally at home in an alehouse, a country rectory, or the King's Court.

Peter Green
John Skelton (London: BC/Longmans, 1960), p. 7

GENERAL

His poetic production shows an extraordinary variety. He moves with ease, sometimes even with mastership, in all the traditional forms of poetry. In his longer poems he is very original, particularly where he uses his characteristic style, the short "breathless rimes," not unknown before him, but never used so largely and effectively as by him. Sometimes they literally chase along, and the reader is carried away by them. . . . Lack of constructive power often spoils the impression of Skelton's poems; but this deficiency is made up for in many cases by an immense vivacity and by the originality of the ideas. His satires against the clergy in general, and, particularly, those against Wolsey, are remarkable for their boldness. Of all the poetical successors of Chaucer in England Skelton is by far the most original.

A. Koelbing
"Barclay and Skelton. Early German Influences on English
Literature," *CHEL*, vol. III (1908), pp. 78-79

This double tradition [learned and popular] which Skelton followed reveals the twofold sources of his eloquence. On the one side he cultivated the new style with its ornate and aureate diction, tending in verse towards a regular numbered meter and in prose towards a clearly defined sentence structure; and on the other, he followed the old native tradition of a free alliterative long line, easily passing into a loose prose, and already in *Piers Plowman* used for bombastic and magniloquent effects, which on Skelton, under the impulse of an unrestrained vatic enthusiasm, cross the bounds of eloquence into rant and even nonsense. There can be no doubt that Skelton was seriously seeking in both of these directions for a method by which he could attain to a high style. He felt keenly the two tendencies of English expression in his day. As a scholar and a courtier, he was naturally attracted by the polished terms of the courtly aureate style. As *regius orator* and as plain speaker, he doubtless felt an equal admiration for the exuberant and ornamental popular style, which he must have known not only as a literary tradition, but also from the dithyrambic oratory of some of his eloquent contemporaries. For the popular style was never without its representatives. The pulpit kept it alive, and its influence always ran parallel to that of the classic ideals and models of eloquence. [1915]

George P. Krapp
The Rise of English Literary Prose (New York:
Frederick Ungar, 1963), pp. 284-85

The weak stomach will be turned by it [*Elynour Rummyng*]: but those with a gizzard for strong meat will find it a remarkable piece. I do not speak of it as a precursor of the "realistic" school of poetry: it is more valuable than that. It is the processional manipulation of vivid impressions, the orchestration, the mental rhythm which strikes me. So far from calling it a realistic poem, I would call it one of the few really abstract poems in the language. Its esthetic effect is that of a *good* cubist picture (or any picture dependent on form for its value).

Richard Hughes, ed.
Poems by John Skelton (London: William Heinemann, 1924), p. xiv

His style shows in the same way the lack of balance in his nature. He resorts to mystifications and to jargon as did the decadent grammarians of the late Roman time, or as did a gallic spirit restless as his, but finer than his— François Villon. He pours out lists longer than those of Lydgate, whole catalogues of Greek myths and Latin authors; and these he intermingles with homely proverbs and with colloquialisms. Everything is in excess; he cannot call Wolsey or Garnesche names without emptying the dictionary of thieves' lingo; and he hurls opprobious epithets without pause or choice of weapon. Never is there in his work what Elton terms the "precision of insult" attained by the Roman or by the eighteenth-century English satirist. Skelton aims not at clarity but at speed, not at form but at fluency; and the race of his metre, the rattle of his epithets and allusions, suit the narrowly personal and occasional character of his work. But that a temperament has run away with an intellect we may judge from his University honors, from the praise of Caxton and of Erasmus, and from a very few words of his own. It was no incompetent literary critic who said of Chaucer that "no word he wrote in vain," and of Lydgate that "it is diffuse to find the sentence of his mind."

E. P. Hammond
English Verse Between Chaucer and Surrey (Durham, N. C.:
Duke Univ. Pr., 1927), p. 339

. . . There is in Skelton's skimble-skamble that peculiar elfin quality which belongs to the highest romantic genius. In the individual intensity of this fantasy, as of his rough-and-tumble satire and of his descriptive passages generally, there is small scope for tradition. Indeed his work is almost a conscious protest against the old; or rather it is anarchical, for he has not, and does not care to have, any new poetic to take its place. The most tangible expression of his rebellion is in the verse form.

G. Gregory Smith
The Transition Period (Edinburgh and London:
William Blackwood and Sons, 1927), p. 29

It is little wonder that "beastly" Skelton presented such a problem to later ages which had little knowledge of the literary tradition behind him. We now recognize that the convention in which he works is not new, but is to be found in the monkish tradition. His very characteristic line is the short line of mediaeval Latin poetry. His manner is essentially the manner of the satirical monk or priestly writer, with its inveterate tendency to Scriptural burlesque. So ingrained was the habit that we should not perhaps take it for burlesque at all, any more than the kindred trick of dropping out of English into Latin, and assembling all the fantastic odds and ends of language in one long breath.

George Kitchin
A Survey of Burlesque and Parody in English (Edinburgh:
Oliver and Boyd, 1931), pp. 31-32

As a literary artist, it is difficult to escape the conclusion that Skelton is an oddity, like Blake, who cannot be really fitted into literary history as an inevitable product of the fifteenth century. There is every reason for the existence of Hawes or even Barclay as the moribund end of the Chaucerian tradition; it is comparatively easy to understand Elizabethan poetry as a fusion of the Italian Renaissance and native folk elements; but the vigour and character of Skelton's work remains unpredictable.

Indeed, the tempo of Skelton's verse is consistently quicker than that of any other English poet; only the author of *Hudibras*, and in recent times Vachel Lindsay, come anywhere near him in this respect.

All Skelton's work has this physical appeal. Other poets, such as Spenser and Swinburne, have been no more dependent upon ideas, but they have touched only one sense, the auditory. The Catherine-wheel motion of Skelton's verse is exciting in itself, but his language is never vaguely emotive. Indeed, it is deficient in overtones, but is always precise, both visually and tactually.

If we accept, and I think we must, a distinction between the visionary and the entertainer, the first being one who extends our knowledge of, insight into, and power of control over human conduct and emotion, without whom our understanding would be so much the poorer, Skelton is definitely among the entertainers. He is not one of the indispensables, but among entertainers —and how few are the indispensables—he takes a high place.

W. H. Auden

"John Skelton," *The Great Tudors*, ed. K. Garvin (London: Ivor Nicholson and Katson, 1935), pp. 58, 62, 66-67

Looking back over the long range of his work, one is bound to admit that he never entered the promised land, though at times he obtained something of a Pisgah-sight of it. His work is full of unmistakable sign-posts: his poetry, filling to overflowing its mediaeval channels, strays here and there into fascinating rivulets which soon peter out among the sands. Skelton never rises far above tradition, but for all that he had done with it. At last a poet had arisen who could squeeze out its juice to the very last drop. That he was content with that is his misfortune and our own, yet it would be ungrateful to wish him elsewhere, in more fortunate times. He has a solid achievement of his own to stand upon, and criticism will dig a pit for itself if it ventures to border on the patronizing.

L. J. Lloyd

John Skelton (Oxford: Basil Blackwell, 1938), pp. 138-39

... Both beauty and subtlety are incidental, are perhaps even accidental in Skelton's poems. They are by-products. Of what? It is hard to put it precisely. Anyone reading Skelton can see just what he was aiming at, but the proper word for it, the exact, just phrase is, somehow, elusive. Fun, satire, energy? Energy is perhaps nearest it. There is fun, it is true; Skelton has an astonishing eye, an astonishing gusto. But the scenes he chooses are often not intrinsically funny. It is rather that he deliberately makes them funny, that he sustains the reader's amusement with his own energy of vision. ... This ability, then, to make one laugh at anything is not so much the character of a humorist as of an orator; it is a way not of increasing perception, but of exerting power.

G. S. Fraser
Adel. (December, 1936), pp. 158-59

Skelton is between two ages, and a genuine love of learning like that of the older continental humanists struggles with only partial success against a distrust of the newer philosophies and the religious difficulties they involved. On the one side is his classical reading, differing little from that of the pupils of Guarino; the testimony of Erasmus; his retention—in company with the more conservative English and Italian humanists—of the older "solid" education; his confessed admiration for "humanyte." On the other is his blindness to Italy and perhaps his lack of enthusiasm for Greek. Cutting across these lines and confusing the issue are his private hatreds, of Wolsey, of Lily, of Lutherans, of all desecrators of the Church. As he grew older his prejudices hardened and his hatreds grew fiercer, till it becomes increasingly difficult in the criss-cross of "humanyte" and mediaevalism to form a clear conception of where Skelton stood. Faced with the question of whether he was a humanist, he might be tempted to reply that he had always loved "fresh Humanyte." Presented with a curriculum from the school at Ferrara, he would have given it his complete approval, with the caution that so much Greek must not interfere with the pupils groundwork in grammar and rhetoric. But when he thought of his arch-enemy Wolsey endowing a college for the new learning and founding a chair of Greek, of Bilney misled by the Protestant-Humanism from Germany, he would have forgotten all the attractions of the new study and damned it outright. There, too, lies the danger for the modern critic of Skelton—one cannot be any more certain of his attitudes than he was himself. Humanism is not a tag which can be tied to one group of scholars and denied to another. It was a developing doctrine of surprising latitude. Skelton stands with one foot over its boundary.

Ivan A. Gordon
John Skelton (Melbourne and London:
Melbourne Univ. Pr., 1943), pp. 100-101

"Doggerel" his ragged rhymes may be, and ribald they often are; but they are alive. Skelton is looking at life, not at books and dead conventions. There is real passion in his onslaught on Wolsey in *Why come Ye not to Court?* and real tenderness as well as buffoonery in *Philip Sparrow.* Even the ink-horn terms in which, like Hawes and Barclay, he indulges, show that learning has revived in England. The sap is rising again: the Renaissance is in sight.

Herbert J. C. Grierson and J. C. Smith
A Critical History of English Poetry (London:
Chatto and Windus, 1944), p. 50

Skelton's belief in poets as the first priests, his reverence for poetry as an independent science, his belief in the Platonic theory of inspiration, his estimate of the function of satire, and his interest in, and dicta concerning matters of poetic technique, clearly rank him with the humanists. That his philosophy should contain mediaeval elements, and his practice be burdened with mediaeval motifs and stylisms might be expected; for in the days of the early humanists, new techniques had not yet been found, and the next hundred years saw only bitterness on that subject. Skelton was not the man to work out a technique equal to the glory of Renaissance thought, but, as far as he did reach, holding largely to the forms and motifs he inherited, he grasped. Further, one of the strongest characteristics of humanists, both early and late, was their interest not only in Greek, but in the vernacular. To all the humanists of England, the English language was brutish, barbarous, or unpolished; and with one accord they set about enriching it. Moreover, they did enrich it; and, in spite of such abuses as might derive from excessive zeal . . . or as might inspire a mid-century reaction against ink-horn terms, they succeeded in creating a medium worthy of Shakespeare and Milton.

In his translation of Diodorus in 1485, Skelton uses upwards of *eight hundred words*, ten, twenty, fifty, a hundred, and even three hundred (and more) years earlier than the first dates recorded for these words, or for individual senses of them by the *NED* [*New English Dictionary,* Oxford Univ. Pr.]. For hundreds of other words, *NED* already credits Skelton with the first use in English. . . . Where there are so many, it is reasonable to suppose that Skelton did actually invent some of the words which Elyot and others used after him. And it is reasonable to suppose that when he fusses with a word, underlines it, or supplies an alternative, the term is in his opinion new or uncommon. Further, whatever anyone may think of the claim of this rude, rough, railing poet to be called a humanist, in enriching the English language he certainly acted like one.

F. M. Salter
PTRSC (May, 1945), pp. 120, 122-23

Skelton was neither a humanist nor a dunce—though most humanists, I fear, would have dubbed him the latter; he was a man of the Renaissance. In type, he stands beside the Renaissance lords of the vernacular. His sense of kinship with the Roman poets gives him the same Cellinesque swagger. He has the same devotion to his mother-tongue. Even his feuds are an Italian fashion. In all his work he reveals the budding national pride from which Christendom was to blossom violently into a new Europe. And in his devotion to the things of this world, in his healthy robustness of perception, in his independence, in his satirist's clearsightedness—in his very vulgarity, he expresses the English counterpart of the earthly, Catholic paganism of the High Renaissance.

H. L. R. Edwards
Skelton (London: Jonathan Cape, 1949), p. 23

At their best, then, Skelton's lyrics have dropped the generalization from a place of prime importance. In its place appears an interest in getting the details of characterization and of experience. These details are expressed, not through a close analysis of the elements or through means of an extended metaphor, but through almost a riot of images which seem to have little connection or co-ordination but each of which expresses some facet of the experience; and by the accumulation of such facets a rounded, full communication of the experience is occasionally attained.

Alan Swallow
PQ (January, 1953), p. 41

As with Dunbar again, the secret lies partly in the amplitude of the abuse, in keeping it up so long, in simply holding the floor; the abuse pours out in a torrent, sweeping the derided object away with it and submerging all distinction. It is, of course, mainly a matter of vocabulary with Skelton, but the rapid tumbling metre and the clattering rhyme reinforce the ribald effect.

James Sutherland
English Satire (Cambridge Univ. Pr., 1958), pp. 28-29

I have not seen any explicit recognition of how much Skelton's work owes to proverbial language, and in doing so, to the whole way of life and cast of mind which finds its expression in proverbial language. . . . His verse draws on the proverbial kind of expression for a good deal of its vivid metaphorical wealth, and for something of its whole attitude toward its subject—bold yet unassuming, essentially down-to-earth. It uses the clichés of ordinary people (which are not clichés at all, because instead of making the mind gloss over the plain facts, they bring it abruptly up against them) but it is using these in order to assimilate the whole idea which ordinary people form of reality. To notice Skelton's reliance on the proverbial expression is not to notice a literary trick or a literary routine, but to notice, at its most easily recognizable point, the essential quality of what was creative in his mind.

What Henry James called "felt life" seems to operate in the texture of his language with a quite special freedom and directness; and when that language moves, as it often does, beyond plain speech, it moves . . . less toward wit and argumentation, than toward the proverbial gnomic solemnity of the traditional and popular mind. The result is no mere mirror of life, no mere Skeltonic realism, but something of an embodiment of life's permanent contours and essential vitality. Much may be absent from Skelton, but this, with the deep refreshment which it brings, is not absent.

John Holloway
The Charted Mirror (London: Routledge
and Kegan Paul, 1960), pp. 17, 23-24

We can now begin to appreciate Skelton's response to literary traditions. Having completely accepted in *Bowge of Court* the conventional object of anti-court satire, he could have been expected to accept also the compact set of techniques conventionally hurled against it. He could have written a letter to a relative or friend, warning him wittily and explicitly of evils of the court. But such a letter would have been old-fashioned; it would have challenged neither the skill of the poet nor the wit of the reader. So Skelton chose the oldest of devices, the allegorical dream-vision, and used it to compose the freshest of satires. And nearly two decades later, in attacking the weak king, and his foolish use of counsel and wealth, Skelton chose not to write another *speculum principis,* nor even another *Regement of Princes;* once more he blended hackneyed object with hackneyed techniques to concoct an unprecedented mixture of great satiric power.

We must note very carefully one characteristic of Skelton's mixtures. Their ingredients come from two sources. The objects attacked by both *Bowge of Court* and *Magnyfycence* derive principally from *rhetorical* works in which arguments—along with the whole panoply of allusions, "colours," exempla—support explicit warnings, chastisements, complaints; but no works wholly devoted to attacking precisely these objects had yet appeared in which arguments were themselves actions, in which didactic goals were achieved wholly by means of fictions. Furthermore, these fictions derive from conventions not heretofore used as the principal means of attacking these particular objects. As a result of combining these elements, the poet can conclude *Bowge of Court* by denying any rhetorical intention; he can rely completely on his fiction, eschewing any explicit condemnation of his object. On the other hand, the chorus which ends *Magnyfycence* is far more direct, more "rhetorical," because the conventions of the morality play provided the author with characters whose function was to enunciate the meaning of the work.

A. R. Heiserman
Skelton and Satire (Chicago: Univ. Chicago Pr., 1961), pp. 126-27

JOHN WYCLIF

ca. 1330-1384

John Wyclif, philosopher, theologian, and reformer, was educated at Oxford University. He became Master of Balliol College in 1360. He held the rectorships of Fillingham (1361-1368), Ludgershall (1368-1384), and Lutterworth (1374-1384), quite apart from other canonries and prebends, while he was still for the most part teaching and lecturing at Oxford. In 1371 he entered the royal service and was a member of the delegation which went to Bruges in 1374 to confer with Pope Gregory XI's legates concerning the Statute of Provisors. His loud cries for reform and his bold views on civil and ecclesiastical dominion together with his eucharistic doctrines alarmed the clergy, and he was accused of heresy in 1377-1378 and again in 1382, when his teaching was finally condemned as either heretical or erroneous. He retired to Lutterworth, and died there of a paralytic stroke on December 28, 1384. His influence on Reformation thinkers, particularly John Hus, is marked, and he must be credited with inspiring the first translation of the Bible into English (after 1378). His printed works on philosophy and theology in Latin and English run to over forty volumes; many other writings remain in manuscript.

H. E. Winn, ed., *John Wyclif, Select English Writings* (1929)

H. B. Workman, *John Wyclif* (1926) 2 vols.

PERSONAL

He controverted every doctrine he considered mistaken, and advocated every doctrine he considered true, not so much for the sake of the doctrine itself as for the sake of the doctrine's effect upon the spiritual condition of those who held it. He had, one may venture to assert, a higher interest than even the interest of Truth.

Henry W. Clark
History of English Nonconformity, vol. I (London:
Chapman and Hall, 1911), p. 67

The old-fashioned, popular, idea of Wycliffe as an early John Wesley, primarily concerned to promote the evangelisation of the masses, gives a very false idea of his activities. Wycliffe was primarily a university professor, with far more affinities in character and ability to Peter Abelard, than to John Wesley or Peter Waldo. The predominant powers in his personality were intellectual, not spiritual: and it is curious that one in whom the intellectual side so predominated—one, for instance, who wrote a treatise on the true nature of prayer and made it consist solely in a completely moral life—should have kindled the genuine religious flame which burnt for a generation in Lollardy. It is curious both that one who was so much a scholar and so little a saint should have inspired men willing to be burnt for their faith, and that his followers should have lost so soon and so completely his guarded sense of intellectual balance.

Margaret Deanesly
The Lollard Bible (Cambridge Univ. Pr., 1920), pp. 225-26

Wyclif's personal character was beyond the reproach even of his enemies. His intense moral earnestness is evident on every page. On his own confession he was passionate, and like other passionate men often failed to maintain a due balance in speech and thought, in spite of a severe intellectual outlook and training. But to this same note of passion we owe the forceful, nervous style of his English writings, which entitles him to a high place among our early authors. Of an indomitable will-power which defied sickness and difficulty there can be no question. That Wyclif was built for battle may be conceded, nor was he careful to count the number or quality of his foes. In the fearlessness of his courage he is the equal of Luther, without, however, Luther's supreme opportunity at Worms. In the higher moral courage he was the superior of Luther; Wyclif would never have consented to the pitiable condonation of Philip of Hesse. He lacked, however, Luther's warm emotions. His humour is rare and generally acid. . . . Poetry, music, singing, architecture made no appeal to him. But for the downtrodden, the serf, and the poor his sympathies were unbounded, and well out in the midst of arid, scholastic reasoning. Probably, it is true, they were impersonal sympathies, bitterness against wrong in the abstract rather than sorrow for one of the wronged. Wyclif would have wept over Jerusalem, but could never have gone into the wilderness to find the one lost sheep. Owing to his identification of being and knowing, the poignant sense of individual transgression is lacking. The man of to-day may laugh at Luther's struggles with a personal devil; but one secret of the success of Luther lay in his consciousness of the reality of sin, just as one secret of the failure of Wyclif lay in his doctrine that sin is but a negation—"that it has no idea." Thus in the earnestness of his life he stood almost alone, for the interest of others in reform was too often that of politics and greed. Hence the failure of his proposed reformation inasmuch as it was little more than an external movement, with suitable environment for the spread and development of his ideas. Wyclif was a mighty, but isolated force; the Reformation, on the contrary, formed part of a movement larger than itself.

Herbert B. Workman
John Wyclif, vol. II (Oxford: Clarendon Pr., 1926), pp. 321-23

While Wyclif was philosophically a realist, temperamentally he was an individualist. Without violating his realism, he might have come down to earth and given us a doctrine of an ideal visible church as a spiritual body, corresponding to Calvin's classical treatment of the Church catholic. With a more than Calvinist emphasis on the church predestinate and invisible, he falls into almost unrelieved individualism in his references to the church on earth. Each man's salvation is a concern merely of God and his own soul. If emphasis is put upon the priesthood of the laity, it is often mainly to weaken the claims of the priesthood of the clergy, and with no discoverable content of spiritual responsibility or social solidarity.

John Thomas McNeill
JR (July, 1927), p. 463

Calamitous as were the efforts of Wycliffe as a practical reformer, his life and teaching yet deserve at least as much study as they have received. Whatever mistakes he made as a political strategist, he still remains one of the most remarkable figures of his age. His vitality and the fearlessness of his thought—the very qualities which interfered with his success in action

—shine beneath the dust and tarnish of nearly six centuries. Time has reduced most of his great contemporaries to vague, scarcely discernible shapes; Wycliffe, inspite of the enormous gaps in the evidence, lives, if as a force more than as a man.

K. B. McFarlane
John Wycliffe and the Beginnings of English Nonconformity
(London: English Universities Pr., 1952), p. 188

GENERAL

Neither in style nor in power . . . have his English works any special note of distinction. The style of his sermons ranks higher than the early version of the New Testament, commonly ascribed to him, and it would not be surprising to find that, like many other medieval works, they had undergone some revision by a faithful disciple. In these English works there is a strange mingling of simple directness and ruggedness; their true significance lies in their instinctive feeling for their large audience. Wyclif had proved his power over an academic world, democratic in itself, and so he easily passed to a more democratic public still. . . .

J. P. Whitney
"Religious Movements in the Fourteenth Century,"
CHEL, vol. II (1908), p. 66

To call him [Wyclif] "the first writer of English prose" is merely an unconscious aposiopesis, and an equally unconscious confession of ignorance. If there be added to it, "of whom the writer or speaker ever heard," it might, no doubt, be admitted *pro tanto*. The tracts attributed to, and certainly in some cases written by, Wyclif show, as one *might* expect, a certain advance in facility of handling, and, as one *would* expect, a certain greater advance still in violence. All bad language has a positive tendency to vivacity, though also to monotony. I do not know whether any German or English "enumerator" has ever counted the number of times the word "cursed" occurs in Wyclif's tracts. And the abundance, enthusiasm, and popularity of Wyclif's wandering preachers must have done something for our speech. But "father of English prose" is, as applied to him, one of the silliest of these usually silly expressions, and is perhaps most frequent in the mouths of those who also consider him—and perhaps really mean by it—"father of English Protestantism."

George Saintsbury
A History of English Prose Rhythm
(London: Macmillan, 1922), p. 58

He has been justly and appropriately called a master pamphleteer. He would have made a first-class journalist. He had all the qualities of both. His writings abound in the sort of rough-and-ready but striking statements that catch the public eye and attract the necessary attention.

He was a master of *argumentum ad hominem*. He made ready use of the spice of irony and sarcasm. He had a vigorous opinion on every subject of the day and his output and industry were enormous. It would be unfair to expect him to be in addition both profound and precise as we must expect of a theologian and philosopher. No one expects the pamphleteer or the journalist to be either. If, once they have achieved their object, they take the edge off their early outbursts, they are to be commended rather than blamed. It required an honest and courageous mind to do that. John Wycliffe had both.

George C. Heseltine
Great Yorkshiremen (London and New York:
Longmans, Green, 1932), p. 227

The work of Wyclif cannot be squeezed into a single formula. No sect or school remained in England to embody his influence with completeness; it was in another country that they were to find the fullest expression and by the death of another man that they were to receive the seal of martyrdom. In most of his thought Wyclif was a typical scholar of the fourteenth century. His erudition and his manner of using it, his knowledge of the Bible, of the Fathers, of the great schoolmen of the West, mark him as a late schoolman with the defects and the qualities of a later schoolman. Though he deplored the dominant tendencies of theological thought since St. Thomas, he combated his opponents with their own weapons, and never showed more relish for his work than when he piled subtlety on subtlety and refinement on refinement. There were contemporary thinkers with whom he was in sympathy: to Bradwardine and Fitzralph in particular he directly acknowledged his debt. But his master was St. Augustine. "John, sone of Augustine" his disciples called him; and his references to St. Augustine not only far outnumber his references to any other writer, they give a faithful indication of the source from which he drew the essentials of his interpretation of Christianity. . . . The prevailing quality of Wyclif's mind is often said to be rationalism. This is true if by rationalism is meant not a reliance on reason to the disparagement of faith, but a reassertion of the reasonableness of the Christian faith. Wyclif tried to rescue the orthodox from a combination of intellectual scepticism with unreasoning acceptance of ecclesiastical authority, by a return to the older opinion that, in so far as they touch, faith and reason support each other. Like most rebels, therefore, Wyclif conceived that he was calling for the return to a healthier outlook of an earlier age. In the dissolution of St. Thomas' synthesis of reason, the Bible, and Church custom and belief, Wyclif does not fall back on ecclesiastical authority. He proposes to reestablish equilibrium by the more arduous method of adjusting Church custom and belief so as to agree with a reasoned interpretation of the Bible, for the Bible is the most authoritative statement of God's law.

Bernard L. Manning
"Wyclif," *Cambridge Medieval History*, vol. VII (1932), pp. 505-6

Wyclif was one who united high abstract speculation with practical experience, and could see where theory and rule of thumb agreed; one whose doctrines had grown out of his environment, and who therefore revealed to the Englishmen of his time the hitherto only half-conscious needs of their environment. His weakest point, perhaps, was that asperity which he himself confessed publicly with regret. . . . But this Englishman was the first man of outstanding talents, learning, and moral character who saw straight into the practical solution of the problem. He realized, as some at least of those others would probably have realized if they had lived on into those days when hopes deferred had made the heart sick, that the hierarchy was essentially incapable of reforming itself, and that the pressure must come from without; from the laity, in some form or other.

G. G. Coulton
Medieval Panorama (Cambridge Univ. Pr.;
New York: Macmillan, 1938), pp. 489-90

. . . In his Latin *Sermones*, collected probably in retirement during the last five years of his life, he set forth his ideas on the art of preaching, and, indirectly, of prose-writing in general . . . his teaching represents an important contribution, not only to homiletics, but to critical theory as well. He is dealing, it is true, with spoken, as opposed to written, language; but his basic principles are applicable to all forms of prose composition; and they constitute an epoch-making departure in the development of English prose theory. Now for the first time a direct attack was being made on the false rhetoric cherished throughout the Middle Ages. . . . That system, originally inspired by the New Sophistic of post-classical times, had embodied much that ran counter to classical tradition and good taste; and Wyclif, with characteristic energy, challenges the whole position. In so doing he was doubtless animated by the promptings of his own native genius. But probably he drew inspiration also from Augustine's *De Doctina Christiana* . . . in which an attempt had been made to counter Sophistic in its earlier stages by adapting the teaching of Cicero. Faced with the same problem Wyclif puts forward the same fundamental doctrines, shorn however of their details and their systematic form. And in his insistence on the need for plain and simple utterance in accordance with both speaker and hearer, as well as on the avoidance of all artificial emotional devices whether rhetorical or rhythmical, he was essentially at one with Aristotle in his opposition to Gorgianic prose, when the latter declared clearness and propriety to be the two fundamental virtues of good speaking and writing. In this way did Wyclif unconsciously revive in England certain elements of the teaching of classical antiquity of permanent value. Incidentally he also distinguished between the principles of composition in poetry and prose, a service no less valuable at this particular date. Notable as was his achievement, however, his immediate influence was but slight. . . . Yet he had accomplished work of lasting importance; he had revealed the secret of all good prose, and the foundations on which later masters of English were to build.

J. W. H. Atkins
English Literary Criticism: The Medieval Phase (Cambridge
Univ. Pr.; New York: Macmillan, 1943), pp. 149-51

Wyclif was . . . essentially a critic and satirist, lashing out at the abuses which were so obvious to him. But to counteract the evils of the day he made two positive contributions. Conscious of the ignorance of the laity, ground down by tyrannical priests, he conceived the idea of translating the Bible into English in order that the ordinary literate layman might himself study the Scriptures and form his own judgments. Assisted by some of his followers. . . , the whole Bible was translated into English during the last few years of Wyclif's life, and copies soon began to circulate. This stupendous task, carried out in the teeth of considerable opposition and danger, represents Wyclif's greatest work for the Church. His other positive contribution was the assembling together of a body of disciples and enthusiasts who were prepared to go about the country, as the early friars had done, preaching the Gospel to all men wherever they might make themselves heard. . . . As they went out they took copies of the Scriptures in English with them and laid much stress on the Bible as the sole standard of faith and action. Their positive preaching of the Gospel was undoubtedly mixed with a good deal of vulgar criticism of monks, friars, bishops and rich clergy . . . and some of them stimulated social unrest by encouraging the demands of the disaffected labourers; but the fact remains that Wyclif was able to inspire a band of enthusiasts ready to face danger and hardship in the cause which they believed to be right. . . . With all his faults Wyclif succeeded in lighting a candle which burnt steadily through many years of trial and which is by no means extinguished at the present day.

John R. H. Moorman
A History of the Church in England (London: Adam
and Charles Black, 1953), pp. 121-22

. . . It will probably not be mistaken to regard him as a thinker not unlike Marsilius of Padua: perverse, that is, and even confused as a metaphysician or pure theologian, but abounding in radical views and new methods of debate, and with a capacity amounting to genius for propounding the germinal ideas that were to dissolve the medieval church more than a century after his death.

David Knowles
The Religious Orders in England, vol. II, The End of the Middle Ages (Cambridge Univ. Pr., 1955), pp. 98-99

The most natural way of speaking, when our feelings are not deeply aroused, or when we are not trying to make an emotional impression of some kind, is to come out with the main idea at once, and then if necessary qualify it or modify it, and pass on to related ideas. Before the end of the fourteenth century, John Wyclif in his sermons had evolved a simple and unlaboured style of this kind for the exposition of the scriptures, and he carried the same directness and determination to be understood into his controversial writings. . . . What moulded Wyclif's prose was above all his consciousness of the humble listener, not there to be impressed, but to be helped and convinced. Preaching and talking frequently to such men and women, Wyclif was never tempted to put words before matter; indeed, he was under constant pressure to ensure that his words expressed the matter clearly and simply.

James R. Sutherland
On English Prose (Toronto: Univ. Toronto Pr., 1957), p. 14

By his repudiation of papal and ecclesiastical authority, his confidence in the sole sufficiency of Holy Scripture, both as a revelation of the Christ and as a rule of life for every man, and his demand for a Bible open to the people, Wyclif anticipated the most fundamental protestant convictions. For good or for ill these convictions were to mould the character and help to determine the destiny of the English-speaking peoples throughout the world. The man who first set them forth was in a very real sense the spiritual ancestor of Bunyan, and Baxter, and Whitfield. Whatever his faults and whatever his limitations, he has a title to his countrymen's respect.

May McKisack
The Fourteenth Century 1307-1399 (Oxford: Clarendon Pr., 1959), p. 517

. . . Wycliff exhibited in a very marked degree the scholastic tendency of carrying theories and doctrines to their furthest logical point. At intermediate stages of development his theories and doctrines represent Reform; carried through to their furthest logical point they become Radical Dissent. . . . For Wyclif the Reformer, Holy Scripture is a weapon which he uses in order to reform the medieval Church. For Wyclif the Radical Dissenter, Holy Scripture is a weapon which he uses in order to eliminate completely any organized Church whatsoever, Catholic or Protestant.

Edward A. Block
John Wyclif Radical Dissenter (San Diego, Calif.: San Diego State College Pr., 1962), pp. 48-49

ELIZABETHAN
AND JACOBEAN LITERATURE

Irving Ribner, editor

ROGER ASCHAM
1515-1568

Born in Yorkshire in 1515. Served in household of Sir Anthony Wingfield.
Entered St. John's College, Cambridge, in 1530. Awarded B.A. in 1533.
Elected fellow of his college. Awarded M.A. in 1537 and appointed Reader
in Greek. Named Lecturer in Mathematics in 1541. Named Public Orator
at Cambridge in 1547. Sided with Sir John Cheke in support of Anglicizing
pronunciation of Greek. Presented *Toxophilus,* his first publication, to
King Henry VIII in 1545. Awarded pension by the king. Appointed tutor
to Princess Elizabeth in 1548, continued to serve her in this capacity after
her accession to the throne. Visited Lady Jane Grey in 1550. In same
year became secretary to Sir Richard Moryson, ambassador to the
Emperor Charles V. Travelled with Moryson to various places on the
Continent, including Louvain and Venice. Became Latin Secretary to
Queen Mary in 1553. Married Elizabeth Howe in 1554. Appointed
Prebend of Wetwang in 1559. Died in 1568. *The Scholemaster* published
posthumously by his wife in 1570.

J. A. Giles, ed., *The Whole Works of Roger Ascham* (1864-1865), 4 vols.

W. A. Wright, ed., *The English Works of Roger Ascham* (1904)

By way of summary, Ascham believed in and was capable of the historical
truthfulness that made Italian humanists like Polydore Vergil and Paulus
Æmilius superior to most Northerners; he was primarily interested in
and abreast of his time in discerning historical causes; he showed an unusual
freedom for the sixteenth century in his method of organizing his material;
and, though somewhat conservative, he was aware of the trend away from
certain stylistic devices. Judged by his theory of history and his brief essay
into the field, Ascham, had he written a full-scale account *de suo tempore,*
would have roughly measured up to the highest level of humanistic history
writing in the mid-sixteenth century.

Walter F. Staton, Jr.
SP (April, 1959), p. 137

Though not the only successful example of vernacular prose from early
Tudor times, *Toxophilus* won particular acclaim from Ascham's contemporaries because it stood without a native rival in its kind. No one had
previously brought so much learning or literary talent to the writing of a

treatise on a pastime. Nor had any author created more vivid passages expressing his delight in observing the marvels of his immediate surroundings. And, even more significantly perhaps, Ascham had achieved his aim of showing other Englishmen how to order the matter of prose discourse in the most effective manner.

In arranging his material, he relied on three interrelating and mutually reinforcing structural patterns, all deriving from classical theory and example. Basically, he depended upon a three-part arrangement characteristic of treatises on sport ever since the divisions were first suggested by the *Cynegeticus*, a discourse, attributed to Xenophon, on hunting the hare. The second ordering pattern, since his end was to persuade men of the value of shooting, he took from rhetorical theory, the first half of *Toxophilus* being constructed upon the recommended scheme for the deliberative oration. Finally, he cast the work, in imitation of Platonic and Ciceronian examples, as a dialogue, a form eminently suited in the humanist view to both deliberative thought and technical exposition. Before him no writer in English, not even Elyot or More, had fully realized the capabilities of dialogue for such purposes. Ascham blends all three patterns, moreover, with such apparent ease that the reader, as should be the case whenever art succeeds in concealing art, is seldom fully aware of the intricacy of the artifice. . . .

But most significant in shaping the distinctive character of Ascham's treatise [*The Scholemaster*] were the acknowledged contributions of Sturm and the unacknowledged, though equally evident, contributions of Elyot and Quintilian. That these three authors, in addition to Plato and Cicero, should have had a marked influence upon *The Scholemaster* is not surprising. Quintilian has more to say on education than any other classical writer, and the discovery of his entire *Institutio Oratoria* by Poggio early in the fifteenth century inspired much of the theory and practice of the great humanist teachers of Italy. . . .

Close as Ascham is in ideals, therefore, to contemporaries like Erasmus, Vives, and Elyot, he tends with Sturm to stand apart from these earlier humanists through his emphasis on form rather than content. . . .

Ascham's discussion of the meters of Plautus and Terence leads to his most famous, if not necessarily most salutary, contribution to Elizabethan literary theory and practice. In meter and verse, he warns, the two Roman dramatists are not to be followed because they lived before Virgil and Horace, who "by right imitation of the perfect Grecians, had brought poetry to perfectness also in the Latin tongue" (III, 248-49). He had often discussed this subject with Watson and Cheke; they had agreed that contemporary English versifiers, like the wisest Roman poets, should "follow the best examples" rather than that "rude beggarly rhyming, brought first into Italy by Goths and Huns." Though otherwise commendable, the poetry of Chaucer, Thomas Norton of Bristol, Wyatt, and Surrey was marred by their having "been carried by time and custom to content themselves with that barbarous and rude rhyming" (III, 250). . . .

This argument that vernacular poetry should be written, after the custom of the ancients, in quantitative measures, led to considerable speculation and experiment until the turn of the century, when the Campion-Daniel "debate" over rhyme marked its end as a living issue. Nor was the controversy, in spite of the many prosodic horrors it produced in the interest of the antirhyming party, the purely academic curiosity that some literary historians have taken it to be. The theorizing and experimentation did lead to deeper understanding of the principles governing English versification and to intelligent substitution of fit native equivalents for standard Greek and Roman metrical forms. . . .

Ascham's contribution to prose style, then, was to point out and illustrate various means of molding the sentence into a more harmonious and orderly unit of artistic expression. His attempt to render the vernacular eloquent was not entirely successful because he does tend to overwork the Gorgianic figures in the most obvious situations. As a consequence, although one may no longer call him without qualification an immediate begetter of euphuism, the force of his example undoubtedly lent authority to stylistic experimentation and may even have led to some of the schematic, though certainly not the metaphorical, excesses of Lyly and his followers. At the same time Ascham, for those who knew how to profit from his example, pointed the way to a firmer and more graceful manner of expression.

Lawrence V. Ryan
Roger Ascham (Palto Alto, Calif.: Stanford Univ. Pr., 1963),
pp. 69-70, 261, 265, 273, 283-84

SIR FRANCIS BACON
1561-1626

Son of Sir Nicholas Bacon, Lord Keeper of the Great Seal. His mother was one of the learned daughters of Sir Anthony Cooke. At the age of twelve entered Trinity College, Cambridge and began his life-long rebellion against Aristotelian philosophy. Left Cambridge in 1575 without taking a degree. In that year entered Gray's Inn as a law student. Between 1576 and 1579 served abroad on the staff of Sir Amyas Paulet, ambassador to France. Became a barrister in 1582. Entered Parliament in 1584. Championship of rights of Parliament in opposition to the court won him the disfavor of Queen Elizabeth. In spite of powerful family connections was unable to obtain any important political office during her reign. Participated in the prosecution for treason of the Earl of Essex who had been his friend. Began to thrive under King James I. Knighted in 1603. Became

Solicitor-General in 1607, Attorney-General in 1613, Lord Keeper of the Great Seal in 1617, and Lord Chancellor of England in 1618. Created Baron Verulam in 1618, Viscount St. Albans in 1621. In 1621 was arraigned before Parliament for accepting bribes. Defended the practice. Deprived of his office, fined, condemned to prison at the King's pleasure. Released from prison quickly and fine was remitted. Retired to estate at Gorhambury. Died of pneumonia in 1626, probably contracted while he was performing refrigeration experiments with snow.

James Spedding, R. L. Ellis, and D. D. Heath, eds., *The Works of Francis Bacon* (1857-1859), 7 vols.

Catherine Drinker Bowen, *Francis Bacon: The Temper of a Man* (1963)

PERSONAL

Like almost all representative Renaissance thinkers, he was inspired with the Faustian urge. In this context may be mentioned one of the most significant and impressive elements of his doctrine; whose motto is "Knowledge is power," and its aim the *regnum hominis*. It is the pragmatic utilitarianism of the Baconian philosophy which is here first and most adequately stated. Bacon strikes an entirely new note, which derives directly from the heightened zest for life characteristic of the Renaissance, but which before his time had not been heard in its full strength. For the first time the philosopher meets us not as a sedentary figure closeted away from the affairs of the world, not as a mere onlooker who seeks truth for its own sake, but as a being possessed by a passionate impulse to action, who places his knowledge at the service of practical ends and assigns to it as its greatest task the subjection of nature to the will of man. Bacon has established a vital connexion between theory and practice, knowledge and life, and has done so not, like his less-gifted later followers, by degrading knowledge, but by assigning to it a mission of the highest order. In this, Bacon's thought and feeling are entirely modern, and there is no vestige of medievalism left.

Rudolf Metz
in *Seventeenth Century Studies Presented to Sir Herbert Grierson*
(Oxford: Clarendon Pr., 1938), p. 30

There was a poet somewhere in Francis Bacon. His own tremendous visions for the betterment of science and law show plainly that imagination, in a more Coleridgean sense, was one of his strongest qualities. And the sheer magnificence of his style looks in the same direction. But we are not now discussing that question. Caught in a philosophy which regarded literature as inferior since it was fiction, rather than fact, and himself dedicated with all his energies to a lifelong search for fact, Bacon relegated narrative and dramatic art to a category of play, which was insulting enough. But there, at least, such art could disport itself harmlessly. If it trespassed outside the bounds of that category it became potentially one of the acutest of perils and might be tolerated, watchfully, only if it kept on its good behavior as a servant of thought and action. The world was objectively real; poetry dealt with the unreal. There can be no doubt where Bacon's conscious, continuous allegiance lay. There might be moments when he grew weary of the world and lamented, in the words of the Psalm, that he was but a pilgrim here. At such moments the unreal worlds of the theater might seem to him closer to man's true goal in Heaven. But the moods passed, and Bacon resumed with characteristic determination his campaign for a better place for himself and for deluded humanity in the here and now. This, I suggest, explains such minor waverings as may appear in his estimate of literature (including drama) and, above all, the dominant condescension, bordering on suspicion and contempt, with which he treated it in most of his work.

Paul H. Kocher
Essays on Shakespeare and Elizabethan Drama in Honor of Hardin Craig (Columbia, Mo.: Univ. Missouri Pr., 1962), pp. 306-7

Essays

Whoever has taken the pains to read the *Essays* in the order and form of their original publication must inevitably have been struck, on passing from the essays of 1597 to those of 1612 and then to those of 1625, by several outstanding differences in method and style. In the first place, as compared with the essays of 1597, those of 1612 and 1625 exhibit a marked tendency toward greater fullness and coherence in the development of particular ideas, so that instead of being mere collections of juxtaposed maxims without connective elements, they are now for the most part closely articulated compositions. . . .

The problem of how to account for the changes which have just been described has naturally presented itself to more than one of the many students of the *Essays*. Of the solutions which have been offered I shall mention only two. The first—that of Macaulay—is essentially a psychological explanation: if the style of the later essays—for example, "Of Adversity" (1625)—is superior "in eloquence, in sweetness and variety of expression, and in richness of illustration" to that of the earlier—for example, "Of Studies" (1597)—the primary reason is that with Bacon the usual order of mental development was reversed, so that his "fancy" came to maturity late, long after his "judgment" had been fully formed. The second explanation—that of M. Pierre Villey—attributes the new elements in the later essays, particularly the increase in coherence and in the number of images, "examples," and personal reminiscences, to an external influence—the *Essais* of Montaigne. . . .

Both of these explanations I believe to be incorrect, and for much the same reason: both err through assuming that the elements which distinguished the later from the earlier essays constituted a manner of writing not before practised by Bacon. The truth of the matter, on the contrary, is that all of these elements, in varying proportions, are to be found in works of Bacon antedating not only the essays of 1612 but also those of 1597. Whoever will read such productions as *An Advertisement touching the Controversies of the Church of England* (1589), the famous letter to Burleigh (cir. 1589), and *Certain Observations made upon a Libel* (1592), to say nothing of the *Meditationes Sacræ* and the *Colors of Good and Evil*, published with the *Essays* of 1597, will find abundant evidence that the habit of writing coherent, well-planned discourses, enriched with figures, "sentences," and "examples," so far from being a comparatively late development, the result of a psychological change or of the reading of Montaigne, was in reality an essential part of Bacon's literary equipment from the first. . . .

Ronald S. Crane
in *Schelling Anniversary Papers* (New York: Century, 1923),
pp. 95-96, 98-99

GENERAL

There is only one other author of nearly equal importance with Lipsius and Montaigne in the history of the establishment of the Attic tradition—Francis Bacon. He was not quite the first professed Anti-Ciceronian in England. Thomas Nashe and Gabriel Harvey undertook a vigorous attack during the nineties against both Ciceronian Latin and the ornate vernacular style of Lyly and his school, each of them seeking an escape from formalism through the method of extravagance and licentious freedom of style; and there are interesting similarities between their efforts and those of some Continental "libertines" of the same period. But neither of these writers had philosophy or authority enough to lead his age, and their attack on tradition was soon lost sight of in the great success of Bacon's more imposing offensive movement. . . . Bacon's great service to English prose was that he naturalized a style in which ingenious obscurity and acute significance are the appropriate garb of the mysteries of empire; and by means of his example the Tacitean strain became familiar to many English writers who were not sufficiently trained in Tacitus himself to imitate his style directly.

Morris Croll
in *Schelling Anniversary Papers* (New York:
Century, 1923), pp. 137, 143

But what can be asserted with confidence, I think, is that Bacon's desire to separate religious truth and scientific truth was in the interests of science, not of religion. He wished to *keep science pure from religion*; the opposite part of the process—keeping religion pure from science—did not interest him nearly so much. . . .

To Bacon the logic-spinning of the schoolmen was a kind of forbidden knowledge; it was a presumptuous attempt to read the secret purposes of God, and to force his works into conformity with the laws of the human mind. This was for him the real *hubris,* this metaphysical arrogance, which "disdains to dwell upon particulars" and confidently explains all things by syllogism. The true humility is the attribute of the Baconian scientist, who is content to come forth into the light of things, and let nature be his teacher. . . .

Nothing is more characteristic of Bacon than his distrust of the "meddling intellect," which interposes too soon with its abstractions and distorts nature instead of explaining her.

Basil Willey
The Seventeenth Century Background (London:
Chatto and Windus, 1934), pp. 29, 35-36

Bacon's claim to be *"buccinator novi temporis,"* accepted for three hundred years, is not likely to be disputed. He was the prophet, if he was not the founder, of modern scientific rationalism. Modern rationalism, of course, is not the only form that can be taken by the exercise of the reason. It is the exercise of reason towards a particular end in a particular way. The aim is the understanding and mastery of the material world; the method is a scrupulous examination of how things work and how they influence each other—what we now call the scientific method. Both aim and general method were defined by Bacon. The purpose of knowledge that he returns to repeatedly is "the benefit and use of man," "the endowment and benefit of man's life," "the serious use of business and occasions." The method proposed is "a laborious and sober inquiry of truth," "ascending from experiments to the invention of causes, and descending from causes to the invention of new experiments"; and he notes as "the root of all error," "too untimely a departure and too remote a recess from particulars." And the scope of rational investigation is universal: "For that nothing parcel of the world is denied to man's inquiry and invention." These quotations from *The Advancement of Learning* (1605) sufficiently indicate the main directions of his thought.

We must, it is true, beware of exaggerating Bacon's *direct* influence on the development of modern science or of confounding him with a nineteenth-century Rationalist. Not only was he not himself an experimental scientist, he was either ignorant or contemptuous of the major scientific discoveries of his own time; and he was without a glimmer of perception of what was to be the supreme scientific achievement of the seventeenth century—the development of mathematical physics. But his ignorance of science did not prevent him from clarifying the ideals that seventeenth-century scientists were to find congenial. . . .

[T]he characteristically Shakespearean manner, depending as it does on the maximum range of sensitive awareness, is diametrically opposed to the Baconian manner, which represents a development of assertive will and practical reason at the expense of the more delicately perceptive elements of the sensibility. You see this especially in Bacon's images taken from Nature. In my own reading of Bacon I have only found one passage that indicates any sense of the creative life behind the natural phenomena that he observes. And in this of course he points forward to the eighteenth century. To Shakespeare and the majority of his contemporaries "Nature" indicated a world of non-human life to which man was bound by intimate and essentially religious ties. By the beginning of the eighteenth century "Nature" had come to mean simply the daylight world of common sense and practical effort. Man had ceased to feel "the filial bond" binding him to all that is not human, and assumed without question that his part was simply to observe, to understand and to dominate the world of "matter." Almost as much as his explicit philosophy, Bacon's prose style is an index of the emergence of the modern world.

L. C. Knights

Explorations (London: Chatto and Windus, 1946), pp. 93-94, 101-2

When we compare Bacon with Shakespeare, we are not, I think, comparing a mind naturally and chiefly intellectual and analytical, with a mind naturally poetical. Bacon's mind sheered off from the labour of philosophical analysis; nor was his mind of the scientific quality which was being exhibited and laboriously employed by the makers of scientific method and discovery in his own time. He was naturally impassioned and imaginative; he was quick, in the words he used of King James but which are really a description of himself, to "take flame and blaze from the least occasion presented, or the least spark of another's knowledge delivered." He himself distinguished between the mind apt in resemblances, lofty and discursive, and the mind apt in distinctions, steady and acute; and he belonged himself to the first sort. He left off the writing of the *New Atlantis* to push on with "Natural History"; but he knew his way about in Atlantis better than in his scientific investigations, where he easily got himself lost. He knew what he wanted, and showed us Atlantis; he could not even apply his own rules for getting there. . . . He could not carry his imaginative thought into the detail and trial of analytical labour; he had little head for mathematics; and he could not depart so far from his images without stumbling or losing vitality and clarity. For the same reason, he could not, like Descartes, withdraw himself from the world; brooding and puzzling in front of a stove would not facilitate his kind of thinking. Hobbes was content to be a dependent of a noble family; Bacon must move between the Court, York House, and his splendid Manor of Gorhambury. He was to be Lord Chancellor; but he had worked at his profession of the law reluctantly and against the grain; he was a better and happier Lord Chancellor than he was a working lawyer. He could write of the new science like a Lord Chancellor; we cannot say with any accuracy that he contributed to scientific knowledge. He needed the stimulus of great scenes, great affairs, of wide vistas and splendid prospects to release the peculiar power of his ample mind.

D. G. James
The Dream of Learning (Oxford: Clarendon Pr., 1951), pp. 23-25

It is at this point that Bacon's true significance emerges. Although his vaunted methodology could lead nowhere and his "science" was at best questionable, he was a born propagandist. He made a powerful case for that bifurcation of nature and grace, arguing on secular grounds the principle which Ockham and Calvin had argued on religious grounds. As the second book of the *Novum Organum* shows, his cumbersome methodology for exploiting man's franchise for natural knowledge is often ludicrous, but his powerful defense of that franchise provided a rationale for some of the most characteristic thought of the seventeenth century. . . .

The antirationalistic—that is, the antischolastic—bias of Bacon's thought, though not as deep as he believed, was what most impressed his contemporaries and immediate posterity. His contempt for the system-spinning abstractions of the Schoolmen is matched only by his confidence in the possibilities of man's emancipated intellect. Once he abandons the futile and impious search for first causes, relinquishes the effort to make theology rational and knowledge moral, and shakes off the dead weight of scholastic authority, he can then proceed to the observation, description, and control of natural processes.

Herschel Baker
The Wars of Truth (London: Staples Pr., 1952), pp. 169-70

In his views on communication, rhetoric, and the behavior of the rhetorical imagination, Bacon has saturated communication with psychology. Communication must rely upon all the faculties of the mind. It engages the whole man. So far as I know, no modern scholar or scientist, whether he be psychologist, linguist, or rhetorician, has so explicitly and comprehensively imbued communication with psychology. One is tempted to say that Bacon is not merely modern; he is ultra-modern.

Karl R. Wallace
QJS (December, 1956), pp. 405-6

The main points of this paper are three: (a) Bacon's interest in allegory and myth tended to preserve through a bleak silver age the golden thread of imagination whereby poetry could still bind, by an idealistic verisimilitude, images of things into that "unity of effect" which he recognized as the persuading heart of poetry; (b) his linking of divine illumination and poetry, and separation of poetry and "philosophical" knowledge, gave poetry credit different in kind, and not merely in degree, from the scientific registers of information; and (c) his acknowledgment of the large role Imagination played in both poetry and rhetoric, authorized its importance in matters political and ethical, segregate and congregate, no matter what the vehicle.

John L. Harrison
HLQ (February, 1957), p. 108

His main achievement is the conception of a programme for a scientific age, and a method of carrying it out. This is the function of a statesman of such an age, a man who guides the aim of science, which has become the primary instrument in modern life. He is the first example of the new kind of statesman required for organizing a society in which scientific activity and human life are one. As human activities become more and more scientific, the leadership of mankind will devolve more and more on such men, who are not primarily scientists, but statesmen of science, who understand and foster it, and guide its utilization for the benefit of the human race.

J. G. Crowther
Francis Bacon, First Statesman of Science
(London: Cresset Pr., 1960), p. 2

In the *Novum Organum,* the arrogant heart of the *Great Instauration,* Bacon glibly cites the *Advancement* of fifteen years ago as proof that he is no enemy of humanistic studies and need not waste words asserting the fact now. He apologetically designates that work, revised and done into Latin, to be a part, however imperfect, of the *Instauration.* But in his exasperation at the inability of traditional disciples to penetrate the complexities of external nature, Bacon changes his position in the second of his two principal philosophical works to one unquestionably hostile to many of the finer things of life. . . .

Natural philosophy itself tends to become the Prima Philosophia which, in the *Advancement,* united the branches of natural, divine, and human philosophy, so that in an incredible aphorism (Book I, CXXVII) Verulam declares that he means all knowledges, including ethics and politics, to be reinstituted according to the inductive method developed for studying such phenomena as heat and cold, light, and vegetation. Instead of distinguishing the knowledges as lines or veins, Bacon here foretells the current dismal entropy.

It is not a question of his sacrificing scales of values descended from antiquity, but of his allowing them needlessly to be swept into insignificance by the passion to interrogate nature. It is not so much that he divorces some medieval marriage of faith and the world as that he preserves a medieval division between them while wanting, like ourselves, to give full play to each. In the *Advancement* and its narrative offshoot the *New Atlantis* Bacon brings natural philosophy down into the theater of man's life. The completed *New Atlantis* (had not science drawn him away from that work) would have given scientific research its distinct place in an ideal commonwealth. Bacon's mature humanism, more than the scientific preoccupations of his old age and retirement, gives him relevance to a society (and an Academy) in which the two cultures are mutually exclusive. "Let there be . . . ," he wrote in a moment of anticipation of Sir Charles Snow,

> (and may it be for the benefit of both) two streams and two dispensations of knowledge; and in like manner two tribes or kindreds of students in philosophy—tribes not hostile or alien to each other, but bound together by mutual services;—let there in short be one method for the cultivation, another for the invention, of knowledge.

Edmund H. Creeth
Papers Michigan Academy of Science, Arts, and Letters
(1962), pp. 647-48

It is the scope of his inquiry for which we have to thank Francis Bacon. In science he made no single discovery. His celebrated "forms" have proven useless to laboratory workers. Moreover it is nonsense to claim him as father of the inductive method. The inductive method goes back as far as Aristotle. Yet it is to be remembered that the seventeenth century was an era not of definite discoveries but of inspired guesses, large speculations impossible to prove experimentally until the necessary precision instruments and mathematical techniques should be developed. These inspired leaps and guesses were actually the forerunners of theories which later became accepted and part of general knowledge. To read Bacon on the winds, on heat, light, the ocean currents and the cosmos is to find oneself bewildered by the conjunction of folklore, notions from the ancient Greek philosophers, medieval superstition and inspired sudden reaches into the scientific future.

Catherine Drinker Bowen
Francis Bacon: The Temper of a Man (Boston: Little, Brown, 1963), p. 9

FRANCIS BEAUMONT
1584-1616
and
JOHN FLETCHER
1597-1625

FRANCIS BEAUMONT was born at Grace Dieu in Leicestershire, the youngest son of a Justice of Common Pleas. Entered Broadgates Hall, Oxford in 1597 at the age of 12. Left without taking his degree. Entered Inner Temple in 1600. Poem *Salmacis and Hermaphroditus* was published anonymously in 1602. Made the friendship of Ben Jonson. Around 1606 wrote *The Woman Hater* for Children of Paul's. Produced *The Knight of the Burning Pestle* in 1607. Began collaboration with John Fletcher around 1608. Shared lodgings with him in the theater district. Collaborated on about seven plays. Married heiress Ursula Aubrey in 1613.

JOHN FLETCHER was born in Sussex, the son of a clergyman, the Vicar of Rye, later Bishop of Bristol, Worcester, and London. Cousin of poets Phineas Fletcher and Giles Fletcher, the younger. May have attended Corpus Christi College, Cambridge, but evidence for this is uncertain. May have written for Queen's Revels company before 1608. Wrote *Faithful Shepherdess* around 1608. Began collaboration with Beaumont at that time. After Beaumont's death continued collaboration with others: Massinger, Jonson, Field, Daborne, Middleton, Rowley, Shirley and perhaps Shakespeare. Chief collaboration with Massinger. Wrote almost entirely for King's Men.

A. Glover and A. R. Waller, eds., *The Works of Francis Beaumont and John Fletcher* (1905-12), 10 vols.

The work of Beaumont and Fletcher escapes from the tyranny of Jacobean incertitude into a world of its own creating. It is bound neither by the weight and horror which oppresses the tragedy nor by the compensatory pragmatism which binds the comedy to realistic portraiture. It evades the great questions (except as debating topics) and it endows with remoteness all emotions, so that the strongest passions fail to engulf us, however fiercely the characters seem to be shaken by them. Through the tragi-comedies and the early joint tragedies in particular, there is transfused a colour of such singular beauty that we accept enchantment as we do a dream or a fairy-tale, not seeking in these plays, as in the great Jacobean tragedies, implicit answers to our urgent doubts, but escaping into them as into the moonlit stage of an exquisite opera-set, become suddenly real and co-extensive with life itself. Upon this stage and in this clear, remote radiance all the events of life take part and types of character of nearly as wide a range as can be found in all the rest of the Jacobean drama; the air is full of reverberant rhetoric, melting cadences of word and music, clear, sweet pathos and sentiment more noble than can be readily found in the world outside. So bright is it, so self-contained, this sanctuary from the agonies of spiritual tragedy and the cynicism of observant comedy, that it dims the real world, bewilders our faculties and comes near to laying asleep in us the uneasy sense of sleepwalking illusion. . . .

There is, of course, enough consistency of character to make it superfi-cially convincing; even a fairy-tale fails of its consummation if there is no sufficient evidence that these things are happening to people reasonably like those we know. The emotions must be strange enough to give us the sense of escape, but the people who experience them must be like enough to persuade us that it is we in them who achieve that escape. And so the fairy-world of Beaumont and Fletcher is, even at its most fanciful, peopled by beings who act plausibly most of the time and only rarely strain our credulity. But the distinction between them and those other people of the earlier Jacobean drama is that, with Beaumont and Fletcher, we have an impression that the motives have been supplied after the situations and emotional crises have been determined upon; they have been thought-out carefully and articulated delicately but, nevertheless, they are only part of the apparatus of illusion, made to conceal the real springs of the machine, which are situation and action. . . .

But in general we abandon quite early the demand for homogeneousness of mood, thought and character, abandon the unsuitable effort to think of the plays as organic growths or to see in each its individual spatial form and look instead at the bewildering variety of beauty in situation, episode, sentiment and language. We are bewildered, dazzled, intoxicated by cadence, variation, unexpected change of action, of sentiment, of tempo until we lose the power of integrating this magic world into which we have strayed and surrender ourselves to a beauty which, however it be rooted in falsity, bears again and again a singular and lovely flower. Whether it be the excellence of the structure, the rapidity and variety of the movement in comedy and the sudden breathless turns of fate in the serious plays; whether it be the vigour and effectiveness of the characters in the later tragedies, the brilliance and variety of those in the comedies, the perfumed beauty of certain isolated, pathetic figures in the tragi-comedies and tragedies; whether it be the solid vigour of individual speeches, the long passages of sustained dialogue or the poignant snatches of verse and image; whether it be the spellbound atmosphere that holds the romances or the gaiety and geniality of the comic plots and comic interludes, enough is here to satisfy us—once we have admitted the dispersal of the elements, the disintegration of mood, character and thought, which sets these writers and those who entered their territory apart from the strict Jacobean tragedy and comedy.

Una Ellis-Fermor
The Jacobean Drama (London: Methuen, 1936), pp. 201, 207, 212

I do not mean that Fletcher's pre-eminence was purely an accident, or that the decline of Jacobean drama was without cultural implications. Fletcher's ascendancy in Shakespeare's company marked the victory of the private theater sensibility in the once public playhouse. From a broadly popular art the English drama rapidly diminished to a courtly diversion performed for a "select" and sophisticated audience. Yet in a larger perspective Fletcher did not radically alter the development of the stage. He represents instead the final stage of a long-continuing evolution that transformed the drama from an amateur communal undertaking in provincial cities and towns into a capitalistic enterprise, a very skilled, professional, and commercial entertainment centered in the metropolis of London and influenced to varying degrees by the taste and patronage of the court. Only during the relatively brief score of years when Shakespeare's genius flowered did the drama become artistically significant and retain its popular character. For he alone had the comprehensiveness and fecundity to create many plays of truly universal appeal that did not require an intellectually sophisticated audience and yet met the highest standards of disciplined and refined taste. It is not quite accurate to say that Shakespeare's art prospered at the Globe because it expressed the views of the predominantly middle-class audience. Shakespeare won his audiences by sharing with them a vision of life that transcended the parochial views of any particular class. And because he brought the relatively crude art of the popular stage to an unparalleled level of aesthetic achievement, he unwittingly helped to extinguish it.

Robert Ornstein
The Moral Vision of Jacobean Tragedy (Madison, Wisc.:
Univ. Wisconsin Pr., 1950), pp. 164-65

His characters are not defined by personal qualities of speech like Shakespeare's or Jonson's: they speak an unaffected easy verse, which, except in the occasional tirades, is free of rhetorical devices. The broad farce of *The Woman's Prize* may demand a heightened diction and the politer exchanges of *The Wild Goose Chace* a cooler one; but in his comedies, unlike his tragi-comedies, Fletcher is neither ranting nor raucous. His characters do not indulge in sets of wit in the old manner, but in more natural exchanges; except for his simple soldiers and his few fops, no one has any special marks of speech. Repetition and parenthesis, the easy movement of an oiled sentence, give to the comedies their air of lightness and insubstantial elegance: the older style is occasionally glanced at, with a few mocking quotations from *Hamlet* or *The Spanish Tragedy*. . . .

The style of Fletcher's plays and the whole mode in which they were conceived look forward to that of Restoration comedy; they retained their great popularity till the end of the seventeenth century. Their difference from the plays of popular writers like Dekker and Heywood is hardly greater than their difference from the satirists' work of Jonson or Middleton. Here the appeal is both to the sympathy and the ironic disclaimers of a small group of gallants, wits or cavaliers: the standards are those of contemporary good manners. Yet these are not social comedies in the old sense, for there is no feeling of the structure of society in any of them. The comedy of individual relationships is presented within a single group, that of the gentry and their servants. The scene may be England, France or Spain; the City, Court and Country are no longer valid divisions. The individuals who constitute this world have no roots; they are allowed to play out their jests in the anterooms of great houses, with no particular suggestion of day or night, winter or summer, the real flavour of London, Paris or Madrid.

Fletcher's is an inward world; not the world of tragedy, but none the less of *pathos* rather than *ethos*, a world of motive and of sentiment. Protean changes of mood are the method of conducting the story forward; the intrigues are for the most part loosely woven, compared with Chapman's or Jonson's, yet they are skilfully calculated to keep the interest of the audience without absorbing it. The sentiments, tone and air of witty comedy count for more than the action, but the two are in general well balanced.

M. C. Bradbrook
The Growth and Structure of English Comedy (London:
Chatto and Windus, 1955), pp. 184-85

In Fletcher's major plays we are never allowed to think only in one way about anything: the antithesis between strange action and easy conversational dialogue mirrors the clash in judgments. Even when its happy endings are most strenuously achieved, Fletcher's drama always withdraws from a final judgment: it is too sceptical ever to be rebellious: it refrains from assertion as from challenge. And in the plays of his maturity this judiciously balanced effect is achieved through his use of the possible though peripheral situation, the thing that could conceivably happen—with explosive consequence—in the court and the city. *The Faithful Shepherdess* was an experiment which exhibited, but could not give full existence to, his characteristic mode of vision. . . .

The easy eloquence of his set speeches, his adroit hand in the management of pathos, his command of the courtier's conversation—all these things are as evident as the limitations which are at least as frequently pointed out. So, too, is the clarity of his language: indeed Fletcher is the easiest to read of English playwrights before Shirley, his talented disciple in the reign of Charles I. It is this very clarity of language that has, I think, disguised the complexity of Fletcher's approach to his characters and themes. No more than those dramatists of his time whose work commonly seems to exist on a higher level did he present a dramatic action to be taken in one way only. His comedy at its best, and that is surely in *The Humorous Lieutenant*, has a deep vein of irony; his work in tragicomedy is ambivalent in the portrayal of character and subtle in its conception of an action controlled by a dual impulse; his tragedies—though as tragedies narrowly circumscribed—are firm and logical structures dependent on a valid functioning of the creative imagination. In the very eccentricity of his hypotheses, he must have compelled his audience to think. Yet all this is conveyed in a language that is easy, relaxed, crystalline, so that the contrast between what is apparent and what ultimately emerges constitutes a mannerism.

Clifford Leech
The John Fletcher Plays (Cambridge, Mass.:
Harvard Univ. Pr., 1962), pp. 47, 137

Beaumont and Fletcher might have written truly moral tragedy. I would suggest that they failed to do so because of their very attachment to a past social ideal which may never have fully existed except in men's minds, and because the ethical paradoxes they examine are related only to artificial—and ultimately unimportant—patterns of social conduct, and never to the larger problem of the relation of good to evil in the world. There is, moreover, no real working through of these paradoxes in their plays, no evidence of real intellectual and emotional involvement, what Eliot has called a struggle for harmony in the soul of the poet. The paradoxes which form the central conflicts of their plays are resolved by dramaturgy, the clever manipulation of situation, with a masterly control of shock and suspense. There is no real quest for moral certainty in their plays, only the facile reduction of artificially contrived paradoxes, with no attempt to resolve moral issues.

The Maid's Tragedy rings its many changes on the themes of honour, love and friendship, values dear to the Elizabethan world of Wilton and

Penshurst, but in this play reduced to a specious shallowness. Amintor is torn at first between his love for Aspatia and his loyalty to the king, two conflicting absolute values, and we must remember that Beaumont and Fletcher are as conservative as Heywood in their doctrine that the king, no matter how evil he may be, must be unconditionally obeyed. Amintor must sacrifice the honour of his betrothed for his loyalty to the king. When he learns that Evadne is the king's whore, he is again torn between duty and honour, for he cannot oppose the king who has made him a cuckold. The shallowness of the ideal of honour to which these characters so thoroughly are committed is revealed by Evadne: she has married Amintor to preserve an honour which in truth already has been forfeited, and to do so she must destroy the honour of her husband by making him a cuckold. In the same way Amintor must be a knowing bawd to his wife in order to preserve his own honour because to reveal his cuckoldry is to destroy his reputation and thus his honour. Honour here is a meaningless pretence.

Irving Ribner
Jacobean Tragedy (London: Methuen, 1962), pp. 16-17

RICHARD BROME

ca. 1590-1652?

> No records of early life in existence. Probably born around 1590. Name first appears in Introduction to Ben Jonson's *Bartholomew Fair* (1614). A servant and disciple of Jonson. Mentioned as playwright in 1623 in office-book of Sir Henry Herbert, Master of the Revels. Wrote plays for various London companies, performed at Red Bull and Salisbury Court theaters. Assumed to have died in 1652 or 1653, although we have no certain evidence.
>
> *The Dramatic Works of Richard Brome* (1873), 3 vols.
> C. E. Andrews, *Richard Brome: A Study of His Life and Works* (1913)
> R. J. Kaufmann, *Richard Brome, Caroline Playwright* (1961)

It does not seem to be oversubtilizing to conclude that the rôle played by the Antipodean scenes in helping Peregrine recover his wits was intended by Brome to suggest a theory of comic catharsis. Comedy, in other words— though it may carry a stark madman only this side or folly-wards of sanity— may directly administer to human sanity generally by engrossing the mind in an elaborate scheme of incongruities and enabling it to perceive through them the omnipotence and ubiquity of imperfection.

The second concept underlying Letoy's Antipodean scenes is that the method of comedy need not be strictly realistic in the sense of reflecting things as they are with the fidelity of a looking-glass. If the main purpose of comedy is psychological adjustment through engrossment in life's general incongruity rather than ethical correction through the exposure of specific deformities, it requires only a basic orientation in the actual and beyond this may distort life even to the extent of "being the world turn'd upside-downe," to quote the description which the curate, Quailpipe, gives of Letoy's play. Although it is possible to discover in the Antipodean scenes of Brome's *tour de force* such an implicit plea for distortion in comedy, it must not be forgotten that Brome nowhere formulates the principle of distortion as applicable to all comedy, that he presents Letoy's play within a framework drama that has realistic elements not inferior to those in his previous comedies, and that in his prologue he calls attention to his choice of "low and home-bred subjects" in the realistic tradition of Jonson, Dekker, and Chapman. Hence, his departure from traditional comic theory is by way of indirect and tentative suggestion rather than through a rationale fully stated and aggressively advanced.

Joe Lee Davis
SP (October, 1943), pp. 525-26

A close study of his extant canon of fifteen comic plays is proof that he achieved a very coherent body of work, and that this work is built out of a predictable talent for transposing an internally consistent set of moral convictions into effective dramatic statement. Brome displays the prime dramatic knack for finding the fable, the actable image, the theatrical gesture which can make his conventional social attitudes the more potent for being dramatized. . . .

His plays, individually and altogether, reflect and embody an attitude toward, and a criticism of, the life of his time. This attitude is a complex one presented in comic modes with conventional distortions and concessions. If social comedy derives its form from the theater, it derives its subject matter and its informing vigor from life. Its *themes* are the *preoccupations* of the times; its repeated types are modifications of (or even disguised equivalents for) its representative social classes, its pressure or splinter groups. Comedy's aim is comprehension of what is going on, and a contribution to the ordering of society along stabilizing lines of good sense, charity, and justice. . . .

Brome's plays are far less self-repetitive than Shirley's and show more versatility in comic invention than Fletcher's. Brome is a master craftsman whose substantial gifts are delimited primarily by three characteristic practices: He was overfond of farcical horseplay; he could not intensify his language for crucial scenes; and his studies under Jonson gave him predispositions for serious satire without either Jonson's massive learning and intellect or his carefuly documented moral views. As a result, to state the adverse case in its strongest form, when Brome attacks general vices or perversions there is sometimes a thin, parroting quality, a suspicion of incomplete sincerity, an uncertainty as to convictions, and a general stiffening of language. One suspects the speech or the situation has been devised for dramatic convenience. The Jonsonian mantle was too long and of too heavy fabric; Brome entangled himself and walked falteringly in it. It is not too much to say that, given to mirth-making as he was, Broome was sometimes embarrassed by the obligations he felt to thicken the texture of his plays by exhortation or serious satire. . . .

Richard Brome was the last representative of the conservative moral tradition in the theater at a time when the position he represented was still contemporary and not yet reactionary. Besides being a social conservative actively interested in giving dramatic expression to his beliefs as to what constituted the "good society," Brome is also one of the last masters of the art of analogical thinking—the art which enabled the dramatic construction of Shakespeare and his major contemporaries. T. S. Eliot, though an immeasurably better poet, is theatrically a direct descendent of Brome.

Brome's two basic dramatic forms were realistic comedy (with many specialized variations) and his own sly adaptations of popular tragicomedy. In *The Queen and Concubine* Brome established a pattern of social, political, and ethical views. These views are formally patterned in the play by Brome's own deliberate intention; the fabric is carefully woven. In *The Queen and Concubine* he made his most earnest (though not most successful) attempt to find artistic means for stating his convictions about the non-acquisitive sense of responsibility and the disinterested love (*Agape*) which are the informing concepts of his best work.

R. J. Kaufmann
Richard Brome, Caroline Playwright (New York:
Columbia Univ. Pr., 1961), pp. 1, 36-37, 88

SIR   THOMAS   BROWNE
1605-1682

Born in London. Attended Winchester from 1616 to 1623. Entered Broadgates Hall, Oxford (later called Pembroke College) in 1623. Took B.A. in 1627, M.A. in 1627. After brief period of medical practice journeyed abroad. Studied medicine at Montpellier, Padua, and Leyden between 1631 and 1634. Received M.D. degree from University of Leyden. Returned to England. Lived for a time in Halifax, Yorkshire where he wrote *Religio Medici*. Settled in Norwich in 1637. Remained there for rest of his life practicing medicine. Married in 1641. Became father of ten children, only three of whom grew to be adults. Royalist throughout civil war, but took no part in politics. Testified at a trial of witches in 1664. Knighted in 1671 on occasion of a royal visit to Norwich. Bequeathed his skull to be kept in the city hospital at Norwich after his death in 1682.

Geoffrey Keynes, ed., *The Works of Sir Thomas Browne* (1928-1931), 6 vols.

J. S. Finch, *Sir Thomas Browne* (1950)

Religio Medici

Religio Medici is broadly an "informal essay," but that term is far too vague and too modern for our purposes. . . . In the last quarter of the sixteenth century there emerged in all the literary languages of Europe a new prose style, which developed hand in hand with the rise of rationalism and its new moral and scientific attitudes. It grew out of a revival of interest in the Stoic writers of the first Christian century, especially Seneca, and it caused both a revival of Stoicism and an imitation of the "Attic" style cultivated by the Stoics. Like its classical model it was an anti-Ciceronian movement. It rejected the oratorical, or "Asiatic," style, with its copiousness, rhetorical balance, floridity, and flowing ease. The movement was begun on the Continent by Muret, Lipsius, and Montaigne, and in England by Bacon. All of them had rejected the philosophical rigidity and complacence of the High Renaissance. . . .

In other words Browne is a religious romanticist. His thought lacks the sharp outlines of Calvin's or Bacon's or Hooker's. Like all these he draws a separating line between the natural and the revealed, but he does it in a different way. Calvin draws the line in order to separate lost man from sovereign God; Bacon draws it in order to mark off a workable field of knowledge; Hooker draws it to safeguard both the uniqueness of the Bible and the validity of the Christian experience. Browne is closest to Hooker, and he needed the vast theological edifice of the Middle Ages, like a cathedral of many periods and styles, where Aristotle and Augustine meet; but whereas Hooker had derived from Scholasticism a coherent and rational philosophy, Browne loves to roam in other regions of it—the mystical. The noteworthy thing is that he draws less from Thomas Aquinas than from Tertullian.

"I love to lose myself in a mystery; to pursue my reason to an *O altitudo.*" That is probably the key to the whole. One returns to the passage which is built up around this sentence with a deepening conviction that it explains everything in Browne. Here he first uses those two symbols which seem to have captured his imagination more than any other: the mystical circle of God whose center is everywhere and whose circumference nowhere, and the divine adumbration—*Lux est umbra Dei.* He uses both again and again. . . .

So where Hooker speaks of the eternal reason, "laid up in the bosom of God," or Calvin of the divine decree, Browne takes refuge in two unthinkable paradoxes. In these obscurities, he tells us in this early passage in *Religio Medici*, it is good to sit down with "an adumbration; for by acquainting our reason how unable it is to display the visible and obvious effects of nature, it becomes more humble and submissive unto the subtleties of faith; and thus I teach my haggard and unreclaimed reason to stoop into the lure of faith." This falcon metaphor is a beautiful and, it seems, a daringly inverted one, with its notion of soaring reason flying at the sun to be enticed to earth by the lure of faith. But we see Browne's bent. Bacon, setting the method of scientific investigation for the future, points out how clumsy were the Schoolmen's logical tools beside the infinite subtleties of nature and taught his generation to track her by keeping the eye on the object and trusting to the mind and senses in combination. But Browne is first poet and then scientist. And in the realm of imagination, which was his peculiar domain, reason and sense alike were "haggard" and unreclaimed.

William P. Dunn
Sir Thomas Browne: A Study in Religious Philosophy
(Minneapolis, Minn.: Univ. of Minnesota Pr., 1950),
pp. 38-39, 54-55

The *Religio Medici* is beautifully composed and expressed; it is a work of art. He prepared manuscripts for private circulation, eight copies of which still survive. But to publish any work about religion in the seventeenth century was to invite controversy and this he certainly wished to avoid. He knew that "a man may be in as just possession of Truth as of a City and yet bee forced to surrender; 'tis therefore farre better to enjoy her with peace, then to hazzard her on a battel" [I, 6]. Browne was the reverse of pugnacious and this may well be why, for seven years, he refrained from publishing; as soon as the pirated edition appeared in 1642 the heresy hunt began. Sir Kenelm Digby wrote his *Observations upon Religio Medici* between 19 December, when he received a copy sent to him by the Earl of Dorset, and 23 December, when he returned the copy with his commentary. Alexander Ross printed his attack on the authorized edition in 1645; it was entitled: *Medicus Medicatus: or the Physician cured by a Lenitive or Gentle Potion: with some Animadversions upon Sir Kenelm Digbie's Observations on Religio Medici*. But when we read the *Religio* we know that the hunters were on a false trail. It is not a work of controversy; the heresies Browne describes are recorded as part of his endeavour to explore the relations between his faith, his temperament and his profession. . . .

In Part I of *Religio Medici* Browne's central theme is his religious belief.

It is a work which could only have been written by this one man at this one time; highly individual and characteristic, it also reveals a conception of the world and of the cosmos impregnated with classical and medieval ideas, modified by notions coming to birth in the seventeenth century. A part of the attraction of all Browne's writings is this combination, a markedly individual mind and style vividly expressing the thought of a particular time. . . .

Joan Bennett
Sir Thomas Browne (Cambridge Univ. Pr., 1962), pp. 54, 98

Another stylistic trait in *Religio Medici* related to the dichotomous mode of procedure but existing in whole periods rather than in phrases is a form of sentence pattern which I shall call the metabolic style. It consists of Browne's taking us in a single sentence from a very low point in subject matter, diction, and rhythm, up to a high point; then, beginning at a high point and bringing us down. . . . This stylistic trait gives the effect of building up and breaking down in a series of changes in energy—alternating anabolism and catabolism. The pattern is well suited to the doctor's thoughts on generation and decay, man and God, this world and the next. In a half sentence he swings us up from the trivia of everyday life to the throne of God, often with optimism, concealed pride, and certitude; then the opposite movement takes us down, often with humility and deep irony. . . .

Frank R. Huntley
Sir Thomas Browne (Ann Arbor, Mich.:
Univ. Michigan Pr., 1962), p. 122

GENERAL

From what we have seen of Browne's nonchalance toward his own truth-seeking and of his burning confidence in the judgments of God, we can posit the two poles of his attitude toward controversy. On the one hand he rejects consistency where it inhibits intellectual growth, and on the other he reminds himself that God is not bound to defend his own creature's partial vision of the truth. . . . As if human considerations would not deter him from dogmatism, there are always the ways and the thoughts of God, which are not the ways and the thoughts of man. . . .

Amid the violent controversies of his day, Browne could afford to be moderate and reasonable, for he felt that "a good cause needs not to be patron'd by passion, but can sustain itself upon a temperate dispute." Heresies had no terror for this man, who continued to exercise "a wary and pious Discretion." He would not be disturbed by winds of doctrine in which he could discover "nothing that may startle a discreet belief." The men he held to be most inimical to truth were not those who disagreed with him but "those vulgar heads that look asquint on the face of Truth, and those unstable Judgments that cannot consist in the narrow point and centre of Virtue without a reel or stagger to the Circumference." But even as he condemns, he brings succour. He too has known the intellectual difficulties common to men. . . .

Margaret L. Wiley
The Sutble Knot (Cambridge, Mass.: Harvard
Univ. Pr., 1952), pp. 152-53

Browne shared with so many men of his age the belief that the world was approaching its end. But he does not believe, as Raleigh and others believed, that because the world had grown old it was in decay. There is an optimism in this book which is not found in Raleigh or in Donne, and this appears nowhere more clearly than in his remarks upon death. It has no terrors for him. In one place he tells us, "There are few that fear the face of death less than myself," and in another he says that it is not death he fears so much as the disfigurement of death, and adds with cheerful irony, "Not that I am ashamed of the Anatomy of my parts . . . whereby I might not call myself as wholesome a morsel for the worms as any." It is worlds removed from the tormented reflections of Donne upon mortality. So confident is Browne of salvation, he tells us, that he has fixed his contemplations on Heaven and almost forgotten the Idea of Hell. And so his imagination lingers not upon the gruesome trappings of death but upon the strange processes of nature, the mysteries of an incorporeal soul in a corporeal body, and the life beyond death.

He cannot be called a mystic, but the world he lived in and practiced his experiments upon seemed to him a divine world, the visible world a picture of the invisible. He collects his divinity not from the word of God but from His works. Between the visible and the invisible worlds there was continual traffic, traffic of devils as well as of angels, so much so that those who disbelieve in witches, he held, "not only deny them but Spirits; and are obliquely and upon consequence a sort not of Infidels but Atheists." . . .

But the attempt to set up Browne as a modern man of science, even in that age when the medieval and the modern were still inextricably mingled, is beyond my power. His aims and many of his conclusions are modern, yet in method and in style nothing could be more remote from the course that science was taking when Browne wrote his book. In spite of what he says in the first book, he delights to parade the authority of the ancients, classical and medieval. The *Vulgar Errors,* it has been said, "is the twilight of the medieval gods." Albertus Magnus and other "learned and authentic fellows" make almost their last appearances as serious authorities on matters of science. He cites them even if he contradicts them, so lingering at his task of demolition and killing his errors as if he loved them. . . .

The danger with a man like Browne, no very clear or profound thinker yet with a style so elaborate, is when the matter is not answerable to the style, when the reader becomes aware of a discrepancy between the poverty of the thought and the pomp of language and cadence expended on it. In *Urn Burial* his themes are all commonplaces: the decay and dissolution of all material things, the vanities of man, the transience of the monuments of human power, time and immortality, life and death. But they stir and provoke his mind as he turns them over and over, looks upon them now from one surprising angle and now from another, and makes what was old seem new by the obliquity of his vision and the strange majesty of his style.

F. P. Wilson
Seventeenth Century Prose (Berkeley, Calif.: Univ.
California Pr., 1960), pp. 73-74, 79, 85

ROBERT BURTON
1577-1640

> Born in Leicestershire. Entered Brasenose College, Oxford in 1593. Elected a student of Christ Church in 1599. Took B.A. degree in 1602. Lived at Christ Church for remainder of his very uneventful life. Took a degree in divinity in 1614. Became vicar of St. Thomas' Church in Oxford. Held various other church livings, but rarely left Oxford. Published *Anatomy of Melancholy* at Oxford in 1621. Wide popularity led to many editions. Wrote a Latin play, *Philosophaster,* acted at Christ Church in 1618 but not printed until 1862. Contributed Latin verses to various anthologies.
>
> H. Jackson, ed., *The Anatomy of Melancholy* (1932), 3 vols.

Burton also defends himself by reciting the attacks made on Seneca. . . . Thus Burton might have claimed the example of Seneca and the Stoics for the jumble which he accumulated, but ordered in general with great ceremony. For his style he claimed the authority of Seneca. In practice Burton alternates between clipped and tumbling expression, cutting his speech into short clauses, "foaming out synonymies"—the amplification which Hoskins calls "accumulation." These manners, which are allied in effect, are relieved by a more connected, but still loose, type of discourse. Burton runs the full gamut of Senecan style, to which he adds his own exuberant amplification.

George Williamson
The Senecan Amble (Chicago: Univ. Chicago Pr., 1951), p. 200

The Robert Burton who emerges from the "Digression of Air" is an alert, inquisitive man, well posted on the contemporary scene, actively interested in science and especially in the exciting new astronomy. He knows few of the answers, but all of the questions. There is no reason to picture Burton as an extremely profound thinker, but neither ought we take too seriously the Burton of legend—a quaintly amusing academic odd-fellow, a sort of Lamb-in-the-library. . . .

Thus we see that Burton was widely acquainted with astronomical writing. His knowledge, however, was wider than it was deep: his handling of the great astronomers shows him to be frequently inaccurate. . . .

Many of these errors are obviously as much the result of carelessness as of ignorance. Burton's fine unconcern with accuracy in quotation and citation of authorities, and his slipshod habits of revision, make such things inevitable. Very often a sentence that was simple and clear in the first edition will accumulate so many subordinate clauses in the course of time that its meaning becomes quite distorted—a patchwork method that is frequently responsible for the peculiar charm of the Burtonian style.

Granted that his mistakes are often accidental, it remains true that Burton is not too interested in the technical aspects of astronomy. There is added technical data in every edition, but until the fifth it is scanty and not very significant. In 1638 Burton sets down for the first time scientific objections to the new system to bolster his earlier argument from analogy. Throughout he opposes the Ptolemaic system, distrusts the Copernican, and shows respect for the Tychonic. At one time he seems to favor Origanus' idea of earth's rotation, but in the end he is the partisan of no system.

All this is understandable enough, considering that Burton was not an astronomer but merely a layman with a great deal of intellectual curiosity. He is really interested in broad outlines and implications, not in questions of technical superiority. As a result he devotes much of his space to the provocative theory of infinite worlds, continuing to read and write about this intriguing idea all his life, though he has rejected it from the first. . . .

In the end Burton's approach to these baffling new problems is that of the professional man, the physician of melancholy. For a mind oppressed and weighted down by care, there is no more delightful remedy than to speculate on these mysteries occasionally, or to investigate the various fields of knowledge. Our author himself is such a one.

Robert M. Browne
MLQ (June, 1952), pp. 145-47

Beyond his talents as a raconteur and a man of learning, Burton has an infallible sense of the dramatic and a real literary skill. His characterization of himself in the first sentence of the *Anatomy* as an actor intruding himself "upon this common theatre of the world's view" is accurate; the reader seldom loses sight of Burton throughout the three volumes. There is a personal, subjective touch almost totally lacking in the other writers on melancholy. . . .

Burton's style is, however, highly functional; it is always appropriate to the subject matter. His statement that he respects matter, not words, can be understood in the sense that the content governs the choice, arrangement, and rhythm of the words; he is at the opposite pole from the euphuist. He acquaints the reader with this functional aesthetic when he compares his style to a river which runs sometimes swift, sometimes slow; sometimes direct, sometimes winding. The river flows as the terrain requires; his style flows "as the present subject require[s]" (I, 31). He uses at least three distinct styles (with many variations therein) to express three different kinds of subject matter.

Burton sometimes writes the prose of purely scientific communication, seeking only to present facts objectively and clearly; in this he comes closest to the prose of Bright, Wright, and Adams. This type is best exemplified in Partition I, Section I, Membrane II, in the eleven subdivisions of which he writes a detailed account of the anatomy of the body and of the soul. . . .

When Burton changes his role from that of the scientific communicator to that of the Christian satirist, his prose also changes. He no longer seeks simply to inform but to startle the reader, to stir the emotions with an impassioned description of the evils of this world. The style becomes harsh in rhythm, sound effects, and imagery. The staccato rhythm is achieved through Burton's piling up of verbs, adjectives, and nouns with a minimum of connectives. . . . The imagery compares men to animals—and not of the lap-dog variety at that, but greedy wolves or vicious tigers. . . .

Burton has a third distinct prose style which may be best described as lyrical. This, in common with his vituperative style, makes a direct appeal to the emotions. But the appeal, of course, is a different one; it is highly sensuous and seeks to please, not to startle.

William R. Mueller
The Anatomy of Robert Burton's England (Berkeley, Calif.:
Univ. California Pr., 1952), pp. 26-29

Burton goes beyond the English tradition most distinctly in his insistence that the disease of melancholy is not only an individual, but also a national, problem. Although he has much in common with his predecessors in his treatment of the "six non-natural things," of perturbations of the mind, and of the body-soul relationship, he adds a new dimension to the study of melancholy when he writes of the causes, symptoms, and cures of the disease in relation to state and church. He sees in the disease not only physiological and psychological aspects but also sociological implications. . . .

The *Anatomy* itself illustrates Burton's belief in the practical value of scholarship. Excluded from positions of political and ecclesiastical authority in which he might put his accomplishments and acquirements to use in the direction of public affairs, the scholar may at least offer his services to his fellow men through his writings. This is precisely what Burton, lacking more effective means of serving society, has done. Penned up in his study, he has absorbed the wisdom of the ages from many books. He has winnowed out the best that has been thought and said (his winnowing is, to be sure, very imperfect) and has presented his knowledge and his wisdom in a form which was particularly palatable to his generation.

The *Anatomy* is a work of scholarship. One finds in it information and opinion which the author has assembled from the works of many others. There is no pretense of originality. Although the book as a whole is highly original, the author claims merely that "the method only is mine own . . . we can say nothing but what hath been said, the composition and method is ours only, & shows a Scholar" (I.23). Burton seems to have no ambition to be an original thinker, an intellectual leader. But there is pride in his claim to scholarship. This quotation is less modest than might be apparent to many twentieth century readers. . . .

Yet Burton is not a wholehearted partisan of science. Among the tribulations of humanity is "*Curiosity,* that irksome, that tyrannizing care, *nimia sollicitudo, superfluous industry about unprofitable things and their qualities,* as *Thomas* defines it: an itching humour . . . to know that secret which should not be known, to eat of the forbidden fruit. . . . For what matter is it for us to know how high the *Pleiades* are, how far distant *Perseus* and *Cassiopea* from us, how deep the sea, &c? We are neither wiser, as he [Eusebius] follows it, nor modester, nor better, nor richer, nor stronger, for the knowledge of it. *Quod supra nos nihil ad nos.* I may say the same of . . . Astrology . . . Magick . . . Physick . . . Alchemy . . ." (I.420-21). The effect of this passage, which comes from Burton's review of the causes of melancholy, is somewhat neutralized by the enthusiasm with which he later recommends the study of scientific subjects (in moderation) as a cure for melancholy. . . .

But it is not possible that the writer of a work on a scientific subject could be wholly dubious of the value of science. Where would Burton draw the line between defensible and indefensible scientific study? He never draws it for us, but it is not hard to see what distinction he would make. Cosmology, alchemy, and to some extent astrology, however interesting they may be, are finally futile and frustrating. But Burton never shows any doubts concerning the value of the applied sciences: metallurgy, agriculture, navigational mathematics. These contribute to the well-being of man. Medical science is justifiable because it relieves the physical sufferings of man. Psychology relieves his mental miseries and furthermore has ethical value in that it teaches man to know himself and to exercise rational self-control.

Burton's norm for the judgment of science, then, is the same as Milton's, the norm of usefulness (*Paradise Lost,* VIII, 167-78). Every body of knowledge is to be approved which has either practical or moral value. But Burton is dubious, though not altogether condemnatory, in his attitude toward those sciences which are most remote from human needs.

Lawrence Babb
Sanity in Bedlam (East Lansing, Mich.: Michigan
State Univ. Pr., 1959), pp. 33, 56, 74-75

There is nothing eccentric in the elaborate division and subdivision of the *Anatomy.* Parallels can be found in many a work of his age. It is an elaborate arrangement, but it is a logical one. Each of the three partitions is divided into sections which are divided into members which are sometimes divided into subsections. I will only say that of the three partitions the first considers the kinds, causes, symptoms, and prognostics of melancholy; the second, the cure of melancholy; and the third is devoted to a detailed examination of two especially important types of melancholy— love melancholy and religious melancholy. Because he proceeded by a logical method, because each of the many facets of his argument is allotted its rightful place, he was able in successive editions to add new evidence without having to rewrite and without spoiling the structure of the whole.

F. P. Wilson
Seventeenth Century Prose (Berkeley, Calif.:
Univ. California Pr., 1960), p. 37

Nothing shows his [Burton's] quality better than the long "Satyricall Preface" in which Democritus Junior explains his pseudonym and purpose and, from his college window, surveys the mad world as it reels or rushes by. Given an invincible sanity and clarity of vision—and Burton has affinities with Lucian, Chaucer, Erasmus, Rabelais, Montaigne, and Shakespeare—no satire can be more effective than the mere cataloguing of what men feel and do, their carnal and worldly lusts, the fantastic objects, public and private, that they pursue, the follies and crimes they commit in the pursuit, the whole topsy-turvy scale of values and motives that society disowns and maintains. "If it be so that the Earth is a Moon, then are we also giddy, vertigenous and lunatick within this sublunary Maze." From the panorama of life as it is Burton turns to consider what it might be, and it is characteristic of his common sense that his Utopia—more or less enlarged in later editions—is not a chimerical commonwealth but a practicable improvement on what already exists. His proposals range from broad streets to hospitals and pensions for the aged and infirm, from the thorough cultivation of all land to the abolition of monopolies, from the suppression of extravagance in building and dress to the curing of idleness, "the *malus Genius* of our nation."

But though Burton is here and everywhere a realistic satirist, a detached observer of the human comedy, he is much more than that. He does not, like some modern psychologists, worship a particular idol of the cave, nor does he start with the tacit invocation, "Now, Muse, let's sing of rats." His subject is the soul, body, and whole life of man, and he writes as both a divine and a physician. The *Anatomy* proper begins with a contrast between the original endowment and felicity of "Man, the most excellent and noble creature of the World, the principal and mighty work of God," and the present miseries, inherited from Adam, of the wretched being who is in many ways inferior to the lower animals. That contrast is seldom absent from Burton's mind and, since he feels as well as thinks, it is tragic as well as comic. . . .

Even a summary sketch of Burton cannot fail to suggest his sanity of mind and largeness of heart, his love of life and of human beings, his capacity alike for robustious or bitter laughter and for sensitive exploration of the darker places of the soul. His matter is never dull, but more than half of our pleasure is in his manner, the revelation of himself. He would have written in the international language—as Browne intended to write the *Pseudodoxia*—if the mercenary stationers had not shied at a Latin treatise. While feeling grateful for that blessing, we may wonder how such a scholar happens to be conspicuous not only in his own period but in the whole range of English prose for colloquial naturalness, garrulous spontaneity, and juicy vigour. Burton has his moments of eloquence (and he wrote passable verses which Milton may have read), but he is not, like some famous contemporaries, a poet in prose. No English author, however, certainly no author of a long didactic work, has more variety of tone on the prose level. His flood of slangy, proverbial, and picturesque language is nearer to Nashe and Dekker than to Cicero or Seneca. Burton piles up all the critical complaints that might be brought against his irregular, homespun writing, but his self-depreciation is really a satire on other men's affectations, and he did not fail to revise his style in successive editions—though he did often fail to verify his references and to catch multiplying misprints.

Douglas Bush
English Literature in the Earlier Seventeenth Century, 2nd ed.
(Oxford: Clarendon Pr., 1962), pp. 296-97, 300-301

THOMAS CAMPION
1567-1620

Entered Peterhouse, Cambridge, as Gentleman Pensioner in 1581. Left without taking degree in 1584 and entered Gray's Inn for the study of law in 1586. Never practiced law. Probably served under Earl of Essex in expedition to aid King Henry IV of France in 1591. Later took a degree in medicine, probably at a continental university. Began to write poetry while at Gray's Inn. Five poems appeared in a surreptitious edition of Sidney's *Astrophel and Stella* in 1591. Others circulated in manuscript. Published volume of Latin epigrams in 1595. With Philip Rosseter produced *A Book of Airs* in 1601. Composed lyrics for solo songs to be sung with the lute. In 1602 published prose treatise, *Observations in the Art of English Poesy.* His argument for quantitative rather than qualitative verse inspired a defence of rhyme by Samuel Daniel. Between 1607 and 1613 wrote four masques. Published two more collections of songs for which he wrote both words and music in 1613 and 1617.

P. Vivian, ed., *The Works of Thomas Campion* (1909)

Campion's recognition that pauses as well as syllables must be counted to fill the time periods of a metrical pattern is a real contribution to prosody. It is a corollary of his preliminary assumption that the metre of poetry, like that of music, is based on a succession of time periods felt to be equal. The rhythm heard against this regular metrical pattern is that of the words as pronounced in ordinary speech: that is why Campion is interested in the "natural" length of syllables, although he fails to appreciate the extent to which words owe their stresses and quantities to their functions in the sentence. The metrical measure, like the bar of music, can be divided among any number of time values, provided the total duration remains constant. The "iambic licentiate" may contain feet of three syllables instead of the ordinary two, and the "English elegiac" may contain feet of several different types: the constant element is not the dispositions of the syllables but the duration of the foot. The result may only be free blank verse, but Campion has tried to include in his system of prosody what most systems have not mentioned, the variety of rhythm which distinguishes interesting from monotonous verse.

It is curious that, having started to time verses and got very near to a perception of the equality of time in feet of different patterns, he should have been deflected into a discussion of feet in terms of the classical longs and shorts. The great variety of consonant groups in English should have warned him that there were many classes of long and half-long syllables. He did not consider that Greek quantity might have been arbitrary, and that such arbitrary division of all syllables into long and short might be permissible in a language like Latin, which has few heavy blocks of consonants, but would not work in a language like English. Modern barring makes it more obvious than sixteenth-century scoring, but it is still strange Campion did not remember the time periods in music can be broken into notes of more than two different values. From that he might have perceived more than two lengths of syllable were possible. But his classical training blinded him, and his one published experiment in quantitative metre set to music is marred by following the example of the French neo-classicists and restricting himself to two time values. The metre he chose for his experiment was sapphic.

Bruce Pattison
Music and Poetry in the English Renaissance
(London: Methuen, 1948), pp. 130-31

Self-conscious in the attempt to unite poetry and music, Campion was also a theorist of prosody, publishing in 1602 his notorious *Obseruations in the Art of English Poesy,* which drew forth Samuel Daniel's *Defence of Rhyme.* Campion's teaching has been much misunderstood; the older view, represented by his editor Vivian, that Campion failed to understand the difference between quantity and accent and that in his actual practice, "what was accentual verse when read, became quantitative verse when sung," has now been modified. Miles Kastendieck, who brought a scholarly training in both music and poetry to the study of Campion, has successfully shown that Campion's theory was based upon a recognition of the presence of both accent and quantity in English, and that his application of principles of music to prosodic theory made a new and remarkable achievement rather than the confused and reactionary document which earlier critics had seen in the *Obseruations.* Campion was merely the culmination of a movement, which had begun as early as Sidney, of seeing music and poetry together, but Sidney had not the benefit of the great English musical renaissance on which to draw. . . .

When Campion stuck to the rules of classical versification, as in "Come let us sound the praises," he had to confine himself to notes of only two different time values in the music. He must have realized that in English there are more than two units of length for a syllable, and in his setting of the poems which he called "ear-pleasing rhymes without art" he utilized this fact. The relationship between the versification and the music in Campion is difficult to explain for the reason that he wrote both, and quite possibly there was interaction between them in the process of composition. . . .

It is not merely in the matter of rhythmical freedom and variety that Campion's musical method in poetry is significant. He knew that the movement of poetry and its sounds are inextricably entwined. He comments in the preface to the *Two Bookes:* "The light of this will best appeare to him who hath paysed our Monasyllables and Syllables combined, both of which, are so loaded with Consonants, as that they will hardly keepe company with swift Notes, or give the Vowell conuenient liberty."

It is this scrupulous care and sensitiveness to the movement of the line, the inflectional effects suggested by music, and the concern for the convenient liberty of the vowel that has made some of Campion's ayres among the most successful lyric poems in the language.

Hallett Smith
Elizabethan Poetry (Cambridge, Mass.:
Harvard Univ. Pr., 1952), pp. 280-81

Campion's doctrine [in *Obseruations in the Art of English Poesy*] is far removed from the crudities of Harvey and Spenser: he knows that dactylic metres are unsuitable to our language and feels, with a musician's sensibility, that five feet in English are equivalent to six in Latin. He is not in the least deceived by spelling; "we must esteeme our sillables as we speake, not as we write." Yet when all is said his theory has very little to do with English practice, even his own. Thus in analysing the line

Men that do fall to misery, quickly fall,

he explains that the syllables *to miser-* are a "Tribrack." So they are; but stress-accent on the first of *misery* has been ignored as if it had nothing to do with the movement of the line. Yet his temporary concern with quantitative metres bore delightful fruit in "Rose-cheekt Lawra come." I suspect that a poetic impulse towards the unrhymed lyric came first and the theory was devised to mitigate the innovation. Campion (quite erroneously) thought he could not swim without these classical bladders. And they are not at all becoming. He adopts the humanistic attitude in all its boastful ignorance: everything before Erasmus, "Rewcline," and More is to him "illiterate Monks and Friers," and rhyme in its metrical use must be bad because it is listed as a mere figure in the books of rhetoric. . . .

His [Campion's] poetry is as nearly passionless as great poetry can be. There are passions somewhere in the background, but a passion, like a metre, is to Campion only a starting-point: not for moral or intellectual activity but for the creation of a new experience which could occur only in poetry. By the time he has finished, the original, the merely actual, passion hardly survives as such: it has all been used. This happens as much in his religious as in his erotic pieces. The Christian life becomes an idyll or a romance. . . . Campion is fond of words like sun, beams, sunlike beauty, "a streame that brightly flowes" and, for contrast, of groves and shadows. Yet perhaps aural experience means more to him than visual—"silent" days, the "peacefull" western wind, "musicke" which is the beloved's "Eccho" and "beauties simpathie" (*Book of Airs*, 10). In one place (IV. 6), if I have not misunderstood him, he suggests that light exists only in order that beauty's "grac't words might better take," as if the visible woman were merely an accompaniment to the audible woman. Certainly, unlike many of his sex, he thinks it a pity that a woman should be silent: "Awake, thou spring of speaking grace, mute rest becomes not thee" (III. 13). No further development along the same line was possible after Campion. Indeed, when we read the description of his masques, we may feel that civilization itself, soon after his time, lost some of the elements which made such art possible. He "makes mouths at our speech."

C. S. Lewis
English Literature in the Sixteenth Century (Oxford:
Clarendon Pr., 1954), pp. 434, 556-57

All of the poems we have examined are marked by an almost classical firmness and clarity of outline. The usual form in each strophe is statement, counterstatement, and conclusion, something like a syllogism in logic. Such a form combines contrast and balance within a logical framework—like all "classical" forms it allows elements to appear in all their uniqueness and difference while still insisting on their interrelations. Campion's music, too, exhibits this quality. The *canzona* form, especially, blocks out balance and contrast in clear sections; moreover, in Campion's hands, it frequently shows subtle interrelations between parts—when, for example, a contrasting theme shades off into an analogue of the theme it originally contrasted. In their clear logical structure, these songs resemble the Petrarchan sonnet as it was handled by Sidney. Or, perhaps the genre they most resemble is the epigram.

Campion had a penchant for the epigrammatic, as the number of his Latin epigrams or the plethora of epigrams used as examples in *Observations in the Art of English Poesie* show. Moreover, he repeatedly compared the air to the epigram: in the preface to *A Booke of Ayres* he wrote, "What Epigrams are in Poetrie, the same are Ayres in musicke, then in their chiefe perfection when they are short and well seasoned"; and in the preface to *The First Booke of Ayres,* "Short Ayres, if they be skilfully framed, and naturally exprest, are like quicke and good Epigrammes in Poesie, many of them shewing as much artifice, and breeding as great difficultie as a larger Poeme." The qualities of the air which he meant to stress are, of course, its limited range of thought and emotion, its polish, and its brevity, but we can extend his remarks to include other elements. Epigrams are terse, to the point, without repetition: so are the airs. Epigrams usually have a logical structure and build clearly toward a climax in the last line —a climax deliberately held back till the end when it either intensifies what precedes it or gives it a new twist: so do most of the airs ("I must complain" is an especially good example). The trick of the epigram is to prepare for the ending from the start, but to hide the preparation so that the ending seems at first surprising but then immediately after seems inevitable: we have seen that it is this quality which Campion takes pains to stress in his musical settings.

Walter R. Davis
Criticism (Winter, 1962), pp. 98-99

THOMAS CAREW

1594?-1640

> Second son of the eminent lawyer, Sir Matthew Carew. Entered Merton College, Oxford, in 1608, left with B.A. in 1611. Spent brief period studying law at Middle Temple. Became secretary to Sir Dudley Carleton. Remained in his service from 1613 to 1616, accompanying him on his missions as ambassador to Venice and to the Low Countries. Dismissed from service in 1616 for writing satire against Lady Carleton. Went to France in 1619 in service of Sir Edward Herbert (later Lord Herbert of Cherbury). Received position at court in 1628. Associated with prominent literary figures of his age. Remained in service of King Charles I until his death. His masque, *Coelum Britannicum*, was presented and printed in 1634. His *Poems* were published in 1640.
>
> R. Dunlap, ed., *The Poems of Thomas Carew* (1949)

Jonson did so much to give its accepted form to one genre, the masque, that nobody who worked in it after him escaped his influence. Carew's single masque, *Coelum Britannicum,* can scarcely be understood without reference to the conventions—antimasque, song, allegorical figures, ethical, social and celestial themes—established or developed by Inigo Jones's greatest collaborator. Because the type is so special, and raises many problems not strictly poetic, we shall narrow our task even further here by noting only that *Coelum Britannicum* shows a specific indebtedness to some of Jonson's masques—especially to *Pleasure Reconciled to Virtue*— as well as an over-all resemblance in structure and aim. Nor should it be forgotten that Carew, who left us no plays, would probably never have turned his hand to this bastard form of "entertainment," and so would not have revealed a substantial talent for lofty blank verse and sharp satirical prose, if Jonson had not shown him the way.

Most of the other genres practiced by Carew recall Jonson. They may be divided into categories for which there are Jonsonian precedents: tributes to the work of friends, epistles of friendship, compliments to those in a high position, obituary pieces, and lyrics. The narrow range at once reminds us how much of Jonson we shall be leaving out. It was in the lyric alone that Carew surpassed Jonson in both range and volume.

Rufus A. Blanshard
SP (April, 1955), p. 197

We needn't be embarrassed about Thomas Carew. What distinguishes him from other avowed disciples of Donne, and from Donne himself, is precisely his attention to "design" and "consent of parts." Not that he gives up the conceits, but that he orders them. It is this control that makes his extravagance seem somehow reasonable, his coruscations calm, his digressions calculated. Whether it is a typically "metaphysical" quality is questionable; but Carew fits better than most of his contemporaries the statement of John Crowe Ransom's that "the impulse to metaphysical poetry . . . consists in committing the feelings in the case—those of unrequited love for example —to their determination within the elected figure." The election and the commitment, which will be the subject of this paper, were so important to Carew that his friend Suckling, to whom such care smelled of the lamp, called his muse "hard bound." It is possible that Carew, a craftsman in the Jonsonian sense, will outlast natural, easy Suckling.

Some of the master figures of the Renaissance rhetorics are useful to recall. Carew, hard bound or not, could scarcely have written poems to fit them, any more than a dramatist could spin a tragedy out of the *Poetics*. But certain of the figures apply to a remarkable number of the shorter poems, and of passages in the longer poems. This means both that Carew was a traditional poet, and that a handbook like *The Arte of English Poesie* is a storehouse of persistent as well as ephemeral devices. Puttenham's names and definitions of four organizing, image-producing figures supply a more exact basis for categorizing and discussing Carew's effects than any terms in the modern vocabulary. The four figures are *Hypotiposis, Icon, Parabola,* and *Allegoria.*

Rufus A. Blanshard
Boston Univ. Stud. in Eng. (Winter, 1957), pp. 214-15

That is, the distinguishing mark of Carew's work seems to me to lie not in its narrow circle of interest—and this point can be exaggerated—or its neat Jonsonian architectonics and lucidity. It lies in its unexpected tendency to expand: to keep its vision broad. Thus Momus's satire is more playful and general than bitter; thus a fairly long masque can be worked out coherently, and its verse can with no sense of forcing incorporate glowing imagery; thus a tribute to a dead girl can unobtrusively evoke the thought of Christ and of salvation; and thus amorous verse can be given similar richness and significance by its overtones. This manner of approaching poetry is indeed not that of a neo-classic like Jonson; and neither, as Carew uses it, is it that of a passionate, introverted writer like Donne. It is that of the Elizabethans of the last two decades of the sixteenth century, and especially of the Petrarchans and Neo-Platonists, of whom Spenser was the chief figure. It is nevertheless the manner of Carew's work almost three-fourths of the time, writing in a social and literary environment distinctly opposed to it in spite of the affected Platonism which surrounded Queen Henrietta . . . Hence I offer the following speculation about Carew's development as a poet. I cannot possibly prove it; but it seems a reasonably satisfactory manner of accounting for the special quality which marks his work. I suggest that at an early age he knew well Spenser and other Petrarchan sonneteers, English as well as continental; and that he found their way of writing amorous verse so congenial that neither Donne's revolt against it nor the neo-classic mode of the court wits could kill its influence on his way of approach to poetry. I suggest further that from these same writers, with now the powerful influence of Donne added, he soaked up the sense of a cosmos in which macrocosm and microcosm, physical world and spiritual, body and soul, were interwoven and at all points analogous; and that again his later environment, though it kept him a shallower person than the men he followed, could not destroy the older attitude. I suggest that if we pull out of the body of Carew's work all the poems whose roots lie in this older tradition we shall have, with the exception of "A Rapture" and a number of small though exquisite things like the best epitaph for Lady Mary Villiers ("This little Vault, this narrow roome" [54]), all of Carew's best work: a point which seems to reinforce my theory.

Francis G. Schoff
Discourse (January, 1958), pp. 22-23

We have pictured Thomas Carew most often as a lyrical poet who sings with mellifluous accents of love and beauty. It would be quite accurate to summarize in this way three fourths of his total poetic achievement. But it is necessary to recognize that some of Carew's work does not at all fit into the category of the lyric—seems, in fact, to be poetry at the furthest possible remove from such a performance as *Aske me no more*. Nothing could be more surprising in a first reading of Carew than to discover, in the middle of the 1640 edition, the verse-epistles he addressed to Ben Jonson and to John Donne. Here is no lyrical style polished to perfection, enriched by an exclusive choice of golden images and heightened by the dominant inspiration of the singing voice, but a rough colloquial style, well adapted to angular imagery and to a comparatively uninhibited rambling of the speaking voice from one topic to the next. It is as if the reader were suddenly to be dropped from a higher to a lower plane of poetic discourse.

Surprising as this contrast between styles may be, it is quite understandable both in terms of the distinction we have made from time to time beween two possible voices of poetry, and in terms of certain traditional attitudes Carew was always likely to assume toward his craft. The dictum that the style is the man holds no more true in his case than it does for the majority of Renaissance poets. One has an overwhelming impression that Carew always kept in mind the genre in which he was to write. In this respect, he is not only a true "Son" of Ben, but also an inheritor of certain classical precepts tracing back to Horace and Quintilian. . . .

But except for a few uninspired translations of the Psalms, Carew does not attempt to embrace higher worlds or to affirm sanctions beyond this present life. He is too much in love with mortal beauty ever to forego it, despite his recognition of its inability to satisfy the longings of the heart. Nor is this earth-bound existence the only limiting factor in his work. He had also to reckon with a hard-bound muse, unaccustomed to flights into the empyrean on the wings of a lofty genius. What we find in Carew's work is a diligent, unassuming technique which depends in many cases upon extensive revision for the sake of exactness in the choice of words. These are the limitations, if you will, of even his finest poetry.

Edward I. Selig
The Flourishing Wreath (New Haven, Conn.:
Yale Univ. Pr., 1958), pp. 146-47, 176

GEORGE CHAPMAN

ca. 1559-1634

Born in Hitchin, Hertfordshire, in 1559 or 1560. Probably attended Oxford, perhaps Cambridge as well, but we know nothing specific about his education. Probably served as a soldier in the Low Countries sometime before 1594. In that year his earliest work, *Shadow of Night*, was published in London. Has been connected with a coterie of intellectuals known as "The School of Night" although there is no certain evidence that such a group ever existed. Knew Walter Raleigh, Thomas Harriott, Christopher Marlowe, and other intellectuals of his day. In 1595 published another volume of poetry, *Ovid's Banquet of Sense*. Was writing plays for the Lord Admiral's Men by 1596. In 1598 published a translation of the first seven books of Homer's *Iliad* and his completion of Marlowe's *Hero and Leander*. Continued to write comedies for Lord Admiral's Men. First tragedy, *Bussy D'Ambois*, printed in 1604. In 1605 collaborated with Ben Jonson and John Marston on *Eastward Ho*. Landed in prison with Jonson for offending the crown in the play. Again in difficulty over *Conspiracy of Biron* in 1608 which offended French ambassador. Wrote actively for the stage until 1613. Complete translation of *Iliad* appeared in 1611. In financial difficulties because of the death of his patron, Prince Henry, in that year. Masque for marriage of Princess Elizabeth acted at

Lincoln's Inn in 1613. *Whole Works of Homer* published in 1616. Had come under the patronage of Robert Carr, Earl of Somerset, following the death of Prince Henry. Fell into financial troubles again with Somerset's fall. Last years were unhappy ones. Quarrelled with Ben Jonson. Between 1619 and 1622 forced to defend himself in long chancery suit. Died in London.

Thomas Marc Parrott, ed., *The Comedies of George Chapman* (1914), *The Tragedies of George Chapman* (1910)
P. Bartlett, ed., *The Poems of George Chapman* (1941)

PLAYS

All Chapman's tragedies may be described as dramatic studies of the interaction between a great man and his society. There are four main elements at work in this interaction: in the hero, his moral nature (his goodness or badness), and his outward role, as soldier, rebel, or servant to the king; ranged opposite to him in society are two kinds of men, the mouthpieces of Chapman's ideas on social order, or the hypostases of various kinds of social corruption. The plays are built up from the innumerable conflicts and harmonies which arise amongst these elements. This schematization suggests that Chapman's plays, like Marlowe's, tend, if we are thinking of them in terms of the contribution made by characterization to the total play, to be grouped round a single great figure. In the plays that bear their names, it is Bussy and Byron, and, in *The Revenge of Bussy,* Clermont d'Ambois, who hold our interest, while the other personages, ambitious prince, ideal king, political schemer, are more important for what they represent in relation to the protagonist than for what they are themselves.

Peter Ure
The Age of Shakespeare (London: Penguin Books, 1955), p. 323

Chapman came to tragedy twenty years too late, after the Spenserian dream of chivalry had become something of a joke to skeptical Jacobean minds. By training and inclination he was a humanistic scholar, steeped in classical philosophy, and dedicated to the pursuit of the heroic in literature if not in life. As the great translations of Homer testify, he could so immerse himself in the grandeur of antiquity as to appear immune to contemporary anxieties. But his drama, which is more closely attuned to the temper of the age, reveals the vulnerability of his humanistic idealism. His comedy descends rapidly from the superficial satire of *An Humourous Day's Mirth* to the cynical depths of *The Widow's Tears.* His tragedies span the poles of Jacobean disillusion from the bitter scorn of *Bussy D'Ambois* (1604) to the meditative Stoic resignation of *Caesar and Pompey* (1612-13). There are, of course, many echoes of Marlowe and of Elizabethan melodrama in his earliest tragedies, yet even in *Bussy* we can trace a confused attempt to unite Elizabethan convention and Jacobean vision, to dramatize through hackneyed theatrical devices the essential political and moral issues of the time. Only late in his career as a tragedian did Chapman free himself completely from the heritage of Elizabethan revenge melodrama and then the price of victory was dullness. His last plays are upright Moralities, noble in thought and sentiment, but only incidentally or coincidentally dramatic in conception. . . .

Dangerous as it would be to identify Chapman with his Stoic heroes, I cannot but feel that he shared their spiritual isolation and their sense of alienation from an unworthy society. Like Milton fallen on evil days he despairs of worldly reformations, and yet he too discovers within himself the paradise which has been elsewhere destroyed. He does not find security, however, through a return to Elizabethan beliefs, nor does he burn his books and renounce his classical learning to embrace salvation. Although in *Byron's Tragedy* knowledge illuminated the way to error, in *Caesar and Pompey* Chapman with Cato follows the light of reason beyond reason itself to the faith that looks through death.

Robert Ornstein
The Moral Vision of Jacobean Tragedy (Madison, Wisc.:
Univ. Wisconsin Pr., 1960), pp. 47, 83

Critics traditionally have pointed to Chapman's weakness in character portrayal, and they have compared him unfavourably to Shakespeare in this respect. Such a comparison does grave injustice to Chapman, for it slights the particular quality of his own dramatic artistry. Chapman was not a naturalistic dramatist. He was never concerned with portraiture of character as a significant end in itself. The wide division among critics of *Bussy D'Ambois* may come in part from a failure to recognize that none of the characters in this play was designed as a realistic portrait from life, but that each performs various thematic functions within the total design, and that these functions are often incompatible with one another in terms of psychological verisimilitude. All together they constitute the ethical statement which is the primary concern of the play. Bussy, Monsieur, Tamyra, and the rest may at times be used to comment with the voice of Chapman on the events of the play in terms inconsistent psychologically with the moral positions for which they already have been made to stand. What results is a sometimes confused and always difficult play, more gratifying perhaps to the reader in his study than it has ever been to an audience in the theatre. Part of this difficulty may have resulted from Chapman's failure adequately to work his philosophical substance into the total structure of his play, his tendency to present it in set speeches which themselves are highly poetic, but which are not well integrated into the dramatic action. Chapman, in short, found it difficult to adapt his concept of the dramatist's high philosophical mission to the requirements of a popular stage.

Irving Ribner
Jacobean Tragedy (London: Methuen, 1962), p. 23

It is characteristic of Chapman, thinking as he did about poetry, to embody the tragedy of a Herculean hero overcome by fate in a fiction which seemingly tells quite another story. For the more ignorant members of the audience there is a story of bloodshed, intrigue, and supernatural doings in a contemporary court. But the original audience for this play included a large proportion of more knowing spectators, for Chapman wrote *Bussy D'Ambois* for one of the "private houses". . . .

These more sophisticated spectators might be expected to share the author's delight in meanings artfully concealed beneath a deceptive surface. The play which resulted from this way of writing cannot be called an unqualified artistic success; the disparities between surface meaning and symbolic meaning, particularly in the conjuring scenes, too often suggest a *tour de force*. However, Chapman's procedure has its merits. Not only are there individual passages of high poetic quality, but the very disparities just referred to make a certain positive contribution to the meaning. Purity of motive and corruption of act are brought out by the ambiguity of every major incident: the decision to go to court is both a capitulation and a defiance, the duel both outrageous and noble, the affairs with Tamyra both culpable and ideal, the association with Behemoth both a dabbling with evil and a mystical pursuit of the hidden truth. Together these paradoxes present the moving dilemma of a great-spirited man who attempts to live by a heroic code in a world dominated by Machiavellian policy.

The difference between Marlowe's and Chapman's portrayals of the Herculean hero appears constantly in the imagery of the two plays. The most brilliant images in *Tamburlaine,* such as that of the hero in his chariot, scourging tyrants, give form and concreteness to the hero's situation. They inevitably interpret that situation, but above all they present it. The poetry of *Bussy D'Ambois* characteristically works towards a different end. Its most brilliant images are those which make some thought about the hero concrete—the sea of his energy, which is both wild and yet contained within bounds—the fire of his spirit, which has the various qualities of a torch borne in the wind, a beacon, a falling star, a thunderbolt, and which, after death, returns to a world of fire. Marlowe's images keep the hero himself before our eyes; Chapman's focus the mind's eye on a problem of the heroic nature.

E. M. Waith
The Herculean Hero (New York: Columbia Univ. Pr., 1962), pp. 110-11

OTHER WORK

The Elizabethan age was at the crossways and that is expressed by the impulse to find expression in dramatic forms which presented various conflicting tendencies. Chapman is essentially of his age, and that is the reason, with his obscurity—Janet Spens well remarks on his overlooked kinship to Donne—why he has been unduly neglected. But in recent times Donne has come into his own. His significance is understood. It seems time that Chapman also should be recognised as a fit interpreter to us of the inner life of his time. The very fact that his genius was not dramatic, but so intimately personal, adds to his significance. The more clearly the Elizabethan age stands out as the greatest age of England the more we are called upon to contemplate Chapman. . . .

Evidently Chapman's first published poem [*The Shadow of Night* in 1594] called out natural complaints of its obscurity, for in the Dedication to his next poem, *Ovid's Banquet of Sense,* published in the following year, Chapman observes rather querulously, "I know that empty and dark spirits will complain of palpable night." In the *Banquet of Sense,* which seems to have obtained some popularity, the shadows are certainly not so thick; it is a collection of rather frigid sensuous conceits with a few passages of beauty, as in the description of Corinna bathing and sitting on a bank singing to her lute, in which Chapman follows, afar off, the Renaissance manner of Marlowe and Greene.

A few years later Chapman testified to his love and admiration for Marlowe, and reached his chief excellence in this field, by completing the *Hero and Leander.* It was scarcely a happy thought—as though Browning undertook to complete Keats's *Hyperion*—yet the close contact of Marlowe seems to save Chapman from his besetting sin of obscurity and infelicity. He had something of Marlowe's delight in physical loveliness, though little of Marlowe's fine aesthetic feeling and quick perception; Chapman always reflects, deliberates, sets forth what he considers the ethical side of things. In the continuation of the *Hero and Leander* there is both beauty and gravity, and the two qualities are combined in a fairly harmonious way. Here Chapman was held in check by the need to live up so far as possible to the standard set by Marlowe. There was really more of himself in the earlier (1595) *Ovid's Banquet of Sense.* . . .

However strange it may seem, Chapman's comedies are all the better for the slight value placed on them. They escaped the tortured elaboration to which his poems were subjected, as well as the fine but often misplaced eloquence he put into his tragedies. In allowing himself to be reckless, almost burlesque, the pattern he fashioned might be extravagant or fantastic, but the verbal texture became simple and to the point, yet instinctively betraying the poet's touch. He even revealed a vein of humour, apart from preceding Jonson in the delineation of "humours." In 1599 was published *An Humorous Day's Mirth*, his first mainly prose comedy extant. It is less absurd than the previous play, and there have been traced in it, influences both from Lyly and Jonson. But it comes to us in a corrupt shape, and it is as careless as *The Blind Beggar*; both show a disregard of moral canons, surprising in so lofty and punctilious a moralist, but they are farcical in conception, and we may remember that, as Janet Spens says on Chapman's behalf, "farce is essentially immoral."

Havelock Ellis
Chapman (Bloomsbury: Nonesuch Pr., 1934), pp. 5, 14-15, 18

DUBIOUS AUTHORSHIP

Alphonsus Emperor of Germany was performed at the private theatre at Blackfriars before Queen Henrietta Maria and the Prince Elector, i.e., the Palsgrave Charles Lewis, son of the "Winter King," on May 5th, 1636. Fleay [*English Drama,* Vol. II, p. 156] speaks of this performance as a revival, but we have no knowledge of an earlier performance. . . .

I . . . will simply state that I am unable to find the slightest trace of Chapman's hand in it. Fleay, following Wood and Winstanley, ascribes it to Peele. This seems to me, *prima facie,* very plausible, at least as regards the firm form of the play, which may well have been revised later. Mr. J. M. Robertson ("Did Shakespeare Write *Titus Andronicus?"* pp. 123-31) has recently pointed out some interesting parallels between this play and Peele's known and suspected work. . . .

Alphonsus did not obtain the honor of a second quarto, and was never included in the various collections of Elizabethan drama. It was first reprinted and edited by Karl Elze . . . in 1867.

Elze's edition . . . was of real value in bringing this curious and interesting play again before the public, in calling attention to the numerous "Germanisms" which mark its style, and in particular, in emending and restoring the extremely corrupt German speeches which in the original quarto are printed in black-letter.

T. M. Parrott
Anglia (July 28, 1907), pp. 349-50

1. Like *Alphonsus* many of Chapman's plays centre round some individual whose name appears in the title.

2. Many of Chapman's plays have the setting and peculiar atmosphere of the early seventeenth century continental court, with its intrigue, deceit and flattery. This is present in *Alphonsus*.

3. Intrigue is the mainspring of Chapman's drama. He seemed enamoured of plot in which a subtle and politic mind works upon the ingenuous if courageous "simpleton" to compass its purpose, which is usually Machiavellian ambition or revenge. In his study of contemporary European politics Chapman found plenty of material for the construction of such subtle, undermining intrigues as he liked. . . .

To sum up: I believe that the original play was wholly or in part by Peele, incorrectly called "John Poole" in the Stationers' Register entry; that it was rewritten for royal performance by Chapman, and that he was assisted in this revision by a German collaborator.

Harold M. Dowling
NQ (May 29, 1933), pp. 366-67

JOHN CLEVELAND
1613-1658

Born in Leicestershire, son of a clergyman who had moved there from Yorkshire. Was student at Christ's College, Cambridge, receiving B.A. 1631, M.A. 1635, contemporary there of John Milton and Henry More. Became fellow of St. John's College, Cambridge, and reader in rhetoric in 1634. Opposed election of Oliver Cromwell as parliamentary member from Cambridge in 1640. Moved to Oxford in 1643. Was Judge-Advocate of Newark in 1645-1646, and defended that town against the Scots. Lived for some years supported only by friends in various parts of England. Between 1647 and 1649 contributed to various journals, most notably the *Mercurius Pragmaticus.* Imprisoned at Yarmouth in 1655-1666 on vague charges. Released from prison after an appeal to Cromwell. First edition of poems appeared in 1647. Died at Gray's Inn in 1658.

John M. Berdan, ed., *The Poems of John Cleveland* (1911)

The absence of any serious emotion in Cleveland's verse, other than his satire, leads one to doubt, as Professor Saintsbury has doubted, whether Cleveland ever wrote "serious" verse in one sense at all. His true bent lay in satire, into which he put his heart, though with partial success; he wrote amatory verse in the spirit of one who plays a game, and knows he plays it cleverly and to the liking of his age; with the result that, lacking emotion, his love poems seem to caricature their own cleverness. *The Hecatomb to his Mistress* lends cogent support to this impression, both in its explicit statements and in the nature of its verse. As if to settle all doubt, *The Rebel Scot*, his most famous satire, surprises us with its passion and vigor; its conceits, lashed by the force of his fury, crush his opponents with fantastic abuse. It is significant that there is in Cleveland not a single one of the poignant lyric flights which charm us in the least of the Metaphysicals and beguile the critical sense of the most determined haters of the conceit. The truth is that Cleveland, like the bee in his *Fuscara,* is a confectioner of conceits in his amatory verse, and therefore not an inheritor of the most characteristic Donne manner, but rather of the Italian cast which that manner received at the hands of Crashaw. For no other reason does his verse, when it is praised, receive the epithet "pretty." This of course does not apply to his satire, which uses the conceit in the more genuine Donne manner.

The peculiar talent of Cleveland seems to lie in his skill with the witty image and phrase. Here he puts the heritage from Donne to individual use.

George Williamson
The Donne Tradition (New York: Noonday Pr., 1958), pp. 171-72

Cleveland stands pre-eminent as a satirist of real distinction and original-ity, the founder of a new department of English literature. He is the first English writer of partisan verse, purely political in his aims.

This last is his true significance in the history of literature, but he would not have wished to be remembered for that alone. A writer at once learned and witty, consciously bold in his conceits, an ingenious practitioner in an age of competitive ingenuity among poets, he would have wished his work to be judged as a whole. And indeed it is best looked at that way, for the daring metaphors and elaborate conceits of his love poetry are echoed and developed in his political squibs and satires. The same virtues flash out of his verses and the same weaknesses obscure them whether he is celebrating a mistress or excoriating a political enemy.

C. V. Wedgwood
List. (May 8, 1958), p. 769

For one whose cadences moved so unevenly and uncertainly despite their intermittent smoothness and exactness and whose metrical range was so limited, Cleveland had an exceptional influence upon the Restoration satiric couplet. Dryden and Butler both learned from him how to speed up, lighten, roughen, and dramatize a caustic or burlesque line. Oldham studied his rhythm to effect its whiplash sharpness. To no other English satirist prior to 1660 could they look for such brilliant examples. Joseph Hall, Marston, and Donne were too irregular and harsh for their tastes.

Wither was too flat and dull. Although Dryden mentioned Waller and Denham as his models, he could not find in their work couplets adequate for his needs. Their "turns," their easy and pleasing meter with its liquid measures and graceful balance and antithesis would not serve for the plunging, thrusting lines of his satires which required a more virile and varied music. Certainly Oldham could find no one before him who handled the curse with such vigor and flexibility. Nor did Butler have any recent English burlesque poet to follow except Cleveland since the last important one had been John Skelton in the sixteenth century. . . .

Hence, it is clear that Cleveland's meter pointed ahead in two different directions. At the end of one line of influence lay such satires as *The Medal* and *Absalom and Achitophel* with their swift, stinging half-lines pivoting on balance and antithesis, incisive pauses, and crisp rhymes all tending toward a firm but resilient cadence. At the end of the other line lay the burlesque *Hudibras* with its tumbling rhythms, clownish rhymes, and tricky elisions all leading to loose and at times reckless numbers. No two types of meter could be farther apart or less likely to be practiced by the same poet.

In Cleveland's work, however, they function side by side, for while on the one hand he was refining his couplet in accordance with the standards of Waller and Denham, on the other hand he was still bound to the Elizabethan convention of roughness. Symmetrical polysyllabic lines that divide neatly in the middle and stop sharply at the end are surrounded by dissonant monosyllables, distorted accents, and careless verses that avoid balance or closure. From the standpoint of satiric meter, then, his poems are a mixture of the old discords and the new harmonies and demonstrate forcibly the metrical uncertainty that existed at mid-century before the rough elements burst into burlesque and those composing smoothness eased their way into formal satire. Although clearly not an original or artistic handler of the heroic couplet in long passages or whole poems, he was a successful innovator within the scope of individual lines and couplets, one from whom the Restoration poets learned more than they realized and borrowed more than they were willing to acknowledge.

John L. Kimmey
PQ (October, 1958), pp. 410-11, 423

RICHARD CRASHAW
1612-1649

Born in London, the son of an anti-Catholic clergyman. Entered Charter-house School in 1629. Enrolled at Pembroke College, Cambridge, in 1631. Took B.A. in 1634. Became fellow of Peterhouse in 1635. Was friend of poet Abraham Cowley. Became associated with Nicholas Ferrar at the lay religious community of Little Gidding. With triumph of Parliamentarians, expelled from his Cambridge fellowship in 1643 along with other high church Anglicans. Lived at Leyden in Holland for a while. Returned to England briefly. In 1645 went to Paris where he became a Roman Catholic. Introduced to Pope. Given position at shrine of Loreto in 1649. Died shortly after his appointment.

L. C. Martin, ed., *The Poems of Richard Crashaw* (1927)

We have already suggested in our comparison of Crashaw's *Sospetto* with Marino's poem the direction of the impulses and the nature of the vision which enabled Crashaw to kindle to poetic life the artificial forms springing from the study of rhetoric and from Marino. But much as this spirit depended for its growth on Crashaw's own inner growth, and highly individual as his work became, he did not advance alone here any more than in his earlier technical studies. Just as the school of rhetoricians and poetical craftsmen had developed the technique of the ingenious metaphor, so another school of craftsmen had been studying how to turn ingenious wit to the use of quickened meanings. These were the emblematists, the makers of *imprese*, the designers of allegorical tapestry. As we have already said when we spoke of Crashaw's reading, his study of emblems cannot be referred to a distinct stage in his development; but as we shall see in the course of this chapter, emblematic figures appear in his translations from Marino and are woven through and through the texture of his hymns. Thus we may link the emblematic mode of thought in him with the deepening of his religious vocation and with his concentration as an artist upon religious themes. . . .

The spirit of the *impresa* is present, too, in Crashaw's symbolization of concrete sense adjectives as well as in his images. "Soft" becomes in Crashaw's poetry a pure adjective of sentiment and "white" passes through a sense of radiance or brilliance—perhaps with some recollection of "candidus"—to become a pure symbol of "exaltation." Here the moral and intellectual impulse is tied up with Crashaw's special quality as an individual,—with that intensity with which he flings himself upon sentiment. On this side it is related to the notable abundance in his poetry of luscious abstract adjectives of sentiment, "gratious," "sullen Cypresse," "sweetly-killing dart," "glorious," "delicious." And yet in general nature the impulse to such sentimental abstraction has much in common with the *impresa*.

And so, taking all the forms we have just illustrated, we may think of the *impresa* and the *impresa*-like image as another special and ingenious mode of expression into which Crashaw forced his art and which, despite its essential imaginative limitations, was made to give scope for Crashaw's ampler utterance once his imagination had transformed it.

As Crashaw develops, his imagery, or as perhaps one ought now to say, his symbolism becomes almost schematic, almost a private scholasticism. Repetition of imagery must be found in any poet writing in this field and trying to describe the ineffable in some ideal form, on any level, as we see, for instance, in Vaughan's images of darkness and light or Shelley's of moonlight and light on moving water. In Crashaw not only images of such scope as *flame* and *sacrifice* but those of more limited connotation like *nest* and *blushes* become elements in a supersensuous scheme. This repetition derives in him both specifically from the emblem and *impresa* and generally from that system of thought which sees this world as one vast alphabet of the other, a system of thought central elements in which are the symbolism of the Mass and the transitional interpretation of the *Song of Songs*. This mode of imagery, much as it has in common with Marino and with the rhetorics in its pure form, has related itself definitely to a universe of coherent meaning in which Marino and the rhetorics do not participate.

Ruth C. Wallerstein
Richard Crashaw (Madison, Wisc.: Univ. Wisconsin Pr.,
1935), pp. 114, 125-26

These conceits are undoubtedly focal points of Crashaw's experience; but what elements are united in them? Their elements are sensations and emotions. Yet, in a sense, they are metaphysical, for it is the intellect that operates the union. It is by a logical device that he unites in them the sensation of love and the sensation of pain. This is the peculiarity of his conceits, sharply differentiating them from those of Donne, Herbert or Vaughan. The intellect is operative, not before or after, but only in the moment of apprehending the image. By its means he contrives images which satisfy his emotional needs. The images of the ascetic Crashaw are far more predominantly sexual than those of Donne, who had known the pleasures of sensuality, or of Herbert, who never seems to have desired them. He constantly identifies the processes of conception, birth and fostering, with the love that unites God and the saints. The function of the intellect in his poetry is to give logical coherence to his perception of identity between these things.

Joan Bennett
Four Metaphysical Poets (Cambridge
Univ. Pr., 1953), pp. 104-5

To sum up, then, I should say that it is not primarily for the strangeness of his imagery that Crashaw is to be impugned. It is a genuine achievement that he should have been able so frequently to avoid invoking anything like a stock response, that he should lead us into unfamiliar and unusual areas of feeling, and to that extent the strangeness of his imagery is surely justified. We could even say that in this respect he is a better poet than he has been given credit for being. What should concern us, however, is the evident disproportion between the weight of his imagery and the slightness of the theme upon which it is made to depend—a slightness which is the poet's own responsibility and in no sense inherent in the subjects which he chose. I have admittedly dealt only with *The Weeper* but it would be easy enough to show that the weaknesses I have tried to indicate appear elsewhere with some frequency, that they are seemingly inveterate in all but his simpler poems (and there are few of those). Those weaknesses might perhaps be accounted for most benevolently in terms of ineptitude, an inability to master and have charge of the materials and means he chose to use; and certainly the nature of his whole approach discloses ambitions so ample as to indicate that he must have been lacking in proficiency: no imagery we can conceive of could stand the strain of conveying such absolute emotions and so rhapsodic a tone for such long periods without breaking down. But even if we take as charitable a view of his work as this we have to admit that Herbert and Donne (I am thinking now of his divine poems) do not make such misjudgments, devout as they also are, and that he cannot rank with them. And if we lean more towards accuracy than charity we have, I am afraid, to admit that it is not only artistry that makes them superior to him, but integrity as well.

John Peter
Scrutiny (October, 1953), pp. 272-73

SAMUEL   DANIEL

1562-1619

Born near Taunton in Somerset. Entered Magdalen Hall, Oxford, as a Commoner in 1581. Left after three years without taking a degree. In 1585 published a translation of a tract by Paulus Jovius. Accompanied the embassy of Lord Stafford to France in 1586. Visited Italy. After 1590 became tutor to William Herbert, son of the Earl of Pembroke at Wilton House near Salisbury. Became part of the circle of Mary Herbert, Countess of Pembroke, sister of Sir Philip Sidney. Under her patronage wrote tragedy, *Cleopatra*, in 1593. In 1597 or 1598 became tutor to Anne Clifford, eleven-year old daughter of the Countess of Cumberland at Skipton in Yorkshire. In 1602 wrote *Defence of Rhyme* in reply to Thomas Campion's attack on use of rhyme in poetry. Upon accession of King James I was preferred to the favor of Queen Anne by Countess of Bedford. Wrote various masques performed at court. Had some difficulties in 1604 over his play, *Philotas*, which seemed too favorable to the late Earl of Essex. Became a groom of the Queen's Privy Chamber in 1617. Discharged from court in 1618 for visiting Sir Robert Floud, then in official disfavor. Retired to farm at Beckington in his native Somerset. Lived there quietly until his death.

A. C. Sprague, ed., *Samuel Daniel: Poems and A Defense of Rhyme* (1930)

A. B. Grosart, ed., *The Complete Works of Samuel Daniel* (1885-1896), 5 vols.

POETRY

The love element in the sonnets is therefore merely conventional; it is an opportunity for Daniel to achieve the expression of a gentle melancholy characteristic of him, to celebrate the lasting power of verse against the ravages of time and barbarism, and to show that the themes and devices which had been used so much by the French and Italian sonneteers had as much grace and dignity in English as they had in other tongues.

The personality of the speaker and the conceits of his arguments, which Sidney had dramatized so vigorously, are left very quiet and colorless in Daniel's poems. Yet these sonnets have an attraction of their own, and the reader of Elizabethan poetry finds himself stopping over sonnets of Daniel's almost as often as over those of any of his rivals. The explanation is that Daniel has made his sonnets effectively lyric instead of dramatic. He chooses the form of the sonnet characteristic of Surrey, with three well-marked quatrains and a couplet. He polishes the conventional themes and situations; his diction is clear and formal; and his emotion is untempered by irritation, argument, or the sudden turn that marks individuality of feeling. Instead of speech, his poetry approaches incantation, but it eschews rhetorical decoration and is self-consciously modern. He even rejects the poetic practice of Spenser. . . . Daniel's preference for the feminine ending, one which he outgrew and renounced in his later revisions of the sonnets, ties the versification of the sonnets to that of *Rosamond*. In the sonnets it provides a variety of movement and relieves the calm and even pace of his lines, especially at the beginning of a sonnet, where the tone is often hushed and incantational. . . .

The simple eloquence for which Daniel strove is achieved even in the process of making the declaration of indifference to literary fame and artistic renown. The same protestation by Sidney had a dramatic purpose; in Daniel's fourth sonnet it serves to give piquancy to the plain and humble modesty of his style.

Essentially, the love situation in Daniel's cycle is merely a pretext for the poetry. The most common theme in the series is the eternity of verse, which is asserted in seven of the sonnets. The lady is a chaste goddess; she reconciles chastity and beauty; and though the lover speaks of his "youth and error," his "blush and error," and "this error" in referring to his love, there is no such conflict between desire and reason as Sidney had utilized in his sonnets. It is quite clear that the love in the *Delia* situation is a "spotless love" and a "chast desire." The despair of the speaker that he is unsuccessful in his love provides the justification for the elegiac tone of the poems; it is serving the same purpose as the old *Mirror for Magistrates* device of the complaining ghost serves for *Rosamond*. There is no analysis of the despair, no real attempt to show its nature or causes; the mood is sustained because it is a fruitful one for reflective lyrics on the passing of time and beauty, the appropriate one for Daniel's characteristically quiet and chastened style.

Hallett Smith
Elizabethan Poetry (Cambridge, Mass.: Harvard
Univ. Pr., 1952), pp. 158-59

In 1591 we reach a sonneteer who matters. In that year Newman's edition of Sidney's *Astrophel* included twenty-eight sonnets by Samuel Daniel. . . . In the following year Daniel published his sequence *Delia* which omitted a few of those printed by Newman and added many others, bringing the total up to fifty-five. *Delia* stands in a different class from the rest of Daniel's work: if he had written nothing else we might hear less of Daniel but we should certainly hear less of "the prosaic Daniel." For assuredly those who like their poetry "not too darn poetical" should avoid *Delia*. It offers no ideas, no psychology, and of course no story: it is simply a masterpiece of phrasing and melody. To anyone who complains that it is a series of commonplaces we can only reply, "Yes, but listen". . . .

The truth is that while everything Daniel says would be commonplace in a prose abstract, nothing is commonplace as it actually occurs in the poetry. In that medium all the Petrarchan gestures become compulsive invitations to enormous sorrows and delights. And it really matters very little that he is so heavily indebted to Desportes. A poetic translation is always to some extent a new work of art. In the large, objective kinds, in epic or tragedy, the degree of novelty is limited, because situation, characters, and architectonics are common to both handlings. But in so small a poem as a sonnet a seemingly trivial change may alter an image, or an implied image, in such a way as to alter the lighting of the whole piece. . . .

Though Daniel's poetry is often uninspired, sometimes obscure, and not seldom simply bad, he has two strong claims on our respect. In the first place, he can at times achieve the same masculine and unstrained majesty which we find in Wordsworth's greater sonnets, and I believe that Wordsworth learned it from Daniel. (The two poets had much in common and Daniel would have liked *Laodamia*.) And secondly Daniel is, in the nineteenth-century sense of the words, a poet of ideas. There had of course been ideas in Chaucer, and Spenser: but I think those poets felt themselves to be simply transmitting an inherited and accepted wisdom. There are, again, plenty of ideas in Donne, but they are, in my opinion, treated merely as the tools of his peculiar rhetoric: he was not interested in their truth or falsehood. But Daniel actually thinks in verse: thinks deeply, arduously, and perhaps with some originality. This is something quite different from Dryden's power of neatly poetizing all the stock arguments for the side on which he is briefed. Dryden states: Daniel can doubt and wrestle. It is no necessary quality in a poet, and Daniel's thinking is not always poetical. But its result is that though Daniel is not one of our greatest poets, he is the most interesting man of letters whom that century produced in England.

C. S. Lewis
English Literature in the Sixteenth Century (Oxford:
Clarendon Pr., 1954), pp. 491-92, 530-31

The attempt has been made in this paper to discuss those features of Daniel's diction, versification, and imagery that are characteristic of his style. Some of these qualities help explain the epithet "well-languaged" that has been long attached to his name. These and certain other features have fixed on him the less enviable label of "prosaic." His diction is largely drawn from what Dr. Johnson called "general nature." It is therefore "pure" in that it has escaped the extinction that particularization generally suffers. Daniel shows no particular concern with the details of common life, nor does he reveal any fondness for nature for its own sake. He is primarily a humanist and moralist. Avoiding archaisms, he shows a fondness for Latinate diction in his revisions, in his frequent use of privatives with Latin prefixes, and especially in his *in*-compounds, many of which he himself coined. Although he has an exceptional sense of structure, balance, and verbal precision, his language sometimes lacks force and vigour, owing partly to an increasing fondness for connective devices that increase the complexity of his sentences and reduce the concreteness of his diction. But in a great many cases he exhibits a remarkable smoothness of versification and an exceptional gift for making the transition to the play of abstract ideas from very limited sensuous detail. Some of the better poems after 1599 are partially sustained by his metaphor of the building or mansion, an image that reinforces his admirable quality of calm and dignity. Although not rich in vigour, fire and passion, he frequently manages to move, without exciting. In many such instances, his gift is for the pathetic, not the tragic. Most often his poetry is addressed to the understanding rather than to the emotions. And in these instances his low-pitched tone of seriousness acquires an eloquence that inspires genuine admiration.

Cecil C. Seronsy

MLR (October, 1957), p. 497

Defence of Rhyme

The part played by beauty of poetic form in making purposes articulate (making subjects manifest) is integral, as seen by Renaissance didactic theory. When Daniel says that we need not copy classical measures, since we admire the Greeks and Latins "not for their smooth-gliding words, nor their measures, but *for their inventions,*" he is saying something much closer to "for their imaginative ordering of reality" than to "for their prose content." And in fact this is part of a defense of just such formal poetic elements as smooth-gliding words; it is, after all, part of a *Defence of Ryme*. There is no inconsistency here, given the understandings I have outlined. These made it possible to see poetry as didactically useful through its aesthetically satisfying form; a thing cannot be useful if it cannot get born. Daniel's treatise is one of the most impressive and exciting critical documents in English because of his peculiar gift for seeing stability in mutability, without sentimentality and without compromise. His is a defense of *"whatsoever* force of words doth moove, delight, and sway the affections of men,*"* cogently argued on the grounds that these habits must change with times, conditions, and the different "idioma" of different languages (in Gregory Smith, II, 363-65). Yet the purposes thus differently habited are the living souls of poems, and not mortal. To turn such understandings of the didactic theory into mere praise of "the thought-content" of poems is foolishness.

Though it is fatal to forget the role of the imagination in bringing conceptions to birth, it is also falsifying if we forget the role of the judgment in writing and reading poetry. Daniel does not wish to see a poet "smoothe up a weake confused sense" in order to delight the ear, "seeing it is matter that satisfies *the iudicial.*" That it is the reader's judgment which finds satisfaction in the conceptions which a poet can beget is not in the least inconsistent with high praise of the imagination such as Puttenham's. The writer's own judgment has passed his invented matter as satisfying, before the reader ever sees it, before it has found expression; it is the intellect which contemplates forms.

Rosemond Tuve

Elizabethan and Metaphysical Imagery (Chicago: Univ. Chicago Pr., 1947), pp. 391-92

No one can claim that any one of these critics, or even all of them taken together, succeeded in stating fully how language can be handled so as to serve as such a material. Between them, however, they at least touch upon all the necessities of a consideration of metre. All are acutely conscious of words, most of them listen carefully to their sounds, and Gascoigne, King James, Sidney for a few moments, Puttenham, Campion and Daniel make real contributions to the subject of metre proper. They are aware of the principal problem of the subject: the problem of how to make words, which are used in poetry for their meaning-reference, serve also, without wrenching them from their natural utterance, to indicate a form independent of the meaning, though not contradictory of its emotional effect, a form which can give pleasure in itself and also, at best, deepen the meaning. They realize with increasing clarity that such form must be rhythmical, and that it must be an organization of time. They wrestle with this problem of time in speech and, taking many falls, yet return to the struggle and score some points. They learn to take help from music and therefore become subtly sensitive to lyric-forms. They find in this connection the part that silence, whether as pause or as rest, can play in organizing sound into rhythmical arrangements of time. Finally, they begin to see how attributes of syllables other than their duration can be used to emphasize these arrangements and bring out their significance.

Catherine Ing
Elizabethan Lyrics (London: Chatto and Windus, 1951), p. 64

Daniel asserts [in the *Defence of Rhyme*] that the different conceptions of wisdom and excellence in the world are but one, "apparelled according to the fashion of every nation." This notion of identity in the midst of diversity is the product of a mind profoundly moved by a vision of history. In the historical process all matters of whatever importance will pass away—even Campion's quarrel with rhyme as Daniel asserts in his closing sentence: "But this is but a Character of that perpetuall revolution that wee see to be in all things that never remaine the same, and we must herein be content to submit our selves to the law of time, which in a few yeares wil make al that, for which we now contend, *Nothing*.". . .

Throughout the *Defence* is this theme of the law of time, with its fatal revolution of events and its superiority over the fixed judgment of an age. One feels that Daniel's perceptions as a critic grow out of a view of human history in which he sees all things undergoing perpetual change and yet in the larger pattern of recurrence all remaining the same. By such a measure he is able to see literary canons as perpetually changing fashions, while at the same time the excellence of man's performance, or at least man's potential, is about the same in all ages. Ironically in the *Defence* this basically classical view serves to shake the calm of infallibility for classical literature.

Cecil S. Seronsy
SP (July, 1957), p. 407

THOMAS DEKKER
1572-1632?

Born in London around 1572, probably of Dutch origins. Nothing known of his education. Probably began writing plays for Philip Henslowe as early as 1594. Between 1598 and 1602 wrote for Lord Admiral's Men, Earl of Worcester's Men, Lord Chamberlain's Men, and Children of St. Paul's. An attack upon Ben Jonson in *Satiromastix* (1601) involved him in the War of the Theatres. In 1604 collaborated with Jonson on entertainment to celebrate the entry of King James I into London. Began to write prose pamphlets on a great variety of subjects. Prepared Lord Mayor's pageant in 1612. Imprisoned for debt in 1613. Remained in prison until 1619. Wrote remarkable series of prison pamphlets. Upon release continued to collaborate with various dramatists until death, probably in 1632. Wrote or had a hand in some forty plays.

Fredson T. Bowers, ed., *The Dramatic Works of Thomas Dekker* (1953-1961), 4 vols.

A. B. Grosart, ed., *Non-Dramatic Works of Thomas Dekker* (1884-1886), 5 vols.

PLAYS

It is wonderful that a man who was the veritable Dickens of his own times was capable of writing two such plays as *Old Fortunatus* and *The Sun's Darling*. They are both charming, and steeped in romance. In them, as Charles Lamb remarks, poetry "simply oozes from Dekker's finger tips," and there is a quality of rare freshness about the dainty lyrics with which they are scattered. The Pleasant Comedy of *Old Fortunatus* is built upon an old fable. Poor and very patient, Fortunatus is offered by Fortune his choice between wisdom, strength, health, beauty, long life and riches, and unfortunately he chooses riches, for

"This age thinks better of a gilded fool, than of a threadbare saint in wisdom's school . . . The rich are wise . . . Gold is the strength, the sinews of the world." So Fortune gives the old man riches. "Thou shall spend ever, and be never poor."

But the gift is the undoing of both Fortunatus and his sons, and the giver of the gift mocks continually at their disasters, calling them "servants of a bright devil." Meantime in a charming song we see the true inwardness of the play. For those who pursue gold, and gold alone.

> Virtue's branches wither, Virtue pines

and more than that:

> Vice doth flourish, Vice in glory shines.

This play seems wrongly named a comedy. It is so grim, but of course there is a love-story also. Mr. Addington Symonds points out: "Among the poet's most perfect achievements are the scenes in which Orleans indulges a lover's lunacy in a passion of wild fancies." Orleans considers the whole world mad and he the only wise man left. He is enamoured to a perfect frenzy. This play which is really almost a masterpiece should be much more widely known.

Constance Spender
CR (August, 1926), pp. 336-37

Dekker, the most traditional of Elizabethan writers, was by nature little of a dramatist and practised intermittently. His plays have moments of tenderness, gleams of pathos, but the general effect is too often amorphous and blurred. His work is mingled with that of others and often survives in a poor state. The titles of forty-two of his plays are recorded; seventeen remain of which five are entirely his own—*Old Fortunatus, The Shoemakers' Holiday, The Whore of Babylon, If it be not a good play, the devil is in it* and *Match Me in London*. In plays where he collaborated, the other partner seems generally to have influenced the plot. Dekker tried all the popular forms, and he wrote for the men's and the boys' companies over a period of more than thirty years. His drama falls roughly into three divisions: the early popular comedies, including *Old Fortunatus, Patient Grissel* and *The Shoemakers' Holiday*; the citizen comedies written with Middleton and Webster; and after an interval, the final tragic lyric mode of *The Witch of Edmonton*, inconsequently joined with some poor fustian. . . .

It is significant that Dekker's finest work is either in lyric form or in prose. His generous and unforced humanity and his deep vein of piety show up best in his pamphlets, which are incomparably superior to anything he wrote for the stage. His style has always the merits of easiness and simplicity, but the blank verse lacks pulse and power. His range is so wide that no one consistent impression remains. The prose speech of his clowns is the most distinctive of all; this was generally true, of course, and is well marked in the early Shakespeare. From the antithetical wit of Shadow in *Old Fortunatus* (a style roughly equivalent to that of Speed in

Shakespeare's *Two Gentlemen of Verona*) Dekker steadily progresses towards colloquial ease. . . .

As his early plays echo Marlowe and Greene, Dekker's middle verse reflects Shakespeare. For formal passages he is addicted to couplets: his imagery is always unobtrusive. His is precisely that simple, lucid, unplanned style which was essential to establish a norm. He is interested in proverbs and in the contrast of foreign speech with English, but language is a tool that has grown into his hand: he does not seek, like Jonson, to polish it.

The delicate fancy and rough vitality of Dekker were quenched by six years' imprisonment in the King's Bench (1613-1619), after which he wrote but little. His pamphlets and pageants continued to appear, but his final comedies are sorry affairs. *The Witch of Edmonton*, a tender and barbarous story, has nothing of comedy in it but Cuddy Banks's jests.

Dekker could not achieve formal structure. The simple contrast of Maid, Wife and Widow in *Patient Grissel* is a traditional one. In *Westward Ho!* and *Northward Ho!* with the aid of Webster he had tried symmetrical grouping of characters, and had speeded up the love-intrigue. In his last plays, *The Wonder of a Kingdom* and *Match Me in London*, he allows three or four pairs of lovers to a play. . . . It is curious that as Dekker in his old age overcrowded his intrigues and multiplied plots in an attempt to follow the style of Jonson and his "sons," Jonson himself turned back to those old moralities which Dekker had drawn on in his youth.

M. C. Bradbrook
The Growth and Structure of English Comedy (London:
Chatto and Windus, 1955), pp. 121, 129-30

Perhaps the nature of the final compromise [in *The Shoemakers' Holiday*], which brings out the best in the social hierarchy as well as in love, honor, and the working-festive life of the "gentle craft," can best be seen in the feasting imagery, some examples of which I have already quoted. There have been several false starts towards the final concept of the communal banquet. The only agreement Lincoln and Mayor Oteley can achieve over their "sundry" feasts, as we have seen, is that it is a "shame / To join a Lacy with an Oteley's name." Hammon, the hunter of his "dear," having lost his venison, expects to "find a wife," only to become ironically the prey at Oteley's "hunter's feast." Switching the hunt to Jane, his "poor famish'd eyes do feed on that / Which made them famish" (III.iv.5), but he is finally excluded altogether from the shoemakers' banquet, as he is excluded from the harmony and festivity of love itself (v.ii.91), because he has not been willing to sacrifice station to love. His is a false quest, not without appeal, but clearly misdirected. Before the final banquet a preliminary feast is held during which Eyre dominates and becomes the envy of those who have more money but less gaiety. Margery's suggestion to "put on gravity" (iii.iii.11) is found unacceptable and Rose is advised to marry "a grocer," since "grocer is a sweet trade: plums, plums." And so Hodge and Firk, as I have indicated, conceive of the feast of life in sensual terms only. . . .

This kind of dream, so full of childlike personification, is, of course, quite different from the aristocratic dream of ideal love, but it, too, rests on the borderline between innocence and irresponsibility. The final shoemakers' banquet, while satisfying these appetites and giving gaiety its due, places controls upon the impulse to take a prolonged vacation. When the pancake bell rings, the shoemakers can be "as free as my lord mayor," shut up their shops, and make holiday, and it may seem that the holiday will "continue for ever"; but in fact it will cease and come again under the cyclical restrictions and discipline of nature and under the sanctions of a social decorum.

Harold E. Toliver
Boston Univ. Stud. in Eng. (Winter, 1961), pp. 216-17

General

It follows from this, then, that when Dekker reveals the preoccupations of his generation, either in thought or dramatic technique, he will do so, in the main, unconsciously, that he will not, like Chapman or Ben Jonson, offer a reasoned and coherent group of principles either moral or aesthetic in opposition to the trend of contemporary social or literary development. Up to a point, in fact, his work resembles rather that of Middleton in its steady reflection of what came to his notice and the absence if not of satirical humour, at least of the satire which attempts reform. But it is only up to a point that we can find in Dekker's work the clear mirroring of the Jacobean world that Middleton's comedy offers, for Dekker, though he has apparently no artistic creed, has an intermittent moral code which seems to derive rather from a simple, but genuine, though unformulated, mysticism—the very quality, indeed, that Chapman indicates in Strozza in *The Gentleman Usher*. But he is utterly without Chapman's systematic reasoning, that built upon this a coherent body of principles. Dekker's mysticism, though it is as different from the brooding spirit of the age as is Chapman's own, escapes in flashes, moments of bright faith which, since they are entirely spontaneous and never forced, have, paradoxically, a security which Chapman's firm declarations sometimes lack. He has not, therefore, in his response to his material or to the mood of his generation, the consistency of either Chapman or Middleton; not Chapman's consistent principling, not Middleton's consistent detachment. With Ben Jonson, of course, he offers no comparison (except in his use of somewhat similar material for some of his comedies); he never appears to have taken himself or his art seriously enough to have evolved any explicit aesthetic creed, much less to preach. His comedy, then, reflects clearly enough the circumscribed world of immediate events and persons, with momentary escapes never long maintained, but never quite abandoned, into a wider universe of the spirit. But at no time, I think, is there fusion or synthesis of the two.

Una M. Ellis-Fermor
The Jacobean Drama (London: Methuen, 1936), p. 119

One large segment of Dekker's work comprises his pamphlets on the recurring plague. . . . To think of accounts of the plague is to think of Defoe, but while Defoe writes as a social historian, marshalling his facts and statistics into a sober analysis, Dekker is a reporter, humorist, and poet who, with a mixture of personal emotion and artistic detachment, seizes upon whatever has immediate human interest. Both writers accept the plague as a divine punishment for sin, but the later *bourgeois* moralist does not ring such poetic changes upon the eternal contrasts between health and disease, exuberant vitality and sudden extinction, the marriage-bed and the grave. Dekker is much closer to the medieval and pictorial tradition of the Dance of Death; *The Meeting of Gallants* carries us back, in its setting if not in its quality, to the *Pardoner's Tale*. Dekker's Jacobean imagination is kindled into macabre intensity by the lurid horrors of wholesale mortality and corruption, yet even the plague does not check his flow of robust humour and racy slang and puns. In *The Wonderful Year,* after visions of the charnel house and crawling worms, come the *fabliau* of the cobbler's wife who made a death-bed confession of her affairs with neighbouring husbands and then recovered, and the anecdote, told with such dramatic verve, of the bold tinker who came sounding through a country town and, to his great profit, buried the Londoner's corpse which the villagers were afraid to approach. In a very different key Dekker speaks out against the people of London who have had the means and the will to escape from the trials of their fellow citizens and have carried the pestilence into the country.

Douglas Bush
English Literature in the Earlier Seventeenth Century 1600-1660
(Oxford: Clarendon Pr., 1945), pp. 40-41

THOMAS DELONEY

ca. 1543-1600

Almost nothing is known of his life. May have attended grammar school in some provincial town. It has been suggested that he came from Norwich, but this is uncertain. Worked as a silk weaver. Began work as popular journalist around 1580. Wrote ballads, one on the defeat of the Spanish Armada in 1588. Wrote pamphlets and novels designed to glorify merchant guilds.

F. O. Mann, ed., *The Works of Thomas Deloney* (1912)
M. E. Lawlis, ed., *The Novels of Thomas Deloney* (1961)

Taken by himself, the Deloney character is very simply constructed, . . . His movement is almost linear, his impact on the reader simple and direct.

But in the final analysis we must remember that he exists in a dramatic context, which means that he has certain definite relationships with other characters. These relationships often have surprisingly complex implications. One thinks of the scenes involving Richard Casteler, Round Robin, Long Meg, Gillian, and the Dutch girl whom Richard eventually marries. In the central theme of marriage there are strong suggestions of irony, now light and playful and now bitingly satirical. We identify with Meg, in her conversations with Richard, despite her weakness and his strength. But the introduction of Robin and Gillian produces an astringent effect. Robin qualifies our involvement with Long Meg through his cynical, detached remarks. Gillian, though by herself a sympathetic character, is caught up in a situation much like Long Meg's; and at times Deloney treats this double portion of pathos as a doubly serious matter, while at other times he sees in it elements of comedy and even of farce.

In such scenes Deloney reveals an attitude toward the people he wrote about, the lower-class apprentices and the middle-class tradesmen, that is quite different from anything else one comes across in Elizabethan literature. In every line of his novels there is the calm assumption that tradesmen are eminently worth writing about.

Merritt E. Lawlis
*Apology for the Middle Class: The Dramatic Novels of Thomas
Deloney* (Bloomington, Ind.: Indiana Univ. Pr., 1960), pp. 106-7

Deloney's novels contrast so strongly with *Euphues,* and with other Elizabethan novels, that the reader immediately recognizes them as something new, as a different order of fiction. *Jack of Newbury* (1597 or 1598) is the first really dramatic novel in English. It is dramatic in every sense. A story more vivid and exciting would be difficult to find. Deloney's vision of life is dramatic: he chooses to write about people of action, people in the act of accomplishing certain material things. Perhaps his basic attitude toward people is what attracted him to the drama and what then led him to make his novels dramatic in the sense of drama-like.

To understand Deloney's use of the play form, all one has to do is contrast Shakespeare's use of the novel form. When Shakespeare borrows from Thomas Lodge's *Rosalynde* and Robert Greene's *Pandosto* for *As*

You Like It and *The Winter's Tale,* he takes not only the incident but the actual wording. Yet it is clear that he already knows what genre he is going to write in: it is the play. Different as the play is from the novel, especially in Elizabethan times, there is not the slightest tendency in Shakespeare to write in the manner of Lodge and Greene. Whatever he uses he "makes his own," as we say, because the novel and the play are so different in form and structure that his act of creation is not diminished by the extensive literal borrowing.

Deloney's indebtedness to the drama is of another kind. He never filches a whole scene; nor does he copy the dialogue word for word. He likes the dramatic form so well that he simply takes it over. He puts a scene before us the way a playwright does; and, especially in the first three novels, he seldom analyzes omnisciently in his own words. Although *Jack of Newbury* begins with omniscient analysis, the point of view quickly changes; and we rarely get Jack's thoughts any longer. Instead, we are an audience viewing a stage, and we know only what we see and hear. . . .

Deloney employs dialogue so naturally, and so much the way we are accustomed to it in the twentieth-century novel, that his achievement at first escapes us. More than four-fifths of *Jack of Newbury* is in dialogue form. The story begins with two brief paragraphs of introduction. Then comes a chorus-like interchange, a distant "quoth one" and "quoth another." But before long Jack is sitting on a cushion beside the widow, his employer; and what we "hear" is an intimate conversation as racy and colloquial as a scene from *The Alchemist.* Some chapters, like Chapter X of *Jack*—the wonderful episode in which Tweedle gets sweet revenge on Mistress Frank—are entirely in dialogue except for a brief comment at the beginning and the end. . . .

Whether the scene to be emphasized is comedy or tragedy, Deloney always manages to be vivid. His focus is on the details of everyday life. The dialogue, in fact, is so concrete that it is a mine of information about the artisans of the Elizabethan period. Love and marriage are the main topics of conversation; but since Deloney is a materialist to the core, his characters talk freely of money, food, and other business and household matters.

Merritt E. Lawlis, ed.
The Novels of Thomas Deloney (Bloomington, Ind.:
Indiana Univ. Pr., 1961), pp. xii, xiv-xv

JOHN DONNE

1572-1631

Son of a prosperous London merchant. Mother the daughter of John Heywood, granddaughter of the sister of Sir Thomas More. Brought up as a Catholic. Studied both at Oxford and Cambridge. Entered Thavies Inn as Law student in 1591. Studied at Lincoln's Inn from 1592-1594. Lived the life of a man about town. Travelled on the Continent. Took part in the Spanish expeditions of the Earl of Essex in 1596 and 1597. Early amorous and satiric poetry written in 1590's. Made secretary in 1597 to Sir Thomas Egerton, the Lord Keeper. Had become an Anglican. Secret marriage to Anne More, niece of Egerton, led to Donne's imprisonment and dismissal from office. Brought an end to his career in public service. Suffered financial hardships until about 1615. Depended upon various patrons. Went abroad with Sir Robert Drury in 1611-1612. Became a member of Parliament for Taunton in 1614. From 1616 to 1622 was Reader in Divinity at Lincoln's Inn. Wife died in 1617 after having given birth to twelve children, five of whom survived. Travelled to Germany as part of Lord Doncaster's embassy in 1619 and 1620. In 1621 appointed Dean of St. Paul's by King James I. In 1624 named Vicar of St. Dunstan's in the West. Seriously ill in 1623-1624. During plague of 1625 lived in Chelsea with Magdalen Herbert, wife of Sir John Danvers. Most of his poems printed posthumously in 1633 and in later years.

H. J. C. Grierson, ed., *The Poetical Works of John Donne* (1912), 2 vols.

T. Redpath, ed., *Songs and Sonnets of John Donne,* (1956)

Helen Gardner, ed., *John Donne: The Elegies and Songs and Sonnets* (1965)

Geoffrey Keynes, *A Bibliography of Dr. John Donne,* 3rd ed. (1958)

PERSONAL

Donne's acceptance of the established Church is the most important single event of his life, because it involved all the powers of his mind and personality. His youthful sympathies must have been with the persecuted Romanists, and his Satires contain bitter allusion to "pursuivants," tormentors of Jesuits; the odious Topcliffe is mentioned by name in some manuscripts. But he was familiar with the fanaticism as well as with the learning of Jesuits; and later he decided that the first of these was the hardest affliction of Christendom, though the second was to serve him well. No one can say exactly when he left one Church for the other; it was a gradual process. . . .

Donne, then, accepted the Church of England because it was truly Catholic. He rejoiced to discover a Reformed Church which cultivated the Fathers and was slow to come "to a final resolution" in "particulars." He wanted tradition but without its errors: Aquinas, but not the scholastic nonsense; the Fathers, but not their mistakes.

Frank Kermode
John Donne (BC/Longmans, 1957), pp. 27, 31

To the student of Donne's sermons, interest in *Pseudo-Martyr* [written in 1609] goes well beyond those passages in which Donne seeks to clarify his personal position. For this treatise contains arguments, of both political and theological nature, which were to be voiced in his pulpit years. Many times in his sermons he returns to what he states in *Pseudo-Martyr* to be the basic corruptness of the Church of Rome, as manifested primarily in three "errors"—1/ the debasing of secular magistrates and the exalting of ecclesiastics; 2/ the misconception of their doctrine of good works, with its views that a man can in the eyes of God go beyond the call of duty; 3/ the belief that there is a purgatorial state, the torments of which may be escaped through the superabundant merits and sufferings of the martyrs.

William R. Mueller
John Donne: Preacher (Princeton, N.J.: Princeton Univ. Pr., 1962), p. 20

It is generally supposed that John Donne as a young man was of loose moral character, and that his acceptance of ordination was a penitent repudiation of his former way of life. According to Walton, "some irregularities of my life" were a reason given by Donne for not taking Holy Orders earlier than he did; he records him saying, "I cannot plead innocency of life, especially of my youth," and Walton himself says: "He was by nature highly passionate. . . ." The student of his life and works must make up his own mind on this matter. The prodigal returning home to Lincoln's Inn as preacher is an exciting spiritual drama, but one must pause to consider how likely it would be for a responsible governing body to appoint him, so early in his ministry, if his character was notorious. . . . The charge of immorality must be held not proven if it rests solely on the interpretation of his poems.

Frederick A. Rowe
I Launch at Paradise: A Consideration of John Donne, Poet and Preacher (London, Epworth Pr., 1964), pp. 21-23

All that we can say is that Donne had enough amatory experience to be able to write his poems. . . . Our overall conclusion should be that the most successful of the poems have the ring of authenticity, that we are hearing the many-mooded voice of experience, but that, unfortunately for the biographer, it is a hopeless task to extract from such nebulous, volatile, and mercurial matter lost facts, specific episodes, faceless and nameless mistresses.

One final excess must be dealt with—the excess of insisting that Donne had no youthful excesses, of crediting him with no mistresses at all. This is an attractive stance to the sophisticated and to English professors. . . . It is altogether wholesome to take every opportunity to point out that genius—the best genius—not only modifies for purposes of art the raw material of

life; it can even perform the miracle of creation *ex nihilo*: imagine perfectly
what others can report only from experience.

Edward Le Comte
Grace to a Witty Sinner: A Life of Donne (London:
Victor Gollancz, 1965), pp. 52-53

GENERAL

Donne's love-poetry is a very complex phenomenon. The two dominant
strains in it are these: the strain of dialectic, subtle play of argument and
wit, erudite and fantastic; and the strain of vivid realism, the record of a
passion which is not ideal nor conventional, neither recollected in tran-
quillity nor a pure product of literary fashion, but love as an actual,
immediate experience in all its moods, gay and angry, scornful and rapturous with joy, touched with tenderness and darkened with sorrow—though
these last two moods, the commonest in love-poetry, are with Donne the
rarest. The first of these strains comes to Donne from the Middle Ages,
the dialectic of the Schools, which passed into mediaeval love-poetry
almost from its inception; the second is the expression of the new temper
of the Renaissance as Donne had assimilated it in Latin countries. . . .

What, then, is the philosophy which disengages itself from Donne's love-
poetry studied in its whole compass? It seems to me that it is more than a
purely negative one, that consciously or unconsciously he sets over against
the abstract idealism, the sharp dualism of the Middle Ages, a justification
of love as a natural passion in the human heart the meaning and end of
which is marriage. The sensuality and exaggerated cynicism of so much of
the poetry of the Renaissance was a reaction from courtly idealism and
mediaeval asceticism. But a mere reaction could lead nowhither. There
are no steps which lead only backward in the history of human thought
and feeling. Poems like Donne's Elegies, like Shakespeare's *Venus and
Adonis*, like Marlowe's *Hero and Leander* could only end in penitent outcries like those of Sidney and Spenser and of Donne himself. The true
escape from courtly or ascetic idealism was a poetry which should do justice
to love as a passion in which body and soul alike have their part, and of
which there is no reason to repent.

And this with all its imperfections Donne's love-poetry is. It was not for
nothing that Sir Thomas Egerton's secretary made a runaway match for
love. For Dante the poet, his wife did not exist. In love of his wife Donne
found the meaning and the infinite value of love. In later days he might
bewail his "idolatry of profane mistresses"; he never repented of having
loved. Between his most sensual and his most spiritual love-songs there is
no cleavage such as separates natural love from Dante's love of Beatrice,
who is in the end Theology. The passion that burns in Dante's most
outspoken elegies, and wantons in the Epithalamia, is not cast out in "The

Anniversary" or "The Canonization," but absorbed. It is purified and enriched by being brought into harmony with his whole nature, spiritual as well as physical. It has lost the exclusive consciousness of itself which is lust, and become merged in an entire affection, as a turbid and discolored stream is lost in the sea.

This justification of natural love as fullness of joy and life is the deepest thought in Donne's love-poems. . . .

Herbert J. C. Grierson, ed.
"The Poetry of Donne" in The Poems of Donne, 2 vols.
(Oxford: Clarendon Pr., 1912), vol. II, pp. xxxiv, xxxv, xlv, xlvi

John Donne was twenty years younger than Ralegh. He belonged to another generation. Yet he is separated from the Elizabethan poets by more than time. His poetry takes up into itself the conventions and gifts of his age. Yet it transmutes these qualities into something unique, different from anything in his contemporaries or followers. For this reason he is difficult to study either as an Elizabethan or as a seventeenth-century poet. Yet if he must belong to one age or the other, he belongs more closely to the seventeenth century. The only poems published in his life-time appeared in 1611, 1612, 1613. His great career as Dean of Saint Paul's was from 1621 to 1631. To be sure, his love poetry, *The Elegies* and *The Songs and Sonnets* as well as some of *Satires* and *Letters* belong in part to the 1590's. . . .

In spirit, however, Donne is separated from the Elizabethan world. There are various reasons for this separation. First of all he is isolated by the quality of his personality. Furthermore he took pains to withhold his verse from the stream of popular publication. None of his poems strayed into the verse collections of the late Nineties and early 1600's, as did Ralegh's. In his letters in which he sometimes enclosed copies of his verses to his friends, he besought their secrecy and specified that the manuscript poems must not come to print. . . . Another thing which separated Donne and contemporary secular poetry was a persistent preoccupation from childhood with religion. This sensual, worldly and fashionable young man of the Nineties carried always with him a teasing bewilderment about religious beliefs. . . . Thus the Elizabethan ingredients were mixed in John Donne in proportions so different from their proportions in men like Ralegh and Shakespeare that the resulting personality is hardly contemporary, in the spiritual sense of the word.

Esther Cloudman Dunn
The Literature of Shakespeare's England (New York:
Charles Scribner's Sons, 1936), pp. 158-60

Already we have given a short account of Donne's early predisposition to disregard authority; the spirit of his writings complementing this disregard is no less significant than an awareness of self as the supremely important and interesting fact of life and the instrument of our conceptions of divinity and truth. Perhaps it is most easily sensed in *Songs and Sonets*, against which the charge has been laid so frequently that in more ways than one they respect authority all too little. They are free enough from an overt dependence upon tradition. But his other works, including the *Anniversaries* and particularly the essays and sermons, may seem to reflect an excessive reverence for the past. This may be said, however, only because marginal note, allusion, and reference make obvious Donne's familiarity with old writers (and new ones too, for that matter). Thus, in considering his various writings one must appreciate the varying demands imposed upon the author by different forms of discourse: a sonnet is not written according to the rules of tractarian controversy, nor should a sermon follow the outlines of a pamphlet. But in the face of the psychological facts one can hardly admit the notion of marked cleavage in personality between the poet who in a manner most perverse supplicates the goddess of love, and the "saint" who prolongs a rather unseemly doubt about his own salvation. Though it would be folly to announce that Donne "broke" with the medieval world and freed himself entirely from its influences, it would be no less absurd to hazard that a catalogue of his medieval doctrines could not be drawn up as conveniently from the heretical verses of his youth as from the copia of his later years wherein those "engines" of medieval learning worked so energetically. Early or late, it is imperative to note that the energy of the poet's own active soul is the one dominant, kinetic force, an energy that was more abundantly released and given direction by the influence of the new philosophy.

With the recognition that this spirit controls Donne's writings, it may be said that it affected his attitude toward authority in a number of specific ways. It brought to his poems an amazing originality; it encouraged an attitude of tolerance and respect for all sound opinion gathered from his various learning and rich experience; it led him to practice discriminating and critical methods of scholarship; and finally, it caused him to seek in conscience, rather than in the varying opinions of men, the criteria of authentic religious experience. [1937]

Charles M. Coffin
John Donne and the New Philosophy (New York:
Humanities Pr., 1958), pp. 216-217

Donne's search was for a love which would triumph over spatial and temporal limits by admitting those who shared it to a world of happiness surpassing anything experienced in the natural world, a love which would not suffer from any antagonism between mind and body, or body and soul. Time and again he is disappointed of this well-nigh unattainable ideal. But he is aware of another release from bodily limits, another entry into a vaster world, and an ultimate, harmonious union between body and soul:

all these are offered by death. Love and death are brought together in Donne's lyrics in an unvoiced comparison of their power to release man from human limitations. There is scarcely one poem among the *Songs and Sonets* in which the theme of death does not occur, either in the title (*The Funerall—The Dissolution—The Expiration*), or in the forceful opening phrase ("When I dyed last"—"As virtuous men passe mildly away"—"Who ever comes to shroud me") or as a sudden discordant note after a beginning voicing the confident pride of satisfied love. There is nothing necrophilic about this use of the theme of death. Donne never writes as the disappointed lover who longs for the grave's obliteration of his pangs. Rather he implies that death will open a way to that plenitude of which love has so often cheated him. . . . At the time he wrote most of his love poems, death seemed to his conscious mind to be a counter-attack upon the lovers, turning to defeat their victory over time and space. At this period of his life, human love offered him the natural and fitting way of allaying his desire to transcend all limitation. If *The Extasie* and *The Undertaking* are addressed to Anne More, he attained his difficult ideal on his marriage to her in 1601.

M. M. Mahood
Poetry and Humanism (London: Jonathan Cape,
1950), pp. 101-2

Donne had a different conception of the function of imagery from that of these other poets. The purpose of an image in his poetry is to define the emotional experience by an intellectual parallel. It is as essential to follow his reasoning when reading, as it is to respond to Keats' sense perception of dethroned Saturn when

> Upon the sodden ground
> His old right hand lay nerveless, listless, dead,
> Unsceptred; and his realmless eyes were closed.

Keats' sensuous impression is identified with the thing he wants to express; Donne, on the other hand, identifies his intellectual analogy with his emotion. A great part of the value of his poetry, to those who enjoy him, lies in the demand he thus makes on the imagination in the sense in which Coleridge defines it: "judgment ever awake and steady self-possession with enthusiasm and feeling profound or vehement."

Donne's reader must be capable, not only of feeling and thinking at the same time; but even of simultaneously sharing an emotion and enjoying a joke. He must move as easily as Donne himself from the mood of the first stanza of *The Sunne Rising* to that of the last; or from the sardonic temper of the opening lines of *The Relique* to the poignancy of what follows.

Joan Bennett
Four Metaphysical Poets (Cambridge Univ. Pr., 1953), p. 31

In this review of Donne's *Elegies, Satires* and *Letters to Severall Personages,* what are the chief qualities we have noticed? Language such as men do use; deliberate rejection of traditional ornaments, images, diction, and of the conventionally beautiful; drama (one may wish, perhaps, that there had been more of it); occasionally—two qualities, these, which Donne shares with Ben Jonson—a vivid realism in imagery and in often satirical description, and a grave and weighty, though often witty, treatment of moral ideas; but, above all, wit: often deliberately outrageous and impudent and coat-trailing, often breath-takingly ingenious in the discovery of comparisons and analogies, but nearly always, in one way or another, argumentative, sequaciously, rigidly, scholastically argumentative, whether in the defence of preposterous paradoxes or in the mock-serious devising of hyperbolical compliments. Little that can be regarded as the direct expression of personal experience, or, indeed, of more than a part, a small part, of the poet's self; little that is more than half-serious; little that is what a modern reader is accustomed (perhaps too accustomed) to call "sincere." A pervading detachment, an impression of one playing, albeit with remarkable skill and strenuousness, a kind of elaborate game. Certainly not, except accidentally, and in so far as he often employs philosophic or theological concepts, a primarily philosophic or metaphysical poet, but as I have insisted, sometimes a dramatic, though more often an argumentative, a wittily argumentative or dialectical, one.

> J. B. Leishman
> *The Monarch of Wit* (London: Hutchinson, 1959), pp. 139-40

There have been times when critics, their ears attuned to poetry that is "regular" or "correct" in movement and avowedly separate from speech, have criticized Donne and his followers for "harsh ruggedness" of rhythm. In fact, however, the characteristic Metaphysical handling of verse movement reproduces the natural stresses and intonations of the speaking voice and plays them against the exigencies of whatever verse poem is being used. In *The Sunne Rising,* Donne employs a complicated and difficult stanza form, but he uses its rhymes and varying line lengths to obtain a remarkably natural effect.

> Jack Dalgish, ed.
> Introd., in *Eight Metaphysical Poets* (London:
> Heinemann, 1961), p. 7

A good many critics have noticed the difference in quality and in poetic method between these "La Corona" sonnets and the "Holy Sonnets" proper, but the essential difference has not, I think, been adequately defined and evaluated. The "La Corona" sonnets seem generally to be regarded as inferior, because of their highly intellectual cast; and this difference is usually explained by the supposition that they were written earlier than the other sonnets—according to Grierson, sometime around the years 1607-9—at a time when Donne's religion was, presumably, still largely an intellectual concern. But the present study will, I hope, suggest another solution: that the "La Corona" sonnets are different from the other "Holy Sonnets" because they are based upon a different kind of meditative tradition. There is no need to postulate any difference in the dating of their composition: whenever they were written, poems composed according to the meditative methods of the corona would tend to differ fundamentally from poems developing out of the *Spiritual Exercises* of St. Ignatius Loyola. We have already seen this kind of difference in Southwell's various poems on the lives of Mary and Christ; and, at a much higher level of poetic value I think we can see essentially the same distinction in Donne's sonnets. I have argued . . . that the finest of the "Holy Sonnets," proper, represent the carefully integrated work of all the powers of the soul within the borders of a single sonnet; and in particular that several of them show a powerful development from vivid composition of place, through devout analysis, to impassioned colloquy. It seems inevitable that such a procedure should result in a powerful union and compression of forces within an individual poem.

But no such process is operating within the individual sonnets of the "La Corona" sequence; for, properly speaking, there are no individual sonnets here. We have one poem, one corona, held together by its repetition of lines, by its consequently interlocking rimes, and by its unbreakable sequence of events. Its method, as announced in Sonnet 1, is the twining of an endless wreath of praise: the twining of a mind that winds its way from paradox to paradox, sometimes seeing the spot, sometimes crying out sharply, but always enveloping the scenes and the cries in a rich sinuosity of intellectual analysis. The metaphor of twining is carried out even in the rime: for the use of repeated lines leads to a linkage of rime between the couplet that concludes each sonnet and the whole octave (abba, abba) of the next: thus the "high, nigh" which concludes Sonnet 1 is echoed by the "nigh, die, lye, trie" of Sonnet 2, and so on in every sonnet, returning to the octave of the first. More than this, the rime-schemes of lines 9-12 in each sonnet show an intertwining alternation, except for the seventh, where the scheme is the same as in the sixth: in Sonnets 1, 3, 5 the rime is cddc; in 2, 4, 6 it is cdcd. These are small effects, but they play their subtle, half-realized part in weaving the whole corona.

Louis Martz
The Poetry of Meditation (New Haven, Conn.:
Yale Univ. Pr., 1962), pp. 110-11

By presenting love as natural, Donne makes it spiritual. The overt spiritual element is the idiom of Christianity. Like Christianity, his love is relational.

This sounds obvious: but most earlier lyric poets except, occasionally, Shakespeare, had written of love as something happening inside themselves (e.g. Petrarch); or as a means to a Platonic end; or as an idea, or accomplishment—a thing or accident external to the lover, or as a vehicle or continuum for sensation, beauty and so on. Donne was the first lyrical poet effectively to treat love as the nexus between two persons. Shakespeare's language is dominated by verbs, Milton's by substantial phrases; Donne's is dominated by personal pronouns.

J. B. Broadbent
Poetic Love (New York: Barnes and Noble; London: Chatto and Windus, 1964), p. 222

In the traditional interpretation of the storm-calm topic, then, good and evil aspects of Fortune were presented, the moral being the council of perfection that a man should maintain equanimity in both. Donne transforms this theme into a dramatic form by not so much contemplating fortune as experiencing it and writing out of that experience. For this he uses the verse letter as a sort of dramatic monologue, rather in the manner of Ovid's *Heroical Epistles*. Moreover, as in Lucan, the calm is simply one of Fortune's ironies and Fortune herself is wholly malevolent. Instead of adding to this a moral in contempt of the world, as was usual in the tradition, Donne accepts the fact that the tragic intensity of man's frustration and despair are the marks of his humanity. Like some of the Jacobean dramatists, he acknowledges that the passions are the source of our discontent but sees in them also a measure of human greatness. Consequently his poems are not a moral syllogism, two different events with a moral conclusion. The very form of the description expresses what it feels like to live under the rule of Fortune.

B. F. Nellist
MLR (October, 1964), p. 515

MICHAEL DRAYTON
1563-1631

Born at Hartshill in Warwickshire. In 1573 entered the service of Sir Henry Goodere at Polesworth, where he served as a page. There he seems to have acquired an interest in poetry. In 1580 entered the service of Sir Thomas Goodere. Returned to service of Sir Henry in 1585. Lived most of life under noble patronage. Wrote sonnets to "Idea" to younger daughter of Sir Henry Goodere. Her friendship with the poet continued after her marriage to Sir Henry Rainsford in 1595. In the early years of the seventeenth century wrote plays for Children of the King's Revels at Whitefriars. Had meeting with Shakespeare and Jonson at Stratford in

1616. Associated with most of the prominent literary men of his era. Involved in founding of the Royal Academy. Buried in Westminster Abbey.

J. W. Hebel, ed., *The Works of Michael Drayton* (1931-1941), 5 vols.

B. H. Newdigate, *Michael Drayton and His Circle* (1941)

I have chosen to examine the revisions of a poet who is supposed to have undergone a sort of conversion or development with regard to precisely the tenet of poetics which is here in question. Drayton's sonnet revisions between 1594 and 1619 should be revealing, since by the latter date his imagery is by common consent admitted to be more concise, colloquial, and original, more like that of Shakespeare or the Metaphysicals. Since his images do show this change in nature, we should expect these revisions to be evidence for the generalization that Drayton outgrew an earlier admiration for intrinsically decorative images, an admiration often seen as a point of difference between "Spenserian" and seventeenth-century poetic.

So far as I can discover from an examination of every cut, change, or addition of an image in the six editions of the sonnets, the evidence does not allow this generalization but some very different ones. Two are pertinent to a consideration of images especially distinguished for their sensuous nature or function.

One generalization is that Drayton's general basis for keeping or cutting seems to be: is the logical structure of the sonnet clear, and do the images sharpen or blunt the meaning? He rejects or retains or adds seemingly without regard to the decorative or undecorative stuff of the figures. If sonnets with Petrarchan conceits, rhetorical elaborations, images using conventional poetical objects, do not successfully unite these elements into poems with clear meanings, they are thrown out. But if sonnets with intellectually complicated conceits, dissonant images, and harsh, surprising, learned, scientific, homely image-content, fall short of a similar structural success, those sonnets are thrown out too. That is to say, Drayton learns a good deal about keeping decorum, about that more excellent integration of form with poetic subject which theorists had praised time out of mind, and he becomes increasingly aware of the sonnet's proper differences from other genres. But with direct regulation of content of images this developing artistry seems to have had little to do.

Drayton does develop certain moods which are less apparent in earlier sonnets, does appear to become increasingly convinced of certain general truths about love and ladies in the statement of which pretty images would be of no great help. This leads to the second observation on the revisions as a whole. Quite regardless of the content of the images, the defiant sonnets, or those in which he would rather cure his love than keep it, impress us as sonnets containing "metaphysical" imagery. When one stops to examine them, one frequently finds the new elements to reside not in images but in concepts, syntax, meter (especially arrangement of pauses). These newly accentuated moods seem to induce the choice of certain poetic subjects—a satirical comment on this, a mocking argument about that— which make Drayton find use sometimes for a kind of imagery resembling that of the Metaphysicals in structure and tone. It would be hard to make a case for image-*content* as the changing factor. But the correlation between changing points of view, on Drayton's part, and an impression of likeness to the Metaphysicals, on ours, is marked and provocative.

Neither of these observations about Drayton's revisions seems to me to fit into the shift in poetic usually postulated, from a sixteenth-century acceptance of imagery as decorative embroidery to a later more functional conception of imagery, born of rebellion against "poetical" objects and diction. The point is a point not only about Drayton but about what really happened to imagery during this period. For we cannot say that there was such a shift but that he did not share in it; his poems *do* show the changing character to account for which this fundamental shift in poetics has been argued by critics.

Rosemond Tuve
Elizabethan and Metaphysical Imagery (Chicago:
Univ. Chicago Pr., 1947), pp. 69-70

Any familiarity with strong tunes clear in repetitive rhythmical outline may give a composer or singer such certainty, and a poet brought up, as Drayton was, in an age when the air used with art the simple certainties of popular music might well feel safe in relying on tunes or their equivalents to carry a form through any resistance of words in their ordinary use. . . . Drayton was writing when the confidence engendered by reliance on tunes was well established. He used an equivalent for a tune—phrases of very strongly marked rhythmical structure occurring at obviously important points in the stanza. They established a movement from which it was impossible for other phrases to break free.

This is, in general, probably the most permanently valuable gift of music to metrical practice. Unlike words, musical signs can give a sure notation. Length, loudness, all the degrees of comparative importance among syllables, and the linking of syllables into rhythmically satisfying phrases can all be indicated by music with absolute certainty. Words are kittle cattle, and a writer not completely sure of their tricks and their manners may hesitate before he goes far in experimenting with them. If, however, he may rely on his experimentation's being supported by musical notation, he has an ally strong enough to bring him mastery over words. I am sure that the fact that many of the poems of the Elizabethan age had their first publication through singing is a major cause of the bold and free experimenting with metrical forms which shows itself in every song-book and miscellany of the time. A poet could experiment with some hope of success, and dozens of poets did in fact experiment with great success.

Catherine Ing
Elizabethan Lyrics (London: Chatto and Windus, 1951), pp. 146-47

The most ambitious of Spenser's followers is Michael Drayton, who published in 1593 a group of eclogues modeled on *The Shepheardes Calender* and called *Idea The Shepheards Garland Fashioned in Nine Eglogs.* Drayton plans his series with the same objectives of variety in style and mood, contrast of type, and seriousness of aesthetic and moral purpose which characterized Spenser, and in many instances the imitation is more direct and specific. His second eclogue, for example, is a debate between age and youth, and his third is a panegyric on Elizabeth under the name of Beta, filling out the rest of her name from Spenser's Eliza in the April eclogue. His first and last eclogues are complaints, as are Spenser's.

Drayton republished his pastorals in 1606 and 1619. He is especially interesting to the student of the history of English poetry because of the revisions he made for the edition of 1606. Some of these, at least, were made before 1600, as the revised versions appear in *England's Helicon* of that year. Drayton, in revising, cuts down the religious imagery, transforms his style into something more balanced, epigrammatic, and classical. He removes some of the archaic language, but on the whole, instead of moving away from discipleship to Spenser, he clearly moves closer to his master. This is a significant point, and Drayton provides the natural link between the pastoral tradition of the Elizabethan and the more domesticated and yet more classical school of the seventeenth century with its Browne, Herrick, and Milton. . . .

Drayton is the most interesting of the followers of Spenser in pastoral, and he illustrates well enough the survival of interest in pastoral poetry, even though the style of it changed, on into the seventeenth century. But Drayton was not so popular among his contemporaries as some other writers of pastoral who might be mentioned. The popularity of the pastoral lyric has already been demonstrated in the discussion of *England's Helicon* (1600). . . .

The qualities of his masterpiece, "Since ther's no helpe, Come let us kisse and part," Drayton must have learned by going back and studying *Astrophel and Stella;* in writing it he carried farther than Sidney had done the Sidneyan traits of particularization of the event, shift of pace and tone, dramatization by the use of colloquial language in a "poetic" context, and the convincing result from the lady's point of view which gives an impression of *energy* to the reader. In this sonnet we have the utilization of the direct speech of the lover, its colloquial reality reinforced by the actuality of the situation in "Now at the last gaspe" and the development of a beautifully controlled picture in the Cupid series. The dramatic surprise in the couplet is softened and made appealing by the feminine ending, and the poem succeeds on just the grounds which Sidney had alleged for this kind of poem. Drayton is no longer depending upon variety and decoration for his effect; he is producing a concentration and energy, a directness and probability, for a triumph toward which Sidney had showed the way.

Hallett Smith
Elizabethan Poetry (Cambridge, Mass.: Harvard
Univ. Pr., 1952), pp. 59-61, 162-63

Michael Drayton (1563-1631) is also a poet only half Golden, but in quite a different way from Greville, Davies, and Daniel. They began with Gold and moved away from it; he began with Drab, constantly relapsed into it, and in his old age, when the Golden period was over, at last produced his perfect Golden work, so pure and fine that no English poet has rivalled it. His weakness is the very opposite of Daniel's; he was in a sense too poetical to be a sound poet. His sensibility responded almost too quickly to every kind of subject—myth, the heroic past, tragic story, and (most of all) the fruitful, sheep-dotted, river-veined, legend-haunted expanse of England. He had an unquenchable desire to write poetry about them all, and he always seemed to himself to be succeeding because he mistook the heat which they aroused in him for a heat he was communicating to the reader. He himself has told us (in the *Epistle To Henry Reynolds)* how at the age of ten he hugged his "mild tutor" begging to be made into a poet, and how the good man granted his request, in typically sixteenth-century fashion, by starting him on Mantuan. In that scene we have what is essential in Drayton the man: a man with one aim, devoted for life to his art, like Milton or Pope. If the Muse regarded merit he would have been one of our greatest poets.

C. S. Lewis
English Literature in the Sixteenth Century (Oxford:
Clarendon Pr., 1954), p. 531

SIR THOMAS ELYOT
ca. 1490-1546

Son of Sir Richard Elyot, justice and attorney-general to queen consort of King Henry VII. Details of education uncertain. Early biographers claimed him as student at both Oxford and Cambridge, but no records are extant. Extremely proficient in the learning of his age. Named Clerk

of Assize on Western Circuit in 1511. Served on Commission of the
Peace for Oxfordshire in 1522. Became Sheriff of Oxfordshire and Berk-
shire in 1527. A friend of Sir Thomas Cromwell. Knighted in 1530. Served
as ambassador to the court of Emperor Charles V in 1531 and 1535.
Member of Parliament for Cambridgeshire in 1542. Published *The
Governour* in 1531, with dedication to King Henry VIII. Served as
Sheriff of Cambridgeshire and Huntingdonshire in 1544.

H. H. S. Croft, ed., *The Governour* (1883), 2 vols.

To sum up, our analysis of the sources for the *Governor* reveals that Elyot
drew most of his ideas from Plato and Aristotle, from Quintilian, Plutarch,
and Cicero among the ancients, and from Petrarch, Erasmus, Castiglione,
Pontano, and Patrizi among the writers of the Renaissance. More space in
the *Governor* is actually given, however, to the historical tales which illustrate Elyot's points and "recreate the reders" than to the ideas themselves.
Plutarch's *Lives* was by far the most important source for these examples,
though Sir Thomas frequently utilized Biblical stories and borrowed also
from Pliny, Xenophon, Tacitus, Suetonius, and Valerius Maximus. One
gets the feeling, indeed, that Elyot's primary aim in Books II and III was
to recount as many episodes from ancient history as possible; his definitions of virtues supply only a unifying framework, and a not very satisfactory one at that. Elyot succeeded mainly in retailing to his fellow
Englishmen popular versions of ancient and Renaissance philosophy and
history.

Stanford E. Lehmberg
Sir Thomas Elyot, Tudor Humanist (Austin, Tex.:
Univ. Texas Pr., 1960), p. 91

Elyot concluded chapter 2 with a promise to include in future all the material he found which might be "apt to the perfection of a iuste publike
weale," one in which all men were to be virtuously occupied. Since he
continued, throughout chapters 1 and 2, to demand that a king rule with
justice and wisdom, act for the common welfare, avoid tyranny, and bring
England to excellence as a public weal, he was certainly not trying to
support the absolute power of the king. . . .

When he was writing the *Governour* perhaps Elyot even had a hope that
Henry VIII would read his entire book and, as a consequence, would be
persuaded not to act like the absolute ruler who follows his personal convenience and his own appetites. In 1531 when the work was published,
Henry had not yet taken any irretrievable step in his break with the universal church. But whether that conjecture is true or not, even in the opening
chapters of *The boke named the Gouernour* Elyot was laying a firm
foundation for a complete structure of limitations on the king's power—

limitations which a king should set up by his own virtue, wisdom, and concern for the public weal.

Pearl Hogrefe
SP (April, 1963), pp. 138-40

In the history of English literature Sir Thomas Elyot occupies an important, albeit secondary, position. Although his works have real limitations —ideas that are largely derivative, a subject matter and approach largely restricted to the expository, and unsteadiness in execution—they nevertheless represent a genuine contribution to English letters. Taken as a whole, their importance is perhaps more historical than strictly literary, and yet two of them at least—*The Book Named the Governour* and the Platonic dialogue *Of the Knowledge Which Maketh a Wise Man*—continue to be read with the kind of pleasure attendant upon prose that is artistic as well as instructive. If Elyot's works display a certain unsureness in structure and style, some allowance must be made for the fact that they were written in the vernacular near the beginning of our Modern English period. Moreover, the deficiencies are offset, as often as not, by a vigor of expression, a moral intensity, and a power when the need arises to raise argument to the level of eloquent pleading.

Elyot's main accomplishment—and a very considerable one it is—was in fashioning for the sixteenth and succeeding centuries the ideal of the English gentleman: the true-nobleman-in-office, a man of virtue and good manners trained in the full program of liberal studies and employing his talents to the benefit of his country. Although various traditions, some of them native, came together to make up this ideal, its final shape took place at the hands of Sir Thomas Elyot, in his *Book Named the Governour* and in the lesser writings which promote the same end, books like the *Image of Governance* and the two translations, *The Doctrinal of Princes,* and *The Education or Bringing Up of Children.* The ideal gentleman is not born but made, and what makes him is the right kind of training. Elyot's second main accomplishment (really a part of the first) was in constructing a lastingly valid program of education in virtue and knowledge which is based on an extensive study of the liberal arts and which stresses Greek and Latin literature. It is the first fully elaborated program of its kind in Renaissance England, and it is the basis for all future programs of English education which aim at the same frankly aristocratic goals.

Elyot's writings are openly didactic in purpose, and in fact it was Elyot's desire, as it was Milton's, to be a teacher of the English nation. A man of wide learning himself, he set out to share his learning with as large an English audience as possible by composing his works in the vernacular. The subjects of his teachings range from medicine to language, poetry, moral philosophy, and educational and political theory, and his knowledge of them derives from the best sources that were available at the time: classical literature and the literature of Renaissance humanism. This points to the third major accomplishment of Elyot, his compiling and disseminating, through his original writings and translations, of some of the most valuable discoveries—or rediscoveries—made during the revival of learning which we call the Renaissance. Elyot's own favorite author and philosopher was Plato, and through incorporation of Plato's ideas in his own discussions of politics, ethics, and psychology he did a great deal to establish the authority of Platonism in English Renaissance thought. This last accomplishment alone would be enough to earn for Sir Thomas Elyot a lasting place among English authors.

John M. Major
Sir Thomas Elyot and Renaissance Humanism (Lincoln, Nebr.:
Univ. Nebraska Pr., 1964), pp. 271-72

JOHN FORD
1586- after 1638

> Baptized at Islington, April 17, 1586. Member of old Devonshire family. Son of prominent lawyer. Probably matriculated at Exeter College, Oxford, in 1601, but not certain. Entered Middle Temple on November 16, 1602. Expelled in Hilary Term 1605/6 for failure to pay buttery bill. Reinstated June 10, 1608. Among members admonished in 1617 for wearing hats in hall instead of traditional lawyers' caps. Received a bequest of ten pounds upon the death of his father in 1610. Elder brother, Henry Ford, bequeathed him the yearly sum of twenty pounds in return for surrender of properties. Literary activity appears to have begun while he was still a student at Temple. Came under the patronage of the Duke and Duchess of Devonshire. Wrote *Fame's Memorial* as elegy on Duke's death. Published in 1606. Wrote other prose tracts. Began to write for theater around 1621 when he collaborated on *Witch of Edmonton* with Thomas Dekker and William Rowley. No record of his death. May have lived on after Restoration.
>
> William Gifford, ed., *The Dramatic Works of John Ford* (1827), 2 vols.
> M. J. Sargeant, *John Ford* (1935)

The Broken Heart, in its careful psychological exposition, of Penthea and of Orgilus particularly, is fine enough to win fame for any dramatist; but if others of Ford's plays have perhaps numerically more weaknesses, if one chooses to count them, I believe they also have less of that air of melodrama that is felt throughout *The Broken Heart*. The play, I suggest, has to *'Tis Pitty* much the same relation as Webster's *Duchess of Malfi* has to *The White Devil*. Of *The Broken Heart* as of *The Duchess of Malfi* it is fatally easy to say that it is quieter, more restrained, more poetic than the play with which it is being compared; one should surely add that it is also less credible and in both subject and treatment essentially less dramatic. . . .

Ford's achievement was that within the limits of the dramatic tradition of his time and without even relying extensively on soliloquy, he went so far towards a pure concentration on states of mind. . . .

The passion of which Ford most frequently writes—of which Jacobean and Caroline dramatists most frequently write—is tragical love; but we should remember also the grief of Huntley, the regret of Ithocles for his youthful impetuosity, the quiet scorn of Castamela for her brother's easily-induced change of mood, and the scenes in which Warbeck, Biancha and Calantha, particularly, meet death. Ford's range of emotion is not really as narrow as some might pretend. It is noticeable, in fact, that if he has a preference, it is for those at the end of the emotional scale that is opposite to violence; he consciously chooses again and again as his principal characters men and women whose emotions are not of the obvious kind and who are at first glance not likely to provide good dramatic material. For his success with them he deserves all the more credit. His women, particularly, are probably second only to Shakespeare's; they are certainly far above those Massinger heroines of whom Arthur Symons so rightly said (in his introduction to the "Mermaid" selection) that they are always talking about their virtue as if it were something "detached and portable"—as if virtue were "a sort of conscious and painful restraint" (pp. xxii, xxvii).

H. J. Oliver
The Problem of John Ford (London and Melbourne:
Univ. Melbourne Pr., 1955), pp. 70, 124-25

Ford's three characteristic tragedies, *Love's Sacrifice*, *The Broken Heart* and *Perkin Warbeck* . . . are remarkable in their comparative indifference to event, in their cultivation of the static scene, in their approach to uniformity of mood throughout the drama, and above all in their suggestion of a total vision of human life in which vicissitude has become irrelevant. From Lessing's viewpoint they are defective writings indeed, for Ford has given scant attention to the study of processes. They are, most strangely in the playhouse, analogues in effect to that Grecian urn in which Keats found only arrested movement, fairness of attitude but no imaginable end. Of course, the plays were to be acted, and they had to have plots. The characters die and sometimes kill. But a reader who makes his way through them for the sake of the dying and the killing will have little satisfaction. Defying the natural limitations of drama, Ford aims at a form of spatial perception. When we first read his plays, what remains most persistently in our minds is a series of static groupings. . . .

We shall see that he is much nearer to the psychological drama of character and action in *Love's Sacrifice* than in the other two tragedies yet in all of them the movement is towards the moment of stillness. It is no coincidence that these most remembered moments are those when death is imminent or just past. Here Ford, with his urge towards a cessation of movement, is necessarily the poet of death. . . .

Above all, he was a poet, not only in his conceptions but in his words. The playhouse of Charles I's time did not encourage an older-fashioned rhetoric, or the use of the compressed or violent image. The tone of the speaking had to be quieter, more attuned to the narrower, more courtly audience. But Ford knew how to secure the moving power of imagery, especially the imagery drawn from life, while assiduously cultivating a simple fluency and melody of language. He resisted the tendency of his time to break down the structure of blank verse: his lines are more regular, less often run-on or with feminine endings, than those of most Caroline playwrights. He knew that the exalted presentation of humanity needed a language that was manifestly different, though not wholly divorced, from that of the nearest actuality. He was writing in a time when poetic drama was in decay, and he showed what could be done by a playwright whose purpose needed poetry but would have been ruined by an ostentatious display of the merely "poetic." As a model of style, if for no other reason, he has an enduring value.

Clifford Leech
John Ford and the Drama of His Time (London: Chatto and Windus, 1957), pp. 74-75, 122-23

It is not accidental that many of the terms applied to Ford's drama are usually reserved for criticism of the plastic or pictorial arts, for in his finest plays the sound and fury of melodramatic conflict give way to the relative stasis of ceremonial gesture. Moments of intense feeling are recorded; sensationalism and violence intrude. But the total impression is of a tranquility and delicacy far removed from Webster and Tourneur. The aim in such plays as *The Broken Heart* and *The Lady's Trial* is not to hold a mirror up to nature but to capture an ultimate "ritual" expression of love and aristrocratic "noblesse." The protagonists of earlier tragedies were noble in their individuality—in their refusal to bow before circumstances. Ford's most admirable characters, however, seem to lose their individuality at climactic moments. Their nobility in the face of death springs not so much from depth of character as from an aristocratic awareness of the role which they must play—of the need to subordinate all personal feeling. They seem to realize that dying well (like living well) requires art and knowledge. They become, so to speak, artists within a work of art crystallizing through studied attitude the aristocratic values of their society; they make the aesthetic expression of virtue a virtue in itself.

To recognize Ford's method of stylization is perhaps to understand why his attempts at comedy are unsuccessful as well as indecent. His Elizabethan and Jacobean predecessors used clownish simplicity as a ground burden to the sophisticated "divisions" of courtly love. They contrasted the artificial posturing of romantic heroes and heroines against the more realistic (if somewhat burlesqued) affections of maids and servants. Ford's comic characters are also coarser-gained than his heroes, but they are not realistic or satiric social types. They do not bring the sounds and smells of workaday London into the perfumed corridors of Veronese palaces. Instead they are caricatures—at times grotesque ones—of his romantic protagonists. It is as if Ford, knowing the true proportions of his delicate lovers, deliberately distorts them for comic and moral contrasts, to create lewd antimasques to romantic tragedy. The vulgarity of the gutter candidly reported (as in Marston) has at least a natural and earthy vitality. The vulgarity of the boudoir, burlesqued by a writer who had no comic talent, is more often than not simply disgusting.

Earlier dramatists were more uneven in their artistic achievement than Ford, but he alone wrote plays like *Love's Sacrifice* that are both delicate and gross, finely wrought and carelessly patched together. Only in *The Broken Heart* does one feel that he perfectly executed his artistic intention. In *'Tis Pity* his reach exceeded his grasp; his techniques were not refined enough for the moral and aesthetic complexity of his subject. Although the chronology of Ford's plays remains problematical, *'Tis Pity* seems to me the earlier of the tragedies. Far more successful artistically than *Love's Sacrifice*, it is notwithstanding less mature in its characterizations and less sophisticated in its themes than the other tragedies. It lacks the concern with aristocratic codes of behavior that marks Ford's later plays and it is the only one which pretends to an ideological significance in the manner of earlier Jacobean plays.

Robert Ornstein
The Moral Vision of Jacobean Tragedy (Madison, Wisc.:
Univ. Wisconsin Pr., 1960), pp. 202-3

If the movement of Ford's tragedies is from an Arcadian setting to a more and more realistic one, *Perkin Warbeck* would appear to be the final stage of his development, for now he casts his moral paradox against the background of his own country and shows it destroying the lives of characters whose actuality the audience cannot doubt. In placing the history of England upon his stage, Ford was following a well-worn dramatic tradition, although one which had been moribund for a quarter of a century; in reviving the history play he wrote with the examples of Marlowe and Shakespeare to guide him. Like them he was interested in the political implications of his story, and *Perkin Warbeck* is an exemplary lesson in the ethics of kingship. Henry VII is set up as a model ruler, with James IV and Perkin Warbeck to emphasize his perfection. What gives this play its particular effect, however, is that the audience is never allowed to embrace the virtue of King Henry with any sense of affirmation; it seems unimportant and unconvincing in the light of Perkin's tragedy.

What is paradoxical about *Perkin Warbeck* is that this most realistic in setting of all Ford's plays is the play in which Ford most effectively questions the very nature of reality. In answer to the ancient question of what makes a king, the play offers the efficient ruler, Henry VII, but it offers also Perkin Warbeck, the impostor with all the outward signs of royalty, who has come himself to believe in his own royalty and who dies a martyr to his own belief. Towards the pretender is directed all of the audience's sympathy, with the loving fidelity of Lady Katherine Gordon to make his tragedy more poignant. The world's justice is triumphant at the end, with a restitution of peace and harmony in England, but it has been purchased by the betrayal of Perkin by the Scottish king, and when Perkin goes to the gallows convinced of his own truth the audience is left in a state of doubt and ambivalence. It cannot really choose between the values of Perkin and King Henry; it is unable finally to distinguish appearance from reality.

Perkin Warbeck more than anything else is a play about the impossibility of belief, a motif emphasized in the treachery to his king of Sir William Stanley with which the play opens and repeated in the treachery of Sir Robert Clifford to his friend. Where can one place his faith in a world in which those a man loves most may turn against him? Perkin is a liar, but in his fidelity to his own pretence he attains a glory greater than that of any other in the play. The alternative of truth is exhibited in the sordid role of Lambert Simnel. We leave *Perkin Warbeck* with the feeling that reality may, after all, be only what we think it is, that there is no truth of which man can be certain, and that we may attain some victory by a heroic persistence even in a false pretence. *Perkin Warbeck* cannot answer the questions which it poses. As surely as *'Tis Pity She's a Whore,* it is the tragedy of man's inability to find certainty, to understand reality or to grasp his own position in the universe. This is why *Perkin Warbeck* is entirely characteristic of Ford, and not, as is sometimes argued, something alien to his ordinary dramatic mode. It is a perfect expression of the Caroline scepticism for which Ford stands, the product of a search for

moral order which can only resolve itself in paradox, and never in the
kind of certainty attained by those Elizabethan forebears whom Ford so
assiduously imitated and in whose company he longed in vain to be.

Irving Ribner
Jacobean Tragedy (London: Methuen, 1962), pp. 174-75

'Tis Pity is obviously Ford's best play. It is more open in its designs on
an audience than either *The Broken Heart* or *Love's Sacrifice*. It is infinitely
more vigorous and courageous than *Perkin Warbeck*. It makes a reasonable
attempt to state boldly and vigorously Giovanni's claims. The attempt,
however, is in good measure doomed from the start. Plays must inevitably
refer to a moral framework, and though they don't of course have to adopt
uncritically the moral standards they find in respectable society, there is
no sense in deliberately and wantonly controverting these. A playwright
who is even tempted to do this will inevitably feel the pull of "normal"
values, and unless he is good enough to balance these seriously and acutely
against attractions of the Giovanni-Annabella kind, the moral framework
and form of the play will be, as here, unbalanced. The critical intelligence
which should be brought continuously to bear on Giovanni and Annabella
is never alert enough to cope with the vigorous challenge which they
certainly do make. They get away with far too much of the author's
unqualified approval.

T. B. Tomlinson
A Study of Elizabethan and Jacobean Tragedy
(Cambridge Univ. Pr., 1964), p. 274

JOHN FOXE
1517-1587

Born in Lincolnshire. Educated at Brasenose College, Oxford. Became
a fellow of Magdalen College in 1538. Resigned in 1545 because of his
extreme Protestant views. Became a tutor in the family of the Duke of
Norfolk. Began to publish theological tracts in support of the Reformation.
Ordained a deacon in 1550 by Bishop Nicholas Ridley. During reign of
Queen Mary became an exile on the Continent. Published first book of
Actes and Monuments in Latin at Strassbourg in 1554. Expanded version
published at Basel in 1559. Returned to England after accession of Queen
Elizabeth. Published English version of *Actes and Monuments* in 1563.
Various other editions followed. Held various church livings in the last
years of his life. Wrote theological treatises directed against Roman
Catholics.

S. R. Cattley, ed., *Actes and Monuments* (1837-1841), 8 vols.

What John Foxe's *Actes and Monumentes* did to justify the place accorded to it in its own time beside the Bible should now be clear. By the time James came to the throne the Book of Martyrs and the stream of annals, chronologies and histories in similar vein had gone far to establish in the public mind a familiar legend of the nation's history, of the part which its rulers had played in the working out of its destiny, and so too a quite definite conception of the part rulers might be expected to play henceforth. Foxe, of course, had not originated this legend, certainly not single-handed, but he had put the current elements of the legend together in a single connected narrative which the Elizabethan regime and its supporters accepted at once as the most convincing statement of their position in their continuing struggle with the powers opposing them at home and abroad. The book provided a circumstantial account of the events which had led directly to the queen's accession. In the stories of the Marian martyrs, with Elizabeth's own story for climax, it presented in the most vivid dramatic terms the essence of the faith presumed to have been established in the national Church by her authority.

It framed these stories in an account of ecclesiastical history which purported to show that this faith was the same for which the martyrs of the primitive Church had died, the same which had been brought uncorrupted to Britain in the beginning directly from the apostles. This account of Church history the book also linked to a history of the long succession of native rulers down to Elizabeth, shown as owing their authority directly to divine appointment and prospering or not, and their people with them, according as they heeded their vocation to defend the faith and the people in the faith, or suffered themselves to be misled by false counsellors, or overborne by misbelieving usurpers and invaders. And to conclude, the book made plain that by all the signs to be found in scripture and history the will of God was about to be fulfilled in England by a prince perfect in her obedience to her vocation, ruling a people perfect in their obedience to her authority.

That is to say, Foxe set the apocalyptical conception of England which he brought back from exile at the death of Mary in a valid historical perspective focussed on the place and function of kingship now devolving upon Elizabeth. The course of events in Elizabeth's long reign, not least her own dazzling performance in the role appointed her in the Book of Martyrs, impressed that conception more and more deeply on the public mind. Elizabeth, who probably did not need Foxe to instruct her in the lessons of history, exploited the gifts of personality and the arts of showmanship at her command to counteract the disruptive effects of religion among her subjects by attracting their devotion to herself as queen and exciting their pride in being, like herself, above everything else English.

The effect was to make them, in spite of their religious differences, more conscious of England as an entity by itself and of themselves as a people set apart from all others.

It was also to give greater meaning to that body of fact and fable concerning the national past which a thriving book-trade was putting into print for all to read.

William Haller
The Elect Nation: The Meaning and Relevance of Foxe's "Book of Martyrs" (New York: Harper and Row, 1963), pp. 224-25

But though he is by no means sparing of adjectives, Foxe is still more effective through the skill with which he selects striking and dramatic detail. He has the authentic Elizabethan genius for the unforgettable detail, especially of the homely, dramatic order. Richard Bayfield burning three-quarters of an hour, fixed, unmoving in prayer, is an impressive enough spectacle without the terrible detail of the burned left arm rubbed off unconcernedly by the right. No one thing more constantly contributes to the dramatic quality of his narrative than this; indeed, in this as in so many elements of his vast book Foxe proves himself a storyteller of quite remarkable power, one of the greatest of a great age. And no dramatist of the time has a sharper eye for the dramatic gesture than Foxe. . . .

In this exploitation of the physical details of the martyr's suffering Foxe easily challenges comparison with the masters of the martyr cult in the seventeenth century. It is customary to see in the detail with which the later writers contemplate the sufferings of the martyrs one of the most characteristic manifestations of the baroque influence in literature. But Foxe is no less appreciative of the sensuous and dramatic possibilities of the extremes of physical torment. In general, too, he illustrates the baroque tendency to develop its material in the round, with sensuous fullness and material substance. There is a certain solidity, a certain literal and immediate and fully presented realism in Foxe's handling of detail, that leaves very little indeed to be imagined. But it should be added that the emphasis is primarily upon the physical appearance rather than upon the psychological or emotional or even nervous elements involved. In other words, the baroque movement has advanced as far as the complete exploitation of physical pathology in Foxe. By and large, the exploitation of the nervous and the emotional remains for the next century.

Helen C. White
Tudor Books of Saints and Martyrs (Madison, Wisc.: Univ. Wisconsin Pr., 1963), pp. 160-62

GEORGE GASCOIGNE
ca. 1535-1577

Born at Cardington, Bedfordshire, of old and noble family. Had early schooling in Westmoreland. Was a student at Trinity College, Cambridge, between 1547 and 1555, exact period uncertain. Entered Gray's Inn, London, in 1555. While at Gray's Inn wrote two plays, *Supposes* and *Jocasta* (with Francis Kilwermesh). In 1558 served in parliament as representative from Bedford. Barred from parliament in 1572 because of charges brought against him. Left Gray's Inn. Lived dissolute life at court. Had financial difficulties. In 1571 married Elizabeth Breton, mother of the poet, Nicholas Breton. Involved in legal difficulties with her second husband over her divorce and control of her property. Returned to Gray's Inn in 1563 for short period. He was left 195 pounds per annum in land upon the death of his father, but was still in financial difficulty. Imprisoned for debt in 1570. Left England in 1572 to serve in the Netherlands. Captured by Spaniards. Returned to England in 1574. Sent back to Netherlands as observer in 1576. Time spent in writing until death in 1577. Wrote novel, *The Adventures of Master F. J.*; long poem, *The Steel Glass*; morality play, *The Glass of Government*; literary criticism, *Certain Notes of Instruction*; many short poems of great metrical variety.

J. W. Cunliffe, ed., *The Complete Works of George Gascoigne* (1907-1910), 2 vols.

C. T. Prouty, ed., *An Hundreth Sundry Flowres* (1942)

C. T. Prouty, *George Gascoigne, Elizabethan Courtier, Soldier and Poet* (1942)

PROSE

Leaving now these rather unprofitable speculations, let us consider the literary aspects of the novel. It is curious that writers on Elizabethan fiction have so often passed over *The adventures of master F. J.* with a mere reference or a brief comment on the Italian title of the second edition. As a matter of fact, it is not only much more entertaining than *Euphues,* for instance, but it shows that the art of fiction had been highly developed in England some years before the appearance of Lyly's work. And in that art Gascoigne was superior to Lyly, for he recognized that a novel must first of all be a story and not a series of elegant essays on love and friendship. His novel has an excellent plot, fully developed and adequately motivated, embellished with a diversity of scenes and incidents, yet all restricted to a four-months' visit at a country estate. His conversation is life-like and witty, and its tone has a convincing reality. Finally, the characters, because drawn from the life, are intensely real. The tale is an unrivalled picture of the daily activities and amusements of an Elizabethan noble's household. In this respect it is almost unique in its period.

It is just this adherence to realism which shows Gascoigne's originality and independence of his models. His work is modern in its presentation of the complete *mise-en-scène* in which the characters are placed. We walk with them in the park, we listen to their conversation at dinner, we are present at their dances and evening amusements. The method is that of Jane Austen—a few characters set in a restricted scene and slowly turned about until all sides of their natures are shown. The action rises slowly and logically to an inevitable conclusion.

On the other hand, the traits of this work show that Gascoigne was acquainted with the best fiction of his day. He had absorbed elements from many sources. The love intrigue, the basis of his plot, is the principal feature in the *novelle* of Boccaccio, Bandello, and Cinthio. The election of kings or queens to rule the evening's amusement is at least as old as Boccaccio's *Filocolo* and occurs in many later works in the Renaissance. It was also a common feature of the life of the nobility at this time. The habit of including poems in narrative belongs to the pastoral type, such as Montemayor's *Diana* and Bembo's *Asolani*. For the use of letters, so skilfully introduced by Gascoigne, there are fewer sources. In the *novelle* they are almost entirely lacking and they are hardly more frequent in the pastoral romances. It is interesting to note that Belleforest, in his translation of Bandello, adds both letters and poems to several of the tales. The story of Dom Diego and Ginevra la Blonde, translated (with the letters and poems) by both Painter and Fenton (1566, 1567) is quite likely to have been read by Gascoigne, as it was very popular in his time. It is, incidentally, of about the same length as his story.

Leicester Bradner
PMLA (June, 1930), pp. 546-47

George Gascoigne was more than "the first conscious purist in his art." With wit and energy he sought to solve a wide range of urgent Elizabethan literary problems. To his credit stand the first English prose comedy, translation of the first tragedy from the Italian, the first mask and regular English satire, the first critical English treatment of prosody.

What of his artistry in prose fiction? Many would agree that *The Adventures of Master F. J.,* with its humorous exploration of Elizabethan country-house life, is the age's most entertaining short narrative. If *"The Adventures* (1573) are original fiction," said C. S. Lewis, "they rise to some importance as our earliest novel or (longish) short story."

Its originality as imaginative fiction has long been questioned. In 1575 some contemporaries apparently regarded the piece as a sort of *roman à clef,* probably libelous, although Gascoigne himself then denied the charge and ridiculed the idea. Among critics since 1891 has emerged a view, now almost standard, that some version of a *roman à clef* idea (there is no agreement) must be correct, and that consequently *The Adventures* should be read not as imaginative fiction but instead as a disguised account of a historical love affair. Sweepingly, Gascoigne's latest editor asserted that "the tale is autobiographical"; that "a true understanding of the merits . . . rests upon a realization that it is an account of actual events, told by one of the chief participants [Gascoigne himself]," and that "the situation, the characters and events are drawn from life and are thus not creations."

The evidence seems to me to be inadequate either to prove this kind of "drawing from life" or indeed to sustain solidly any *roman à clef* hypothesis. I seek to show that *The Adventures* should be read and enjoyed as an ingeniously conceived and wittily executed work of original imaginative fiction.

R. P. Adams
PMLA (September, 1958), p. 315

POETRY

As we have noted in connection with Gascoigne's earlier attempts at satire, his vein is English. The conventional classical and Italian satire of the courtly life in comparison with the rural existence was imitated by Wyatt, but Gascoigne looks to *Piers Plowman* and the Malvern Hills, not to Italy and its already decadent society. . . .

While the conventional satire of Italy and Wyatt's "John Poins" are limited rather closely to the social world of the upper classes, *The Steele Glas* ranges over the whole of contemporary life. Likewise, the principle of Wyatt's satire is limited. His reasons for eschewing the court are personal; it is his inability to dissemble and his personal disgust of hypocrisy of which he writes. *Piers Plowman* is objective, in that it presents the omnipresent vitiation of morality that results from the pursuit of Lady Meed. Gascoigne also deals in the larger issues; each man is driven by "Surcuydry" to seek his own advancement, and in this search he abandons all morality, all justice, truth, and social responsibility. Petrarch, Ariosto, Alain Chartier, and Wyatt ring the changes upon the familiar theme of the busy, worldly man's desire for a country retreat. It is equally valid and trite in any society and at any time. Langland and Gascoigne both were aware of the social upheaval of the times in which they lived. To both, the ideal lay in the smooth functioning of social responsibility within the medieval hierarchy.

In method as well as point of view, Gascoigne is close to Langland. His points are emphasized by significant details of ordinary life. The entire conclusion portraying the ideal world deals not in generalities or philosophical abstractions. . . .

Specific, too, are his charges against the knights, soldiers, lawyers, and merchants. He knows their tricks from bitter experience, and his satire is pungent because of this realism.

There are, of course, variations from the method of Langland. Gascoigne is not imitating directly; so we do not expect to find the biblical quotations, the dramatic scenes of real life, or the allegory which are so much a part of *Piers Plowman*. Gascoigne adds the classical examples of virtuous life, which are a part of the conventional satire of Italy. He imposes a variety of rhetorical devices, and of course he employs blank verse. . . .

It is not, however, in the mechanics of poetry that we may find the true merit of *The Steel Glas*. However interesting may be Gascoigne's hesitant use of the new medium, the matter is far more unusual than the manner. Satire did not flourish in the great days of Elizabethan literature, and one reason may lie in the social status of the creators of that literature. George Gascoigne came of an old family, well established in the medieval tradition. To him the changing social pattern was an upsetting force that prevented his following the accustomed pattern of life. He therefore felt the force of change strongly enough to cry out upon it. On the other hand, this same transition which stifled the feudal families was favorable to the emergence of men from the lower classes. To these men the age was one of opportunity, and what cause had a Marlowe, son of a Canterbury shoemaker, to cry out for a return to the virtues of a rigidly stratified society? George Gascoigne was proud of his family tradition and his right, as the eldest son of a knight, to the title of "armiger." But in the new world of the Tudors the significance of family was not what it had been; hence Gascoigne looked back to the days when the world was well ordered, when the eldest son of a knight would have fared better.

C. T. Prouty
George Gascoigne (New York: Columbia Univ. Pr., 1942), pp. 249-51

It is by now apparent, perhaps, that the long section in *The Steel Glas* following the introduction of the priests is nothing more nor less than an elaborate bidding prayer. It is just as apparent that Gascoigne thought of it as such, including it in his sermon as was not infrequently done by the preachers of his day. . . .

Thus Gascoigne follows the form and customary sequence of the bidding prayers, with considerable elaboration and special petitions, such as that referring to the universities and the final one for himself. He makes it the peroration or application of the sermon, the call for action. In so doing he deviates from the usual custom of putting the biddings at the beginning of the sermon or just before it, but his change is remarkably well suited to his purpose, and in putting them last he is, wittingly or unwittingly, following the suggestion made by St. Justin Martyr, the man who seems to have instituted the practice.

Thus Gascoigne's satire calls for action. It lies not only in the picture of a corrupt society as seen in the glass, but also in the picture of a reformed clergy who may through unceasing prayer reform this society. And this reformed clergy, these praying priests of the order of Melchisedec, are the priests of the Establishment—not the extremist Protestant preachers of Flanders and Liegeland, such as he had known in his military experience, nor yet those who are "Romainelike" and *"Esteme their pall,* and habyte overmuche."* Likewise in his satire he attacks the corrupted clergy, as many had done before, and as Spenser and Milton especially were to do after him. He indicates that he is familiar with the tradition of this satirical attack and with the fact that the bidding prayers were derived from the teachings of St. Paul. He was well aware of their common and frequent use among the English clergy of his own day.

Though it is verse satire consciously inspired, according to the writer, by the Roman satirists, *The Steel Glas* is just as consciously built upon well known, if loosely applied, rules for the structure of the sermon. Its style is just as consciously homiletic; and the introduction of the bidding into the work, aside from its being properly placed in a sermon, is most effectively employed as a call to reformation, a stroke of genius indeed. And since these devices of the preacher were all perfectly familiar to Gascoigne's readers, they doubtless gave those readers the satisfaction which comes with recognition as they read. If the poet owed Lucilius his inspiration for verse satire, his steel glass, he owed even more to the preachers of his day and to the liturgical tradition assumed by the Establishment.

T. B. Stroup and H. W. Jackson
SP (January, 1961), pp. 59-60

Gascoigne's metrics are generally very regular, and it would seem, at first glance, quite foolhardy to suggest he was trying to reproduce the versification of *Piers Plowman,* but somehow falling into blank verse by mistake. . . . Daniel was not the first to use the words *stress* or *accent,* but he was the first to use the terms consistently, apparently recognizing just what was involved. Though such poets as Gascoigne had already mastered metrical regularity, they were not thoroughly aware of what they had done; the practice preceded the theory. . . .

It is my conclusion that Gascoigne, not understanding completely the basis for the versification of either *Piers Plowman* or the verse practiced in his own day, made an approximation of the old verse form, using the metrical system currently available to him. It would seem that metrically *The Steele Glas,* like so much in sixteenth century literature, reveals more than one influence. In the verse of other sixteenth century poets Gascoigne had examples of alliteration and heavy caesura—both perhaps showing the indirect influence of the medieval native tradition. In addition Gascoigne was probably influenced consciously and directly by *The Vision of Piers the Plowman,* a recently published specimen of that same native tradition.

Stanley R. Maveety
SP (April, 1963), pp. 172-73

ROBERT GREENE
1558-1592

Baptized at Norwich on July 11, 1558. Entered St. John's College, Cambridge in 1575. Took B.A. in 1580. Moved to Clare Hall. Took M.A. in 1583. During Cambridge years was friend of Thomas Nashe, Gabriel Harvey, Abraham France. Granted M.A. by Oxford in 1588, probably at Brasenose College. Probably travelled abroad, chiefly in Italy. Earliest literary work, *Mamillia*, entered in Stationers' Register in October 1580. Continued to write romantic fiction throughout life. Connections with theater seem to have begun around 1586, when he came to London after deserting the wife he had married in 1584. In London took as mistress the sister of the notorious criminal, Cutting Ball, later hanged at Tyburn. Had son named Fortunatus. Lived Bohemian life, earning living by pen. Wrote plays for various dramatic companies. Quarrelled with actors. Died on September 30, 1592, supposedly of surfeit of Rhenish wine and pickled herrings. Died in squalid room, after writing letter to deserted wife to beg her forgiveness. Requested that landlady, Mrs. Isam, place a garland of bays on his dead body. Buried in the New Churchyard, near Bedlam, London.

J. C. Collins, ed., *The Plays and Poems of Robert Greene* (1905), 2 vols.

A. B. Grosart, ed., *The Complete Works in Prose and Verse of Robert Greene* (1881-1886), 15 vols.

Nicholas Storojenko, *Robert Greene, His Life and Works*, tr. Hodgetts, ed. A. B. Grosart (1881)

PLAYS

Much more important for the assimilation of romance to drama was Greene's attempt to put on to the stage stories of love adventure; and it was Greene rather than Lyly who first achieved impressive success in writing comedies that had a serious and substantial tale of human lovers as their core.

Even in *Orlando Furioso* the doughty deeds are subordinate to the love-story. . . .

There is a similar dramatisation of love adventures, with play on suspense and surprise, in Greene's two best works, *Friar Bacon and Friar Bungay* and *James IV*. The story of the latter in particular resembles that of several of Shakespeare's romances and romantic comedies, notably that of *Cymbeline*. . . .

In all these love-tales that Greene dramatised there is, however, a striking absence of one outstanding romantic characteristic—courtship. There is no love-making at all in *Orlando*. . . .

However, if there is this one large omission in Greene's dramatisation of romantic love-stories, in most other respects his stories reveal the marks of their kind. Much of their action, for instance, derives from a situation in which love is subjected to some heavy and unusual strain. . . .

Again, these love-stories are whole-heartedly romantic in that they make no pretence to verisimilitude. . . .

As we should expect, the convention of disguise and mistaken identity is much exploited in these romantic stories. . . .

More than his successors—and probably to a large extent through the influence of Marlowe's *Faustus*—Greene also makes a considerable use of dream, magic, and the supernatural in the fabrication of his stories of romantic make-believe.

With love-stories of this sort, deliberately extravagant and far-fetched as fairy-tales, prodigal in their employment of accident and coincidence, and frequently dependent on magic and the supernatural, it follows, as a corollary true also to romance, that the motivation is usually of a quite incredible kind. . . .

On the surface also, in the creation of personality, Greene's dramatic art is weak; for all the stimulus of dramatic presentation, most of his characters are as insipid and indeterminate as those of *Arcadia*. Yet there is a difference between Orlando and Angelica, woodenly passionless and incommunicative even in what should be their moments of greatest stress, and some of the principal characters of *Friar Bacon* or *James IV*. What—in advance of Lyly—Greene was beginning to achieve was a certain sort of animation; he was learning to breathe at least the life of feeling into his lovers, and in Margaret, Dorothea and Ida he created figures of emotion, sentiment and, to some extent, of intelligence, with whom we can at times sympathise. . . .

Finally, the spirit of Greene's work, which is gentle, full of grace, goodness, mercy and justice, owes much more to the romantic than it does to the classical tradition. There is little suffering and barely a glimpse, except perhaps in Ateukin, of wickedness in its all too real forms. The few bad characters, such as they are, receive their deserts; the virtuous and innocent are ultimately vindicated and rewarded in a system of poetic justice; and there is always the happy ending where all is made right in an atmosphere of forgiveness and reconciliation. T. H. Dickinson, the editor of Greene's plays in the *Mermaid Series,* was not far out when he described Greene's art as one of "contemplative repose and genial humanity," and essentially the spirit of his comedies is that of Shakespeare's, though it is simpler, cruder and less thoughtful.

On many important counts then, Greene is quite as significant as Lyly in the assimilation of romance to English drama and in the creation of a comedy of delight after Sidney's own heart. But there is this great difference between Shakespeare's two predecessors in romantic comedy: whereas the plays of Lyly are now chiefly of historical interest, a text for scholars and critics, Greene's *Friar Bacon* and *James IV* still compare favourably with all but the pick of Shakespeare's comedies and still merit stage-production.

E. C. Pettet
Shakespeare and the Romance Tradition (London:
Staples Pr., 1949), pp. 56-66

Although the basic plot of their comedies was a love story, neither Greene nor Shakespeare saw love as an isolated phenomenon in human life. For both, it is a power with connections which reach into every sphere of human activity; its qualities and the behaviour it provokes are a reflex of life as a whole. Its characteristics are self-denial, unselfishness, complete loyalty; its essence is giving. In the plays of both, therefore, the love story is set invariably in a larger context from which the difficulties of the lovers in part derive. The nature of this and the dramatic emphasis it receives may vary, but it is always present. . . .

In most of Greene's and Shakespeare's comedies, the barrier between the lovers reflects some delusion or spiritual blindness in one or both of them as well as in the characters who surround them. Indicative of this are the conscious and unconscious violations of one's nature which is basic in many of the comic situations. At certain points their handling of this idea is similar. Pretences and delusions of all kinds flourish. . . .

This scene from *Friar Bacon* is of greater significance for the hint it provides of Greene's comic attitude, and its basic similarity with Shakespeare's. At certain points in their works both dramatists make the audience aware of the dramatic illusion itself. The use of disguise and the nature of the various "roles" some characters play is part of this but it may also be seen at work in the devising of whole scenes. John Palmer has noticed that Shakespeare frequently has a character or group of characters standing as intermediary between the audience and part of the action:

in the letter scene in *Twelfth Night,* Malvolio's gullibility is witnessed and commented on by Maria, Sir Toby, Sir Andrew and Fabian behind the garden hedge; when Benedick and Beatrice are caught in the snares laid for them by Hero, Claudio, Don Pedro and Margaret, the trappers are on hand to witness their success; when Titania is enamoured of Bottom, both Puck and Oberon are there to enjoy her delusion, and Puck is present to provide a commentary on "what fools these mortals be" as the four lovers play out their farce. In the scene from *Friar Bacon* mentioned above, Bacon himself and Edward stand between the audience on the one hand and Margaret, Lacy and Bungay on the other in much the same way as do Maria, Don Pedro, Puck and the rest. "Sit still, my lord, and marke the comedie," says Bacon to Edward, and this, in effect, is what both Greene and Shakespeare are saying to their audiences: "Mark this comedy within the comedy, watch both the players and their audience." We are no longer detached spectators, we are drawn into the world of both comedies; we feel that we may be "on either side of the hedge."

Greene carries this device a stage further in *James IV*, in which the story of James and Dorothea is set within the framework involving Oberon, the king of the fairies, the misanthropic Scotsman, Bohan, and his two sons, Slipper and Nano. The fragility and suppleness of the limits of drama are stressed; the gap between audience and action becomes blurred as Oberon steps out of the framework to save Slipper from the results of his knavery, or as Nano accompanies Dorothea on her journey. The "reality" of Dorothea's sufferings, or of Ateukin's evil, or of James' lust is at once shattered and reinforced; and the audience are simultaneously distanced from and brought closer to the world of the play. Even at the end of the play, when Greene drops the framework material, Nano, who stepped out of it at the beginning of the play, is present as its representative to sound the last note of the play.

Norman Sanders
in *Early Shakespeare* (New York: St. Martin's Pr.,
1961), pp. 41, 43, 50-51

Ultimately, the play [*Friar Bacon and Friar Bungay*] celebrates natural order. The carefully planned structure which accomplishes this was a great advance in the technique of Tudor drama, and is typical of stagecraft which taught "the only Shake-scene in a country" more about the making of plays than he learned from any other predecessor. Whatever Greene may have been like during the last unhappy and ungenerous months before his death, there is a generosity of spirit in *Friar Bacon* which again and again reminds us of Shakespeare. The rugged, frequently eloquent verse often rings of the English countryside—as it does, for example, when Serlsby promises Margaret his "forty kine with fair and burnish'd heads,/With strouting dugs that paggle to the ground" (x, 62-63)—and the play as a whole implies that human beings are created with a natural propensity for good. In *Friar Bacon*, the courtly virtues of magnanimity and gentleness are seen as natural human resources, and are celebrated in the cumulative effect of the plot. To delight in such virtues may be said to reveal them in the playwright himself, and since everything we know about Greene's life is so generally sordid, it is only fair to point out that this play, in eschewing misanthropy and in praising humanity, is typical of his best writing for the Elizabethan stage.

Daniel Seltzer, ed.
Friar Bacon and Friar Bungay (Lincoln, Nebr.:
Univ. Nebraska Pr., 1963), p. xxi

PROSE

Of all the Euphuists, Robert Greene was the one most fascinated by the rhetorical possibilities provided for literature by science. Similies and allusions drawn from the storehouse of natural history appear on almost every page of his work. One counts references to more than thirty animals, forty minerals and precious stones, fifteen reptiles, thirty birds, fifteen fish, twenty trees, fifteen insects, and sixty herbs in the corpus of his prose romances. The number of his allusions must total almost a thousand—a staggering mass of material for such a mercurial mind to retain. What is the origin of all this learning? . . .

The only method of search consists of a check of Greene's information against all possible sources to determine whether or not his facts are orthodox, whether or not they were part of the intellectual atmosphere. For writers like Greene, the air was foggy with information, but fogs settle and information crystallizes in books. If we cannot find Greene's references in books, we must for the moment attribute them to his invention. Greene's method of invention can be indicated briefly by studying one group of his references. . . .

Greene's lore about precious stones consists, then, of a small number of traditional facts and a great mass of data invented according to the conventional categories. The same method holds true for all his other scientific matter. When he discusses birds, he uses eleven conventional facts; the rest of his material is invented according to set rules. He tells us of a certain number of birds that change the color of their plumage, of the friendships and hostilities of birds, and of the differences between the habits of young and old birds. A similar method carries over to the other groups, but on only a few occasions does he use orthodox material.

Don Cameron Allen
PMLA (December, 1938), pp. 1007-11

This brief analysis of Greene's borrowing from Wotton has been enough to demonstrate something of Greene's purpose as a novelist. It is clear that in no case did he borrow from Wotton for the sake of explaining motivation or supporting argument. He was looking for ornament, and where Wotton's phrasing was not sufficiently ornamental, Greene still further embroidered it.

John S. Weld
SP (April, 1948), p. 170

Greene's *Groats-Worth of Wit bought with a million of Repentance* (1592) might almost be classed among pamphlets: but in so far as it is fiction at all, it is realistic. Greene is anxious to parade rather than to conceal the autobiographical element in his story of Roberto and passes finally into direct confession. The historical interest with which we follow Greene when he paints the misery and conscious degradation of the first professional playwrights, and the famous attack on the "vpstart" Shakespeare, will always ensure readers for the *Groats-Worth*. As a work of art it is a slight thing. The style, generally free from euphuism, is lively enough, and the portrait of the old usurer is effective coarse painting.

C. S. Lewis
English Literature in the Sixteenth Century
(Oxford: Clarendon Pr., 1954), p. 427

Greene, by the standards of any age, was a plagiarist, and a plagiarist by the carload in his first novels. During his period of literary apprenticeship, if one can use so dignified a term to describe it, he was no conscientious apprentice. Rather, he was a literary quilt maker. How many works help account for *Gwydonius* I do not know, but two of the major ones, certainly, were his own earlier *Mamillia* (1583) and Pettie's *Petite Pallace*. And from a few such sources he may well have patched together the entire novel. The use of his own work was perhaps legitimate though not to his credit as an artist; the use of Pettie transcends any Elizabethan notions about legitimate "imitation." Both works he apparently knew suffciently well to skip at will from part to part, seizing on whatever would fit his needs; at times, instead, he may merely have inserted additions into his draft as he ran across appropriate passages in the two earlier works.

Robert W. Dent
HLQ (February, 1961), pp. 151-52

FULKE GREVILLE
1554-1628

Born at his father's estate, Beauchamp Court, in Warwickshire. Entered Shrewsbury School in 1564, along with Sir Philip Sidney, his life-long friend. Entered Jesus College, Cambridge, in 1568. Served in the Court of the Marches of Wales in 1576. Accompanied Sidney on embassy abroad in following year. Named Secretary for Wales in 1583, Member of Parliament for Warwickshire in 1592-1593, 1597, and 1603. From 1598 served as Treasurer of the Navy. Knighted in 1597. Held in high esteem at Elizabeth's court. Was able to support many men of letters. Entertained Giordano Bruno on visit to England in 1583. Upon accession of King James I went into retirement. Occupied himself with revising his earlier poems and with writing the two plays *Mustapha* and *Alaham*. After Death of William Cecil in 1612 returned to public life. Became Chancellor of the Exchequer in 1614. Active as member of Privy Council. In 1621 named Baron Brooke of Beauchamp Court. Continued to serve at court well into reign of Charles I. Died of a wound inflicted by a servant who believed he had been unjustly excluded from his master's will.

Geoffrey Bullough, ed., *Poems and Dramas of Fulke Greville* (1945), 2 vols.

PERSONAL

Our first impression of Greville, drawn from his plays, poems and prose, is of a man whose mind houses more conflicting ideas than was usual even in his age of intellectual doubts. He abhors war (which destroys all but the military virtues of courage and force), yet he despises alike the processes and the achievements of human art and reason; he holds this world's fame and honour a gilded dream, yet despatches contemptuously the retreat of the stoic. . . .

A mixture of bitter asceticism which, when it touches learning and art (and especially art), is sadistically vindictive and of astute and penetrating analysis of the motives, feelings and experiences of man in his political and religious life, Brooke's qualities as a dramatist could almost be prejudged from his other writings. Almost, but not quite. We might, indeed we almost certainly should, anticipate from the poems and the sonnets the severe and disillusioned survey of the "wearisome condition of humanity," the soundness of his thought on broad issues of statecraft and the nature of civilization, the acuteness of his penetration into men's motives and processes of thought, especially into the motives of public men and the thought processes of religious or semi-religious men; we might even have anticipated the obscure concentration of style in which all this is expressed. What surprises us in the plays, in *Alaham* to some degree but notably in *Mustapha*, is the passion which there gives depth and volume to the expression of these thoughts, bringing, as in the similar case of Donne, an unwonted clarity and inevitableness of utterance at the moments of supreme fusion of feeling and thought. Granted that these plays were not, of course, written for performance, that they were, in fact, nothing more than contributions to the late Senecan revival begun by Daniel and passing through Alexander to Greville, yet they have certain dramatic qualities, more I think than those of either of the other two exponents. The relatively simple Senecan scheme limits his character list and the convolutions of his story; for this perhaps we may be thankful. His passion, which was a little like Marlowe's in that it could fasten itself upon an abstraction and was relatively independent of the stimulus of character or personality, gave intensity to themes some of which in other hands might have been arid as the desert sand—the conflict between the rival parties at an oriental court, the struggle to overthrow one tyrant and set up another, the accompanying reflections on monarchy, democracy, the relations of the state and the individual, loyalty, honour, religion and, most promising of all, the relations of the governing power and the state religion, the part played by state religion in the control and even the oppression of the people. . . .

Dramatic power is, then, I think, not lacking in these plays but the quality which cuts them off effectively from the theatre is Greville's peculiar, characteristic style. Had he intended (as how should one who so despised the arts intend it?) to produce practical theatre plays, his habit of writing would probably have hindered him against his will. As he did not so intend, there is no curb upon it and it shows all the marks of closet-writing at any time and in any form. It separates immediately from that of his fellow-dramatists, the working theatre-men, as the style of Browne's *Hydriotaphia* separates from that of Jeremy Taylor's sermons, not only because of the different musical and imagistic qualities of the writers, but because of that major distinction between writing which does not have to refer itself to a public and writing, whether drama, sermon, polemic or narrative, which does.

Una M. Ellis-Fermor
The Jacobean Drama (London: Methuen, 1936), pp. 192-95

GENERAL

In the main Greville is closer to Spenser and Sidney. (He quoted or was quoted by Spenser.) With them he shares the pseudo-Platonic conception of love, and like them has moods in which the beloved is identified with Ideal Beauty (I, III, X). Love is the "mortall sphere of powers diuine" (IX); it is "placed aboue these *middle* regions" (XVI); Myra transcends the mutability of things (VII); the name Cælica suggests the same feeling, common enough already in foreign poets of the Petrarchan school. It is noteworthy, however, that the platonising poems are mostly near the beginning of the cycle; when after dropping this manner he takes it up again, in LXXXV, Platonism is assimilated to Christianity, as in Spenser's later *Hymnes*. . . .

Yet even in these poems the differences between Sidney and Greville are more striking than the similarities. When Greville takes over an idea from his friend he often gives it a twist; sunny becomes saturnine, passion becomes irony; at times he seems almost to be giving his friend the lie direct. This is not imitation, but deliberate rivalry, adaptation of another mood and personality.

Nothing could show more clearly the essential difference in temperament between the two friends than their sonnet sequences. Both begin with an ideal conception of love; both suffer frustration; and both turn their desires to heaven. But while *Astrophel and Stella* is remarkable for its harmony of tone, *Cælica* is bewildering in its diversity; and as Croll declares, "It is indeed a fair question whether *Cælica* is a cycle of love or of anti-love.". . .

The view of war is precisely what we might expect of one with Greville's dual attitude to life. He hates war both for its destructive results and for its root in evil desires; he even seems to suggest that the true Christian will be pacifist; war comes from the Fall. But once again he proves himself a realist. Having to live as a fallen being in a fallen world, he makes the best of it. Hence he sees war as occasionally necessary both for national advancement and purification; since he declares that the Christians' failure is due to their vacillation between their professed and the worldly point of view, it might seem that he preferred a completely wicked activity to a half-hearted inaction. But in lamenting the divisions in Christendom he is following Sidney. A Crusade would be the most just of all wars.

He seems to feel that this end would justify any means; his real object of scorn is the hypocrisy, the unenlightened self-interest, of the Western European leaders, Catholic and Protestant alike.

Geoffrey Bullough
Poems and Dramas of Fulke Greville (New York:
Oxford Univ. Pr., 1945), vol. I, pp. 44-45, 70

But if Greville was cut off from a soldier's life of action, his writings show he continued throughout his career to be fascinated by it, and by the nature and problems of war. He considered war chiefly in four separate works: the *Life of . . . Sidney, A Treatise of Monarchy*, "sonnet" CVIII of *Caelica*, and, especially, *A Treatie of Warres*. These various writings examine war from three points of view. "Souldiers," after all, had honored Sidney, "and were so honoured by him, as no man thought he marched under the true Banner of *Mars*, that had not obtained Sir *Philip Sidney's* approbation." In his friend, Greville saw war ennobled and idealized: "Learning, and Honour . . . brought . . . into the Court, and Camp"; "he revived that ancient, and secure discipline of order." Through Sidney also, as Greville presents him in the *Life*, war is shown to be an instrument of order, and of the "true religion," employed by Elizabeth as Protestant and English princess. Thus, as might be expected, Greville's treatment of war, in the biography, reflects primarily the devoted friend and patriot; and it is developed, so to speak, on the level of the individual and the state. Approximately fifty-five stanzas in *A Treatise of Monarchy* discuss war chiefly in terms of political maneuvering: balance of power, mutual aid pacts, the importance of military strength, the threat of Rome as political entity. In *Caelica,* CVIII, and in *A Treatie of Warres,* finally, Greville considers war within a larger frame of reference; and it is particularly in the *Treatie* that he draws together every aspect of the problem. In this poem he deals with war, not merely on a personal or patriotic basis, nor as a political absolutist with misgivings; the *Treatie of Warres,* taking those points of view into consideration, subordinates them to one of rigoristic voluntarism, which regards war primarily in terms of man's role within a divine scheme.

Hugh N. Maclean
HLQ (February, 1958), pp. 96-97

To sum up: in a tentative list of Greville's works in order of composition, the *Caelica* sonnets to c.lxxxvi would come first, followed by *Mustapha, Alaham,* and *Antonie and Cleopatra,* and *A Treatise of Monarchy* in its first form. *Caelica* was probably begun in 1577-80, the plays were completed by 1600-01, and *Of Monarchy* developed from the plays, the sections "Of Church," "Of Lawes," "Of Nobility," "Of War," "Of Peace," and "The Declination of Monarchy" existing in some form at the time the *Life of Sidney* was written. Then follow the later treatises as a group, *A Treatie of Warres* and *An Inquisition vpon Fame and Honour* probably preceding *A Treatie of Humane Learning* and *A Treatise of Religion.* The revision of the plays, and the final sonnets of *Caelica,* also belong to this period. While some parts of the pattern are now beyond recovery, and the details can only be conjectured, the general stages of the sequence proposed seem to be in accord with the evidence available.

G. A. Wilkes
SP (July, 1959), pp. 502-3

GEORGE HERBERT
1593-1633

Member of a very distinguished family. Fifth son of Richard and Magdalen Herbert, younger brother of Lord Edward Herbert of Cherbury. After the early death of his father reared by his mother who was a friend of John Donne. She married Sir John Danvers in 1609 and died in 1627. Distinguished himself as scholar at Westminster School. Received his B.A. from Trinity College, Cambridge, in 1612, M.A. in 1616. Made a fellow of his college in that year, Reader in Rhetoric in 1618. Between 1620 and 1627 served as Public Orator of the university. Ordained a deacon in the Church of England around 1626. In 1630 named Rector of Bemerton, near Salisbury. Ordained as a priest. Friend of Nicholas Ferrar. Never published his English poems, which were intensely personal and were circulated in a manuscript that was sent before his death to Ferrar to be either burned or printed.

F. E. Hutchinson, ed., *The Works of George Herbert* (1945)
Margaret Bottrall, *George Herbert* (1954)

The poetry of George Herbert is so intimately bound up with his beliefs as a Christian and his practice as a priest of the Church of England that those who enjoy the poetry without sharing the beliefs may well feel some presumption in attempting to define the human, as distinguished from the specifically Christian, value of his work. The excuse for such an attempt can only be the conviction that there is much more in Herbert's poetry for readers of *all* kinds than is recognized in the common estimate. That his appeal is a wide one is implicit in the accepted claim that he is a poet and not simply a writer of devotional verse; but I think I am right in saying that discussion of him tends to take for granted that admirers are likely to be drawn from a smaller circle than admirers of, say, Donne or Marvell. Even Dr. Hutchinson, whose superbly edited and annotated edition of the complete Works is not likely to be superseded—it would be difficult to imagine a better qualified editor and introducer—even Dr. Hutchinson remarks that, "if to-day there is a less general sympathy with Herbert's religion, the beauty and sincerity of its expression are appreciated by those who do not share it." True; but there is also much more than the "expression" that we appreciate, as I shall try to show. Herbert's poetry is an integral part of the great English tradition.

The significance of Herbert's "homely" imagery—pointing as it does to some of the central preoccupations of his poetry—is something that we need to get clear. But before taking up this question—or, rather, as a way of taking it up—I should like to bring into focus another aspect of his imagery. As well as metaphor and simile Herbert uses symbols and allegory. Now whereas metaphor conveys its meaning directly from common experience, in symbolism there is usually an element of the arbitrary. *The Church-floore* is an obvious example:

> Mark you the floore? that square & speckled stone,
> Which looks so firm and strong,
> Is *Patience*.

But this arbitrary use of symbols is not characteristic of Herbert. Much more often his verse (like Bunyan's prose) gives life to its symbolic figures and allegorical situations, so that they appear as something immediately experienced, and carry their meaning with them. Even the highly emblematic poem, *Love Unknown,* has a matter-of-fact quality that makes it something more than a monument to a bygone taste. In *The Pilgrimage* the allegory is completely realized in terms of the actual. . . .

This use of vivid allegory—tied down, as it were, to the actual and immediate—represents one aspect of Herbert's method. In poems such as *Vertue* and *Life* ("I made a posie, while the day ran by") we have the opposite and complementary process, where natural objects, without ceasing to be natural, have a rich symbolic meaning. In the lovely lines of *Vertue* the rose is no less a real rose, "angrie and brave," for being at the same time a symbol of life rooted in death. It is here that we see something of the significance of Herbert's consistent use of homely and familiar imagery. We may recall Coleridge's account of the genesis of the *Lyrical Ballads:* "Mr. Wordsworth was to propose to himself as his object to give the charm of novelty to things of every day, and to excite a feeling analogous to the supernatural, by awakening the mind's attention from the lethargy of custom, and directing it to the loveliness and wonder of the world before us." It is "the things of every day" that Herbert's poetry keeps consistently before us; but instead of invoking a rather adventitious "charm of novelty" or exciting "a feeling analogous to the supernatural" (one thinks of *Peter Bell*), he sees them in direct relation to a supernatural order in which he firmly believes.

L. C. Knights
Explorations (New York: George C. Stewart,
1947), pp. 112, 135-37

Like any Renaissance personal "device," Herbert's motto *Lesse then the least of Gods mercies* is obscure until we know its context or source. This source is in Jacob's speech in Gen. xxxii. 10 (the chapter in which he wrestles with God and is given the name Israel), when in fear of his brother Esau Jacob prays for God's help and reminds Him of His promise:

> I am not worthy *of the least of all the mercies* [marg. note: Hebrew: I am less than all, &c.] and of all the truth, which Thou hast shewed unto thy servant; *for with my staff I passed over this Jordan.*

To Herbert's sensitive conscience, his Jordans never stayed crossed, and though his poems are "The Church" he tried in all humility to build, though they are the very purified speaking heart which was the altar to be built "on that day when ye shall pass over Jordan," yet even so his poetry is also the long record of his agony of spirit at seeing his failures to think, be, and write as a "very member of Christ," an altar and tabernacle of Heavenly Love. There were rare occasions when he dared to think he had "passed over this Jordan with his staff," had learned how at most to begin to build that altar on the farther side of Jordan upon which the workman's tool was not to be lifted. "Jordan, I" and "II" are two such occasions. It is quite clear that Jordan, Christian symbol of redemptive purification and of entrance into union with Christ as Heavenly Love incarnate, was Herbert's own symbol for this complex of ideas, and that he thought of poetry as both the means and the fruit of such a union.

The symbol was a "public" one. We have observed in Herbert's own poems its manifold and deep implications; it should be made clear that such a complex of metaphorical meanings was also "public," and no mere idiosyncrasy, born of chance tie-ups between a number of Bible verses. Because it was public it was understood, and not only subtle but moving.

Rosemond Tuve
A Reading of George Herbert (London:
Faber and Faber, 1952), pp. 196-97

Herbert's poetry is the expression of an ardent temperament with a single emotional outlet.

With the exception of a few didactic poems interpreting the doctrine or ritual of the Church, all his poetry is spiritual autobiography. The devotional poet, perhaps even more than the love poet, is exposed to the danger of confiding in his public instead of writing poems. His problem is to build a structure that will stand alone, independently of either the reader's or the poet's private concerns. It is here that the "Donne tradition" is salutary. Within that tradition the structure of a poem is normally dialectic. Herbert states his premises with precision, usually by means of an image, in the tone of a prose argument. The reader is never befogged; the words represent clear-cut ideas which are the medium through which the poet's emotion is conveyed as well as, often, the cause of the emotion. Herbert knows and states what he thinks, as well as what he feels, about, for example, death and immortality or the relation between God and the soul. This does not mean that his poems are arguments designed to persuade the reader. Herbert takes the reader's intellectual assent for granted. He writes for his fellow-Christian. The substance of each poem is emotional, but the emotion is rooted in thought. As the reader absorbs the poem he becomes aware of that fusion between thought and feeling which constitutes the poet's belief.

Suspension of his own irrelevant incredulities is easier than it is with poetry whose intellectual structure is less self-sufficient.

Joan Bennett
Four Metaphysical Poets (Cambridge Univ. Pr., 1953), pp. 56-57

I do not wish to overemphasize the example of Sidney. It would be more accurate to say that the evidence of Herbert's poetry points toward this hypothesis: that as Herbert developed in spirituality he found that the mode of Donne did not accord with the ideal of simplicity that he set for himself under the guidance of those spiritual masters in whom he found his own center of being. Consequently, he turned toward modes of poetry which accorded with this ideal: and where, more appropriately, than toward that love-poet who had himself spoken as one who sought simplicity?

Meanwhile, Herbert's love and mastery of music would have led him to those airs and madrigals which everyone was singing, and which developed a neatly patterned simplicity based on the fact that they were designed to be sung. Echoes of Elizabethan lute-songs ring throughout the *Temple*, in such motifs as the lover's address to his heart or his lute, and in the similarity between Herbert's handling of stanza-form and that found in E. H. Fellowes' superb collection, *English Madrigal Verse, 1588-1632*. It is important to notice how closely those dates, which represent the period of the flourishing of English song, accord with the dates of Herbert's birth and death (1593-1633); the *Temple*, appearing in 1633, may be seen as a culmination, a fulfillment, of the greatest era of English music: these poems are full of sounds and sweet airs plucked from the surrounding atmosphere. . . .

Herbert's *Temple* displays a structure built upon the art of mental communion, and so designed, beyond any doubt, by George Herbert himself. The early Williams manuscript contains the skeleton of the same structure which the published *Temple* displays; Walton gives, from Duncon's own testimony, the picture of Herbert handing to Duncon his book of "spiritual Conflicts" for delivery to Nicholas Ferrar; and Ferrar himself, in his preface to the *Temple*, explains the lack of the usual introductory matter by his desire to present the work to the world "in that naked simplicitie, with which he left it." But the best evidence lies within the *Temple* itself.

Consider first the structure in the large. Is there any significance in the tripartite arrangement of "Church-porch," "Church," and "Church Militant"? Certainly the first two parts are much more closely related than the last two. And certainly the "Church Militant," in many respects, may seem to represent a rather desperate effort to salvage, if only by way of appendix, a very early poem. It has undergone careful revision, and it is deeply influenced by the themes, the idiom, and the management of pentameter couplet, found in Donne's *Anniversaries*; indeed the division of the poem into five parts by means of a refrain very strongly suggests the example of the *First Anniversary*. Yet it has, I believe, a function in the whole volume. . . .

So the whole *Temple* grows from this sacrament, the other images cluster around it, the strings and pairs of poems issue from and return into it, throughout this body of conflicts, until near the close of the "Church" we feel this central Image asserting itself with a stronger and stronger dominance. We have struggled toward what might be called a sacramental plateau, matching the section which I have called the sacramental introduction. The movement toward this "plateau" is marked, about thirty poems from the end of the "Church," by a tightly connected sequence of four quite different poems: "The Search," "Grief," "The Crosse," and "The Flower." The unity here is most remarkable in the answer which the last stanza of "The Flower" provides for the opening queries of "The Search."

Louis Martz
The Poetry of Meditation (New Haven, Conn.:
Yale Univ. Pr., 1962), pp. 272, 288-89, 309

ROBERT HERRICK
1591-1674

Born in London, the son of a goldsmith. In 1607 was apprenticed for ten years to his uncle, Sir William Herrick, also a goldsmith. Broke apprenticeship in 1613 to enter St. Catherine's College, Cambridge. Took B.A. in 1617, M.A. in 1620. After 1620 lived in London and associated with various men of letters including Ben Jonson. In 1627 took part in an expedition to Isle of Rhé as Chaplain to the Duke of Buckingham. In 1629 became the Vicar of Dean Prior near Exeter in Devonshire. During eighteen years as a rural minister wrote most of his poetry. Removed from Dean Prior by Parliamentary government in 1647. Probably spent the next fifteen years chiefly in London. In 1648 his single volume *Hesperides and Noble Numbers* (two volumes in one) was published in London. Never published again. Restored to living of Dean Prior in 1662. Lived there quietly until his death.

L. C. Martin, ed., *The Poetical Works of Robert Herrick* (1956)
F. W. Moorman, *Robert Herrick* (1910)

In these ambiguous metaphors Herrick resolves formally, with respect to an afterlife, what he cannot resolve logically: the tension between his Christian and Dionysian views. This is, however, only one way in which he deals with this problem. In "Corinna," as both Cleanth Brooks and S. Musgrove have noted, the pagan ceremony of spring "receives its due," while the Christian ceremonies, which provide the implicit framework of the poem's world, temporarily retire into the background. But it will not do, I think, to maintain (as Musgrove does) that the relationship established here is generally true of Herrick's world—that is, that his universe is dominantly Christian and that the mass of secular poems express the "mind on a holiday," or merely "indicate a preference for certain kinds of social behaviour" (*The Universe of Robert Herrick*, pp. 13, 15). The paganism goes deeper than this, as the previous analyses indicate. Herrick's verse moves in two worlds, which are imperfectly coordinated. Some poems bring into focus the ceremony of natural regeneration, the ceremony of Dionysus. There, as in "Corinna," Christianity may be in slight abeyance ("Few Beads are best, when once we goe a Maying"), it may sanctify the results of the natural process (as the priest does after the green-gowns have been given), or it may disappear entirely ("All love, all liking, all delight / Lies drown'd with us in endless night"). In other poems the imagery may suggest to varying degrees a Christian transfiguration of the natural process—as in the references to the holy sisterhood of "The Funerall Rites of the Rose," or to praying and the "even-song" in "To Daffadills." Other poems, especially in *Noble Numbers*, focus upon Christian ceremony; and there one finds more narrowly Christian ways of coordinating the two realms, as in "The Transfiguration" or "The School or Perl of Putney," poems on which Musgrove relies heavily. In the large, *Noble Numbers* complements *Hesperides* just as the Christian imagery complements the pagan—and it is surely no accident that *Hesperides* is the better volume.

However the two realms may be related for Herrick the Anglican priest, they are not in fixed relation for Herrick the poet. Rather, the Christian and the qualified Dionysian are two perspectives upon a reality that transcends them both and so cannot be expressed by either symbolism alone. Herrick is feeling for a harmonious middle realm, "Part Pagan, part Papisticall," that may present a variety of reactions to this complex and rather fluid world before him. To this end the attempts to create his own eclectic myth of the garden of the Hesperides, aided by what we presumptuously call a "modern" sense of myth's ability to order the facts and demands of the human situation.

Thomas R. Whitaker
ELH (March, 1955), pp. 30-31

So far we have examined only one aspect of Herrick's verse, the warm, vibrant sensuality which colours and moulds poem after poem in *Hesperides*. We must now glance at an equally significant facet—the consummate technical skill which he brings to the practice of his art. He is not only responsive to the colours, shapes, smells, sounds, tastes and textures of the world, but acutely sensitive also to the properties and potentialities of language: the weight of words; the sensuous values of consonants and vowels; the melodic flow of verse; the varied shapes of metrical patterns; the way in which verbal rhythms can be adjusted to correspond with a shift of emotional mood; the means whereby a poem's tone can be made lighter or darker; the extent to which a poem's texture can change in sympathy with the unfolding of its logical and emotional argument; the orchestral resources of our tongue, which draws upon Anglo-Saxon and Romance elements. A knowledge of these and kindred factors must be inborn in a poet or acquired by constant labour; and few verse-writers have shown more accomplishment than Herrick in the management of those devices which all need to master if their poems are to survive the whirligig of fashion and the collapse of political systems.

His poetic technique is, on the surface, lucid and straightforward, exhibiting little of the daring ingenuity and complexity so much prized by the Metaphysicals, or of the learned artistry which distinguishes Milton's early work. In his diction an easy grace and fluency mingle with a homely strength, although in his more formal poems his vocabulary tends to be richer and more elaborate than in his personal lyrics. One of his favourite devices is to introduce a Latinism quite unexpectedly into a passage largely made up of common everyday words, thereby varying the simplicity of the language and breaking the gentle flow of monosyllables by a heavy polysyllable.

John Press
Herrick (London: Longmans, Green, 1961), pp. 15-16

As to the form of our poem ["Delight in Disorder"], I wonder why critics so eager to read poems "closely" and so alert to questions of structure have failed to see that the idea of wild civility is reflected by two features of our poem: its syntax and its rhymes. In this "sonnet of couplets" in each of which (except for the first and the last couplet) one piece of clothing is enumerated, six rhymes out of seven are only approximate (dress: wantonnéss; thrown: distractión; there: stomachér; thereby: confusedlý; note: petticóat; tie: civilitý), the final one being a perfect rhyme (art: part)—a rhyme structure and a syntactic structure, that shows in itself wildness tamed: the final couplet contains the predicate which the series of enumerated nouns made us wait for and formulates the artistic creed of the poet, the finality of which is reflected in the perfect rhyme. Metrical perfection (indeed "precision" at the moment when "precision" is only half-heartedly endorsed in the couplet) wins out in the end over approximation.

Up to this point we have deliberately ignored other poems of Herrick's concerned with women's dress as well as the sources of "Delight in Disorder" (both categories are discussed in L. C. Martin's edition). As to the sources, the immediate model, Ben Jonson's "Song" inserted in the play *Epicoene or the Silent Woman* shows one indumentary detail (no enumeration of several pieces of clothing) in the service of a plea for natural simplicity addressed to his lady:

> Give me a look, give me a face,
> That makes *simplicity* a grace;
> *Robes loosely flowing,* hair as free;
> Such *sweet neglect* more taketh me
> Than all th'adulteries of art.

Here Ben Jonson is echoing similar pleas for simplicity found in Neo-Latin poems of the type (cf. the edition of Jonson's play in *Yale Studies in English* XXXI, p. LV):

> *Neglectim* mihi se quae comit amica
> Se det; et ornatus *simplicitate* valet.

We recognize as the central *topos* the paradox of "sweet neglect" which, whether applied to woman's appearance or not, has ancient precedents in Ovid's *neglecta decens* and Cicero's (advice to the orator) *quaedam etiam negligentia est diligens*. But in contrast with the praise of the natural and the simple of the sources Herrick praises the art hiding behind apparent neglectfulness. For instance, another poem of his "Art above Nature, to Julia" (l. c., p. 202) seems to be a direct rejoinder to Ben Jonson's poem, from the title to the proclamation in the end (in which the very rhymes of Jonson are used: heart: art):

> I must confess, mine eye and heart
> Dotes less on Nature then on Art—

a point of view shared by Burton in a passage of his *Anatomy* in which there is also found an enumeration of beautiful "coutrements" more tempting then "barbarian homelinesse." Thus Herrick sees art, if not in the barbaric, in the wild and his "wild civility" is, as it were, a synthesis of "art superior to nature" and "barbarian homlinesse."

Leo Spitzer
MLN (April, 1961), pp. 212-13

Noble Numbers is certainly not "religious metaphysical" nor except in some isolated instances meditational; rarely is it emblematic. Still less does it support the cliché of Herrick the pagan-priest, for what is classical in *Noble Numbers* had long since been acclimatized and enfranchised. Such symbolism as it employs is of the most deeply absorbed and received kind; its figurative mode is essentially metaphorical. It can only be described generically as the "poetry of devotion" and it is very inclusive of its kind. It happens to be largely didactic and affective, approaching "common devotion." It grows more distinctive, humanistically, on the comparatively few occasions when the devotions grow more "private," and when they grow more symbolic. It grows most original when Herrick's peculiar quality, the *ingenu* quality, grows marked, and when Herrick's devotional muse follows in the path of his secular one. By its inclusiveness it catches us up to the recognition of the existence of much seventeenth-century devotional poetry that, failing our exigencies, has been politely ignored, poetry even of Herbert, *The Church Porch*, even of Donne, *The Lamentations of Jeremy*.

Nor, finally, should one be unrespectful of the particular power of *Noble Numbers*, a power that has gone completely unrecognized. Conventional as much of it is, much has undergone a sea change into something particularly immediate, personal, local, simple, and humane. But to speak of Herrick's simplicities is never to suggest naïveté. Herrick's is an achieved simplicity, a certitude of matter and manner both. Nor is it suggested when one says that Herrick humanized devotion that he minimized the incarnational beyond the characteristic habits of his time. Indeed, one of his distinguishing qualities is that, even at his most incarnational, he succeeds at many points in his intention to humanize it. He domesticates the mystery.

Miriam K. Starkman
in *Reason and the Imagination*, ed. J. A. Mazzeo
(New York: Columbia Univ. Pr., 1962), pp. 26-27

THOMAS HEYWOOD
ca. 1573-1641

Born in Lincolnshire. Probably the son of a clergyman of an old Cheshire family. May be the Heywood who entered Emmanuel College, Cambridge, as a pensioner in 1591. Left without taking degree, perhaps because of the death of his father in 1593. Appeared in London as a writer of plays. Earliest known publication is an Ovidian love poem, *Oenone and Paris* in 1594. Wrote regularly for Philip Henslowe. Plays produced by Lord Admiral's Men, later by Earl of Worcester's Men. During long career had "either an entire hand, or at least a main finger" in some 220 plays. Published *Apology for Actors* in 1612. Wrote prose histories. Between 1631 and 1639 prepared Lord Mayors' pageants. Wrote history plays such as *Edward IV* and *If You Know Not Me;* domestic tragedies such as *The English Traveller* and *A Woman Killed with Kindness*. Tried formal Roman tragedy in *The Rape of Lucrece*. Dramatized classical mythology in *The Four Ages*, sophisticated romance in *Royal King and Loyal Subject*, adventure in *Fortune by Land and Sea* and *The Captives*. Wrote realistic studies of lower class life in *The Wise Woman of Hogsdon* and *The Fair Maid of the Exchange*.

R. H. Shepherd, ed., *The Works of Thomas Heywood* (1874)

A. M. Clark, *Thomas Heywood, Playwright and Miscellanist* (1931)

Two central characters, as we have seen [in *A Woman Killed With Kindness*], fail to meet the demands of honor when faced with a crisis. Frankford also faces a crisis, and we may expect him to face it with honor. And so he does—yet his reaction to his crisis holds its own surprises. The situation he faces has been set up in conventionally melodramatic terms: cuckolded by his protégé, warned by his servant, he plots to catch the sinners *in flagrante delicto*. It is the sort of problem common in Elizabethan and later drama, and usually leads to a bloody resolution.

The "unwritten law" justifies a husband in taking immediate revenge on an erring wife and her lover; it has even, in drama, justified prolonged and ingenious revenge. Mistress Frankford has betrayed her honor as a wife; Wendoll has betrayed his as a friend; we may expect Master Frankford to uphold his honor as a husband. This he does not do, because he is bound by larger standards. It is as a Christian that he reacts, not as a husband. He refrains from killing the lovers in their bed because—unlike Hamlet —he does not wish them to go to judgment in the flower of their sin; he is grateful to the maid who keeps him from murdering Wendoll. He gives his wife time to repent fully, and when she has repented, on her deathbed, he forgives her. He acts, in short, consistently as a Christian, in relation to a high concept of Christian honor. In this respect he differs notably from all other characters in the play. . . . Death is the customary reward of betrayal, but Frankford is not governed by the narrow code of Sir Francis.

Yet despite his high standard of honor, he is not a flawless character, and his goodness does not suffice to lighten the import of the play— because it is largely ineffectual goodness. Frankford may be virtuous, but he is not perceptive, and failure of perception can be as disastrous in its effects as failure of goodness. The tragedy which befalls Master Frankford is in a sense his own fault. It is he who insists on the virtue of Wendoll and who presses Wendoll to accept an intimate place in his family; it is he who urges his wife to be kind to the new member of the household. Despite the fact that he behaves with high honor, he is brought to the forcible and bitter realization that he cannot trust his own perception and judgment. . . . Frankford's characterization presents the problem of perception from a different angle: he is the false perceiver rather than the false object of perception.

In the main plot of *A Woman Killed with Kindness,* then, the theme of honor is closely linked to that of appearance and reality. Two characters who appear to be honorable turn out to be dishonorable; the other major participants in the action consistently judge them wrong. A third principal, honorable though he is, cannot distinguish between goodness and the mere shape of goodness in others. If we take these three as typical representatives of humanity, the suggested picture is dark indeed: treachery where faith is to be expected, evil men judged and rewarded as virtuous, the good man blind in his goodness. The deathbed forgiveness scene does nothing to relieve the essential gloom.

P. M. Spacks
MLQ (December, 1959), pp. 325-26

We have in Heywood, therefore, a dramatist who wrote easily and quickly, if not always thoughtfully, who knew his own limitations and kept well within them, who had no particular social, moral, or religious axe to grind (at least not to the extent of turning his plays into treatises—"studious for thy pleasure and profit" seems to sum up quite well his attitude towards his audience), who had intimate knowledge of and respect for the acting profession, and who was concerned above all things with writing for the stage, not for the study.

. . . Once the play has started, Heywood seems to have no objection to using any and every stage device in the manipulation of his plot, and it is on this ground, I feel, that the most serious accusations may be leveled against him as a dramatic artist. . . . [He] was often too readily dependent on swift changes of location, coincidence, accident, disguise, nonrecognition between closely related characters, dumbshow, and all the other paraphernalia by means of which a plot could be kicked along if it showed signs of flagging.

. . . The rapid interchange of serious matter and broad comedy, indeed buffoonery, is a prominent feature of Heywood's art, and it is interesting to note that although he had no illusions about the capabilities of those in the audience who preferred the second element, he nevertheless acknowledged their right to be supplied with this kind of entertainment and in some measure approved of it.

. . . An examination of Heywood's art places him fairly and squarely in the company of those Elizabethan and Jacobean dramatists, some known, many others anonymous, who, while having a flair for the theater, rarely rose to the heights of great drama, often plumbed the depths of bad drama, but in general managed to keep to the broad road of drama which could at least be relied upon to provide a company with its bread and butter. They could never become specialists in any kind, for the simple reason that they were called upon to write all kinds. Having no particularly profound outlook upon life, they would tend inevitably to produce work which in the last resort could be called uninspired.

Arthur Brown
*Essays on Shakespeare and Elizabethan Drama in
Honor of Hardin Craig* (Columbia, Mo.: Univ. Missouri Pr.,
1962), pp. 329-39

The most prolific dramatist by far of the entire Elizabethan and Jacobean period was Thomas Heywood, having had a hand, by his own account, in some two hundred and twenty plays. His career, like that of George Chapman, spans the final years of Elizabeth's reign, all of that of James, and extends in fact through most of the Caroline era, for Heywood lived until 1641, surviving into an age when the plays he had written at the beginning of his career were already an anachronism. The greatest of his achievements, *A Woman Killed with Kindness,* was written probably in the same year as Chapman's *Bussy D'Ambois,* but here the parallel between the two men ends, for Heywood remained the apostle of a Renaissance cosmic optimism throughout his long career. He is still, however, entirely a product of his times, for while his writings show a constant reaffirmation of order and degree, of traditional moral values in traditional terms, into his greatest plays there sometimes creeps, perhaps in spite of his avowed didactic purposes, a reflection of the contradictions and ambiguities of his time.

It is probably because his outlook is so different from those of his greater Jacobean contemporaries that Professor Ellis-Fermor omitted Heywood from her classic study of the Jacobean drama. He stands indeed apart from the dramatists we are considering, but if we would have a proper estimate of the moral climate of Jacobean tragedy he cannot be ignored. Although he left no monuments like those of Webster or Middleton, he probably enjoyed a greater popularity than either of them, and he continued to write for the stage after both were dead. Heywood is important because he may illuminate for us a facet of the moral and intellectual milieu of Jacobean tragedy of which we can have no awareness while we restrict our vision to the greater artistic achievements of his contemporaries. Heywood is one who doggedly continued to assert the moral values of an earlier age in a new world in which they no longer had great meaning.

Charles Lamb may have most perfectly summed up the significance of Heywood when he called him a prose Shakespeare. He has been celebrated for the realism of his scenes of Elizabethan life and for the gentle sentimentality of his romantic plots; he may be even more important as one whose imitation of Shakespeare led him to reflect in more prosaic terms a moral viewpoint which we associate with the greatest plays of his master. Like Shakespeare, Heywood was conservative. He saw the universe as the ordered creation of a loving God, every part of which was related to every other, and all joined together in a great cosmic harmony. His tragedies, like Shakespeare's, are concerned with evil as a violation of this order, and they end with the restoration of order by the working out of evil itself in accord with a divine providence. What in Shakespeare emerges, however, as the poet's comprehensive vision of human destiny, conveyed in striking emotional terms, appears in Heywood in the terms of the Elizabethan devotional and homiletic tract.

Irving Ribner

Jacobean Tragedy (London: Methuen, 1962), pp. 50-51

RICHARD HOOKER
1554-1600

> Born at Heavitree, Exeter. Educated at Exeter Grammar school. Patronized by John Jewel and Edwin Sandys. Entered Corpus Christi College, Oxford, in 1573. Took B.A. in 1574, M.A. in 1577. Became a fellow of the college in 1577, Deputy Professor of Hebrew in 1579. Entered holy orders in 1581. Preached a sermon at Paul's Cross in same year. Granted the living of Drayton Beauchamp in 1584. Became Master of the Temple in 1585. Married Joan Churchaman in 1588. Lost a son in 1589. Resigned from the Temple Mastership in 1591. Became Rector of Boscombe and Prebendary of Netheravon in 1591, Vicar of Bishopsbourne in 1595. Lost another son in 1597.
>
> John Keble, ed., *The Works of Richard Hooker*, rev. R. W. Church and F. Paget (1888), 3 vols.

But while the *Ecclesiastical Polity* is rightly hailed as a masterpiece of literature, it is a no less notable contribution to English theology. It covers a wide range of subjects, and there is scarcely an aspect of classical theology on which it does not touch. Not only does Hooker concern himself with Church order and Church discipline, not only does he expose the weaknesses of his opponents' case, but he discourses, in the least political but most notable part of his book, on the doctrines of the Incarnation and the Person of Christ, he examines the Liturgy and the Creeds, and sets forth the Anglican teaching on prayer and the Sacraments. Biblical exegesis moves side by side with quotations from the Fathers, and nowhere is there a division between matters of administration and matters of doctrine.

Theology, however, is no longer the queen of the sciences, and even students of literature are perhaps in the minority. But Hooker has two principal claims on the public, the first of which lies in his contribution to political philosophy. His was not an original genius; as we have seen, he owes much to his predecessors, and even his own ideas were often contradictory and in need of elucidation and development. Like Burke, he had a vivid sense of the process of history, and esteemed it his duty to preserve the best of one age and pass it on to the next. In nothing was he more truly English; he was not a comet unexpectedly streaking across the sky and commanding our whole attention till it sinks to oblivion. He was rather a known constellation which sheds an understanding light about it, and at which we do not too often look because we know it is always there, a symbol of the clear order of Eternity, above our fever and malice. It was Hooker's function to link the political theory of an intense age with the past and the future, and with the eternal laws which underlay it.

His first contribution, then, to political philosophy is his conception of the Natural Law, which leads to his contractual theory. If here, again, he is not entirely original, these ideas, with their corollaries of "consent" and the "rights of the people," were to form a main stream of political thought, flowing from him to Hobbes, to Locke and America, to Rousseau and France, with world-shaking consequences.

F. J. Shirley
Richard Hooker and Contemporary Political Ideas
(London: Society for the Propagation of Christian Knowledge,
1949), pp. 224–25

The real problem which thus confronted Hooker and many others was how to maintain a political system in which secular and ecclesiastical powers co-operated in the sense of the second type of political philosophy. Or, in other words: it was necessary to refute the exorbitant claims of all those people who believed in a newly discovered source of revealed law and who arrogated to themselves the right to a final decision in all matters affecting the conduct of life. This was a double task: because there was first the claim of the newly established churches to be better repositories of revealed truth than the Church of Rome and secondly the growing conviction that divine law could simply override and dispense with natural law. . . .

Hooker's opposition was roused, in the last analysis, by the Puritan attack on natural law and the disparagement of reason. He saw that Puritanism was both an appeal to and a justification of the irrational elements in human nature. And when he set to work to state his counter-argument, he was probably aware of the fact that the human mind was standing at one of the crossroads of its history. Hence the weighty words with which he opened the Preface to the *Laws of Ecclesiastical Polity:* "Though for no other cause, yet for this; that posterity may know we have not loosely through silence permitted things to pass away as in a dream. . . ."

Hooker therefore went back to that medieval thinker who—though for different reasons—had built up a case against Augustinianism. He began his great work with a summary of Thomistic philosophy which takes up the better part of the first book. Most of the arguments are telescoped to such an extent that to a reader unacquainted with the main principles of Thomism they may fail to carry conviction. But Hooker's philosophically inclined sixteenth-century reader must have quickly grasped what he was trying to do. The summary was made in Hooker's own language, not encumbered with any philosophical pedantry or technical jargon, and bears witness to the extent to which the grandiose system of Thomistic philosophy had been assimilated by Hooker. He could write about these matters with ease and grace, probably forgetting half the time that he was propounding philosophy, thinking that he was merely briefly expounding what everybody knew or ought to know. What to him, at any rate, had become so familiar as to be obvious rather than a matter for controversy.

Peter Munz
The Place of Hooker in the History of Thought
(London: Routledge and Kegan Paul, 1952), pp. 15, 39, 49

His great work, *Of the Laws of Ecclesiastical Polity,* was a refutation of the Puritan position, essentially an exaggerated fideistic one, that church authority, independent of the state, is assigned to a council of presbyters who hold their commission as an external prerogative granted by positive enactment of Holy Scripture and that Holy Scripture alone is the sole rule for church government, discipline, and ritual. Hooker reduced the Anglican-Puritan controversy to first causes. He founded his defense of the government and the subsidiary interests in the Church of England on the nature of law, on the hierarchy of laws, and on the law of reason proper to man. Neither to Scripture alone nor to the law of reason alone does Hooker assign the authority for ecclesiastical polity, but rather to the harmony of both faith and reason. To counteract the inherent fideism of the Puritan opposition and to restore the reason-faith balance of Christian humanism, Hooker resorted to an emphasis on reason characteristic of the scholastical-dialectical tradition. His position, therefore, in the history of Renaissance Christian humanism is obviously unique. As a Protestant theologian trained in the grammatical-rhetorical tradition and in positive theology, he tends to emphasize faith; however, to refute an exaggerated fideism, he draws largely upon the scholastical-dialectical tradition for a thought content that emphasizes, with reservations, reason. Yet to communicate that thought content, that *inventio,* he employs the balanced rhetorical style and exegetical method proper to the broad concept of grammar, both of which characterize the grammatical-rhetorical tradition. By relating the balances of both traditions and by integrating them in the organically constructed and artistically designed *Polity,* Hooker marks a significant development among the Protestant exponents of Renaissance Christian humanism. . . .

Not only is this emphasis on the intellect consistent with the total balanced content of the *Polity* and proper to the reason-faith balance which Hooker aimed to re-establish, but it governs the intellectual fiber of the style employed in the defense. Designed architectonically as a forensic oration, the *Polity* is an eminent, pratical commentary on the type of rhetoric proper to the grammatical-rhetorical tradition as it developed under Cicero, Quintilian, and St. Augustine and as it was resuscitated by the Renaissance Christian humanists. Emphasis is always given to *inventio,* which is drawn primarily from the resources of the scholastical-dialectical tradition; *dispositio* and *elocutio* are always subordinated to the content. Moreover, the style itself is completely functional and appropriate to the intellectual and balanced character of the content. The diction points to the nature of the thing nominated; the imagery, the use of rhetorical devices, and the rhythm further the idea; and the Ciceronian period reflects the universal order and teleological design of the hierarchy of being and of laws.

Sister M. Stephanie Stueber
PMLA (September, 1956), pp. 811-12, 819

BEN JONSON

1572-1637

Born in London, the posthumous son of a minister. His mother married a bricklayer after his birth. Sent to Westminster School, probably by William Camden the antiquarian. Left in 1589, probably without finishing. No record of his ever attending a university. Worked for a time as a bricklayer, probably apprenticed to his stepfather. First mentioned in Henslowe's *Diary* in 1597. May have served as a soldier in the Low Countries for a while. Probably had become an actor. Had married. Contributed to Thomas Nashe's play, *Isle of Dogs,* in 1597. Imprisoned for his share in the work, which offended the authorities. In September 1598 killed actor Gabriel Spencer in a duel. Imprisoned, but escaped hanging by reciting "neck verse." In 1598 Lord Chamberlain's Men, probably at the suggestion of Shakespeare, produced *Every Man in His Humour.* Other plays followed. Became involved in War of the Theaters. Began to write masques under King James in 1603. Offended the King in *Eastward Ho,* written in collaboration with Chapman and Marston. Imprisoned again. Period of great comedies began with *Volpone* in 1606. Wrote for various companies. Became the leader of a group of writers who gathered at Mermaid Tavern and Devil Tavern. Patronized by various noblemen, including the Earl of Pembroke, Lord d'Aubigny, and the Countess of Bedford. In 1612 and 1613 went abroad as a tutor to the son of Sir Walter Ralegh, then imprisoned in the Tower. A folio of his works was printed in 1616. Granted a pension by King James in same year. Received honorary degrees of Master of Arts from both Oxford and Cambridge. In summer of 1618 took a walking trip to Scotland. Had conversations with Drummond of Hawthornden. Books and manuscripts destroyed by fire in 1623. Suffered a stroke in 1628. In the same year succeeded Thomas Middleton as Chronologer of City of London. Final plays were failures on stage. Quarrelled with Inigo Jones. Bedridden in last years. Died in Westminster. Buried in Westminster Abbey.

C. H. Herford, P. Simpson, and E. Simpson, eds., *Ben Jonson* (1925-53), 11 vols.

PLAYS

This will mean, not that Shakespeare's spring from the feelings or imagination and Jonson's from the intellect or invention; they have equally an emotional source; but that Shakespeare's represent a more complex tissue of feelings and desires, as well as a more supple, a more susceptible temperament. Falstaff is not only the roast Manning-tree ox with the pudding in his belly; he also "grows old," and, finally, his nose is as sharp as a pen. He was perhaps the *satisfaction* of more, and of more complicated feelings; and perhaps he was, as the great tragic characters must have been, the offspring of deeper, less apprehensible feelings: deeper, but not necessarily stronger or more intense, than those of Jonson. It is obvious that the spring of the difference is not the difference between feeling and thought, or superior insight, superior perception, on the part of Shakespeare, but his susceptibility to a greater range of emotion, and emotion deeper and more obscure. But his characters are no more "alive" than are the characters of Jonson.

The world they live in is a larger one. But small worlds—the worlds which artists create—do not differ only in magnitude; if they are complete worlds, drawn to scale in every part, they differ in kind also. And Jonson's world has this scale. His type of personality found its relief in something falling under the category of burlesque or farce—though when you are dealing with a *unique* world, like his, these terms fail to appease the desire for definition. It is not, at all events, the farce of Molière: the latter is more analytic, more an intellectual redistribution. It is not defined by the word "satire." Jonson poses as a satirist. But satire like Jonson's is great in the end not by hitting off its object, but by creating it; the satire is merely the means which leads to the aesthetic result, the impulse which projects a new world into a new orbit. In *Every Man in his Humour* there is a neat, a very neat, comedy of humours. In discovering and proclaiming in this play the new genre Jonson was simply recognizing, unconsciously, the route which opened out in the proper direction for his instincts. His characters are and remain, like Marlowe's, simplified characters; but the simplification does not consist in the dominance of a particular humour or monomania. That is a very superficial account of it. The simplification consists largely in reduction of detail, in the seizing of aspects relevant to

the relief of an emotional impulse which remains the same for that character, in making the character conform to a particular setting. This
stripping is essential to the art, to which is also essential a flat distortion
in the drawing; it is an art of caricature, of great caricature, like Marlowe's.
It is a great caricature, which is beautiful; and a great humour, which is
serious. The "world" of Jonson is sufficiently large; it is a world of poetic
imagination; it is sombre. He did not get the third dimension, but he was not
trying to get it.

T. S. Eliot
Selected Essays 1917-1932 (New York:
Harcourt, Brace, 1932), pp. 137-38

Yet in spite of his learning, Jonson was fortunately not academic in habit
nor pedantic in style. Art in his work had freed itself from the restraints of
scholastic theory; the Induction to *Every Man out of his Humour,* his first
manifesto, contains a definition of his new type of comedy, and a justification of his departure from classical models. He transported Art from the
Schools to the boards; he had no single solution to propound, no fixed
model to offer, but instead a series of experiments and a continuous stream
of discussion upon them, with alternative definitions. At the same time he
sought constantly to defend his Art, so that the inductions, epilogues and
incidental comments in his plays furnish the most complete theory of the
drama which the age produced, based not upon scholastic arguments but
upon practical experience. His parody of old-fashioned parts, such as the
amorous, the martial and the tyrant's, in the scene of *Poetaster* where the
boys rehearse before the players, depends upon a practical knowledge of the
way to build a traditional play, and is comparable with the mechanicals'
parody in *A Midsummer Night's Dream,* or Hamlet's condescending catalogue of the King, the adventurous knight, the lover, the humorous man, the
clown and the lady. He has all the old playtags at his tongue's end.

Jonsonian comedy more than qualified for the ironic definition of Horace,
in the Satire which Jonson so often relied upon: for much of it was in prose.

> Some people have questioned whether comedy can be called
> poetry: for neither in language nor plot has it the fire or the force
> of inspiration, and save for the regular beat of the rhythm, it might
> as well be prose.
>
> *Satires,* I.IV.

"Deeds and language such as men do use" were Jonson's materials. He
agreed with few of the professed critics, who all, from Sidney to Bacon,
conceived that the poet's function was to build a brave new world, a second
Creation in which the limits of the first were transcended. "Our erected wit
maketh us to know what perfection is, and yet our infected will keepeth us

from reaching unto it," Sidney observed; and to Bacon "the use of this feigned history hath been to give some shadow of satisfaction to the mind of man in those points wherein the nature of things doth deny it, the world being inferior to the soul." These are justifications at once Platonic and Christian; poetry restores man to his original self, brings back the Golden Age and rediscovers his true kingdom. . . .

Jonson's "humours and observation" were to his city audience so familiar as to be startling. He presented the unexpected and freshly collected habits of Cockney streets and taverns in a form that was dignified with all the requirements of art. The shock to his contemporaries must have been as great as the pleasure, much like to the shock of Donne's familiar style in love-poetry. The growth of London, and in particular the growth of its under-world, a class of professional sharkers, had been depicted in the earlier pamphlets of Greene and Nashe, largely by a refashioning of traditional material. Jonson drew from the life. . . . The basis of the play [*Every Man out of his Humor*] is in fact the analysis and dissection of identity. Action is secondary, and the number of roles is such that it cannot be devoloped. The stage is crowded with a parade of eccentrics, and the catastrophe is the destruction of all their pretensions. A fine court lady cannot distinguish a gentleman from a clown; and an elegant fop is left in the debtor's prison. Each character assumes a role which is stripped from him; and the role varies from the horseplay of Puntarvolo with his dog to the deadly earnestness of Sordido with his halter.

M. C. Bradbrook
The Growth and Structure of English Comedy (London:
Chatto and Windus, 1955), pp. 105-6, 142-43

Briefly, I believe that the essential unity of Jonson's comedy is thematic. In each of his major plays he explores an idea or a cluster of related ideas through a variety of characters and actions. And the central expression of the unifying idea is usually not in a fully developed plot but in a fantastic comic conceit, an extravagant exaggeration of human folly, to which all of the more realistically conceived characters and incidents have reference.

Ray L. Heffner, Jr.
in *English Stage Comedy*, ed. W. K. Wimsatt
(New York: Columbia Univ. Pr., 1955), p. 75

Fully to enjoy what Ben Jonson has to offer we need, in the first place, to understand an individual tone and accent that can only be defined in terms of the union of opposites. The manner is remarkably individual, yet informed with a strong sense of tradition: its appeal is to a common wisdom. A marked classical bent is combined with an Englishness that can digest erudition. A mode of expression that is grave, weighty, and sententious moves easily into high-spirited buoyancy. The voice of an insistent moralist is also that of a successful popular entertainer and the author of some of the best farces in the language. . . .

Now, it is certainly true that Jonson was a very learned man, that his plays were nourished by his familiarity with the Latin authors, and that he believed passionately in the moral function of the poet. It may also be assumed that when a creative writer theorizes in language as vigorous and telling as Jonson's, the critical theory is a rationalization of something intrinsic and fundamental to his art. Jonson's classical bent, his concern for the unities, and so on, is an expression of his own vigorous and simplifying vision of life, of his feeling that saying something effectively is largely a matter of not saying too much. His didactic insistence is neither the sermonizing of a pedant nor the camouflage of a popular writer conscious of Puritan hostility to the stage; it expresses his sense of comedy as essentially a serious art. Jonson, in short, appealed to the Ancients not only because he felt for them the respect of any classically trained mind—a discriminating respect, it must be added—but because they conferred authority on deeply congenial modes.

Yet that is only half the story. The best of Jonson's plays are living drama because the learning and "classical" elements are assimilated by a sensibility in direct contact with its own age. The judgement, the operative standards, are those of a man who has read and thought, but the material, however transmuted, is supplied by direct observation. . . .

Jonson's world, though complete in itself, is not a large one. You cannot live in it for long at a time. In a sense its very completeness is against it. Nothing breaks through from the hidden world of longing or suffering; the prevailing mode is never disturbed by unexpected sympathies or glimpses of paradox. There is little in the plays that you can dwell on, as you find yourself dwelling on a play—or a few lines—of Shakespeare's, or a poem— or a few lines—of Blake's, so that new aspects of human nature (your own nature among others) and new possibilities of being are continually revealed. Exclusion was the condition of Jonson's achievement. But the best of his plays have qualities common to all great literature. They define with precision a permanent aspect of human nature. For what they isolate for sardonic inspection is a form of folly which, however grotesque in its dramatic representation, in Sejanus, Mammon, or Meercraft, is not confined to fools; it is simply the folly of inordinate desire. And although this, deeply considered, is a theme for tragedy, there is also a rightness in the particular form of Jonsonian comedy, in which simplified figures seem to blow themselves up until they burst, and schemes, contrived with a remarkable and persistent ingenuity topple like a house of cards.

L. C. Knights

"Ben Jonson, Dramatist," in The Age of Shakespeare,
ed. Boris Ford (London: Penguin Books, 1955),
pp. 302-4, 315-16

Furthermore, the humour figures were amusing, if distressing, because they knew little. These Romans are frightening because they may know much. The courtiers of *Cynthia's Revels* have nothing under their children's artificial faces and elaborate clothes. Beneath Livia's cosmetics and the men's tunics lurk, or may lurk, many concealed plans. The uncertainty increases the torment. The difference indicates a major shift of emphasis. Since the happy assumptions about the availability of truth in *The Case Is Altered*, the eye, of course, has been praised as the instrument for detecting disguises. Here its abilities shrink. Not one among the Romans understands the whole imbroglio; the most vigilant are liable to error. The voice deceives as much as ever when—another function of Tiberius' letter—from Capri the Emperor's accents sound in the Roman Senate with the complete assurance of winning what they desire. Deprived thus of reliable allies, reason must become a hit-or-miss game of chance in which no throw of the dice can be final until the last, catastrophic cast. This mode fits with the tragic theme of Fortune's wheel twirling in lottery princes and peoples, although fortune lives in the population and not as a goddess apart. Direct references stress these plottings, for example: "steepes his words, / When he would kill, in artificiall teares" (II. 422-23); "Their faces runne like shittles, they are weauing / Some curious cobweb to catch flyes" (III. 23-24); "For, night hath many eies, / Wherof, though most doe sleepe, yet some are spies." (V. 169-70) The trickery, blending well with the darkness, animal cunning, portents, and cosmetics, runs throughout and bolsters the dramatic themes. Suitably, for tragedy Jonson abandoned the clarity of the comic truth and by action and imagery summoned darker forces. Even here, contributing to the special tone of this complex work, he does not analyze psychological drives but keeps to what can be observed. This thorough grasp of surfaces ensures the tragedy its firm, if limited, outlook. . . .

In *Sejanus* and *Catiline* night falls as the dimming of human insight before tragedy. Here the approach of dark becomes an accentuation in the comic pattern. It represents how an inevitable process catches up the deluded. Mistakes, close to unforgivable error, create a tragedy; in petty individuality and in choosing the false standards lies the ridiculous. If one prefers hearing the still, sad music of humanity, the classical tempo in *Volpone* may sound repugnant, but this predilection merely tells one that audiences remain somewhat behind Jonson as connoisseurs of comedians. With disguise so convincingly pervasive, the eye cannot guide one, but this shift occurs because of the change in defining personality. Despite an undeniable cleverness, the clients are so obsessed that they see only what they wish, and, since it nearly amounts to the same thing, what Volpone wants them to. The voice continues to mislead when shaped by the rhetoric of Volpone and Voltore. There is, then, no accountable force to deliver moralizing speeches and to round off all corners nicely. Viewed in this way, the rationale of the play must be accepted as largely negative; judgments have to be brought from outside the dramatic frame by the audience roused through what the stage denies them.

John J. Enck
Jonson and the Comic Truth (Madison, Wisc.:
Univ. Wisconsin Pr., 1957), pp. 102-3, 124-25

It is Jonson's explicit intention to sport with follies on the stage so that they will not become—or remain—the crimes of real life. This does not mean that Jonson is not "realistic"; it does mean that he is not naturalistic. The characters that he presents on the stage are *like* characters one might meet in real life, but they are not the same. Jonson's typical use of psychologically oversimplified characters—the "humor" characters—implies a deliberate limitation on characterization that is both artistic and didactic, qualities which for Jonson are inseparable. And even in such a generally pleasant and indulgent spectacle as that provided by *Every Man In His Humour,* one can see that society could be corrupted and ruined if it included a sufficient number of Stephens, Kitelys, Matthews, and Bobadills. . . .

But what *humors* finally means for Jonson is *manners,* as he himself often indicates. Indeed, in the Prologue to *The Alchemist*, he specifies that humors is simply a fashionable term for manners: ". . . whose manners, now called humours feed the stage. . . ." The humors are the simplified, often caricatured, manners of men; from this it would follow that the comedy of humors is for all practical purposes a comedy of manners, specifically, a comedy concerned with the manners of men in society. . . .

Two differences we have specifically noticed: the battleground in Jonsonian tragedy is the state, not the universe; and history is the guiding and shaping force. For Jonson the tragic muse is really the muse of history, and the tragic poet becomes the poet of history. Shakespeare's and Webster's major tragedies would have been great tragedies even if the history on which they are based had really been fiction; but if Tiberius, Sejanus, Cicero, and Catiline had never actually lived Jonson would simply not have written his plays, which are specifically designed to recreate on the tragic stage certain events whose significance lies precisely in the fact that they did occur, one signifying a period of social decay, the other suggesting the temporary salvation of society. . . .

In some of the earlier plays it has been possible to discern two groups of characters—those whose realistic presentation carries a symbolic value, and those whom we might describe as more or less purely realistic. Thus Volpone and Mosca as opposed to Voltore, Corvino, and Corbaccio; Face and Subtle as opposed to their victims; Dauphine, Truewit, and Clerimont in contrast to the gulls; and earlier, and on various levels, the controlling figures of

Brainworm, Asper, Macilente, Carlo Buffone. That is to say, there has been one group of characters that we might describe as poet-figures, set up in opposition to another group of characters whose quintessence they expose.

In reviewing this particular point, I wish to insist that the poet-figures are also realistic figures and that their symbolic identity does not "make" any particular play but enriches the satirical comedy in which they appear. For example, I am not aware that any previous critic has insisted that Subtle must be regarded as a symbolic figure for the comic artist or that alchemy represents comic art. That Subtle is such a figure and that alchemy does have such a significance seems to me undeniable. Virtually all critics have agreed that *The Alchemist* is a thoroughly masterful play, even without recognizing just how masterful it actually is.

C. G. Thayer
Ben Jonson: Studies in the Plays (Norman, Okla.:
Univ. Oklahoma Pr., 1963), pp. 18-21, 114-15, 157-58

POETRY

Ben Jonson is a very great poet—more finely endowed, I think, than any who succeeeded him in the seventeenth century—and he read deliberately and widely. It was to be expected, therefore, that the effects of his reading would be in some manner present in his verse. Dryden said of him that he was a learned plagiary of all the ancients: "you track him everywhere in their snow." But this, the common view, violently distorts the sense in which Jonson is "traditional"; it not only makes him appear to owe to the Greek and Latin writers a mere accumulation of thoughts and phrases, it completely hides the native springs of his vitality. The aim of this chapter is to correct the perspective, to show that Jonson's art is intimately related to the popular tradition of individual and social morality.

L. C. Knights
Drama and Society in the Age of Jonson (London:
Chatto and Windus, 1937), pp. 179-80

When Senecanism had become a fashion and the superficial idiosyncrasies of style were being imitated, when the roughness and conscious carelessness, encouraged in reaction to the circular smoothness of Ciceronian periods, were used as excuses for bad writing, especially in verse, Jonson criticized it and those "who thinke those things the stronger, that have no Art" as severely as he had the Ciceronians. Vives, Bacon, and John Hoskyns did the same. . . .

The poems of Jonson other than those that are written in any of the four genres traditionally associated with the classical *sermo* owe their excellence to the intentions and the qualities of language of the plain style, which were beginning to be extended to genres that had habitually employed the *genus floridum* and the *genus grande*. The incursion by the plain style into the subjects of the high and middle styles in the sixteenth century was not a result of an entirely new stylistic strategy as much as it was simply a further step in the direction that the plain style had traditionally taken. The step, however, was an important one, and Jonson took it as decisively in poetry as Erasmus, Vives, and Lipsius had done in rhetoric. . . .

Jonson's "To Heaven" is one of the finest religious poems of the seventeenth century. The rhythm and its qualification of feeling . . . exhibit fully the classical conventions of prosody restrained to the formal demands of the English couplet. The poem is a religious and moral meditation, and the style, developed for this purpose, provides a method of introspection. Jonson does not attempt to isolate the religious experience in order to suggest its mystical qualities, but places it, as he does secular love, in the context of his entire personal experience:

> Good, and great GOD, can I not thinke of thee,
>> But it must, straight, my melancholy bee?
> Is it interpreted in me disease,
>> That, laden with my sinnes, I seeke for ease?
>>> (ll. 1-4)

Jonson addresses God in the secular language of contemporary psychology. . . . The reasons Jonson gives for his rejection of the Petrarchan hero reveal the attitudes which give his love poetry its power. He places the experience of love in the context of his experience as a whole. Hence, he is not preoccupied with isolating it in order to give it more emphasis than it would ordinarily seem to have; he does not wish to strip from it the ethical and circumstantial world in which it must take place. To do so would be to distort the truth. Real lovers exist in a real world. Hence, love is only one of their problems, and their feelings about it are greatly complicated by the others. This is why Jonson's poems seem to be less expressions of love than statements about it. They take into account his age and his appearance, both of which he may reasonably expect to give him difficulty. His first intention, however, is to tell the truth about himself and to take his chances (which, according to Drummond, seem to have been pretty good).

Wesley Trimpi
Ben Jonson's Poems: A Study of the Plain Style (Stanford, Calif.: Stanford Univ. Pr., 1962), pp. 47, 191, 205-6, 209

GENERAL

Like his predecessors in pulpit and poetry, Ben emphasizes two feminine sins almost to the exclusion of all others. Goody Polish, however, one of the most consistently evil and dangerous of his characters, is a babbler. Her "humour" is talk, and most of her fellow characters in *The Magnetic Lady* are misled by her copious flow of language into underestimating her capacity for serious evil. It may well be that Ben, like the preacher Bromyard and his own Morose in *The Silent Woman*, thought that talk was evil enough without additional sins, even though he furnished Polish with an abundance of the latter. Lady Politick Would-be also has the sin of verbosity and causes Volpone acute agony; indeed, Jonson's typical Elizabethan habit of abbreviating the names of speakers in his plays makes Lady "Pol." certainly a pun—a pun repeated in *The Magnetic Lady*, for Polish is also "Pol." With these and other characters in the comedies as exceptions, Jonson's satire is directed against pride first and lechery second. . . .

Chief emblem of pride in Jonson's opinion was extravagant personal adornment. . . .

In considering Jonson's classicism from the angle of form and structure, then, the question again arises: is classical form that which arises from imitation of the ancients, or is it construction that is carefully proportioned? If it is the former, Ben Jonson is surely less of a classicist than his reputation would indicate. There are, I think, only two verse forms in his poetic writings which can be shown to be directly indebted to classical models: his adaptation of the elegiac distich, used in the Prologue to *Volpone* and in "To Sir Robert Wroth," and his adaptations of the classical ode, especially the Pindaric ode. Both these forms were altered by the addition of rhyme, and, of course, they were *accentual* rather than *metrical* verse. All the remaining verse patterns in the nondramatic poetry had already been naturalized in English; Ben's favorite, the heroic couplet had been made a truly English form by Geoffrey Chaucer himself, and even Edmund Spenser, whose importance in shaping the poet Jonson seems to me to have been grossly underrated, used it in "Mother Hubbard's Tale." Hence, although related to the Latin distich, the heroic couplet, as Jonson used it, cannot be said to be a classical imitation. The couplet with alternating lines of five and four stresses, however, like those in the Prologue to *Volpone*, is almost certainly a return to the ancients instead of a continuation of an English tradition. The latter form, though, is not of any great importance in subsequent English literature, nor did it play much of a part in Ben's own writings. His real contribution to the classical verse in English literature is the ode, represented by the piece to Cary and Morison, one of his most ambitious attempts in poetry.

George Johnston
Ben Jonson: Poet (New York: Columbia Univ.
Pr., 1945), pp. 73, 75, 154-55

Bearing in mind the varied nature of Jonson's critical activities—the dramatic criticism, the literary theorizing and judgments of his earlier years, together with the later classical studies of the *Discoveries*—what can now be said of his critical achievement as a whole? As a literary theorist, in the first place, he has been loosely described as "a champion of the rules," an early advocate of those constricting doctrines bound up with the later neoclassical system. Yet nothing in reality could be farther from the truth. Actuated throughout by a profound respect for the ancients, at no stage did he recommend a slavish following, to be attained by means of fixed and mechanical rules. In this matter he would probably have agreed with Bacon that "to make judgment wholly by their rules is the humour of a scholar (pedant)." What he strove for, in view of current extravagances, was a return to the ordered harmony, the spirit, of the ancients, to those permanent and fundamental principles that had inspired their art; and in this sense alone can he be regarded as a classicist.

J. W. H. Atkins
English Literary Criticism: The Renaissance
(London: Methuen, 1951), p. 333

Jonson, then, characteristically establishes and maintains a comic tone largely, though not solely, by means of diction. Without the aesthetic distance and the comic detachment which this diction gives us, the actions in most Jonsonian plays might well be unbearably sordid or sinister or pathetic. But, by means of epithets, allusions, metaphors, and precisely chosen words, Jonson gives us the proper comic perspective: cold, hard, and merciless, yet clear, free of cant, and massively controlled.

The actual words we hear constitute one of Jonson's major ways of revealing characters simultaneously as the human beings they are supposed to be in the plot and as the lower (or higher) beings they are associated with by means of the imagery. Volpone, a Magnifico of Venice, thinks of himself at one time as a fox and at another time as Jove. This double vision reveals a comic disproportion: a Magnifico of Venice is ludicrously unlike either a fox or a Greek god. Through the use of such startling juxtapositions Jonson hoped to force us to see Volpone in a new light or with a new emotion. The contrast of Volpone's actions with the associations normally expected of a man, a god, and a fox makes us both laugh at him and judge him morally.

To gain such an ironic perspective, Jonson habitually used the devices typical of a small and sometimes misunderstood group of writers who celebrate their allegiance to an ideal world by creating the perversions of the idea. Thus, Swift created his Lilliputians and Yahoos; Baudelaire his Black Mass; and Poe his sick heroes morbidly concerned with decaying beauty and terror.

Edward Partridge
The Broken Compass (London: Chatto and Windus, 1958), p. 225

The identity of language with character, in Jonson, leads to an especially acute concern for decorum, the law which demands that a character speak like himself at all times. Mimicry, however, introduces a complication: a violation of decorum, so to speak, on the part of the character, who is straining *not* to speak like himself, *not* to play his proper role. The playwright then has the task of observing decorum while his character is offending against it. And this he may do either by insinuating, through the texture of the language, that all is false, or else by intermingling the "true" and "natural" in his character's speech with the unnaturally appropriated expressions, the forms of wantonness. The latter is Jonson's more usual procedure. . . .

The most obvious trait of Jonson's style, its realism, thus brings to a climax a process toward which comedy had been moving for generations, perhaps since its origins. Jonson, strenuously seeking to copy "nature," displays an increasing preoccupation with lifelike speech, a growing suspicion of "literary" sounding language, except where this becomes an object of satire, and a closer and closer attachment to the kind of familiar subject matter for which everyday language is appropriate. And this, as we have seen already, without sacrificing the techniques of inflation that end by turning "realistic" talk into a transfigured babble.

In his programmatic effort to evolve a vital comic speech out of the raw materials of heard conversation, Jonson hence forms one of the pillars of the comic tradition.

Jonas A. Barish
Ben Jonson and the Language of Prose Comedy (Cambridge,
Mass.: Harvard Univ. Pr., 1960), pp. 92-93, 274

THOMAS KYD

1558-1594

Born in London, the son of a scrivener. Studied under Richard Mulcaster at Merchant Taylors' School in London. No evidence that he attended either university. Probably followed his father's profession as a scrivener. By the summer of 1593 Kyd had been in the service of some nobleman, presently unknown, for about six years, but had lost the lord's favor. Shared a room with Christopher Marlowe in 1591. Arrested for atheism in 1593. Tortured on the rack. Probably acquitted of the charge, but left in disgrace and poverty. Dead by December of 1594. Mother filed legal renunciation of the administration of his estate. At some time appears to have been patronized by Mary Sidney, Countess of Pembroke, for whom he wrote *Cornelia*. This and *Spanish Tragedy* are the only plays which can be attributed to him with certainty.

F. S. Boas, ed., *The Works of Thomas Kyd* (1901)
P. Edwards, ed., *The Spanish Tragedy* (1959)

The consensus of scholarly opinion will be found to contain, at times ambiguously, two distinct propositions: (1) Kyd's use of the chorus is Senecan;

(2) the figures which compose the chorus—one of them or both—are Senecan. We may reserve comment on the first proposition until later. The second proposition, however, is entirely unconvincing, for ghosts are essential to medieval traditions in tragedy, and personifications like Revenge are quite exclusively medieval. Kyd's use, furthermore, of an *induction* immediately suggests some connection with earlier nondramatic poetry. And finally, whatever the virtues or weaknesses of the argument that Senecan creations are models for Kyd's Ghost and Revenge, it is only an argument by analogy. The analogy, moreover, is one upon which the most cautious scholars have insisted with no great degree of severity; Cunliffe, for instance, sums up his remarks on Kyd's play by saying that distinctive features of Seneca's mode of treatment are wanting.

Our present attack on the subject aims to present what seems to be a more convincing analogy; it maintains that the Ghost of Andrea and Revenge are adaptations of stock characters in the medieval metrical "tragedies." It holds that the Ghost is a variation on the ghosts who, in the metrical tragedies, come back to this world to recount their "falls"; that Revenge is one of the supernatural beings of medieval literature who act as guides, interpreters, and interlocutors, in the "marvelous journeys"—journeys which might be like that of a ghost back into the world. It recognizes that *The Spanish Tragedy* is more than a dramatization of the metrical tragedy in its narrowest form, that is, more than a dramatized recital of Andrea's unhappy death; but it argues that certain popular "tragedies" were likely to pay more attention to embellishments of ghosts and guides and marvelous journeys— features of Kyd's dramatic machinery—than to Chaucer's "certain story" of him that is

> y-fallen out of heigh degree
> Into miserie, and endeth wrecchedly;

and that Kyd's adaptation of tragical machinery is quite in line with earlier adaptations.

Howard Baker
Induction to Tragedy (Baton Rouge, La.: Louisiana
State Univ. Pr., 1939), pp. 108-9

Elizabethan revenge tragedy properly begins with Thomas Kyd's extant masterpiece, *The Spanish Tragedy* (1587-1589) which presented revenge in kind—blood-revenge, the sacred duty of the father to avenge the murder of his son—and from that sensational theme derived its popularity. Sensational though the central motive proved, it was a universal one, appealing to all classes of people and to all time. . . .

A specific source is customarily presupposed for *The Spanish Tragedy*, but it has never been found, and very probably no detailed source for the entire story ever existed; for if this hypothetical source be disregarded, the roots of the play are found in Seneca's tragedies, the Italian and French *novelle*, possibly in the Renaissance Italian tragedy, and certainly in the old Teutonic story of Hamlet as told by Saxo Grammaticus and translated by Belleforest. . . .

To a certain extent, however, the debt to Seneca has been exaggerated. Actual insanity in Seneca is limited to the madness sent by Juno upon Hercules, a situation which has no possible parallel in *The Spanish Tragedy*. Somewhat closer to Kyd's conception are the divine "madnesses" of Medea and Deïanira, but the origin of Hieronimo's insanity does not actually come from the Roman tragedian. . . . The most specific contribution of Seneca to the dramatic form of *The Spanish Tragedy* is the ghost; yet it has been noted how Kyd was gradually led away from the Senecan construction so that his supernatural chorus became superfluous and even intrusive. The interest in the play is on the revenge on Lorenzo (and only incidentally on Balthazar) for a Horatio murdered in plain view of the audience, not the revenge on Balthazar for the ghost of Andrea, with whom Hieronimo is entirely unconnected.

Yet the general influence of Seneca on the writing and the original conception of the play cannot be denied, for such an influence was unavoidable at the time. . . .

Kyd, as is shown by *The Spanish Tragedy,* was a brilliant inventor of dramatic incident. . . . Kyd, the ever-spectacular, broke wide with tradition and introduced into the action of the play itself a ghost who acquaints his son with the true facts of his death. The classical drama had employed ghosts as omens of disaster and, as in *Agamemnon* and *Troades,* to demand vengeance; but, it must be emphasized, never as actors to reveal the murder to the unsuspecting revenger-to-be.

Fredson T. Bowers
Elizabethan Revenge Tragedy (Princeton, N. J.: Princeton
Univ. Pr., 1940), pp. 65, 73-74, 89-90

But what an Elizabethan might think of Hieronimo's actions in real life may be irrelevant to the meaning of *The Spanish Tragedy*. Hieronimo may still be a sympathetic hero in spite of Elizabethan indignation against private revenge. The cry of *Vindicta mihi*, and the pause it gives Hieronimo may be more of a dramatic than a moral point. Hieronimo, robbed of the law's support, rocks for a moment in indecision before determining that at all costs the murderers must die. The indecision, and then the determination, are dramatically most important and effective; but the cause of the indecision (the inappropriate promptings of Christian ethics) is not important. Kyd has won sympathy for Hieronimo in his sufferings; there is no sign, at the end of the third and the beginning of the fourth Act, that Kyd now wishes the audience to change their sympathetic attitude, even though orthodoxy would condemn the private executioner. Kyd creates, and successfully sustains, his own world of revenge, and attitudes are sanctioned which might well be deplored in real life. The moral world of the play is a make-believe world; the gods are make-believe gods. In this make-believe world, the private executioner may be sympathetically portrayed and his Senecan gods may countenance his actions. And all this may be, however strongly Kyd himself disapproved of private vengeance. I remarked that *The Spanish Tragedy* was an un-Christian play, and so it is. But it is not written to advocate a system of ethics, or to oppose one. If its moral attitudes are mistaken for the "real life" attitudes of the dramatist, then the play has an appalling message. But if the play is seen as a thing of great—and skilful —artificiality, with standards of values which we accept while we are in the theatre, there is no problem at all about sympathizing with the hero. The play had power enough to lull an Elizabethn conscience while it was being performed.

Philip Edwards, ed.
Thomas Kyd, *The Spanish Tragedy* (London, 1959), pp. lix-lx

As a pioneering attempt at a drama of action, Kyd's *Spanish Tragedy* could hardly fail to be flawed. It opens with a ghost who seeks a niche in the underworld, then abandons his quest to assume an entirely different role. Its transparent subplot sacrifices characterization to morality. Its characters spout rhetoric, occasionally maunder, and sometimes appear to be puppets of the plot rather than fully-realized people in an autonomous world. The catastrophe contains more sensation than motivation: there is no justification for the death of Castile, and the Viceroy's credulity in giving Hieronimo the fatal knife is as questionable as the moral necessity of the use to which that knife is put. And Andrea's ghost and Revenge are neither large nor awful enough to conjure up the inexorable forces which rule a tragic universe.

Critics have traditionally grown fat by battering on these weaknesses, but they have done so by refusing to recognize the play's central strengths. Kyd was a more-than-competent dramatist; as the first English tragedian to write dramatically, he could not help making mistakes, but those he makes pale to insignificance beside the exciting swirl of action and emotion that encloses them. It is the contention of this article that Kyd, far from imitating the Senecan revenge play per se, consciously translated it into the idiom of the young Elizabethan stage; that the characters he created can stand as living people both within and without the dramatic pattern; that almost nothing in the play is gratuitous; and that *The Spanish Tragedy*, which has often been blasted as a disorganized amalgam of Senecan convention and cheap sensationalism, is in fact unified by triple threads of meaning, morality, and motivation which bind its disparate parts into a comprehensible and effective dramatic whole. . . .

The Spanish Tragedy is many things. It is a theatrically conceived essay on the moral dilemma of the avenger. It is a study of Machiavellism in action. It is a treatise to the effect that nobility confers obligations, not exemptions from moral responsibility. It is a superbly handled exercise in dramatic irony. Finally, it is an object lesson in the imperishability of justice. For even as Hieronimo bewails his impotence and Belimperia chafes in forced inaction, the mills of the gods are grinding towards moral resolution.

Michael H. Levin
SEL (Spring, 1964), pp. 307, 323

THOMAS LODGE
1558-1625

Born in London, the son of a prominent member of the Grocers' Company who had been Lord Mayor of London. Educated at Merchant Taylors' School in London and at Trinity College, Oxford. Took B.A. in 1577. In 1578 entered Lincoln's Inn as a law student. Began his literary career with *Defence of Plays* in 1580, an answer to Stephen Gosson's *School of Abuse* (1579). Served for a time as a soldier. Took part in an expedition to South America in 1591. Gave up his literary career for the study of medicine. Took M.D. at Avignon in 1600 and another one at Oxford in 1602. While abroad became a Roman Catholic. Practiced medicine in London until his death.

Edmund Gosse, ed., *The Complete Works of Thomas Lodge* (1883), 4 vols.

Rosalynde is not only on this account the best-known, but is also intrinsically the most interesting of his romances. The story is too familiar to need detailing. Its origin, as is also well known, is the *Tale of Gamelyn*, the story which Chaucer intended putting into the mouth either of the cook, or more probably of the yeoman, and the hero of which apparently belongs to the Robin Hood cycle. The interest centres round the three sons of Sir John of Bordeaux, who retains his name with Lodge and is Shakespeare's Sir Roland de Bois, and whose youngest son, Lodge's Rosader and Shakespeare's Orlando, is named Gamelyn, and the outlaw king, Lodge's king of France and Shakespeare's Duke senior. The entire pastoral element, as well as the courtly scenes of the earlier portion of the novel, are Lodge's own invention. His shepherds, whether genuine, as Coridon and Phoebe, or assumed, as Rosalynde and Rosader, are all alike Italian Arcadians, equally polished and poetical. Montanus, a shepherd corresponding to Shakespeare's Silvius, is a dainty rimester, and is not only well posted in the loves of Polyphemus and Galatea, but can rail on blind boy Cupid in good French, and on his mistress too—

> Son cuer ne doit estre de glace,
> Bien que elle ait de Neige le sein.

Thus Lodge added to the original story the figures of the usurper, Rosalynde, Alinda (Celia), and the shepherds Montanus (Silvius), Coridon (Corin) and Phoebe, while to Shakespeare we owe Amiens, Jacques, Touchstone, Audre, and a few minor characters; whence it appears that Lodge's contribution forms the mainstay of the plot as familiar to modern readers. Moreover, in spite of the stiltedness of the style where the author yet remembers to be euphuistic, in spite of the long "orations," "passions," "meditations" and the like, each carefully labelled and giving to the whole the air of a series of rhetorical exercises, in spite of the mediocre quality of most of the verses, if we except its one perfect gem, the romance yet retains not a little of its silvan and idyllic sweetness.

W. W. Greg
Pastoral Poetry and Pastoral Drama (London:
A. H. Bullen, 1906), pp. 146-47

A Looking Glasse shows the influence of *Tamburlaine* and, perhaps, of *The Spanish Tragedy,* but does not give any indication of the threat of the Armada. The play makes frequent reference to the London life of Lodge's time, and an allusion to an attempted invasion, or even a threatened one, would have been, by the nature of the play, easy, natural, and suitable. The flexibility and variety of the verse as compared with that of *The Wounds of Ciuill War* argues the influence of *Tamburlaine.* There is reason for believing that the similarities between *A Looking Glasse* and *Doctor Faustus* originated in the former play, but the date of *Doctor Faustus* is so uncertain that this probability offers little help in determining the date of *A Looking Glasse.* The purpose and construction of *A Looking Glasse* closely resemble those of *The Wounds of Ciuill War.* Both are didactic in aim, the earlier play being concerned chiefly with politics, the later, with morals, and both consist of a number of loosely connected scenes which deal with the events of a historical period rather than with the character of an individual or a group of individuals. Both plays, too, introduce scenes from low life although they are primarily concerned with persons of lofty station. In type *A Looking Glasse* is like such plays as *The Coblers Prophesie.* It deals with the presentation of sin, warning, and final repentance brought about by characters from the lower order of society. It is a step beyond *The Three Ladies of London* in the progress from the religious interlude to the pure drama, although it belongs essentially to the class of R. W.'s play, for its direct concern is with a moral problem, and its characters, for the most part, represent moral ideas rather than human individuals. Lodge seems to have started his dramatic writing after his return from the Canaries in 1585, and *A Looking Glasse* cannot have been separated from *The Wounds of Ciuill War* by a very great interval.

N. Burton Paradise
Thomas Lodge: The History of an Elizabethan
(New Haven, Conn.: Yale Univ. Pr., 1931), p. 151

Apart from its significance in literary history as one of the earliest pamphlets and first attempts at realism, the *Alarum* has considerable importance as a historical and social document. It comments sharply on the confused money economy of the time. The aristocracy were land-rich and money-poor; the habit of borrowing was well-nigh universal among them. Sons and heirs aped their fathers, and from both, the usurers reaped a goodly harvest. The usurers were not content to take the ten per cent interest legalized by Parliament in 1571, and the devices to evade the statute were numerous and ingenious. Thomas Lodge saw clearly the social and moral significance of the abuse. He saw how it undermined the moral character of both the usurer and the borrower, and how it was undermining the position of the landed aristocracy.

Edward A. Tenney
Thomas Lodge (Ithaca, N. Y.: Cornell Univ. Pr., 1935), p. 93

Lodge learned from Nashe, . . . the trick of making a satirical prose pamphlet lively and readable, and it may be that the experiment of verse satire did not catch on readily because many of its functions were served by the prose tracts. The reader to whom satire appealed could turn to the Martin Marprelate tracts, to Greene's cony-catching pamphlets, or to the lampoons of Nashe and Harvey. Lodge refers to Nashe as the "true English Aretine," and his influence and example were powerful. Had he expressed himself in verse satire instead of prose pamphlets, the experimental beginning made by Lodge, with its proper form the pentameter couplet, might have flourished in the mid-nineties.

As it is, Lodge's four satires in *A Fig* (numbered, through an error, 1, 3, 4, and 5) are too mild for their purpose and too general. The most effective passages are those which are reflective and philosophical. Lodge is more concerned, in *A Fig for Momus,* with friendliness, good counsel, solidarity among writers, than he is with anatomizing the body politic or operating on its visible sores. (Even the eclogues are addressed to friends, to Spenser, Drayton, and Daniel, for example.) He has felt the quality of Horace more than that of Juvenal and Persius, and his chief distinction as a writer of verse satire must be that he is one of the first in English to use for the purpose the heroic couplet.

Hallett Smith
Elizabethan Poetry (Cambridge, Mass.: Harvard
Univ. Pr., 1952, pp. 222-23

Others may want high seriousness, or irony, or social awareness. Lodge offers nothing of that kind. He hardly offers even passion; only gestures, delightfully graceful gestures, symbolical of it. By varying line-lengths and artful disposition of the rhymes each stanza is a delicate surprise: when the pattern has been repeated often enough to be familiar, the poem ends. But it seldom seems to end just for that reason. Each poem has shape in the sense that the thought, or rather the playing at thought, progresses and comes to a full close. All these virtues can be illustrated from Rosalynde's "Loue in my bosom" alone. There is aural surprise in the mono-rhymed quatrain towards the end of each stanza and aural suspense, long but just not too long, while we wait for the feminine rhyme from one stanza's end to another's. There is a progression from complaint in the first two, through revolt in the third, to submission in the last. We are not left asking, as so often in a Drab lyric, why it ends where it does. In "Phoebe sate" there is a wonderful minuet of rhymes. The freshness, the illusion of spontaneity which in all these lyrics so refreshes the reader, depends on filling the highly sophisticated form with all the silly-sooth of love-making, with flowers, birds, lips, sun, and shade. They are of course, as they were intended to be, trifles. That is one reason why only an artist could have made them. In large, serious works there are so many means besides poetic art with which to hold a reader's attention.

C. S. Lewis
English Literature in the Sixteenth Century (Oxford:
Clarendon Pr., 1954), p. 490

JOHN LYLY
1554-1606

Born in Kent. Son of the Registrar of Canterbury Cathedral, grandson of William Lyly, humanist friend of Colet and Erasmus and author of a standard sixteenth-century Latin grammar. Entered Magdalen College, Oxford, as a Commoner in 1569. Took B.A. in 1573, M.A. in 1575. Was unsuccessful in his attempt to get royal nomination to a fellowship. Entered the service of the Earl of Oxford around 1578. Lost his favor in

1582. His novel, *Euphues: The Anatomy of Wit*, was published in 1578, and became a best seller. A sequel appeared in 1580. Became Assistant Master of Children's companies at Chapel Royal and St. Paul's. Member of Parliament in 1588 and 1589. In 1589 became involved in the Marprelate controversy on the side of the Anglican bishops. Hoped for a position as Master of the Revels, but was never awarded it. Addressed petitions to Queen Elizabeth in 1595 and 1598. Sat in four parliaments between 1589 and 1606. Died disappointed and in relative poverty.

R. W. Bond, ed., *The Complete Works of John Lyly* (1902)

G. K. Hunter, *John Lyly: The Humanist as Courtier* (1921)

Euphues

The notion that things contain within them their own contraries, or the power to work contrary effects, occurs so often in *Euphues* and in its sequel that by virtue of sheer frequency of repetition it comes to be felt as a major insight. It is an insight to which Lyly's disjunctive imagination is peculiarly sympathetic, and to which his analytic syntax admirably lends itself. The grammatical subject may be made to govern two verbs, each expressing a contrary action ("the Sunne doth harden the durte & melt the waxe"), or one verb may control two antagonistic object phrases ("fire maketh the gold to shine and the straw to smother"). In each case a thing splits up into its mutually antipathetic halves.

Many of Lyly's antitheses take the form of paradox, either in the sense that they propose an idea repugnant to common sense or in that they point out mutually conflicting properties in the same thing. Such paradoxes range from the banal to the startling. . . .

Lyly, who is fascinated by this elementary paradox, is at pains to make it as extreme, as *outré,* as possible. Grammatically, he does so by making his antitheses sharp, by pitting every term as rigidly as possible against its mate. Two comparatives are better than two positive adjectives, because they double the distance between the antithetic terms, and superlatives are best of all, since they drive the terms as far apart as they will go:

> The fine christall is sooner crazed then the harde marble, the greenest Beeche burneth faster then the dryest Oke, the fairest silke is soonest soyled, and the sweetest wine tourneth to the sharpest vineger, the pestilence doth most ryfest infect the cleerest complection, and the Caterpiller cleaueth vnto the ripest fruite. . . .

Here, underneath the not necessarily in itself paradoxical idea that the most precious things are also the most perishable, lies Lyly's paradoxical principle that like engenders unlike: the fairest silk lends itself more quickly to soiling, the sweetest wine is ready at a moment's notice to become the sharpest vinegar, and the greenest beech defies all natural law by burning faster than the driest oak, because in Lyly's world if things do not already defy the proprieties they must be made to do so. The precarious closeness of extremes must be constantly stressed, and it does not much matter whether the illustrative instance conforms to everyday experience or violates it. Both kinds of instance, in fact, are necessary in order to establish precedents on a sufficiently massive scale. If we recognize the illustration as a commonplace, we are being reminded that even humdrum things contain the principle of self-contradiction within them. If the example strikes us as exotic, we are being reminded of the extremes to which nature will go in the propagation of paradoxes.

Such paradoxes often turn on the antagonism between substance and appearance. A recurrent figure is the one contrasting an ugly exterior with a precious interior or the reverse, a fair face with a vile heart, an outer semblance belied by an inner essence, as in the cases of the gold, the kernel, and the toad. The moral is always the same: that the more absolute of its kind a thing may appear to be, the more certain it is that somewhere within it lies its own antithesis, its anti-self.

Jonas Barish
ELH (March, 1956), pp. 20-22

If we are to treat *Euphues* biographically, all we can say, I suspect, is that the book reads like the pipe-dream of a disappointed don. The contrast between Athens and Naples, the University and the metropolis, is an essential part of the contrast between learning and experience, wit and wisdom. In the person of Euphues, Lyly manages to have it both ways (as he had signally failed to do in real life). Plunging into experience Euphues becomes a notable figure in the great world; Lucilla (not only charming, but an heiress) falls in love with him at first sight, bewitched by his wit. But he sees through the world of courtship, and returns to his University, entitled to lecture others on all kinds of topics. He becomes "public reader in the University, with such commendation as never any before him; in the which he continued for the space of ten years, only searching out the secrets of nature and the hidden mysteries of philosophy, and having collected into three volumes his lectures, thought for the profit of the young scholars to set them forth in print, which if he had done, I would also in this his *Anatomy* have inserted" (I. 286). We are spared the three volumes of lectures because Euphues, increasing in sanctity even beyond the status of a "public reader," turns to divinity, and vanishes from sight in a cloud of Biblical references. The book obviously bears some relation to Lyly's hopes of an Oxford fellowship. If he had been told at the time of his application that he had not enough experience to fill the post, we might regard *Euphues* as a demonstration that he now knew quite enough about experience and its fruits. But to suppose this would be to suppose too far. Euphues and Lyly are alike, but they are not identical. It seems fair to infer that Lyly was like his hero in certain characteristics; that he fancied himself as a wit and as a scholar, that he laboured under a sense of injustice, that he felt himself entitled to stand aside and castigate both court and university. But with what immediate aim he expressed these attitudes in *Euphues* we cannot tell. . . .

Lyly is the most famous of the dramatists who wrote for the sixteenth century boys' companies, and his plays can be seen to take up all those aspects of child-acting which I have discussed above; they show a unique skill in using the talents that were available and in avoiding the areas where the weaknesses would show. Lyly's plays do not develop quickly by means of "strong" emotional entanglements. They rather proceed by means of a series of static tableaux. They do not raise our expectations by mystery or surprise. They rather show how elegantly the movements we expect can be performed. They do not involve parts that it would be difficult for boys to play, and regularly include a number of page roles where the boys need only to be themselves. They never concentrate the action round a single character or give any one speaker a high proportion of the lines—such as Shakespeare gave to Richard III or Hamlet. They concentrate instead on the consort of voices, the quick and witty dialogue where voice chimes with voice, idea picks up idea and image begets image.

G. K. Hunter
John Lyly: The Humanist as Courtier (London: Routledge
and Kegan Paul, 1962), pp. 61-62, 103

PLAYS

It was a schoolmaster writing for the choristers of St. Paul's Cathedral School who first devised for himself a distinct and individual comic form, and who propounded a practical as distinct from a text-book theory of comedy. The work of John Lyly, if designed for fashion, is rooted in the Schools. In his Prologues he follows the tradition of Udall in seeing his plays as recreation; but he also submits them to the judgement of the audience. For the audience had changed its character: the court was patron and arbiter, and the players, with the author, were not improving their equals but soliciting applause of their betters. Lyly is not striving to impose a meaning, but invites a variety of interpretation. The plays signify "what you will" and should be taken "as you like it." The audience's demands, however various, will all be met. These players, though still schoolboys, are now professionals; their motto "Placere cupio," "We hope to please you.". . .

The learned Lyly defies the theorists, Sidney included, and claims his right to mingle the kinds. On the other hand, the unity and consistency of his style and temper exceed those of any other Elizabethan writer. His rhetorical artificial patterns of alliteration, antitheses and simile have an almost steely strength, and on the surface, his plays would appear to have far less variety than the academic drama. The smooth enamel of his style, the formal grouping of his characters and the simplicity of his action are stiffened by further restraints which he proudly acknowledges. . . .

There remained the possibility of various interpretations of his deceptively simple comedy. Here disagreement among the spectators still persists —which is clearly what Lyly designed. He avoids a final significance: and draws the audience within the circle of the play by inviting them to complete it with their judgement. He presents an open field for their "exercises," only making plain that there is room for all, and that he has "mixed mirth with counsel and discipline with delight." Lyly's humility, that of the true artist, is the natural consequence of his own unwavering sense of design. Each spectator may adapt the work to suit his own imagination. Constantly in his prologues he uses the image of a dream. Dreams are at once private and messages from beyond the world, free from the logic of daytime existence, and yet a commentary upon it, open to many interpretations. . . .

The norm in Lyly is the courtly speech of Euphuized gentlewomen. His plays are among other things conversational models. There is also a great variety of jargon which appears for its comic effect: in *Gallathea* the jargon of alchemists—which Chaucer before him and Jonson after him found equally fascinating. Here, too, there are seamen's terms, and huntsmen's terms in *Midas*. The proverbs of rustic fools at quarterstaff are set against the rapier-wit of the quarrelsome pageboys. Delicate songs are mixed with boisterous jests; "variety" was a rhetorical requirement of which Lyly was conscious, for he praised the sonnets of Thomas Watson precisely for this quality. Such artifice did not allow much development, and the long set tirade which appears in *Campaspe* and *Midas* is only a little less formal than the language of the earlier *Sapho and Phao* and *Endimion;* but in his latest plays, Lyly moved nearer to the diction of common life.

M. C. Bradbrook
The Growth and Structure of Elizabethan Comedy
(London: Chatto and Windus, 1955), pp. 39-40, 50

If Lyly saw these comedies and felt unsatisfied by the way they dramatized love, he may have been attracted to the hesitancy and indirection of the allegorical speeches which suggest a sense of delicacy about the speaker's feelings, for these foreshadow the more artful dialogues of hesitant lovers in his early comedies.

These dialogues, Lyly's major contribution to the technique of dramatizing love, occur in four of his comedies: *Campaspe, Sapho and Phao, Gallathea,* and in modified fashion in *Mother Bombie.* He constructed circumstances unfavorable to the lover's disclosure of his true sentiments and in conflict with his desire to speak his mind. When the lovers confront one another, each speaks enigmatically, in part from fear and in part from sensitivity to the delicate nature of love. This tension between unfavorable circumstances and desire creates dialogue in which each assertion is tentative and each response quivering, and this dialogue, by not mentioning love directly, captures an unmistakable sense of what it is like to be in love, sometimes poignantly and sometimes wittily.

As he reworked these muted dialogues in his early plays, Lyly improved them by refining the unfavorable circumstances which inhibit speech. . . .

These special dialogues of love were innovations that arose, it seems to me, from Lyly's experience in writing novels, and by examining the relation of these dialogues to the uses of language in the two novels about Euphues, I wish to show that Lyly's sense of language rather than his insight into love influenced his technique of composing dialogue and set his scenes of courtship apart from the dramatic tradition of the 1560's and 1570's in England.

Robert Y. Turner
ELH (September, 1962), pp. 278-79, 284

CHRISTOPHER MARLOWE
1564-1593

Born Canterbury. Baptized February 26, 1593. Son of a member of the Cordwainers guild. Attended King's School, Canterbury. At the age of seventeen entered Corpus Christi College, Cambridge, on a Parker foundation scholarship. Granted B.A. in 1584, M.A. in 1587 after request by Queen's Privy Council that degree be granted in spite of his absence from Cambridge on government business. Came to London after taking M.A. degree and associated with various men of letters; wrote for several theater companies including Lord Pembroke's Men and Lord Admiral's Men. Spent brief time in Newgate prison in 1589 as a result of a brawl in which William Bradley was fatally stabbed by Marlowe's friend, the poet Thomas Watson. On May 9, 1592, ordered to post bond as surety to keep peace. Accused of atheism by Thomas Kyd in May, 1592. On May 18, 1592, arrested at the estate of Thomas Walsingham at Scadbury, Kent. Ordered to be in daily attendance upon Privy Council until disposal of his case. Stabbed by Ingram Frizer in a tavern at Deptford on May 30, 1593.

C. F. Tucker Brooke, ed., *The Works of Christopher Marlowe* (1910)

R. H. Case, ed., *The Works and Life of Christopher Marlowe* (1930-33), 6 vols.

Irving Ribner, ed., *The Complete Plays of Christopher Marlowe* (1963)

John Bakeless, *The Tragicall History of Christopher Marlowe* (1942)

PERSONAL

Marlowe's diction, profiting from richness, attains its speed by means of polysyllables and its resonance by means of proper names. Whenever these two join forces at the end of a line, the emphasis is particularly strong, as *Tamburlaine* will repeatedly demonstrate. It is a far cry from the homely archaism of Surrey, where one verse often bogs down into ten harsh monosyllables, to what Nashe aptly termed "the spacious volubilitie of a drumming decasillabon," where the mouth-filling Latinate phraseology is continually amplified by mythological and geographical reverberations. All this is kept under firm control by the line itself, which—largely through Marlowe's avoidance of run-overs—becomes a syntactic as well as a metrical unit, coinciding with a single clause from a periodic sentence of as many as a dozen lines. By piling one such unit on top of another, he builds up those larger structures of discourse which, therefore, ought to be called verse-sentences rather than verse-paragraphs. When Nashe speaks of botching out verses with "ifs" and "ands," he indicates how the momentum of a speech can be suspended by conditional clauses and prolonged by a series of double predicates and appositional phrases. Their effect is to pad the sharp grammatical skeleton; whence the Elizabethan term for padding, "bombast," is applied not merely to actors' costumes but to their locutions. Again, when Nashe speaks of "the swelling bumbast of bragging blanke verse," he illustrates how Marlowe keeps an internal balance by modifying nouns with participles. The adjective is energized by the verb when he characteristically substitutes "shining" for "bright" or "mounting" for "high" or "fainting" for "low." The parts of speech, like the spheres that form his cosmos, are ever-moving. . . .

[From] what we know of Marlowe's own character, we may fairly suppose that he threw a good deal of himself into these monomaniac exponents of the first person: egoists, exhibitionists, infidels, outsiders.

As Marlowe progresses from Tamburlaine and Barabas to Edward and Faustus, the mask seems to fit more closely; the viewpoint is more sympathetic, and fear is mellowed by pity. After his imaginary flights through the realms of higher policy, he comes back with Faustus to the scholar's study. He has pursued ambition, the wish to outsoar one's fellow men, as well as revenge, the animus against them. Between the active voice of Tamburlaine and the passive voice of Edward, between the scourge of sadism and the self-torture of masochism, Barabas is the equivocating figure who unwittingly contrives his own punishment. The triumph symbolized by the chariot is easy and unrealistic; but there is poetic justice in the caldron; and Marlowe's deepened concern with suffering propounds its final symbol in the hell-mouth. Among the reiterated images that carry his peculiar impetus through his various writings, probably the most typical recurrence is the constellation of "topless towers" and "quenchless fires." Both of these complementary phrases impose concreteness on the idea of infinity: unlimited construction, ambition, pride; unlimited destruction, purgation, suffering. The underlying antagonism between civilization and nature has its *locus classicus* in Faustus' vision of the Trojan holocaust, and again in the frescoes that adorn Hero's temple:

> Loue kindling fire, to burne such townes as *Troy*.   (I,153)

Fire is so standard a trope for love that Racine's lovers speak casually of *nos feux*. Doubtless its primitive symbolism was phallic. However, the taming of fire was the crucial step toward human culture, as prefigured in the myth of Prometheus, the fire-bringer. Freud finds an analogy for this in the curbing of the sexual instinct, and asserts that the findings of psychoanalysis "testify to the close connection between the ideas of ambition, fire, and urethral erotism." In *The Tragedy of Dido*, where the fiery imagery culminates in an actual pyre, the Promethean theft is associated with all-consuming and unrequited passion, when the Queen begs Aeneas to "quench these flames."

Harry Levin
The Overreacher (Cambridge, Mass.: Harvard
Univ. Pr., 1952), pp. 13, 157

Tamburlaine

It is possible, however, to find two polar positions in Marlowe's view of the world. There is at one end an emphasis upon the limitless potentialities of mankind which we find in *Dido* and the first part of *Tamburlaine,* and not so much diminished in the second part as some writers have supposed. At the other end of the spectrum there is that sense of human limitation and defeat, what Una Ellis-Fermor called the "mood of spiritual despair," which we find in *Edward II* and *Doctor Faustus* (*The Jacobean Drama,* 1936, pp. 1-5). That these were Marlowe's final plays seems very likely; most commentators today would place *Doctor Faustus* as the later of the two, and if we may make any guesses about *The Massacre at Paris,* we must suppose that it belongs with these final works, perhaps, as I shall suggest, between *The Jew of Malta* and *Edward II.* The second part of *Tamburlaine* shows the first faint signs of change from the confident optimism of the first part, and it seems to have been followed by *The Jew of Malta,* a play which stands midway between the two extremes of Marlowe's vision. If we could know it fully, it might emerge as the play in which the values of *Tamburlaine* are first held up to scrutiny and found wanting. Certainly the Machiavellian view of the world so proudly asserted in *Tamburlaine,* is in *The Jew of Malta* subjected to some ridicule. . . .

When Marlowe wrote the first part of *Tamburlaine* in 1586 or 1587, he did something which never before had been done in English drama. He took a historical figure—praised in a long series of humanistic historical accounts as a successful ruler and as one who had stemmed the Turkish advance over Christian Europe at Ankara in 1402, an instrument of Divine Providence whose cruelty was the visitation of punishment upon evildoers —and he framed a play which would exalt such a figure by revealing his steady movement towards the conquest of the world. His play became an episodic sequence of scenes each of which was designed to make more clear the greatness of his hero. Marlowe, in fact, applied the episodic technique of the miracle drama to a secular figure, and he used him as the symbol of a way of life which denied every Christian premise dear to the Elizabethan establishment. The first part of *Tamburlaine* makes no pretense at being anything other than a heroic celebration of the ruthless conquering hero's triumph, "the man of humble birth," as F. P. Wilson has written, "who rises from victory to victory to the noon or meridian of his fortunes, where the dramatist leaves him a happy warrior and a happy lover" (*Marlowe and the Early Shakespeare,* 1953, p. 19). This conception is Marlowe's initial view of Tamburlaine, and if in the second part some elements intrude to diminish the hero's brightness, we must remember that the sequel is a later addition which represents a further stage in Marlowe's growth, and that the first part was conceived entirely independently of it.

Marlowe approached his historical subject not with the Christian view of history as the working out of God's purposes on earth, but rather with the premises of the classical historians he had read at Cambridge. He seems to have been influenced in particular by Polybius, who in his history of Rome had exalted individual prowess, seeing historical event as the product of human ability and will in a world ruled only by a blind fortune. The greatness of the true hero of history lay in his ability to assert his individual will in opposition to fortune and to master it for as long as possible. Finally he must be cut off by death, and this being so, he must accept his end with stoical resignation and fortitude. Of this human ability to master fortune the first part of *Tamburlaine* provides a supreme example, while the second part depicts the inevitable triumph of death in spite of human prowess. In Marlowe's hero there is also the Machiavellian ideal of the lawgiver, the superman who by his own *virtù*, his power of mind and will, can arrest the processes of decay to which all civilizations are subject and create new nations. While doing so he stands outside of all morality.

In Tamburlaine we have also the static quality of the movers of Roman history. He is at the play's beginning a fully drawn man of destiny, and he passes from one static scene to the next as he goes about his conquest of the world, the dramatist never displaying change or development in his hero's character. His end of world conquest is implicit in his initial characterization—an end from which nothing can deter him, not even the tears of the Zenocrate he loves. He must destroy her native city because it is in his nature to do so. The Virgins of Damascus must be slaughtered because his unalterable principles of warfare decree it. The play is concerned not with development of character, but with its revelation. In this, as I have suggested, Marlowe was following the historical method of Polybius, whose subject was the conquest of the world by an initially complete but ever expanding Rome.

The addition of a second part to *Tamburlaine* could not change the conception of the first; it certainly could not make of it, as Roy W. Battenhouse has suggested (*Marlowe's Tamburlaine,* 1941), the first movement of a ten-act morality play illustrating God's punishment visited upon a blasphemous infidel. The subject of the sequel is the death of the hero, and in George Whetstone's *English Mirror,* which may well have been Marlowe's principal source, Marlowe would have read that "this great personage, without disgrace of fortune, after sundry great victories, by the course of nature died." This view of Tamburlaine's death is in accord with a general treatment of the subject by humanist historians, going back at least to Poggio Bracciolini who had told the story of Tamburlaine in his *De varietate fortunae,* written between 1431 and 1448, close to the events themselves of Tamburlaine's career. They had seen him as the superman who had mastered fortune for as long as it was possible for any man to do so, that is until death finally had triumphed. His death could not be viewed as a punishment for his life, but rather as the necessary culmination of his greatness, for he was cut off, as classical historians held that the great man should be, at the very peak of his glory. Marlowe's Tamburlaine until the moment of his death is a reflection of the same humanist ideal of the superman by the light of which Machiavelli shaped his *Life of Castruccio Castracani* (1520, printed 1532), and whom he envisaged as the saviour and unifier of Italy.

Marlowe's hero dies only because all who live must die. His conquests are undiminished; the one son incapable of following in his footsteps has been destroyed, and his two remaining sons are ready to complete their father's domination of the world. That historically they did not do so, but instead brought about the dissolution of their father's empire, is a consideration outside the scope of the play.

Irving Ribner
Essays on Shakespeare and Elizabethan Drama in Honor of Hardin Craig (Columbia, Mo.: Univ. Missouri Pr., 1962), pp. 92-95

The last moments of the play [*Tamburlaine*] appeal to the spectator's pity by insisting on the tragic limitation of Tamburlaine as a human being. "For Tamburlaine, the scourge of God, must die" is comparable to Achilles' lines: "For not even the strength of Herakles fled away from destruction, / Although he was dearest of all to lord Zeus. . . ." But the play's dominant appeal is to the wonder aroused by vast heroic potential. The very paradoxes of Tamburlaine's nature excite wonder, and this was supposed in Marlowe's time to be the effect of paradox. Puttenham, in his familiar *Arte of English Poesie,* calls paradox "the wondrer." Tamburlaine's "high astounding terms," for which the Prologue prepares us, clearly aim at the same effect. Many years later, Sir William Alexander, the author of several Senecan tragedies, wrote that the three stylistic devices which pleased him most were: "A grave sentence, by which the Judgment may be bettered; a witty Conceit, which doth harmoniously delight the Spirits; and a generous Rapture expressing Magnanimity, whereby the Mind may be inflamed for great Things." The last of these three he found in Lucan, in whose "Heroical Conceptions" he saw an "innate Generosity"; he remarked the power of "the unmatchable Height of his Ravishing Conceits to provoke Magnanimity." Marlowe was undoubtedly influenced by the style of the *Pharsalia,* the first book of which he had translated, and in any case Alexander's words might justly be applied to *Tamburlaine.* The epic grandeur of the style, with its resounding catalogues of exotic names, its hyperboles, and its heroic boasts and tirades, "expresses magnanimity," that largeness of spirit so consistently ascribed to the great hero. Alexander testifies that such a style may inflame the mind "for great things," and general as this description is, it serves well for the feeling aroused by the play. Another name for it was admiration.

E. M. Waith
The Herculean Hero (New York: Columbia Univ. Pr., 1962), p. 87

Tamburlaine is the most solid and unflawed of Marlowe's plays: more consistent in quality than *Dido* or *Faustus,* more whole and substantial than *The Jew of Malta,* and more vigorous in imagination and sustaining power than *Edward II.* The two parts together make an impressive achievement; the work, one would say, of a man writing with full confidence in his powers, and with assurance, poise, and singleness of mind.

The apparent singleness of mind also informs the work with an apparent singleness of moral purpose which, judged by Christian or humanitarian or liberal standards, is an evil one: to find it anything else involves either misjudgments of the plays or dissociation from those standards. But the singlenesses referred to *are* only apparent. In the moral purpose the diabolonian predominates, and in the whole mind it has a prominent place, though in neither is it exclusive. There is, in fact, beneath the ringing speeches and triumphantly sensational episodes, a basic instability: a to-and-fro movement in which the feelings alternately support and recoil from the protagonist, and which gives the plays something of the character of an unevenly matched debate.

J. B. Steane
Marlowe, A Critical Study (Cambridge Univ. Pr., 1964), p. 62

The comparatively limited point that Marlowe does effect in *Tamburlaine* is one which can be seen clearly enough, but which is often obscured by attempts to set the play in a line of development leading directly to Shakespeare. For it is a point that Marlowe was led to make not despite his limitations but because of them, and it consists in a clear though still stiffly uncompromising recognition of the essential sterility at the heart of his hero's ambitions. This is a different issue from the more negative one of an over-simple control in the verse, though it is certainly related. Briefly, the point is that there is a tendency in the play initially to see energy as vitality, a life-giving activity constantly supporting the hero; but, almost contemporaneously, there is an opposing tendency to see it in life-denying terms, as something brutal, limited, ultimately sterile. After the Fortune's wheel speech early on, these tendencies gradually become more at odds until, with the Damascus scenes, Marlowe's early calm has deserted him and the question he put so clearly and confidently early on—"What of the hero who is not prepared to submit to what is nevertheless and all the time the logic of necessity?"—has become more urgently personal. The surviving interest that we have in the play today centres on this movement from a slightly too rigid control at the beginning to turbulence and alarm near the end.

T. B. Tomlinson
A Study of Elizabethan and Jacobean Tragedy
(Cambridge Univ. Pr., 1964), p. 53

The Jew of Malta

The Jew of Malta is a tragic farce, at once both terrifying and absurd. The world it exhibits, by its wide dissimilarity to life as we know it, is ludicrous beyond the bounds of comedy; yet it frightens by reason of a certain logical relationship with reality. If certain conditions governed the world as we know it, it would be exactly like the Malta ruled by Ferneze and terrorised by the Jew Barabas. Chief among these conditions would be the conviction, acknowledged or concealed, of all such a world's inhabitants, that the material order comprised the whole of existence. Throughout his first two tragedies, Marlowe never lets us forget the existence of worlds other than the visible—the Heaven which Tamburlaine's pride impels him to defy, the Hell into which Faustus is plunged by his despair. In *The Jew of Malta* there is no such impingement of one order of being upon another. The play depicts a world which has cut itself off entirely from the transcendent. The God invoked by Barabas is a "Prime Motor," who has set the machine in motion and left it to run as best it may. There is no possibility here of intervention by the Divine Justice that pursues Tamburlaine or by the Divine Mercy offered to Faustus.

Such contraction of the drama's scope to mundane, social matter, almost unparalleled in tragedy, imparts a feeling of constriction to the opening scene. Tamburlaine and Faustus are both physically and mentally restless; the one marches over great areas of the eastern hemisphere, the other, "to prooue *Cosmography*," moves invisible over the length and breadth of Europe. In contrast, *The Jew of Malta* has for its setting an island of the land-locked Mediterranean; and Barabas is content to remain in his counting-house where the wealth of many lands is compressed into the "little room" of his jewels. By comparison with Marlowe's earlier plays, *The Jew of Malta* shows an impoverishment in the character of the hero, as well as in the play's setting. Where Tamburlaine and Faustus sought to control, the one by conquest and the other by knowledge, Barabas is satisfied to plunder:

> What more may Heauen doe for earthly man
> Then thus to powre out plenty in their laps,
> Ripping the bowels of the earth for them,
> Making the Sea their seruant, and winds
> To driue their substance with successfull blasts?
>
> 145-9

The Jew turns his back upon the coloured splendours of his Mediterranean world, content with the reflection of fire and sea and sky in the precious stones which comprise his wealth. If any of an artist's delight in form and hue remains in Barabas's praise of his treasure, it has been contaminated by the worldly sense of values which is inimical to art. And although he holds a king's ransom in his hand when the play opens, Barabas is soon forced to admit that he has no hope of a crown; no principality awaits this Machiavellian. Thus in comparison with Tamburlaine and Faustus, the Jew appears a shrunken figure, withered in body and mind.

M. M. Mahood

Poetry and Humanism (London: Jonathan Cape, 1950), pp. 74-75

Granted that Marlowe is more interested in the morally black Barabas than in his morally neutral or mixed milieu, what is the nature of that interest? I should say that it is primarily that of the popular entertainer; and that we shall get nearer the truth about the play if we ourselves are less "terribly serious" about it, and think a little less in terms of moral philosophy and a little more in terms of native sports. There was bear-baiting, bull-baiting, and, their theatrical equivalent, devil-baiting. Behind the latter lies a long tradition, with the "Vice" figures of the interludes bustling aggressively and triumphantly among men until their final pre-ordained discomfiture. The aggression of the Vice figure was not originally deadly. He pestered by placing boards under the earth where the farmer must dig, or by setting neighbors at loggerheads, but he succeeded in killing neither bodies nor souls, so that in a sense he was frustrated—"baited"—even before his final downfall. (The last was sometimes absentmindedly neglected by the interludists.) The appeal was primarily comic. The comic action persisted, elaborated after the example of classical comedy of intrigue, even when its results became deadly and gave us the peculiarly mixed quality of a certain type of Elizabethan "tragedy."

In Marlowe's play the devil is baited in the form of a Machiavellian Jew. If the sport was to be any fun, the "baitee" must seem dangerous. In the game-ring, an amiable bear or a listless beast would not do—the game-masters must occasionally be clawed and the bull-dogs gored and tossed. The same principle applied in the theatre. The devil-figure must have his ups and downs, so that an audience might greet the "ups" with glee, "laughing all in one voice at any notable act of cozenage," and the "downs" with pious approval. Marlowe is not mocking the popular audience in *The Jew of Malta,* but conspiring hand-and-glove with it. He supplied the best devil-figure thus far conceived—in his agile-minded, arrogant, ruthless, lethal Barabas.

Alfred Harbage
TDR (Spring, 1964), pp. 53-54

Edward II

In *Edward II* it is made quite clear that the characters not only carry the emotional burden of the play, but also sustain its plot; on the other hand, it is equally clear that the plot is not solely dependent on what they do. Marlowe has struck a balance between a plot whose events are directed by its hero and one which develops independently of him and reacts upon him. It is true that the King sets certain events in motion, but he has also to maintain a passive role in the plot. This plot is broken up into a great many separate episodes, most of them quite short, but we can follow it as a close-knit, coherent and logical chain of cause and effect, for in all the episodes the person and character of the King are in some way involved.

Thus Marlowe made an appreciable advance towards what is commonly described as "character-drama," but he was not equally successful all along the line. He was so intent on creating a fast-moving plot, especially in the earlier part of the play, that he did not leave himself enough room to develop the emotional significance of particular moments and to work out his situations in an unhurried way. The scenes follow one another much too quickly, and there are too many of them; they do not take root in our memory, as do the scenes in Shakespeare's histories from *Richard III* onwards, which by themselves form pictures with a symbolic impact and remain unforgettable in our minds as miniature plays in their own right. For all his skill in complicating the plot, the composition, especially in the first two-thirds of the play, is hurried and breathless, and nothing is carried through to its proper conclusion. For long stretches the language is entirely factual and its choice is determined by the practical consideration of keeping the plot moving; it supplies information, instruction, explanation, question and answer, and is all the time concerned solely with externalities. There are moments, indeed, when the emotional atmosphere begins to grow more intense, but the poetic power which is necessary to translate it into words almost at once fades away. We get no further than isolated outbursts of feeling, which are too abruptly handled and do not impart their tone to the accompanying dialogue in the scene.

Wolfgang Clemen
English Tragedy Before Shakespeare (London:
Methuen, 1961), pp. 155-56

In *Edward II* Marlowe was chiefly interested in the character of the King, but while the political significance of the play is only intermittent, it is not casual. Edward is a king, his failings are the failings of a ruler, and the crisis of his reign is political. Marlowe recognizes that the sins of the man cannot be separated from the sins of his government. The play presents man's personal failure, and there is no sense that this failure may be related to causes outside himself. Marlowe did not conceive the existence of a divine plan in which the miseries of this particular reign might in due time be forgotten in a restored prosperity; and his explanation of the fall of Mortimer was not so much that he deserved to suffer for his overweening ambition as that he had been suddenly brought low by the turn of Fortune's wheel. . . . On the other hand his attitude to rebellion was entirely orthodox. The choric Edmund refuses to join the English lords in their revolt; and when, later, he has been persuaded to withdraw his allegiance, he swings violently back again to hysterical, self-disgusted loyalty. . . . Except for Mortimer, whose motive is ambition, the rebels are careful to explain that they intend no harm to the King himself: their purpose is only to retrieve him in his own despite from the unmanly toils of Gaveston. . . . In spite, however, of the purity of these sentiments, Marlowe gives no hint of the historical patterning we find in Hall or Shakespeare. He never suggests that the crime of rebellion against Edward may provoke heaven to anger which future generations will have to expiate.

M. M. Reese
The Cease of Majesty (London: Edward Arnold, 1961), pp. 80-81

A graphic representation of the structure of *Edward II* would show the intersections of at least five lines, each corresponding to the rising and falling fortunes of a major character. The diffusion of interest, due to Marlowe's choice of a weak and unusually inactive protagonist, has been noted by every critic. Edward, more often than not, is the victim of the series of schemes which form the episodes of the play, and the importance thus robbed from him attaches to the perpetrators of the schemes. Yet the play is less episodic than *Tamburlaine*. An effect of interlocking is achieved, partly by the simple device of preparing in one episode for the episode to follow, but even more by revealing (and in some cases creating) an intricate net of relationships between the King's chief friends and enemies: Gaveston, the Spencers, the barons. Queen Isabella, and Mortimer. Furthermore, the effect of this structural coherence is strongly reinforced by the repeated expression of a very limited number of emotions. Not only is the play consistently serious in tone, but it is dominated by grief and the desire for revenge, only two of the emotions traditionally considered proper for tragedy. The firm control of this pattern of emotional response is one of the chief artistic merits of the play.

. . . The design of the play differs from that of *Tamburlaine* not only in being more complex but in the total impression it gives. Where Tamburlaine seems to open up ever wider prospects up to the moment of the hero's death, *Edward II* closes down until the focus is upon a prison, a death-bed, a bier. *Tamburlaine's* chief emotions are related to vast human potentiality, with only a final moment of regret that all is not possible, while in *Edward II*, all the emphasis falls on the pathos and horror of predicaments in which man is inextricably caught.

E. M. Waith
TDR (Spring, 1964), pp. 60–61, 76

Doctor Faustus

It is the loss, then, of this sense of unity, of this harmony between his mind and the universal forces surrounding him, which is the essence of spiritual tragedy, and it is of a loss of this kind that *Faustus* is the record. We feel in this play that the protagonist (and the poet himself whom he so closely shadows) has lost his sense of secure contact; his lines of communication are broken. The central idea of the play is an idea of loss. Marlowe does not tell us precisely what this is, for the plain reason that he did not know. The catastrophe is too recent; *Faustus* is written hard upon the heels of the event. But the passionate agony of the play is an agony of loss and it finds a fitting form for its expression in the medieval idea of a lost soul. . . . He offers in *Faustus* a series of explanations, some of which seem, in the light of his earlier and of his later work, to be the true ones, some of which contradict these and are a kind of apostasy in which Marlowe denies his fundamental creed. Most deeply of all he resents and blames that servitude to the dry and barren learning which he rightly perceives has led him somehow astray, though the error is too complete for him to see what it is that he should have followed in its stead or, even, at this stage, to hope for a recovery of the way. This he expresses very truly as the loss of the soul—the cutting off of the personality from its natural sources of inspiration and of faith. What these sources are, he does not know and cannot tell us; only, of the loss there is no question; the pain reveals the presence of disease, but does not diagnose it. In his further attempts at diagnosis he, as often as not, gives what must have appeared to him later as an altogether wrong explanation: he accepts, with a half-cowed and sometimes almost frantic submission, the conventional idea that it is his rejection of the superstitions of his contemporaries that has ruined him. It is here, I think, that there is apostasy.

Una M. Ellis-Fermor
Christopher Marlowe (London: Methuen, 1927), pp. 62-63

But in spite of all . . . similarities, *Faustus* is different from *Tamburlaine* in one significant respect: it shifts the emphasis from the strength of the self to its weakness, from victory to defeat. *Tamburlaine* may be called a drama of exultation which happens to end in death, whereas *Faustus* is a drama of spiritual death which happens to begin with exultation. The latter drama is, among other things, an utterance of Marlowe's fears for his own destiny as a free-thinking rebel from the laws of a Christian cosmos. But the important fact is that an unfolding in Marlowe's nature now leads him to choose the theme of the helplessness of even the most titanic human ego before God. He could not have written *Faustus* without feeling this impotence far more keenly than he did in the earlier play. Tamburlaine's arrogance is indeed overthrown—if death in the midst of victory be an overthrow—but Marlowe depicts his fall with none of the agonizing truth, the intensity of personal realization, which characterizes that of Faustus. As has been said, *Tamburlaine* stresses the success of ambition, *Faustus* its failure.

We must observe, however, that though Faustus confesses his weakness in the hands of the Deity, he remains unreconciled. He is led shrieking off, shattered by superior power but without love in his heart. Tamburlaine has the same disposition to look upon God as a repressing force, potentially an enemy. *Hero and Leander* speaks of Fate rather than God. In fact, nowhere in Marlowe is God considered a dispenser of love and mercy; at most, he is legislator and judge who effects justice upon earth. For Marlowe, as for many other men, the way to see God as love might have been through the worship of beauty. He was intensely spiritual, as most poets are spiritual, in that the outward and visible impressions of beauty in women and in nature created in him states of exaltation which rose far above the physical world which gave them birth. They differed from the religious ecstasy only in not being directed towards a Supreme Being. Had Marlowe considered beautiful forms as the immediate products of the Creator's hand and looked consistently beyond them to that Creator, he would have been the most religious of men. That he failed to do so is a tragic circumstance for which the Elizabethan view of Christianity was probably responsible. Religion in that era still taught men that the world of the senses, whereby beauty must enter in, belonged to the Devil; so that in order to love God it was necessary to scorn the world. This dichotomy appears significantly in *Faustus* when Helen, the incarnation of earthly beauty, is summoned up to seduce Faustus from his desire for God.

The recognition of the powerlessness of the self before God has important, if indirect, consequences for Marlowe's relations with men. It constitutes an advance towards greater fellow-feeling for mankind, for the sense of one's own weakness is the strongest incentive for associating oneself in act, sympathy, and thought with others of the race, while the sense of strength has the contrary effect.

In the main, however, *Faustus* is still basically unsocial as being a colloquy solely between Faustus and the ruling powers of the universe, in which other human beings drop away and are forgotten. It is left for the later dramas to give to the idea of human society its proper emphasis.

Paul H. Kocher
Christopher Marlowe: A Study of His Thought, Learning and Character (Chapel Hill, N. C.: Univ. North Carolina Pr., 1946), pp. 306-7

There is no denying the fact that in *Doctor Faustus*, Christopher Marlowe, whatever his personal views of Christianity may have been, has fashioned a play that is thoroughly Christian in conception and import. Christianity was of course explicit in Marlowe's source, the English Faust-Book. But in adapting that meandering collection of anecdotes about the famous German magician, Marlowe gave it a new, concentrated, intellectual shape in reorganizing his material along the more sophisticated lines of philosophical and theological concepts of evil. As a result, his play carries much more meaning than simply, "Don't sell your soul to the devil." The moral of the English Faust-Book is little more than that.

. . . the interesting thing is that when one looks at the way in which

Marlowe has chosen to present *his* Doctor Faustus, as contrasted with the Faust-Book presentation, it is clear that the theological ideas and concepts involved in the Augustinian definition of moral evil are transposed *directly* into dramatic language and action. One does not have to look behind the words and actions to discover Faustus' pride, the willfulness of his falling from God, or his egoistic ambition to become his own god; they are outwardly and directly manifest in everything he says and does.

. . . The suffering which grows out of that choice is as spiritual as the evil which produces it, an agony of the mind and will. It is an agony which, by reason of the poetic and dramatic skill which created it, has become an unforgettable part of the English dramatic tradition. In its own time, it stands unmatched as an expression of deep human fear and torment; no other protagonist in surviving plays of the contemporary stage has been represented in so intense a state of suffering over so spiritual a loss . . . no figure in early Elizabethan tragic drama had ever been driven to such torment by the prospect of the damnation of his immortal soul.

Douglas Cole
Suffering and Evil in the Plays of Christopher Marlowe
(Princeton, N. J.: Princeton Univ. Pr., 1962), pp. 194, 196, 231

Doctor Faustus tends to come apart in paraphrase. It can be turned into a fable about a Modern Man who seeks to break out of Medieval limitations. On the other hand, when one retells the story in religious terms, it tends to come out as though it were Marlowe's source, *The History of the Damnable Life and Deserved Death of Doctor John Faustus*. The truth is that the play is irreducibly dramatic. Marlowe dramatizes blasphemy, but not with the single perspective of a religious point of view: he dramatizes blasphemy as heroic endeavor. The play is an expression of the Reformation; it is profoundly shaped by sixteenth-century religious thought and ritual. But in presenting a search for magical dominion, Marlowe makes blasphemy a Promethean enterprise, heroic and tragic, an expression of the Renaissance.

The emergence of a new art form puts man in a new relation to his experience. Marlowe could present blasphemy as heroic endeavor, and the tragic ironies of such endeavor, because he had the new poetic drama, which put poetry in dynamic relation to action—indeed he himself had been the most important single pioneer in creating this form, in *Tamburlaine*. This creation, in turn, depended on the new professional repertory theatre to which, when he came down from Cambridge in 1587, he brought his talents, and his need to project possibilities of human omnipotence. The London theatre was a "place apart" of a new kind, where drama was not presented as part of a seasonal or other social occasion but in its own right. Its stage gave a special vantage on experience. . . . Marlowe, with characteristic modernity, calls his play just what we call it—a form. He has an audience which includes gentlemen, to whose patient judgments he appeals. In this new situation, blasphemy can be "good or bad."

C. L. Barber
TDR (Spring, 1964), pp. 91-92

GENERAL

... Marlowe was the Moses who led the way to the promised land, though he did not live to enter it. He is the first English poet using drama who possesses intellectual energy. The Jacobeans thought of him as a great primitive. They speak of his "pure elemental wit," of his raptures being "All air and fire, which made his verses clear." He was to them what Bacon seemed to be to the early members of the Royal Society. He forged the New Instrument which was to change for ever the character of dramatic verse. The suppleness and flexibility with which Spenser had transformed the rigidity of mid-sixteenth-century verse began to be made available for the stage. But Marlowe's verse has pace and resonance. He held the attention of wit and groundling alike, and was the first Englishman to make of tragedy a form of art that was both popular and serious.

... yet Marlowe's chief interest lay in morality. To say that he was more interested in moral ideas than in dramatic character is to say little, for it is true of most of these dramatists. . . . Few dramatists, perhaps only Webster and Middleton, share some of Shakespeare's power of expressing a play's moral intention in and through characters that can be mistaken for creatures of flesh and blood. . . . But to expect in Marlowe's plays or in Elizabethan or Jacobean drama in general a realistic representation of human character comparable to what is found in some fifteenth- and sixteenth-century paintings is to expect what is not there and seriously to misinterpret what is there. In Marlowe there is a strong infusion of the morality play.

F. P. Wilson
Elizabethan and Jacobean (Oxford: Clarendon
Pr., 1945), pp. 100-101

Marlowe's development, then, as a poet, is through a "discandying" period when he is under the spell of Spenser and writes the lyrically sweet lines of *Dido, Queen of Carthage* to the powerful reverberations of *Tamburlaine*, stressed and structured upon bombast and blood, thunder and the distant. A transitional period wherein the poet throws off the mighty line and finds great poetry in native English accents, idioms, and cadences, comes with *The Jew of Malta*. Marlowe then denudes his verse so completely that *Edward II* might be called a play almost completely bare of ornament. Tumultuous passions are subdued under a dispassionate rhetoric with the result that an entirely new kind of dramatic poetry comes to the English stage. But, to my mind, it is our good fortune that Marlowe decided the method of *Edward II* was not to be his future way, and we have the soaring achievement of *Faustus*, which can be termed only a play of awe.

Harry Morris
TDR (Spring, 1964), p. 154

JOHN MARSTON

1576-1634

Christened October 7, 1576, at Wardington, Oxford. Son of John Marston, a Shropshire lawyer, and Maria Guarsi. Entered Brasenose College, Oxford, 1591. Admitted to Inner Temple August 2, 1592. B.A. Oxford, 1594. Residence at Inner temple around 1595. Father died in 1599, leaving his son his law books. Resided at Inner Temple in 1596, 1597, 1599, 1600, 1601. Departed finally in 1606. Published verse satire, *Pygmalion's Image and Certain Satires*, 1598. *Scourge of Villainy* in same year under pesudonym W. Kinsayder. 1599, second collection of satires published. Writing for Lord Admiral's Company by September 28, 1599. Engaged in War of the Theatres with Ben Jonson. Wrote for Children of St. Paul's. 1606, worked on city pageant for King James and King Christian of Denmark. Wrote *Entertainment* at Ashby-de-la-Zourche in 1607 while living in Coventry. Probably began study for the ministry at this time. Committed to Newgate prison June 8, 1608, probably for minor infraction about which nothing is known. At St. Mary's Hall, Oxford, in 1609. Ordained priest December 24, 1609. Victim of Highway robbery at Knightsbridge August 10, 1616. Appointed to living of Christchurch in Hampshire October 10, 1616. Died June 25, 1634.

A. H. Bullen, ed., *The Plays of John Marston* (1887), 3 vols.

PERSONAL

No one, I think, can study Marston's work without deciding that his problems were often subjective ones, what the kindly psychiatrist calls "personality difficulties." He must have been a strange young man and perhaps, like most real neurotics, a very tiresome one too. At all events we should not advance him (as we might Dekker or Middleton) as an exemplar of "normality." But if there is a certain fascination about his personality there is much more to interest a critic or historian in the Muse he chose to serve—that angular, exacting, and capricious figure whom he called "iust *Rhamnusia*" and "grim *Reproofe*.". . .

Marston himself, of course, was not an innocent victim. He chose her and indeed perhaps created her, a monster that he could not control. To that extent his own literary life has a touch of the retributive about it: he sups a poison tempered by himself. But any reader of his plays must be conscious

tastes of his spectators. Marston's plays were written for the exclusive patrons who attended performances at the private theatres. In much the same manner as the dramatists of the Restoration, he stimulated the jaded tastes of his frivolous and sophisticated aristocratic audience—an audience that lacked a feeling for true tragedy, an audience that was pleased with sensationalism, satire, exaggerated emotions, and sententious declamation. Marston was able to satisfy these needs; he included, moreover, a gratuitous display of his own morbid tendencies, for he found his audience receptive to the cynical, the tortured, and the perverse. For the modern reader Marston remains interesting primarily for his self-revelation. Eventually he abandoned the stage and entered the church, but we do not know whether he resolved in his new surroundings the conflicts that are evident in his writings. All that remains is the work of his earlier years—a testimonial of the turbulent emotions of a distressed spirit.

Samuel Schoenbaum
PMLA (December, 1952), pp. 1072, 1078

VERSE AND SATIRE

Marston, in spite of his limitations and his superfiicial ugliness, is a very interesting writer. He has things to say which are said by no other poet of his time, and they are pertinent, not only to that time, and hence to an understanding of Shakespeare at the most interesting period of his career, but also to the present day.

But Marston's manner of expressing himself has always given trouble. In his own time, Ben Jonson made fun of his style in *The Poetaster*, and everyone who has since paid any attention to it has found it turgid, ugly and obscure. This is largely true, but we should not rest content with the mere statement: there are many ways of being turgid and obscure, and Marston's way is worth investigating, for from it we can learn a good deal about Elizabethan poetry. . . .

Marston knew what *ought* to be said, but his sensitivity was only half-developed; he knew the analytical meaning of words, but was unaware of their connotations; as a result his poetry is dry, it lacks overtones, it walks unnaturally on stilts, and only very rarely does it give that impression of ease and control which we find in poetry that is complete. . . .

It is particularly regrettable that Marston was only half a poet, since he seems to have been aware, although his crudity of expression frequently conceals it, of the chief poetic currents of his time. Indeed his linguistic vices are an important symptom of what was then happening to language. Just as the superficial rhythms of *Euphues*, though uninteresting in themselves, were of major importance in training the Elizabethan ear for its later rhythmic triumphs, both in prose and verse, so the publicity which Jonson and others gave to the atrocities of Marston's vocabulary prevented other poets (as it later prevented Marston himself) from making similar mistakes. Marston's style was an object lesson, and Shakespeare, among others, probably benefited by it, as he benefited by Euphuism. A man who, like Marston, is continually experimenting with words is bound to have a stimulating effect on his poetic contemporaries, even though his experiments are rarely successful.

Theodore Spencer
Criterion (July, 1934), pp. 582-84

John Marston's work in verse satire is, perhaps, as exemplary as anything he was ever to do of the purposes that unified the fashionable poets at the end of the sixteenth century. In taking up the "Satyre's knottie rod" in 1598, he assumed a stance, a voice, and a state of mind ideally suited to a vociferous declaration of his individuality. This gesture was to exert a permanent influence on his literary career. Although he was soon prevented from publishing verse satires by the Order of Conflagration of 1599 and although his literary efforts after that year were almost wholly dramatic, once he had turned to satire he never abandoned it. It will be increasingly clear, indeed, that his work in verse satire constituted an apprenticeship in the literary methods and techniques that were to be the foundation of his efforts in the drama. . . .

All in all, Marston's efforts in the verse satires are most profitably seen in the context of an almost pretentious aim to elevate and dignify this "new" genre. His multifaceted persona, his chameleon-like language, his battery of devices for exposing and ridiculing deformity, and his careful articulation of a constructive attitude toward it—all this is subsumed by the purpose of setting forth what Marston believed to be a mature response to the contemporary world. This response is extremely complex, as we shall see when Marston has improved on his means of communicating it. But even here, despite a strikingly roughhewn quality, we must conclude that he knew what he was about. The pieces fit, though they may rattle a bit: the parts cohere, though the coherence is undeniably difficult to grasp and difficult to hold. . . .

It is the tempering and directing influence of Neo-Stoicism in almost every facet of Marston's work that justifies our attention to it. Marston was neither an original nor a particularly forceful thinker. But he seems to have been widely read among the Stoics and Neo-Stoics; and his personal synthesis of Stoic and Christian ideas, however diversely derived, was integral to his practice as a writer. His considerable debt to Seneca and Montaigne has long been recognized. One of the most striking features of the plays is that before 1603 they are freighted with quotations and parallel passages from Seneca, while after 1603 they are full of allusions to Florio's Montaigne. But his debt to Epictetus and to others, though far more elusive, is probably more profound. He does not, as far as I know, quote Epictetus anywhere; in fact he only briefly acknowledged having read him by signing *Certain Satires* with the name "Epictetus" and by twice alluding to him in such a way as to suggest that Epictetus was for him something of a model or guide. . . .

Finally, this is what all the roles cultivated, ideas articulated, problems faced, and fashions attacked add up to: a particular way of confronting the world of the late Renaissance in England, a particular way of charting its directions, of measuring its failures, of responding to its immediate surfaces. It is, finally, the expression of this attitude toward his world that best explains Marston's long-range aims as a writer and that best accounts for his success with his educated audience.

Yet not the least interesting aspect of Marston's work is that his satire evolves so clearly from the explicit tracing out of this view in the verse satires to the expression of it in wholly dramatic terms in the last satirical comedies. Had he not abandoned literature for the church, like his contemporaries he too might have embraced more diversity in time, just as he might have written a play of more importance than *The Malcontent*. But he did not. Our compensation is found in the remarkably unified canon he has left and the light it sheds on him and his time.

Anthony Caputi
John Marston, Satirist (Ithaca, N. Y.: Cornell Univ. Pr.,
1961), pp. 23, 50, 58-59, 250

ANDREW MARVELL
1621-1678

Born in Winestead-in-Holderness, Yorkshire, on March 31, 1621. Educated at Hull Grammar School, of which his father was master. Matriculated Trinity College, Cambridge, Dec., 1633; received B.A. in 1638. Left Cambridge, 1641.

After Trinity College, Cambridge, Marvell travelled on the continent as tutor and companion during the Civil War period. During 1650-1652 he was tutor to Lord Fairfax's daughter, Mary, at Nunappleton House, York. He became Assistant Secretary for Foreign Tongues in 1657, Milton having recommended him four years earlier. From 1659 to his death he was a member of parliament for Hull. He was spokesman for policies of toleration (as in *The Rehearsal Transposed*, 1672-1673), and satirist against Charles II. His poems were published posthumously in 1681 by his "widow," actually his landlady seeking reimbursement for his debts.

H. M. Margoliouth, ed., *The Poems and Letters* (rev. 1952), 2 vols.
Pierre Legouis, *André Marvell, poète, puritan, patriote* (Paris, 1928); revised, abridged, and translated by Legouis as *Andrew Marvell* (1965)

Horatian Ode

I would begin by reemphasizing the dramatic character of the poem. It is not a statement—an essay on "Why I cannot support Cromwell" or on "Why I am now ready to support Cromwell." It is a poem essentially dramatic in its presentation, which means that it is diagnostic rather than remedial, and eventuates, not in a course of action, but in contemplation. . . . Cromwell is the usurper who demands and commands admiration. . . .

Cromwell is the truly kingly man who is *not* king—whose very virtues conduce to kingly power and almost force kingly power upon him. It is not any fumbling on the poet's part which causes him to call Cromwell "a Caesar" before the poem ends, even though he has earlier appropriated that name to Charles. *Both* men are Caesar, Charles the wearer of the purple, and Cromwell, the invincible general, the inveterate campaigner, the man "that does both act and know." Cromwell is the Caesar who must refuse the crown—whose glory it is that he is willing to refuse the crown—but who cannot enjoy the reward and the security that a crown affords. The tension between the speaker's admiration for the kingliness which has won Cromwell the power and his awareness that the power can be maintained only by a continual exertion of these talents for kingship—this tension is never relaxed. Cromwell is not of royal blood—he boasts a higher and a baser pedigree: he is the "Wars and Fortunes Son." He cannot rest because he is restless Cromwell. . . . These implications enrich and qualify an insight into Cromwell which is as heavily freighted with admiration as it is with a great condemnation. But the admiration and the condemnation do not cancel each other. They define each other; and because there is responsible definition, they reinforce each other.

Cleanth Brooks
English Institute Essays, 1946 (New York:
Columbia Univ. Pr., 1947), pp. 151-53

The poem . . . begins with an overmastering sense of the virtue of Cromwell's sheer force and personal energy in themselves. It ends with a justification of force as the sole instrument which can either create order or maintain it once it is established. And so great is the significance of order that Marvell is at first ready to allow Cromwell's very success as sufficient proof that his force is heaven's flame. In this view Marvell is at one with Waller's almost contemporary poem and with Dryden's poem on Cromwell's death. And they were all in harmony with that weary, practical belief in the absolute priority of order by which, partly through the medium of Hobbes, many even of the Royalists who had fought longest and given most were soon to be reconciled to the apparently accomplished fact of Cromwell's triumph and England's meteoric rise to international significance. . . . The opening lines of the *Ode* mark, then, a turn of feeling about 1650 away from loyalty to the old order, a turn which it was seemingly Cromwell who had aroused in him, though he hopes Cromwell may be the instrument of a constitutional order and not of a dictatorship. . . . Marvell's view of Cromwell's success and of the new order he will be instrumental in creating is at once humanized and made more terrible . . . by a passionate, though in part a blinding, religious intensity. There is in the lines on Cromwell and the state just such a confident belief in Cromwell, if not yet such a certainty that in the new order the kingdom of God is at hand. . . .

Ruth Wallerstein
Studies in Seventeenth-Century Poetic (Madison, Wisc.:
Univ. Wisconsin Pr., 1950), pp. 278-80

But the moment we enter upon Mr. Brooks's exegesis we see that, far from making a disinterested inquiry into the evidence provided by the poem, he is forcing the evidence to fit an unspoken assumption—namely, that a sensitive, penetrating, and well-balanced mind like Marvell could not really have admired a crude, single-minded, and ruthless man of action like Cromwell. . . . Mr. Brooks's special pleading begins with his gloss on the first lines. . . . To the unprejudiced reader, the lines say that, in these troubled times, the young man of spirit must leave bookish and poetical pursuits for military action. . . . [But] the critic has already made up his mind about the poet's view of Cromwell, and, instead of taking "forward" in its common and natural sense, must grasp at a pejorative possibility [i.e., presumptuous]. . . .

Since I cannot follow much of Mr. Brooks's reading of the earlier stanzas, I cannot follow such an explanation [as irony in the last]. Nothing in the wording seems to me to carry the faintest trace of irony; it is as straightforward a statement as we could have, however little we like it. Nor do I see how irony could pass at once into what Mr. Brooks accepts as eulogy without the slightest hint of a change of tone. . . . instead of twisting Marvell's plain words into irony, and thereby molding him into the likeness of a modern liberal, we really must accept the unpalatable fact that he wrote as an Englishman of 1650; and, in regard to what seems to us a strange assertion, we must say that he is indulging in some wishful thinking —Cromwell is so great a conqueror that even the Irish must share English sentiment and accept the course of history.

Douglas Bush
SwR (Summer, 1952), pp. 364-65, 373

The complexity of Marvell's vision and the tensions in the poem ["An Horatian Ode"] are those we feel in the work of Machiavelli. They result from a perspective on politics as an activity which cannot be entirely subsumed in the categories of traditional ethics. . . .

In the last analysis, man is moral but society is not. Any group is such for particular ends, and the only ethically unambiguous sphere is that of individual morality. This is the vision which is expressed in the "Horatian Ode." The poem does not express unresolved personal feeling any more than *Oedipus Rex* expresses an unresolved personal feeling of Sophocles about whether or not to side with Oedipus or with Fate. We are in a realm analogous to that of tragedy where we are compelled to recognize that the judgments concerning justice and injustice, good or evil, that we employ in our daily life cannot be easily or unambiguously applied when the context in which we use them is no longer the living room, but the state, the world, or the universe.

This is the perspective from which Marvell regards the central events of the Great Rebellion. Cromwell is the embodiment of two of the major dimensions of the Machiavellian new ruler the man of *virtù* who creates a state from chaos, the central figure of *Il Principe,* and the legally self-binding new ruler of the *Discorsi,* who, having consolidated his power tries to establish the rule of good laws and good customs enforced by good arms. It would seem that the "Prince" for whose arrival Machiavelli yearned, who, like his Moses, would be a new prince in a new state with new laws, finally arrived on the stage of history, but on the English and not the Italian stage. He comes fulfilling the prophecy of that greatest of unarmed prophets, Machiavelli himself, as if in fulfillment of the archetypal model Machiavelli had created. It seems to me that some of the awe and excitement the "Horatian Ode" communicates flows from Marvell's shock at finding this theoretical figure fulfilled in reality, not in distant Italy, but in his own time and country.

Joseph Anthony Mazzeo
JHI (January-March, 1960), pp. 16-17

The moving stanzas on the death of Charles are the major cause for the consistent misinterpretation of the ode. They are set against all the stanzas which praise Cromwell, and the result is a conflict which, critics have said, Marvell mastered by his poised detachment. Yet the movement of the poem is in no way determined by an opposition between Charles and Cromwell; Charles is merely an incident in a narrative which begins with Cromwell's extraordinary past and ends with the promise of his glorious future. . . .

The ode reveals that Marvell had become Cromwellian, and had no confidence in government solely by parliamentary committees and a Council of State, but it does not therefore follow that Marvell had put on party blinkers, or was blind to the degeneracy of the age. Far from being inconsistent with his faith in Cromwell, Marvell's earlier lines to Lovelace seem to me to spring from the very sense of disaster which made Cromwell necessary:

> Our Civill Wars have lost the Civicke crowne.
> He highest builds, who with most Art destroys,

And against others Fame his owne employs.
I see the envious Caterpillar sit
On the faire blossome of each growing wit.

At any time, and most of all in times of crisis, the political poet's duty was to squash his own envious caterpillar and to seek to know the good of the state. In finding therefore a simpler message in the ode than others have found, I do not seek to make Marvell's view of Cromwell more naive, or the fusion of emotions less real. Cromwell is a usurping Caesar —more so than ever—but Marvell's opinion of Cromwell's success is that God must have willed it, inexplicable as that may be, and that he (the poet) must write to validate God's will, not to oppose it. Those who would view such an argument as a poor rationalization offered in defense of the status quo—and the Presbyterians did so view it, declaring that evil permitted by God was no justification for persisting in it—disregard the strength in the seventeenth century of the sense of providence, and the century's devotion to the idea of a poet who spoke with supreme, not personal, authority. The final lines of the ode, which seem to glance at the same possibility of Cromwell's overthrow with which the poem began, are certainly a secular justification of force, but they are not cynical. Practical necessity is contained within a total view of divine order.

John M. Wallace
PMLA (March, 1962), pp. 44-45

OTHER POEMS

[In the Mower poems] Man has sinned, and brought Death into the world. He has infected all Nature with his own "luxurious" vice: every flower has learnt deceitful allurements . . . the same sins against which the poet had to encamp his mind. But the detail with which these horticultural crimes are described suggests anything but indifference: the interest is that of a gardener. The wit of the writing is directly opposed to the Puritan asceticism it claims to advocate: it is airy and fanciful. . . .

Then suddenly the standards of Nature are more seriously invoked; they are equally far from asceticism, but instead of the elaborate fancies of the garden they have a fresh sensuousness. . . .

The elegance and wit of the poem depend at first on pretending to denounce what is really enjoyed in a "witty" manner; but the conclusion gains its power from the resolution of the discord. It is as delicate as the beginning and more satisfying. Neither attitude is rustic: and the Mower's occupation is only relevant in so far as he makes a clean sweep both of the narrow ascetic and the mere fine gentleman.

M. C. Bradbrook and M. G. Lloyd Thomas
Andrew Marvell (Cambridge Univ. Pr., 1940), pp. 39-41

"The Garden" is a poem of the anti-genre of the naturalist paradise. Marvell therefore rejects the naturalist account of love, and with it that Platonism which was associated with the delights of the senses. The poets of the Renaissance were profitably aware of the possible antitheses in Platonic theories of love, just as they were aware of Plato's argument against their status as vessels of the truth. . . . Nothing is more characteristic of Renaissance poetry than the synthesis of spiritual and erotic in poetic genre and image. . . . [Genre and anti-genre] not only co-exist, but suggest each other. Marvell could pass with ease from the libertine garden to the garden of the Platonic *solitaire,* soliciting the primary *furor* of spiritual ascent. . . .

"The Garden" stands in relation to the poetry of the gardens of sense as the *Hymn of Heavenly Beauty* stands in relation to the *Hymn of Beauty.* It is poetry written in the language of, or using the "norms" of, a genre in a formal refutation of the genre. In fact, this was a method Marvell habitually used, sometimes almost with an affectation of pedantry.

Frank Kermode
EIC (July, 1952), pp. 228-29

"To his Coy Mistress," as it is written to here [1. 37], is merely a superior *carpe diem* piece. But with the "am'rous birds of prey" image (1. 38) the poet goes beyond that theme in a way that leads me to believe that the address to the mistress and the exhortation to sport are merely a device, a road traveled many times before, the purpose of which it is to bring the poet to the point where he can express what he has seen beyond. The answer Marvell here provides to the time problem he has so wittily presented is action; but this action as the imagery progressively defines it is not mere sporting with a fleshly mistress. First of all, we must note that the poet now is acting from his place of repose, into which he has slipped almost unnoticeably. . . . the poet and his mistress hang in the air, as is characteristic of birds of prey, seeing, observing the earth beneath them in full perspective before they strike. Then, the action which is to be performed is destructive. For if man can create, he can also destroy. . . . In "To his Coy Mistress" man, because he can choose when to destroy his own hour, because he need not submit to the "slow-chapt pow'r" of time (11. 39-40), at least has the satisfaction of knowing he exercises control over time. The image in lines forty-one and forty-two modifies the figure we have just been examining quite as radically as that figure modified the "sport us while we may." In rolling all of their energy (strength) and beauty (sweetness) into a little world which did not exist before (ball), the poet and his mistress will be acting creatively. Out of their defiance of time, their snatching of their fate from his hands and holding it firmly in their own, they have given their destiny a shape; and so something is born. To act creatively, to give birth is not easy. Pleasures must be torn, not indulged in. Surely the imagery here, the putting of the lover's strength (male) and the beloved's beauty (female) into a ball (round and perfect, like a fresh soul) and tearing their pleasures through the iron gates of life (the pangs and and trauma of the sudden emergence of new life) is meant to suggest birth. The pun on sun (*sun-son*) in the final couplet confirms this interpretation. The poet is saying that, although we cannot, as Joshua could, make the sun (time, the winged chariot) stand still, yet we can through the exercise of our creative powers make our son (posterity and hence immortality) move forward.

John Wheatcroft
BR (December, 1956), pp. 49-50

The garden is the Garden of Innocence; it is the place where man "walk'd without a Mate." But the poet who is looking at it, although he can *imagine* himself to be the innocent Adam, *knows* all along that he is the fallen Adam. Because he is both Adams he can make *The Garden* a microcosm of the sinful world as well as a symbol of Eden. That is why the laurel in the first stanza can represent both the "green" innocent plants and the futility of human fame, and the fruits in the fifth stanza represent both innocence and sexuality.

Lawrence W. Hyman
ELH (March, 1958), p. 21

In the whole description of her relationship with the living animal the Nymph has kept herself in the background, minimizing the depth of her feeling and indeed comparing herself disadvantageously with the animal (she "blushed" at its whiteness). Even in death the white fawn will transcend her: for while her own final destiny is not mentioned, she is assured that he will dwell in Elysium with the other white animals that embody purity. The animal that has "stayed" with her (faithfully) is asked not "to run too fast" toward Elysium—a graceful conceit: even in death the deer will preserve its natural fleetness. And even in the monument to be erected after her death the figure of the fawn will be of "alabaster" that never can be "as white as thee," but whiter than the "marble" that will perpetuate her own figure. While the relationship between mistress and animal will be expressed by the position of the fawn's image at her feet . . . , the mistress will remain forever the human mourner rather than the traditional owner. The Nymph will become a Niobe, endowed, if not with the boastfulness, with the disconsolate feelings of that "unhappy" mother.

. . . We understand now the particular tone of our "Complaint" in which the protagonist tells her story in an "inner monologue" of rather simple, direct words which contrast with the sophisticated examples of metaphysical wit. This stylistic contrast reflects the inner contrast between sadness and beauty: the sadness of disillusionment is reflected convincingly by the simple speech, not unknown to Marvell, while the miraculous metamorphosis into sensuous beauty finds its expression in the mirages of wit.

Leo Spitzer
MLQ (September, 1958), pp. 241-43

GENERAL

Marvell's poetry varies in the degree of its simplicity; but, at its simplest, it is not easy. He has several styles, but all of them rely, in ways more or less implicit, upon evanescent shades of meaning in a rapidly changing vocabulary, and upon those larger categories of thought, which are not at first sight very obvious to the reader of the present day. It is more usual to read him incompletely than to misread him, but his fine workmanship demands and repays a close analysis.

M. C. Bradbrook and M. G. Lloyd Thomas
Andrew Marvell (Cambridge Univ. Pr., 1940), p. 26

Wordplay is integral to Marvell's imagery. . . . It is important to recognize not only its general prevalence in the age but the logical and strict character of it in Marvell. Upon a mistaken interpretation of it depends much of the warping of Marvell in recent criticism. His images and plays upon words have been interpreted as free association, notably by Mr. Empson but by others also in Mr. Empson's school of criticism; and his puns and double meanings have been held to impart a light or cynical tone. To these critics who have exploited Marvell's "ambiguity" we owe a fresh awareness of the great number of double meanings in him. But they have perverted both his substance and his tone. In his poems, though many emotional currents flow into the making of a poem and into the words of which it is made, the result is not a "stream of consciousness." In the finished poem a context has been set up which determines the specific meanings of the words, often suggesting several meanings but ruling out many possible others. And though, as in passages of *Upon Appleton House,* wordplay may be the instrument for conveying a fantastic half-seriousness of tone, it does so precisely because in a normal context in the seventeenth century and in Marvell such language has the utmost seriousness of tone, whether in tragedy or in the certainly not gay comedies of Ben Jonson. Wordplay is with Marvell so ever-present a habit because it expresses his philosophical irony and paradox.

Ruth Wallerstein
Studies in Seventeenth-Century Poetic (Madison, Wisc.:
Univ. Wisconsin Pr., 1950), pp. 168-69

That moral seriousness which is the second noteworthy element in Marvell's poetry pervades almost everything that he wrote. We can discern it most clearly in the poems where he overtly rejects the pleasures of the senses and even of the arts, but it informs so apparently slight a poem as *Clorinda and Damon* in which Damon thrusts aside the temptations proffered by Clorinda:

C.	Near this, a Fountaines liquid Bell
	Tinkles within the concave Shell.
D.	Might a Soul bath there and be clean,
	Or slake its Drought?

Moreover, his concern for social order, his feeling for the unspoiled life of the countryside, and his admiration for the values fostered by great country houses rooted in local tradition give his poetry a fine, mature dignity. A humble gratitude for God's bounty informs his sense of Nature as a divine theatre alive with symbols and hieroglyphs, a sense which is implicit in the Garden poems and explicit in *Bermudas* where, after enumerating the luxuriant fruits and trees, Marvell proclaims the true glory of the islands. . . .

His inner harmony and balance are reflected in the tone of his voice. Like Ben Jonson, whose influence, coupled with that of Spenser, came if not to supplant at least to temper the extravagance of his early Clevelandism, Marvell speaks with the unaffected ease of a man sure of his place in society talking to his equals. We find in him a courtly elegance, a poised, alert wit, an urbane irony that never degenerates into a cheap cynicism, a fierce passion far removed from the licentious insolence of the Restoration song-writers, and an assured sense of values which frees him to relish the small joys of life without guilt because he has made his peace with things of great account.

Finally, we must consider the element of lyrical delight, but for which metaphysical wit becomes frigid and moral strength mere wooden didacticism.

John Press
Andrew Marvell (London: Longmans, Green, 1958), pp. 18-19

With the exception of George Herbert, Marvell is the most considerable of Donne's followers. But his strength is quite different. He is, as I suggested, far more carefully and absorbedly a craftsman in poetry; and this went with a different poetic stance. It matters not a jot that his love poems are thin in comparison with Donne's; there is, after all, little outside Shakespeare's sonnets that can stand that comparison. The difference is between kinds of poets: between the poet whose first concern is to judge and the poet who, above all, synthesizes. The vitality of Donne's poetry depends on his knack of taking on everything that comes with the same immediacy, accuracy and full, tough intelligence. At the end of any of Donne's poems the forces have been resolved and ordered in such a way as to make you believe that a similar readjustment of the feelings have taken place in the poet himself. It is, in a sense, a poetry of action. Marvell, however, is always a little further outside his subjects. His extraordinarily civilized sophistication is a fixed quantity. With it he weighs and judges his material with such dispassionate fairness as to leave you, as a final and lasting taste, with the mature subtlety of his judgment. Unlike Donne and Herbert, he never writes a poem which shows him in the process of attaining his maturity. It is, rather, a quality without which he would not have been able to begin to write. Marvell's detached and sophisticated wit may be infinitely more subtle and less stereotyped than that of the Augustan Man of Sense, but it is of essentially the same kind. In achievement, if not chronologically, he is the last of the School of Donne.

A. Alvarez
HdR (Autumn, 1960), p. 428

It is difficult to claim for Marvell the import or seriousness we habitually expect of the very great or of the specifically "religious" poets of the seventeenth century. The first remain unquestionably central to our literature. The second have a permanent lien on our attention, for they patently draw upon an idiom which has always given us classic ways of expressing our largest ideas. Marvell, who fits neither category, necessarily suffers. We remain relatively unaware that he is one of the great Christian poets of his century. And we are still less aware that, unlike Herbert or Crashaw, he illuminates the dominant Christian themes in ways which, since Wordsworth's spiritualization of nature, should be perfectly familiar to us. We have not gone to Marvell for this order of significance and, not seeking, we have not found it.

This is not really surprising. For Marvell often cultivates the mannerisms of the minor poet working in minor modes upon minor themes. One is easily tricked by his deceptive transparency and polish into regarding his finest lines as the exceptional flourishes of a sensibility which delighted in surfaces but shunned depths. Like the good but minor poet, he is abundantly facile within the limits of a given tradition. His Caroline urbanity and grace, his metaphysical wit and sophistication, appear less as original gifts than as felicitous drawings upon current stock. He almost cries out to be placed in literary histories as a kind of exquisite miniaturist.

John D. Rosenberg
Boston Univ. Studies in Eng. (Autumn, 1960), p. 152

PHILIP MASSINGER
1583-1640

> Born in Salisbury. Son of a gentleman in the service of the Herbert family. Patronized himself by Philip Herbert, fourth Earl of Pembroke. Entered St. Alban Hall, Oxford, in 1602. Left in 1606 without taking degree. May have written poem on London plague while still at Oxford. Began to write plays for Philip Henslowe around 1613. First published play *The Virgin Martyr* (1622) in collaboration with Dekker. Collaborated also with Field, Daborne, and Fletcher. Wrote for the King's Men from 1613 until his death, except for the period from 1623 to 1625 when he wrote for the Queen's Men. Very prolific writer, but never prospered. Often forced to borrow money from Henslowe.
>
> F. Cunningham, ed., *The Plays of Philip Massinger* (1871), 4 vols.

A dramatist who so skilfully welds together parts which have no reason for being together, who fabricates plays so well knit and so remote from unity, we should expect to exhibit the same synthetic cunning in character. Mr. Cruickshank, Coleridge, and Leslie Stephen are pretty well agreed that Massinger is no master of characterization. You can, in fact, put together heterogeneous parts to form a lively play; but a character, to be living, must be conceived from some emotional unity. A character is not to be composed of scattered observations of human nature, but of parts which are felt together. Hence it is that although Massinger's failure to draw a moving character is no greater than his failure to make a whole play, and probably springs from the same defective sensitiveness, yet the failure in character is more conspicuous and more disastrous. A "living" character is not necessarily "true to life." It is a person whom we can see and hear, whether he be true or false to human nature as we know it. What the creator of character needs is not so much knowledge of motives as keen sensibility; the dramatist need not understand people; but he must be exceptionally aware of them. This awareness was not given to Massinger. He inherits the traditions of conduct, female chastity, hymeneal sanctity, the fashion of honour, without either criticizing or informing them from his own experience. . . .

What may be considered corrupt or decadent in the morals of Massinger is not an alteration or diminution in morals; it is simply the disappearance of all the personal and real emotions which this morality supported and into which it introduced a kind of order. As soon as the emotions disappear the morality which ordered it appears hideous. Puritanism itself became repulsive only when it appeared as the survival of a restraint after the feelings which it restrained had gone. When Massinger's ladies resist temptation they do not appear to undergo any important emotion; they merely know what is expected of them; they manifest themselves to us as lubricious prudes. Any age has its conventions; and any age might appear absurd when its conventions get into the hands of a man like Massinger—a man, we mean, of so exceptionally superior a literary talent as Massinger's, and so paltry an imagination.

T. S. Eliot
Selected Essays (London: Faber and Faber, 2nd ed., 1934), pp. 212-14

Taken . . . in its proper context of the Jacobean theatre, Massinger's plotting is remarkable for its adroit handling of its raw material, improbable, melodramatic, not to say incredible, as much of that was, and its dexterous adaptation of this to the limitations of the prevailing theatrical conventions. In short, for their time and kind, Massinger's plots are very carefully considered and precisely jointed and deserve to the full the praise they have received.

The close dovetailing of his plots and the cold calculation expended on the contraction, expansion, and emphasising of the events is, to be sure, only one result of the care and thought Massinger bestowed on every feature of his dramaturgy. . . .

Wherever he does most strikingly fail in plotting, it almost always involves a fundamental principle which seems to have governed every aspect of his work, a certain trait in his character which makes it absolutely necessary for him to introduce the moral viewpoint at no matter what cost to anything else. For him, artistic conscience always succumbs to the conscience of the moralist. . . .

Where the woman of virtue is common in Massinger, the corresponding man of virtue is rare, at least in the leading role. I mean the man whose primary concern is the pursuit of a self-conscious virtue-ideal. The nearest Massinger comes to such a type is the virtuously Stoical (but tediously pessimistic) Antiochus, the hero of *Believe As You List*. . . .

The heroes whom Massinger wishes us to admire have the public virtues of courage, sensitive honour, candour in word and deed, sense of duty, decision. The noblest of them are all, appropriately, soldiers—in effect, exponents of the knightly virtues. But in addition Massinger's heroes are men of definite competence in their station and office: if their ends are tragic, their *hamartia* is never official ineffectiveness. Thus Sforza is an efficient prince and an able and successful advocate with his sovereign, the Emperor Charles; and Leosthenes is not only a brave warrior but a master of the art of war.

But the good qualities in these characters can be defeated, temporarily or altogether, by passion, violence, and rashness. The overwhelming of virtue by such intemperance provides a tragic interest in *The Duke of Milan* and *The Fatal Dowry*. In plays such as *The Picture, The Renegado,* and *The Maid of Honour,* in which the principal male character emerges from the conflict of his good qualities with his passion, the interest lies precisely in the conflict. . . .

The differences between Massinger and Shakespeare as regards their diction might be summed up briefly in general terms as follows: where Shakespeare is precise, Massinger is vague; where Shakespeare is tense, Massinger is slack; where Shakespeare is terse, Massinger is diffuse; and where Shakespeare is concentrated, Massinger is dilute. That is the crux of the matter. In Massinger the high degree of condensation, the packed significance and suggestiveness, we know from Shakespeare and expect from many of his lesser brethren, is gone, and the effect of his verse upon the reader or audience is of a considerably reduced impact. . . .

Massinger, in short, is not a poet. Only rarely is there any "compelling emotion" behind his work. His periodic structure is a prose-form. His ideas are prose-concepts, springing not from Feeling but from Intellect. . . .

T. A. Dunn
Philip Massinger (London: T. Nelson, 1957),
pp. 56, 74, 119, 246, 266

Time and again one finds that Massinger's tragicomedies turn upon problems of conduct. No one would suggest that the very gentle *Great Duke of Florence* was primarily a didactic play. Yet the crisis of the play is the favorite's decision to lie to the king about the beauty of Lidia and to get the young hero to cover up as well; the importance of the play from the moralist's point of view is the degradation which deception brings the two men. And all this is handled within a comedy whose tone is as light as possible. As one reads the plays, one soon gets into the position which Massinger as censor himself seems to take, and one takes a keener pleasure in the plays as plays because of this moral viewpoint. One watches closely for the telltale strokes which give away the flawed man—for, as I have said, Massinger is careful not to broadcast his disapproval at the beginning of the play. It is true that it is much more difficult to identify oneself with Massinger's rigid code of honor, but then there are difficulties in accepting Jane Austen's. *The Fatal Dowry* (before 1620) is a good example of a play which improves greatly when one sees oneself as a juryman. The play tells how the incorruptible Charalois, whom no cruelty could weaken, is destroyed by generosity—the gift of a fortune and a faithless wife. Again Massinger sets his hero in a corrupt society, this time a mercantile society, moved only by money values. Rochfort is so moved by Charalois' nobility in a degenerate age that he frees him from prison, pays his debts, and weds him to his daughter Beaumelle. Charalois finds her in bed with young Novall and kills her. The question which the play sets, taking it over from the source, is whether Charalois should have pocketed up his wrongs in gratitude to the father Rochfort, who had done so much for him. The audience is asked to judge.

Philip Edwards
Essays on Shakespeare and Elizabethan Drama in Honor of Hardin Craig (Columbia, Mo.: Univ. Missouri Pr., 1962), p. 348

THOMAS MIDDLETON
1580-1627

Born at St. Lawrence in the Old Jewry, London. Christened April 18, 1580. First publication in 1597, *The Wisdom of Solomon* paraphrased. Entered Queen's College, Oxford, in April 1598. Published satires in 1599. Mentioned in Henslowe's Diary in 1602 for the first time. In 1603 married niece of Dr. Roger Marbeck, Provost of Oriel College, Oxford, daughter of a clerk of Chancery, and sister of an actor, Thomas Marbeck. Collaborated with various dramatists. Wrote city pageants. Collaboration with William Rowley began about 1612. In later years devoted more time to civic entertainments than to plays. In 1620 attained office of Chronologer of City of London. In 1624, *The Game at Chess* offended the Spanish ambassador. Caused Middleton to appear before the Privy Council along with the actors of the play. Died in parish of Newington Butts.

A. H. Bullen, ed., *The Plays of Thomas Middleton* (1885-6), 8 vols.

But Middleton's comedy is not, like the comedy of Congreve, the comedy of a set social behaviour; it is still, like the later comedy of Dickens, the comedy of individuals, in spite of the continual motions of city merchants towards county gentility. In the comedy of the Restoration a figure such as that of Moll Cut-Purse [in *The Roaring Girl*] would have been impossible. As a social document the comedy of Middleton illustrates the transition from government by a landed aristocracy to government by a city aristocracy gradually engrossing the land. As such it is of the greatest interest. But as literature, as a dispassionate picture of human nature, Middleton's comedy deserves to be remembered chiefly by its real—perpetually real—and human figure of Mill the Roaring Girl. That Middleton's comedy was "photographic," that it introduces us to the low life of the time far better than anything in the comedy of Shakespeare or the comedy of Jonson, better than anything except the pamphlets of Dekker and Greene and Nashe, there is little doubt. But it produced one great play—*The Roaring Girl*—a great play in spite of the tedious long speeches of some of the principal characters, in spite of the clumsy machinery of the plot: for the reason that Middleton was a great observer of human nature, without fear, without sentiment, without prejudice.

The man . . . remains inscrutable, solitary, unadmired, welcoming collaboration, indifferent to fame; dying no one knows when and no one knows how; attracting, in three hundred years, no personal admiration. Yet he wrote one tragedy [*The Changeling*] which more than any play except those of Shakespeare has a profound and permanent moral value and horror; and one comedy [*The Roaring Girl*] which more than any Elizabethan comedy realizes a free and noble womanhood.

T. S. Eliot
Selected Essays (London: Faber and Faber, 2nd ed., 1934), pp. 168-70

Middleton's tragedies are as similar in their methods of construction as they are different from the plays already considered. Rowley's name appears on the title page of *The Changeling*, but it is difficult to see the possibility of his sharing in the main plot, for its unity is of a kind which not even the most sympathetic collaboration could achieve.

The connection between the two plots of this play is, however, very carefully worked out. It is indicated even in the title, *"The Changeling,"* which describes both Antonio, the innocent, and Beatrice-Joanna, the inconstant woman (a usual meaning—*vide Anything for a Quiet Life*, 2. 1. 71, and *N.E.D. sub verb.*).

The construction of the play is masked by the greater naturalism of the treatment. Compared with the characters of earlier plays, Middleton's are fuller, more natural and human. Their motives and actions may be conventionally "Italianate" (they have vestigial remains of the Revenge code in the melancholy of Tomazo the revenger and the appearance of the ghost), but their feelings and responses are normal. Beatrice-Joanna's famous outburst, when the murderer demands possession of her as a reward:

> Why 'tis impossible thou canst be so wicked
> Or shelter such cunning cruelty
> To make his death the murderer of my honour—

(3. 4. 121 ff.)

is only the most obvious illustration of Middleton's interest in the way the mind works. Deflores' brief plea to the man he has cuckolded, when he hears Beatrice-Joanna crying out in futile anger:

Let me go to her, sir—   (5. 3. 112)

is so assured of his right to calm her that the husband can but send him in.

The construction of the play is, however, partly dependent on themes: briefly it may be described as a study in the conflict of passion and judgment, and of the transforming power of love. All the characters (save Alsemero) are entirely at the mercy of their feelings, which are instinctive and uncontrollable. Judgment is blinded, so that the characters practise all kinds of deception and self-deception to gain their ends. Love is "a tame madness," a kind of possession which seizes upon a man and "changes" him so that he is no longer recognizable. In the main plot the themes are worked out naturalistically; in the subplot the use of the madmen, and of more literal transformations, as well as more farcical action, makes a kind of phantasmagoria. The key words are "change," "judgment," and "will" (in the sense of instinctive desire, often of sensual desire, as in Shakespeare).

Muriel C. Bradbrook
Themes and Conventions of Elizabethan Tragedy
(Cambridge Univ. Pr., 1935), pp. 213-14

When Middleton, perhaps as a result of association with Rowley, turned to tragedy through the intermediate stages of such tragi-comedies as *A Fair Quarrel*, the experience of a long period of comedy writing remained with him. The peculiar quality of Middleton's tragedy, the grimness, the plainness, the absence alike of romance, pathos, passion or heroism, derives thus directly from the long training in matter-of-fact and unemotional observation, culminating as it does in the wide but precise satire of *A Chaste Maid*. It is not merely, then, that his range of character and episode has been widened, that his theatre technique has become familiar to the point of oblivion, though both of these advantages undoubtedly came to him, as to Shakespeare, through a long period of successful comedy preceding his tragic work; above all, he understands, in the later half of his career, that those very elements that at one time seemed to point only to a comic universe may now be present in the midst of tragic events, not in detached and significant contrast only, but intimately associated, not only as parts of the plot, but as indispensable constituents of the total mood. Some of his contemporaries (Chapman, for example, and Ben Jonson) demonstrate in alternate plays their capacity for tragic and for comic work. Some, the tragi-comedy writers, Fletcher, Beaumont and Massinger (occasionally also Chapman), blend the comic with the near-tragic so closely that though "it wants deaths, which is enough to make it no tragedy, yet it brings some near it, which is enough to make it no comedy." But Middleton's process, like Shakespeare's, goes as far beyond the second as the second goes beyond the first. He shows the sternest tragic issues intimately blended with comic ones, with characters that are themselves hardly capable of tragic passion, that yet play an indispensable part, not only in the direct disposal of events, but indirectly through their effect upon the central characters, and contribute vitally to the colouring of the final impression. The countryman who brings the asps to Cleopatra, the porter of Macbeth's castle, Emilia in *Othello,* the grave-diggers and Osric in *Hamlet,* not only come from a comic world, but bring it with them, unsubdued, when they enter tragedy and modify thereby the mood, the conduct, even, it may be, the very nature of the tragic figures. This principle of extending and modifying tragedy by the intimate associa-tion of comedy, Middleton carried, I think, perhaps further than Shake-speare. For in Middleton's tragedies, the levelling effect of the one mood upon the other goes so far as to obscure the tragic effect at first glance. The constant, not the occasional, presence of the coarse, the impercipient, the shallow and the callous renders the whole more cynical, diminishes, not the sufferings of the main figures, but the dignity of the sufferings. Had *Troilus and Cressida* been focussed upon the death of the two lovers it would have achieved something like the balance of tragic and comic mood in Middle-ton, though not, even so, Middleton's synthesis. The significant thing is that, even had it been so altered, Thersites' summary would still be valid: "All the argument is a cuckold and a whore." A grey light results from this even balancing of tragic and comic; the colours subdue each other and the mood is neither heroic nor genial, pathetic nor gay, but something in which each impulse strives with its opposite and comes to equilibrium in frustrated denial. But the resulting atmosphere has a stillness and clarity in which we see with startling sharpness the details of the processes at work upon the minds.

Una Ellis-Fermor
Jacobean Drama (London: Methuen, 1953), pp. 139-40

The *Chaste Maid* is not a simple play, and the powerful impression it leaves is achieved, it seems to me, largely by means of a tension maintained be-tween disparate elements: the essential brutality of the content of the play is counterpoised by the laughter which informs the dramatist's treatment of his chilling material. In effecting and sustaining this recalcitrant balance, Middleton is well served by his irony—an instrument peculiarly fitted to the expression of the cruel and the comic alike. Thus we laugh at what, under other circumstances, might horrify us.

But there is another factor, as yet unsuggested, that contributes to the complex effect produced by this extraordinary play. As the action unfolds, we gradually perceive that Middleton's realism has taken on an added dimension—a dimension to which the Elizabethan comic dramatist does not often aspire. The life of the play overflows the artificial bounds of stage narrative; becomes, as it were, a fragment out of time. In the London of *Michaelmas Term* Easy meets Quomodo for the first time; Follywit in the *Mad World* and Witgood in the *Trick* set in motion their intrigues in the opening scenes. But situations introduced in the *Chaste Maid* existed before the play's beginning: Moll and Touchwood junior have already accepted one another. Mistress Allwit has borne Sir Walter six children in the course of a decade. In Elizabethan comedy the dramatist will of course provide necessary background information concerning his principal figures (Witgood's previous dealings with his uncle, for example), but in the *Chaste Maid* the characters' pasts have a concreteness beyond the immediate needs of the action. We learn much, for example, about the Yellowhammers. Maud was "lightsome and quick" two years before her marriage and took dancing lessons from "a pretty brown gentleman"; her husband is descended from the Yellowhammers of Oxfordshire, near Abington, and many years back had a child by Mistress Anne ("he's now a jolly fellow, / Has been twice warden"); for eight years Tim stumbled over *as in praesenti* in his grammar, only to go on to impress the gentleman commoners in the hall at Cambridge by eating his broth with a silver spoon. Even minor personages are portrayed with a scrupulous particularity. We are told of the Welsh courtesan's red hair, we hear her speak in her native tongue, we learn that she is from North Wales and lost her maidenhead at Brecknockshire.

As we follow the movement of the play, we are aware—as we are not with the earlier City comedies—of the passage of time and the changes wrought by the succession of events; finally, we can envision a future for some, at least of Middleton's characters. Sir Walter travels his rake's progress to the Knights' ward. Mistress Allwit, "as great as she can wallow," longs for her lover's return and pickled cucumbers. Time passes: her infant is born and christened; the "good founder" casts her off and is himself cast off; in the end the Allwits look ahead to a different life as they prepare to take a house in the Strand and let out lodgings. The result of the dramatist's consciousness of time is an illusion of reality so persuasive that it is scarcely vitiated by the fantastic elements in plot and characterization.

Samuel Schoenbaum
in *Studies in the English Renaissance Drama in Memory of K. J. Holtzknecht*, eds. Josephine W. Bennett, Oscar Cargill, and Vernon Hall
(New York: New York Univ. Pr., 1959), pp. 306-8

His ironically detached, unheroic view of life was not attuned to the heroic passions of early tragedy; his psychological and sociological interests could not embrace the epic cosmological themes of Marlowe or Chapman. While his contemporaries pondered man's tragic relation to the universe, Middleton studied the comic relation between human appetites and the social environment which conditions them. Significantly, he did not return to tragedy until it had acquired a shape more pleasing to his talent; however much he learned from Shakespeare or Jonson, he drew his immediate inspiration from *The Maid's Tragedy,* a play which heralds the romantic and psychological bias of later Jacobean tragedy. . . .

We might even say that regardless of the tastes of his audiences, Middleton required a wild and bloody denouement in *Women Beware Women,* for having denied a genuine capacity for tragic emotion to his characters he had at last to submerge their personalities in melodrama to make them seem like tragic figures. Because they were not born to play tragic roles, he had to slaughter them wholesale to create a superficial impression of tragic doom. . . .

Whether Middleton's tragedies are more objective or less critical of life than those of Jonson, Tourneur, and Webster is not an easy question to answer. It seems to me that Middleton is unique among the tragedians not so much for his "clinical detachment" as for his total indifference to the ideal in human nature. If he actually portrayed the destruction of innocence without stirring any pity or compassion in his readers, his plays would strike us as perversely deficient in moral sensibility. We do not object to his pitilessness because he convinces us that ultimately his characters deserve no pity, that their virtue is easily debased because it is superficial or counterfeit to begin with, and that there is no trace of the spirit in their carnal passions. Thus even when his plays blaze like diamonds they are cold to the touch.

Robert Ornstein
The Moral Vision of Jacobean Tragedy (Madison, Wisc.:
Univ. Wisconsin Pr., 1960), pp. 171, 191, 199

Thomas Middleton's plays are remarkable for a naturalistic technique which is almost unique in his age. It appears in the almost journalistic realism of his comedies of London life, and among his tragedies in a depth of psychological penetration and insight such as we find only in Shakespeare. . . .

I would suggest . . . that the realistic technique, not only of *The Changeling,* but of *Women Beware Women* as well, is merely the instrument by which Middleton effects a larger thematic design, and that in both plays the main plot and sub-plot are united by a common theme. Middleton is concerned not so much with the complexities of human character as with the nature of evil in the world, and each of his tragedies in its own way provides the emotional equivalent of a statement about man's relation to evil. In this sense the tragedies of Thomas Middleton . . . are profoundly moral works. They embrace a more comprehensive view of human life than ever could be encompassed in the psychological study of an individual, no matter how intense or revealing. . . .

Middleton is Christian in his point of view, but we must recognize that his Christianity is of a distinct kind; it is neither that of Heywood nor of Tourneur. Heaven and hell are always present in Middleton's cosmos; the limits of good and evil are always clear and well defined, and the sinner must inevitably suffer divine retribution. At the end of *The Changeling* there is a vindication of divine justice with the emergence of a new moral order; evil has been purged from society and new life is ready to begin. That we do not find such tragic reconciliation at the end of *Women Beware Women* may be the mark of an increasing pessimism combined with a broadening social range which causes the dramatist at last to see all of human society as corrupt and destined for destruction, with no redeeming qualities in man to offer any hope for the future. We do not have in *Women Beware Women* any of Shakespeare's faith in the heroic capabilities of man or of Heywood's belief in the power of love and human goodness to destroy evil. There is no suggestion of a divine providence guiding the affairs of men, in spite of their own indirection, to a rebirth of good, and there is little of Tourneur's confidence in a true felicity to be attained in heaven. Middleton's attention is fixed steadily on hell.

Irving Ribner
Jacobean Tragedy (London: Methuen, 1962), pp. 123-25

As a whole the play [*The Changeling*] makes an impact probably greater than any other of Middleton's. It has the directness of outlook which characterizes *Women Beware Women*; it also seems to me more vital than this play because the peculiar structure allows a statement not of one thing only, viz. the unreality of the apparently real, but also of the frightening energy of the forces at work within the situations Middleton is describing. Beatrice and De Flores in particular, and on a more general plane Vermandero's castle with all it contains and stands for, its beauty and its "labyrinths," have a passionate intensity unequaled elsewhere in Middleton except perhaps in individual characters. Though the play rarely swerves from the vein of naturalistic writing which makes Middleton such an original figure in the Jacobean drama, it has at the same time an imaginative depth and force comparable to Webster's.

Indeed what we have been observing in *The Changeling* is a depth of focus unique in Jacobean (and probably any other) drama. The play is not to be placed in the richly evocative line of Shakespearean development; its meaning and significance are the result of a fresh start in Jacobean enquiry and one which depends a good deal on unswervingly naturalistic attitudes in the verse and dialogue. Yet a term like "naturalism" is after all wrong or inadequate for Middleton's work as a whole and certainly for this play. Here as nowhere else we are presented, not with a flat, naturalistic surface, but with the spectacle of a single complex image—Vermandero's "castle"— dominating a whole drama. Not only do we look at and admire the progress of the action; at the same time we, as it were, look down through the surface of this dominant image into the complexity of its internal structure. Where in other plays—Tourneur's, some of Marlowe's, Shakespeare's—we watch and participate in the growth of a network of inter-connected images, in *The Changeling* we are presented with something which is much more clearly a single complex image, a product of the whole play which grows in depth like a gradually expanding sphere, the surface of which is firm but also clear enough for us to gaze into the complex centre. The play is therefore unique, though linked with *Women Beware Women* in obvious ways. Together with the rest of Middleton's work it separates itself off from Jacobean drama generally; while at the same time it preserves, within the Middleton *œuvre*, a separate and distinct identity.

T. B. Tomlinson
A Study of Elizabethan and Jacobean Tragedy
(Cambridge Univ. Pr., 1964), pp. 207-8

THOMAS NASHE
1567-1601

Born at Lowestoft. Entered St. John's College, Cambridge, as Sizar in 1582. Took B.A. in 1586. Probably in London by 1588 when *Anatomy of Absurdity* was published. Stayed at Carisbrooke Castle with patron, Sir George Cary, in 1592 and 1593. Offended London City authorities with *Christ's Tears over Jerusalem* in 1594. Probably became involved in Marprelate controversy as pamphleteer. In 1595 lived at the Dolphin in Cambridge. Lived for short time with his printer, John Danter. Published *Unfortunate Traveller* in 1594. Collaborated with Ben Jonson on play, *Isle of Dogs,* in 1597. Gave offence to authorities. His lodgings searched by order of the Privy Council. While Jonson was imprisoned, Nashe fled to East Anglia. Visited Yarmouth. Mentioned as dead in 1601, although just when death occurred is not certain.

R. B. McKerrow, ed., *The Works of Thomas Nashe* (1904-1910), 5 vols., rev. F. P. Wilson (1958)

The champion of the anti-Martinists, Mar-Martin Junior, who silenced Martin and held him up to public scorn, is thus confirmed to be Thomas Nashe, the Elizabethan satirist, whose terms "laid in steepe in Aquafortis & Gunpowder" later to be used against the Harveys, owe their inspiration to Martin's "tapsterly termes." In matching wits and words with Martin,

Nashe toughened his sinews for his bout with the son of the halter-maker. He himself in an offhand way vouches the information that he wrote *An Almond*, though the more skeptical of our modern scholars shrug their shoulders and say, "It can't be so." But even if Nashe had not admitted his authorship, the style of the tract reveals him as the author.

Donald J. McGinn
PMLA (December, 1944), p. 984

The chief characteristic of Nashe's prose is its alertness to the possibilities of metaphor. The impression given by reading Nashe is that of an extremely alert mind always conscious of the medium of expression, playing upon it as a complex instrument. Indeed it is no exaggeration to assert that the metaphorical possibilities of language form the essential subject-matter of the prose. . . .

The theme is of interest to Nashe chiefly as an excuse for darting imagery. Much Elizabethan prose has this quality, but none of his contemporaries indulge so consistently as Nashe in metaphorical pyrotechnics. . . .

At the same time the dexterity is something more than merely verbal. Apart from sheer metaphoric zest the performance aims at giving the reader the sense of immediate physical action. It is a prose which has indeed largely abandoned that "choiceness of the phrase, and the sweet falling of the clauses, and the varying and illustration . . . with tropes and figures" (to quote the familiar complaint of Bacon in *The Advancement of Learning* about sixteenth-century prose), but instead of anticipating Bacon's ideal prose with its "weight of matter, worth of subject, soundness of argument, life of invention, and depth of judgment," Nashe offers a series of particular physical impressions which are chiefly concerned with movement of some kind. Where the underlying idea is static or abstract it is endowed by the imagery with movement and solidity; where it is already one of physical movement, that life and movement is extended and exaggerated for Nashe's grotesque purposes. There is certainly "life of invention," but hardly of the kind demanded by Bacon or exemplified in his own prose. Imagery, taking it at a conveniently simple level, is the placing of two elements in a particular equivalence. The art of reading consists very largely in the comprehension of such equivalences of language.

A. K. Croston
RES (April, 1948), pp. 90-91

From these various pronouncements of Nashe some idea may now be gathered of the place he occupies in critical history. Of orthodox judgments and doctrines he provides ample traces; yet the most striking feature of his work is the divorce existing between his earlier orthodoxy and his later general practice. In other words, the development in his ideas concerning literature and literary expression in particular. In matters of poetry he shares the limited views of many of his contemporaries; but in treating of style he is an individualist, announcing confidently the changes that seemed to him inevitable. And in so doing he reflected the changing ideals of his age, those principles of realism and individualism that were breathing fresh life into the popular drama. Herein then lies his most valuable contribution to critical doctrine. Something more than a mere voice from the underworld of letters, he presents his views in enthusiastic and forcible fashion, thereby sounding an alarm against fixed rules and standards, and claiming for natural instincts their due place in literary ventures.

J. W. H. Atkins
English Literary Criticism: The Renascence
(London: Methuen, 1951), pp. 186-87

It was natural that Nashe, a writer responding fully in his sensibility to the new world, but not yet fully conscious of what it meant to be a bourgeois, should write a book like *The Unfortunate Traveller*, perhaps the most remarkable picaresque story in our language. *The Unfortunate Traveller* is a hotch-potch; it has no central core to it. It is the story of the adventures of a young man, Jack Wilton, who has almost all the characteristics of the outcast rogue. He is the servant of a nobleman and therefore has a certain place in society, but in no sense does he "belong" to that society or feel himself in any way morally bound to its standards. The sense of "not belonging" is increased by sending him to the Continent for all his adventures. I emphasize this point because it is what determines the form of the picaresque novel, its casual shapelessness. It is a series of incidents held together by no informing plan, by nothing save the presence of the hero, who is himself a vagabond whose life has no centre and no pattern.

Behind *The Unfortunate Traveller* there is no consistent moral attitude beyond a concern in getting out of awkward situations, and a rather superficial anti-Catholicism; but there is a powerful curiosity (vigorous rather than consistent) about the sixteenth-century world and a remarkable attempt to get the physical "feel" of that world on to paper.

It is not surprising that the early picaresque stories lacked a consistent moral standpoint which might have given them pattern, for the social outcasts with whom they dealt were not yet a conscious class with a conscious ethic. Nashe's Jack Wilton, like Rabelais' Panurge, is an utterly irresponsible character who gets his vitality from his irrepressible determination to hold his own in a world for which he has no respect. But until bourgeois man had a clearer idea both of what he stood for and of what he was up against his social and literary adventures were bound to be a series of disconnected skirmishes lacking a central significance.

Arnold Kettle
An Introduction to the English Novel (London:
Hutchinson's Univ. Library, 1951), vol. I, pp. 24-25

In its careful cultivation on the wayward and the unexpected *Pierce Penilesse* has some of the qualities of the medley poem and is more like Byron's
Don Juan than almost anything written in the interval between them. In
both works the author dramatizes his own personality in that of the hero
and comments on his own times. In both he emphasizes the apparent disorder of his work and makes the same excuse. . . .

This excuse does not mean, however, that Nashe had no literary precedents in mind when he wrote it. Had he been pressed to account for his
apparent formlessness, he would probably, I think, have pointed to the
writings of the Roman satirists and especially to the example of Juvenal.
He had announced his intention of being "satyricall" in the *Anatomy of
Absurdity*, and the fact that Greene in his *Groatsworth of Wit* actually addresses him as "yong *Iuuenal*, that byting Satyrist" would seem to indicate
that he saw some Juvenalian features in Nashe's work. Nor was he wrong
to do so. Like Nashe, Juvenal has often been criticized for weak powers of
construction. Moreover, some of the devices they use are similar; both are
fond of the dramatic effect that can be derived from a sudden transition from
indirect to direct speech and back again. . . . Inheriting the two traditions of
satire, the classical and the mediaeval, Nashe marries them to each other.
Pierce Penilesse is the fruit of their union, resembling both in some ways,
yet fundamentally like neither. Two features in particular distinguish it from
its literary parents: first, the deliberate infusion into it of a personality;
secondly, the absence from it of that moral fervour which Juvenal and
Langland have in common. For Nashe, by the time he comes to write *Pierce
Penilesse*, satire is neither a vehicle for despairing protest, as it had been
for Juvenal, nor an impassioned plea for reform, as it had been for Langland, but rather a stage, a convenient platform, on which he can exhibit his
virtuosity as a writer. . . .

In most of his writings he has no subject in the sense that he is not wholly
absorbed in what he is saying, not concerned solely with conveying the
nature and significance of something he is deeply interested in. Instead of
his eye being fixed on a topic, it is fixed on himself writing about that topic,
on the kind of figure he is cutting in the public eye, on the effect he is making. The way he says a thing counts for more with him than the thing said.
It is for this reason that he is, and always has been, a minor writer.

G. R. Hibbard
Thomas Nashe: A Critical Introduction (Cambridge, Mass.:
Harvard Univ. Pr., 1962), pp. 63-64

GEORGE PEELE
ca. 1558-1596

Born in London. Son of a maker of pageants who was a clerk of Christ's Hospital. Educated at Christ's Hospital grammar school. Studied at Oxford. Took B.A. in 1577, M.A. in 1579. Returned to Oxford from London in 1583 to direct a performance of two Latin plays by William Gager. Spent the remainder of his life in London. Wrote for the stage. Associated with Marlowe, Nashe, and Greene. Seems to have lived a fairly profligate life. Supposed exploits and practical jokes circulated in a book called the *Jests of George Peele*, printed in 1605. Earliest play, *Arraignment of Paris,* acted before Queen Elizabeth by Children of Chapel Royal. Prepared several pageants for London guilds. Buried in the Parish of St. James, Clerkenwell, in London.

C. T. Prouty, ed, *The Life and Works of George Peele* (1952—in progress)

*The Old Wive's Tale**

The extant version of *The Old Wive's Tale* is seen to represent a playhouse revision of the comedy to make it capable of performance by a smaller company than that for which it was first written. The play is usually dated about 1590-1, and the quarto was issued in 1595. During the intervening years it formed part of the repertory of the Queen's Company. It is interesting therefore to watch the history of this Company and to find that the Queen's men spent a good deal of time during these years touring the provinces. *The Old Wive's Tale* is one of a number of plays given over to the printer by the Queen's men soon after their arrival back in London in financial straits in 1594. There can be no reasonable doubt that it is the provisional text that we have.

Adaptation of plays for provincial performance was no uncommon practice. A company would have fewer players in the provinces, and during 1590-1 the Queen's Company toured in two separte bands. One of them seems to have combined temporarily with Sussex's, but the other must have been very much smaller than a full London company. Beyond the fact that the cast was usually somewhat limited in size, there is unfortunately little evidence of the kind of performances the country towns were likely to get. Possibly they often had to be content with shorter pieces than the London audiences, but, however common abridgement was, that can hardly account for the unique brevity of *The Old Wive's Tale*. A play as short as this may perhaps have been fobbed off upon some of the less remunerative towns, or this text may possibly have been prepared for a particular occasion when a very short play was required. That can only be conjecture. What is clear,

* Variously spelled as *Wives, Wife's, Wives', Wive's*

however, is that there are unmistakable signs of cutting and adaptation; and what is less obvious, but at least probable, from the general state of the text, is that the abridgement was of a very thoroughgoing nature.

The play as we have it may represent little more than the bare bones of Peele's original play, and this must affect our view of it as a dramatic work. While the author charmingly reflects in the tale itself the *naïveté* of the old woman who tells the tale, I believe that Peele intended her to pick her muddled way through all its legends in much more leisurely fashion, and that however deliberately he may have contrived the impression of confusion and unsubtle juxtaposition of episodes, a great deal of what seems like the abruptness and incompleteness of his treatment of the story is the accidental result of abridgement.

Harold Jenkins
MLR (April, 1939), pp. 184-85

The most interesting problem of the play [*The Old Wives' Tale*] is not the date but the interpretation. Until recently critics have been unanimous in describing it as a burlesque of romantic comedy, the genre which begins with *Clyomon and Clamydes* and reaches its climax with *A Winter's Tale*. According to this view *The Old Wives' Tale* is the first literary satire, an early *Knight of the Burning Pestle*. Lately, however, there has been a tendency to regard it as a serious attempt at romantic comedy with the addition of satirical bits, such as the characterization of Huanebango. Today, indeed, its confused and absurd action makes it sound like ridicule. If so, however, it is ridicule more subtle than was usual among Elizabethan playwrights. . . .

The alternative to accepting the literary satire theory is not rejecting *The Old Wives' Tale* as a poor play. Let us grant that there is no disputing the mediocrity of its characterization and verse. Structurally, also, it is apparently bad: the two plots weave around each other with the seeming purposelessness of a dream. But here may be the clue of what Peele had in mind when he wrote it. . . .

Its sources are drawn from the fairy tales of folk lore. Peele may have heard the two Irish tales of "Beauty and the World" and "The King of Ireland's Son" related by his mother while the family was gathered around the hearth at home. In spirit the play is not very far removed from *The Arraignment of Paris*. The *Arraignment* appealed to a more sophisticated audience only because for proper appreciation the classicism of its mythology required a bookish education and because the closeness of its adherence to court-of-love philosophy gave it the inner-circle touch. *The Old Wives' Tale* is the *Arraignment* brought down to the hearthside level. It is the sort of thing the Children of the Chapel might have done extremely well if they had ever stopped playing grownup and acted for a while as children.

If it is accepted on these terms and not judged by the standards of either the romantic comedy or the literary satire, it begins to develop excellences which before were defects. One of these is the fitting dialogue of the homely characters: the three pages, Madge, Clunch, Wiggen, Corebus, the Church-warden, and the Sexton. . . . Deserving of special note also are the songs, effective, like all of Peele's, because of their extreme simplicity. But the par-ticular excellence of the play is still its dream quality. Bits of folk lore flicker in and out like fragments of memory of the days when the world was young. It is significant that Peele caused Madge, the storyteller, to go to sleep. The play, if done in today's experimental theater, could be applauded as expres-sionistic. In the dramatist's own day it may not have appealed to the gallery of the public play house, which looked for something more esoteric, but the groundlings should have liked it, and when they stop cracking nuts the groundlings of any age are not to be ignored.

David H. Horne
The Life and Minor Works of George Peele (New Haven,
Conn.: Yale Univ. Pr., 1952), pp. 89-91

Of Peele's five dramatic works, *The Old Wives' Tale* stands out as the most successful. In all the others he so playfully imitates themes and forms of his contemporaries that he ends up with no more than a pastiche. *The Arraign-ment of Paris*, for all of its graceful pageantry, never does harmonize the pastoral theme of unrequited love and the mythological one of the fate of Paris. And, though *David and Bethsabe* has some exotically sensual love poetry and some striking insights into sin and expiation, it never does quite reconcile its morality-play account of David and Bethsabe's sin and its *Tamburlaine*-like handling of the battle scenes. But in *The Old Wives' Tale* Peele seems able to use his playfulness to greater advantage, and, as a result, he has fashioned one of the freshest and most quixotically charming of Elizabethan comedies. A very important secret of his success is his resource-ful use of different literary worlds—a method he may have learned from Lyly. However, Peele goes beyond Lyly, and, in fact, most of his other contemporaries, for he does not stop at simple contrast but has these differ-ent worlds interact upon one another and blend together. . . .

To begin with, the humor of speech and subject matter is really one mani-festation of a much broader interplay that results from the interaction of folklore and many other literary worlds. This more inclusive interplay ex-presses itself in the relationship between characters and in the presentation of individual characters.

In the first type, characters from widely different literary worlds find com-mon ground, and, despite their apparent differences, accept one another readily. . . .

The second type of interplay depends more upon complex and shifting interaction of literary worlds and seems to individualize the characters. Peele takes stock types, like the folklore heroine, the enchanter, or the *miles gloriosus,* and has them constantly echo themes, lines, or actions of stock characters from other Elizabethan literary worlds. The result of this constant echoing is that each character becomes a composite of types and evokes in the audience varied feelings associated with the literary worlds from which he is drawn. Yet each character is more than the sum of his parts, for the various echoings make the characters more distinctively individual than they might otherwise be.

Herbert Goldstone
Boston Univ. Stud. in Eng. (Winter, 1960) pp. 205-7

In *The Old Wives'* Tale there is no need for information, orderly sequence of plot, or dramatic connexion, since the enchanted princess "as white as snow and as red as blood"; her two brothers, who seek her; the wicked enchanter; the wandering knight; the beggar with his two daughters, one fair and curst, the other foul and patient; the Spanish Knight with his two-handed sword have been met with by the audience many times before the play began. They had no need to play an action: merely to display themselves for what they were. "When I was a little one, you might have drawne me a mile after you with such a discourse."

So, whether as the result of the actors' cutting or not, when the Two Brothers meet Erestus, the enchanted knight—who is also addressed as "the white bear of England's wood" (a title from medieval romance) and once as "Father Time,"—he does not need to be told their story, but can ask at once "Is she fair?" In performance, this seems perfectly natural; the perplexity felt by a reader melts away. When, through simultaneous setting, the audience is released from the confines of place, they cannot be tied to narrative progression.

The fluid life of such plays, like that of ballads, belonged within folk tradition, where the marvellous must always be familiar, though it cannot be rational. Recognition of the familiar and delight by the unexpected must be evenly balanced for the audience to be "rapt." Consistency of mood, the power to absorb the fancy and lull the feelings, binds simplified characters together in a fantastic action, dependent on riddles and magic shews. Each figure was so familiar that as he came forward to give his sequence, it would have been natural for the audience, if pleased, to demand a little more—to cry for the braggart to come back; in Bottom's phrase, "Let him roar again." In fact the first sequence of the boastful Spaniard, Juan y Bango (Huanebango) may have been inserted as an addition in this way; it is somewhat out of key with the rest of the play, the Clown is given a different name in it, and it contains specific literary allusions which place it in or about 1591. The core of the play consists of adventures familiar from tales of wandering knights, many of which had been turned into plays; but the groupings of these characters are drawn from medley plays, which the Queen's Men had given at other times. In these plays there is no narrative sequence: instead, variety of spectacle effects unity of mood or temper.

M. C. Bradbrook
ES (October, 1962), pp. 324-25

OTHER PLAYS

Nevertheless, even apart from its lyrics, one of which is in its way unsurpassed, the play [*The Arraignment of Paris*] contains passages of real grace in the versification. The greater part is written either in fourteeners or in decasyllabic couplets with occasional alexandrines, in both of which the author displays an ease and mastery which, to say the least, were uncommon in the dramatic work of the early eighties; while the passages of blank verse introduced at important dramatic points, notably in Paris' defence and in Diana's speech, are the best of their kind between Surrey and Marlowe. The style, though now and again clumsy, is in general free from affectation except for an occasional weakness in the shape of a play upon words. . . .

With regard to the general construction of the piece it is hardly too much to say that the skill with which the author has enlarged a masque-subject into a regular drama, altered a classical legend to subserve a particular aim, and conducted throughout the multiple perhaps rather than complex threads of his plot, mark him out as pre-eminent among his contemporaries. We must not, it is true, look for perfect balance of construction, for adequacy of dramatic climax, or for subtle characterization; but what has been achieved was, in the stage of development at which the drama had then arrived, no mean achievement. The dramatic effects are carefully prepared for and led up to, reminding us almost at times of the recurrence of a musical motive. Thus the song between Paris and Oenone, just before the shepherd goes off to cross Dame Venus' path, is a fine piece of dramatic irony as well as a charming lyric.

W. W. Greg
Pastoral Poetry and Pastoral Drama (London:
A. H. Bullen, 1906), pp. 22-23

The four canonical plays of Peele thus show a strong resemblance, particularly in structure. In each is a large number of plots, four stories being used in *The Arraignment of Paris, The Old Wives Tale,* and *David and Bethsabe,* and five in *Edward I.* Moreover, in each there is extraneous material. In much the same way every play shows structural weakness because the dramatist failed to combine and order his plots to the best advantage. In *The Arraignment* and *David and Bethsabe* the plots are not well integrated because the main threads of action are spliced, not interwoven; one plot ends before another begins, so that each play gives the effect of presenting not one story but several. Though in *Edward I* and *The Old Wives Tale* the merging of the plots is more successful, the plots are developed by fits and jerks so that the effect of a smoothly running story is destroyed. A serious and fundamental lack of unity is characteristic of every play known to be by Peele.

A discursive, haphazard, chronicle type of structure is indeed the norm to which Peele's dramas conform, and a further element of weakness is the incoherent development of the individual plots. In *The Arraignment* the fate of Paris is left in doubt; in *Edward I* the Mortimer-Ellen story and possibly also the Edward-Baliol story lack conclusions; the development of the Erestus-Venelia plot in *The Old Wives Tale* is unsatisfactory; while the David-Bethsabe and the Absolon-David plots in *David and Bethsabe* show various defects in development. In working out even a single story, Peele was apt to burden the action with useless incidents or to arrive at a weak and straggling conclusion.

Closely allied with the incoherent development of the single plots is a faulty proportion in dealing with certain scenes. In *The Arraignment* too much space is allotted to the reception of the goddesses by the rural deities; in the same way excessive emphasis is placed on the Robin Hood scenes in *Edward I*. *The Old Wives Tale* gives several examples, notably the *dénouement,* in which the action is developed in a very sketchy fashion. On the other hand, humorous scenes are overemphasized. In *David and Bethsabe* the climax of the love affair of David in the death of Urias is related in a chorus, while the scene in which Urias is made drunk is over-elaborated.

To what, then, may we attribute the popularity of Peele's plays in his own day? The answer is that Peele understood the tricks of the stage of his time. Pageant effects appear in all his dramas, and no play contains less than three songs, while *The Arraignment* originally had eleven.

One other characteristic of Peele is his fondness for balancing one plot against another. In *The Arraignment* Paris' desertion of Œnone is balanced by Thestylis' ill-treament of Colin. In *Edward I* the duel of Edward and Lluellen is balanced by the duel of David and Mortimer. In *The Old Wives Tale* the Huanebango-Zantippa plot is contrasted with the Corebus-Celanta episodes, while in *David and Bethsabe* David's adultery is paralleled by Ammon's incest.

A. M. Sampley
PMLA (September, 1936), pp. 699-700

May we not assume that it was the Bible's bathing-scene, with its intrinsic similarity to contemporary poetic themes, that first stirred Peele's imagination and attracted him to the subject of *David and Bethsabe*? And do we not then, as we continue to read the play, see that Peele is not merely out to give us a *de casibus* play on David's sins of the flesh and the divine punishment for them, nor just to chronicle a Bible story? He is also out, in the Ovidian fashion, to show us the beauties of the flesh and of the senses—"The *Love* of King David and *Fair* Bethsabe"—and he does it through the very texture of his poetry.

A modern reader, especially if he is trying to squeeze the play in under such labels as "Miracle play" or "Biblical Chronicle," is likely to find Peele's poetry incongruous with his dramatic subject. An Elizabethan, presented at the very opening of the play with a scene familiar from tapestries and poems, is bound to have seen through the Bible episode the Ovidian mythological one—each by itself and both together. What we—if we forget pre-conceived expectations derived from subject and supposed "genre"—may, then, take with us from the play, is a sense of the rich eclecticism that we find in so much Renaissance poetry. Or, perhaps "comprehensiveness" is a better word for what we have seen in *David and Bethsabe*: a power of holding together within one frame both classical and biblical myth, making the two one.

Inga-Stina Ekeblad
ES (April, 1958), pp. 61-62

SIR WALTER RALEGH
1552?-1618

Born in Devonshire. Attended Oxford but left in 1572 without taking a degree. Joined his half brother, Sir Humphrey Gilbert, in an expedition against the Spaniards in 1578. Helped suppress Desmonds in Munster, Ireland, in 1580. Came to court as protégé of the Earl of Leicester. Won the patronage of Queen Elizabeth. Granted many privileges, including a License to export woolen goods. Explored the coast of North America from Florida to the Carolinas. In 1585 sent settlers to occupy Roanoke Island, but they deserted the colony in the following year. Made various attempts to colonize Virginia, which he had named in honor of Queen Elizabeth. Introduced potatoes and tobacco into England. Became a friend of Edmund Spenser in Ireland. Banished by Elizabeth because of his secret marriage to Elizabeth Throckmorton, one of her maids. Went on an expedition to Guiana, explored the coasts of Trinidad, and sailed up the Orinoco river in 1595. Took part in an expedition against Cadiz in 1596 and an attack upon the Azores in 1597. Stripped of his offices upon the death of Elizabeth in 1603. Imprisoned in the Tower of London on charges of conspiring against King James I. Lived with his wife and son in the Tower, where he wrote the *History of the World,* published in 1614. Released to lead an expedition in search of gold along the Orinoco river. Returned to England in 1618 after losing his fleet in a storm, many of his men dead of disease. Had angered the Spanish minister by the destruction of the Spanish town of San Tomàs. On demand of the Spanish minister the old sentence against him was revived and he was beheaded in 1618.

Agnes M. C. Latham, ed., *The Poems of Sir Walter Ralegh* (1951)

PERSONAL

Our résumé of Ralegh's opinions on chronology brings to a close a survey of his beliefs in terms of the principal Elizabethan meanings of "atheism." On God and the soul, on personal and political ethics, on natural philosophy, and lastly on chronology, where no hint of "men before Adam" prevails against scriptural authority, Ralegh holds staunchly to orthodox positions. Charges of atheism, in any sober Elizabethan sense except perhaps the ethical, cannot be made to stick. There is, of course, ample room for misunderstanding (apart from the inevitable distortions of personal dislike or distrust) in confusion of meanings, as in the debate with the Reverend Ralph Ironside; or in the conflicting attitudes of the age toward scientific studies; or in the independence of judgment which Ralegh reserves to himself in matters where "the Scriptures are silent, and it is no point of our saving belief." But the man revealed in these chapters is obedient to the religious code of his day, yet anxious to define and if possible to enlarge the limits of free intellectual inquiry. . . .

Finally—and briefly, since this entire study is pertinent to the question— I find little agreement between the doctrines credited to the "School of Night" and the opinions of Ralegh that can be derived from his own speeches or writings. The doctrines of the "School," as variously described by proponents of the theory, imply more radical departures from orthodox religious thought than I have been able to find in Ralegh. He had a driving curiosity, abetted by an impulsiveness of temperament, which led him to seek knowledge where he could find it; but these very qualities make him a poor candidate for a coterie. In his studies he commonly sought practical ends: improved navigation; better ships; a more effective cure-all in physic; success in politics; a stronger empire—and personal power. When he is meditative and speculative, as he often is and in the grand manner, he keeps within the limits of a serious, even somber, ethic and an orthodox religion.

The fundamental difficulty of the "School of Night" theory, of course, goes back to Shakespeare's text. Those who propound the theory find an allusion in *Love's Labour's Lost* and develop to the utmost the topical possibilities of that play, with the result that, as in most studies of Elizabethan topical allusions, identifications abound and conflict. I find no personal allusion in the King's scoffing rejection of Berowne's praise of his "black" lady, and I believe that other evidence for a "School" has been applied too selectively to be convincing. The great value of studies of the "School of

Night" has been the light they have thrown upon some literary relationships and theories in the flourishing last decade of the sixteenth century. That value remains even when we abandon attempts to organize these impermanent and often casual associations into formally opposed coteries, and to discover in Shakespeare's play topical allusions of a subtlety one would be surprised to meet in Elizabethan literature.

Ernest A. Strathmann
Sir Walter Ralegh: A Study in Elizabethan Skepticism (New York:
Columbia Univ. Pr., 1951), pp. 218, 270-71

GENERAL

If the passages I have stressed are reflectively considered it will be obvious how discriminating is Coleridge's judgment, and what a great achievement the early Elizabethan style really was. These writers carried out a work quite as heavy, though less noticeable, than that of their successors: and the new lyric school of the nineties was only possible because foundations had been laid for it. In bringing rhythmic forms to a greater flexibility and resilience, and in developing a pure and sonorous vocabulary, they prepared the way for the rich complexity of the dramatists and the "metaphysicals." The revolt from what later seemed a heavy and formal way of writing was partly the result of the greater malleability and stability of the language which that style had brought about, and which offered a firm basis for variation and experiment.

Ralegh was one of the pioneers. His characteristic accent, representing his technical contribution to English verse, was slow and emphatic, open vowels weighted by rich alliteration:

> Oblivion laid him down on Laura's hearse.

But he did not always move in such heavy brocade: in his songs he developed varieties of tempo rather than sound-patterns. *The Lie,* for instance, is built on parallel clauses and a slightly varied refrain, which comes in at the end of each stanza like a dagger thrust, and emphasizes the brute energy of the vituperation. The matter of the poems shifts more in the method of approach than in the method of presentation. By control of the tempo (i.e. "total rhythm"), Ralegh gets all the contrasts which a later poet would have expressed by imagery or description.

M. C. Bradbrook
The School of Night (Cambridge Univ. Pr., 1936), pp. 78-79

The book [*The History of the World*] made its immediate appeal, not least because of a personal illumination we can find in hardly any historian. The narrative is always apt to be lit up by some tersely vivid citation from experience. This is what I saw done in the French wars. This is the true doctrine of defense, whether by land or sea; and I can illustrate it by what I saw in "eighty-eight," the great Armada year, and by my own taking of Fayal. He breaks off his discussion of the wars between Rome and Macedon to compare English and Roman soldiers in valor. He takes occasion, when telling of the Amazons of classical legend, to glance at an old sneer against himself, who had also brought back a rumor of Amazons.

But when all is said, it was by its style, so laden with music and solemn reflection, that the book won such acceptance, and most of all from the few who have been Ralegh's peers. His influence on Milton's style has never been considered; it is greater, I believe, than that of any other English prose writer. If you ask for literal proof, there are particularities which reappear in *Paradise Lost,* such as the warfare waged between Griffins and Arimaspi, for the former's hoarded gold. But the real proof lies in the cadence, the mingling of imagination and of personal pathos. Keats has observed that in Milton there is a pathos found in no other writer, of an allusive and almost muttered kind, passed off in parenthesis, where none but another poet would note it:

> rocks and stones had ears
> To rapture, till the savage clamour drowned
> Both voice and song (nor could the Muse defend
> Her son). . . .

Every student of Milton's work knows how this utterance in an undertone, as if to himself, will startle in some prose passage of a very different kind. I know no other writer who has it, of this precise quality, except Ralegh. In the Preface to the *History* are sentences which, quoted to a sensitive ear without indication of their context, might be guessed immediately and wrongly as the work of Milton.

Edward Thompson
Sir Walter Ralegh, Last of the Elizabethans (New Haven,
Conn.: Yale Univ. Pr., 1936), pp. 256-57

The breadth and depth of Ralegh's genius are best revealed in his prose, into which he put more of his heart and soul than went into his brilliant verse—and which alone he intended for the English nation and for posterity. The difference is worth repeating; it is the difference between the bagpipe and the organ. Ralegh was a daring and accomplished master of both. The one is dashing, shrill, and provocative; the other of a sonorous dignity which few English writers have equalled. One famous sentence of Ralegh's stands in all good anthologies as the *ne plus ultra* of prose eloquence, matchable with the best of Sir Thomas Browne or De Quincey:

O eloquent, just, and mighty Death! whom none could advise, thou hast persuaded; what none hath dared, thou hast done; and whom all the world hath flattered, thou only hast cast out of the world and despised: thou hast drawn together all the far-stretched greatness, all the pride, cruelty, and ambition of man, and covered it all over with these two narrow words, *Hic jacet!*

This is the rich and solemn melody to which is set nearly all of Ralegh's formal prose. . . .

What the gipsy palmists say of the lines of the two hands might be said of the two sides of Ralegh's work. One shows the spirit with which he was born, and which never ceased to be fundamental in him—a high romantic spirit. The other shows what he made himself when under the influence of courtly feud and self-seeking. The lower voice sounds often in what he wrote on impulse without view to publication. We hear the higher voice when he looks beyond the court and writes consciously for posterity. Prose is then his language, and he speaks a noble tongue. His greatest prose writings—the *History of the World,* the *Discovery of Guiana,* and the *Last Fight of the Revenge*—are splendid monuments of his romantic spirit. They show him to have been a deeply original thinker and moralist, a glorious patriot, and an enthusiastic amateur of the marvels of life.

C. F. Tucker Brooke
ELH (June, 1938), pp. 101-3

While I believe *The Ocean to Cynthia* presents an interesting document to the psychologist, I have no wish to treat it as a mere record. It is a poem, or at least a lump of poetry, *madre d'oro.* The breaks, the fragmentariness and incoherence may also indicate that Ralegh is feeling for a form he never found, that he is not even sure what kind of poem he is trying to write.

But because of its apparent spontaneity, and the crowd and huddle of images of a kind we do not find in his other poems, because it touches depths few of his other poems reach, it seems fair to ask what light this poem throws on the nature of Ralegh's imagination; of his imagination, that is, as it found expression in words, and not in clothes, ships or colonies. It suggests that the poet in him responded to power and vastness in nature, to its creative and destructive force; that he finds in it an energy which answers to his own. Negatively it suggests that the power and vastness of the ocean hardly touch him. It is true that *The Ocean to Cynthia,* in spite of its title, is about something steadfast which has been shaken, something growing uprooted. But it can be demonstrated that almost nowhere in his other poems is there a reference to the sea that is more than conventional. The same is true of the prose.

Joyce Horner
EIC (July, 1955), pp. 206-7

JAMES SHIRLEY
1596-1666

Born in London. Baptized in the parish of St. Mary Woolchurch. Entered
Merchant Taylors' School in 1608. Left in 1612. Appears to have attended
Oxford for a short while and to have left without taking a degree.
Matriculated at St. Catherine's College, Cambridge, in 1615. Took B.A.
in 1617. Probably wrote narrative poem, *Echo and Narcissus*, while at
Cambridge. Entered clergy. On June 1, 1618, married Elizabeth Gilmet
of St. Albans, daughter of a prominent family. Several children born.
Was Master of St. Albans Grammar School by January 1621. Left the
post in July 1624 following conversion to Roman Catholicism. For a
while was a student at Gray's Inn. Began to write plays in London.
Earliest one, *Love Tricks*, written in 1624. Wrote for the Cockpit theater
under the management of Christopher Beeston. Named Valet of the
Chamber to Queen Henrietta Maria. Went to Ireland in 1623 when the
London theaters were closed because of the plague. Wrote for the Dublin
theater. Published plays in Ireland. Made trips back to London in 1637
and 1638. Upon return to England in 1640 began to write plays for
King's Men at Blackfriars. Supported Royalist cause during the Civil War.
Retired to obscurity in London after the triumph of Parliamentary forces.
Returned to teaching school. Little known of his life after the Restoration.
Driven from home by the Great Fire of London. Died on the same day
as his wife, probably as a result of the fire. Both buried in a single grave
at Church of St. Giles in the Fields, London.

W. Gifford and A. Dyce, eds., *The Dramatic Works and Poems of James
Shirley* (1883), 6 vols.

Dramatic romance—distinguished from romantic comedy chiefly by stress
upon surprising revelations of the plot rather than upon the depiction or
development of character—is Shirley's most frequent, though not most
fruitful field. It is, moreover, the type in which Shirley's work most closely
approximates the work of Fletcher. Slightly suggested in the masque and
pastoral elements of *Love Tricks*, in the maiden-page of *The Wedding,* and
in the miracles of *St. Patrick for Ireland,* this Fletcherian type is thoroughly
exemplified in the oracle, the disguises, and the surprising dénouement of
The Arcadia; in the incognito, the extravagance, and the startling resolution
of *The Bird in a Cage;* in the concealed identity and kaleidoscopic changes
of *The Coronation;* in the exchanged positions of Giovanni and Thomazo
in *The Gentleman of Venice;* in the shifting love, the maiden-page, and the
successive revolutions of *The Doubtful Heir;* and, finally, in the blending
of surprise and of suspense in the double imposture of *The Court Secret.*
Slight as several of these romances are, they are lacking neither in interest
nor in poetic charm. At their best, they have a tensity of climax and an

unexpectedness of outcome that hold one breathless. Whatever their weaknesses, they demonstrate at least Shirley's mastery of romantic plot.

Arthur Nason
James Shirley, Dramatist (New York:
A. H. Nason, 1915), pp. 393-94

In comedy Shirley produced two types of plays: comedies of manners, and romances. . . . With one exception the scenes of the former are laid in London—the lively London of Charles I—and the characters are those whom Shirley knew well from experience: men about town, not necessarily court figures, of considerable wealth and wit. . . . In the romantic comedies, fourteen in number, he turned to Mediterranean settings and staged his action almost invariably in court. These plays are properly tragi-comedies, the consequences of their serious main plots being averted only by surprise endings in the final act.

Shirley considered *The Cardinal* (1614) his finest achievement. The student will find in it rather striking reminiscences of Webster's *Duchess of Malfi,* but it must be granted that the work is not entirely unworthy of its model. . . .

He was not a first-rate poet, not as fine as [John] Ford, for example, and incapable of Ford's poignancy and depth. But he possessed, by way of compensation, the virtues of balance, of smooth diction, of skill in plot construction; his plays are both easily read and interesting. In spite of his chronological position, he deserves to be remembered among the greater writers of his age.

Edd Winfield Parks and Richmond Croom Beatty, eds.
The English Drama (New York: W. W. Norton, 1935), pp. 1364-65

The foregoing similarities, since they equate peculiarities that are not found elsewhere in the early drama, seem hardly to be accidental ones. But, regardless of the extent to which Steele and Cibber may have been indebted, these resemblances are characteristic of the many points of contact between Shirley's practice of sentimentalism and that of the eighteenth-century comic playwrights. Not only Beaumont and Mistress Wilding, but approximately one-half of Shirley's principal comic characters are, in their marked esteem of virtue, the forebears of the Amandas, the Bookwits, the Lady Easys, and the Bevil Juniors of the later sentimental school; their dominant characteristic is a self-realized and confident awareness of the fundamental goodness of mankind, a factor that explains the invariable triumph of conscience in Shirley's plays. Basically, there is one major difference that distinguishes the true sentimentalist from the playwright who occasionally indulges in a sentimental device: the former bases the entire thematic conception of his dramaturgy upon the doctrine that goodness, being inborn, is the ascendant attribute of human nature; the latter merely exploits a phase of this doctrine to the extent that it advantages the mechanics of his plot. By this yardstick, Shirley, who at almost every opportune crisis stressed the ascendant quality of inborn human goodness, often emphasizing it beyond its importance to the plot, was, in the manner of the eighteenth-century playwrights, a deliberate sentimentalist. But it cannot be argued, *a priori,* that he wrote sentimental comedy. The restrictions imposed upon him as a moralist were external ones; the Caroline audience would undoubtedly have hissed a thoroughly sentimental comedy from the boards. Only by means of forceful insinuation, as Cibber later recognized, could the idea of sentimentalism infiltrate the English comedy of manners and undermine, as it eventually did, the established tradition of indelicacy. Of this principle, Shirley was the first self-conscious advocate.

Robert R. Reed
Anglia (1955), pp. 169-70

SIR PHILIP SIDNEY
1554-1586

Born at Penshurst, father's estate in Kent. Son of Sir Henry Sidney, soldier and courtier. Entered Shrewsbury School in 1564. Entered Christ Church, Oxford, in 1568. Engaged to Ann Cecil, daughter of Lord Cecil, 1569. Match broken off. From 1572 to 1574 travelled abroad. Served in the train of his uncle, Robert Dudley, Earl of Leicester. Met many European dignitaries, including Peter Ramus, Hubert Languet, Johannes Sturm. Painted by Veronese in Padua. Attended reception at Kenilworth for Queen Elizabeth by the Earl of Leicester in July 1575. Engaged to Penelope Devereux, daughter of the Earl of Essex. Match broken off for reasons unknown. Went abroad again in 1577 as ambassador to the Emperor of Germany and Elector Palatine. Met Edmund Campion in Prague. In 1579, wrote the masque, *Lady of May* for the entertainment of the Queen by Leicester at Wanstead. Associated with Fulke Greville, Edward Dyer, and other literary figures. As part of the Areopagus club, interested in the use of classical quantitative meters in English verse. Quarrelled with the Earl of Oxford. In 1583 wrote *Defence of Poesy* in answer to Stephen Gosson. Banished from court in 1580 because of tract advising Queen against marriage to Duc d'Alençon. Retired to Wilton house, the home of his sister, the Countess of Pembroke. There completed the first draft of *Arcadia.* In 1580 Penelope Devereux married Lord Rich. *Astrophel and Stella* circulated in manuscript. Knighted in 1583. In the same year married Frances Walsingham and entertained Giordano Bruno. Went to Holland in 1585 as the Governor of Flushing. Served in campaigns against Spanish. Died of wounds received at the Battle of Zutphen. None of his work published during his lifetime.

A. Feuillerat, ed., *The Complete Works of Sir Philip Sidney* (1922-1926), 4 vols.

W. Ringler, ed., *The Poems of Sir Philip Sidney* (1964)

M. Wallace, *The Life of Sir Philip Sidney* (1915)

The New Arcadia

The *New Arcadia* is not an epic; for it has no formal invocation, it is written in prose, it introduces pastoral elements, it lacks a supernatural machinery. In all these points, however, it has the consistency of conscious art, and is in perfect harmony with the author's critical theories as described in the *Defence of Poesie*. Again, in its enormous complexity the *New Arcadia* is remote from the simple and noble outlines of the Homeric epic. Its subject matter, however, is heroic; for from the Renaissance point of view love is a theme appropriate to epic no less than to romance, and in the *New Arcadia* there are also the other stock themes of heroic poetry—adventure, war, and great national and even international events. Again, the narrative technique —the beginning *in mediis rebus*, the reporting by dramatic narration "things done in former time or other place," the scrupulous avoiding of unnecessary breaks, particularly in critical scenes—is precisely that which Minturno demands in the epic and is perfectly consistent with what Sidney requires in tragedy. Finally, in its structure it has in general the single great action and causal connection of events on which Minturno puts his greatest emphasis. The art of the *New Arcadia is* more conscious than that of the *Old,* and more consistent with the author's theories. Its structure is no less appropriate to the epic, its subject and above all its narrative method are conspicuously more appropriate, than those of the original version. That Sidney regarded the *Old Arcadia* as an heroic poem there is little or no evidence. There is strong reason for believing he so regarded the *New Arcadia*. . . .

The *Arcadia* is not a treatise about public and private virtue. Still less is it an idle tale, composed "to beguile a summer's holiday." Nor is it merely a composite work of varied texture, as Mr. Zandvoort suggests. It is an heroic poem which makes noble conduct beautiful. In both versions, to be sure, the lessons are numerous and quite as definite as is required by Sidney's theory. In the first draft, however, they are to be found in theoretical discussions no less than in the deeds of the characters and in their fates. Only in the revised work do the examples of men in action assume the importance that they have in the *Defence of Poesie*. The teaching is especially plain in the narrative of events prior to the main story, where time after time it is made clear by comparison or contrast. In the fable, too, the same method is often used, notably in the account of Amphialus; and at all times we judge men's behavior by the ideal standards which are so unmistakable in the episodes. In fact, just as these digressions help us to understand the course of events in the main action, so do they enable us to view the events from the author's ethical point of view. The teaching is deliberate, but even in the episodes it is unobtrusive; and to call the *Arcadia* a treatise is to overlook its pervading beauty.

Kenneth O. Myrick
Sir Philip Sidney as a Literary Craftsman (Cambridge, Mass.: Harvard Univ. Pr., 1935), pp. 149-50, 295

But the submission to convention is by no means a passive process, even if the poet does it so naturally that he never thinks of doing anything else. The convention, whether it involve setting, as in the pastoral, or tone, as in the elegy, or technique, as in the sestina, must obviously be freshened by continual re-examination so that it is re-made every time it is used . . . the convention has stimulated, has even created, those feelings. Once the poet has set himself the task of writing an amorous complaint, that deep melancholy which lay beneath the surface glamor of Elizabethan existence and which was so characteristic of Sidney himself, begins to fill the conventional form with a more than conventional weight. It surges through the magical adagio of the lines; they have that depth of reverberation, like the sound of gongs beaten under water, which is something characteristic of Sidney as of no other Elizabethan, not even Shakespeare.

The most famous of the poems in the *Arcadia,* in fact the only one which is at all well-known, is the sonnet in book three beginning "My true love hath my heart and I have his." The theme of the poem, the exchange of hearts, is a common one, and in the sestet, at least, it is expressed in a commonplace fashion, but there are two things about it which make it memorable: the monosyllabic simplicity of the diction (only twelve words are not monosyllables), and the flawless movement of the rhetoric. The poem is a perfectly drawn circle, ending most contentedly where it began: "My true love hath my heart, and I have his." This particular movement is something new in English sonnet writing; it is one more example of the continual experimenting which make the poems in the *Arcadia* such a striking revelation of what could—and sometimes of what could not—be done with the English tongue.

Theodore Spencer
ELH (December, 1945), pp. 267-68

The two great influences on Sidney's romance are the *Arcadia* (1501) of Sannazaro and the *Ethiopian History* (fourth century A.D.) of Heliodorus. There are of course others; Malory possibly, *Amadis* probably, and Montemayor's *Diana*. But Montemayor is himself largely a disciple of Sannazaro:

it is from Sannazaro and Heliodorus that the two kinds of fiction which Sidney is fusing really descend. . . .

The elaboration of the style, always, of course, most noticeable to those who have no taste for the matter, seems to me to lessen as the book goes on. But even at its most elaborate it does not exclude reality, though it is usually a heightened reality. Most of the characters are, no doubt, types and much that happens is improbable; but Sidney contrives to let us know very well the sort of people he is talking about. His artificiality is not of the kind which needs to be carefully protected; whenever he pleases he can drop into simplicity and no shock is felt. . . .

Yet characterization is not Sidney's main interest. The heart of the *Arcadia,* the thing for which it exists, which wrung from Milton even in his anger an admission of its "wit and worth," is its nobility of sentiment. We can almost say of Sidney as Johnson said of Richardson, "You must read him for the sentiment." Sidney assumes in his readers an agreed response to certain ideals of virtue, honour, friendship, and magnanimity. His conception of love is a Platonic elaboration of medieval *Frauendienst* —the theory, later expressed by Patmore, that erotic love can be a sensuous appetite of intelligible good. Hence he can speak of noble women as having "throwne reason vpon our desires and, as it were, giuen eyes to Cupid" (I. i). . . . And the second alternative is to be taken seriously. A lover is not to be suspected of self-deception when he says

the roote of my desire
Was vertue cladde in constant loues attire (1593, III).

At the same time, there is no notion that love has a right to override all claims. Infinite, so to speak, in one direction, it is, in another, rigidly bounded by different parts of the pattern of honour. It leaves the laws of friendship sacred. . . . Everything proposed for our admiration in the *Arcadia* is on that level, everything is good and fair and beyond the common reach. It was not written for a democracy. And though this exaltation may strain a modern reader it is never itself strained, never rings false like the later heroic drama. We can hardly doubt that it was among the lofty romances which Milton acknowledged as his textbooks of love and chastity, replete with those beauties whereof "not to be sensible argues a gross and swainish disposition."

C. S. Lewis
English Literature in the Sixteenth Century (Oxford: Clarendon Pr., 1954), pp. 333, 337-39

When Sidney revised the original *Old Arcadia* into the incomplete *New Arcadia* published in 1590, he elaborated his presentation of characters and ideas, his style, and, most saliently, his plot. Sidney actually changed his plot proper very little, but he did change his manner of presenting it, from *ab ovo* to *in medias res*. And he made really sizeable additions, which doubled the bulk of the book and changed its character, in the form of over a dozen episodes not integral to the plot. One of them is the captivity episode of Book III (itself longer than the original Book III), a mixture of moral temptation, tragedy, and medieval siege. To Book I he added three long amorous episodes, and, to Book II, nine interwoven short stories that involve the heroes' exploits before they came to Arcadia.

The most striking effect of these additions is, of course, complication: a simple and direct story became a complex book full of episodes weaving in and out of each other; a romance became a work that "is at once a romance and a treatise." But this complication is also, I believe, an amplification whereby the matter of the original main plot is diffused, reflected, moralized, and generally clarified in the many new episodes.

Walter R. Davis
SP (April, 1960), p. 123

Astrophel and Stella

Sidney's complaint poems also show a sharper psychological probing than Spenser's do; they depend less upon tone and more upon the dramatic expression of the speaker's feelings. The passion mounts to a genuine climax, as in the striking line

And stop mine eares lest I growe mad with Musicke.

This is not surprising in view of Sidney's sonnets, and the reader of the pastoral poems in *Arcadia* can also find the conflict between reason and passion which is a major motif in *Astrophel and Stella*. . . .

If the criteria of historical significance (i.e., influence) and of intrinsic value be considered together, certainly the sonnet cycle of Sir Philip Sidney, *Astrophel and Stella,* is the most important of Elizabethan sonnet cycles. It was written sometime about 1581-1583, published in a pirated edition in 1591, and finally issued with the authorization and textual supervision of Sidney's sister, the Countess of Pembroke, in the 1598 folio edition of the *Arcadia.* It circulated in manuscript copies, several of which have survived, and it was known to readers of poetry even before its first publication in 1591. *Astrophel and Stella* shares with Spenser's *Shepheardes Calender* the honor of inaugurating one of the greatest ages of English poetry. . . .

The significance of the Astrophel-Sidney identification lies in the fact that it solves the problem of the relationship between poet, subject matter, and reader. The professions of "sincerity," of plainness, of lack of art, are directed to the lady; she is not only subject matter but also a reader, within the framework of the convention of the sonnet cycle. The role of Astrophel is of course directed at Stella. The reader, an outsider in this situation, must go around through the lady's position to approach the poet. How much of her presumed attitude does he share? Not her coldness to the lover, perhaps; the sonnets, if successful, will move the reader even though they fail in their professed purpose of moving the lady. If the reader is persuaded, if he shares the emotion attributed to Astrophel, then there is the emotional ground for the control of decoration and "similitudes." As we recall, the force of a similitude, or the value of decoration, is not to prove anything to a contrary disputer but only to explain to a willing hearer. For Stella, then, unvarnished plainness and simplicity. For the reader, who goes beyond Stella in his sharing of the speaker's feelings, all the similitudes and decoration that the emotion will maintain. But the reader must partly share Stella's position, and so far as he does he will believe in the artlessness and simplicity of the poet, and the great feat of hiding art by art will be achieved.

Hallett Smith
Elizabethan Poetry (Cambridge, Mass.: Harvard
Univ. Pr., 1952), pp. 52, 142, 152

The exploration of Sidney's own personality is the subject of most of his serious sonnets. He views himself from many angles: as a literary artist, as a diplomat in the service of his country, as a soldier, as a cultured humanist, as a sincere practising Christian. His passion for Stella is, of course, the recurrent theme of every poem, and the problems to which it gives rise in relation to his activities, interests, and beliefs decide the character of his writing.

The sonnet tradition required that Stella should be endowed with all the womanly virtues. Accordingly she is chaste and fair; she exercises a beneficent influence upon those around her; above all, she inspires the poet to noble and unselfish conduct. Even in physical appearance she is a blood-relation to the Délies, the Dianes, and the Olives who populate the works of the *Pléiade*, and may trace her descent back to the incomparable Laura. But a closer inspection of Sidney's sonnets reveals a treatment of her character, and especially of the poet's reactions to it, which is markedly individual. . . . These hints and implications do not, and could not without violating the tradition, make up a sustained attack upon courtly love. Most often, Stella is described as in LXXI, as "Perfections heire," the embodiment of virtue and beauty, who strives "all minds that way to moue." As such she fulfills the part of the beloved in Plato's Symposium, and should guide the lover by ascending stages to the realm of pure ideas. Nevertheless in certain moods Astrophel is far from glad at having become involved with her at all: not because he meets with discouragement; not even because her marriage to another man stands in his way; but because he finds that his preoccupation with her distracts him from more serious concerns. The Platonic lover is, in effect, being driven to neglect his Plato. This is made very clear in the confession that, to a trusted observer, and even to himself in calmer moments, the affair appears disruptive and degrading, and that the experience may be resolved into nothing more than an overmastering infatuation of the senses. The lucid self-examination in sonnet XVIII completes the picture. The school of Petrarch had seen the beloved as the joint work of nature and heaven: Sidney finds that the lover too is a beneficiary of these powers, while his very love has robbed him of the means to repay his debt. . . . The sestet is a final bitter commentary on the moral confusion induced by passionate love. . . .

The principal theme of *Astrophel and Stella* appears, then, as a study of the inner conflicts that romance precipitates in the personality of a contemporary man. . . .

Since the expression of a complex personality was the driving force of Sidney's sonnets, it is to be expected that metre and diction should display an extraordinary range and flexibility. The Tudor pioneers of the sonnet had been largely concerned with the primary need to evolve a standard poetic diction and standard verse-rhythms. For them the simplest epithets and the purest English terms were the best. Sidney had already grasped the rudiments of their technique in the sonnets of *Arcadia*: he was free now to strike out for himself and invent his personal idiom. In *Astrophel and Stella* he coined such compounds as "rose-enameld skies," "past-praise hue," "long-with loue-acquainted eyes"; employed technical and somewhat recondite words like "quintessence," "metamorphosed," "demurre," "flegmatike"; and indulged in elaborate word-play and burlesque alliteration—

> Of touch they are that without touch doth touch (IX)

> Into your rimes, running in ratling rowes (XV)

Even more striking was his use of colloquialisms and current speech-rhythms. To a certain extent Wyatt had practised these methods in his sonnets, but he was never so confident of his medium as to ring the changes we find in *Astrophel and Stella*:

> Guesse we the cause, what is it thus? fie, no:
> Or so? much lesse: how then? sure thus it is: (LXXIV)

> What, he? say they of me, now I dare sweare,
> He cannot loue: no, no, let him alone. (LIV)

Sidney's metres are in fact so closely associated with speech-rhythms that they can hardly be considered separately.

J. W. Lever
The Elizabethan Love Sonnet (London: Methuen, 1956), pp. 71, 74, 86

Long-standing and firmly conventional forms of expression are one motive for the ornate style of the *Arcadia* poems. But there are more precise causes to be found in Sidney's own presentation of idealized love. I have said that he does not allegorize love as transcendental religious yearning in the manner of Dante or record its evolution towards piety in the manner of Petrarch, but for Sidney love is, nevertheless, a mode of worship. The difference is that for him beauty and virtue never became totally and exclusively symbolic. They prompt impulses identical or similar to those associated with religious adoration, which in its turn informs the language of amorous praise. . . .

What is evident in the opening statement of *Astrophel and Stella* governs, to a greater or lesser degree, the majority of its poems. For the sake of direct contact between the mind of Astrophel and that of the reader and for the sake of careful blocking out of Astrophel's thinking, Sidney has adopted a plastic style, shifting from formality to spontaneity, balance to variety, rhetorical amplitude to understatement or the conciseness of wit. And there is an analogy to these procedures in the total scheme of the sequence. It is, to repeat, compounded of several styles. . . .

There is no set pattern to the occurrence of these styles; the effect of their varied appearance, reappearance, and intermixture is to give us what C. S. Lewis calls an "anatomy of love," an imitation of the varied moods and mental operations of a poet-lover, introspective, despairing, confident, adoring, reproachful, jealous, angry, joyous, or resigned. It is axiomatic that for all of these no single mode of expression would be adequate, and it is particularly certain that the stylized consistency of the *Arcadia* verse would be a disaster. Yet in its place ornateness is appropriate. . . .

It is clear enough that *Astrophel and Stella* is a tissue of shifting moods and states of mind, a kaleidoscope of the lover's sensations. What is less clear is the persistence of Astrophel's need to look into himself, to assess the ground he stands on, to question and establish the geography of his emotions.

Robert P. Montgomery, Jr.
Symmetry and Sense: The Poetry of Sir Philip Sidney
(Austin, Tex.: Univ. Texas Pr., 1961), pp. 54, 85-86

GENERAL

Philip and Mary Sidney were not the first or the last patrons of letters in England; but they lived at a time when patronage fitted the current opinions on the nature of poetry, and when the poets most needed the enlightened and critical encouragement that they provided. So they took the occasion to shape and guide the poetry of the Elizabethan age towards a fullness of achievement that, in the 1570s, only they foresaw.

John Buxton
Sir Philip Sidney and the English Renaissance
(London: Macmillan, 1954), p. 32

Such then are the main contents of Sidney's *Apology for Poetry,* a work which has rightly been valued as one of the outstanding performances in English criticism and one which inaugurated a new phase in critical history. It has been described as an epitome of Renascence theory; but this description can be misleading if it is taken to mean nothing more than a summary reproduction of classical and Italian doctrine. What gives to the work its undoubted value is its originality, the skill with which Sidney has drawn on earlier teaching, selecting, adapting and fusing together ideas gathered from many sources, in order to set forth ultimately his own conception of poetry, independently arrived at. Thus apart from the Italians, he makes use of Plato and Aristotle, Horace and Plutarch; but, like Horace, he subscribes to the authority of no one school of thought. His treatment throughout is of an eclectic kind; his conclusions are the result of personal reflection as well as wide reading; and upon them is stamped the impress of a lofty personality. At the same time it cannot be doubted that Platonic influence played a considerable, perhaps a predominant, part in shaping his views, owing to some affinity of spirit. To him poetry was a natural human activity enabling men to sing of beauty and truth, and to satisfy their longings for a world transformed, thus nurturing in them what was good and noble. Moreover, so far from being merely an instrument for moral teaching, it was a concrete and inspiring revelation of human ideas, and thus, in a sense, a criticism of life. This, then, with its element of permanent truth, was the substance of Sidney's message to an age perplexed and even hostile. With the traditional objections boldly faced, with claims put forward for a place for poetry in the intellectual and social life, and with attempts made at a serious treatment of the poetic art, that message constituted a vindication of poetry, individual and unique in kind, which restored to poetry something of its ancient prestige and meaning, and was calculated to bring enlightenment and reassurance to his own generation.

J. W. Atkins
English Literary Criticism: The Renascence
(London: Methuen, 1951), p. 137

ROBERT SOUTHWELL
ca. 1561-1595

Born in Norfolk. Educated at Douai, and Paris. Served as Prefect of
Studies at English College in Rome. Member of the Society of Jesus.
Ordained priest in 1584. Asked to be sent to England in spite of the
law which made it an act of treason for a priest ordained later than 1577
to spend more than forty days in England. Returned to England while the
Babington conspiracy was being fomented. Had no part in the actual
plot. Lived in hiding. In 1589 became chaplain to the wife of the Earl of
Arundel. Arrested in 1592. Spent the remainder of his life in prison.
Examined thirteen times. Tortured seven times. Executed by hanging.
Poems largely written while in prison. Books began to circulate widely
after death.

A. B. Grosart, ed., *The Complete Poems of Robert Southwell* (1872)
C. Devlin, *The Life of Robert Southwell* (1956)

Thus the Jesuit was, to all appearances, the first to introduce into England
the post-Trentine literature of "Tears." But this should lead to no mistake
as to the contents of his own pieces of this description. Far from indulging
in unrestricted sentimentality, in gushing emotion of the late eighteenth
century type, he remains true to the spirit of the Italian meditation, which
is predominantly intellectual. Mary, indeed, insists on weeping for weeping's sake; yet if the fountain of tears is opened up anew whenever it seems
to run dry, this is done not through an appeal to the weeper's heart, but
to her mind, suitable reasons being provided as an inducement to further
dolefulness. This character is persistent throughout the transformations of
the piece. From the beginning, the influence of theological thinking is
uppermost in the questions and answers, arguments and dictinctions, which
make up the imaginary dialogue. It leads away from real life, to an abstract
consideration of ideas in themselves; and from this again there is an easy
transition to the over-ingenuity which was to be Southwell's main literary
fault in his early years.

Pierre Janelle
Robert Southwell, the Writer (New York:
Sheed and Ward, 1935), p. 190

In content Southwell's poetry is always religious. It is natural to connect
the more tragic pieces with the horrors of his imprisonment and repeated
tortures, but the connexion is by no means certain. "Dyer's Phancy" is
clearly concerned with the pains of the spiritual life itself. Southwell writes
much about the inner conflict, and here his poetic moral theology (as a
confessor he may have talked differently) brings him close to Fisher. All

sin seems to come from the sense, all beauty to belong to the soul—"A briefe wherein all marveyles summed lye." Life is a perpetual conflict

> where halues must disagree
> Or truce of halues the whole betraye.

Death parts "two ever-fighting foes." I do not remember that he ever refers to the resurrection of the body. Hence long before he came into the rackmaster's hands, he may have wished that "Sampson's leaue" (that is, Sampson's dispensation from the prohibition of suicide) "a comon lawe were made." Probably the sweetness of his own nature shielded him from a real knowledge of the *mala mentis gaudia*.

Southwell's work is too small and too little varied for greatness: but it is very choice, very winning, and highly original. We never read him without wondering why we do not read him more. He has (in some poems) certain metrical peculiarities which, if I dealt with at all, I should have to deal with more largely than they deserve. For they are not characteristic: at his best, and most typical, he writes with almost Augustan smoothness, relieved occasionally by an internal rhyme: the greatness of the matter and the masculine precision of phrase save him from dullness.

C. S. Lewis
English Literature in the Sixteenth Century
(Oxford: Clarendon Pr., 1954), pp. 545-46

Although his book [*An Epistle of Comfort*] had the aspect of defiance stamped on it by circumstance, intrinsically it is a work of rare value and scholarship. It revived in the language of his own day the grand tradition of English medieval devotion, like the restoring of a great Cathedral window before the art of those glowing colours had been forgotten.

Christopher Derlin
The Life of Robert Southwell (London:
Longmans, Green, 1956), p. 145

"I Die Alive" is constructed upon elaborate antithesis, and that the most fundamental of all: life and death. Balanced syntax and structural parallels are met commonly in Elizabethan verse, and for this reason the charge that Southwell's art is more than his matter must be anticipated. Many poems that rely heavily upon the devices of rhetoric appeal more by their wit than by their feeling. . . .

Perhaps the first thing that strikes our attention about the total poem ["O Life! What Lette Thee"] is the play upon antithesis already mentioned; perhaps it is the metrical regularity. I am not sure that these do not go hand in hand. But after we have read the poem, which progresses through three and a half stanzas of almost perfect iambics, we have the feeling that somewhere the measure had not run so smoothly. If we search again, we find that the first two lines are the place. But whether we read the poem again or not, the irregularity has served its purpose. As I make out the scansion, "O life! what letts" and "O death! what drawes" are each double spondees. These four opening syllables of each of the first two lines carry a great deal of the poem's emotion. First we are moderately moved by the conjunction of the lamenting "O" with the word "life," ordinarily a word to be associated with joy. Then the paradox, which asks that life be taken quickly away, develops our pity. The long, soul-fed plea for death which follows puts us in the same state of suffering as the poet. Continued life is tedious, and the tedium is echoed in the near-perfect iambic measure of the rest of the poem.

Southwell achieves his greatest tension in this poem through the paradox implied in the feast image. He wishes the banquet to end. All the joy, the festivity, the *life* which we associate with feasting is denied; instead, through the mystical sacrament of communion, especially in its sense of *last* supper, Southwell looks forward to dining with Christ in Heaven. But this tension, inherent in the single symbol, is extended through use of the feast image in two other places as well.

Harry Morris
Tulane Studies in English (1961), pp. 24, 26-27

But to what extent does the advice found in the *Rule* leave its traces in Southwell's poetry? Certainly the Jesuit insistence upon the close inspection of every slightest motion of the mind inspires that excellent gnomic poem, "Losse in delayes"; certainly the conception of life as an interior combat lies at the core of "Mans civill warre," stirring it to considerable subtlety of imagery and thought; and the central aim of all Catholic self-analysis—to discover the image of God within man—lies behind the poem "Looke home," with its foreshadowing of certain lines in Marvell's "Garden." . . .

Yet these poems only describe the need for self-analysis: they do not present, with quivering intensity, the very act of analysis as the poems of Donne and Herbert do. Southwell, we must concede, never shows in his poetry the introspective power that he reveals in his Latin prose remains. Only here and there, usually under the dramatic guise of Peter, the Magdalen, the Prodigal Son, or King David, do we catch some hints of an intense self-awareness—and these hints do not bear any great resemblance to the introspective manner of Donne and Herbert. Even Southwell's meditation "Upon the Image of death" remains very largely within the tradition of the poems in the *Paradise* on this theme; it plainly echoes "Saint Barnard's" famous poem, while its stanza-form, with the use of refrain, is exactly that of "Respice finem" (poem 22). Nevertheless, Southwell's meditation on death shows a much greater concentration on specific details, and a much stronger personal note, than one can find in the general precepts of these two poems. We may say, then, that his poems in general show a greater tendency toward the analysis and representation of inner states than one can find in the religious and didactic poetry of the miscellanies. His poems point the direction which religious poetry is soon to take; but they remain on the rim of the mind.

All this may be found in the one poem by Southwell where specifically Ignatian methods of self-analysis can be clearly seen at work. It is the poem "A vale of teares," a poetical representation of the two "preludes" advised by St. Ignatius (pp. 23-4) for the second spiritual exercise of the First Week: a "meditation upon sins." At the same time, it represents a vivid application of the senses of sight and hearing, and displays a threefold movement in accordance with the workings of the three powers of the soul: the preludes, as we might expect, anticipate the development of a full exercise.

Louis Martz
The Poetry of Meditation (New Haven. Conn.:
Yale Univ. Pr., 1962), pp. 206-7

EDMUND SPENSER
1552-1599

Born probably in London, of a poor family, possibly related to the noble family of Spencer of Althorp. Educated as a "poor boy" at Merchant Taylors' School under Richard Mulcaster. Entered Pembroke Hall, Cambridge, in 1569 as Sizar. In the same year, earliest poems appeared in *Theatre of Voluptuous Worldlings*. Took B.A. in 1573, M.A. in 1576. Friendship with Gabriel Harvey probably began at Cambridge. In 1578 became Secretary to the Bishop of Rochester. In 1579 Secretary to the Earl of Leicester. Associated with Sidney and Dyer at Leicester House. Affected by their interest in reforming English poetry. Published *Shepherds Calendar* in 1579, dedicated to Sidney. In 1580 became Secretary to Lord Grey of Wilton and accompanied him to Dublin. In 1581 made a Clerk in the Irish Court of Chancery. Bought houses in Ireland, held various other positions. Visited by Sir Walter Ralegh at Kilcolman Castle, Cork, in 1589. Revisited England with Ralegh. Arranged for the publication of the first three books of *Faerie Queene* in 1590. *Four Letters* published by Gabriel Harvey in 1592. Involved in law suits with Lord Roche in 1572 and 1574. Married Elizabeth Boyle in 1574. Revisited England in 1595. Published the last three books of *Faerie Queene* and reprinted the first three. Returned to Ireland in 1597. In 1598, during Tyrone's rebellion, took refuge in Cork when Castle Kilcolman was destroyed. Sent back to England with messages from the besieged garrison in Ireland. Died in Westminster, frustrated and in poverty.

E. Greenlaw, C. G. Osgood, F. M. Padelford, and R. Heffner, eds., *The Works of Edmund Spenser: A Variorum Edition* (1932-1949), 10 vols.

The Faerie Queene

The basic allegory of the *Faerie Queene* is the most important element in its structure, and this is one reason why allegory meddles with any reader of the poem. "I labour to pourtraict in Arthur, before he was king, the image of a brave knight, perfected in the twelve private morall vertues, as Aristotle hath devised, the which is the purpose of these first twelve bookes." The twelve moral virtues are to be twelve allegorical figures, to each of which a book will be devoted; and all twelve virtues will be united in Arthur, who is to appear at some critical point in each book, thus symbolizing the union of all the ideal qualities in the perfect knight, and structurally tying the twelve books together. Such in barest outline is the allegorical scheme, which simply and neatly gives an architectonic structure to the poem as conceived at one point during its composition; if the *Faerie Queene* had been carried out thus fewer would complain that Spenser's sense of form is so inferior to Dante's and Milton's. That this scheme was not strictly realized is owing as much to the nature of poetic allegory as to the fact that sections written earlier are included without sufficient revision. His scheme might have succeeded in mural painting; it is not well adapted to poetry.

The moment Spenser embodies Holiness in Redcross, the knight has to move, act, talk, meet situations; in so doing he is necessarily going to be courteous or discourteous, just or unjust, chaste or unchaste, qualities which are relegated by the new scheme of the poem to other books. Consequently, in practice as distinct from theory, more and more the principal knight in each book becomes an epitome of the gentleman, with the quality which he represents merely emphasized in him and in the nature of his experiences. . . .

The opening two books of Spenser's poem embody explicit or implicitly all that he has to say on the great central issues. In them he is concerned with fundamental principles of human conduct; he establishes the relationship between man and God, as well as between man and his fellows. The problems of evil and free will enter inevitably with the need for action; likewise, the problems of love, friendship, justice, courtesy. From the ethical, moral, religious, even psychological points of view, the four remaining books contribute little that is new; they are primarily elaboration and specific application of the central position set forth in the careers of Redcross and Guyon, variations on many of their emotional, social, moral crises of choice and action. Only the Britomart-Artegall love story, with its corrolaries, among these repetitive themes attains special stature. . . .

The ambitious conception of the *Faerie Queene* and his own temperament make it impossible for Spenser to treat love merely in human terms; and the importance of love in the Platonic scheme encourages him to formulate what is a kind of philosophic myth drawn from various not entirely reconcilable sources. Venus and Cupid assume many masks in his poetry. Often merely decorative, idyllic figures, often signifying wantonness, on occasion they have deeper meaning. In a fine passage on the inexhaustibility of life, which may have suggested the "salmon-falls" and "mackerel-crowded seas" in Yeats' *Sailing to Byzantium*, sea-born Venus is the ancient symbol of fertility, the sea the source of life. Usually the sun is the generating principle, and life's origin is some form of immaculate conception. In the *Gardens of Adonis* where Belphoebe's twin, Amoret, is nurtured, Spenser attempts to explain the genesis of life as imposition of form on matter (he was, however, no Aquinas) in an allegory which shows how early cosmological and scientific theories, while dwindling into pseudo-science, remain the substance of poetry. There are other accounts of creation in *Colin Clout* and, more Christianized, in the *Hymnes*. We need not lose ourselves in the intricacies of neo-Platonic, Lucretian, Ovidian, Biblical interfusion in Spenser's thought, since it is enough to stress the persistence of his concern with the origin of life, the variety of his poetic exploration of this question, and a few clear-cut beliefs which emerge. That many are commonplace does not invalidate the quality of his belief.

Primary among these is that love, being the only principle capable of reconciling opposites, is the sole explanation of the origin of life, and the sole means of maintaining it. Through love, life rises from chaos into form and meaning; without the perpetuation of love, it disintegrates into anarchy and oblivion. . . .

Spenser is the artist's poet. With the catholic taste for all the arts and unconcern about demarcations typical of the Renaissance, his poetry is filled with paintings, tapestries, architectural designs, musical instruments, mosaics, engravings, strange machines, fragments of statuary, ancient relics. His great Dragon Sin, wheeling through the end of the First Book of the *Faerie Queene*, might be constructed after a Leonardo fantasy; it anticipates by a quarter of a century some of the machine effects designed by Inigo Jones for the costly masques of the Stuarts. This interest in other forms of art often clutters Spenser's poetry, yet it is the source of much power and beauty besides mere decorative effect. The *Faerie Queene* may at times appear to be a series of versified didactic statements to which are appended decorative medallions, but we must distinguish between pictorial effects which exist almost for their own sake, and those which embody in concrete terms the central meaning of the poem. . . .

Spenser learns more from Chaucer than judicious selection of current dialects—the importance of skillfully handled syntax, the metrical value of the short syllable, effective for melodic purposes and for swift-moving, effortless narrative. With an equal predilection for description and meditation, like Chaucer he is capable also of dramatic narration when it suits his purpose. As he matures Spenser becomes more restrained in his borrowings, more skillful in adaptation, in taking over language principles rather than special practices. And with a swiftness more remarkable, though less famous, than Marlowe's lightning development of blank verse, Spenser molds a style that is rich, varied, fluid, adaptable to racy, homely satire and to conversational directness, as well as to the elegant formality of the *Amoretti* or the lofty idealism of the *Faerie Queene*.

W. B. C. Watkins
Shakespeare and Spenser (Princeton, N. J.: Princeton
Univ. Pr., 1950). pp. 113, 150, 207, 229, 266

In the preceding contrasts I have tried to suggest what may be termed the outlines of Book II [of *The Faerie Queene*], its narrative shape and something of its intellectual structure. This outline was seen to be determined by the revelation, in Canto viii, of that creative Love which underlay the superficially destructive indifference of Fortune. The first six cantos are dominated by a hero whose temperance is Aristotelian— a natural, aristocratic virtue rendering its possessor immune to inner struggle and temptation. This certainty of instinct is needed for the knight who must withstand the Acrasian sorceries of flesh, but it is not sufficient for other kinds of sorcery. Canto vii dramatizes the insufficiency of Aristotelian temperance, the innocence and limited wisdom resulting from reflexes so easy, so assured. Cantos viii-xi disclose the workings of a different kind of temperance: the Christian virtue, supernaturally infused, accessible to all, but gained and retained by each with difficulty. Canto xii, as we shall see in the final chapter, recapitulates the contrast.

Such a change in attitude toward the sources and values of existence as occurs midway through the poem requires a corresponding change in the enemies of existence, requires also the appearance of a justicer —Arthur—more suitable by nature to cope with the new problems. It is not that Guyon and his Palmer are inadequate to the conditions imposed by their quest, but that they are chosen to fulfill a special and limited kind of quest, that the excellence demanded of them almost necessitates the accompanying limitations, that the quest itself paradoxically entails problems beyond its scope and beyond the powers of its patron. . . .

I have tried to suggest, through examples of "conspicuous irrelevance," something of the way in which Spenser's allegorical method works. The emphasis has been on the dual perspective produced by his manipulation of fable and poetic action, on the consequent difference between the world the characters see and the world the readers see. These are the ways in which the poet expresses his poem. The mention of Elizabeth brings us now to a different issue, one which is perhaps more central to the problem of allegory: the intention, imagination, and personality of the poetic speaker, the way in which the poem expresses the poet. The relations between Belphoebe, Elizabeth, Gloriana, and Arthur reach beyond simile, description, canto, and book to the symbolic center of the *Faerie Queene*. We may remember, in this connection, another "irrelevant" passage, Canto x, in which the Artemisian perspective of myth and Penthesilean perspective of history were also set against each other. These conflicting perspectives are woven into the heart of the poem. They belong to Spenser's total poetic vision, and the phrase "poetic vision" implies a seer as well as something seen. Fable and poetic action are what they are, not merely because words evoke images of things rather than the things themselves; the images they evoke are of things in the poet's soul, not of things in the objective world. . . .

Harry Berger, Jr.
The Allegorical Temper (New Haven, Conn.:
Yale Univ. Pr., 1957), pp. 62-63, 160

. . . All that Tasso says can be said of *The Faerie Queene*, with one important qualification. It is an image of the world—but an image of the interior world. The conflicts, enterprises, deeds of valour and love are not there as a mimesis of the outer world in which these events physically occur. They are an image of the inner world—a huge panorama of man's inner experience, political, military, social, erotic, moral, and religious. The forest is the *selva oscura* of man's life; the characters do not need to be dramatized and individualized. Primarily they are not individuals, but aspects of our experience, as in dreams. Here we pass from the outer organization of the poem to the inner, from structure to allegory. . . .

But a better term, as Greenlaw has suggested, would be historical allusion. And the best way to deal with it is to appreciate it where it is evident, for what it is worth, as part of a crowded and complex pattern, one of the elements which helps to give such density to the whole; and to be at no great pains to look for it where it does not make its presence plain. . . .

. . . The attempt to read Book I [of *The Faerie Queene*] as a transcript of Tudor history is strained and uncertain; but clearly a strong strain of allusion to the English reformation runs through it. The Red Cross Knight is Holiness, fighting against the temptations and errors that must universally beset such a virtue. But he is also, more intermittently and imprecisely, English religion (why else should he bear St. George's cross?) struggling against the conspiracies and misdirections of the time, as Spenser saw them. But he is not always Holiness as an achieved state; he is often the universal *miles Christianus,* the militant Christian who must struggle and learn and seek to perfect himself in his journey through the world. Similarly, three themes (not unrelated but certainly distinct) stand behind the figure of Arthur—Magnificence, the historic might and glory of Britain, and the Earl of Leicester. Artegall's adventures are sometimes those of an abstract and general justice, sometimes those of Lord Grey in Ireland.

We have already spoken of the ambiguity of Britomart in another context—of her way of stepping beyond her allegorical rôle. But what is her allegorical rôle? She represents Chastity, in Spenser's special sense of the word, but not exclusively that. She represents also a quite complex Renaissance ideal of female *virtù* (*virtù* meaning strength and energy, not virtue) which Spenser was familiar with through the virago heroines of the Italian epic, and which has nothing to do with chastity at all.

We are of course meant to admire both equally; but there are times when this kind of dual or multiple significance can introduce a moral ambiguity as well. Duessa in Book I is the embodiment of falsehood, outwardly fair but in reality hideous and deformed. When she reappears in Book V a whole cluster of notions connected with Mary Queen of Scots has become attached to her. She is still falsehood, and still to be rejected, but she is also misguided beauty, and a decided element of sympathy for the unhappy queen as a woman has crept into the *significatio.* I do not wish to enter into the vexed question of the Bower of Bliss at this point, except to remark that it cannot represent a simple concept. The idea sometimes put forward that Spenser was secretly on Acrasia's side is obviously wrong; but it could hardly have arisen if the allegory of the bower were a totally unambiguous affair. There *is* an element of indulged and happy voluptuousness in the description of Acrasia's abode, that takes us back to Tasso's Armida, Spenser's principal source. And Armida at the end of the *Gerusalemme Liberata* is not rejected but forgiven.

Frequently, then, more than one theme lies behind the same image, and this is one of the features of *The Faerie Queene* that assimilates it most closely to the dream. . . .

Spenser's conscious, rational moral position is not ambiguous. It is perfectly clear; and a large part of anything we can mean by his heart went into it. But his sensibility was in imperfect accord with it, and this is shown by the fact that the image has assumed an independent life that in part works against the theme. . . .

There are those for whom beauty associated with any kind of moral dubiety at once ceases to be beauty. But for Spenser beauty is always beauty, whatever its tendency. His moral principles are clear and well-established, received for the most part from religion and the civil tradition; but they are not co-extensive with his poetry. The poetry is too wide for them. His heart was very much in his morality; but it was in other things too. Much that is poetically important in *The Faerie Queene* is morally indifferent; and some things that are poetically important tend to run counter to the morality that is consciously invoked.

Graham Hough
A Preface to "The Faerie Queene" (New York:
W. W. Norton, 1963), pp. 98-99, 130-33, 165

Spenser was of course first of all a Christian. There is nothing in Plato or Plotinus that corresponds to the descent of God into the flesh and His sacrifice for mankind. But it is idle to ask whether Spenser was a Christian Platonist or a Platonic Christian. . . . But both Platonists and Christians identify the highest with ultimate good and ultimate beauty, both find material existence in comparison shadowy and poor, both urge man to break from the bounds of earth toward the celestial. The Sapience who sits in God's bosom in the *Hymne of Heavenly Beautie* has been variously interpreted as the Holy Ghost, Christ, the Sapience of the Book of Wisdom, and the Platonic Heavenly Venus, and she has qualities of each of these. Since Spenser does not tell us specifically which she is, he no doubt intends what is common to all, a wealth and wisdom of which this world's riches and knowledge are only a token, an entity associated with God yet not altogether beyond the apprehension of the purified human soul. The high "Ideas . . . which Plato so admyred" are ranged in the celestial realm between the souls of the happy and the Powers and Dominations of the Bible. The Hill of Contemplation from which the Red Cross Knight sees the New Jerusalem is likened to Sinai, the Mount of Olives, and Parnassus.

Spenser's system of love, as even so cursory a study shows, reaches upward from this world but keeps foothold within it. Examined as a logical construct, it disintegrates at once into a conglomeration of inconsistencies and even absurdities. But it has a coherence of another kind. The poet was attempting to justify by the authority of literature, the wisdom of the ancients, and revealed religion his deep feelings about the relationships of man and woman and man and God. He saw a likeness between the love that draws the sexes together, producing noble deeds and perpetuating the race, and the love that draws man to God and fills the world with beauty. . . .

This hunger for complexity, for binding into one the multiple and for revealing the multiple in the one, shows itself in almost every aspect of Spenser's technique. The stanza which he invented for the poem is itself such a various unit. Its closest relatives are the Italian ottava rima (*abababcc*), rhyme royal (*ababbcc*), and the stanza used by Chaucer in the *Monk's Tale* (*ababbcbc*). In the first two forms the final couplet rhymes independently of the rest; the *Monk's Tale* stanza lacks a clear-cut conclusion. By adding an alexandrine rhyming with *c* to this last verse pattern, Spenser introduces metrical variety and at the same time supplies an ending which is linked to rather than separated from the remainder. Stanza is joined to stanza by frequent echoes in the first line of one of the sound or thought of the last line preceding it, and analogous links tie together canto with canto and book with book. To the amalgamation in his stanza of Italian and English forms Spenser adds a Vergilian touch by occasionally leaving a verse unfinished in the manner of the *Aeneid*.

The invention of the names of the characters of *The Faerie Queene* betrays a similar habit of mind. They are designedly derived from different languages: Pyrochles is Greek, Munera Latin, Alma Italian (and also both Latin and Hebrew), Sans Foy French, the first half of Ruddymane English. Many of the names are portmanteaus into which Spenser has stuffed a multiplicity of meanings. "Britomart," for example, reminded his Elizabethan readers of Ariosto's heroine Bradamante as well as of Britomartis, the chaste daughter of Carme whom ancient myth identified with Diana, while at the same time the etymology "martial Briton" must have been inescapable, for Boccaccio calls Britomartis "Britona, Martis filia."

The key ideas of his moral teaching are expressed by as many different symbols as the poet can imagine: the power which binds the disparate or antagonistic is represented by the figure of Concord flanked by Love and Hate; by the hermaphrodite Venus and the snake about her legs whose head and tail are joined together; by the lady Cambina, her team of angry lions, her Aesculapian rod, and her cup of nepenthe. These reciprocal processes of unification and multiplication reflect a conception of the universe which makes it all one, yet unimaginably rich.

There is a plenitude of story in *The Faerie Queene*, martial, amatory, and domestic; myth, fairy tale, chivalric adventure, and anecdote. Some of these tales Spenser invents himself; others he borrows from biblical, classical, medieval, and contemporary sources. . . .

Within *The Faerie Queene*, the unit is the book or legend. It is made up of episodes and "allegories" invented to illuminate its theme. Typically, a book begins with an encounter between new characters and those of its predecessor, there is a climax or shift of emphasis approximately at midpoint, and the end is marked by some great action. Apart from these loose formal characteristics, however, the constituent elements are not sequential in their arrangement; they are truly episodic, obeying no law of progress or development. Rather, they are so placed as to produce effects of variety and contrast. They are tied not to each other but to the principal subject of discourse, and to this they contribute analytically or comprehensively, directly or by analogy, by affirmation or denial.

In Spenser's poem, intention is the soul, while the stories, characters, symbols, figures of speech, the ring of the verse itself constitute the body. . . . Only from the made body can the form be inferred, however, and this is the kind of inference that Spenser expects of his readers. One may take hold of the meaning of a book almost anywhere in it, for it is everywhere there.

Each book of *The Faerie Queene*, I have tried to show, announces itself as an "imitation" of a particular literary model appropriate to its meaning. Each defines a moral problem by reference to an ideal world in which the problem does not exist, investigates it in terms of the oppositions and paradoxes which create it, and expresses those oppositions and paradoxes in a wide variety of ways, among them a political dimension. Each presents its resolution in a central episode which portrays the goodness, harmony, and fruitfulness of which this world is capable. And each recognizes that since such a resolution is of this world it must be tentative only. . . .

For none of the books of *The Faerie Queene*, therefore, is a true conclusion possible. The powers of darkness may for a time be held prisoner, seen in their true horror and rendered impotent, but since they are of earth's essence they will again break free and threaten destruction, night, and chaos. Despite that ever-present threat, indeed because of it, the created world remains beautiful, various, and fecund, and man may hope that when his own strength cannot avail to keep it so the grace of God will come to his aid. So much of victory is all that can be expected as long as the Red Cross Knight serves Gloriana and Mutabilitie fulfills her natural function. Beyond, and really beyond the bounds of *The Faerie Queene*, St. George unites forever with Una in that final Sabbath when all things rest upon the pillars of Eternity.

William Nelson
The Poetry of Edmund Spenser (New York: Columbia
Univ. Pr., 1963), pp. 114-15, 140-41, 145, 297, 314

GENERAL

The skillful employment of the colours of rhetoric gives closeness of texture to style, but their principal use is for variety, and in this respect also Spenser may be compared with the earlier poets, and still more with the two writers of elaborate prose in his own time, Lyly and Sidney, who weary the reader by their constant recourse to two or three figures, while Spenser, though he has his favourites, uses a wide range. . . . The violent "high style" of *The Teares of the Muses* may not be admired, but few English poets of the time could do the like, and fewer before it. There is great variety within *The Shepheardes Calender*, and in *Muiopotmos* Spenser indulged the play instinct that is an element in all art. "Spenser seems to delight in his art for his own skill's sake. In the *Muiopotmos*, see the security and ostentation with which he draws out and refines his description of a butterfly's back and wings.". . . By this time he had his English at will, and enjoyed it; he had advanced from *The Shepheardes Calender*, in which his rhetorical training is so obvious as at times to overcome his taste, and in which E. K. delights to point out "a prety Epanorthosis . . . and withall a Paronomasia," or "a patheticall parenthesis, to encrease a carefull hyperbaton," to *The Faerie Queene*, where the style is not only gorgeous in certain passages and magnificent in others, but is varied at will from page to page with figures which seem inevitable.

This variety of style was not fortuitous, but controlled by the principle of "decorum," which links style closely with kind, form, and subject. . . .

The operation of the principle of decorum may be watched in Spenser's use of the colours of rhetoric—the oratorical questions and exclamations of *The Teares of the Muses*, the "epic" similes of *The Faerie Queene*, the homely proverbs of *The Shepheardes Calender*—and more easily in his choice of similes and metaphors—those of hunting and hawking to suit the knightly subject of *The Faerie Queene*, those of country pursuits and pastimes for the mouths of his shepherds, those of the arts to fit the person of each of the Muses. It was the true appreciation of this artistic principle, the understanding that figures are not valuable in themselves, but only in their time and place, and that their purpose is not mere decoration, but the elucidation and impression of the mood and subject, that gave the new poets greater success in the application of their rhetorical acquirements, just as it was the rhetorical practice that gave them greater control over language than their elders, and greater facility and copiousness than their modern descendants. They were drilled in good expression until it became a habit, and the habit of observing decorum was not the least useful part of the discipline. . . .

Spenser had to remake the English language for his own high purposes, and he developed a style peculiarly Spenserian—a style which is easily recognized as his and no one else's. He had also to make his own discoveries in versification and find his own solutions to its problems. The two processes are really one. The poet's indulgence in or avoidance of inversion, his habitual speed, his lofty vein or downright simplicity, the pointedness of the periodic rotundity of his phrase, his sense of tone and his taste in language—all these affect his choice of metres and his treatment of them; and conversely, his temperamental feeling for rhythm, his power of sustaining it, his capacity for blending and varying it, are all factors governing his choice of words and disposition of phrases. In good poetry meaning, style and verse all work together to produce the unified expression, the effect, for which the poet is striving. It is the unity of effect that is notable, and noticeably new, in Spenser's work, a unity all the more remarkable that diction, style, and verse were, at once and together, the object of experiment and invention. . . .

The method of *The Faerie Queene* is, to display each virtue completely in all its forms and phases, not as a simple characteristic, but as defined by the various trials and experiences operating to its perfection, by the various actions proper to its possession, and, negatively, by the diverse vices and defects opposed to it. A single exemplar is not enough. Guyon and the Palmer present Temperance arising from two different moral bases, highmindedness and restraint; Britomart and Belphœbe and Amoret, different conceptions of chastity—that which depends on strength and faithfulness, that which is a noble fastidiousness removed from common frailty, and that which is a natural attribute of womanly character. Spenser drives home his lesson by repeated variations, adding additional illustrations by additional characters and episodes. Sir Calidore, to take the simplest instance, represents Courtesy: his principal task is to restrain malice and evil speaking—the "Male-Bouche" of the chivalric allegorists —he also teaches mercy and mildness, championship of woman, tenderness to the sick, politeness to honest inferiors. Cruelty, haughtiness, inhospitality, treachery, insincerity, are his opposite, though not necessarily his personal opponents in the story. Tristram and the Hermit show that Courtesy, though rightly "named of court," belongs to "the gentle blood" and not to worldly position; the Savage Man, that goodwill and right instinct are its primary conditions. . . .

The lesson of *The Faerie Queene* is the same throughout: society must be held together by concord or Friendship, the individual must be controlled by Temperance, the state by Justice. The recurrent victory of the trained and disciplined knights over "the rascal many" was more than an inheritance from the aristocratic Middle Ages, or an echo of Tudor statesmanship, or a memory of Irish insurrections. All these were in Spenser's mind, but they were contained within the greater idea, the necessity of stability. The rabble is crushed because it is a rabble, incapable of constant policy of united action. . . .

To seek and bring home the purest honey of beauty and delight from all the fields and gardens of art was a great work for England, but it was not enough for the deep and ambitious mind. Poetry for Spenser was to be an efficient cause of action in the world, and so *The Faerie Queene* was a political tract as well as a fine story. That was for Spenser's own contemporaries: but, beyond that, for all time there should remain the moral doctrine of the poem, working on the minds of men and inspiring them to right thinking and right doing. England then and for ever should have the purest doctrine of life gathered and stored for her use and benefit. Spenser took for his subject all that concerns man in all his faculties and desires and relations, and expended all his native power and all his acquired knowledge and skill on the construction of the ideal and on its embellishment. Feeling, intuition, tradition, learning, the sense of beauty and the sense of right and the sense of divinity, all combined in that idea; the philosophy of the ancients, the teaching of the Church, the custom of English nobility, were fused together.

W. L. Renwick
Edmund Spenser (London: Edward Arnold, 1949),
pp. 72-73, 75, 97, 158-59, 171, 180

The argument of the *Shepheardes Calender* is the rejection of the pastoral life for the truly dedicated life in the world. For Spenser, this means the life of the heroic poet whose high religious calling is to serve the Queen by inspiring her people to all virtuous action. Upon the level of merely private allusion, the poem may refer covertly to Spenser's circle of friends, to local gossip and other topical matters; but such allusion is carefully submerged, being occasional, digressive, and extrinsic to the poem's unity. Upon another level, the personal, the poem records Spenser's progress from his apprenticeship to pastoral poetry towards the heroic poem. Like the Red Cross Knight, he is a "clownishe younge man" described in the letter to Ralegh who "rested him on the floore, vnfitte through his rusticity for a better place" until the Faery Queen appoints him his task. (A year after the *Calender* appeared, Spenser started to write *The Faerie Queene*.) This level of meaning is transmuted through the pastoral conventions into an allegory of human life within the order of Nature. Through the device of the calender, human life is seen in the perspective of the fall and the Nativity: the one bringing the state of death out of which man must escape through rejecting the pastoral Paradise, the other promising rebirth which he may gain through seeking the truly dedicated life in the world. . . .

Book I [of *The Faerie Queen*] outlines the poem's pattern: The four stages of Red Cross Knight's action: (i) his fall through Duessa's witchcraft, (ii) his redemption through Arthur's grace, (iii) his regeneration through Una's faith, and (iv) through slaying the dragon, his restoration signified by marriage to Una, contain the action of the whole poem.

The first stage is described in Book II which shows, as we have seen, how virtue aided by grace may prevent the knight's fall. The second stage is shown in Book III in the redeeming power of chaste love displayed in the female Arthur, Britomart, who descends into the dungeon to save Amoret. The third stage is treated in Books IV and V. In Book IV there is displayed the "regeneration" of the flesh through love which is preparatory to marriage: then in Book V the "regeneration" of England by the defeat of the enemies who stand between her and her glorious destiny, and therefore between Artegal and his marriage to Britomart. The fourth stage is reached in Book VI which projects the vision of the restored lovers joined in delight. If the pattern of Book I were further fulfilled, Book VII would treat the knight's next stage when he returns to the world to serve the Faery Queen. That the cycle of action from fall to restoration may start over again gives the theme of Mutability. . . .

The simultaneous awareness of the power of virtue and the wretchedness of life drives the poem [the *Faerie Queene*] into metaphor. Consequently its central visions are always twofold: Una is veiled, woman's beauty is combined with the serpent's tail in Error and Duessa, the glorious Lucifera as the fallen Faery Queene, Florimell and the false Florimell, Amoret bound, Venus with the snake wound around her feet, Isis and the crocodile. By exploring these visions the poem moves towards an image of man seen perfected in Arthur and also the image of Nature. As Arthur appears in the various knights, Nature appears in her various forms, from that original vision of the Faery Queen and the primary vision of Una to Belphoebe, Amoret, Florimell, Britomart, Colin's damsel surrounded by the graces and maidens, until Nature herself appears in the Mutability Cantos. We see this unfallen Nature in opposition to fallen Nature, her counterpart in the twofold vision. Since this nature is both without and within man, we see unfallen man in the images of virtue at one with nature opposed to fallen man in the images of vice. Once we see that opposition upon all levels, Nature is redeemed, and therefore man. It is in this sense that Spenser delivers in his poem a golden world.

A. C. Hamilton
The Structure of Allegory in "The Faerie Queene" (Oxford: Clarendon Pr., 1961), pp. 46-47, 128-29, 222-23

SIR JOHN SUCKLING
1609-1642

Born at Whitton, near Twinkenham, Middlesex. Descendant of old Norfolk family. Matriculated at Trinity College, Cambridge, in 1623. Left without a degree. Studied for a brief period at Gray's Inn, London. In 1628 left on a grand tour of the continent. Visited France, Germany, Italy, and Spain. Returned to England in 1630. Knighted in 1630. In 1631 accompanied Marquis of Hamilton to Germany and served with him under King Gustavus Adolphus of Sweden in the Thirty Years War. On return to London became famous as a gambler, lover, and wit. Invented the game of cribbage. In 1638 spent a large fortune on staging of the play, *Aglaura*. Raised a troop of a hundred horsemen in 1639 at his own expense. Led them to Scotland in the Royalist cause. Completely defeated. Ridiculed by the Puritans in London. Fled to Paris in 1641 after involvement in Royalist plot. Died there in poverty, perhaps by suicide. *Fragmenta Aurea* published posthumously in 1646.

A. H. Thompson, ed., *The Works of Sir John Suckling* (1910)

POETRY

An examination of the major portion of Suckling's love poetry has indicated that although he was one of the principal court poets of the reign of Charles and Henrietta, he seldom wrote in praise of the new cult of the *précieuse*, which the Queen had introduced from France. In practice, he either ridiculed it or ignored it. He was fully conscious of the ideas represented by this new Platonic movement, and in his plays are many allusions to the group. His usual expression in love poetry was guided by a "libertine" naturalism which he derived directly from Donne, whose poetic disciple he was, and from the minor *libertin* poets in France, of whom he had firsthand knowledge. Because of his popularity during the latter part of the century, his is not the least important place in the history of skeptical naturalism which may be traced throughout the Restoration.

O. H. Fletcher
ELH (December, 1937), p. 298

The speaker [in "Why So Pale and Wan?"], presumably a gallant, experienced in the ways of love, is advising a foolish young man how to behave toward his beloved. If the younger man aspires to be like the speaker, he ought to accept the advice. Thus far the young sinner (or another fond lover, has not been able to win a lady by the brilliance of his repartee or the attractiveness of his manner. He is not behaving properly, for he is pale, dull, and mute—the conventional signs of an unrequited lover. He is unrealistic, too obviously passionate, and too clearly worried about his passion.

However, the rhetorical situation is not all that simple. Quite likely the speaker also intends to have his words overheard by women, just as the Petrarchian complaint, for instance Wyatt's "My lute awake! perfourme the last Labor," was calculated to be heard by the cruel mistress. . . . And Suckling's speaker gains a certain impish advantage if his words are supposed to deflect toward all coy mistresses. He is, in effect, threatening that men will withdraw their attentions if ladies do not behave realistically; beyond a certain point the coy mistress is not worth any more effort.

Historical evidence verifies this theory of a "double audience" for the poem because the song is sung in Act IV of Suckling's play, *Aglaura,* by a gallant named Orsames, a young "antiplatonic" lord, a cynical libertine, who scoffs at the "new religion in love." He does not sing the song to a fond lover; rather he sings it to the platonic ladies, Semanthe and Orithie. While they await the arrival of the queen, they ask Orsames to sing. He at first refuses because his voice is hoarse from walking out at night in his shirt serenading his mistress. After he sings, he says that this was a bit of advice given to a friend fallen into a consumption, and Orithie says that she could have guessed it was the product of Orsames' brain even if she had not been told. To be sure, most Elizabethan plays use songs strictly for ornament, but in this play Suckling explicitly connects the song with the dialogue; the rhetorical situation, therefore, presupposes the presence of the ladies.

What I have called a "double audience" in the poem is different, nevertheless, from a dramatic monologue such as "My Last Duchess" where *x* speaks to *y* but *x*'s words are intended to be heard by a public audience; we judge the speaker's statements differently than does his immediate audience, *y*, as in Suckling's poem; yet the full meaning is directed to a much less restricted group of readers. Browning intends to have his poem read by an undifferentiated audience; Suckling intends his song to be overheard by the platonic ladies. Thus Orsames' song is not only advice to a fond lover but a pose of the gallant and a threat to any coy mistress—if she does not return a man's love, if she does not react as a flesh-and-blood human being, she will be left behind. She will be the rejected one and the gallant will find a woman who will satisfy him.

The doubleness of the rhetorical situation is one of the reasons why this poem is so charming and playful. It gives us, the general readers or third audience, a special detachment, and it probably contributes to the conventional character of the speaker. The whole of the reader's relation to the poem is like a window-peeper watching an eavesdropper hearing a conversation. . . .

The language expresses the speaker's thought with the utmost economy and concision. . . . The language also reveals the strategy of the speaker, for in the first two stanzas he is careful to be gentle. He merely questions and does not force an open admission in a plain statement, and he chooses the colloquial, deferential request, "Prithee," four times in ten lines. The word has just the right feigned delicacy for this part of the argument. Then at the turn, he switches from questions to bold, short commands, from trochaic meter to a spondee followed by iambs, from deferential requests to a common oath (but not so common as to be vulgar). The phrasing is similar to the pattern of the first two stanzas, but every detail deviates as far as possible from the established form. Even the double rhyme, *take her, make her*, occurs in the second, fourth, and fifth rather than the first and third lines. These sharp deviations contribute to the brilliant surprise of the last stanza, and our expectation of another repetition such as "Prithee why so pale," along with the trick of the rhymes, especially focuses attention on the last line. Instead of repetition the listeners get surprise and a common oath. Contrast the closing lines with a revision made for an eighteenth-century setting of the song, where all the piquancy, the saltiness (to use Quintilian's phrase) is taken out. It is insipid.

L. A. Beaurline
Texas Studies in Lang. and Lit. (Winter, 1963), pp. 558-60, 562

PLAYS

The chief characters in the tragi-comedy of *Aglaura* are Platonics and anti-Platonics. All the ladies belong to the former group, and as they have the sovereignty, their arguments are the most authoritative. Aglaura herself upholds the new code in its more difficult aspects. . . . Thus in his plays, as in his poems and letters, Suckling's polite allegiance to the new philosophy is amply demonstrated.

Only in his plays could Suckling do justice to Platonic dialogue. He seized the opportunity with eagerness. *Aglaura* is little more than a tissue of ingenious arguments. Of course, the new social mode offered the logical stimulus to such discourse; its fashions were beautifully precise, and its methods of reasoning had been carefully formulated. By Lyly's similitude contests Suckling may well have been influenced. But he owed the formal symmetry of his dialogue, so opposed to Lyly's whimsical twists and turns of fancy, to the discipline of Platonic conventions. . . .

Suckling wrote a single comedy, *The Goblins* (1638). The play is memorable, despite its lack of dramatic merit, for its pronounced emphasis on anti-Platonic views. Suckling was quite aware of the sources of comic effect inherent in the artificial attitudes of the new religion. Although, as a favored courtier, he could never indulge his comic muse with real freedom, in *The Goblins*, under cover of a thin comic intrigue, he ventured to laugh more heartily and more indiscreetly than in his other plays. In *The Goblins* the Platonic pageant is no longer insured at its face value; its agreeable illusions are perceived as such.

Kathleen M. Lynch
The Social Mode of Restoration Comedy (New York:
Macmillan, 1926), pp. 70-71, 90

HENRY   HOWARD,   EARL   OF   SURREY
1517?-1547

> Of royal blood, being descended from Edward the Confessor through his father and from Edward III through his mother. At thirteen became the companion of Henry, Duke of Richmond, bastard son of King Henry VIII. In 1532 married Frances Vere, daughter of the Earl of Oxford, went to France in train of the king. In 1535 lived with his wife for the first time. Present at the trial of Ann Boleyn. In 1536 served against the Pilgrimage of Grace rebels. In 1537 imprisoned at Windsor for striking a courtier who had accused him of sympathy with the rebels. In charge of the defense of Norfolk against invasion in 1539. Created Knight of the Garter in 1541. Imprisoned in Fleet in 1542 and again in 1543 for breaking windows and failure to observe Lent. Served in various military engagements. Wounded at Montreuil in 1544 after exposing himself to unnecessary danger. Began to displease the crown. Arrested and charged with treason in December 1546. His quartering of his arms with those of Edward the Confessor had been interpreted as a promotion of his own claim to the throne. Beheaded on Tower Hill, January 21, 1547.
>
> F. M. Padelford, ed., *The Poems* (1928)

The Italian sonnet, as Petrarch uses it, automatically breaks into the octave and the sextet, the octave stating the general condition and the sextet giving the concrete application. As the Elizabethan sonnet consists of three quatrains and a couplet, there is no such mechanical break; the idea, therefore, is developed through twelve lines, closing with an epigrammatic couplet. The difference is obvious even in the translations from Petrarch. Wyatt's couplet is not complete in itself, whereas Surrey's may be detached as a quotation. That this form originated with Surrey is very doubtful, since it was used by Wyatt, although with a slightly different rime-scheme, by Grimald, and by several of the Uncertain Authors; Surrey's use of it, however, in all probability gave it currency. It was Surrey's fortune to be accepted as the representative of the age,—the age when for the first time since Chaucer, the language had become relatively fixed in the forms of the words, and when the poetic technique had passed beyond the obviously experimental stage. . . .

For precision and felicity of phrase Surrey need not shun comparison even with the great French poet of his age. The documents in evidence have here been given the reader, that he may form his own judgment. It will be a matter of surprise, however, if the verdict, to some measure at least, does not justify the Elizabethans in their estimate of Surrey. . . .

But this freedom in placing the stress is characteristic of all our great blank verse. And the reason why in the history of the literature blank verse is so late in developing is because it thus combines in itself so many utterly diverse and antagonistic elements. Before it could be written an author must have arisen who in himself combined the movements of the English tradition, the Medieval Latin, and humanism. Logically such a combination was not possible until the second generation of the reign of Henry VIII, the generation of the Earl of Surrey.

It is this union of the separate influences that makes Surrey's work so important.

John M. Berdan
Early Tudor Poetry (New York: Macmillan,
1931), pp. 522-23, 526, 541-42

It is generally recognized that style is Surrey's predominating poetical virtue, and that his refinement of poetic diction contributed much to the improvement of English poetry. The language of poets was archaic when Surrey began to write, but he discarded the archaic language and the pedantic words of which his immediate predecessors had been so ridiculously fond—words for the most part forcibly reft from Latin or French —and created a new poetic diction. Alliteration, so consonant with the writing of all former English poetry, he retained. To the modern ear alliteration is at times too much emphasized in his verse, but his use of it is for the most part delightful. Although he also retained the occasional use of such archaisms as *eke*, the prefix *y*, and the old suffix *en* and often used a phrase or expression typically Chaucerian, Surrey's diction is vivid, direct, and euphonious. In contrast to his predecessors, he recognized the necessity of accepting a fixed rhythmical standard for a word and not varying its value and balance entirely at the need of the poet. And having set up a standard for himself, he was careful to place the tonic accent only on the even syllables; except when introducing proper names into his verse, he used the trochee commonly only in the first foot.

Edwin Casady
Henry Howard, Earl of Surrey (New York:
Modern Language Assn. of America, 1938), p. 225

Nearly all that is good, and some things that are bad, in the Drab Age, can be found in Surrey's poetry. He can, in poulter's, give us specimens of its lumbering clownishness—

> Unhappy hand, it had been happy time for me
> If when to write thou learned first uniointed hadst thou be.

But he also contributed to our poetry a certain smooth and controlled dignity or propriety: and if the word "politeness" rises to our lips we need not reject it, for the Drab Age has certain real affinities with that of the Augustans. He does not warble woodnotes nor thunder in high astounding terms nor wanton in luscious imagery: when he reminds us of the Elizabethans at all, he reminds us of "well languaged Daniel" or sober *Nosce Teipsum*. He can make trifles pleasing by their neat structure and by the ease and consistency of his language. Once or twice he goes higher than this. Metrically, he is one of the great road-makers. If we adopted the ludicrous principle of judging poets not by their own work but by their utility to their sucessors, he would have to rank not only above Wyatt but above Chaucer and Milton; perhaps above Shakespeare too. By any sane standard, however, he is merely a man who served his generation well and has left one or two poems of permanent though moderate, value.

C. S. Lewis
English Literature in the Sixteenth Century (Oxford:
Clarendon Pr., 1954), pp. 234-35

No such contrast has been applied to the work of Surrey, whose lyrics are for the most part awkward and uninteresting. But it must be owned that amongst the sonnets themselves two incompatible approaches to writing may be distinguished. One is that of the industrious but uninspired craftsman, imitating the technical devices of Wyatt with certain improvements, and like him undergoing a phase of apprenticeship to the Italians. The other is the approach of a genuine poet whose verse, though without any temperamental brilliance, yet has an appeal of its own. In all the sonnets ostensibly concerned with love, Surrey is either experimenting quite cold-bloodedly with verse technique; or else he is using his Italian model as a mere spring-board for his own reflections, which really have nothing to do with the thought-patterns of the sonnet. It is only in another—and almost certainly later—group of his sonnet compositions, not relating to sexual love at all, that we find a true and satisfying interplay of form and subject-matter.

J. W. Lever
The Elizabethan Love Sonnet (London: Methuen, 1956), p. 38

While the relation between Wyatt and Surrey was close enough to be called a community of ideas on religious matters, Surrey does not stand in the line of development of Wyatt's best verse. There remains the further argument to be considered that Surrey nevertheless deserves prominence in that he is in the line of development of the best Humanist thinking. That, as a translator of *secular* Latin verse, Surrey is an important figure in early Tudor humanism, and, in particular, that as the "father of English blank verse" he deserves to be approached with respect, are propositions that come to us almost with the force of tradition. Yet it is remarkable that a disproportionately small degree of interest has been shown in what is apparently so valuable. There is no reliable edition of Surrey's translations and some of the very first questions of an unprejudiced enquirer have still to be answered.

Here, then, is a case where scholarly work is required before a critical judgement can be made, or rather, before the last touches can be given to the irresistible critical judgement. For all the scholarship in the world could not affect the verdict that whatever these translations are they are not poems. . . .

The task of translation set Surrey back rather than drew out undeveloped poetic powers. After so many examples of too easy flow in the poulter's measure, it may seem unfair to complain that Surrey's translation of Virgil is too static. This failure to make the lines move, however, is not merely a question of skill in handling the "straunge metre." Surrey's *vocabulary* is itself a dead and dreary selection from the language.

H. A. Mason
Humanism and Poetry in the Early Tudor Period (London:
Routledge and Kegan Paul, 1959), pp. 248, 251

JEREMY TAYLOR
1613-1667

> Born in Cambridge, the son of a barber. Educated at Perse School, Cambridge. Entered Gonville and Caius College, Cambridge, in 1626 as a Sizar. Distinguished himself as a student. Took holy orders in 1633, M.A. degree in 1634. Made a reputation as a substitute preacher at St. Paul's Cathedral in London. Attracted attention of Laud who sent him to Oxford for further education. Became fellow of All Souls College, Oxford, in 1636. From 1638 to 1642 was rector of Uppinham. Married in 1639. Received D.D. degree from Oxford by royal mandate in 1642. Served as chaplain to the household of King Charles I. Captured by Parliamentary forces in 1645. After release lived under the patronage of the Earl of Carbery at an estate in Carmarthenshire, Wales. Here he did most of his writing. *Holy Living* published in 1650, *Holy Dying* in 1651. In 1655 imprisoned

briefly for reasons unknown. In 1658 given a lectureship at Lisburn in Ireland. In 1660 became Bishop of Down and Connor in Ireland. Fought with Presbyterians. Lived in Ireland for the rest of his life. Buried in cathedral at Dromore.

R. Heber, ed., *The Works of Jeremy Taylor*, rev. C. P. Eden (1847-1854), 10 vols.

C. J. Stranks, *The Life and Writings of Jeremy Taylor* (1952)

It will have been obvious from our study that Taylor was a man of his age who had his fair share of human failings. There is evidence in his writings to support Chillingworth's suggestion that Taylor slighted the arguments of his opponents; a good example of this is to be found in some of his criticism of the Roman Church, where he is sometimes guilty of arguing from the particular to the general. There are instances when he may be accused with justice of special pleading, of using his sources uncritically, and of expressing views which his arguments could not sustain. His controversial writings particularly provide illustrations of his failure in these directions. Yet these shortcomings may be attributed to faults of temperament rather than of character. Taylor possessed the intuition of a poet rather than the logic of a philosopher. Having found an answer to a problem by intuition, his logic was not always able to support it. He was, by nature, a practical rather than a systematic theologian; his main interest lay in devotional not speculative divinity. In short, his conception of piety had a marked and increasing influence on his whole theological outlook.

H. Trevor Hughes
The Piety of Jeremy Taylor (London: Macmillan, 1910), p. 153

Taylor does not derive his peculiar doctrine of original sin from the Bible. Rather, he finds in scripture an interpretation of the human infirmity which he has observed about him. Because his sources are so free, his understanding of the human predicament can move paradoxically in two directions—expressing itself on the one hand in flashes of bitter satire and on the other in an attitude of far-reaching tolerance for diverse opinions.

Although Taylor was beguiled by no hope that human ignorance might eventually be overcome, he was aware that progress toward knowledge was possible. His thought, therefore, is marked by appeals to human reason, to scripture, to the practice of the ancient church, and to mystical intuition. Over and beyond these, he seems to have regarded a certain submission to the discipline of the Church of England and the practice of the holy life as ways by which the intellectual problems of faith might be skirted completely. Indeed, the concept of holy living may be regarded as Taylor's major theme, and as it is the only adequate preparation for holy dying, so to it repentance is the only possible approach. . . .

I arrive at two conclusions—the first, the suggestion of a definite (but not rigid) link between these three styles and Taylor's major themes. Careful study of all his work reveals that upon his imagination the ideas of piety and repentance, the beauty of the liturgy, and the pathos of the life of Christ worked most profoundly. The afflatus which these themes produced is to be linked to the periodic, Ciceronian style by the very nature of Taylor's treatment of them. His approach is for the most part neither polemic nor analytical. Rather, it is rhapsodic—free in form—with development achieved not by logical succession of ideas but by accumulation of ideas around a central concept. Such development leads to smoothly rounded, self-contained periods in which high emotion is given ample expression. But an equally powerful influence on Taylor's style was his sense of human sin, his resentment at Catholic interpretation of doctrine, and his hostility toward casuistry and speculation. These ideas found expression in a curt style which preserved the movements of a critical, active mind and was, at the same time, in its peevish brusquerie, an appropriate vehicle for the expression of personal impatience.

We are on safe ground as long as we regard Taylor's several styles as natural expressions of his thematic material and as well-nigh perfect reproductions of the tone of his thinking. Less certainly can it be said that Taylor turned from one style to another as a means of conveying the deeper significance of his material. In other words, we must not make the relationship over-subtle by supposing that Taylor had an audience of metaphysically-inclined friends to whom he sought to communicate a level of heightened consciousness in extraordinarily subtle prose. His constant use of the established literary forms suggests that he was writing for the same comparatively simple audience that his predecessors for three centuries had addressed. Much of his work was composed for families uprooted by the Civil War; the sermons were preached in a small country church—or if in London, in a tiny chapel in the oldest section of the city. Of all those close to Taylor, perhaps only Anne Conway and Henry Vaughan (whose relationship is problematical) were capable of responding to very acute prose.

J. R. King
ES (October, 1956), pp. 201, 208

CYRIL TOURNEUR
1575-1626?

Almost nothing known of his life. No records of birth or education. Published *Transformed Metamorphosis*, allegorical poem, in 1600. May have been the author of a prose pamphlet, *Laugh and Lie Down* printed in

1605. Usually regarded as the author of *The Revenger's Tragedy*, printed in 1607 as acted by King's Men. Has been disputed by many scholars and is still uncertain. Was associated with the Vere family. In 1609 published a funeral elegy on the death of Sir Francis Vere under whom he had served as a soldier in the Low Countries. In 1611 published *Atheist's Tragedy*, one play which can be attributed to him with certainty. Is associated with other plays. Lost play, *The Nobleman*, written in 1610 or 1611. Employed by Vere and Cecil families as an emissary. Arrested in 1617 by order of the Privy Council. Reasons not known. Released under the bond of Sir Edward Cecil. Accompanied Sir Edward on an expedition to Cadiz in search of Spanish treasure ships in 1625. Disease ravaged ships. Many sailors put ashore at Kinsale. Presumably was among these and died there of disease.

A. Nicoll, ed., *The Works of Cyril Tourneur* (1930)
I. Ribner, ed., *The Atheist's Tragedy* (1964)
R. A. Foakes, ed., *The Revenger's Tragedy* (1966)
P. B. Murray, *A Study of Cyril Tourneur* (1964)

Tourneur's images suggest continually that the court society he depicts has grossly perverted the natural, accepted standards of living. His spokesmen are depressed minor gentry; he identifies Nature and neglected innocence with the old-fashioned manor. A number of metaphors emphasize this point of view (vengeance is "murder's quitrent," for example); while to the court world of bribery and prostitution, with its shifting false appearances—the cosmetics, the torchlight, the jewels, the masks and revelling repeatedly pictured in the action and the poetry—Tourneur opposes his abiding reality, the skull. Such a contrast is essentially traditional. Much of the treatment is contemporary; from *The Malcontent* and the disciplined irony of Jonson's *Volpone* (1605), for example, comes Tourneur's general plan of a society of vicious humours which draws to itself a disguised avenger-satirist who hastens its inner tendency to dissolution. But his central metaphors of disguise or transformation also reach back, through Jonson, to popular tradition. And his satiric tirades gain vigour and assurance from the custom of the Morality plays dealing with social abuses, where the Deadly Sins disguise themselves from the other actors, but address the audience directly in mocking terms of frankness. What Tourneur himself contributes is a uniquely strict attention to his images, both as emblems and realities, and to his words, both as sounds and as clusters of meaning.

L. G. Salinger
The Age of Shakespeare (London: Penguin Books, 1955), p. 344

Although the author calls his play [*The Revenger's Tragedy*] a tragedy, the dramatic types that participate in the ironic reversals are, it would seem, associated more properly with farce. They are not so much living characters as embodiments of abstract qualities, symbols of lust and ambition, chastity, and hypocrisy. Even Vindice, the protagonist, is unreal: a fiercely energetic incarnation of the spirit of revenge. The figures who make up the play lack variety and complexity; they have neither nobility nor humanity. Plotting and counterplotting, betraying each other and themselves, they are puppets hurled from one situation to another, automata whose misfortunes stir sardonic mirth rather than terror or compassion. Painted with the broad strokes of carricature, they are fantastic creations: monstrous, it is true, but also amusing. . . .

If the characters and situations are often broadly comic, the language is not of the kind usually associated with farce. The verse is, indeed, Jacobean blank verse of the great period before the decadence: poetry of an order encountered most frequently in the supreme tragedies of the age. Such is the impression that remains with the reader—in spite of the careless alternating between verse and prose; in spite of the naïvely aphoristic couplets that jingle discordantly in the most splendid passages; in spite of lines that are too long or too short, of syntax that is occasionally awkward, of metre that is at times impossible. . . .

This curious fusing of blank verse of tragic grandeur, farcical situations, and melodramatic violence sets the play apart from the rest of Jacobean drama, gives it indeed a status that is unique. *The Revenger's Tragedy* may perhaps be best described as macabre art and, one might add, the sort of macabre art usually associated with the Middle Ages. For, although the background of the play is Renaissance Italy, the point of view suggests more often the medieval heritage. A heritage that was always close to the Elizabethans, it was to exert a profound influence upon the literature of the Jacobean age—a time when many thinking men were given to skepticism, looking back with melancholy to the past rather than hopefully awaiting the future.

Samuel Schoenbaum
Middleton's Tragedies (New York: Columbia
Univ. Pr., 1955), pp. 23-28

Inspired by the literary and scholarly idealism of Renaissance humanism, Chapman and Jonson find their tragic fables in the pages of history. Untouched by their classicism, Tourneur finds the materials of tragedy in the popular myth of Italianate evil, which had already become a common property of the stage. It is a tribute to Tourneur's powers that with all our knowledge of dramatic convention we still feel that *The Revenger's Tragedy* expresses an intensely personal view of reality, though we know its setting is the Italy of the *novella* and of Elizabethan Protestant imaginations, the Italy described so vividly by Ascham and others as a sink of atheism, luxury, and sensual abandonment. In other Jacobean tragedies, Italianate settings are used more or less as backdrops for such glorious villains as Brachiano or Ferdinand. Tourneur's characters, however, do not transcend the Italianate; they epitomize it. His imagination triumphs over nature and reality by distilling the essence of Italianate horror, by pre-empting and refining a conventional image of sensuality and violence.

At the same time that Tourneur's genius presents the Italianate image in all its lurid perfection, his artistic discipline (a rare attribute in Jacobean dramaturgy) makes it difficult to penetrate beyond the image to the mind that created it. Other Jacobean playwrights universalize the action of their dramas by philosophical reflection. Tourneur admits none in *The Revenger's Tragedy* unless we call Vindice's choric commentaries "philosophical." Other dramatists use traditional parallels and correspondences to enlarge their dramatic scene; their characters, vehicles for philosophical and moral attitudes, are archetypal Stoics or politicians. Tourneur's allegorical method of characterization paradoxically denies universal importance to such automata of evil as the Duke and Lussurioso, for though they personify particular vices they are no more than samplings of a depraved world. They cannot vary or develop; they cannot step momentarily out of character to comment on their world because their existence in the reader's imagination depends upon the consistent pulse of the vicious passion which they embody.

Actually Tourneur suggests the existence of his dramatic universe not by philosophical expansion of his immediate scene, but by the use of perspective. He draws a group of characters who are, depending upon their prominence in the play, "large" or "small," distinct or vague. . . . Tourneur cannot convince us that his tragic universe holds a mirror up to nature, but he skillfully creates an illusion of depth in his two-dimensional scene by suggesting that the Duke's court extends and merges imperceptibly with a larger world which, if brought into the foreground, would be no different from the group of sensualists which Tourneur examines in detail.

Robert Ornstein
The Moral Vision of Jacobean Tragedy (Madison, Wisc.:
Univ. Wisconsin Pr., 1960), pp. 107-8

In Tourneur's tragedies the evil characters outnumber by far the virtuous ones, and their evil is so complete and all-embracing as to leave no room for compensating virtues of any kind; they are shocking in the absoluteness of their depravity. In the same manner such virtuous characters as Castiza or Charlemont are so completely free from sin that they lose all illusion of humanity. It has been suggested that Tourneur was so influenced by current Calvanistic doctrine that he came to see the vast majority of mankind as utterly depraved, with only a few saints who could aspire to heaven. It is obvious that he stresses the world's evil in terms of the gluttony and sexuality for which Puritans had a particular horror, and he does dwell upon the terrors of death which were their constant concern.

But the horror of the body and its pleasures, coupled with a constant concern with death in its most terrible forms, need not be confined to Jacobean Puritanism. These were common features also of medieval asceticism, closely associated with the tradition of *contemptus mundi*. The bitterly satirical portrait of Langebeau Snuffe in *The Atheist's Tragedy* certainly makes it difficult to believe that Tourneur himself could have belonged to any Puritan sect. The rigid division of the characters into good and evil, rather than furnishing evidence of a doctrine of the damned and elect, may simply reflect the rigidity of an allegorical method. Tourneur's characters are never meant to convey the illusion of reality. One like Lussurioso is simply a symbol of lechery, and he contains little which is not a part of this symbol. Castiza or Castabella are symbols of chastity, and they cannot be anything but absolutely virtuous. To find Calvinistic doctrine in Tourneur may also be to find in his characters a degree of verisimilitude and psychological development which simply is not in them. The enormity of their evil may reflect not a doctrine of man's total depravity so much as the dramatist's desire to shock his audience into belief. He may be relying upon a type of exaggeration which is a common feature of moral *exemplum*. Sin must be writ large.

The Revenger's Tragedy is not, as it has so often been regarded, a savage melodrama in which a cynical, embittered adolescent expresses the omnipresence of evil and his own hatred for humanity. The play embodies a distinct moral vision, and this involves more than a belief in the inevitability of divine retribution or in the futility of human vengeance. If the play's action is an ingeniously related series of ironic reversals, these are meaningful only in terms of the larger religious principle which governs the total play: the self-destructive quality of evil and the final insignificance in the light of eternity of man's very life on earth. The scorn for the world which Eliot has called mere adolescent cynicism reflects a profoundly religious view of life, for *The Revenger's Tragedy* is a dramatic statement *de contemptu mundi* which uses the very symbols by which this philosophy of worldly withdrawal and heavenly contemplation had expressed itself in the Middle Ages. . . .

To this central theme of the impermanence and imperfection of all human institutions in the light of eternity, all of the parts of the play contribute. It calls for characters who are symbols of vanity and waste; it infuses the action with an irony which underscores the futility of all worldly aspirations, and it runs as a leading motif through the poetic imagery, with its constant playing upon impermanence, time and change.

This central theme is supported by the unique quality of Tourneur's dramatic verse, whose rapidity of movement T. S. Eliot has noted: "His phrases seem to contract the images in his effort to say everything in the least space, the shortest time." The total play provides the emotional equivalent of the statement that life is brief and fleeting, full of the evil of a corrupt and decaying world, hastening always towards inevitable death. To seek the things of the world is only to involve one's self in the evils of the world, to sin, to suffer its consequences and to die, for man's most careful plans may be frustrated by fate with a gruesome irony. The only reality worth man's efforts is the heaven which lies always ahead and which may be attained by the kind of withdrawal from life and cultivation of one's own piety which is mirrored in Castiza and Antonio. From the conviction of heaven's reality springs the sense of reconciliation at the end.

Irving Ribner
Jacobean Tragedy (London: Methuen, 1962), pp. 74-77

The energizing forces in Tourneur's play, the vitality that makes it more than a piece of nicely controlled irony, are centred on the sins condemned: murder, lust, gluttony, adultery, incest—the list is considerable, and a familiar one to readers of late Elizabethan drama. That Tourneur's attitude is not as healthy or as richly affirmative as Shakespeare's goes without saying. On the other hand Shakespeare himself, like all the major Elizabethan dramatists, saw the health and vitality of life most clearly and most richly when he was writing also about its tragic and chaotic possibilities. It is clearly basic to the Elizabethans that tragedy is a form which, leading to destruction and death, liberates at the same time life and energy. Rather than any concept of tragic loss or the "regenerative" force of love, it is this *paradox* of death and life, informing a given play from its opening scenes onwards, which is at the heart of the Elizabethan tragic vision.

Broadly, there are two aspects of *The Revenger's Tragedy*—related but also distinct—which display activating vitality and energy of a kind which offers something more rewarding than a mere sense of "control." The first is the treatment of traditional Revenge situations and themes; the second a movement away from comparatively simple moral attitudes of this kind towards the more complex, near-metaphysical wit we noted briefly in the last chapter. Certainly it is clear that Tourneur does not develop the traditional Revenge plot as Kyd tended to do—informing it at key points with a Hamlet-like introspection from the hero. His attitude is, rather, to make a substantial issue of the neatness and precision of the moralistic Revenge plot, but to lead from this at key points to attitudes and verse which are the reverse of simple and which rely, more clearly even than Shakespeare's commonly do, on a recognizably "metaphysical"

wit. The opening lines of the play, with their rapidly telescoping irony—
"grey-haired adultery," "royal lecher," "juiceless luxur"—are typical.

Tourneur relates these two strands of development in his play—clearly
they are both kinds of "wit"—though he keeps them at the same time
recognizably distinct. The key to a true reading of *The Revenger's Tragedy*
is in the movement of attention we are constantly forced to make between
the almost naïvely simple clarity of Revenge morality on the one hand,
and the richer, more complex wit of metaphysical or near-metaphysical
verse on the other. Even within a single speech, such as Vendice's opening
soliloquy, a couplet movement in the verse, re-enacting in smaller compass
the simple structure of a Revenge morality, jostles up against and mingles
with the more complex lines. Tourneur is a great dramatist in that, while
he senses the limitations of the convention he is using, his wit is not dulled
or bewildered by this (as Webster's, for instance, very often is) because
at the same time he also sees firmly and richly areas of experience beyond
the merely conventional. This I think is why the conventional side of his
writing has a lightness, vivacity and precision which none of the other
Jacobean tragedians—and hardly even Kyd or Marlowe—can achieve. If
Tourneur had been merely conscious of rounding off an exhausted convention, or of seeing its limitations, he would have been either a much duller,
or a much more confused writer than he is. As it is the vivacity of his
Revenge writing both springs from, and in turn enables him to formulate
more surely, his grip on experience outside the simple Revenge convention.
Seeing Revenge clearly leads Tourneur outwards to "metaphysical" writing;
this in turn lends sureness of purpose to the Revenge structure itself.

T. B. Tomlinson
A Study of Elizabethan and Jacobean Tragedy
(Cambridge Univ. Pr., 1964), pp. 109-10

THOMAS TRAHERNE
1637?-1674

Discovered just at the end of the nineteenth century, and not published
until 1903 and 1910, Traherne has been less well known than other seventeenth-century meditational poets. His poetry and poetic prose *Centuries
of Meditations* indicate his intense devotion and self-consciousness. Incidental prose and letters remain unedited. He took three degrees at
Brasenose College, Oxford, and served as a chaplain to the Keeper of the
Seals.

H. M. Margoliouth, ed., *Thomas Traherne's Centuries, Poems, and
Thanksgivings* (1958)
Gladys I. Wade, *Thomas Traherne* (1946)

POEMS

The charm of these meditations, a charm they have exercised ever since their publication over an increasing circle of readers, has its root in the intimacy of the revelation we are privileged to share. In the beginning they were written solely for Mrs. Hopton, intended for no other eye than hers. They contain the most complete expression of Traherne's philosophy, because it was the purpose of their writing to present the unity and glory and reasonableness of that philosophy to one incapable of achieving it for herself. The lucidity and the completeness of the presentation are due in part to the limitations of the one who was to read them; the fervor and passion of it to Traherne's desire that she should share with him a "great enriching Verity."

One of the dominant ideas is that Traherne's own philosophy should be set forth. Now one aspect of it, now another passes in review; now the nature of God, now the nature of man, now man's relationship to God and to his fellow creatures, or the mystery of God becoming Man in the person of Christ.

The other dominant idea is that the path for sinful and stunted man to the attainment of his full stature is found by opening the door of nature; that a serious reverent study of simple natural things, even the most ordinary, will lead him who follows it to the very throne of God. The *Centuries* are molded by the pressure of these two ideas, as they are quickened by emotion—by a companionable human love for a friend as well as by the still white heat of another passion that is the vital fire of all Traherne writes.

Gladys I. Wade
Thomas Traherne (Princeton, N. J.: Princeton
Univ. Pr., 1946), pp. 183-84

Few of the poems of Thomas Traherne can be said to be in the tradition of Horace's second epode, although they represent a logical enough development of the *beatus ille*-themes in some respects. The poetry of this Anglican minister is the deeply personal record of a man who penetrated beyond mere argument to a fountain of spiritual bliss. For this reason it is more concerned with the results of this achievement, than with the various steps leading to it. Traherne's chief and only concern was with felicity, and so in him we have the most extreme example of the type of *beatus vir* which is here referred to as the Hortulan Saint.

In Traherne's conception of felicity, neo-Platonic ideas outweigh the neo-Stoic. The picture which he draws of the *beatus vir* is almost entirely free of negative characteristics. His happiness is not derived from an absence of misery, but from a positive enjoyment of life, which in its turn is based upon a neo-Platonic purification of sense experience. Speaking in terms of themes, this means that Traherne focussed on the themes of the Earthly Paradise and on the mystic vision of the *beatus vir*, rather than on the Stoic themes of contentment and obscurity.

Maren-Sofie Røstvig
The Happy Man (Oxford: Basil Blackwell, 1954), p. 295

The images Traherne chose, up to his last enraptured outbursts on infinity, are all the circle images so dear to the imagination of his century, the sphere, the globe, the ring; his concept of infinity does not force itself out of the circle of perfection until it has been made communicable to men in forms they can recognize and revere. Only when he was ready to transcend his own limitations was Traherne ready to abandon the unconscious image of the old, limited universe. . . .

For Traherne, finite man with his infinite capacity was a great and wonderful creation, deliberately made finite to be the fixed measure of created things. Such a man, so significantly endowed, deserved to be measured for his salvation against the infinity of space. . . .

Infinity of space was his image of the spiritual infinity of God's goodness; only by understanding and accepting infinite space could man approach ultimate union with the infinitely infinite God.

Rosalie L. Colie
HLQ (November, 1957), pp. 80-81

The thirty-seven poems of the Dobell Folio MS, which are scrupulously written in Traherne's own hand, constitute a complete five-part meditation which fulfills all the major conditions of a Jesuit exercise. It consists of an opening "composition of place" (four poems), followed by a second prelude or "pre-meditation" (six poems), and finished by a three-part analysis "according to the three powers of the soul"—the memory, the understanding, and the will (eight, ten, and nine poems). So skillfully has Traherne ensured the continuity of these sections that it would not always be easy to fix the demarcation between them had not the titles of the poems indicated the exact lines of division. . . . One may regret that Traherne did not leave a title for the whole sequence which, there can be no doubt, was a sustained effort on a single theme. In general terms, the meditation examines the relation between God and His creatures, exploring thereby the conditions on which earthly and eternal bliss may be obtained and to the end that the Christian poet's life may be made joyful and serviceable. But within this broad outline regeneration is the governing motif and Traherne has taken for his text Mark x. 15: "Whosoever shall not receive the kingdom of God as a little child, he shall not enter therein." To read Traherne's poetry as, first and foremost, a solipsistic or Neo-Platonic document is to miss at once the catholic foundation of his art and it is only a knowledge of his basic form which can enable us to assess confidently Traherne's modifications of traditional Christian thought.

John Malcolm Wallace
ELH (June, 1958), pp. 80-81

The title given to Traherne's miraculously recovered manuscript, *Centuries of Meditation,* was not of his own devising, and it partly obscures the intention of the book. It suggests that we have here a series of devout and personal reflections, upon which we can ponder if we choose to do so; but it does not convey the sense of urgency that runs through the whole work.

Traherne's purpose, as he clearly states it at the beginning, was to expound his own tested method of achieving felicity. It is the record of a successful quest, but at the same time a guide-book. It was designed for his friend Susannah Hopton, a Royalist lady earnestly given to pious pursuits. Assured of her personal interest, Traherne wrote freely about his own spiritual experiences in childhood and since; but the autobiographical passages are not mere reminiscences; they are subservient to his declared intention, that of charting the road to joy which he had himself discovered and trodden.

Margaret Bottrall
CQ (Summer, 1959), p. 126

"It is of the nobility of man's soul that he is insatiable," wrote Thomas Traherne. As Herbert embodied all the themes of the poets of content, Traherne was the seventeenth-century climax of the poets of aspiration. Mystic as he was, he seemed to the critics who discovered his poetry in the nineteenth century to have lived apart from his time in a timeless universe, as remote from the discoveries of his age as his own works remained for more than two hundred years. We know now that Traherne was deeply affected by the discoveries of the new science and the implications of the new philosophy. When he saw eternity in a grain of sand, he was speaking not only mystically but microscopically. The worlds unnumbered through which his God was known were his heritage from both the Platonists and the telescope. In the *Centuries of Meditations* he spoke metaphorically of the impact of learning upon him in his university days: "I saw that there were things in this world of which I never dreamed, glorious secrets. . . . There I saw into the nature of the Sea, the Heavens, the Sun, the Moon, and the Stars, the Elements,

Minerals, and Vegetables. All which appeared like the King's Daughter, all glorious within."

But training in science and philosophy served only to heighten youthful intuition. Even in childhood he was engrossed with the two concepts that are most persistent in his prose and poetry: Eternity and Infinity.

Marjorie H. Nicolson
The Breaking of the Circle (New York:
Columbia Univ. Pr., 1960), pp. 196-97

GENERAL

The cornerstone of Traherne's concept of life is his unfaltering belief in the immanence of God. It was a truth that he had unconsciously accepted before he had learned anything else of his environment. Consequently, like Wordsworth, he felt the innocence and sanctity of childhood and its peculiar, intuitive appreciation of the highest truths. In the early years of life God is especially near to one. . . .

Traherne, however, fails to account for these spiritual powers of childhood as explicit as does either Vaughan or Wordsworth. The explanation for them was the child's nearness to the life in the unseen world whence he came; the soul comes to this world trailing clouds of glory. But Traherne is less certain of pre-existence. . . . Nevertheless, Traherne is just as sure of the child's superior insight. Calling himself in infancy a little stranger, he says: "My knowledge was Divine. I knew by intuition those things which since my Apostasy, I collected again by the highest reason," and asks: "Is it not strange, that an infant should be heir of the whole World?" This one thought fills the first thirty pages of Traherne's poems, and really underlies them all.

Elbert N. S. Thompson
PQ (January, 1929), pp. 98, 99

These reflections on his own early experiences lead Traherne to certain profound convictions or intuitions, to a conception of God, Man, and Nature which is both intensely philosophic and intensely poetic. He insists that God can only be known through the creation; that the creation only becomes significant . . . when it is mirrored and recreated by the mind of a man, which is more divine than its object; that man's duty is perpetually to recreate the world and to present it as an acceptable offering to God; and that happiness, felicity, consists in seeing the world as God sees it, feeling that all things are working together for good.

. . . as in his attitude to the doctrine of original sin and in his view of the cause and purpose of the creation, Traherne's fundamental intuitions, his fidelity to his own experience, seem to drive him beyond the bounds of orthodox Christianity. At times he seems very near to Pantheism, that doctrine which the Church has always looked upon with extreme disfavour, since its logical consequence is that good and evil are equally manifestations of God, and that God himself is no more than the *rerum natura*, the nature of things. Traherne, however, is able to preserve the conception of a God who is both immanent and transcendent; he never admits or recognizes the existence of any necessary evil in the creation, and moral evil he attributes entirely to man's misuse of his free will, often explicitly declaring that Heaven and Hell are within us. . . .

J. B. Leishman
The Metaphysical Poets (Oxford Univ. Pr., 1934), pp. 194, 197

If Traherne had indeed been as great a poet as he was a prose writer, he would have stood with Blake and Wordsworth. And he does not. Yet many of his gifts were not inferior to theirs; indeed he seems often astonishingly to have anticipated them, in phrase as well as in thought. Traherne had many of the essential gifts of a great poet. He had the greatest, for he had in the highest degree all that we mean by vision. No man ever lived in a vaster world than Traherne, or beheld more magnificent drama in the cosmos; no man ever saw beauty with clearer eyes, and beauty in one of its rarest forms; no man ever worshipped more truly the beauty he beheld, or served it with more complete devotion. He had passion and sincerity; he had culture and breadth of experience, access to all the treasures of books and contact at many points with the world of man; he had originality and intellectual force, so that nothing he wrote could be trivial or commonplace.

Yet he failed to be a great poet. Primarily, I believe it was because he never perceived the true function of poetry. He turned to it by a sort of instinct, and because his hero David was also a poet. Yet he did not ever perceive the creative power of the poetic imagination. . . .

Another error followed on this first one—his misunderstanding of form. He saw, and rightly, that the vision of beauty is the essential quality in poetry; he saw that words misused can obscure the vision. That perception saved him from many of the faults of his age; and his "Author to the Critical Peruser" anticipates in many respects Wordworth's famous preface. Where Traherne made his mistake—and Wordsworth was not quite innocent of it—was in thinking that one plain word was as good as another for the uses of poetry; that the function of words was negative, merely not to refract the visionary light. But as the greatest of poets have shown, this light will shine only through song. There is no virtue in mere plainness and simplicity.

Thus for Traherne there is not a vital connection between form and content; content may be the spirit of his work, but form is not the body shaped by that spirit, only a dress, embroidered and arranged with some care. The divine puts on the poet's dress, as Thomas Traherne says, "to win Acceptance. For we all descry When Precepts cannot, Poems take the Ey." The precepts are the thing, the verse a concession to human weakness.

Gladys I. Wade
Thomas Traherne (Princeton, N. J.: Princeton
Univ. Pr., 1946), pp. 194-96

HENRY VAUGHAN
1621-1695

> Born in Brecknockshire, Wales. Entered Jesus College, Oxford, in 1638. Left without taking a degree in order to study law in London. Served with the Royalist forces during the Civil War. Studied medicine at some unknown time. Practiced medicine for some time at Brecknock and later at Newton-by-Usk where he lived quietly for the rest of his life. Published a rendition of Juvenal's tenth satire in 1646, *Olor Iscanus* (*Swan of the Usk*), in the following year. Greatest work appeared in two parts of *Silex Scintillans* in 1650 and 1655.
>
> L. C. Martin, ed., *The Works of Henry Vaughan* (1957)
> F. E. Hutchinson, *Henry Vaughan* (1947)

HIS CONVERSION

The chief explanation for the change in Vaughan's views between 1654 and 1673 almost certainly resides, as in the case of his earlier conversion, in the political developments of the time. The Commonwealth, let us recall, came to an end five years after the publication of the second *Silex Scintillans*. The Restoration was a happy event for the Royalists. And when we consider that Vaughan was less than forty years old, it becomes almost inconceivable that he should fail to respond to new conditions affording, among other benefits, a liberation of spirit that challenged retirement. His medical career, which in 1673 had extended for "many years," shows his adjustment to these better times, which was as natural as his previous reaction to political ostracism.

The account of Vaughan's religious conversion becomes, then, a simple and understandable story. During and immediately after his residence in London, the young law student indulged his poetic impulses in imitative experiments with various literary forms and themes. Results of these first attempts he later saw fit to publish, along with a Latin translation, as the *Poems* in 1646. In the meantime, the frustration of his study of law proving an incentive to literary effort, he continued to write with growing earnestness. Although his interest in conventional themes continued, as the true import of the war became manifest Vaughan, disturbed by the social and political confusion, was impelled to turn his poetic attention also to themes relating to the conflict and frequently to infuse into other expressions his concern about the moral issues of the strife. In 1647 such writings—probably along with some translations—had accumulated considerably, and on 17 December he wrote a dedication with a view to publishing the work when sufficiently augmented. Having been attracted to the sacred writing of George Herbert, however, Vaughan was already experimenting with religious themes, and he now began to find relief for his increasing perturbation not only in secular compositions which more overtly attacked the prospering Parliamentarians (and were therefore unpublishable) but also in pious verses reflecting the manner and mood of *The Temple*. His dejection deepening as the signs of a Royalist defeat increased, he turned more and more to Herbert as a source of inspiration and guidance and eventually came to devote his literary talent chiefly to pious compositions. The final overthrow of the monarchy and the execution of the King supplied the impulse of 1650 to bring forth the sacred verse as appropriate testimony to the efficacy of Christian faith during the current triumph of evil.

E. L. Marilla
RES (January, 1945), pp. 21-22

"Regeneration" is formed out of an endeavor to convey insight into the initial stages of the mystic way, termed Awakening, Purgation, and Illumination, and it ends in a prayer for that death of the self which is rebirth in God. These four quantums constitute its broad structures, while the archetypes of the quest or night journey, and the *magnum opus* of the spiritual alchemists inform its progression and imagery. Included in this large frame are the essential matter and meaning of Vaughan's whole work. "Regeneration" is the map of his country. . . .

The implication in [the last] stanza is that beyond all a man can do the attainment of the final goal of the mystic way is an act of Grace. To be sure, he must strengthen his will, once he has awakened to reality, in order to undergo the rigors of the purgative way. Otherwise there is no hope at all. But even so, ultimate union is "not of him that willest or runneth but of God which hath mercy" (Rom. ix.16). It is the final poignant note in Vaughan that though he desired greatly he was not chosen.

Robert Allen Durr
SP (January, 1957), pp. 15, 28

If we accept the reality and depth of Vaughan's regeneration, in what respects may it be said to have inspired and shaped his poetry?

For one, it gave him something that had been notably lacking in his earlier writing, a vital and engrossing subject. No need to stress that important subjects, and the writer's attitude to them, do not necessarily produce important poetry—often the opposite; but, attracting and patterning the poet's experience towards a magnetic centre, infusing him with seriousness, passion, and urgency, they certainly create some of the indispensable conditions for important poetry. For the first time in his life Vaughan really had something to say for himself as a poet.

Next, one surmises, with some degree of certainty, that it was the urge to communicate his religious experience that at last threw fully open and brought into poetry all the rich world of his private imagination. Particularly because of those qualities of contrast and antithesis that we have already noticed, this world was one peculiarly suited to the expression of the great Christian opposite, while much of its substance—mornings, waters, green things below the earth (all objects of sensibility in the first place)—were readily translatable into spiritual metaphor and symbol. On the other hand, religion was not simply the magic key that unlocked this world; it also enriched it and to some extent ordered it into coherence, transforming its images, which were sometimes conventional and undistinguished, into complex, compelling symbols. The stars and streams of *Silex Scintillans* are the stars and streams of *Poems* and *Olor Iscanus*; but they are something else too, and it is the fire of Vaughan's regeneration that has transmuted them.

E. C. Pettet
Of Paradise and Light (Cambridge Univ. Pr., 1960), pp. 18-19

HIS HERMETICISM

More than any poem in *Silex Scintillans,* "Cock-crowing" is steeped in Hermetic tradition and then sublimated. Vaughan has caught his brother's figure of the *"Candle . . . tinn'd* in the *Elements."* The "house of light" too, simply and inevitably as it appears here, belongs to astrology. . . .

Vaughan always transmutes his Hermetic tradition in some personal and intimate manner. His cock here "dreams of Paradise" because all the creatures in his world—sun, stars, birds, and all of Nature except man— are pictured as belonging in some sort to the Eden-life of which we have spoken, and which symbolises Vaughan's own desire. But meanwhile the cock also "dreams of light" because, acording to Hermetic tradition, he is a "solary" bird, and under the special influence of the sun. . . . And here we are brought to those Hermetic theories of "sympathy," "magnetism," and "influence," which underlie so many of his poems, and are themselves underpropped in his case by a fundamental personal emotion.

Elizabeth Holmes
Henry Vaughan and the Hermetic Philosophy (Oxford:
Basil Blackwell, 1932), pp. 36-38

Henry Vaughan, then, both knew and in some degree used characteristic Hermetic ideas and language. Having said this much, we have perhaps given sufficient importance to the element in his work. There were many Hermetists, but only one Henry Vaughan, nor is he to be confined in the one term, Hermetic. Even the debt to his brother is by no means assured. Parallel passages . . . are the exception, and, if we assume genuinely strong fraternal bonds, remarkably rare. The brothers are distinct, each an individual in his own rights. There is very little in Henry Vaughan to justify the suspicion that he was, like his brother, a seeker for converts to a special order of mysticism. . . .

Henry Vaughan, I believe, was poet first, and Hermetist, if at all, only by a temperamental attraction to a mystic view of man and of nature. A religious man by instinct, a poet and lover of nature besides, what was more natural than that the Hermetic sense of spirit in nature should appeal to him as a reconciliation of the two dominant interests of his life?

Wilson O. Clough
PMLA (December, 1933), pp. 1128, 1129

How far Henry Vaughan shared his brother's interest in the Hermetic literature cannot be gauged. Besides anything he may have read in Thomas's writings, he shows occasional traces of independent knowledge of the writers whom his brother quotes. For instance, he interpolates into his translation of Nieremberg a quotation from "Another Hermetist" besides the one just cited in his original. [There is a] single quotation from Agrippa. . . . He interpolates in Nieremberg a quotation from Paracelsus also, which includes the phrase "the night is the working-time of Spirits," and he turns it to much profit in his wonderful poem "The Night." The preface to his translation of Nolle suggests that he had some acquaintance with Paracelsian medicine, but this would hardly affect his poetry. Professor Martin has shown beyond a doubt Henry Vaughan's indebtedness to the *Hermetica* for a long passage in "The Importunate Fortune," and this clear case makes Professor Martin's other instances probable.

There are enough parallel sentences in Thomas Vaughan's treatises and Henry's poems to show that the elder brother had some acquaintance with the writings of Eugenius Philalethes, but it is unlikely that he followed his brother far into the maze of his blend of theosophy, alchemy, and occult philosophy.

F. E. Hutchinson
Henry Vaughan (Oxford Univ. Pr., 1947), pp. 151-52

The objection suggested here to the Hermetic assumption, however, is not to the Hermetic image as such but to the implication that the use of Hermetic imagery implies a deep-seated Hermeticism, a Gnostic dualism. The source of an image in the history of ideas is one thing; its use by a particular poet in a particular poem is another. Vaughan does often posit an image as intended to be true for its own sake and not merely because it is a convenient scheme by which to demonstrate the truth of something else. But any number of images may be seen as true and still posit the same truth beyond them. The silkworm of "Resurrection and Immortality," for example, is seen in terms that probably owe a lot to Hermetic science. On the other hand, there is little doubt that Vaughan looked upon the silkworm as intended by God to shadow forth transcendent truths; it would have been so intended whether it occurred to the poet or not; for him the universe is an allegory of glory. There is nothing, then, in the formulation, as such, to differentiate traditional Neoplatonic Christian borrowings from the rather heterodox borrowings from Hermeticism. The stuff of Vaughan's imagery can be posited for the double truth—that of its own validity and of the validity beyond—whatever its source. Vaughan's use of Hermetic imagery seems to be the same as that of any other imagery he lighted upon; in fact, he saw the Hermetic image in the same way he saw the allegorical image, and he used it in the same way. But the allegorical image, drawn from Biblical commentary, apparently shaped his use of Hermetic material, and not vice versa.

Ross Garner
Henry Vaughan, Experience and the Tradition (Chicago: Univ. Chicago Pr., 1959), p. 90

GENERAL

Vaughan's chief significance as a nature poet lies, in my opinion, less in the intensity of his appreciation of nature, or in the beauty of his nature passages, than in the scope and character of his interests: it is these that make him so remarkable a precursor of the eighteenth-century romantic poets. Not of course that he broke all the prison bars of his time. Indeed, some of his admirers have harmed him by over-stating his greatness as a nature poet. . . . He rarely finds language to describe, perhaps he did not often perceive, what we think of to-day as landscape beauty. . . . He appreciates spring but not autumn. To him nature seems chiefly appropriate in poetry as the illustration of some religious idea. In many respects, then, he is a child of his century.

And yet his poetry contains many flashes of a liberated spirit. Often he hints at our more catholic and more subtle interest in nature. . . . In all nature about him, he saw—sometimes, at least—a beautiful, harmonious unity. Tree, herb, flower, bird, and even the stones under foot had hidden away in them a "tincture," or "touch," of the divine spirit. They spoke to him of order and obedience and of praise to God, and they occasioned some of his most profound thoughts about life and death.

Alexander C. Judson
PMLA (March, 1927), pp. 155-56

Some readers have professed to discover in Vaughan the traces of an hermetic philosophy of profound depths. It may be there; if so, it belongs not to literature but to cryptography. The mystical element in Vaughan which belongs to his poetry is there for any one to see; it is "mysticism" only by a not uncommon extension of the term. A genuine mystical *statement* is to be found in the last canto of the Paradiso; this is primarily great poetry. An equally genuine mysticism is expressed in the verses of St. John of the Cross; this is not a statement, but a riddling expression; it belongs to great mysticism, but not to great poetry. Vaughan is neither a great mystic nor a very great poet. . . .

T. S. Eliot
The Dial (September, 1927), p. 260

. . . Vaughan muses on the early days of the world and of Christianity in much the same way as Spenser and other poets had mused on the traditional legend of a Golden Age and on the days of Chivalry. . . . The difference is that, while the ideal with which Spenser unfavourably contrasted his own age was formed from the romances and the classic poets, Vaughan's was formed from Scripture. But these reflections on the world's decay also suggested to Vaughan another line of meditation which . . . is to be found in the works of only one other of his contemporaries, Thomas Traherne. He returned, not only to the early days of the world, but to his own early days, to the days of his childhood, in which, so it seemed to him, his soul, not yet corrupted by the ways of the world or dulled by the lethargy of custom, had looked upon the Creation as God intended all men to look upon it, as a wonderful and glorious thing, the garment of God. This idea is expressed in the most famous of all his poems, *The Retreate*. . . . Only in these two poems [*The Retreate* and *Childe-hood*] does Vaughan reveal to us that he had made the new and thrilling discovery which forms the basis of all the thinking of his contemporary Traherne.

J. B. Leishman
The Metaphysical Poets (Oxford Univ. Pr., 1934), pp. 165-68

Whatever the provenience of Vaughan's thought in *The Retreate*, we may be confident that the nostalgia for a lost beauty which inspired the poem is not puerile. Some modern criticism has injected puerility into it, but that fact does not justify Mr. T. S. Eliot in the inference that Vaughan shared the sentimental attachment of certain twentieth century poets for childhood. The psychic infirmity with which Mr. Eliot charges him is, from the historical point of view, almost as recent a phenomenon on the spiritual scene as its diagnosis by Freud. There is no more of it in *The Retreate* and *Childe-hood* than there is in the words of Jesus to which those poems finally go back: "Verily I say unto you, Except ye be converted and become as little children, ye shall not enter into the kingdom of heaven." . . . Mr. Leishman puts the right interpretation on *The Retreate* when he says that it is a vision of "the Creation as God intended all men to look upon it, as a glorious thing, the garment of God." This does not mean that the poem should be read as a classic of "nature mysticism" or "natural religion." It should be read as the work of a poet who, though he may have been as deficient as one of his most sympathetic interpreters says that he was in experience of "the central core of . . . developed mysticism," was no less mature in his outlook upon childhood than the best of his contemporaries. *The Retreate* is a supremely poetic statement about childhood in relation to the soul's possible pre-existence and certain divine origin. It fully corresponded to the best intellectual as well as poetical position of its time upon a matter which then naturally seemed more theological than psychological.

Merritt Y. Hughes
PQ (July, 1941), pp. 498, 499

Turning to the religious poetry, if one goes straight through the two parts of *Silex Scintillans* and the few inferior pieces in *Thalia Rediviva*. . . the immediate impression will, I think, prove disappointing. Vaughan is much greater as a sacred than as a secular poet, but he is also much more uneven. He is writing now with a serious didactic purpose, with the remorseless earnestness of a recent convert. If we contrast the religious with the amatory verse, it is plain that his centre of attention has shifted not merely from profane to sacred love but from art to life—from the question of how to say it, to a deep concern for what he has to say. This is good in the main—there is a new depth and power—but it has its minor disadvantages. There is not the same careful finish; even more, there is not the same deliberate organisation: the individual love poems have a unity which is achieved only now and then in the religious poetry. . . . he lacks the power of impassioned argument in which Donne and Herbert are supreme; there is often no necessary connection, only a causal and casual connection, between thought and thought as his theme develops. And in didactic mood he goes on too long, as if compelled by conscience not to refrain from good words but to commend diligently each lesson that ingenious allegory can wring from the emblematic pages of Nature's book. When he achieves unity and succinctness, as he not infrequently does, it is on a less conscious plane. His religious insight is intuitional not ratiocinative, instantaneous not developing. . . . Thus, the unity of his most powerful pieces, such as *The World* and *The Night*, is an emotional and atmospheric unity, as he recreates through sensory material an intuition of eternal reality; it is a unity in which, as it were, the centre is at each point in the temporal succession of the poem. Quite often, however, Vaughan misses this unity altogether: he will write several good stanzas and then trail off into unnecessary moral amplification, or he will strike out isolated lines or phrases of great beauty and depth, which shine in incongruously drab surroundings.

S. L. Bethell
The Cultural Revolution of the Seventeenth Century
(New York: Roy Publishers, 1951), pp. 133-34

Vaughan brought a new range of experience within the compass of this style. No one else among Donne's followers watched the earth, sky, and water, the birds and flowers with the same emotion, nor with the same delicacy of observation. Vaughan lacked Donne's vigorous and varied awareness of human character and affairs; he lacked Herbert's sobriety and exquisite sense of form, his undeviating control of powerful feeling; but often his poetry has a radiance and a movement which neither of these attempts. Vaughan, who resembles Wordsworth in his nature mysticism, sometimes resembles Shelley in the ecstatic outpouring of his numbers. He is more lyrical than his masters. Perhaps he is less restrained by intellectual perplexity. He could immerse himself in rapturous contemplation of dawn or sunset. Neither Donne nor Herbert could have written *The Dawning*: but Vaughan would not have written it as he did had he not learnt from them and assimilated the metaphysical influence. It is a song of rapture, but with an intellectual ground base.

Joan Bennett
Four Metaphysical Poets (Cambridge Univ. Pr., 1953), p. 88

In general the sound-texture of Vaughan's poetry is plain spun, as his rhythm, especially in his favourite octosyllabic measure, is frequently undistinguished, mechanical, and sometimes clumsy. That said, it is perhaps relevant to notice here that the passage just quoted from *Dressing* draws heavily on the Bible and Herbert, for it is quite likely that its exceptional richness of word music was a carry-over from Vaughan's sources and that when the suggestive force of these echoes was spent he lapsed into his more common, plainer style.

One is forced to go further and admit that, so far as poetic melody is concerned, Vaughan had not a very sensitive ear. Even in those passages where he does achieve some pleasing aural effect one often feels that his melodic line was probably created without much contrivance and perhaps without much awareness. And there are certainly moments when his ear is quite defective. How dangerously close, for instance, he comes to destroying the delightful interchange of *i* and *o* vowels and the delicate *l* alliteration of

> their green branches shoot
> Towards the old and still enduring skies,
> While the low violet thrives at their root
>
> *The Timber*

with the jarring collision of "groves grow" in the immediately preceding phrase.

However, as we have already seen in *The Waterfall,* Vaughan often displays one vital and compelling rhythmical impulse in his poetry. Like so many of the metaphysicals, but more commonly than anyone else except Donne, he frequently creates a dynamic tension in his poems by forcing his predominantly speech rhythms across some fairly elaborate (and, if one likes to use the word, artificial) metrical form of diversified rhyme pattern and line length.

Negatively described, this tension arises from his resistance to the strong mechanical pressure that both his exacting and sometimes intricate rhyme scheme and his often arbitrary variations of line length exert upon his syntax and word-order, his shaping of cadences and placing of pauses. In more positive terms, he gives some potentially rigid, even constricting, metrical form suppleness and motion by freely running his sense across line endings, by employing strong mid-line pauses, and by expressing himself in varied cadences and long sweeps of rhythm extending over many lines, sometimes over an entire stanza.

Often, though not always, this tension between the cross-weaving thread of rhythm and the frame of stanzaic structure is heightened by strong counterpoint between the natural speech stresses and the underlying metrical pulse. Commonly these speaking stresses intensify or weaken the metrical beat, syncopate it, and produce consecutive strong accents. A striking example (though merely one out of many) of this kind of rhythmical effect is to be found in "As Time one day":

> Whére through thíck pángs, hígh ágonies
> Fáith into life bréaks, and deáth díes.

In particular, as we have already noticed in *The Waterfall* and elsewhere, Vaughan has a marked Keatsian habit of weighting the end of his lines with several closely recurrent stresses.

E. C. Pettet
Of Paradise and Light (Cambridge Univ. Pr., 1960), pp. 182-84

JOHN WEBSTER
ca. 1580-1634

No certain records of either birth or death. Probably the son of a merchant-tailor. May have studied at Middle Temple. Man of his name admitted in 1598. First work as a dramatist was collaboration with Munday, Drayton, Middleton, Dekker, Chettle, and Wentworth Smith on various plays for Philip Henslowe. Earliest probably *Caesar's Fall* (now lost) in 1602. Wrote Introduction for Marston's *Malcontent* in 1604. In 1605 collaborated with Dekker on *Westward Ho!* and *Northward Ho!* acted by Children of Paul's. *White Devil* written for Queen Anne's Men probably in 1611. Published in 1612. In 1613 or 1614 wrote *Duchess of Malfi* for King's Men. Not published until 1623. Wrote *Monumental Column* on the death of Prince Henry in 1613. Wrote 32 new characters for the sixth edition of Overbury's *Characters* in 1615. Wrote *Monument of Honour*, a Lord Mayor's Show sometime after 1616. Collaborated on *Keep the Widow Waking*. Is unheard of after 1624.

F. L. Lucas, ed., *The Works of John Webster* (1927), 4 vols.

J. R. Brown, ed., *The White Devil* (1960)

J. R. Brown, ed., *The Duchess of Malfi* (1964)

P. B. Murray, *A Study of John Webster* (1968)

There are few Jacobean tragedies in which innocence and guilt seem as irrelevant as in *The White Devil*. Despite the obliquity in *Bussy D'Ambois* there is a surge of moral passion that exceeds the demands of art and that overwhelms the conventionally contrived dramatic situations. In *The White Devil* the opposite seems true: the scorn and bitterness in its lines seem inadequate to the terror of the dramatic situations; even murders seem, to use Lodovico's phrase, no more than "flea-bytinges." Morally sensitive characters like Isabella and Marcello are weak and ineffectual, too easily silenced, murdered in dumb show or by a casual sword thrust. Those like Flamineo who effectively dissect the corruption of their world are part of that corruption and too perverse in their values to comprehend moral truths. Because their choric commentaries lack the moral accent of Vindice's speeches, we leave the play with the impression that the harshest reality of Flamineo's world is not the ruthless destruction of innocence but the ingratitude of princes and the venality of their underlings. In *King Lear* the perversion of the feudal bond of loyalty by servants like Oswald is a recurrent subject of moral commentary and a symbol of the annihilation of traditional moral and political values. But in *The White Devil* there are no faithful Kents to remind us that in the past servants did not always pander to their masters' wills. In the tragedies of Chapman, Jonson, and Tourneur, the decadence of the present scene is directly or indirectly contrasted with a previous norm of aristocratic values. But in *The White Devil* there is no suggestion that the courts of princes were once less corrupt or that the hunger for wealth, position, and sensual pleasure was not always the norm of human existence.

On the other hand, Webster does not deny the reality of virtue in *The White Devil*. He does not suggest that Isabella's devotion to Brachiano is sham or that Vittoria is the pattern of womanhood. Virtue does exist untainted and uncompromised, but it is impotent and ultimately meaningless—swept away into the same mist that enshrouds the fates of assassins and adulterers. . . .

The moralist teaches men how to avoid catastrophe; Webster is concerned only with how they accept it. The moralist explains the justice of men's falls; Webster does not reassure us that measure for measure is the law of existence. Armed with the doctrine of free will the moralist cannot believe in fatality; but in the hideous mist of error that enshrouds Webster's characters, no man can be called master of his fate, and no choice is clear until circumstances force men's decisions. Webster dramatizes the mystery of the irrational will without moralistic gloss. He offers no simple explanation of why Antonio, who is called a brave soldier, always chooses a coward's way or why Bosola obeys his baser instincts. If critics emphasize the irrationality of Ferdinand's motives rather than the Cardinal's, it is because the Cardinal does not attempt to explain his goals, while Ferdinand calls attention to the nightmarish confusion of his mind. Even as Goneril and Regan have no reason to torture Lear, so Ferdinand has no reason to torture his sister, unless a frenzied egomania is "reason" enough.

Robert Ornstein
The Moral Vision of Jacobean Tragedy (Madison, Wisc.:
Univ. Wisconsin Pr., 1960), pp. 132-33, 141

The fundamental contest in Webster's tragedies, though the revenge plot may disguise this, is not one between good and evil, but one between life and death. And since this is one in which the grave must have the victory, the action of *The Duchess of Malfi* shows not movement and counter-movement but an uninterrupted progression. Webster's interest in life's victims was shown in the new turn he gave to the traditional revenge plot; but it was only when he completely reversed this plot that he clearly discovered, or at least expressed, what I take to be his tragic vision. What moves me in Webster is the tragedy of the passionate human creature which reaches out towards life but advances slowly to decay until its radiance is shrouded in extinction. His is, I think, a smaller and less harmonious vision than Shakespeare's if only because it sees more of death than of life. It stresses suffering, but not reconciliation nor for-giveness.

Harold Jenkins
SS (Cambridge Univ. Pr., 1961), pp. 54-55

In *The Duchess of Malfi* Webster returns to the "mist" which is the world of *The White Devil,* but there is an immediate difference, for the later play opens with Antonio's description of the emergence of order and justice in France, and this conditions what follows, for the audience has seen at the beginning the possibility of a moral order, and nothing in the play can convince it of its impossibility. The two plays are linked by common motifs. Bosola too calls the world "a mist" (V. v, 118). Vittoria in *The White Devil* dies lamenting the corruption of the court: "O happy they that never saw the court" (V. vi, 261), and dying Antonio at the end of *The Duchess of Malfi* prays "And let my son fly the courts of princes" (V, iv, 84). The difference is that Vittoria could not escape the evils of the world, whereas the son of Antonio will have learned how to do so.

The moral statement of *The Duchess of Malfi* is not implicit in the stock apothegms of such virtuous characters as Delio and Pescara which, as has been observed, sometimes bear but slight relation to the action and read—though, by no means, always—like later additions. It is implicit in the total imaginative impression of the play, for *The Duchess* is a unified work, with mood, action, characterization and poetry all carefully shaped together as an assertion of the inherent dignity of man. As part of this total thematic statement the final act is of crucial importance, for its func-tion is to exhibit the effect upon the debased world of the human spirit's triumph in spite of the body's destruction. The particular effect of this tragedy is in its power to generate a tension between our terror of a corrupt, disordered and chaotic universe and our pride in the nobility of the human spirit which enables man to survive and triumph in spite of such a world. In this tension is Webster's moral vision, for the dignity of the human spirit separates man from the baseness of the world, and the need to preserve this dignity affords the true basis of morality. "The ultimate tragedy of Webster's world," writes Travis Bogard (p. 147), "is not the death of any individual but the presence of evil and decay which drags all mankind to death . . . the tragic story is the story of a few who find courage to defy such revelation. In their defiance there is a glory for mankind, and in their struggle and assertion lies the brilliance of Websterian tragedy." But this very sense of glory postulates a value which the evils of the world cannot destroy and which makes man superior to his world. It provides a frame of reference in which the relation of man to the forces of evil becomes apparent, and it leads not to a sense of despair but to one of tragic reconciliation. . . .

The most important unifying element in *The Duchess of Malfi* is Bosola, a character whom critics have found particularly difficult to explain in terms of human psychology. The different roles he assumes as the play progresses may be reconciled to one another only in terms of the play's total thematic design. In the traditional pose of the malcontent he recapitulates the function of Flamineo in *The White Devil,* for he illuminates the evils of the world which will destroy the Duchess. As the instrument of the Arragonian brothers he shows this evil made explicit in action. In the death scene of the Duchess he serves a new and more complex function, for here he plays several roles, each designed to further the symbolism of the total scene. Primarily he is used to help the Duchess overcome her womanly fears and to arouse the spirit of greatness in her; he stands here for the nobility of the human spirit which he had opposed in his role as malcontent. . . . Man's awareness of the insignificance of his pain may help him to rise above it. That "the stars shine still" is a crucial statement of the play, for it is an assertion of the permanence and indestructibility of nature. While the stars shine there is certainty, for we cannot doubt the reality of the universe and of an illuminating beauty which persists in spite of all. The stars are a symbol of hope which defeats the feeling of despair which the horrors of the play may generate. Through the office of Bosola the Duchess is able to assert the dignity of human life and meet her death with the readiness and courage which are her triumph. To know the insignificance of human pain and the certainty of an unextinguishable heavenly light is a means of escape from the horrors of the world.

Irving Ribner
Jacobean Tragedy (London: Methuen, 1962), pp. 108-11

The case for *The Duchess of Malfi,* then, is simply that, centring as it does on the "prison" image of Act IV, it succeeds in presenting a new and particular attitude to living, a fresh statement of the familiar Elizabethan problem of clarity in chaos, vitality in destruction. Moreover Webster's success comes because of, not despite the decadence and disintegration that threaten him at every turn. If we see him merely as clinging to his place on a slippery ladder of decadence, however *high* a place beneath Shakespeare we accord him, we will miss the individuality to which he was led by very force of circumstance. The success of his play lies in the fact that the disintegrating forces at work on and in the early scenes, appearing there as restlessness and energy fragmented, are challenges to Webster, manifestations in fact of the same energizing violence on which he later has to rely in order to build and focus the dominant image: the image of the Duchess placed as both fighting against and responding to her environment. A cruder (and a vaguer) point than any of Shakespeare's, this is nevertheless more than a simple warding-off of decadence, or a point made *faute de mieux*. For his final view of the Duchess image, Webster draws on the very forces he is also seeking to control: the shifting horror of Bosola's "mists of error"; the madmen's vivid and alive presentation of lust and sin; the Duchess's own sense of immediate response to the "heaven" of "molten brass." The result is an image of impressive greatness, but greatness defined partly in terms of anarchy and violence.

Nothing else in Webster is as good as this; nothing else is as clearly a valuable and evaluating statement about the Elizabethan world order. On the other hand, even Webster's best play scarcely competes, I think, with the best of Middleton. Even granting Webster's success in *The Duchess of Malfi*, it is Tourneur and Middleton, writing almost at opposite extremes of the Jacobean age, who dominate drama of the period. Webster wrote one great play, but its structure and development betray too much strain at key points—i.e. even at the points which define its success—for it to carry real weight in the Jacobean era.

T. B. Tomlinson
A Study of Elizabethan and Jacobean Tragedy (Cambridge
Univ. Pr., 1964), pp. 156-57

GEORGE WITHER
1588-1667

Born in Brentworth, Hampshire, of old and wealthy family. Entered Magdalen College, Oxford, in 1603 but left before taking a degree. Imprisoned in 1614 for the frankness of his satire, *Abuses Stript and Whipt*. Imprisoned again for *Wither's Motto* in 1621. Published pastorals, *The Shepherd's Hunting* in 1615. His *Hymns and Songs of the Church*, published in 1623, led to a long quarrel with the stationers. Served as an officer in the parliamentary army. Was captured, saved from hanging by the intercession of Sir John Denham, who claimed that while Wither was alive Denham could not be called the worst poet in England. Imprisoned again in 1660 for a poem called *Vox Vulgi* which has never been published. Released in 1663. Wrote actively until his death four years later.

F. Sidgwick, ed., *The Poetry of George Wither* (1902), 2 vols.

There was apparently not enough of the sycophant in Wither's composition to ensure him a rapid rise in court favour, and failing to obtain preferment, he turned satirical, and in 1613 produced his *Abuses Stript and Whipt*, in the dedication to which he says that, having been provided with no work, he has employed his leisure in observing the vices of the times. Warton says the satires are severe, not witty. They certainly contain none of those pungent personalities such as Dryden and Pope loved to make their adversaries' ears tingle with. Hate, envy, revenge, covetousness, vanity, and the rest of them, receive some hard knocks, but it is always abstract vice that he scourges, never particular men in whom such vices are presumed to be personified. . . .

During his imprisonment in the Marshalsea, he had composed *The Shepherd's Hunting*. This is a pastoral poem in five eclogues. . . . [In the poem is] the splendid panegyric, which extends to one hundred and twenty lines, [and which] has been more frequently quoted than anything else that Wither wrote. . . .

Wither's poetry, at least all that was written between 1613 and 1623, before he sold his birthright for a mess of pottage, is characterised by fine feeling, delicate fancy, true pathos, and singularly sweet versification. He is at his best in the seven-syllabled trochaic measure of *Philarete* and *The Shepherd's Hunting*, but many of his lyrics are only below the best, and have that indescribable charm of the older Elizabethan manner, which he lived long enough to see evaporating into the courtly sprightliness of his later contemporaries. Only one of these keeps its place in the popular anthologies, the "Shall I, wasting in despair.". . . But Wither has the true lyrical note, and the music of more than one song of his "beats time to nothing in the brain" of many a student who knows and loves the treasures that lie buried in worm-eaten volumes. . . .

John Fyvie
Some Literary Eccentrics (New York: James Pott; London: Archibald Constable, 1906), pp. 231, 233-34, 248

The connection between Wither's deterioration as a poet and his exclusively didactic theory is very apparent; but it has not been sufficiently recognized that his didactic disregard for careful artistry was strongly reinforced by principles identifying prophecy and poetry. Little attention has been paid to Wither's citation in *Abuses Stript and Whipt* (1613) of "*Sylvester matchlesse, glory of these yeeres*" as one of the "Muses Darlings" whom he most admires and whose work he desires to emulate (p. 293). Yet Wither developed in a more extreme fashion than perhaps any other English poet the theory of inspiration which has been formulated by Du Bartas and popularized in England through Sylvester's versions of *Urania* and *The Divine Weeks*. He was not content, as some sounder poets were, merely to state the theory; nor did he recognize, as Milton so emphatically did, the necessity of balancing it by an insistence upon human art; he interpreted it in an extraordinarily narrow way, he added some elements of his own to it, and he made a literal attempt to apply it. The doctrine of inspiration as he developed it supported an emphasis upon matter at the expense of manner, and he utilized it to justify all the artistic defects of his own work. The melancholy story of his career has some interest in the context of the seventeenth-century movement in religious poetry, and it affords striking evidence of the dangers which currently popular theory possessed for a minor poet of limited literary tact and sensibility. . . .

Much of the explanation of how Wither came to develop his theory in its extreme form is to be found in the extended studies of the Psalms which he undertook as preparation for the metrical paraphrases published in 1632 as *The Psalmes of David*. He saw the Psalms as at once poetry of the highest order, inspired utterance of the Holy Ghost, and divine prophecy. The idea that the Psalms and other parts of Scripture were poetry and written in verse, in itself ancient and commonplace, and given great prominence by Du Bartas, acquired a new force for him as he set about his work of Psalm translation. . . .

Holding that "all true Poets are Prophetical," Wither reiterates his claims as a divinely commissioned latter-day prophet throughout the work of this long final phase of his career. Because of his millenarian beliefs, he sees himself as a prophet not only in Augustine's sense, but even in something like Origen's, as one who foretells the second coming of Christ, just as the Old Testament prophets had foretold the first coming. He likes to view himself particularly as a John the Baptist. . . . In practice, however, he most often follows his own precedent in *Britain's Remembrancer* and appears in the role of a Jeremiah or a Jonah, since he feels impelled to declare the wickedness of the English people at great length and to issue innumerable warnings of divine wrath and calls for repentance.

Wither's claims as a prophet are not always mutually consistent, but it is clear that he does not intend them to be dismissed as mere poetic fiction. Those which he makes for the pamphlets which are purely personal or ephemeral in design are relatively modest, but he describes a number of the more substantial works as having come to him in the form of a vision like that he describes in *Britain's Remembrancer*.

Allan Pritchard
SP (April, 1962), pp. 212, 217, 221

SIR THOMAS WYATT
1503-1542

Born at Allington Castle in Kent. As a child fought with a pet lion. Entered St. John's College, Cambridge, in 1516, the year of its opening. In 1520 took M.A. and married Elizabeth Brooke, the daughter of Lord Cobham. Served at court under King Henry VIII. Went abroad on various diplomatic missions. On Embassy to France in 1526, to Italy in 1527. Translated Plutrach's *Quiet of Mind* in 1528. Served as Marchal of Calais from 1528 to 1532. Was present at the coronation of Ann Boleyn in 1533. Imprisoned in Fleet in 1534 because of a brawl. Imprisoned in the Tower of London in 1536 bècause of a quarrel with the Duke of Suffolk at the time of Ann Boleyn's downfall. Suspicion arose and persisted that he had been her lover. Released from the Tower and rusticated to Kent. Regaind royal favor. Made Sheriff of Kent and knighted in the same year of 1536. Served on an embassy to Spain in 1537. While there corresponded with Thomas Cromwell, quarrelled with Thomas Bonner, his fellow envoy. Returned to England in 1538. Served on an embassy to Paris and Flanders in 1539. Returned to England in 1540. Imprisoned in the Tower in 1541, accused of dishonesty while in Spain by Thomas Bonner. Tried in the same year and cleared himself with a notable speech. Made a member of Parliament in 1542. Named Commander of the Fleet. Became ill on a trip to Falmouth to meet the Spanish Ambassador. Died at Sherborne in Dorset. Buried at Sherborne.

A. K. Foxwell, ed., *The Poems of Sir Thomas Wyatt* (1923), 2 vols.

Kenneth Muir, ed., *Collected Poems of Sir Thomas Wyatt* (1950)

A. K. Foxwell, *A Study of Sir Thomas Wyatt* (1911)

PERSONAL

A period of Italian influence has been sought in the fleeting visit to Italy of 1527 and a period of French influence in the longer sojourn at Calais during 1528-30. This may be fanciful, but in any case much of the balette-making is likely to have come before. Love is predominantly an activity of youth. I cannot, of course, prove that some of the more awkward sonnets were not early. But it is noticeable, I think, that the awkwardness is at its height in those which most closely follow their originals. And my impression is that these ought to be regarded as mere exercises in translation or adaptation, roughly jotted down in whatever broken rhythms came readiest to hand, and intended perhaps for subsequent polishing at some time of leisure which never presented itself. However this may be, in a sane estimate of Wyatt's achievement, the exotic writing is of little account. . . .

There is but little fundamental resemblance between Wyatt and Petrarch. He does not dwell upon the physical beauty of his lady; you learn little more than that her hair is of "crispid gold." He does not couple her in proud compare of everything that is in heaven and earth; there is but one perfunctory allusion to lilies and roses. Nor of course does he, like Petrarch, veil her in that circumambient penumbra of spirituality. He makes little use of visual imagery. His range of metaphor is restricted and rather conventional. For the most part he is content with the plainest of words, and relies for his effect upon his rhythmical accomplishment. This economy of speech gives him at times a singular plangency. In appeal or reproach every line tells like a hammer-stroke. . . .

Nor does Wyatt at all foreshadow the Elizabethans, with their lavishness, their passion for visible things, their ready flow of coloured utterance. One phrase rings curiously with Sidney—

> A hart I have besidis all this,
> That hath my herte and I have his.

But Wyatt's real affinities, if with any, are with John Donne. He has not Donne's depth of fiery and often turbid thought. His is a soul of lighter make. But there is something of the same characteristic poise. Wyatt, too, can be a psychologist, watching his own emotions in detachment, with a finger on the burning pulse.

E. K. Chambers
Sir Thomas Wyatt and Some Collected Studies (London:
Sidgwick and Jackson, 1933), pp. 122, 129-30

The conclusions that might be drawn from Wyatt's observed habits of revision, then, do not lend much support to the suggestion that awkwardness and roughness resulted from hasty composition and that they would have been smoothed out in revision. Instead, as a reviser Wyatt was interested primarily in compression, the tightening up of the idea, the insertion of additional adjectives ("And to be ruled by mutabilitie" becomes "By forced law and mutabilitie"), but most of all in the improvement of the general strategy of the poem. This involves changes in grammatical mood, shifts in position of words for emphasis (not euphony), and modifications of tone and attitude. There is a vivid awareness on the poet's part, as he looks back at a poem, that it is spoken and dramatic, and that it takes place in a short time and carries its effects very rapidly. . . .

The critics who have described Wyatt's love songs as merely rehearsing over and over again the interminable complaints of the lover have been looking only at the apparent subject matter. They have missed the turns of style and mood which Wyatt so carefully prepared by the rhetorical organization of his poem, by adapting the metrical scheme to his purpose, and by the use of the tantalizing refrain, often in a different tone from the rest of the poem.

Hallett Smith
HLQ (August, 1946), pp. 332, 348-49

GENERAL

Among the Italian authors Wyatt not only chose poor models, but he also selected poor examples of their work. The question naturally arises, why were these particular poems chosen, when the best of the cinquecento was open to him. The answer to this question is clear from the previous analysis. The one characteristic common to all of Wyatt's translations is that the appeal in them is to the mind, rather than to the heart. The emotional sonnets of Petrarch are passed by in favor of those in which a conceit is carefully worked out; the musical strains of Serafino are ignored to translate an antithesis; the moralization of Alamanni and the sentimentality of Aretino are chosen for intellectual reasons. Each work, whether sonnet or strambotto, whether psalm or satire, is in itself a clearly defined unit. The strambotto is not an undeveloped sonnet, but, from the beginning, the author had a clear perception of exactly what he wished to accomplish; nor is the sonnet by chance a sonnet, but it was originally conceived as a sonnet. However trite this may seem to us, only a glance is needed at the works of his contemporaries to realize that it was a revolutionary conception. There is no place here for poems written "to eschew ydelnes," works that are accretions of years brought together because of a common topic, such as Skelton, or Hawes, or Barclay, or Heywood. Wyatt's works are on a different plane of literary art.

This is his great contribution to literature. It is for this reason that the Elizabethans recognized in him the beginning of English poetry, why Puttenham calls him a "lantern of light." And it was perceived even in his own time.

John M. Berdan
Early Tudor Poetry (New York: Macmillan, 1931), pp. 482-83

It seems very probable that when Wyatt didn't write in regular metre it was because he didn't want to. If we take this view we are left with the question, What did he aim at in the so-called "awkward" rhythms? How are we to read the lines? Where we have no fixed metrical scheme to guide us, it seems that the simplest alternative is to follow speech rhythms, and to group the words into rhythm units suggested partly by the sense and partly by convenience in forming the sounds of the words. The speech rhythm we adopt must be affected by anything we really know about pronunciation in Wyatt's time, but it ought not to be based on "rules of pronunciation" derived from the assumption that he wrote in metre.

Before going further I have to say what I mean by a rhythm unit. The experience of rhythm is not the passive recording of some pattern of time intervals but an active process, the process of rhythmization. It is one kind of mental unifying activity: a number of impressions that would otherwise be merely a sequence can, if rhythmized, be perceived as an organized whole. It is perceived as a unit, distinguished from its background; and it has a structure or pattern, depending on the fact that the component impressions are differentiated within the rhythm unit, some standing out and others being subordinate. . . .

In completely metrical verse there is equally a continuous flowing from one rhythmical unit to the next; but because the successive units have the same internal structure—the same number of syllables and pattern of accents—we still have the outline of the rhythmical unit brought emphatically to our attention. Against this suggested background of repeated identical units the writer then introduces deviations for special effects. But his groundwork is the continuous flow throughout the line, with only a slight pause at the caesura.

Now a characteristic of free verse, and of many of Wyatt's irregular rhythms, is that the rhythmical units will not flow continuously from one to another. It is pausing verse instead of flowing verse. In free verse the pauses are largely secured by the typographical device of the line ending. In the verse of *Piers Plowman*, the pause-mark is used, besides the line ending. But these scribal and typographic devices are not always necessary, because sometimes the structure of the successive rhythmical units is itself enough to prevent any flowing of one into the other. . . .

This pausing verse has much in common with plainsong. The music complicates the question by sometimes giving an unnatural or exaggerated accentuation, but the main effect is similar: the words are divided up into rhythmical units of diverse structure which therefore have to be clearly separated from one another by a pause: "As it was in the beginning—is now—and ever shall be." The "parallelism" adopted in the translation of the Psalms further reinforces the tradition of balanced but distinct units as a satisfactory mode of treating language. And, as the *Encyclopaedia Britannica* article on plainsong points out, the absence of a regularly repeated rhythm allies plainsong "with such things as sea-chanties, counting-out rhymes, and the like."

Within this strong English tradition much of Wyatt's verse takes its place, with two (or possibly more) diverse rhythmical units included in one line. In much of his verse, of course, units of similar structure are brought together and then the line flows, becoming regular and metrical. But it seems evident that Wyatt had no conception that the pausing rhythm was in any way incorrect or unsatisfactory. It would not have been beyond his skill to turn it into flowing rhythm had he wished.

D. W. Harding
Scrutiny (December, 1946), pp. 94, 96, 97

The intrinsic poetic merit of Wyatt has little to do with his historical importance. His finest poems are not, as far as we know, translations. They apparently belong to all periods of his life and they have an ease of movement and of versification which is much less apparent in the translations. It has been argued that the translations were early, experimental work; but many of the lyrics in the Devonshire MS were also written early and, though some of them are feeble enough, they are smoother in versification than most of the sonnets. Other critics have suggested that the metrical deficiencies of the sonnets are due to the difficulty of the form and the need to keep as closely as possible to the original. Against this it must be said that Wyatt frequently departs from his originals when it suits him; and that though one might expect awkward inversions for the sake of the rhyme, there seems to be no particular reason why Wyatt, in writing sonnets, should lose the secret of the iambic pentameter. One might expect inexpert quatrains and forced rhymes—but not unmetrical lines. Miss Foxwell thinks that Wyatt based his versification on Pynson's edition of Chaucer; but the metrical awkwardness is common to all Wyatt's contemporaries, and there is no need to search for a particular source. Sir Edmund Chambers has argued that the sonnets "ought to be regarded as mere exercises in translation or adaptation, roughly jotted down in whatever broken rhythms came readiest to hand, and intended perhaps for subsequent polishing at some time of leisure which never presented itself." The difficulty of this theory is that these translations are given pride of place in the Egerton Manuscript, which was Wyatt's own. Nine out of the first fourteen poems, beautifully transcribed, are translations from Petrarch. It is difficult to avoid the assumption, since the poems are probably not in chronological order, that Wyatt set a higher value on these translations than on the many fine ballets in the Devonshire MS, which were excluded from the Egerton. The latter underwent a certain amount of revision and Wyatt's ear seems to have been satisfied with lines which have offended most of his critics.

Kenneth Muir, ed.
Collected Poems of Sir Thomas Wyatt (Cambridge, Mass.:
Harvard Univ. Pr., 1950), pp. xviii-xx

From this examination of Wyatt's translations from Petrarch several points of general interest emerge. The first concerns his selection of poems for translation from the *Canzoniere*. None of the outstanding lyrics, outstanding by modern taste that is, find a place, and indeed he seems to have had an eye more to ingenuity of expression than any other quality. One gathers the impression that he was interested not so much in the thing said as in the way of saying—"l'arte del dire parole per rima." The second point concerns Wyatt's treatment of his original.

The elegance of Petrarch, the technical brilliance of the sonnets, the easy handling of polished conceits, these were the things which principally attracted Wyatt, and in most of his sonnet versions of Petrarch we see him painstakingly following his originals in a largely unsuccessful attempt to reproduce their adroitness in English. Finally I would suggest that there are two kinds of moment at which he is most effective in these translations and adaptations of Petrarch, moments in which he reaches a state of equilibrium between the native and foreign elements in those compositions. The first occurs in a poem like "My galy charged with forget-fulnes," when, in the midst of his struggles with the complexities of a difficult, unfamiliar verse form, a new sense of drama makes itself felt, and gives fresh life to a conventional image. And the second appears when he takes only the general theme of his original, and reclothes it with a joyous sense of freedom in those native melodies which came most easily and naturally to him.

D. G. Rees
CL (Winter, 1955), p. 24

Wyatt's outstanding characteristic, regarded from a formal viewpoint, was his unceasing readiness to experiment, his desire to explore all the possibilities of a chosen medium. We may see his work in the sonnet as falling into three periods: the early phase, when he was groping his way laboriously towards a suitable form; the middle period, to which belong his mature and highly distinctive love sonnets; and the final phase, when his interest in love had declined and the excitements of public life took its place as a theme for personal poetry. In the first period he succeeded in escaping from the morass of fifteenth-century narrative versification and laid the groundwork of Elizabethan lyrical technique. The admirable love sonnets which followed were, historically regarded, the first shoots of the new kind of poetry which attained its full stature in the last years of the sixteenth century. Wyatt's final phase of experimentation virtually established the standard sonnet-form employed by Surrey, which Shake-speare and his contemporaries were to adopt as an ideally suitable instrument.

But Wyatt was, it should now be clear, something more than a praise-worthy technician, a text-book paragon. He was, without any qualifications at all, a true poet. All these formal achievements sprang from the powerful initial impulse which drove him to seek original expression. A man of the new age, he was intensely responsive to the times in which he lived—the hectic, assertive, perilous times of the early Tudors. "Chance" was one of Wyatt's favourite words; Chance was perhaps his presiding deity; but personal dignity also counted for much. It was the only stance that remained ultimately valid, whether one's mistress proved faithless or one's friends became estranged; whether one's benefactors fell from power or one's own head was in peril. Such was the conception that inspired Wyatt's sonnets; and it was a necessary consequence that in writing them the Petrarchan vision of life and of love should be rejected, together with the verse-form through which it was made manifest. If the stages by which the English sonnet replaced it make a pattern in retrospect, this does not mean that Wyatt himself followed any planned or foreseeable course. The aptest description of his methods of work remains that of Saintsbury:

> We seem to be looking from afar at a man walking or running over a course beset with all sorts of visible stumbling-blocks and invisible snares, into which and over which he is perpetually stumbling and tumbling, yet picking himself up and pressing on towards the goal.

There were always fresh difficulties and fresh solutions. But at the end of his short life Wyatt had shown how a Renaissance form devised to express complex personal experience could be adapted to the traditions of his own nation and the outlook of his age. Such an achievement sufficiently vindicates his right to rank as one of the pioneers of Elizabethan poetry, and supports the claim of these sonnets, not to a "text-book glory," but to the sympathy of all who find pleasure in verse.

J. W. Lever

The Elizabethan Love Sonnet (London: Methuen, 1956), pp. 34-36

Prof. Harding says that, for Wyatt,

> the convention of the love-lament offered indirect expression to a range of feelings—depression, protest at bad faith, weariness from unrewarded service—that may have arisen from quite other sources, such as the difficulties and disappointments of his diplomatic work, fluctuations in the King's regard for him, and the hazards of his position as a courtier among intriguing rivals,

and that, in many of his poems, as in the particular case of No. 84 (another poem of category III),

> one motive for writing is to gain relief for his melancholy by giving it external expression.

In respect of "They fle from me," it seems possible to go beyond both these statements. What Wyatt achieves here is a readjustment to his circumstances rather than just the relief of his feelings, and the readjustment comes when he is able to take over and enter fully into the dramatic role of lover. The poet's struggle to get beyond his own troubles and to dramatize them in this way, seems part of the impulse behind the writing of the poem, and an important part of its meaning.

In none of the poems of category I is this struggle to get the better of personal troubles by associating them with a convention, an analysable part of the poem's meaning, but, on the evidence of "They fle from me," it is reasonable to suppose that a desire to achieve this would sometimes at least be part of the impulse to write. This desire succeeds, to judge by the second and third stanzas of "They fle from me," by exploiting the dramatic potentialities of the convention; and success means, in terms of the dramatic role, the adoption of a "manly" attitude to the unfaithful mistress. Perhaps we have a clue in this poem to a psychological account of those "dramatic" and "manly" qualities so often noted in the love poetry of Wyatt.

J. D. Hainsworth
EIC (January, 1957), pp. 94-95

To add yet further to Wyatt's fame is unnecessary; to re-establish Surrey's impossible. My present concern is exclusively with these poets as the first English Petrarchans; and by an examination of their translations and imitations of Petrarch I hope to provide materials on which judgments of their historical importance, intrinsic values, and comparative merits may be made. What I have to say will generally tend to confirm the views of Hallett Smith and J. W. Lever, to both of whom I am indebted. But by judging Wyatt and Surrey only on a part of their work and only in reference to a poet who is greater than either, I may, at times, seem rather to diminish than enhance their reputation. So much sixteenth-century poetry is described, rather vaguely as "Petrarchan" that it seems worthwhile to ask how much of Petrarch's meaning, quality, and style entered English poetry through his first two followers. . . .

Wyatt must receive the major emphasis in an inquiry of this scope, not because he is judged a priori superior to Surrey, but simply because in bulk his Petrarchan poems far outweigh Surrey's. Surrey translated or imitated five of Petrarch's sonnets, though debts to and reminiscences of Petrarch are apparent in other poems. . . . But no less than twenty-five of Wyatt's poems, mainly sonnets, depend on Petrarch; and it is he, therefore, who is the key figure in the history of this first phase of English Petrarchianism. . . .

A comparison of . . . [two Petrarchan] translations illustrates that Surrey's "advances" were made at considerable cost. The English sonnet form, harmony of numbers, pictorial solidity, and an air of agreeable gallantry are his legacy to his Elizabethan successors. But Wyatt, in this instance and whatever he does elsewhere, ushers much of both the meaning and quality of Petrarch's sonnets into English poetry. And this occurs through his attempt at exactness and in spite of that "essential difference" that really does exist, in general, between Petrarch and Wyatt.

Patricia Thomson
HLQ (February, 1959), pp. 86, 92

SHAKESPEARE

Paul N. Siegel, editor

WILLIAM SHAKESPEARE
1564-1616

Christened at Stratford-on-Avon, April 26, 1564. Probably educated at Stratford Grammar School. Married, 1582. First referred to as a London playwright and actor (by Robert Greene), 1592. Probably migrated to Stratford, 1610. First play probably written in 1590 or 1591, last play probably written in 1612 or 1613. Died at Stratford-on-Avon, April 23, 1616. Works published in life-time: *Venus and Adonis*, 1593; *Lucrece*, 1594; *Titus Andronicus*, 1594; *2 Henry VI*, 1594; *3 Henry VI*, 1595; *Richard III*, 1597; *Richard II*, 1597; *Romeo and Juliet*, 1597; *Henry IV, Part I*, 1598; *Love's Labour's Lost*, 1598; *Henry V*, 1600; *Midsummer Night's Dream*, 1600; *Merchant of Venice*, 1600; *Henry IV, Part II*, 1600; *Much Ado About Nothing*, 1600; *Merry Wives of Windsor*, 1602; *Hamlet*, 1603; *King Lear*, 1608; *Pericles*, 1609; *Sonnets*, 1609; *Troilus and Cressida*, 1609. Member and shareholder of Lord Chamberlain's company of players, which became the King's company after the accession of James I. Plays first collected in 1623, when J. Heminge and H. Condell, members of his company, published the First Folio. This contains all of the plays except *Pericles* now generally attributed to Shakespeare. The standard editions of the separate plays are the New Arden (London: Methuen, 1951-), now almost complete, and the New Cambridge editions (Cambridge University Press, 1921-1962). There are a number of modern one-volume editions of his works. The standard life is Sir Edmund Chambers's *William Shakespeare, A Study of Facts and Problems* (1930).

PERSONAL

Through the efforts of several generations of searchers, one hundred or more records of the activities of the dramatist have been unearthed since Rowe's short account of Shakespeare's life appeared in 1709—more records, in fact, than we have for any other playwright of the time except Ben Jonson. These documents must be the basis for any true picture of the man and his work.

The picture will be far from the complete and colorful one that most admirers of Shakespeare would like to have. It will not reveal his secret ambitions, his bitterest disappointments, or his subconscious desires; it will be a picture lacking in color and details. It will, however, show what the outlines of our conception of Shakespeare must be if the picture is to be related to the man who wrote the plays in the reigns of Queen

Elizabeth and King James I and not to nineteenth- and twentieth-century stereotypes of what an ideal poet should be.

Gerald Eades Bentley
Shakespeare: A Biographical Handbook (New Haven, Conn.:
Yale Univ. Pr., 1961), p. 5

GENERAL

His characters are not merely personified abstractions, but, on the other hand, they are not precisely like real people: for instance, they usually speak in verse. Conventionalism of this kind is so obvious, however, that nineteenth-century critics seem not to have reflected upon its implications; it was usual for them to treat Shakespeare as Ibsen is more appropriately treated: they fastened upon his characters as if they were historical personages, examining their psychology, weighing motives, allotting praise or blame to individual speeches and actions—even attempting to explain problems of character by imaginatively constructing the early life of Hamlet or Othello. There was no attempt to consider the historical anomaly by which a naturalistic drama could so quickly have arisen out of a conventional tradition. Behind the Elizabethan drama were generations of miracle plays and interludes, including "moralities" such as *Everyman;* they had not quite disappeared in the boyhood of Shakespeare himself. More recent investigation has accorded them their proper place as forerunners of the Elizabethan drama, which has been shown to have more in common with its conventional ancestry than used to be suspected. . . .

I have stressed the element of convention in Shakespeare, since it is generally overlooked. But it is necessary also to insist that Shakespeare and his contemporaries worked to no thought-out conventional system; indeed, their conventions are successful just because they are traditional and unconscious. Moreover, being unconscious, they were by no means rigidly adhered to: the Elizabethan playwright varies his position on the scale between conventionalism and naturalism, even in the course of a single play. This rapidity of adjustment is a principal component in Shakespeare's remarkable subtlety. Lapses into naturalism are especially frequent in Shakespeare: they are probably a major cause of his continuous popularity on the stage, and provide color for a psychological approach which would have failed much more signally with, for example, Chapman or Tourneur. A single flash of natural dialogue, breaking the boundaries of convention, will reveal an intuitive understanding of human nature, unshared by his contemporaries. . . .

Characters, without being themselves made up of incompatible qualities, may evoke distinct and separate responses from the audience. Thus Falstaff is (a) amusing, and (b) morally reprehensible; an Elizabethan audience would applaud his wit, but approve his final dismissal. . . . Not only character, but every aspect of the Elizabethan drama, is shot through with this quality of dual awareness. The mixture of conventionalism and naturalism demands a dual mode of attention. Awareness of the play as play implies the dual awareness of play world and real world; upon this depends the piquancy of a play-within-the-play, or of the situation in which a boy plays the part of a girl playing the part of a boy (Julia, Jessica, Rosalind, Viola, Imogen, Perdita).

S. L. Bethell
Shakespeare and the Popular Dramatic Tradition (London:
P. S. King and Staples, 1944), pp. 13-17, 27

THE HISTORY PLAYS

First, this tetralogy to an equal extent with the later tetralogy and more powerfully than the most civilised of the Chronicle Plays shows Shakespeare aware of order or degree. Behind all the confusion of civil war, and the more precious and emphatic because of the confusion, is the belief that the world is a part of the eternal law and that earthly mutability, as in Spenser's last cantos, is itself a part of a greater and permanent pattern. Further, human events as well as being subject to the eternal law are part of an elaborate system of correspondences and hence the more firmly woven into the total web of things. . . .

As powerful as the theme of order in the tetralogy is the continual insistence on cause and effect in the unfolding of history. . . . Again and again, at any great happening, Shakespeare seeks to bring out the concatenation of events. . . .

Shakespeare is more interested in the chain of cause and effect than in the idea that history repeats itself and hence that we may apply to the present the exemplary lessons of the past. But these motives are not absent. . . .

. . . we must think of yet another strain in this tetralogy: that of formalism and stylisation. It is something archaic, inherited from the Morality Play. . . .

But if the Morality Play prompted the formality of Shakespeare's first tetralogy it also supplied a single pervasive theme. . . . In none of the plays is there a hero: and one of the reasons is that there is an unnamed protagonist dominating all four. It is England, or in Morality terms Respublica. . . . England, though she is now quite excluded as a character, is the true hero of Shakespeare's first tetralogy. She is brought near ruin through not being true to herself; yielding to French witchcraft and being divided in mind. But God, though he punishes her, pities her and in the end through his grace allows the suppressed good in her to assert itself and restore her to health. . . .

Finally Shakespeare reinforces the structural unity which the themes of the Morality and of Hall create, by sowing in one play the seeds that are to germinate in the next and by constant references back from a later play to an earlier. . . .

For all the inequality of execution, the vast crowding in of historical incident (some of it inorganic), Shakespeare planned his first historical tetralogy greatly. . . .

However large the apparent differences in style between *Richard II* and *Henry IV,* these plays are connected with a network of cross-references. . . .

Confronted with different styles in *Richard II* and *Henry IV,* we shall have to refrain from calling the first archaic and the second suddenly and miraculously mature, but shall be forced to admit that Shakespeare knew what he was doing from the start and deliberately planned this stylistic contrast. Once we accept this compulsion we shall be the gainers, finding that the plays form a great symphonic scheme.

E. M. W. Tillyard
Shakespeare's History Plays (London: Chatto
and Windus, 1944), pp. 150-61, 234-37

THE ROMANTIC COMEDIES

There are two groups of characters in Shakespeare's comedies:

(1) The young men and women, who dwell in that romantically devised world, of youth, and dreams, and laughter, of which he possessed, and retains, the secret; and

(2) The workaday people, who keep things going—ploughmen, shepherds, servingmen, stewards, waiting-maids—with the unconverted drinkers, jesters, rogues, and odd fellows in a kind of limbo between the two regions—between upstairs and down—all plodding, stepping, tripping, and staggering along in a world of the four elements—of food and drink and sleep and labour. You may study this double world in any of these comedies. . . . All these plays are sweet with music: it is a part of this fairyland, the food of love.

If Comedy laughs, Romance is not to be offended; if Love sighs, Comedy promises to put up with it—to a point! to a point! If the jokes are good, and the sighs are true, there would appear, on this undertaking, to be no reason in literature why they should quarrel. In Romantic Comedy, therefore, the laughers and the sighers live side by side, like good neighbours: on only *one* condition: that neither shall commit excess, or compete for attention at the expense of the other. . . .

. . . there was a tacit understanding at that time between audience and the stage that the entrance of the comic characters indicated a temporary suspension of the romantic or historical fiction on which the serious action was based; that the assumption of a strange country or a different period of history had been dropped. This is the practical explanation of several liberties in more serious plays and even in Tragedies. Such was the Porter in *Macbeth,* with his jokes about Garnett the Jesuit and last year's harvest. No one supposed him to be a porter of ancient Scotland. Here was a primitive convention which Shakespeare maintained.

It is in his power over these two worlds, in his ostensible alternations between Nowhere and England, that Shakespeare's romantic comedies excel all others.

George Gordon
Shakespearean Comedy (Oxford Univ. Pr., 1944), pp. 45-51

In all good New Comedy there is a social as well as an individual theme which must be sought in the general atmosphere of reconciliation that makes the final marriage possible. As the hero gets closer to the heroine and opposition is overcome, all the right-thinking people come over to his side. Thus a new social unit is formed on the stage, and the moment that this social unit crystallizes is the moment of the comic resolution. In the last scene, when the dramatist usually tries to get all his characters on the stage at once, the audience witnesses the birth of a renewed sense of social integration. In comedy as in life the regular expression of this is a festival, whether a marriage, a dance, or a feast. . . .

The essential comic resolution, therefore, is an individual release which is also a social reconciliation. The normal individual is freed from the bonds of a humorous society, and a normal society is freed from the bonds imposed on it by humorous individuals. . . .

The earlier tradition established by Peele and developed by Lyly, Greene, and the masque writers, which uses themes from romance and folklore and avoids the comedy of manners, is the one followed by Shakespeare. . . . We may call this the drama of the green world, and its theme is once again the triumph of life over the waste land, the death and revival of the year impersonated by figures still human, and once divine as well. . . .

Northrop Frye
English Institute Essays, 1948 (New York: Columbia
Univ. Pr., 1949), pp. 60-68

THE SATIRIC COMEDIES

We can perhaps best understand *Measure for Measure* if we regard it as a form of comical satire designed for a popular audience, as *Troilus and Cressida* was the version of the type suited to the taste of an intelligent audience of barristers. The two plays are alike in possessing a background of social disintegration which forms an appropriate milieu for the individuals who are to be satirized. They are alike in attacking lust, the vice against which all the satirists directed most of their barbed shafts. They are alike in the method by which the central figures are presented to the audience.

However, the dramas are in some ways as unlike as the different spectators for which they were written. The complicated structure of *Troilus and Cressida* and the many long passages devoted to the elaboration of ethical and social theory were too heavy for a popular audience. Consequently Shakespeare made the plot which exposes Angelo simple in structure and contrived the philosophical speeches of the Duke and Isabella in such a way that they too advance the plot. Moreover, an ending like that of *Troilus and Cressida* would have confused a popular Elizabethan audience, as it has confused almost every modern reader, just because it is so resolutely consistent with the temper of satire.

Oscar James Campbell
Shakespeare's Satire (Oxford Univ. Pr., 1943), pp. 124-40

THE TRAGEDIES

The tragic hero with Shakespeare, then, need not be "good," though generally he is "good" and therefore at once wins sympathy in his error. But it is necessary that he should have so much of greatness that in his error and fall we may be vividly conscious of the possibilities of human nature. Hence, in the first place, a Shakespearean tragedy is never, like some miscalled tragedies, depressing. No one ever closes the book with the feeling that man is a poor mean creature. He may be wretched and he may be awful, but he is not small. His lot may be heartrending and mysterious, but it is not contemptible. The most confirmed of cynics ceases to be a cynic while he reads these plays. And with this greatness of the tragic hero (which is not always confined to him) is connected, secondly, what I venture to describe as the centre of the tragic impression. This central feeling is the impression of waste. With Shakespeare, at any rate, the pity and fear which are stirred by the tragic story seem to unite with, and even to merge in, a profound sense of sadness and mystery, which is due to this impression of waste. "What a piece of work is man," we cry; "so much more beautiful and so much more terrible than we knew! Why should he be so if this beauty and greatness only tortures itself and throws itself away?" We seem to have before us a type of the mystery of the whole world, the tragic fact which extends far beyond the limits of tragedy. Everywhere, from the crushed rocks beneath our feet to the soul of man, we see power, intelligence, life and glory, which astound us and seem to call for our worship. And everywhere we see them perishing, devouring one another and destroying themselves, often with dreadful pain, as though they came into being for no other end. Tragedy is the typical form of this

mystery, because that greatness of soul which it exhibits oppressed, conflicting and destroyed, is the highest existence in our view. It forces the
mystery upon us, and it makes us realise so vividly the worth of that which
is wasted that we cannot possibly seek comfort in the reflection that all
is vanity.

In this tragic world, then, where individuals, however great they may be
and however decisive their actions may appear, are so evidently not the
ultimate power, what is this power? What account can we give of it which
will correspond with the imaginative impressions we receive? This will be
our final question. . . .

. . . we are left at last with an idea showing two sides or aspects which
we can neither separate nor reconcile. The whole or order against which
the individual part shows itself powerless seems to be animated by a passion for perfection: we cannot otherwise explain its behaviour towards evil.
Yet it appears to engender this evil within itself, and in its effort to overcome and expel it it is agonised with pain, and driven to mutilate its own
substance and to lose not only evil but priceless good. That this idea,
though very different from the idea of a blank fate, is no solution of the
riddle of life is obvious; but why should we expect it to be such a solution?
Shakespeare was not attempting to justify the ways of God to men, or to
show the universe as a Divine Comedy. He was writing tragedy, and
tragedy would not be tragedy if it were not a painful mystery. Nor can he
be said even to point distinctly, like some writers of tragedy, in any direction where a solution might lie. We find a few references to gods or God,
to the influence of the stars, to another life: some of them certainly, all of
them perhaps, merely dramatic—appropriate to the person from whose
lips they fall. A ghost comes from Purgatory to impart a secret out of the
reach of its hearer—who presently meditates on the question whether the
sleep of death is dreamless. Accidents once or twice remind us strangely of
the words, "There's a divinity that shapes our ends." More important are
other impressions. Sometimes from the very furnace of affliction a conviction seems borne to us that somehow, if we could see it, this agony counts
as nothing against the heroism and love which appear in it and thrill our
hearts. Sometimes we are driven to cry out that these mighty or heavenly
spirits who perish are too great for the little space in which they move, and
that they vanish not into nothingness but into freedom. Sometimes from
these sources and from others comes a presentiment, formless but haunting
and even profound, that all the fury of conflict, with its waste and woe, is
less than half the truth, even an illusion, "such stuff as dreams are made
on." But these faint and scattered intimations that the tragic world, being
but a fragment of a whole beyond our vision, must needs be a contradiction
and no ultimate truth, avail nothing to interpret the mystery. We remain
confronted with the inexplicable fact, or the no less inexplicable appear-

ance, of a world travailing for perfection, but bringing to birth, together with glorious good, an evil which it is able to overcome only by self-torture and self-waste. And this fact or appearance is tragedy.

A. C. Bradley
Shakespearean Tragedy (London: Macmillan, 1904), pp. 22-39

There are four major alterations that have to be made in his [Bradley's] picture of Shakespearean tragedy: (1) Shakespearean tragedy conveys a sense of divine providence; (2) this divine providence visits a poetically appropriate retribution upon the guilty; (3) characters and action suggest analogies with the Bible story; (4) there are intimations of the heaven and hell of Christian religion. In short, Bradley's analysis of the Shakespearean tragic universe must be altered to make the order manifested in the course of the tragedies explicitly Christian, its laws the laws ordained by God, the evil within it the consequences of man's fall constantly threatening to overthrow the entire hierarchy of nature. Written when the challenge to Christian humanist values was felt most keenly, the tragedies present most vividly the imperilment of the universal order by man's evil passions, the legacy of his fall, reflecting in doing so the dissolution of the Elizabethan compromise. . . .

The passion which brings about his [the tragic hero's] downfall springs from a force of character that raises him above persons of ordinary clay. That force, that intensity, that Promethean fire, although it enlarges his capacity for suffering and brings it upon him, reveals the possibilities of existence, which we, dozing in our day-by-day routinism, forget. His vitality, the vitality of a Raleigh, of an Essex, and of all those other striking personalities of the new aristocracy who have made the word "Elizabethan" have such vibrant connotations, has potentialities for both good and bad, and the fact that it brings about his downfall does not destroy our awareness of this. . . .

Neither a divinely perfect Christ nor a more than human Adam could become the subject of genuine tragedy, but the association of each with the idea of tragedy must have influenced powerfully the way in which the audience regarded the tragic hero. . . .

If the Shakespearean tragic hero, however, carried with him associations of the suffering and dying god or god king of the pagan fertility cults surviving in semi-feudal Elizabethan England and of the Adam and Christ of Christianity, he also carried with him associations of the scapegoat who embodied the forces of barrenness and evil and was, as Sir James Frazer has shown, identified with or substituted for the divine victim. It is noteworthy that the comparatively innocent heroes Hamlet and Lear are malcontents, persons whose destructive cynicism good Elizabethans regarded with fear and shuddering. Hamlet, clothed in gloomy black, brooding morbidly, obsessed with thoughts of the body's decay and the foulness of sex, is a figure of death. Lear in his madness, seeing humanity as wholly evil, calls for the thunder to destroy all the seeds that produce men. Probing deeply into life and exposing that which the "normal" man would prefer to forget, they, like the guilty heroes, challenge the order of things. It is this challenge to the order of things which makes the Shakespearean tragedies not merely dramatic exempla that comfortably reassured their spectators concerning the rightness of their views but imaginative experiences that shook them up only to renew their basic faith and render it richer and deeper by having been forced to assimilate what Hamlet and Lear saw.

Paul N. Siegel
Shakespearean Tragedy and the Elizabethan Compromise
(New York: New York Univ. Pr., 1957), pp. 82-98

THE TRAGI-COMIC ROMANCES

The stories of *Pericles* and *The Winter's Tale* are remarkably alike. In both the hero loses his wife and daughter just after the birth of his child; in both the idea of a child's helplessness is synchronized with a sea-storm of the usual Shakespearian kind; in both the wife and child are miraculously restored after a long passage of time; and the revival of Thaisa, and the restoration of Marina and Hermione are accompanied by music. These plays are throughout impregnated by an atmosphere of mysticism. The theology is pseudo-Hellenistic. The Delphic oracle and a prophetic dream occur in *The Winter's Tale;* Hermione is restored to Leontes in a "chapel" to the sound of music, Thaisa to Pericles in the temple of Diana, with the full circumstance of religious ceremonial. The goddess Diana appears to Pericles. A reader sensitive to poetic atmosphere must necessarily feel the awakening light of some religious or metaphysical truth symbolized in the plot and attendant machinery of these two plays. . . .

Many of the former elements recur in *Cymbeline*. We have the faithlessness-theme in which Posthumus distrusts Imogen, and Iago is resuscitated in the deceiver Iachimo. Posthumus' very name suggests the birth-theme of the two former plays: like Marina and Perdita he is cast unprotected into a hostile world. Cymbeline's long-lost sons, Guiderius and Arviragus, remind us of the lost children of Pericles and Leontes. We have again the idea of the apparently dead found to be alive. Guiderius and Arviragus think Imogen is dead, and even prepare to bury her. Solemn music sounds at her supposed death. Posthumus, too, is led to think Imogen dead independently. . . . the predominating symbols are loss in tempest and revival to the sounds of music. . . .

. . . on the island of *The Tempest* Prospero is master of his lonely magic. . . .

Prospero's enemies are drawn to the magic island of great poetry by means of a tempest raised by Prospero with the help of Ariel. In Alonso, despairing and self-accusing, bereft of his child, we can see traces of the terrible end of *Lear;* in Antonio and Sebastian, the temper and the tempted, plotting murder for a crown, we can see more than traces of *Macbeth.* But, driven by the tempest-raising power of tragic and passionate poetry within the magic circle of Prospero and Ariel, these hostile and evil things are powerless: they can only stand spell-stopped. They are enveloped in the wondrous laws of enchantment on the island of song and music. . . .

The spirit of the Final Plays also finds its perfected home in this last of the series. Here the child-theme is repeated in Miranda . . . here the lost son of Alonso is recovered. . . . Prospero, like Cerimon over Thaisa, revives, with music, the numbed consciousness of Alonso and his companions; and, as they wake, it is as though mortality were waking into eternity.

G. Wilson Knight
The Crown of Life (London: Methuen, 1958), pp. 14-25

The Comedy of Errors

It is much lighter and funnier than *The Two Menaechmuses.* This mastery is revealed, not so much in the language, though that is perfectly adequate to its modest purposes, as in the consistency with which its farcical limitations are accepted, and in the ingenuity of the plot. This plot really is built like the proverbial "Swiss watch": it is as absurdly neat as Leibniz's pre-established harmony. Comedy of this type, or taste—rationalistic, built on a Latin base—was to be more fully explored in the succeeding age of the Enlightenment, in the innumerable comedies which lighted the theaters of Europe from Molière through Mozart. But Shakespeare was developing in a different direction, not toward the univocal perfection of the geometric diagram, but toward the harmonizing of complementary perspectives; not toward further ingenuity, but toward deeper insight.

Francis Fergusson
SwR (Winter, 1954), pp. 28-29

Love's Labour's Lost

It has no story to tell, or if it has one it tells it artificially. It counts on contemporary occupations with style—occupations now generally forgotten —to keep it interesting; it is Shakespeare's most topical piece. And its purpose, which is literary satire, is one that in the nature of things can never be long popular. That it is brilliant, high-spirited, and verbally masterful does not save it. That its criticism of current affectation and pedantry is so complete as to preserve those vices in their finest form, and to demonstrate their fascination for Shakespeare himself, not the least of whose qualities is a love of language for its own intoxicating sake, does not quite justify it in the human court. And that the texture of its diction and its rhythm is the work of a superb weaver has not seemed to matter with a world which doubtless is right in demanding of poetry that it be other than satin; even the best satin.

Mark Van Doren
Shakespeare (London: George Allen and Unwin, 1941), p. 58

Henry VI, Part I

1 Henry VI develops the general theme of Hall—the retribution on Henry VI for the original sin of his grandfather. The first stage of that retribution consists in the turning of the tables on England by the French; it opens with England in effective control of France and ends with France (almost) completely lost and a French queen about to ascend the throne of England to dominate a boy king and the country. The play looks back to the greatness of Henry V and forward to the rule of Suffolk and Margaret, York's claim, and civil war. The action is far from complete; the internal dissensions and rivalries have still to be worked out. And out of its context, there is no need in the play for e.g. the Mortimer-Plantagenet scene and its genealogy, reported more fully in *2 Henry VI,* or the restoration of York "to his blood," or the Temple Garden scene. The play has, of course, its own unity, but for full appreciation, it should be seen as a unit in a series concerning the events and the dominant themes of Hall's grand conception of the struggle of York and Lancaster.

Andrew S. Cairncross
The First Part of King Henry the Sixth (London: Methuen; Cambridge, Mass.: Harvard Univ. Pr., 1962), "The Arden edition," pp. xlii-xliii

Henry VI, Part II

The most characteristic Shakespearean feature running through all the varied styles is the wealth of association that underlies and permeates the play. . . .

The building up of Henry's "holiness" on a basis of Biblical and religious phrases is the best example of this sustained use of imagery in the field of character, and finds a later parallel in Richard's use of proverb and epigram. In much the same way, the parting of Margaret and Suffolk gathered to itself, along with the natural parallel to Lancelot and Guinevere, and to the story of Dido and Æneas, associations from that of Ovid and his wife, described in the *Tristia.* So the great speech of Young Clifford on finding the body of his father owes much of its tragic quality to the richness of the imagery behind it—imagery shared almost word for word with *Lear* and *Macbeth*, and compounded from representations of the Last Judgement, and associations from 2 *Tamburlaine*, the story of Nabal, and Ovid's *Metamorphoses*.

Andrew S. Cairncross
The Second Part of King Henry the Sixth (London: Methuen; Cambridge, Mass.: Harvard Univ. Pr., 1957, 1962), "The Arden edition," pp. liii-liv

Henry VI, Part III

Thus we have a shapely drama, less comprehensive as a national panorama than Part II, since it contains hardly any scenes representing the commonalty to set beside those of Simpcox and the sham miracle, the armourer and his prentice, or Jack Cade haranguing the rabble; but full of coloured banners and the sound of trumpets, of high words and blazing passion, of hand-to-hand conflicts and ruthless stabbings; and above all rich in character. . . . Bloody Clifford is a revenger whom Marlowe would not have been ashamed to own. The boy Rutland appears in one scene only, but is a pair with Prince Arthur of *King John* (for those who have a taste for little Lord Fauntleroys). Edward, Prince of Wales, is of a different mettle, and of a mould which gave us many other pert and plucky lads, from Edward V in the next play to young Macduff and young Martius. . . . But the three principal figures and most finely drawn studies are Queen Margaret, Richard Crookback and King Henry.

John Dover Wilson
The Third Part of King Henry VI (Cambridge Univ. Press, 1952), pp. xxix-xxx

Richard III

Richard III is Shakespeare's first "heroic" drama. It is built around one figure. From one figure emanate the rays which spread in all directions through the play. This concentration of action-interest upon one single character demands a new technique of composition; the action of the play must be close-knit and compressed.

Richard III moves forward much more rapidly than *Henry VI*. The plot is more coherent and easier to survey than that of the earlier plays. There we had to deal with a concatenation of various events and with numerous disparate motives of action. But in *Richard III* the entire action of the play is dependent upon Richard alone. Even the action of the minor characters derives from him. And, finally, *Richard III* is the first play which gives expression to a powerful human passion.

Subject to this law of concentration and condensation, too, are the images in *Richard III*. The acceleration of movement in the entire play is perceptible in the images, which become briefer (there is no image exceeding four lines). There are no more lengthy conceits and digressions, no long general reflections spun out in detailed simile. . . .

Of course, all this is still in the formalistic and artificial manner, which has attained its height in this play. But all these rhetorical devices, such as antithesis, assonance, symmetry and parallelism are employed in *Richard III* in a more appropriate way than was earlier the case. The firm architecture of style and construction support the forcefulness and at the same time the symbolic significance of the scenes of lament and execration. The conventional stylistic figures, by being suited to the occasion, possess a new vitality. In the great laments these parallelisms and reiterations do not appear inappropriate or unnatural, because it corresponds to the nature of a lamentation to repeat the same thing over and over again.

W. H. Clemen
The Development of Shakespeare's Imagery (London:
Methuen, 1951, pp. 47-49

This notional pattern of historic events rigidly determined by a mechanical necessity is partly paralleled by, partly modified by, the formal patterns of the episodes (or scenes) and the language. By "formal patterns" I mean the unmistakably iterated goings-on in scenes so exactly parallel that if the first *is* passable on a modern stage as quasi-realistic costume-play stuff, the second (repeating it always *more* unrealistically) cannot be. The two wooing-scenes (Richard with Anne and Elizabeth) are the simplest case. . . .

It is not only the iteration of scene that is stylized: the stiffly formal manipulation of echoing phrase and sequence of words within the scenes is even more unrealistic. A closely related parallelism exists in the repeated occurrence of a sort of "single line traffic" in sentences: the classicist's *stichomythia*. One speaker takes from the other exactly the same ration of syllables, and rejoins as if under contract to repeat the form of the given sentence as exactly as possible, using the maximum number of the same words or their logical opposites, or (failing that) words closely associated with them. I describe the game pedantically, because it *is* an exact and scientific game with language, and one of the graces and beauties of the play Shakespeare wrote. . . .

The dramatic ironies of the action run in parallel with these counter-stroke reversals of verbal meaning, and form a kind of harmony.

Those reversals of intention . . . are on precisely the pattern of the repeated reversals of human expectation, the reversals of events, the anticipated reversals (foreseen only by the audience), which make "dramatic irony." The patterned speech of the dialogue—the wit that demonstrates that a sentence is but a cheveril glove, quickly turned the other way—is fundamentally one with the ironic patterns of the plot. "Dramatic irony" here is verbal *peripeteia*.

Richard has grown a new dimension since his abrupt and remarkable development in *3 Henry VI*: he has become a wit, a mocking comedian, a "vice of kings"—but with a clear inheritance from the old Vice of the Moralities: part symbol of evil, part comic devil, and chiefly, on the stage, the generator of roars of laughter at wickednesses. . . . His literary relations with the Senecan "Tyrant" (author of *"In regna mea Mors impetratur,"* etc.) are clear enough; as they are with the Elizabethan myth of "the murderous Machiavel.". . . But only the medieval heritage—from the comic devils with their *Schadenfreude*, and the Vice as comic inverter of order and decency—can fully explain the new Richard of this apparent sequel to the *Henry VI* series.

A. P. Rossiter
Angel with Horns (London: Longmans, Green, 1961), pp. 3-5, 15

Titus Andronicus

Titus Andronicus is no tragedy at all if pity and terror are essential to the tragic experience. Aaron the Moor is the kind of villain concerning whose character there can be no curiosity, and whose deeds therefore cannot be felt as horrible. They do not violate his nature, for there is no nature in him. Nor is Titus an object of increasing pity as his misfortunes mount; he is himself bloody-minded and insensitive, and in fact his misfortunes, rather than mounting, stretch along in a simple series which nothing save ingenuity prolongs. Monstrosities and absurdities abound. Not only is there the butchery of Bassianus, and the descent of Quintus and Martius into the pit, and the mutilation of Lavinia, and the piglike squeak of the nurse as Aaron stabs her, and the amputation of Titus's hand, and the meal of human flesh; there is also the absence of any reason why Chiron and Demetrius in v, ii, should come to Titus's house—any other reason, that is to say, than the author's will to bring them where they can have their throats cut over a basin.

The lack of feeling with which the play is written may have been part of a prescription: the tragedy of blood as a form called only for heaps of death, and sentiment was as much out of place as it is in the modern equivalent, the detective story, which fails as soon as the reader is permitted to have any pity for the victim of poison, bullet, or dagger. The spectator at a tragedy of blood wanted only new shapes of death, and novel devices for revenge.

Mark Van Doren
Shakespeare (London: George Allen and Unwin, 1941), p. 38

The Taming of the Shrew

Bianca's lovers are indeed granted somewhat larger liberty of romantic utterance than are their counterparts in Ariosto's *Suppositi*. . . . But clearly these Anglo-Italian lovers are not yet initiated into the full ritual. They are mostly occupied with planning opportunities to express a faith which has not yet become articulate. Love remains more an intrigue than a religion. Hence the convenience of the classical machinery. Wily, scheming men-servants, disguises to procure mistaken identifications, inopportune coincidences to be encountered by still further reaches of unfeeling cunning —these are the traditional weapons of classical comedy. . . .

Petruchio is different from the wooers of romance, because he remembers the grocer, the butcher, and the tailor. He drags love out of heaven, and brings it down to earth. To the chivalrous, love is a state of worship; to him, it is a problem of wiving. . . . *The Taming of the Shrew* gives Shakespeare momentary ease of the burden of romance; but only by denying its existence. It does not solve his problem; it merely shelves it. But he will return to the facts of Elizabethan experience in the more characteristic mood which we shall find in *A Midsummer Night's Dream*. In the meantime, this at least can be claimed: that though for the moment his mood was to exhibit the love of woman more in the spirit of the Roman marketplace than in that of his own modern Europe, he has at least allowed his artistic sense to make the proper accommodation in the temper of every part of his play.

H. B. Charlton
Shakespearian Comedy (London: Methuen, 1938), pp. 94-99

The Two Gentlemen of Verona

None of Shakespeare's comedies is more deeply infused with romantic elements than *The Two Gentlemen of Verona*. . . .

Yet *The Two Gentlemen* is not merely a romance; it is also a comedy. . . . .

Even at this early stage in his development Shakespeare was capable of standing in conscious and amused detachment from the romantic mode and tradition. So far from the comedy of the piece being merely a matter of inadvertent humour, Shakespeare deliberately uses Speed and Launce —as he later uses Touchstone—to guy romantic sentiment through the realistic and occasionally satiric chorus of the clown. . . . Even in his youthful and most enthusiastic days, when romance was the main inspiration of his work, Shakespeare, with the comprehensiveness of true genius, was capable of smiling at what he cherished.

E. C. Pettet
Shakespeare and the Romance Tradition (London and New York: Staples Pr., 1949), pp. 101-4

Romeo and Juliet

In *Romeo and Juliet* the beauty and ardour of young love is seen by Shakespeare as the irradiating glory of sunlight and starlight in a dark world. The dominating image is *light,* every form and manifestation of it; the sun, moon, stars, fire, lightning, the flash of gunpowder, and the reflected light of beauty and of love; while by contrast we have night, darkness, clouds, rain, mist, and smoke.

Each of the lovers thinks of the other as light; Romeo's overpowering impression when he first catches sight of Juliet on the fateful evening at the Capulets' ball is seen in his exclamation,

> O, she doth teach the torches to burn bright!

To Juliet, Romeo is "day in night"; to Romeo, Juliet is the sun rising from the east, and when they soar to love's ecstasy, each alike pictures the other as stars in heaven, shedding such brightness as puts to shame the heavenly bodies themselves.

The intensity of feeling in both lovers purges even the most highly affected and euphuistic conceits of their artificiality, and transforms them into the exquisite and passionate expression of love's rhapsody. . . .

There can be no question, I think, that Shakespeare saw the story, in its swift and tragic beauty, as an almost blinding flash of light, suddenly ignited and as swiftly quenched. He quite deliberately compresses the action from over nine months to the almost incredibly short period of five days; so that the lovers meet on Sunday, are wedded on Monday, part at dawn on Tuesday, and are reunited in death on the night of Thursday. The sensation of swiftness and brilliance, accompanied by danger and destruction, is accentuated again and again; by Juliet when she avows their betrothal

> is too rash, too unadvised, too sudden,
> Too like the lightning, which doth cease to be
> Ere one can say "It lightens";

and by Romeo and the Friar, who instinctively make repeated use of the image of the quick destructive flash of gunpowder (III. iii. 103, 132; v. i. 63). . . .

And then at the end we see the darkness of the churchyard, lit by the glittering torch of Paris, quickly quenched; Romeo's arrival with his torch, the swift fight and death, the dark vault, which is not a grave but a lantern irradiated by Juliet's beauty, Romeo's grim jest on the "lightning before death," followed immediately by the self-slaughter of the "star-crossed" lovers, the gathering together of the stricken mourners as the day breaks, and the "glooming" peace of the overcast morning when

The sun for sorrow will not show his head. . . .

Caroline Spurgeon
Shakespeare Association Lecture (Oxford Univ. Pr., 1930), pp. 5-9

Shakespeare's sonnet-prologue offers us a tale of star-crossed lovers and "The *fearfull passage* of their *death-markt* loue." *Death-marked* can mean "marked out for (or by) death; fore-doomed." If, however, we take *passage* in the sense of a voyage (and this sub-meaning prompts *trafficque* in the twelfth line) as well as a course of events, *death-marked* recalls the "euer fixed marke" of Sonnet 116 and the sea-mark of Othello's utmost sail, and suggests the meaning "With death as their objective." The two meanings of *fearful* increase the line's oscillation; the meaning "frightened" makes the lovers helpless, but they are not necessarily so if the word means "fearsome" and so suggests that we, the audience, are awe-struck by their undertaking. These ambiguities pose the play's fundamental question at the outset: is its ending frustration or fulfilment? Does Death choose the lovers or do they elect to die? This question emerges from the language of the play itself and thus differs from the conventional, superimposed problem: is *Romeo and Juliet* a tragedy of Character or of Fate? which can be answered only by a neglect or distortion of the play as a dramatic experience. To blame or excuse the lovers' impetuosity and the connivance of others is to return to Arthur Broke's disapproval of unhonest desire, stolen contracts, drunken gossips and auricular confession. Recent critics have, I believe, come nearer to defining the play's experience when they have stressed the *Liebestod* of the ending and suggested that the love of Romeo and Juliet is the tragic passion that seeks its own destruction. . . .

Shakespeare's story conflicts, however, with the traditional myth at several points. . . . Romeo faces capture and death, Juliet the horror of being entombed alive, not because they want to die but because they want to live together. These woes are to serve them for sweet discourses in their time to come. In contrast to this, the wish-fulfilment of the *Liebestod* is accomplished only by the story of a suicide pact. . . .

By itself, the suicide pact offers the audience wish-fulfilment and not *katharsis*. The good cry we enjoy over the worn reels of *Meyerling* bears only a remote relationship to the tragic experience of *Romeo and Juliet*. . . .

[The words] spoken by Romeo after he has drunk the poison reaffirm the paradox of the play's experience at its most dramatic moment:

O *true* Appothecary:
Thy drugs are *quicke*. Thus with a kisse I die.

(V.iii.119-20)

Like the Friar's herbs the apothecary's poison both heals and destroys. He is *true* not only because he has spoken the truth to Romeo in describing the poison's potency, but because he has been true to his calling in finding the salve for Romeo's ills. His drugs are not only speedy, but also *quick* in the sense of "life-giving." Romeo and Juliet "cease to die, by dying."

M. M. Mahood
Shakespeare's Wordplay (London: Methuen, 1957), pp. 56-59, 72

Richard II

It is obvious what a stylized production might make of a play so full of pageantry and symbolism as *Richard II*. Even the brawling of the nobles and the casting of their gages, at the opening of act 4, an episode irritating to the modern reader hoodwinked by naturalistic conceptions of drama, would fall into place as a detail in the design. As for symbolism, three writers have lately independently drawn attention to the sun-image, which dominates the play as the swastika dominates a Nazi gathering. For Shakespeare the sun stood in general as the symbol of royal majesty; but it appears that "the sun emerging from a cloud" was also a personal emblem of King Richard himself, and is actually one of the three badges embroidered upon the robes of his effigy in Westminster Abbey. Whether the dramatist was conscious or not of this fact, he certainly employs sun-imagery with peculiar force and frequency in the play, and theatrical producers might well take a hint from it. *Richard II* ought to be played throughout as ritual. . . .

. . . the heart of the play [is] a sacramental quality in the agony and death of the sacrificial victim, as it were of the god slain upon the altar, which we to-day can only begin to understand by reading a book like *The Golden Bough.* . . .

The fall of Richard fascinated the late medieval and Renaissance world as much by its magnitude and its unaccountableness as by its pathos and the sacrilege it brought to pass. . . .

The second great attraction, then, of the story of Richard of Bordeaux and Henry, Duke of Lancaster, for the men of the fifteenth and sixteenth centuries, was that it afforded, in its spectacle of the "dejecting of the one and advancing of the other," a perfect example of the mysterious action of Fortune, working of course under the inscrutable "providence of God," according to the quasi-mechanical symbolism under which they conceived that action. And this in turn constituted one of the main appeals of *Richard II* for the spectators who first witnessed it. For, though the operations of Fortune were most evident and potent in the lives of the great, everything human was subject to them.

J. Dover Wilson
King Richard II (Cambridge Univ. Pr., 1939), pp. xii-xxii

A Midsummer Night's Dream

A Midsummer Night's Dream shines like *Romeo and Juliet* in darkness, but shines merrily. Lysander, one of the two nonentities who are its heroes, complains at the beginning about the brevity of love's course, and sums up his complaint with a line which would not be out of place in *Romeo and Juliet*:

> So quick bright things come to confusion. (I, i, 149)

This, however, is at the beginning. Bright things will come to clarity in a playful, sparkling night while fountains gush and spangled starlight betrays the presence in a wood near Athens of magic persons who can girdle the earth in forty minutes and bring any cure for human woe. Nor will the woe to be cured have any power to elicit our anxiety. The four lovers whose situations resemble so closely the situation created in *The Two Gentlemen of Verona* will come nowhere near the seriousness of that predicament; they will remain to the end four automatic creatures whose artificial and pretty fate it is to fall in and out of love like dolls, and like dolls they will go to sleep as soon as they are laid down. There will be no pretense that reason and love keep company, or that because they do not death lurks at the horizon. There is no death in *A Midsummer Night's Dream,* and the smiling horizon is immeasurably remote.

Mark Van Doren
Shakespeare (London: George Allen and Unwin, 1941), p. 76

The lyrical sonnet-like verse of *Romeo and Juliet* becomes more happily allied to content and mood in *A Midsummer Night's Dream*. This, the first of Shakespeare's great comedies, presents itself to us as a kind of amalgam of much that had gone before. The lovers' changing affections give us the situation caused by Proteus' inconstancy; the maze of errors reminds us of the comedy of that name, and even the world of Titania is anticipated there in Dromio's

> O for my beads! I cross me for a sinner.
> This is the fairy land. O spite of spites!
> We talk with goblins, owls and sprites.

For the idea of the burlesque play-within-the-play Shakespeare turns to the masque of the worthies in *Love's Labour's Lost*, and perhaps even *Romeo and Juliet* inspires the choice of the Pyramus and Thisbe theme. It is all a tissue of earlier material, and all magnificently new spun. Within the framework provided by Theseus and Hippolyta are set the four lovers, the artisans and the fairies, all bound together by the theme of errors. Through the forest the lovers blunder their distracted way, the artisans not only rehearse a playlet of errors but themselves are carried into the maze. Oberon in his wisdom tries to set things right and only succeeds in making confusion worse confounded, while for Puck the creating of error is his spirit food.

Here Shakespeare first clearly introduces another of his potent preoccupations—the concept of dream and reality; and with it he first boldly sets forth the contrast between seeming and being. From both, much of the inner quality of his later dramas, both comic and tragic, was to arise; both were to be the very stuff of his double vision, of his common-sense view of life, of his identification with the force of Nature. Appearance and reality interplay in these dramas like two themes in a symphony. . . .

Various critics have pointed out that in Theseus we have, as it were, a level-headed commentator on the action, one who is never likely to mistake a bush for a bear. Beyond this, however, we must certainly go. We have just seen Oberon and Titania, and it is precisely these characters whose very existence Theseus would deny; we have just seen young lyric love, uniting with Nature's force, triumph over man-made law, and it is precisely lyric love that Theseus would reject. Besides Theseus there is another level-headed character—Bottom, but Bottom has a fairy's kisses on his lips. Shakespeare's level-headedness, his sublime common sense, cannot be restricted within the ring of Theseus' practicality: it embraces the imagination as well as the ordinary real.

Allardyce Nicoll
Shakespeare (London: Methuen, 1952), pp. 104-6

King John

. . . He [John] proves a genuine leader at a time when Faulconbridge is little more than a racy and attractive adventurer. . . . It is only for the moment in which his personal ambition drives him, in his fear of Arthur, to a criminal act that everything is rapidly transformed: this is the *primum mobile* of his degradation—and Faulconbridge it is who now rises to the status of a ruler or, more exactly, of *the* hero that the King himself had ceased to be. . . .

He . . . [Faulconbridge] remains unstained by Commodity and, having kept a total integrity in the most trying circumstances, finally proves to be himself the natural ruler that John had ceased to be.

Adrien Bonjour
ELH (December, 1951), pp. 270, 272

The Merchant of Venice

Lest at his first appearance the Jew should make too favorable an impression by his Scripture quotations, Antonio is led to observe that the devil can cite Scripture for his purpose; lest the Jew's motive in foregoing interest (for once in his life) should seem like the kindness Antonio takes it to be, Bassanio avows that he likes not fair terms and a villain's mind; and once the Jew has caught the Christian on the hip, every one, from Duke to Gaoler, has words of horror or detestation for him and of compassion for his victim. . . .

Launcelot and Jessica, in separate scenes, are introduced before Shylock reaches home, that, hearing their story, we may side with them, and, when the old curmudgeon appears, may be moved to laughter as he complains of Launcelot's gormandizing, sleeping, and rending apparel out, and as he is made game of by the young conspirators to his face. Here, as Mr Poel has noticed, when there might be some danger of our sympathy becoming enlisted on Shylock's side because he is about to lose his daughter and some of his property, Shakespeare forestalls it. He lets Shylock, in his hesitation whether to go to the feast, take warning from a dream, but nevertheless, though he knows that they bid him not for love, decide to go in hate, in order to feed upon the prodigal Christian. And he lets him give up Launcelot, whom he has half a liking for, save that he is a huge feeder, to Bassanio—"to one that I would have him help to waste his borrowed purse." Small credit these sentiments do him; little do they add to his pathos or dignity. Still more conspicuous is this care when Shylock laments over his daughter and his ducats. Lest then by any chance a stupid or tender-hearted audience should not laugh but grieve, Salanio reports his outcries—in part word for word—two scenes in advance, as matter of mirth to himself and all the boys in Venice. It is exactly the same method as that employed in *Twelfth Night,* Act III, scene ii, where Maria comes and tells not only Sir Toby, Sir Andrew, and Fabian, but, above all, the audience, how ridiculously Malvolio is acting, before they see it for themselves. The art of the theatre, but particularly the art of the comic theatre, is the art of preparations, else it is not securely comic. But the impression first of all imparted to us is of Shylock's villainy —an impression which, however comical he may become, we are not again allowed to lose. . . .

Only twice does Shakespeare seem to follow Shylock's pleadings and reasonings with any sympathy—"Hath a dog money?" in the first scene in which he appears, and "Hath not a Jew eyes?" in the third act—but a bit too much has been made of this. Either plea ends in such fashion as to alienate the audience. To Shylock's reproaches the admirable Antonio, "one of the gentlest and humblest of all the men in Shakespeare's theatre," praised and honoured by every one but Shylock, retorts, secure in his virtue, that he is just as like to spit on him and spurn him again. And Shylock's celebrated justification of his race runs headlong into a justification of his villainy. . . .

E. E. Stoll
Shakespeare Studies (New York: Macmillan, 1927), pp. 264-68

Like other heroines of the comedies, Portia and Nerissa teach their men a lesson by taking advantage of their unawareness. . . .

The ladies' practice on their husbands, though severe, is lightly executed; Bassanio and Gratiano are stretched long on the rack, but they are released before they are pulled apart. Supposing that their wives have remained in Belmont and that they alone know the story of Antonio's trial, their consciences uneasy because the rings are gone but soothed by the certainty that they were given to men and not women, they here occupy that depth of unawareness reserved for Dogberrys, Aguecheeks, Bottoms—and romantic heroes. Poor Orlando will stand there soon, as will Orsino and Bertram. . . .

Indeed, presumably they will come to know more than we do if the letter brought Antonio by Portia explains how it can be that his three argosies—which we were first assured would be lost and then informed were lost in fact—"Are richly come to harbour suddenly." Portia is only the bearer of the good news and can of course have had no actual part in saving the ships: *yet the effect is as though she had saved them.* The sudden, surprising announcement, coming from her after we have been assured that they were lost, makes it seem almost as if she had wrought the miracle. Fabulous when we first hear of her, dazzling in the casket scene, all-knowing and seemingly all-powerful in the court scene, nowhere does she more truly prefigure the ultimate Prospero than in the effect of this closing moment. Antonio's comment on the miraculous news is alone adequate for participant and spectator: "I am dumb."

Bertrand Evans
Shakespeare's Comedies (Oxford Univ. Pr., 1960), pp. 65-67

The trial scene climaxes the action at all the levels of meaning that have been established. As has been suggested, it portrays at the moral level Shylock's degradation to a cur and a monster through his commitment to revenge, and by contrast, Antonio's attainment of the fullness of Christian love through his abjuration of revenge. Allegorically, the scene develops the sharpest opposition of Old Law and New in terms of their respective theological principles, Justice and Mercy, Righteousness and Faith; it culminates in the final defeat of the Old Law and the symbolic conversion of the Jew.

Barbara K. Lewalski
SQ (Summer, 1962), p. 338

Henry IV, Part I

I have suggested that many of the "secret impressions of courage" are contradictions inherent in the type of the braggart captain. For to this type Falstaff unquestionably belongs. He has the increasing belly and decreasing leg, the diminutive page for a foil, the weapon (his pistol) that is no weapon but a fraud, as well as most of the inner qualities of this ancient stage-figure—cowardice and unbridled bragging, gluttony and lechery, sycophancy and pride. Also he is a recruiting officer and (though it be in the *Merry Wives of Windsor*) a suitor gulled. All these traits are manifest, except his sycophancy, which, however, appears in his dependence on the Prince and his wheedling ways with him; and except his pride, which appears in his insistence on his title on every occasion, and in his reputation for a proud jack among the drawers. Lyly's Sir Tophas, Jonson's Bobadill and Tucca, Beaumont's Bessus, Chapman's Braggadino and Quintiliano, the still earlier Ralph Roister Doister, Ambidexter, and Thersites, as well as Shakespeare's Pistol, Don Armado, and Parolles, have most or many of these traits; and these descend to them, if not from the classics directly, from the Italian popular *miles*, Capitano Spavento. The English and the Italian specimens differ from those of Plautus in that they are impecunious, the unwelcome parasites of tailor, barber, or landlady, not the patrons of parasites. Falstaff is both the one and the other. Unlike most braggart captains, however, he is not silly and affected—those qualities were reserved for Pistol—boasts only when he has, not reason, but need to do so, is not beaten and knocked about the stage but keeps a sort of dignity, and is a humorist and wit. It is these circumstances no doubt that have made critics, even of late, declare that the impression of his character is quite different, and is therefore not that of a coward. But all the other traits save paunch and spindle-shanks are also the traits of famous clowns—Panurge, Sosie, Folengo's Cingar, Scarron's Jodelet—and even now a clown not a coward is a rarity on the stage. . . .

The braggart captain, indeed, is incompatible with himself. Cowards do not go to war, or, if driven to it, do not become captains. Or if even that be not beyond the compass of chance and their own contriving, the clever ones do not boast so extravagantly as to rob themselves of credence and engage themselves in undertakings which it is farthest from their wish to approach. The huge and delectable contrasts of the old comedy involve contradictions as huge, and the spectators blinked fact—if indeed they were not blind to it—in the throes of their laughter.

E. E. Stoll
Shakespeare Studies (New York: Macmillan, 1927), pp. 428-31

In *I Henry IV* the serious and comic are not compounded, one out of the other, but are mixed complexly, as crossing strands, and their conjunction is the resolution of the play. . . .

The conspiracy does not have a moral integrity that can survive into the resolution. Further, the conspirators have a major political frailty, feudal separatism. The national traits of the Welshman, the Scotsman, and the Northumbrian are strongly handled; each is made interesting and sympathetic in itself, but, therefore, together they are almost comic as a conspiracy. . . .

Now, as a serious character, Hotspur is brave in war and eager for the reputation of bravery, Honor. This combination is involved in a double complexity. First, it is tragically fatal in that it leads to hasty commitments and unprepared battle (IV, 3; cf. the behavior of Brutus in *Julius Caesar*, IV, 3). Second, Hotspur is a comic humor, as in the conspiracy in Act I, the scene with Kate in Act II, in Wales in Act III, and in his quick envy of Hal. . . . And so the Prince, who, as we shall see, is a figure of resolution with respect to both the serious and the comic actions, and therefore speaks philosophically (not as a character) in both, judges Percy to be comic and mentions him in a breath with Francis the Drawer (II, 4).

It is Hotspur's humor that lays him open to a reversal into the comic action. But after his death, of course, his honor is purged of its comic part, and the Prince then speaks the lines, "Fare thee well, great heart. . . ."

The conjunction of Falstaff and Percy, the comic and the serious plots, is glorious and pitiful. The death of Percy is not very fearful (he has been handled too humorously), but his fate is exceptionally pitiful; and so much the greater is the glory of Falstaff's witty triumph.

Paul Goodman
The Structure of Literature (Chicago:
Univ. Chicago Pr., 1954), pp. 104-8

Falstaff may be the most conspicuous, he is certainly the most fascinating, character in *Henry IV*, but all critics are agreed, I believe, that the technical centre of the play is not the fat knight but the lean prince. Hal links the low life with the high life, the scenes at Eastcheap with those at Westminster, the tavern with the battlefield; his doings provide most of the material for both Parts, and with him too lies the future, since he is to become Henry V, the ideal king, in the play that bears his name; finally, the mainspring of the dramatic action is . . . the choice he is called upon to make between Vanity and Government, taking the latter in its accepted Tudor meaning, which includes Chivalry or prowess in the field, the theme of Part I, and Justice, which is the theme of Part II. Shakespeare, moreover, breathes life into these abstractions by embodying them, or aspects of them, in prominent characters, who stand, as it were, about the Prince, like attendant spirits: Falstaff typifying Vanity in every sense of the word, Hostpur Chivalry, of the old anarchic kind, and the Lord Chief Justice the Rule of Law or the new ideal of service to the state. . . .

Hal associates Falstaff in turn with the Devil of the miracle play, the

Vice of the morality, and the Riot of the interlude, when he calls him "that villainous abominable misleader of Youth, that old white-bearded Satan," "that reverend Vice, that grey Iniquity, that father Ruffian, that Vanity in years," and "the tutor and the feeder of my riots." "Riot," again is the word that comes most readily to King Henry's lips when speaking of his prodigal son's misconduct. And, as heir to the Vice, Falstaff inherits by reversion the functions and attributes of the Lord of Misrule, the Fool, the Buffoon, and the Jester, antic figures the origins of which are lost in the dark backward and abysm of folk-custom. . . . Falstaff possesses a strain, and more than a strain, of the classical *miles gloriosus* as well. In short, the Falstaff-Hal plot embodies a composite myth which had been centuries amaking. . . .

Shakespeare's audience enjoyed the fascination of Prince Hal's "white-bearded Satan" for two whole plays, as perhaps no character on the world's stage had ever been enjoyed before. But they knew, from the beginning, that . . . Falstaff must be rejected by the Prodigal Prince, when the time for reformation came.

J. Dover Wilson
The Fortunes of Falstaff (Cambridge Univ. Pr., 1943), pp. 17-22

Henry IV, Part II

In 2 *Henry IV* Shakespeare repeats the same symbolic morality pattern he had used in the first play, and it is for this reason that Hal must again be educated and won from Falstaff, with little regard to his reformation at the end of *Part I*, and in spite of any inconsistency this may present to modern readers. Hal's contempt for Falstaff is, however, even greater than it had been in *Part I*, and we see little real relish on his part for the antics of Falstaff. The reformation of Hal in both plays is presented primarily as symbolic ritual for didactic purposes, rather than as documentary exposition of historical fact. Falstaff fills the same role of tempter, but, as most commentators have noted, he is far less attractive a figure than in *Part I*, for in addition to his sloth and cowardice, he now symbolizes some of the more loathsome aspects of civil disorder and misgovernment, particularly evident in his relations with Mistress Quickly and Doll Tearsheet, his fleecing of Justice Shallow, and his abuses of his military position for personal gain. Opposed to Falstaff we now have the Lord Chief Justice, a figure inherited from popular legend and from *The Famous Victories of Henry V*. He is, of course, a symbol of sobriety, order, and the justice upon which all good government is based. . . .

We see little of Hal in Falstaff's company in 2 *Henry IV*, and in the few places where they are together Hal shows little joy in the association.

When Hal is crowned, we are entirely prepared for the total rejection of Falstaff which is to follow. The political theme of 2 *Henry IV* is expressed largely in the contrast between Falstaff and the Lord Chief Justice, who face each other in the second scene of the play, and whose antagonism is maintained to the very end. The Justice is the one person Falstaff fears, just as the devil fears God. When Falstaff in 2 *Henry IV* hears finally that Hal has been crowned, as he revels in the thought of the disorder he will now bring to England, he gloats also over the apparent defeat of his old enemy, the Lord Chief Justice. . . .

And similarly the Lord Chief Justice fears for his own life when he hears of the new king, for like everyone else, he assumes that Falstaff has triumphed. . . .

The conflict between Falstaff and the Lord Chief Justice is at the heart of the play. All expect that Hal will choose Falstaff, but instead he chooses the Lord Chief Justice, thus assuring the defeat of Falstaff and the victory of England.

Irving Ribner
The English History Play in the Age of Shakespeare
(Princeton, N. J.: Princeton Univ. Pr., 1957), pp. 176-78

Much Ado About Nothing

The play as a whole is closer to everyday life than *A Midsummer Night's Dream*, with its magical woods, or *As You Like It*, with its fabulous Forest of Arden. But like the other great comedies, *Much Ado* is a holiday from the cares of the world; an entertainment in which humor of several kinds is delicately mingled with both real music and music of the verse. . . .

This festivity (Act II, Scene 1), with its graceful parade of masked couples, its music, and its dance, provides an image of the action of the whole play. . . . When the drum gives the signal, and the maskers, two by two, play out their mocking and wistful flirtations, we can see how all are groping for "true love" behind its thin disguises.

Shakespeare gives this episode a shimmering quality by shifting between prose, verse, and music. The prose of the four masked couples (as beautiful as any Shakespeare wrote) is designed to characterize each pair, and at the same time to provide a rhythmic anticipation of the dance music which soon follows. . . .

Claudio's and Benedick's love-stories are woven together, as the friends mock or help each other, throughout the play. These parallel scenes of elaborate fooling, frankly theatrical as they are, have much of the quality of the masked party. They are also full of insight into love's varied moods, from hearty bawdiness at one extreme to the nostalgia of song at the other. . . .

Benedick's and Claudio's affairs both reach a climax and turning-point in Act III, Scene 2. . . . It looks as though Claudio had lost a bride just as Benedick found one.

By making fun of Don John's efforts, and rendering them harmless in advance, Shakespeare softens the big scene in the church (Act IV, Scene 1) when Claudio accuses Hero. . . . When the Friar leads them all solemnly in, Claudio, Don Pedro and Don John playing their stiff parts, and hiding their real feelings, the procession should recall the masquerade in Act II. . . .

The transition from the comically-deluded world of the play back to everyday reality, where real marriages are possible, is appropriately accomplished by Claudio and Don Pedro, who were partly to blame for the last big mistake. Their nocturnal visit to Hero's tomb is as formal as the masked ball or the wedding-procession, and like those two ceremonious occasions, it is both true and false. For the Hero whom Claudio thought he knew is really dead, while the real Hero "lives in death with glorious fame," as his song says.

Francis Fergusson
Much Ado About Nothing (New York:
Dell Publishing Co., 1960), pp. 6-14

The primary identifying fact about *Much Ado,* I think, is that it is the most realistic of Shakespeare's love comedies written during the reign of Elizabeth. And it is realistic despite the basic improbability (or conventionality) of Claudio's deception by Don John. It abandons completely the romantic landscape, the romantic disguisings, the romantic dialogue of Portia's and Bassanio's Belmont, of Rosalind's and Orlando's Forest of Arden, of Viola's and Duke Orsino's Illyria. In *Much Ado* we enter a dramatic world created in very close imitation of the habitable one we know outside the theater. . . .

The language used to carry the interchanges between Rosalind and Orlando, or between Viola and Duke Orsino, is romantically stylized and tempts us to immerse ourselves in some ideal, golden world of love. The language used for the interchanges between characters in *Much Ado* constantly reminds us of the flow of clever discourse in the best moments of the actual world we all inhabit. And the potency of this language of *Much Ado* is such that it seems capable of generating the natural, this-worldly atmosphere of the play just in itself. It is not the formalized repartee, the carefully contrived and balanced give and take of wit in Restoration comedy. Rather, its special quality is its air of the spontaneous. In *Much Ado* it is as if the characters themselves were inventing in front of us their quick ironic retorts and their exultant gaiety at the accomplishment. . . .

The substance of *Much Ado* is that of the romantic comedies, sex, love, and marriage. But this play's differentiated way of regarding this substance, its sophisticated realism, is certainly intentionally suggested by its title.

David L. Stevenson
Much Ado About Nothing (New York: New American Library, 1964), pp. xxi-xxv

Henry V

Theme and hero clearly called for epic; and the problem was how to use the theatre for this purpose. It was solved by setting a series of heroic episodes or tableaux upon the stage, interspersed indeed for comic relief with lighter scenes, which introduce bragging Frenchmen (at times extraordinarily like Mussolini), rascally camp-followers, or a couple of French ladies making pretty fritters of English, but never for long distracting the attention of the audience from the contemplation of one figure, that of the great King, which, exhibited in a variety of moods and situations, dominates the play as Æneas dominates the *Æneid*. And the epical tone was emphasized by a Chorus, who speaks five prologues and an epilogue. . . .

The background of *Henry V* is war; and its atmosphere, as in most epics, is determined by the poet's attitude towards war. Now war may be conceived in two ways: as man's greatest vocation, the pursuit of Glory, at the risk of one's own life or those of others, and through the ruthless exercise of power; or as one of the greatest of human evils, with its miserable train of blood and anguish, horror and tears. The first, on the whole that of the traditional epic, is once again Marlowe's; the second, represented by Hardy's *Dynasts* and Tolstoy's *War and Peace*, is on the whole modern. Shakespeare gives both, one after the other. Yet there is no sudden transition, no violent contrast or crude incongruity: the change is so natural and inevitable that a spectator will not realize it is taking place; it corresponds with the development of the campaign, and reflects the mood of the nation and the army. . . .

As the ordeal draws near Shakespeare reveals more and more of the man to us, and his humanity is the argument at once of his conversation with the soldiers and of the soliloquy that follows. Where else, too, in English poetry is to be found our English notion of leadership better expressed than in the fourth Chorus, which describes him touring the camp throughout the night, and cheering the "ruined band" by his mere presence, words of comfort being idle mockery in that awful predicament? . . .

Yet Shakespeare has a still finer moment for him, the last before battle, into which he sends his soldiers, no longer as at Harfleur with the war-cry

"God for England, Harry and Saint George!" but with a petition, "How thou pleasest, God, dispose the day! . . ."

It is a statement of the ultimate heroic faith, a faith which, like that of the martyrs, puts him who holds it beyond reach of mortal man.

J. Dover Wilson
King Henry V (Cambridge Univ. Pr., 1947),
pp. xii-xiii, xxvii-xxviii, xli

Julius Caesar

Shakespeare in *Julius Caesar* was interested in two great figures from Roman history, and he treated them with all of the reverence for Rome and the tolerance for Roman political institutions which was so character- istic of the Renaissance, both in England and on the continent. He treated Caesar and Brutus in accordance with the long literary tradition which he inherited: Caesar as the noble hero overthrown by his pride and ambi- tion, and Brutus as the virtuous would-be saviour of his country who, through his own insufficiency and because of the depravity of the Roman people, brings only greater tragedy to Rome. Of the two tragedies, that of Brutus more completely attracted his interest. As an historical dramatist, Shakespeare was fully aware of the political implications of his theme. In the murder of Caesar, however, he did not see primarily a vindication of monarchy as a divinely favored institution. Important as this doctrine may have been to Shakespeare and his contemporaries, it is irrelevant to this play. He saw rather, on the one hand, a lesson in the civil chaos which results when a great and noble leader tries to overthrow long-established institutions and seeks, with the support of the mob, to attain a kingship to which he has no lawful claim. On the other hand, he saw the even greater chaos which results when men of noble instincts violate their own natures and enter into evil so that political good may result. These are the two political issues with which *Julius Caesar* is concerned.

Irving Ribner
JEGP (January, 1957), p. 22

The official Caesar of Shakespeare's play is presented with all the pomp and ceremony of a great public person. Yet he is curiously undercut by our image of Caesar the private man, full of physical infirmities and an irritating insistence on his own dignity. . . .

It is logically true that deafness in one ear does not disqualify a man from political power, but in context it offers an ironic comment on Caesar's omnipotent and superhuman claims. The whole of the assassination scene is shot through with this same irony. While Caesar is claiming the passion- less infallibility of a god, we cannot help thinking of Caesar the man and asking ourselves: Is this a god indeed? or are these claims the pretensions of an ordinary and weak mortal? There cannot humanly be a greatness in the man Caesar equivalent to the greatness he imagines for himself, and in this disproportion lies his fall of pride, which is in the *De Casibus* tradition of medieval tragedy.

There is an interesting series of changes in our attitude toward Caesar from the moment of his murder to the end of the play. In the first confusion after the assassination, we are acutely conscious of the fall of great Caesar. A moment ago he had made his highest and most superhuman claims, and now his body lies at the pedestal of Pompey's statue "No worthier than the dust!" (3.1.116). Caesar the man has been humbled to this, as pride goeth before a fall—we almost feel the inevitability of such a movement, and it points up the vanity of earthly glory. . . .

The ironic interplay between the images of Caesar the man and Caesar the political figure suggests an important distinction between Brutus and Cassius. The shrewd Cassius sees the conspiracy in terms of individual men, whereas Brutus sees it in terms of principles unfortunately embodied in men. Brutus is not concerned with Caesar the man as Cassius is, but only with "the spirit of Caesar" (2.1.167): this is the public Caesar, Caesarism, the principles for which Caesar stands and their potentiality for evil. Brutus considered and rejected the personal argument three separate times in his "orchard" soliloquy (2.1.10-12, 19-21, 28-29). For Brutus the conspiracy will destroy in advance the tyranny that Caesar may bring, with its probable suppression of republican liberties. The murder of Caesar the man, no matter what one's personal attachment, is a necessary means to this end. Cassius, on the other hand, emphasizes the infirmities and tyranny of Caesar the man as if all that were needed to right matters in Rome were the death of Caesar; Cassius does not really seem to be at all concerned with the issue of Caesarism. But the course of the dramatic action reverses Brutus' plan and shows its tragic wrongness, for the conspirators are only able to kill the body of Caesar not the spirit.

Maurice Charney
Shakespeare's Roman Plays (Cambridge, Mass.:
Harvard Univ. Pr., 1961), pp. 67, 73-74, 77

As You Like It

The comedy, then, is less a comedy of dramatic event than a playful fantastic criticism of life: wherein a courtly society being removed to the greenwood, to picnic there, the Duke Senior can gently moralise on the artificiality he has left at home, and his courtiers—being courtiers still, albeit loyal ones—must ape his humours. But this in turn, being less than sincere, needs salutary mockery: wherefore Shakespeare invents Jaques and Touchstone, critics so skilfully opposed, to supply it. But yet again, Jaques' cynicism being something of a pose, he must be mocked at by the Fool; while the Fool, being professionally a fool, must be laughed at by Jaques, and, being betrayed to real folly by human weakness, laughed at by himself. Even Rosalind, being in love, must play with love. . . .

But in truth all the rest of our bright characters are not in earnest. They do but *play* at life in Arden. As Touchstone knew, "cat will after kind"; and, as Shakespeare knew, the world is the world as man made it for man to live in. These courtiers are not *real* Robin Hoods. When the *ducdame, ducdame* has been played out, yet not so as to overweary, Shakespeare gathers up his "fashionables"—as afterwards in *The Tempest* he gathers up the Neopolitan courtiers—and restores them, like so many fish, to their proper element.

Arthur Quiller-Couch
Shakespeare's Workmanship (London:
T. Fisher Unwin, 1918), pp. 127-29

In *As You Like It* the art of comic juxtaposition is at its subtlest. It is to give it fullest scope that the action can be pushed up into a corner, and the usual entanglements of plotting, though not dispensed with altogether, can be loosened. Freedom, of course, is in the hospitable air of Arden, where convenient caves stand ready to receive outlaws, alfresco meals are abundantly provided, with a concert of birds and running brooks, and there is no worse hardship than a salubrious winter wind. This is "the golden world" to which, with the beginning of his second act, Shakespeare at once transports us. . . .

. . . Nothing is neater in the construction of the play than those well-placed little scenes which, by despatching first Orlando and then Oliver to the forest, do what is still required by the story and give the illusion that an action is still going briskly forward, while at the same time they renew our acquaintance with the wicked world. . . .

The contrast between court and country is thus presented and our preference is very plain. Yet as a counterpoise to all this, there is one man in the country-side who actually prefers the court. Finding himself in Arden, Touchstone decides: "When I was at home, I was in a better place." It is no doubt important that he is a fool, whose values may well be topsy-turvy. But in one word he reminds us that there are such things as domestic comforts. And presently we find that the old man whom society throws into the corner is likely in the "uncouth forest" to die of hunger and exposure to the "bleak air." There is clearly something to be said on the other side; the fool may anatomize the wise man's folly. And there is also

Jaques to point out that the natural life in Arden . . . is as cruel and unnatural as the other. . . .

Shakespeare, then, builds up his ideal world and lets his idealists scorn the real one. But into their midst he introduces people who mock their ideals and others who mock *them*. One must not say that Shakespeare never judges, but one judgement is always being modified by another. Opposite views may contradict one another, but of course they do not cancel out. Instead they add up to an all-embracing view far larger and more satisfying than any one of them in itself.

Harold Jenkins
SS (Cambridge Univ. Pr., 1955), pp. 43-45

Twelfth Night

In fact about two-thirds of *Twelfth Night* is in prose, a considerably larger proportion than in *As You Like It.* Yet though the verse of *Twelfth Night* falls below the prose in quantity, it surely surpasses it in quality. Apart from occasional phrases—"sick of self-love," "cakes and ale," "ginger hot in the mouth"—the comic dialogue, excellent as it is on the stage, escapes the memory. There are no such verbal fireworks as in *Much Ado,* no such cascades of gaiety as in *As You Like It.* What we remember best, perhaps, in *Twelfth Night* are bits of verse. . . .

In contrast with the lyrical flow of *A Midsumer Night's Dream* or the graceful eloquence of *The Merchant of Venice,* the poetry of *Twelfth Night* has an almost elegiac quality. Orsino's description of a song he calls for may serve to characterize it:

> Mark it, Caesario; it is old and plain;
>
> . . .
>
> And dallies with the innocence of love,
> Like the old age.

It is the innocence of love that Shakespeare plays with in this comedy, not the fickle fancy of the *Dream* nor the burning passion of *Romeo and Juliet.* This is especially marked in the character and action of Viola, and it is not too much, perhaps, to say that it is Viola who imparts to the air of *Twelfth Night* a fragrance all its own. . . .

There is a strain of gentleness, of sweetness, even of humility, in Viola that distinguishes her from such lively characters as Beatrice and Rosalind. She does not pretend to be master of her fate; she would die a thousand deaths to give her master peace of mind; she is frank to confess that she "had rather go with sir priest than sir knight"; altogether she is the most modest, the most wistful, perhaps the most lovable of Shakespeare's ladies.

Thomas Marc Parrott
Shakespearean Comedy (Oxford Univ. Pr., 1949), pp. 186-87

However fanciful its dreams of desire, the play moves within a context of an almost real world, from one disguise and half-understood intrigue to another, until all its elements are whirled into a complexly related and moving figure. With the constant contrasts and parallels and reversals in character, situation, and intrigue, we find ourselves at last, along with Malvolio and Olivia and Viola and the rest, in a state of real delirium. Until the concluding scene, however, we can largely agree with Sebastian: if we dream, we do not wish to wake; if this is madness, it is still comic madness, and we do not envy the sane. The attempts at false and inflexible authority are being defeated, the pretentious are being deflated, and the very sentimentality of the likable sentimentalists has led them close to biological reality. We are particularly delighted with Viola. Young, intelligent, zestful, she is a realist. She cuts through the subterfuges and disguises of the others with absolute clarity, and she provides us with a center for the movement, a standard of normality which is never dull. In her rejection of the artificial myths of love, moreover, Viola never becomes the advocate of a far more terrifying myth, the myth of absolute rationality. In a completely rational world, Shakespeare never tires of pointing out, what we know as love could not exist. We have never desired such a world.

From the time of her first aside to the audience after she has seen Orsino ("Yet a barful strife!/Whoe'er I woo, myself would be his wife"), Viola directly admits her irrational love. She differs, then, from Orsino and Olivia not in any invulnerability to blindness and passion, but in the clarity and simplicity with which she recognizes and accepts her state. Reason is not abandoned: she rationally admits her irrationality and her inability to cope with the situation. . . .

The entrance of Sebastian is "what we will." It is the most dramatic moment of the play. The confrontation of Sebastian and Cesario-Viola, those identical images, concludes the formal plot and provides the means for the discarding of all the lovers' masks. The moment must be savored and fully realized. As Viola and Sebastian chant their traditional formulas of proof, both the audience and the other characters on the stage undistractedly view the physical image of the duality which has made the confusion and the play. The masks and the play are to be abandoned for a vision of delight beyond delight, in which lovers have neither to wear nor to penetrate disguises since they are at last invulnerable to error and laughter.

Joseph H. Summers
UKCR (Autumn, 1955), pp. 28-29

Hamlet

Is it possible to conceive an experience more desolating to a man such as we have seen Hamlet to be; and is its result anything but perfectly natural?

It brings bewildered horror, then loathing, then despair of human nature. His whole mind is poisoned. . . .

A nature morally blunter would have felt even so dreadful a revelation less keenly. A slower and more limited and positive mind might not have extended so widely through its world the disgust and disbelief that have entered it. . . .

. . . the *immediate* cause of that [Hamlet's inaction] is simply that his habitual feeling is one of disgust at life and everything in it, himself included—a disgust which varies in intensity, rising at times into a longing for death, sinking often into weary apathy, but is never dispelled for more than brief intervals. . . .

I have dwelt thus at length on Hamlet's melancholy because, from the psychological point of view, it is the centre of the tragedy, and to omit it from consideration or to underrate its intensity is to make Shakespeare's story unintelligible. But the psychological point of view is not equivalent to the tragic; and, having once given its due weight to the fact of Hamlet's melancholy, we may freely admit, or rather may be anxious to insist, that this pathological condition would excite but little, if any, tragic interest if it were not the condition of a nature distinguished by that speculative genius on which the Schlegel-Coleridge type of theory lays stress. Such theories misinterpret the connection between that genius and Hamlet's failure, but still it is this connection which gives to his story its peculiar fascination and makes it appear (if the phrase may be allowed) as the symbol of a tragic mystery inherent in human nature. Wherever this mystery touches us, wherever we are forced to feel the wonder and awe of man's godlike "apprehension" and his "'thoughts that wander through eternity,'" and at the same time are forced to see him powerless in his petty sphere of action, and powerless (it would appear) from the very divinity of his thought, we remember Hamlet. And this is the reason why, in the great ideal movement which began towards the close of the eighteenth century, this tragedy acquired a position unique among Shakespeare's dramas, and shared only by Goethe's *Faust*. It was not that *Hamlet* is Shakespeare's greatest tragedy or most perfect work of art; it was that *Hamlet* most brings home to us at once the sense of the soul's infinity, and the sense of the doom which not only circumscribes that infinity but appears to be its offspring.

A. C. Bradley
Shakespearean Tragedy (London: Macmillan, 1904),
pp. 119, 122, 122-28

Hamlet's soul is sick. The symptoms are, horror at the fact of death and an equal detestation of life, a sense of uncleanliness and evil in the things of nature; a disgust at the physical body of man; bitterness, cynicism, hate.

It tends towards insanity. All these elements are insistent in Hamlet. He can describe the glories of heaven and earth—but for him those glories are gone. . . .

It will be clear that Hamlet's outstanding peculiarity in the action of this play may be regarded as a symptom of this sickness in his soul. He does not avenge his father's death, not because he dare not, not because he hates the thought of bloodshed, but because his "wit's diseased" (III. ii. 341); his will is snapped and useless, like a broken leg. Nothing is worth while. After the player has worked himself into a tragic passion in the recitation of "Aeneas' Tale to Dido," Hamlet looks inward and curses and hates himself for his lack of passion, and then he hates himself the more for his futile self-hatred. . . . Death is indeed the theme of this play, for Hamlet's disease is mental and spiritual death. . . .

And it will be clear that the elements which I have emphasized, the matter of Hamlet's madness, his patent cruelty, his coarse humour, his strange dialogue with Ophelia, his inability to avenge his father's death, are all equally related to the same sickness within. The coherence of these elements in the play must be evident. Creative action; love; passion—all these can find none but a momentary home in Hamlet's paralysed mind. . . . The outstanding peculiarities of him are his bitterness, his disillusionment, his utter loss of purpose: and many of his humorous speeches which are often performed as pleasant witticisms, or as playful mock-madness, would be more truly rendered with the scornful stare and grating voice of cynicism.

The impression of the play, as a whole, is not so gloomy as the main theme: if it were, it would not have been so popular. There are many individual scenes of action, passion, humour, and beauty, that take our thoughts from the essentially morbid impact of Hamlet's melancholia. Hamlet himself at times recovers his old instinctive friendliness, humour, and gentleness. We can guess what he was like before. That side of his nature which never quite dies, appearing intermittently until the end, is important: it lends point and pathos to the inroads of his cynicism and disgust. His mind wavers between the principle of good, which is love, and that of evil, which is loathing and cruelty. But too much emphasis has been laid on this element of Hamlet. The popularity of the play is not innocent of misunderstanding. To ignore the unpleasant aspects of Hamlet blurs our vision of the protagonist, the play as a whole, and its place in Shakespeare's work.

G. Wilson Knight
The Wheel of Fire (London: Methuen, 1930,
rev. 1956), pp. 23-30

The sense in which death is the subject of *Hamlet* will become apparent if we compare it with other plays. Macbeth has commerce with Hell, but at the very outset of his career dismisses all thought of the life to come. For Brutus and Othello, suicide in the high tragic manner is escape and climax. For Lear death is deliverance. For Romeo and Antony, poignant loss. For all these, as for their author while he writes and the audience while they watch, death is the end: it is almost the frame of the picture. They think of dying: no one thinks, in these plays, of *being dead*. In *Hamlet* we are kept thinking about it all the time, whether in terms of the soul's destiny or of the body's. Purgatory, Hell, Heaven, the wounded name, the rights—or wrongs—of Ophelia's burial, and the staying-power of a tanner's corpse: and beyond this, beyond all Christian and all Pagan maps of the hereafter, comes a curious groping and tapping of thoughts, about "what dreams may come." It is this that gives to the whole play its quality of darkness and of misgiving. Of course there is much else in the play: but nearly always, the same groping. The characters are all watching one another, forming theories about one another, listening, contriving, full of anxiety. The world of *Hamlet* is a world where one has lost one's way. The Prince also has no doubt lost his, and we can tell the precise moment at which he finds it again. "Not a whit. We defy augury. There's a special providence in the fall of a sparrow. It it be now, 'tis not to come: if it be not to come, it will be now: if it be not now, yet it will come: the readiness is all: since no man has aught of what he leaves, what is't to leave betimes?"

C. S. Lewis
Proceedings of the British Academy (1942), p. 13

The conflict in his soul is insoluble, and the only steps he can make are those which inexorably draw him nearer and nearer to his doom. In him, as in every victim of a powerful unconscious conflict, the Will to Death is fundamentally stronger than the Will of Life, and his struggle is at heart one long despairing fight against suicide, the least intolerable solution of the problem. He is caught by fate in a dilemma so tragically poignant that death becomes preferable to life. Being unable to free himself from the ascendancy of his past he is necessarily impelled by Fate along the only path he can travel—to Death. . . .

There is thus reason to believe that the new life which Shakespeare poured into the old story was the outcome of inspirations that took their origin in the deepest and darkest regions of his mind. . . . It is only fitting that the greatest work of the world-poet had to do with the deepest problem and the intensest conflict that have occupied the mind of man since the beginning of time—the revolt of youth and of the impulse to love against the restraint imposed by the jealous old. [1949]

Ernest Jones
Hamlet and Oedipus (Garden City, N. Y.: Doubleday Anchor,
1955; repr., New York: W. W. Norton, 1949), pp. 178-79

The Merry Wives of Windsor

He [Falstaff] has obvious similarities with the Falstaff of *King Henry IV:* but he is somehow not our Falstaff. For an instance (and it lies at the root), the Falstaff that we know was easy enough with Doll Tearsheet: he would simply not have troubled to intrigue with Mistress Ford or with Mistress Page. He is too English, moreover, to be at home in an Italian comedy (and the plot of the *Merry Wives* is pure Italian). Again, though Bardolph, Pistol, Nym, wear their old names, they are not quite the same people. . . .

Now, in *King Henry IV* these characters had become so individual to us that we cannot understand what has happened. Again I suggest that we shall understand better by casting back and remembering that, to the playwright, these figures—all of them—were, first of all, types . . . Falstaff (Gluttony) with a fat paunch; Bardolph (Drunkenness) with a red nose . . . all types—"Here we are again!" in fine. Shakespeare's mind is working; but the whole Elizabethan drama is in ferment too, yeasting up from type to individual . . . from "the old Vice with his dagger of lath" to tragedy in which passion spins the plot. . . .

Arthur Quiller-Couch
Shakespeare's Workmanship (London:
T. Fisher Unwin, 1918), pp. 127-29

Troilus and Cressida

There are two main themes in the play: the theme of war and the theme of love. The first is represented by Hector, the second by Troilus, and the climax of the action is that both these heroes are destroyed. At the end Hector removes his armor, and Achilles, not even single-handed, but accompanied by a gang of Myrmidons, attacks him in the most cowardly fashion and he is killed without a chance for self-defense. Cressida, the object of Troilus' passionate devotion, after swearing to him that she will be forever true, betrays him the very first night after their separation. The result is that we have, in the case of Troilus, a worse kind of tragedy than death, the tragedy of continued existence after everything that matters has been destroyed. There is nothing here of that inevitability which ennobles the end of *Hamlet*.

The two dastardly climaxes of the action, the murder of Hector and the betrayal of Troilus, are all the more shocking because of the way Shakespeare planned the play. For in *Troilus and Cressida,* almost more elaborately than anywhere else, Shakespeare sets up a standard of conduct which the main action of the play violates. . . .

But Shakespeare does not rely merely on the violation of the conventional standards to give his picture of disruption, he uses another feature of the old story, the character of Thersites, to act as a reviling and denigrating chorus to the whole action. In many previous versions of the story, dramatic and otherwise, Thersites had been described as a railer, and in making him rail, Shakespeare was only giving the members of his audience what they expected. But they can never before have heard such effectively corrosive railing as this. . . .

. . . he is not merely a commentator on the warriors, he is a commentator on the lovers too, and he adds his harsh, grating emphasis to the peculiar bitterness which is so deeply a part of Troilus' emotion. . . .

Troilus and Cressida, though it follows Hamlet chronologically, is obviously not an improvement on it as a play. But it is not the ambiguous failure it has often been thought to be. Indeed, so far as our subject is concerned, it marks an extension of awareness in Shakespeare's presentation of man's nature. Whatever name we give it, whether we call it a tragedy, or a history, a comedy or a "comicall satyre," it describes in a new way the difference between man as he ought to be and man as he is. He ought to be part of an ordered state in an ordered universe; he ought to act according to reason and not according to passion. But these ideals are expounded only to be refuted by example after example: Achilles is a proud and selfish individualist who, when he is finally roused, acts like a bully; Cressida is a whore; and the nobility of Troilus, shining through his own sensuality and the murky lustfulness of his environment, is disillusioned and betrayed.

Theodore Spencer
Shakespeare and the Nature of Man (Cambridge Univ. Pr.;
New York: Macmillan, 1943), pp. 111-21

In *The Wheel of Fire,* G. Wilson Knight, holding that ". . . the Trojan party stands for human beauty and worth, the Greek party for the bestial and stupid elements of man," has declared: "Troy is a world breathing the air of medieval storied romance; the Greek camp exists on that of Renaissance satire and disillusion." Oscar James Campbell, on the other hand, seeing in *Comicall Satyre and Shakespeare's Troilus and Cressida* the play as an expression of *fin de siecle* satire addressed to a sophisticatedly Inns of Court audience, regards both sides as the object of derisive mirth: "The Trojans in *Troilus and Cressida* fare no better than the Greeks. . . . In spite of critics, like G. Wilson Knight, who believe that the Trojans were intended to represent some sort of ideal values, Shakespeare presents them as predominantly irrational and foolish."

There is something of truth in each position. Although the fall of Troy comes from the disregard of reason, with Troy goes something fine and grand. It is true that the conversations of those light ladies, Cressida and Helen, with the leering old sensualist Pandarus set the social tone of a society in which chivalry is a cloak for libertinage and love is not an inspiration but a dissipation. In this Shakespeare is representing the practices of chivalric love at the court of Elizabeth, where they continued as the diversion of the old feudalistic aristocracy although the spirit of chivalric love was gone. . . . Yet, decadent as this chivalric society is, its finest flowers stand in contrast to the besieging Greeks, who represent rude force: the courtly Aeneas to the blockish Ajax; the noble Hector to the base Achilles, who looses his Myrmidons on him while Hector is unarmed; the naïvely idealistic Troilus to the self-assured, brusque Diomed, who knows how to make the woman whom Troilus has placed on so lofty a height stoop to him.

Paul N. Siegel
CR (Winter, 1964), pp. 51-53

All's Well That Ends Well

Bertram's fall is due to ill company: Parolles, or Words, another character of Shakespeare's own invention, is perceived in the end by Bertram himself to be the Lie incarnate, a fact which everyone else has known from the beginning. He is that principal danger of noble youth, the flatterer and misleader, the base companion against whom all books of behaviour issued lengthy warning. . . .

The last scene, which is Shakespeare's improvement of his source, is a "judgment," like those which conclude so many of Chapman's comedies. The most extraordinary stratagems are practised by Diana and Hellen to extract Truth from the Accused. The jewels which are bandied about have symbolic significance; they stand for a contract and an estate of life. The King's gem derived from him to Hellen, and Bertram neither knows nor cares what it is. His own monumental ring symbolizes all he has thrown away. . . .

This jewel, with which he had taunted Hellen, is found at the end to be in her keeping. Hellen too is a "Jewell" (5. 3. 1) which Bertram has thrown away. In this scene the King appears as the fount of justice, as earlier he had been the fount of honour. . . . The likeness with the later play of *Measure for Measure,* which was evidently modelled in part on *All's Well,* is particularly strong in this judgment scene, with charge and countercharge piled up in bewildering succession till they are resolved as if by magic in the appearance of the central figure. The ingenuities of Hellen, like those of the Duke, are not to modern taste but their purpose is conversion.

Bertram's conversion must be reckoned among Hellen's miracles.

M. C. Bradbrook
Shakespeare and Elizabethan Poetry (London: Chatto and Windus;
Toronto: Clarke Irwin, 1951), pp. 164-68

Othello

There is in most of the later heroes something colossal, something which reminds us of Michael Angelo's figures. They are not merely exceptional men, they are huge men; as it were, survivors of the heroic age living in a later and smaller world. . . . Othello is the first of these men, a being essentially large and grand, towering above his fellows, holding a volume of force which in repose ensures pre-eminence without an effort, and in commotion reminds us rather of the fury of the elements than of the tumult of common human passion.

What is the peculiarity of *Othello?* What is the distinctive impression that it leaves? Of all Shakespeare's tragedies, I would answer, not even excepting *King Lear, Othello* is the most painfully exciting and the most terrible. From the moment when the temptation of the hero begins, the reader's heart and mind are held in a vice, experiencing the extremes of pity and fear, sympathy and repulsion, sickening hope and dreadful expectation. Evil is displayed before him, not indeed with the profusion found in *King Lear,* but forming, as it were, the soul of a single character, and united with an intellectual superiority so great that he watches its advance fascinated and appalled. He sees it, in itself almost irresistible, aided at every step by fortunate accidents and the innocent mistakes of its victims. He seems to breathe an atmosphere as fateful as that of *King Lear,* but more confined and oppressive, the darkness not of night but of a close-shut murderous room. His imagination is excited to intense activity, but it is the activity of concentration rather than dilation. . . .

Othello is not only the most masterly of the tragedies in point of construction, but its method of construction is unusual. And this method, by which the conflict begins late, and advances without appreciable pause and with accelerating speed to the catastrophe, is a main cause of the painful tension just described.

A. C. Bradley
Shakespearean Tragedy (London: Macmillan, 1904), pp. 176-77

Othello can be interpreted on three levels, the personal, the social and the metaphysical. In *Lear* and *Macbeth* these three levels are so closely interrelated that it is impossible to make sense of the personal or story level without taking the others into consideration. In *Othello* the interrelationship is less complete: the story can be considered alone, with the result that the other elements often remain unnoticed. Unfortunately without them the story itself is liable to misinterpretation. On the personal level we have a straightforward domestic tragedy—Cinthio's *novella,* in fact, with modifications. On the social level we have a study of a contemporary problem, the clash between the "new man" thrown up by certain aspects of

Renaissance culture, the atheist-Machiavel with his principle of pure self-interest, and the chivalric type, representing the traditional values of social order and morality. That Iago is more intelligent than Othello reflects the usual ambivalence of Shakespeare's judgement. On the metaphysical level we see Othello and Iago as exemplifying and participating in the age-long warfare of Good and Evil.

These various planes of meaning coalesce into something like unity. It appears that to Shakespeare Cinthio's ensign suggested (*a*) the contemporary atheist-Machiavel, and (*b*) the Devil himself. It seems to follow that Shakespeare thought of the "new man," with his contempt for traditional morality and religion, as a disintegrating force seeking to break down the social order that is a part of cosmic order—as, in fact, an instrument (no doubt unconscious) of the Devil in his constant effort to reduce cosmos to chaos. This would be a very natural attitude for a conservative Elizabethan, and to express this attitude is one main function—a general function—of the diabolic imagery in *Othello*: Iago is a "demi-devil" (v, ii, 301), worse than an ordinary devil, a bastard one, and his philosophy is a "divinity of hell."

But Shakespeare's metaphysical interest is not wholly absorbed in the social issue. The problem of good end evil is also presented for itself and in much the same terms as we are familiar with from modern interpretations of *Macbeth*. L. C. Knights has drawn attention to the theme of "the deceitful appearance" in the later play. . . .

Deceitful appearance thus characterizes all the main figures in *Othello*. Where is the evil one? Who is true and who is false? The play is a solemn game of hunt the devil, with, of course, the audience largely in the know. And it is in this game that the diabolic imagery is bandied about from character to character until the denouement: we know the devil then, but he has summoned another lost soul to his side.

S. L. Bethell
SS (Cambridge Univ. Pr., 1952), pp. 71-72

Just as Brabantio has been made to see the marriage in a false light and Cassio has been robbed of his senses, Othello is "unwitted" and made to see Desdemona as a "fair devil" (III, iii, 478) . . . She, who appears "like one of heaven" (IV, ii, 36), has a "young and sweating devil" (III, iv, 42) in her moist palm, the sign of her sensuality. "Devil!" he exclaims as he strikes her (IV, i, 251). Emilia, whom he treats as the madam of the house where Desdemona prostitutes herself, he addresses (IV, ii, 90-92), "You, mistress, / That have the office opposite to Saint Peter, / And keep the gate of hell!"

In seeing the heavenly Desdemona as a fair devil, Othello gives himself over to the devil of cynicism. . . .

. . . Othello, in his bitterness at what he believes to be her final lie, asserts that he killed her and, defending himself against Emilia's charge that Desdemona was "heavenly true" and that he is "a devil" (135, 133), affirms his certitude in terms that confirm his damnation (137-39): "O, I were damn'd beneath all depth in hell, / But that I did proceed upon just grounds / To this extremity." And when the truth is finally revealed to him, he is overwhelmed by the feeling that he is indeed damned. "Will you, I pray, demand that demi-devil / Why he hath thus ensnared my soul and body?" he asks (301-2).

Crushed by the sight of her lying pale on the white marriage sheets, the symbol of her purity, he calls to be transported to hell at once. His words are expressive of what the "Homily of Repentance" calls "Judas' repentance," that is, the overwhelming sense of guilt without faith in the mercy of God which is the heinous sin of despair. The sight of his victim blasts any hope of salvation in him (V, ii, 273-75): "When we shall meet at compt, / This look of thine will hurl my soul from heaven, / And fiends will snatch at it." When he continues, "Whip me, ye devils, / From the possession of this heavenly sight," he is not only expressing his despair but is entering upon the punishments of hell in this life.

In commiting self-murder at the conclusion he is continuing to follow Judas' example. His behavior in his last moments, therefore, would have confirmed Elizabethans in the impression that his soul is lost which they gained from observing the dramatic irony of his offering Desdemona an opportunity, as he supposes, for salvation and then withdrawing it in a rage, not realizing that his own salvation is at issue and forgetting that those who do not forgive will not be forgiven.

In killing Desdemona he had rejected her divine goodness and cast away, he says in his final speech, a pearl worth more than all the world, losing his soul. His last words, however, are not those of heartbreak or of self-torture. They are spoken with the resolution of one who knows his irrevocable fate and the regret of one who knows the preciousness of what he has lost and act as a valediction summing up for us the pathos of the ensnarement of this noble nature.

Paul N. Siegel
Shakespearean Tragedy and the Elizabethan Compromise
(New York: New York Univ. Pr., 1957), pp. 125-31

In all his [Iago's] intimate words to the audience his laughter lurks, modulated to scorn for honest fools or to self-satisfaction as he successfully pursues his sport and demonstrates his point. . . . It is no longer the coarse hilarity of the Vice of old, but if not loud it remains deep. And since his whole action in the play is absorbed into his intrigue, the laughter of the allegorical intriguer spreads throughout his role, gaining in extension what it loses in clamor. . . . At the end, in his comment on the wound he has just received, his gaiety even glints with the impervious immortality of his abstract forbears: "I bleed, sir, but not kill'd." Can we really be sure of his death? He and his more primitive brother Aaron are Shakespeare's only tragic villains still alive after the last word and the last scene. His intimate mood readily falls into focus when we stop peering for the character by way of the motives, but look instead at the *performance* by way of tradition. In this tradition humor is not only the native mood of evil, it is also, along with the hate and the dishonesty, the indispensable predication for the massive operation of deceit. . . .

When William Hazlitt described Iago as "an amateur of tragedy in real life," when Bradley noted as "a curious point of technique" with Shakespeare that Iago's "soliloquies . . . read almost like explanations offered to the audience," and when other critics observe the "histrionic" or "artistic" element in the performance, they all respond to a phenomenon whose real nature, although they do not quite discern it, is by now sufficiently familiar to us. It is once more the homiletic dramaturgy of the moral play, where personified evil demonstrated its destructive operation and preached its own exposure, addressing itself as intimately to its audience as any minister to his congregation or pedagogue to his pupils, with the difference that the dramatized lesson was made trenchant by satire and by action. This method reached its culmination in the Vice and descended from him to the line of villains he fathered. All of them manipulate their victims into comic or tragic confusion in order to exhibit the name and nature of villainy. It is, as we have seen, a declining method, and in Iago it is substantially diminished in its two principal features: the action loses as a demonstration what it gains as an organic plot, and the homily recedes before the enactment of the literal story. But although diminished it remains, exploited by the playwright at the height of his powers.

Bernard Spivack
Shakespeare and the Allegory of Evil (New York: Columbia
Univ. Pr.; Oxford Univ. Pr., 1958), pp. 434-36

Measure for Measure

The essentially realistic character of the main plot, which deals with the fortunes of Claudio, Angelo and Isabella, a plot apparently based upon an episode from real life, was emphasized by Shakespeare's vivid and sympathetic treatment, and its realism was further heightened by the portrayal of the low-comedy characters Mistress Overdone, Elbow, Pompey and Abhorson, and of Froth and Lucio, who, though of better social station, are fitly to be grouped with them. The elements added to the main plot by Shakespeare, which most affect the Duke and Mariana, offer a striking contrast, since those elements were drawn from conventional story-telling, and are thoroughly artificial. By his art in making them plausible, Shakespeare preserved, to a large extent, the illusion of reality produced by the play as a whole. . . .

The machinations of the Duke, his deceptions that good may result, must be judged in the light of romantic and dramatic tradition, which may be studied in other Shakespearean plays. The Duke, in his own person, and in his disguise as a friar, combines the two agencies regularly used for the settlement of dramatic complications in accord with justice: the State and the Church. Neither his character nor his actions can be judged on a realistic basis. His state policies and his moral reforms must be viewed as belonging in the realm of story-telling, not as serious discussion of moral issues, or as a transcript of life. Since he represents supreme authority, whether as Duke or Friar, whether secular or religious, other personages of the plot are not to be censured for entrusting themselves entirely to this guidance. . . .

The true interpretation of the whole play, indeed, depends upon constant realization that while it seems real through the brilliancy and veracity of the portraiture of most of its characters, and through the intensely human struggle of the basic plot, it nevertheless exhibits improbabilities and archaisms which must be judged in the light of early traditions and social usages.

William Witherle Lawrence
Shakespeare's Problem Comedies (New York:
Macmillan, 1931), pp. 119-21

Coleridge thought the pardon and marriage of Angelo not only unjust, but degrading to the character of woman. Yet repentance, intercession and forgiveness are the stuff of Christianity and of the old stories of Christendom. . . .

Angelo, publicly shamed, longing for death, faces an Isabel who can bring herself to say, after an agony of silent struggle, "let him not die." It was not in a spirit of "weariness, cynicism, and disgust" that the Master Craftsman made the whirligig of time bring in revenges like these. . . .

. . . Angelo's sin has been, not in act, but in thought, and human law cannot take cognizance of thought: "thoughts are no subjects." Besides, Isabel is conscious that, however innocently, she herself has been the cause of Angelo's fall. . . . And Angelo is penitent. There can be no doubt what the words of the Sermon on the Mount demand: "Judge not, and ye shall not be judged." That had been Isabel's plea for Claudio. It is a test of her sincerity, if she can put forward a plea for mercy for her dearest foe, as well as for him whom she dearly loves.

Criticism of *Measure for Measure,* from Coleridge downwards, has amounted to this: "There is a limit to human charity." "There is," says Chesterton's Father Brown, "and that is the real difference between human charity and Christian charity. . . ."

. . . in Shakespeare's greatest plays, his greatest characters, for all their individuality, have also an imaginative, a symbolic suggestion. . . . No woman in Shakespeare is more individual than Isabel: silent yet eloquent, sternly righteous yet capable of infinite forgiveness, a very saint and a very vixen. But, first and last, she "stands for" mercy. The Duke is first shown to us as a governor perplexed about justice, puzzled in his search for righteousness, seeking above all things to know himself; and he becomes the arbiter of the destinies of everyone in the play. Is it altogether fanciful to remember once again that *Measure for Measure* was acted before the court at Christmas, 1604. . . . the Feast of the Nativity . . . was—is— celebrated in the Christmas psalm:

Mercy and truth are met together: righteousness and peace have kissed each other.

Shakespeare's audience expected a marriage at the end: and, though it may be an accident, the marriage of Isabel and the Duke makes a good ending to a Christmas play.

> R. W. Chambers
> *Man's Unconquerable Mind* (London:
> Jonathan Cape, 1939), pp. 297-308

King Lear

This is certainly the most terrible picture that Shakespeare painted of the world. In no other of his tragedies does humanity appear more pitiably infirm or more hopelessly bad. What is Iago's malignity against an envied stranger compared with the cruelty of the son of Gloster and the daughters of Lear? What are the sufferings of a strong man like Othello to those of helpless age? Much too that we have already observed—the repetition of the main theme in that of the under-plot, the comparisons of man with the most wretched and the most horrible of the beasts, the impression of Nature's hostility to him, the irony of the unexpected catastrophe—these, with much else, seem even to indicate an intention to show things at their worst, and to return the sternest of replies to that question of the ultimate power and those appeals for retribution. . . . Is it not . . . Shakespeare's judgment on the worth of existence that we hear in Lear's agonised cry, "No, no, no life!"?

Beyond doubt, I think, some such feelings as these possess us, and if we follow Shakespeare, ought to possess us, from time to time as we read *King Lear*. . . .

But do they represent the total and final impression produced by the play? . . .

Its final and total result is one in which pity and terror, carried perhaps to the extreme limits of art, are so blended with a sense of law and beauty that we feel at last, not depression and much less despair, but a consciousness of greatness in pain, and of solemnity in the mystery we cannot fathom. . . .

And if here there is "very night herself," she comes "with stars in her raiment." Cordelia, Kent, Edgar, the Fool—these form a group not less remarkable than that which we have just left. There is in the world of *King Lear* the same abundance of extreme good as of extreme evil. It generates in profusion self-less devotion and unconquerable love. And the strange thing is that neither Shakespeare nor we are surprised. We approve these characters, admire them, love them; but we feel no mystery. We do not ask in bewilderment, Is there any cause in nature that makes these kind hearts? Such hardened optimists are we, and Shakespeare,—and those who find the darkness of revelation in a tragedy which reveals Cordelia. Yet surely, if we condemn the universe for Cordelia's death, we ought also to remember that it gave her birth. The fact that Socrates was executed does not remove the fact that he lived, and the inference thence to be drawn about the world that produced him.

A. C. Bradley
Shakespearean Tragedy (London: Macmillan,
1904), p. 261-305

Bradley pointed out, thirty-five years ago, that the agony in which Lear actually dies is one, not of pain, but of ecstasy. . . .

That Bradley's interpretation is *not* fantastic, but a true perception of Shakespeare's meaning, can be proved, I think, when we examine Shakespeare's sources. . . . We have seen how, wishing to duplicate and reinforce the story of Lear, he chose the parallel story of the blind king from Sidney's *Arcadia*. And it is precisely such an ecstasy of joy, succeeding affliction, which Sidney depicts as killing his old king. . . . Shakespeare reproduces this in the death of Gloucester. . . . Shakespeare then gives the same death to Lear. And, with the extraordinary parallelism which runs through the whole play, both Gloucester and Lear have said that this would be recompense for all their sufferings. . . .

. . . the tradition which Shakespeare's audience (and probably Shakespeare himself) regarded as real and true history allowed a living Cordelia to tend Lear's last hours and to bury and mourn him when dead. Shakespeare deliberately altered this historic tradition; because Lear's desolation over Cordelia dead gave him the symbolic truth he wanted. Yet the moving of Cordelia's lips is the last thing seen by Lear's dying eyes. That also gave Shakespeare the symbolic truth he wanted. . . .

So far is *King Lear* from being a play (as Dr. Johnson said) in which the wicked prosper, that by the end of the play the wicked not only are dead but have already ceased to concern us. The bodies of Regan and Goneril are lying there: Lear does not see them nor heed the news of their death. Edmund's death is announced. "That's but a trifle here," says Albany—though it is not a trifle that before Edmund died he had forgiven his slayer and Edgar had forgiven him. Love alone matters, as Edgar tells the story of his reunion with his father, and Lear bends over Cordelia dead. Gloucester had seen in Lear an image of the great world wearing itself out to nought, and as the world vanishes from Gloucester and Lear and Kent, their "strings of life crack" in a passion of love which, after all they have suffered, they cannot sustain. This world passes away, and the fashion of it, and we are left, as at the end of the *Divine Comedy*, with

> The love that moves the sun and all the stars.
> Love bears it out even to the edge of doom.
>
> R. W. Chambers
> *Glasgow Univ. Publications*, LIV (1940), pp. 44-52

In artistic methods, no less than in basic themes, *King Lear* is an epitome of the age. . . . Professors Spencer and Tillyard have shown how deeply rooted in the thought of the age was the belief, dramatized in *King Lear*, that a breach in the natural bonds of duty, affection, gratitude, and sincerity was of world-shaking importance and would be reflected not only in the domain of man—dethroning his reason and lowering him to the level of beasts—but also in the domain of the state—causing civil war—and in the very stars and elements themselves—causing disorder, eclipses, storms, and tempests. . . . If we study the artistic habits inherited from the Middle Ages, we discover that *King Lear*, in its aesthetic organization no less than in its basic thought, has this same dependence on the repetition, in different domains, of a basic pattern.

The medieval basis for this artistic principle of parallelism was the doctrine of prefiguration. Incidents in the Old Testament were paired with corresponding incidents in the life of Christ. . . . Collections of similar stories, like the famous *Mirror for Magistrates*, had the same purpose of tracing a single pattern in many events.

King Lear is built on this same artistic principle of correspondence or parallelism. Each motif is repeated in as many ways as possible. Each character repeats or balances some other character; each event is the prefiguration of some other event; and structural units are balanced against each other. Further, each theme is repeated in the wit and imagery. Just as the main theme of violation of natural law is explored in three domains—the individual character, the social state, and the wider universe of stars and tempests—so the artistic method may be traced in its three domains—the alignment of characters, the structure of scenes, and the verbal imagery. . . .

Out of extremely complex material Shakespeare created a unity of theme, structure, and texture that is scarcely approached by even the best symphonies.

George R. Kernodle
Elizabethan Studies and Other Essays in Honor of George F. Reynolds
(Boulder, Colo.: Univ. Colorado Pr., 1945), *University of Colorado Studies, Series B*, II (Oct. 1945), pp. 185-86, 191

. . . the medieval world with its communal tradition was slowly dying, and the modern individualist world was bringing itself to birth. Shakespeare lived in that violent period of transition. The old world still echoed in his ears; he was aware of the new as we are áware of the future, that is as an inchoate, semi-prophetic dream. Now it seems to me that that dream, those echoes, fill *King Lear* and account for the sense of vastness which it gives us, the feeling that it covers a far greater stretch of time than can be explained by the action. The extreme age of the King brings to our minds the image of a civilization of legendary antiquity; yet that civilization is destroyed by a new generation which belongs to Shakespeare's own time, a perfectly up-to-date gang of Renaissance adventurers. The play contains, therefore, or has taken on, a significance which Shakespeare probably could not have known, but could only have felt, and without his being aware, he wrote in it the mythical drama of the transmutation of civilization. . . .

The judgement on the new generation is passed by a member of it who does not belong spiritually to it: Edgar. It is remarkable that in the scenes where Lear, the Fool and Edgar are together, it is Edgar, the only sane man, who conjures up the deepest images of horror. For he is of the new generation, and knows it as Lear cannot. When Lear asks him who he is, he replies by giving a portrait of his brother Edmund. . . . That is a picture of an animal with human faculties, made corrupt and legendary by the proudly curled hair. It is a picture, too, of the man of policy in the latest style, who regards the sacred order of society as his prey, and recognizes only two realities, interest and force, the gods of the new age.

Edwin Muir
The Politics of King Lear (Glasgow:
Jackson, Son, 1947), pp. 7, 24

Macbeth

Now all these agencies—darkness, the lights and colours that illuminate it, the storm that rushes through it, the violent and gigantic images—conspire with the appearances of the Witches and the Ghost to awaken horror, and in some degree also a supernatural dread. And to this effect other influences contribute. The pictures called up by the mere words of the Witches stir the same feelings . . . In Nature, again, something is felt to be at work, sympathetic with human guilt and supernatural malice. She labours with portents. . . .

Then, as if to deepen these impressions, Shakespeare has concentrated attention on the obscurer regions of man's being, on phenomena which make it seem that he is in the power of secret forces lurking below, and independent of his consciousness and will: such as the relapse of Macbeth from conversation into a reverie, during which he gazes fascinated at the image of murder drawing closer and closer; the writing on his face of strange things he never meant to show; the pressure of imagination heightening into illusion, like the vision of a dagger in the air, at first bright, then suddenly splashed with blood, or the sound of a voice that cried "Sleep no more" and would not be silenced. To these are added other, and constant, allusions to sleep, man's strange half-conscious life; to the misery of its withholding; to the terrible dreams of remorse; to the cursed thoughts from which Banquo is free by day, but which tempt him in his sleep: and again to abnormal disturbances of sleep; in the two men, of whom one during the murder of Duncan laughed in his sleep, and the other raised a cry of murder; and in Lady Macbeth, who rises to re-enact in somnambulism those scenes the memory of which is pushing her on to madness or suicide. All this has one effect, to excite supernatural alarm and, even more, a dread of the presence of evil not only in its recognised seat but all through and around our mysterious nature. Perhaps there is no other work equal to *Macbeth* in the production of this effect.

It is enhanced—to take a last point—by the use of a literary expedient. . . . I refer to . . . ironical juxtapositions of persons and events, and especially to the "Sophoclean irony" by which a speaker is made to use words bearing to the audience, in addition to his own meaning, a further and ominous sense, hidden from himself and, usually, from the other persons on the stage. . . . It cannot be by accident that Shakespeare so frequently in this play uses a device which contributes to excite the vague fear of hidden forces operating on minds unconscious of their influence.

A. C. Bradley
Shakespearean Tragedy (London: Macmillan, 1904), pp. 337-40

He [Macbeth] inhabits a world which strikes us with the effect of an elder age, yet not with the impression of a remotely distant past. It appears like a ruder, simpler epoch preceding but at times surviving into contemporary time. . . . Indeed, the material furnishings of social and domestic life are sparsely represented in the dramatic architecture of the world which Shakespeare makes for Macbeth. In effect, he gives it its appointed place in time by shrouding it in its own peculiar atmosphere, rather than by stuffing it with appropriate archaeological impedimenta. Its persisting backcloth is the massive masonry of ancient fortress strongholds, surrounded by wind-swept, storm-wracked heaths and vast expanses of wild moorland where rival armies clash in the barbaric fury of hand-to-hand encounter, and brandished steel smokes with bloody execution as it unseams an enemy from the nave unto the chaps. Over it all for the most part is spread the gloom of twilight or the thick blackness of night.

H. B. Charlton
Shakespearian Tragedy (Cambridge Univ. Pr., 1948), pp. 143-44

The play is linked to *Hamlet* in more ways than one: Macbeth's shrinking from the murder of Duncan, and the infirmity of purpose with which his wife charges him, are similar to Hamlet's inability to carry out the instructions of the Ghost—though Macbeth's act is "evil" and Hamlet's (at least in his conscious opinion) is "good." Macbeth also resembles Claudius in that both are murderers and usurpers. Macbeth is (consciously) willing to jump the life to come, and we cannot imagine him on his knees; Claudius tries to repent: but both are led from crime to crime in their attempt to achieve security. Macbeth may, in a sense, be regarded as a humanization of Claudius; Shakespeare wished to get inside the skin of a murderer, and to show that the Poet for the Defense, though he extenuates nothing, can make us feel that we might have fallen in the same way, so that we may even assent to Professor Alexander's application of Donne's words:

> Thou knowest this man's fall, but thou knowest not his wrastling; which perchance was such that almost his very fall is justified and accepted of God.

Though Macbeth is *a miserable, and a banished, and a damned creature, yet* he is God's *creature still and contributes something to his glory even in* his *damnation.*

Kenneth Muir
Macbeth (London: Methuen, 1951, 1963), p. 1

Its opening scenes are dominated less by the human figures in them, than by emblematic images which embody great and indeed terrible forces running through human life, but which appear before us in detachment from the realistically presented characters. Out of a world dominated by these two images, the powers of evil in the witches, and the emblem of revolt in the man of blood, one of the human characters emerges into prominence. At first, this is a prominence which belongs properly to the chief of the king's lieutenants and the saviour of the state.

Yet even from the start, Macbeth is more than, as it were, a plain historical figure. Through his identification with the image of revolt he becomes an icon of one of the great evil potentialities of life. . . .

Macbeth's status as emblem and embodiment of evil is stressed by his formal self-dedication to this as a way of life (Lady Macbeth pursues the same course), and by his ritualized invocation of universal disaster on Nature in pursuit of his own ends. His actions replace the "bounteous nature" of the kingdom under Duncan by a condition of life which, on the level of explicit political affairs, is one of tyranny, fear, spying and continual murder; and at the level of poetic suggestion is one where ordinary life is haunted—no less emphatic word will serve—haunted by the emblematical images of the evil things of night, the armed rider, the violent horses, the Horsemen, even, of the Apocalypse. These spread through the ordinary patterns of life and give it a new quality of unnatural disruption, strangeness and violence.

As the powers of good re-assert themselves, our perspective is shifted once more. We are now invited to see Macbeth's progress through the contours, as it were, of another image, though one again which has had a long history in human thought and society. We are invited to see him as a kind of ritual victim: a scapegoat, a lord of misrule, who has turned life into riot for his limited time, and is then driven out and destroyed by the forces which embody the fertile vitality and the communal happiness of the social group. A vital part of the interest of these closing scenes is Macbeth's own growing consciousness of how what he has done futilely defies these forces, and is sterile and self-destroying.

The element of ritual in the closing scenes, their almost imperceptible relapsing into the contours of a sacrificial fertility ceremony, the expulsion, hunting down and destruction of a man who has turned into a monster, give to the action its final shape.

John Holloway
The Story of the Night (London: Routledge
and Kegan Paul, 1961), pp. 72-74

Antony and Cleopatra

Though the character of Octavius is neither attractive nor wholly clear, his figure is invested with a certain tragic dignity, because he is felt to be the Man of Destiny, the agent of forces against which the intentions of an individual would avail nothing. . . . And to the influence of this feeling in giving impressiveness to the story is added that of the immense scale and world-wide issue of the conflict. Even the distances traversed by fleets and armies enhance this effect.

And yet there seems to be something half-hearted in Shakespeare's appeal here, something even ironical in his presentation of this conflict. Its external magnitude, like Antony's magnificence in lavishing realms and gathering the kings of the East in his support, fails to uplift or dilate the imagination. The struggle in Lear's little island seems to us to have an infinitely wider scope. . . . A painful sense of hollowness oppresses us. We know too well what must happen in a world so splendid, so false, and so petty. . . .

This presentation of the outward conflict has two results. First, it blunts our feeling of the greatness of Antony's fall from prosperity. Indeed this feeling, which we might expect to be unusually acute, is hardly so; it is less acute, for example, than the like feeling in the case of Richard II, who loses so much smaller a realm. Our deeper sympathies are focussed rather on Antony's heart, on the inward fall to which the enchantment of passion leads him, and the inward recovery which succeeds it. And the second result is this. The greatness of Antony and Cleopatra in their fall is so much heightened by contrast with the world they lose and the conqueror who wins it, that the positive element in the final tragic impression, the element of reconciliation, is strongly emphasised. The peculiar effect of the drama depends partly, as we have seen, on the absence of decidedly tragic scenes and events in its first half; but it depends quite as much on this emphasis. In any Shakespearean tragedy we watch some elect spirit colliding, partly through its error and defect, with a superhuman power which bears it down; and yet we feel that this spirit, even in the error and defect, rises by its greatness into ideal union with the power that overwhelms it. In some tragedies this latter feeling is relatively weak. In *Antony and Cleopatra* it is unusually strong; stronger, with some readers at least, than the fear and grief and pity with which they contemplate the tragic error and the advance of doom.

A. C. Bradley
Oxford Lectures on Poetry (London: Macmillan, 1909), pp. 290-92

Shakespeare's Cleopatra had to be acted by a boy, and this did everything to determine, not his view of the character, but his presenting of it. Think how a modern dramatist, a practical man of the theatre, with an actress for his Cleopatra, would set about the business. He might give us the tragedy of the play's end much as Shakespeare does, no doubt—if he could; but can we conceive him leaving Cleopatra without one single scene in which to show the sensual charm which drew Antony to her, and back to her, which is the tragedy's very fount? Yet this is what Shakespeare does, and with excellent reason: a boy could not show it, except objectionably or ridiculously. He does not shirk her sensuality, he stresses it time and again; but he has to find other ways than the one impracticable way of bringing it home to us. . . .

His only choice, then, is to endow her with other charms for conquest: wit, coquetry, perception, subtlety, imagination, inconsequence—and this he does to the full. But had be a veritable Cleopatra to play the part, what other and what better could he do? How does a Cleopatra differ from the common run of wantons but in just such gifts as these? It would take a commonplace dramatist to insist upon the obvious, upon all that age does wither, while custom even sooner stales its infinite monotony!

It is, of course, with his magic words that Shakespeare weaves Cleopatra's charm. . . . This is the woman herself, quick, jealous, imperious, mischievous, malicious, flagrant, subtle; but a delicate creature, too, and the light, glib verse seems to set her on tiptoe. . . .

From wantonness, trickery and folly, Shakespeare means to lift her to a noble end. But, even in doing it, he shirks no jot of the truth about her. . . . But it is not till the supreme moment approaches that she can pretend to any calm of courage. . . .

She is herself to the very end. Her last breath fails upon the impatient

> What should I stay . . . ?

Her last sensation is the luxury of

> As sweet as balm, as soft as air, as gentle!

And what more luminous summary could there be of such sensual womanhood than the dignity and perverse humour blended in this picture of her yielded to her death—suckling an asp?

Harley Granville-Barker
Prefaces to Shakespeare, Second Series (London:
Sidgwick and Jackson, 1930), pp. 203-7, 215-19

This historical attitude to his subject is also responsible for the fact that the play is so much more varied in mood than are Shakespeare's regular tragedies. A convincing picture of the great world cannot be steeped in the consistently tragic atmosphere which envelops *King Lear*. To a detached observer, the life of the great world is never consistently tragic; it is an extraordinary compound of sad and comic, prosaic and poetic. So is Shakespeare's play. There is a great deal of comedy in it; ranging from

the farcical humour of the clown, who brings the means of death to Cleopatra—ironically this illustrates how little the great and their misfortunes
mean to the humble—to the cool satire of the scene on Pompey's galley,
when "the third part of the world" is carried drunk to bed. For these
great people, as Shakespeare sees them, are far from being as dignified
as they wish to appear. Cleopatra herself, during the first half of the play,
is a comedy figure, with her petty feminine vanity, her childish lack of self-
control. Even at the end, when she is on the point of killing herself, she
cuffs her treasurer in a fit of temper because he gives away the fact that
she has been trying to deceive Octavious as to the real amount of her
treasure. Yet, mingled with all this comedy is the grave statesman's wisdom
of the political drama, the tragic pathos of Enobarbus' end, the passionate
lyrical beauty of the love scenes, the supernatural mystery of the sooth-
sayer scenes, or that in which the soldiers hear the fading unearthly music
which betokens the departure of the god Hercules, who had, up to then,
protected Antony's fortunes; while over all glows the light of Shakespeare's
sense of the romance inherent in grand historic events.

David Cecil
Poets and Storytellers (London: Constable, 1949), pp. 19-20

Timon of Athens

Timon's speech on friendship, delivered while he is entertaining his
friends . . . furnishes us with a vital point of reference that we must never
overlook in our interpretations of the play. Whatever doubts we may
have about the authorship of some passages, these sentences are indubitably
Shakespeare. More than that, they breathe the warm-hearted friendliness
and generosity of Shakespeare's own personality. At the same time all the
beliefs expressed in the speech—service and responsibility, class solidarity,
the social nature of good—are medieval beliefs and probably derive to
some extent from traditional moral teaching. This and the fact that they
are given to Timon to proclaim should be sufficient to explode the misconception of him as a blind prodigal who has only himself to blame for all
the suffering that later befalls him. He may, as he himself admits, have
given unwisely; he has never given ignobly . . .

> No villainous bounty yet hath passed my heart;
> Unwisely, not ignobly, have I given.

It is not merely Timon's bounty, the subject of the first Act, that links
him, if as an ideal projection, with the flesh-and-blood gentry of Shakespeare's own time. Like theirs, his wealth is in land; like them, too, he
has been able to keep up a lavish scale of bounty only by mortgaging

his estates to the last acre. And when disaster overtakes him it is not the fairytale disaster of Antonio and Bassanio, but the real disaster that hung over the heads of so many of the Elizabethan upper class: he has mortgaged his lands to the point when he has nothing further to mortgage. . . .

E. C. Pettet
RES (Octber, 1947), pp. 326-27

Coriolanus

The pride of Coriolanus has two very contradictory faculties. It is the tragic flaw in his character and therefore has the well-known power of pride the preëminent deadly sin to produce other faults and destroy good in the spirit of its possessor; but it is at the same time the basis of self-respect in his character and thus has power to produce good in his spirit. Whether destructive of good or productive of good, it is a fierce pride, accompanied by a wrath that makes it work at white heat. The wrath is like the pride it accompanies in not always having the qualities of a deadly sin; it can at times be righteous wrath, directed against human baseness. Hence both the pride and the wrath of Coriolanus can be admirable as well as detestable. Just as taints and honors "wage equal" with the sensualistic Antony, so do they with the proud Coriolanus.

Shakespeare lets us know in the first scene of the play that even among the worst enemies of Coriolanus his honors ask to be balanced against his taints. It is with praise alone that Shakespeare surrounds a deeply flawed but noble hero at the opening of *Macbeth*, and it is with scorn alone that he surrounds such a hero at the opening of *Antony and Cleopatra*; but it is with praise and scorn together, set one against the other, that he surrounds such a hero at the opening of *Coriolanus*, and if the praise does not receive so much dramatic emphasis as the scorn, it is nevertheless honest praise and weighs all the more when we consider that it is offered in defense of Coriolanus by a fair-minded man who has no reason to love him.

Willard Farnham
Shakespeare's Tragic Frontier (Berkeley and Los Angeles, Calif.:
Univ. California Pr., 1950), pp. 219-20

. . . Coriolanus is not only presented as a god and compared to Hercules; he is "like a thing / Made by some other deity than Nature." So extraordinary is he that even his troops, inspired by him, feel themselves to be as much superior to the Romans as boys to butterflies or butchers to flies. Like Menaphon's description of Tamburlaine ("Such breadth of shoulders as might mainly bear / Old Atlas' burthen") and Cleopatra's of Antony ("His legs bestrid the ocean"), this description of Coriolanus is central to Shakespeare's depiction of his hero. His superhuman bearing and his opposition to Rome are the two most important facts about him. . . .

The world which Coriolanus now inhabits is neither the world of the Romans nor that of the Volscians. It is a world of absolutes—the world, as I have already suggested, of heroes. When Cominius comes to intercede for Rome, he refuses to answer to his name, insisting that he must forge a new name in the fire of burning Rome; he sits "in gold, his eye/Red as 'twould burn Rome" (V, 1, 11-15, 63-4). The fierceness of his adherence to his prinicples has translated him almost beyond humanity. . . . Coriolanus has steeled himself to become a Tamburlaine and administer divine chastisement, refusing to be softened by considerations of friendship.

Eugene M. Waith
The Herculean Hero (London: Chatto and Windus;
Toronto: Clarke, Irwin, 1962), pp. 121-22, 137-38

Pericles

Although it is likely that the last three acts are mainly Shakespeare, there is no proof that he handled them seriously enough to justify our basing any elaborate theorising upon them. The scene of Marina's birth (III. i.) does indeed touch the height of Shakespearean art, while the recognition of Pericles and Marina is very fine. . . . If the brothel scenes are ineffective, except in isolation, the end, with the vision of Diana and the recognition of Thaisa in Ephesus, is scanty and ridiculous. . . . On the other hand, there is heard now and then, and perhaps for the first time in Shakespeare, that simple yet strained, remote and magical note that sounds from time to time in the last plays and helps to give them their unique character.

E. M. W. Tillyard
Shakespeare's Last Plays (London: Chatto and Windus;
Toronto: Macmillan, 1938), pp. 22-23

Cymbeline

Examining the bare plots rather than the total impression of the last three plays, we find in each the same general scheme of prosperity, destruction, and re-creation. The main character is a King. At the beginning he is in prosperity. He then does an evil or misguided deed. Great suffering follows, but during this suffering or at its height the seeds of something new to issue from it are germinating, usually in secret. In the end this new element assimilates and transforms the old evil. The King overcomes his evil instincts, joins himself to the new order by an act of forgiveness or repentance; and the play issues into a fairer prosperity than had first existed. . . .

Bearing in mind the very close connection of the last three plays, and arguing back a little from the last two to *Cymbeline*, we cannot doubt that the above account truly represents part of that play's intention. Reading the play without paying special heed to the plot, we have to confess that this intention is very feebly expressed. Half a dozen other things emerge more vividly. . . .

It looks as if Shakespeare knew that what he wanted to express could be expressed through the cycle of prosperity, destruction, and renewed prosperity, and that the complex material of the prose romance was in some ways congenial to his needs. Yet he is unable to adjust his methods to the new wealth of content; with the result that his main concern becomes blurred and remote, and the details become more emphatic than the end it was their business to forward.

E. M. W. Tillyard
Shakespeare's Last Plays (London: Chatto and Windus;
Toronto: Macmillan, 1938), pp. 26-27, 40

The Winter's Tale

This is not to say, of course, that the surface meaning of *The Winter's Tale* generally creates little enjoyment or has little subtlety. Much of it is stamped with Shakespeare's magnificence. Several of the scenes, especially that of the trial, are beautifully organized and filled with exciting action. . . .

Yet however satisfying a great part of the surface meaning, there nevertheless remain many passages and scenes which do not make much sense unless viewed as part of a deeper imaginative world hidden behind the surface. . . .

The symbolism of this play thus revolves around the life-death-life pattern of nature and of human existence. From the playful innocence of youth, man passes into the state of sin and inward death, just as does the Clown who witnesses the death of Antigonus. But the restored Old Shepherd "meets with things newborn." Leontes suffers the loss of Mamillius, and the temporary death of Hermione and Perdita, passing through tempest and fall, in order sixteen years later, as a man old with "experience," in Blake's sense of the word, to be restored to life and permanent peace. His repentance is accompanied by the growth of a new and creative love, itself derived from benevolent nature, assuming bodily shape in Perdita. His paradise at the end of the play is not, like Perdita's, that of a garden, but of a city and a temple, corresponding to the Heavenly City in the New Testament, the Temple of God. There he remarries Hermione, just as Dante meets Beatrice again, and Faust the eternal form of Gretchen . . .

The Winter's Tale is not just a tale of fancy or a charming illustration of a moral platitude, or the utopia of a feeble old man's dream. Its poetry is great and its world is real, however much it has been "hooted at like an old tale."

F. David Hoeniger
UTQ (October, 1950), pp. 12-13, 25-26

The Tempest

How daring and effective a device for the clear presentation of character Shakespeare has made use of parallelisms! Not a character in the play speaks a line out of keeping with what the dramatist tells of his station and opportunities in life: though characters greatly unlike utter similar speeches and do similar deeds, there is always enough difference to accentuate the dissimilarity of those characters. Prospero's analogy to the witch Sycorax is so far from making him like her that it makes him more evidently the learned man, strong through years of study, and her the witch whose power depends on her contract with the devil. When Ferdinand does the tasks of Caliban he is so little like Caliban that he is yet further removed from the savage by his like occupation: Ferdinand piling a great quantity of logs carries them like a prince, and Caliban with his burden of fire-wood is more a serf than ever. Caliban's speech on the noises of the island is more impressive than that of Ferdinand on the mysterious music of Ariel, partly because that of Ferdinand is more conventional; but this very conventionality makes it more fitting to the character of the prince. Ferdinand talks of *music*, and the savage Caliban contrasts himself with him by speaking of *noises*. Antonio calls Caliban a "fish" with the amused contempt of a noble, the more emphatic in contrast with the vulgar astonishment with which the servant Trinculo uses the same word. Miranda and Caliban are both amazed at the appearance of the strangers who come to the island; but how different are their expressions of wonder! The verbal similarity of their exclamations but makes more striking the great difference in the two characters: Caliban's words are full of vulgar fear, but Miranda's have in them something of maidenly reverence. The parallels of the play emphasize the contrasts of the characters in virtue while bringing out their truth to type. The plan of the nobles to murder their victims when they are sleeping, made known in courtly phrases, seems blacker when contrasted with Caliban's similar plan, set forth in language proper to him.

Allan H. Gilbert
JEGP (January, 1915), pp. 73-74

The storm that rages through *King Lear* is now shut up into an episode of seventy lines, in which we see a human society with its gradation of rank—its king lurking unseen in his cabin, its quarrelsome nobles cursing the fate that hangs above their heads, and its men of action vainly struggling against it—brought to sudden and seemingly irretrievable disaster, as the ship splits and plunges into the gulf, amid the anguished cries of all on board. As a picture of appalling catastrophe there is nothing elsewhere in Shakespeare to touch it; and when Lytton Strachey asks for realism, here it is in full measure! So overwhelming is the realism and so convincing, that the dramatist has us completely at his mercy for the wonders he means later to put upon us; and that, no doubt, is in part the purpose of the scene. But it has other and more profound uses. It serves as kind of back-cloth to the Enchanted Island, which we contemplate in all its serenity, magic and detachment in deliberated contrast with the world of reality, the world in which the quarrelsome, brawling, cursing, despairing human race is for ever foundering upon the rocks. It is as if Shakespeare had packed his whole tragic vision of life into one brief scene before bestowing his new vision upon us, as if he reminds us first of the old vision that we may the better appreciate the new. Certainly our sense of the island owes much to our coming upon it with the storm in mind. *The Tempest* begins with the stage-direction "A tempestuous noise of thunder and lightning heard" and ends with Prospero's promise of "calm seas, auspicious gales. . . ."

The change from tempest to calm possesses, however, another purpose also, a psychological purpose. Just as the storm in *King Lear* symbolizes the spiritual and mental condition of the mad old king, so the allaying of the waters about the island is paralleled by a change in Prospero himself. . . .

The Prospero we see at the end of the play is a very humble person, still a little stern with Caliban, Stephano and Trinculo, but pardoning even them, and with a mind that looks forward with penitence rather than exultation to the future. . . .

And though the concluding scene of the play leaves with us an impression of serenity and peace only paralleled by that conveyed in some of Beethoven's latest compositions, it is of peace after storm, a peace which comes to some battered vessel which makes port with difficulty after many perils.

J. Dover Wilson
The Meaning of the Tempest (The Literary and Philosophical
Society of Newcastle Upon Tyne, 1936), pp. 13-22

Henry VIII

Among Shakespeare's history plays *Henry VIII* is conspicuous for its disunity. As the crowd of notable historical personages parades before us, our attention is drawn first to Buckingham, then to Queen Katherine and

Wolsey, and finally to Cranmer. No theme unites their sucessive stories except that most general of tragic themes: how are the mighty fallen! And even this unifying principle does not apply to Cranmer, who narrowly escapes the dismal fate of the other three and ends the play with the triumphant prophecy of the Elizabethan glories to come.

One substitute for continuity in this play is the impressive amount of pageantry. . . . The play is a series of magnificent shows, perfectly suited to the character of the titular hero but tending to make the chronicle even more like a masque than like a tragedy. Whether or not this preponderance of spectacular effect was due to Fletcher, it was a technique with which he was quite familiar, as we know from his other plays.

Eugene M. Waith
The Pattern of Tragicomedy in Beaumont and Fletcher (New Haven, Conn.: Yale Univ. Pr.; Oxford Univ. Pr., 1952), p. 119

The Two Noble Kinsmen

. . . it is, I believe, now generally agreed that Shakespeare wrote Act I, scenes 1-3; Act III, scene 1; Act V, except scene 2, and possibly more, and that he was equally responsible with Fletcher for the characterization and plotting.

The style of the Shakespearean parts of *The Two Noble Kinsmen* . . . is the style of an old man, a style that reveals, to be sure, an expert technique in handling words, and a mastery of incantation, but which has little concern for the tricks that would please an audience, and which is, in a sense, dramatically stagnant.

Theodore Spencer
MP (February, 1939), pp. 255, 276

Sir Thomas More

We shall probably never be able to prove that Shakespeare wrote the Three Pages in *Sir Thomas More*. But a case, which in Greg's words rests on "the convergence of a number of independent lines of argument— palaeographical, orthographic, linguistic, stylistic, psychological—and not on any one alone," can never be *dis*proved and is bound to win acceptance from an ever-widening circle of scholars. Indeed, two recent editors have actually included it in *The Complete Works*. We may say then that it has now been canonized.

J. Dover Wilson
SS (Cambridge, 1956), p. 78

Venus and Adonis

His first narrative poem, naturally, is almost wholly conventional, an exhaustive collection of traditional motives and devices, though he appropriates them, and plies his nimble wit in embroidering them, with as much zest as if they were his own jerks of invention. Shakespeare breathed the same air as other men, and his scent for popular formulas was unusually keen and prophetic. The luxuriant Italianate manner had been naturalized in England, and no immediate foreign contacts were necessary. Not only was every poetical device at hand, there was also Elizabethan fiction. If in Shakespeare's poems action bears to rhetoric much the same proportion as bread to sack in Falstaff's bill, we may remember the technique of Pettie, Lyly, and Greene in their prose tales.

Douglas Bush
Mythology and the Renaissance Tradition (Minneapolis,
Minn.: Univ. Minnesota Pr., 1932), p. 143

The Rape of Lucrece

Shakespeare does not, as Spenser sometimes does, treat rape as a decorative theme, but his handling, in trying to be both serious and decorative, falls between two stools. When Tarquin arrives on his evil errand, three stanzas are given up to the "silent war of lilies and roses" in the face of the hostess. . . . Granting of course that the conceited style was instinctive with most Elizabethans as it cannot be with us, one discerns in this baffling tissue of ingenuities only a clever brain, not a quickened pulse. . . . As often in the early plays, the author has quite forgotten the situation; he is holding the subject at arm's length, turning it round, saying as much as he can about every side of it.

Douglas Bush
Mythology and the Renaissance Tradition (Minneapolis,
Minn.: Univ. Minnesota Pr., 1932), pp. 152-53

SONNETS

In contrast with the relative conventionality of the other Elizabethan sequences, this dramatic "plot"—the poet, his young friend, the rival poet, and "the dark lady"—has seemed to many critics to carry special marks of actuality, and there has been much throwing about of brains (the phrase is something of a euphemism) in the effort to identify the *dramatis personae* as figures in Shakespeare's world. . . . But the one fact is that we know nothing, and the wise reader will ignore the whole business. . . .

Shakespeare, even more than most Elizabethan writers, thinks and feels in images, and his imagery is no less notable for control than for fecundity. The material of his images, like that of his plays and Elizabethan poetry in general, is drawn chiefly from nature and everyday life, from business and law and the fine arts. . . .

The structure and texture of the sonnets combine a disciplined, orthodox formalism with the passionate ratiocination that we associate with the "metaphysical" poets—a strain that was emerging in the early 1590's, notably in Donne and Chapman. On the one hand, Shakespeare's style and rhythm, "the proud full sail of his great verse" (to quote his phrase about the rival poet), are mainly in the grand manner and have a smooth Italianate amplitude and flow, the rhetorical rotundity that we find in the earlier plays. . . . On the other hand, Shakespeare's diction (often monosyllabic) and images can be colloquial and homely, even when his argumentative conceits are most intricate. . . .

Most of the great sonnets are at once self-sufficient units and notes in a complex symphony. . . .

Shakespeare's world is composed of universal elements, beauty and decay, time and death, permanence and flux, truth and falsehood, and love in all its forms, from lust to "charity"; and the changes are rung on these timeless themes by an artist of supreme sensitivity to feeling and thought and word and rhythm.

Douglas Bush
Sonnets (Baltimore, Md.: Penguin Books, 1961),
pp. 9-10, 12-15, 18

The Phoenix and the Turtle

But in *The Phoenix and the Turtle* Shakespeare celebrates love of yet another kind, selfless, sexless, "interinanimating," as Donne puts it—not the marriage of two minds but the union of two souls:

> So they loved, as love in twain
> Had the essence but in one;
> Two distincts, division none,
> Number there in love was slain.

Shakespeare's own adventure in the metaphysical style combines at once the quality of a proposition in Euclid and of a piece of music. It is pure, abstract, symbolical and complete.

George Rylands
A Companion to Shakespeare Studies, eds. Harley Granville-Barker
and G. B. Harrison (Cambridge Univ. Pr.;
New York: Macmillan, 1934), p. 111

The Authorship Controversy

The reasons we have for believing that William Shakespeare of Stratford-on-Avon wrote the plays and poems are the same as the reasons we have for believing any other historical event. . . .

If one can argue that the evidence in Shakespeare's case does not mean what it says, that it has been falsified to sustain a gigantic hoax that has remained undetected for centuries, then one can just as surely argue that other evidence is not to be trusted and that, as Henry Ford said, "history is bunk." That is why the charge that Shakespeare did not write the plays does matter. And that is why, until contradictory factual evidence is unearthed, there appears to be no valid reason to doubt that the official records, the evidence of title pages, the testimony of self-described friends and fellow writers, mean just what they appear to say—that William Shakespeare of Stratford was the author of the wonderful works that bear his name.

Frank W. Wadsworth
The Poacher from Stratford (Berkeley and Los Angeles, Calif.:
Univ. California Pr., 1958), pp. 163-64

Rejected Plays

. . . *The True Chronicle History of Thomas Lord Cromwell* (1602) and *The Puritan; or, The Widow of Watling Street* (1607), are upon their title-pages declared to have been written by "W. S."; a third and the earliest of the three, *The Lamentable Tragedy of Locrine* (1595), is somewhat ambiguously asserted to have been "Newly set foorth, ouerseene and corrected, by W. S.". . . . *A Yorkshire Tragedy*, having been entered to Thomas Pavier upon the Stationers' Register on 2 May 1608, was printed for him later in the same year and is both in the Stationers' Register and on the title-page declared to have been written by "W. Shakspeare." Although the first three plays named were, of course, omitted by Heminge and Condell from the Shakespeare First Folio of 1623, by the latter half of the seventeenth century the "W. S." had been accepted as evidence of Shakespeare's authorship, and all three plays were accordingly included in the Third Shakespeare Folio of 1664, together with *A Yorkshire Tragedy* and three other plays which, though likewise omitted from the earlier folios, had previously appeared in quartos bearing Shakespeare's name.

Of this second group—the four plays which had earlier been printed under Shakespeare's name—only *Pericles* (1609) is today accepted as in large part his. Some modern scholars have perhaps been not unwilling to recognize his hand in a few passages in *A Yorkshire Tragedy*, but none